sparta

a history of mi

by Lyman L. Frimodig and Fred W. Stabley

MICHIGAN STATE UNIVERSITY
East Lansing, Michigan

PREFACE

SPARTAN SAGA has been in preparation for 52 years. The first steps were taken in 1919 when Lyman Frimodig returned to the campus where he had been a brilliant all-around athlete just a few years before.

But let Frim tell about it:

"I returned to the campus on Jan. 1, 1919, as a member of the athletic department. I was hired for the remainder of the school year only, but that six months lasted 41½ years.

"Shortly after my arrival, I received a phone call from one of our old grads requesting information. He wanted to know if MAC had had an undefeated football season prior to 1913 when we were 7-0-0 and beat Michigan for the first time. Being new and unfamiliar with the files, I asked acting director George Gauthier (director Chester Brewer was in military service) where I could find the answer. His response was: 'We don't have any records.' It seems all athletic records had been kept in the office of the chairman of the athletic council, Herman Vedder, an engineering professor. They were destroyed in the fire which consumed the old engineering building in 1916.

"Then, I started digging into newspapers, student weeklies and year books. Finally, I found the answer. The 1913 team was the only one with a perfect mark. But the 1908 team also had gone undefeated with a 6-0-2 card. The ties were 0-0 scores with Michigan and DePauw.

"The hunt for this answer aroused my interest in compiling our athletic records and I decided to go further. Every summer and whatever other time I could spare, I found myself digging. The work was tedious, but it held great interest for me. Current records also were kept with the invaluable assistance of longtime athletic ticket manager Warren Burtt. By the time I retired in 1960, I had practically completed a full story of the sports in which we participated."

That he had. Through the years, Frim had gradually widened his sights from just compiling all-time game scores and event results. He assembled an authoritative list of all-time letterwinners in all sports, developed coaches' records, records with individual opponents and other statistical features and kept many notes about things which he had uncovered in his research.

Even in retirement, he kept after his longtime hobby. In 1965, he enjoyed the first fruits of his work, with the publication of MICHIGAN STATE UNIVERSITY, ALUMNI VARSITY LETTERMEN, a directory of letterwinners in all sports.

The letterwinners list, updated through the 1969-70 school year, is part of SPARTAN SAGA.

SPARTAN SAGA, itself, has undergone an enlargement in scope from the original plan. At first, it was to be a simple records book, listing all-time game and

meet scores in all sports, coaches' records and a few other items, largely tabular. Later, such additions as a brief history of each sport, a Spartan sports chronology, Olympic and Pan-American participants, Chester Brewer and Conference Medal of Honor winners and football bowl game participants were made. In its final form, SPARTAN SAGA has become a veritable encyclopedia of Michigan Agricultural College, Michigan State College and Michigan State University athletics.

The substance of SPARTAN SAGA came from Frim's records and notes, two histories of the institution—HISTORY OF THE MICHIGAN AGRICULTURAL COLLEGE, by Dr. W. J. Beal (1915) and MICHIGAN STATE, THE FIRST 100 YEARS, by Dr. Madison Kuhn (1955)—and an unpublished, but very valuable work entitled A HISTORY OF MICHIGAN STATE SPORTS (1857-1959) by Gary Gildner. The latter was a graduate research project done while Gildner was a student aide in the Michigan State Sports Information Office. In addition, there has been extensive examination of primary source materials, such as the MICHIGAN STATE NEWS, LANSING STATE JOURNAL, LANSING REPUBLICAN, HOLCAD and SPECULUM files by the coauthors. The latter two were early MAC student publications.

Jim Totten, associate university editor and managing editor of athletic publications, assisted with the editing and directed the design, layout and production work for the publication. Bob Brent of the MSU Design Service did the cover. Assistant Sports Information Director Nick Vista assisted in assembling the photos and in editorial functions. Mrs. Carol Howland and Mrs. Patsy Kohagen did most of the typing. Student aides John Viges and Mike Manley did the bulk of the proofreading.

Fred W. Stabley
Sports Information Director
and Coauthor

CONTENTS

Preface	3
The Big Picture	6
Fall Sports	25
Cross Country	26
Football	34
Soccer	66
Winter Sports	73
Basketball	74
Boxing	96
Fencing	102
Gymnastics	112
Hockey	120
Swimming	130
Wrestling	142
Spring Sports	153
Baseball	154
Golf	180
Lacrosse	190
Tennis	192
Track	204
1971 Review	230
Spartan Officials	234
Spartan Coaches	235
All-Time Letterwinners	236
Directory	237

Students engage in "Class Rush," begun in 1863, where they fight to get ball.

The Old Armory, which housed first basketball court, now site of Music Building.

Irving Lankey, cheerleader who wrote the Spartan fight song in 1916.

Star performers on various athletic teams pose for group shot sometime in the 1890s.

THE BIG PICTURE

CHRONOLOGY OF MICHIGAN STATE SPORTS

1855 Michigan Agricultural College is founded, but with no plans for organized athletics of any kind.

1860 Athletic facilities consist of a trapeze and swinging rings hung from campus trees. (Intensive work-study program and faculty opposition cause MAC to lag behind other schools in sports activity.)

1862 Students begin first of many campaigns to get athletics on campus.

1863 "Class Rush" is born. (Two entire classes fight each other to get possession of ball tossed between them.)

1865 Student-run Star baseball team, first organized athletic team of any kind, is born on campus. First outside competition is five-game series with Capital Club of Lansing.

1866 Star baseball team makes road trip, a 16-mile train ride to Mason with four fans. Team later disbands due to graduation of players.

1870 Students renew clamor for athletic program.

1871 Baseball team is organized and makes trip to Detroit to play a game. (Receipts are to pay for return trip, but the game is rained out and Aggie players hitch-hike home.)

1873 Biggest sporting event of the year is a match hunt between sophomore and junior teams on a fall Saturday which bags 79 squirrels, 12 pigeons, 9 quail, 4 turkeys, 6 partridges and 8 ducks.

1877 Most famous early student-run baseball team, The Nine Spots, is organized. It wins 8 of 11 regular season games and then barnstorms Michigan. Team disbands after 1878 season.

1881 Student newspaper, *The Speculum,* takes up crusade against the anti-sports faculty and administration.

1882 *The Speculum* says: "Why can we not form a college athletic association? The matter has been discussed for some time. Why should we be behind other colleges in this respect? At present, our sports are confined to an occasional 'scrub' game of baseball, or a miscellaneous kicking of a football. Why cannot the energy displayed in these games be organized and improved?"

1884 On May 19, an MAC baseball team plays Olivet at Olivet and wins 20-9. (It is the earliest recorded intercollegiate sports event at MAC.)

On June 14, an intramural field day featuring side hold wrestling, collar and elbow wrestling, football, tug-of-war and such track events as running broad jump, 35-pound weight throw, high kick and standing broad jump is tacitly condoned by college authorities. A special feature is a baseball game between MAC and Michigan which Michigan wins 13-3. It is MAC's first home intercollegiate sports event.

1886 A student-run athletic association, with Prof. R. C. Carpenter as advisor, is formed. It is to have control, with the advice and consent of the still-reluctant faculty, of all college athletics.

MAC hosts its first intercollegiate field day, with Olivet and Albion as guests. Track and wrestling events are featured.

1888 MAC, Albion, Hillsdale and Olivet form Michigan Intercollegiate Athletic Association (MIAA). MAC hosts first annual MIAA Field Day.

1889 Drill room of Armory, located where the Music Building now stands, is designated as MAC's first gymnasium.

1890 State Board of Agriculture appropriates $250 to buy equipment for the gymnasium. It is the first money ever given by the MAC administration for sports.

1892 First on-campus running track is installed on field just north of present Women's Gym. (Earlier field days probably were held at Lansing Race Track, which was located on south side of Michigan Avenue near the present-day Red Cedar Golf Course.)

Leander Burnett, State's first bona fide athletic hero, finishes his career. (He was a star pitcher in baseball and a great all-around trackman. In five MIAA field days, he won 37 track and field events, topped by 10 in 1890, and twice was awarded the diamond medal for best all-around performance.)

1896 Football bows in with a regular schedule of four games. (Credit was due in part to a revised academic schedule which switched the traditional long vacation period to the summer. Earlier, this break had come in late fall through the winter to permit MAC students to teach in country schools.)

1897 Bobby Gale, a member of the Detroit Tigers, is hired for $50 by the athletic association to tutor MAC's baseball team for three weeks prior to the opening of his season. Henry Keep, an engineering student, coaches the football team.

1899 Rev. Charles O. Bemies is hired as football coach and head of the Department of Physical Culture. Basketball begins.

1900 First two tennis courts are built north of Morrill Hall.

1902 First swimming pool is installed in new Bath House. Old College Field becomes main outdoor athletic area with running track, football and baseball facilities.

1903 Chester L. Brewer is hired as athletic director and coach of all sports with professorial rank. (This is possibly first such academic recognition given anywhere to a college athletic coach and administrator.)

1904 Ace sprinter Harry Moon, one of first men ever to do :10.0 in the 100-yard dash, competes in U.S. Olympic team trials, the first Aggie to achieve this honor.

1905 Track team beats Notre Dame. (It is first MAC victory in any sport over the Irish.)

1906 MAC athletic association votes to drop out of the MIAA, which the Aggies were rapidly outgrowing.

1908 First undefeated football team elates MAC. The 6-0-2 record includes 0-0 tie with Michigan. Aggies play Notre Dame in basketball for first time and win 33-20. Track team debuts in Big Ten track meet and Ralph Carr wins two-mile.

1909 Fred Tillotson wins another two-mile title for MAC in the Big Ten championships. MAC opens basketball relations with Michigan and beats Wolverines twice. First athletes are sent to Penn Relays.

1910 MAC scores first football victory over Notre Dame, 17-0. Varsity cross country starts.

1911 John Macklin succeeds Chester Brewer as athletic director and head coach of all sports.

1913 MAC has first perfect season in football, 7-0-0, and scores first victory over Michigan, 12-7.

1914 Jack Heppinstall starts 45-year career as athletic trainer.

1915 Macklin concludes MAC career with a 5-1 football season and another victory over Michigan, 24-0. Jerry DaPrato and Blake Miller are first first-team All-Americans. Lyman Frimodig scores 30 points in a basketball game, a record which stands up at State for 35 years.

Aerial shot of State's athletic plant: field house, ice rink, stadium, ball diamonds.

Ralph H. Young, athletic director at State from 1923 to 1954.

President Robert Shaw names stadium in honor of John Macklin, r., in 1935.

Jack Heppinstall, l., in athletic training room in 1927.

Demonstration Hall, site of the Ice Arena where the Spartans play their home hockey games, earlier used for basketball.

1916 Original version of the "Fight Song" is written by cheerleader F. I. Lankey. MAC plays key role in inaugurating Michigan State Intercollegiate Track Meet. MAC wins first team title. First individual MAC winners are Earl B. Sheldon in the 880 and mile, Howard Beatty in the 120 high and 220 low hurdles and Frank Warner in the broad jump.

1917 Lyman Frimodig makes history by winning 10th varsity letter, the all-time high at Michigan State.

1920 The Men's Gymnasium, now the Women's Gymnasium, is opened. MAC joins the NCAA.

1921 The MAC Track Carnival (later the Michigan State Relays) has inaugural in Men's Gym. Basketball and other indoor activities also move to Men's Gym. WKAR begins varsity basketball broadcasts, which may be earliest college athletic broadcasts in the U.S.

1922 Swimming becomes varsity sport. Athletes go to Drake Relays for first time and DeGay Ernst wins the 440-yard hurdles in meet record time of :54.4. Hockey becomes varsity sport. Outdoor arena is located on tennis courts north and east of Morrill Hall.

1923 Ralph Young becomes athletic director and football coach. Football moves from Old College Field to new football stadium with 14,000-capacity stands. WKAR starts football broadcasts, which may be another national first. Chemistry prof Charles D. Ball starts 24-year career as State's tennis coach.

1924 Macklin Field is dedicated in game with Michigan. William D. Frazer becomes first MAC Olympian as U.S. pistol team member.

1925 John Kobs begins 39-year career as State's baseball coach and also becomes first hockey coach. School is renamed Michigan State College. Running track shifts from Old College Field to football stadium.

1926 Teams get nickname of Spartans through Lansing State Journal Sports Editor George S. Alderton. Fencing becomes a varsity sport. Central Collegiate Conference is formed.

1927 Ben VanAlstyne begins 23-year career as basketball coach. Don Fleser bats an all-time Spartan high of .667. State scores first victory at Penn Relays with 880-yard relay team composed of Forrest Lang, Henry Henson, Bohn Grim and Fred Alderman in time of 1:28.4. State joins the IC4A and Fred Alderman becomes Spartans' first champion by taking the 440. Alderman also becomes Spartans' first NCAA champion in any sport by winning the 100 and 220-yard dashes.

1928 Golf becomes a varsity sport. Fred Alderman is a member of Olympic championship 1,600-meter relay team and becomes State's first Olympic gold medalist.

1930 Clark Chamberlain is State's first IC4A cross country winner. Fendley Collins starts 33-year career as wrestling coach.

Football team produces a 5-1-2 mark, best record since 1915, in first season under Jim Crowley. (Excitement raged so high that an 11-car chartered train followed the team to Washington, D.C., for the Spartans' first night game against Georgetown. Georgetown won 14-13.) Basketball moves to new Demonstration Hall.

1931 Hockey is abandoned after adverse weather conditions wipe out entire schedule. Basketball team posts a 16-1 record, best in State's history.

1933 Charles Bachman succeeds Jim Crowley as head football coach. Cross country team wins first of record five straight IC4A team titles.

1934 Football team beats Michigan for first time since 1915 and starts four-game win streak over Wolverines. Tom Ottey wins second straight IC4A cross country title. Stadium officially named Macklin Field.

1935 Boxing becomes a varsity sport with Leon Burhans as coach. Sid Wagner becomes State's third All-American in football and first since 1915.

1936 Walter Jacob wins State's first NCAA wrestling crown. Stadium capacity is increased to 26,000 by lowering field level and building in 12 rows of seats all the way around field on what had been the running track.

1937 After another good season, 8-1, the football team receives State's first bowl bid. Spartans play and lose, 6-0, to Auburn in Orange Bowl, Jan. 1, 1938. Walter Jacob wins first of three straight National AAU wrestling titles.

1938 John Pingel becomes State's fourth All-American in football. State inaugurates NCAA cross country championships, first in a string of 26 straight held on the State campus through 1964.

1939 Cross country wins first NCAA team championship. Charles Schmitter starts as MSC fencing coach, a career still going strong in 1970.

1940 Jenison Field House is dedicated with basketball game against Tennessee. Chet Aubuchon becomes MSC's first All-American in basketball.

1941 Karl Schlademan begins 17-year career as MSC track coach. Identical twins Merle and Burl Jennings win NCAA wrestling championships. Jenison

scholarships for athletes are established. Francis Thalken becomes first fencing All-American.

1942 Charles McCaffree starts 27-year career as State's head swimming coach. Jennings twins do it again, both winning NCAA wrestling crowns.

1943 Regular sports schedules are abandoned during 1943-44 school year due to war. Chuck Davey wins first of four NCAA boxing titles, the only man in college ring history to accomplish the feat. Bill Zurakowski also wins NCAA boxing crown.

1945 Spartan Statue is unveiled. Wrestler Gale Mikles wins first of four straight Walter Jacob awards for scoring most points on team.

1946 First NCAA swim title is won by 400-yard freestyle relay team of Zigmund Indyke, John DeMond, James Quigley and Robert Allwardt.

1947 Biggie Munn becomes head football coach, succeeding Charles Bachman.

1948 Macklin Field seating is expanded to 51,000 to prepare way for Big Ten membership. Michigan State is voted into the Big Ten on Dec. 12, subject to certification by a committee of faculty representatives that it is in compliance with conference rules and regulations. Gymnastics becomes a varsity sport with George Szypula as head coach.

1949 State gets final clearance and officially becomes Big Ten member on May 20, 1949. Spartans are to begin competition in all sports with 1950-51 school year, with the exception of football which will start in 1953. State hits jackpot with three All-American gridders—Lynn Chandnois, Ed Bagdon and Don Mason—the first in 11 years. Mel Stout is State's first NCAA gymnastics champion, winning in parallel bars. Ice Arena is opened.

1950 Hockey is reinstated as varsity sport, with home in Demonstration Hall and Harold Paulsen as first head coach. Football team has 8-1 season and embarks on 28-game winning streak.

1951 Tennis becomes first team to win a Big Ten title. Leonard Brose wins singles and he and John Sahratian win doubles. Everett (Sonny) Grandelius, an All-American halfback in football, is first recipient of two new major annual awards to athletes: Chester Brewer Award and Conference Medal of Honor. Boxing team, under George Makris, wins first of two NCAA team titles. (Other came in 1955.)

Cross country takes first of 12 Big Ten team titles won through 1970. Bert McLachlan and Clarke Scholes each win two titles as State participates in first Big Ten swim meet. George Bender and Gene Gibbons are State's first Big Ten wrestling champs.

1952 Football team posts second straight undefeated and untied season and rates No. 1 nationally on both AP and UPI polls. Biggie Munn is named "Coach of the Year." Six players make All-America. Amo Bessone succeeds Harold Paulsen as hockey coach. Clarke Scholes wins Olympic 100-meter swim title in record time. Dick Berry in epee and Fred Freiheit in sabre are State's first Big Ten fencing champions.

1953 Football begins Big Ten play, ties Illinois for title and is voted Rose Bowl bid. Don Dohoney and LeRoy Bolden are State's first All-Big Ten selections.

1954 State beats UCLA in Rose Bowl thriller Jan. 1, 28-20. Ralph Young retires as athletic director. Biggie Munn becomes athletic director and Duffy Daugherty takes over as head football coach. Baseball team wins Big Ten title. State wins unofficial Big Ten all-sports championship for first time. (Through 1970, State was first five times, second 11 times, third three times and fifth once.)

1955 Football team has 8-1 record, places second in Big Ten and gets Rose Bowl bid. Henry Kennedy is State's first Big Ten cross country titlist.

1956 Spartans win another Rose Bowl thriller on Jan. 2 over UCLA, 17-14, on Dave Kaiser's field goal with seven seconds left on the clock. Macklin Field is enlarged to 60,000 capacity. Soccer becomes a varsity sport with Gene Kenney as head coach. Duffy Daugherty is named "Coach of the Year" for great 1955 campaign. Julius (Hooks) McCoy scores 45 points against Notre Dame for all-time Spartan record which was still on books through 1970.

1957 Macklin Field is renamed Spartan Stadium and doubledecked to raise seating capacity to 76,000. Basketball team, paced by John Green, ties for Big Ten title and goes to semi-finals of NCAA tournament before losing. Jack Quiggle is State's second All-American in basketball. Swim team wins first Big Ten crown.

1958 Forest Akers golf course is completed. Boxing is dropped as a varsity sport. Ron Perranoski finishes Spartan baseball career with all-time high of 21 pitching victories. Forddy Kennedy wins State's first NCAA cross country title and team wins seventh national crown. Gymnastics ties for first NCAA title. Al Sarria is first soccer All-American.

1959 Men's Intramural Building is completed. Basketball wins first outright Big Ten championship. John Green is State's third cage All-American. Biggie Munn is named to Football Foundation Hall of Fame as a coach. Hockey wins first Big Ten title and goalie Joe Selinger becomes State's first hockey All-American.

1960 Former Spartan hockey stars Weldon Olson and Gene Grazia play for U.S. team which scores stupendous upset in winning Olympic Gold Medal.

President John Hannah speaks at the unveiling of "Sparty" in 1945.

Gene Washington, All-American end, 1965, 66, now top pro player.

Herb Washington, Big Ten and NCAA 60-yard dash champion, 1970.

Exterior of press box at Spartan Stadium, one of the largest and most complete facilities of its type in the world.

1961 Golfer Gene Hunt reaches semi-finals of NCAA tournament before bowing 2-1 to eventual winner Jack Nicklaus of Ohio State. Wrestling squad wins first Big Ten team title.

1962 Basketball team registers all-time single game high score for a State team with 118-100 win over Oklahoma.

1963 John Kobs retires as baseball coach and is succeeded by Danny Litwhiler in 1964 season. State loses Big Ten football title and Rose Bowl bid to Illinois in game postponed by assassination of President Kennedy from a Saturday to Thanksgiving Day. Fencing wins first Big Ten championship.

1964 Outfielder Joe Porrevecchio is named to All-Big Ten baseball first team for third straight year. Soccer makes it to NCAA tournament finals, losing to Navy, 1-0.

1965 Football team wins first outright Big Ten title and second national championship with 10-0 regular season record. Daugherty is "Coach of the Year" again, first man ever to be named twice. Eight gridders make All-America first teams. Gene Washington, an All-America end in football, also wins 60-yard high hurdles at first NCAA indoor track championships and also cops first two of six Big Ten hurdles crowns. Track wins first outdoor team title in Big Ten.

1966 Football team loses, 14-12, to UCLA in Rose Bowl Jan. 1. Team comes back in fall with another undefeated campaign marred only by controversial 10-10 tie with Notre Dame in one of college football's all-time great games. Eleven Spartans make All-Big Ten and six achieve All-American laurels. Track team takes first Big Ten indoor title and second straight outdoor crown. Hockey team wins its first NCAA championship.

1967 Grady Peninger, who succeeded Fendley Collins as head wrestling coach in 1963, coaches his team to first official NCAA title ever won by a Big Ten school. A nine-hole golf course is added to the Forest Akers layout. Soccer wins first of two straight NCAA cochampionships. Bob Steele becomes first Spartan to win back-to-back NCAA track titles by taking 440-yard hurdles again in :50.2.

1968 Swimmer Ken Walsh wins two gold and one silver medals with U.S. Olympic team at Mexico City Games. John Pingel becomes first Spartan player to enter the National Football Foundation Hall of Fame. Gymnastics attains Big Ten cochampionship, a Spartan first.

1969 Golf wins Big Ten title to complete State's slam of championships in all sports in which Big Ten has competition. State becomes only school ever to

win team title in every sport. Spartan Stadium gets artificial Tartan Turf surface.

1970 Lacrosse becomes a varsity sport with Robert Kauffman as head coach. Ralph Simpson, in basketball, is perhaps all-time most sensational Spartan sophomore in any sport. He sets Spartan single season scoring mark of 667 points and makes playing and academic All-Big Ten and All-American teams. He then signs million dollar pro contract. Sprinter Herb Washington wins 60-yard dash crown in the NCAA indoor meet in :05.9, a meet record and world record-tying time.

MICHIGAN STATE SUCCEEDS IN THE BIG TEN

Michigan State, the newest member of the Big Ten, also is the only one ever to win a championship or cochampionship in every sport in which the conference sponsors competition.

Spartan teams began Big Ten play in the fall of 1950 in all sports except football. The first team title—in tennis—was won the following spring. The unique sweep was completed with a victory in golf in 1969.

Official championship competition in football didn't begin until 1953 because of advance scheduling practices. The Spartans started right off with a cochampionship with Illinois, won the 1954 Rose Bowl nomination and scored a thrilling 28-20 victory over UCLA in the big Pasadena spectacular. It was the first of three trips State has taken to the Rose Bowl, two of which have resulted in victories.

Michigan State's success in the Big Ten athletic picture is further pointed up by the fact that unofficial all-sports tabulations for its first 20 years of competition in the league show the Spartans to have rated first five times, second eleven times, third three times and fifth once.

Spartan teams have won 36 Big Ten titles and individuals have claimed 223 crowns. The first Big Ten team title was won by tennis in 1951. The most recent was a wrestling victory in 1970. This was an unprecedented fifth straight conference crown won in this sport.

Honors for winning the first Big Ten individual titles are divided among four men—two swimmers and two wrestlers—all of whom won crowns in the 1951 winter meets. The swimmers were Bert McLachlan and Clarke Scholes, later an Olympic champion, and the wrestlers were George Bender and Gene Gibbons. The most recent Big Ten winner was sprinter Herb Washington in the 100-yard dash of the 1970 spring meet.

SPARTANS SHINE IN NCAA COMPETITION

Spartan teams and individuals have achieved great success in National Collegiate Athletic Association competition.

The 1970 edition of NATIONAL COLLEGIATE CHAMPIONSHIPS, an official publication of the NCAA, said this of Michigan State:

"Michigan State, ranked seventh in both team and individual titles, owns the singular honor of having won team or individual honors in the most sports—nine.

BIG TEN ALL-SPORTS STANDINGS SINCE MICHIGAN STATE'S ENTRY IN 1951

Standing	1951	1952	1953	1954	1955	1956	1957	1958	1959	1960
1.	Ill	Ill	Ill	Mich St	Mich	Mich	Mich	Mich St	Mich	Mich St
2.	Mich St	Mich	Mich St	Ill	Ill	Iowa	Mich St	Ill	Mich St	Mich
3.	OSU	Mich St	Mich	Mich	Mich St	Mich St	Iowa	Iowa	Ill	Minn
4.	Mich	Wis	Iowa	Iowa	OSU	Ill	Ill	Ind	Iowa	Ill
5.	Wis	Iowa	Ind	Ind	Wis	OSU	OSU	OSU	Ind	Iowa
6.	Iowa	Ind	OSU	Wis	Iowa	Ind	Ind	Minn	Minn	OSU
7.	Ind	OSU	Wis	OSU	Ind	Wis	Minn	Mich	OSU	Ind
8.	Pur	NU	Minn	Minn	Minn	Minn	NU	Pur	Wis	NU
9.	NU	Pur	Pur	NU	Pur	Pur	Wis	Wis	Pur	Wis
10.	Minn	Minn	NU	Pur	NU	NU	Pur	NU	NU	Pur

Standing	1961	1962	1963	1964	1965	1966	1967	1968	1969	1970
1.	Mich	Mich	Mich	Mich	Mich	Mich St	Mich St	Mich	Mich	Mich
2.	Mich St	Mich St	Wis	Mich St	Mich St	Mich	Mich	Mich St	Mich St	Mich St
3.	Ind	Wis	Minn	Wis	Minn	Minn	Wis	Minn	Ind	Minn
4.	Iowa	Iowa	Iowa	Minn	Ill	Wis	Iowa	Ind	Minn	OSU
5.	Ill	Ill	Mich St	Ind	Wis	OSU	Minn	OSU	OSU	Ind
6.	OSU	Ind	Ill	OSU	Ind	Ill	Ind	Wis	Wis	Wis
7.	Minn	OSU	NU	Ill	OSU	Iowa	OSU	Iowa	Ill	Ill
8.	NU	Minn	OSU	Pur	Iowa	NU	Pur	Ill	Iowa	Iowa
9.	Wis	Pur	Ind	NU	Pur	Ind	Ill	NU	Pur	Pur
10.	Pur	NU	Pur	Iowa	NU	Pur	NU	Pur	NU	NU

MSU SUMMARY: 1st place - 5   2nd place - 11   3rd place - 3   4th place - 0   5th place - 1

18

The Spartans have laurels to their credit in boxing, cross country, gymnastics, ice hockey, indoor track, soccer, swimming, outdoor track and wrestling.

"Ohio State and Michigan have claimed titles in eight different sports, while Southern California, Navy and Oklahoma State have earned first in seven."

State has won 15 team crowns, starting with a cross country victory in 1939. The most recent was wrestling in 1967. Olympic sprinter Fred Alderman gave State its first of 87 individual NCAA titles with victories in the 100 and 220-yard dashes in 1927. The most recent, appropriately, was by another great sprinter, Herb Washington, in the 60-yard dash of the 1970 indoor meet at Detroit's Cobo Hall.

SPARTANS STAR ON THE INTERNATIONAL SCENE

Michigan State men and women athletes have gained berths on U.S. or foreign Olympic teams in every Games competition since 1924. The list of Spartan Olympians now numbers 37.

Twelve have won medals over the years, including six coveted first-place gold medals.

Fifteen Spartans have made it to Pan American Games competition, the first in 1955, with 10 winning honors, topped by six gold medals.

A number of coaches and officials also have served in various capacities in both Olympic and Pan American activities.

University facilities were used for the 1959 Pan American swimming and wrestling team tryouts, and as a training site by the 1960 Men's Olympic swimming team.

Biggest medal haul by any Spartan athlete is that of swimming great Kenneth Walsh, who won two gold and one silver medal in the 1968 Olympics and two gold medals in the 1967 Pan American Games.

Also high on the awards list are gymnast David Thor with four bronze medals earned in the 1967 Pan American Games, and gymnast Ernestine Russell Carter with four gold medals as she represented Canada in the 1959 Pan American Games.

Spartans Ernest Crosbie and Adolph Weinacker (track) and Allan Kwartler (fencing) each were members of three olympic teams.

MICHIGAN STATE ATHLETES ON U.S. OLYMPIC TEAMS
(with medal winners noted)

MEN

Col. William D. Frazer, Pistol, 1924

Frederick P. Alderman, Track, 1928
(gold medal—member of first place 1,600-meter relay team)

Thomas C. Ottey, Track, 1932

Ernest Crosbie, Track, 1932, 1936, 1948

Albert J. Mangan, Track, 1936

Charles P. Davey, Boxing, 1948

George A. Hoogerhyde, Swimming, 1948

Howard F. Patterson, Swimming, 1948

Robert G. Maldegan, Wrestling, 1948

Leland G. Merrill, Wrestling, 1948
(bronze medal—160.5 weight division)

Charles W. Spieser, Boxing, 1948, 1952

Adolph F. Weinacker, Track, 1948, 1952, 1956

Clarke C. Scholes, Swimming, 1952
(gold medal—100-meter freestyle)

Warren O. Druetzler, Track, 1952

Allan S. Kwartler, Fencing, 1952, 1956, 1960

Pearce A. Lane, Boxing, 1956

Choken Maekawa, Boxing, 1956

Weldon N. Olson, Hockey, 1956, 1960
(silver medal, second place team, 1956)
(gold medal, first place team, 1960)

Eugene W. Grazia, Hockey, 1960
(gold medal, first place team)

William A. Smoke, Canoeing, 1964

Gary J. Dilley, Swimming, 1964
(silver medal, 200-meter backstroke)

Douglas S. Volmar, Hockey, 1968

David B. Thor, Gymnastics, 1968

Kenneth M. Walsh, Swimming, 1968
(gold medal, member of first place 400-meter freestyle relay)
(gold medal, member of first place 400-meter medley relay)
(silver medal, 100-meter freestyle)

Peter E. Williams, Swimming, 1968

Donald R. Behm, Wrestling, 1968
(silver medal, bantamweight division)

Joseph R. Puleo, Weightlifting, 1968

WOMEN

Miss Virginia D. Baxter, Figure Skating, 1952

Miss Judy K. Goodrich, Fencing, 1956, 1960

Miss Carol E. Heiss, Figure Skating, 1956, 1960
(silver medal, singles, 1956)
(gold medal, singles, 1960)

Mrs. Marcia Jones Smoke, Canoeing, 1964, 1968
(bronze medal, kayak singles, 1964)

MICHIGAN STATE ATHLETES ON FOREIGN OLYMPIC TEAMS

MEN

David F. Lean, Australia, Track, 1956
(silver medal, member of second place 1,600-meter relay team)

R. Kevan Gosper, Australia, Track, 1956, 1960
(silver medal, member of second place 1,600-meter relay team, 1956)

William Steuart, South Africa, Swimming, 1956

Solomon S. Akpata, Nigeria, Track, 1964

George A. Gonzalez, Puerto Rico, Swimming, 1968

WOMEN

Mrs. Ernestine J. Russell Carter, Canada, Gymnastics, 1956, 1960

MICHIGAN STATE STAFF PERSONNEL IN OLYMPIC GAMES

Ralph H. Young, Associate Track Coach, 1932

John G. Heppinstall, Trainer, 1948

MICHIGAN STATE ATHLETES ON U.S. PAN AMERICAN TEAMS

MEN

Vincent Magi, Baseball, 1955
(silver medal, member of second place team)

Allan S. Kwartler, Fencing, 1955, 1959
(gold medal, sabre, 1959)

Clarke C. Scholes, Swimming, 1955
(gold medal, 100-meter freestyle)
(gold medal, member of first place 400-meter freestyle relay team)

William C. Mansfield, Baseball, 1959
(bronze medal, member of third place team)

Richard N. Berry, Fencing, 1959

Willie J. Atterberry, Track, 1963
(silver medal, 400-meter hurdles)

Joseph R. Puleo, Weightlifting, 1963, 1967
(gold medal, 185 division, 1963)
(gold medal, 181 division, 1967)

James T. Ferguson, Wrestling, 1963
(gold medal, 191.8 weight division)

David B. Thor, Gymnastics, 1967
(bronze medal, all-around)
(bronze medal, horizontal bar)
(bronze medal, side horse)
(bronze medal, floor exercise)

Ernest H. Tuchscherer, Soccer, 1967

Kenneth M. Walsh, Swimming, 1967
(gold medal, member of first place 400-meter freestyle relay team)
(gold medal, member of first place 800-meter freestyle relay team)

WOMEN

Miss Judy K. Goodrich, Fencing, 1959

Mrs. Marcia Jones Smoke, Canoeing, 1967 (Demonstration team)

MICHIGAN STATE ATHLETES ON FOREIGN PAN AMERICAN TEAMS

Mrs. Ernestine J. Russell Carter, Canada, Gymnastics, 1959
(gold medal, all-around)
(gold medal, side horse vault)
(gold medal, balance beam)
(gold medal, uneven parallel bars)

Calvin J. Girard, Canada, Gymnastics, 1959

MICHIGAN STATE STAFF PERSONNEL IN PAN AMERICAN GAMES

John H. Kobs, Baseball Coach, 1955, 1959

Fendley A. Collins, Wrestling Coach, 1955

Charles McCaffree Jr., Swimming Coach, 1959

Charles R. Schmitter, Assistant Fencing Coach, 1959; Armorer, Fencing, 1963

Karl A. Schlademan, Assistant Track Manager, 1963

Gayle B. Robinson, Trainer, 1967

William A. Smoke, Canoeing Manager, 1967

James E. Bibbs, Women's Track Coach, 1967.

THE CHESTER L. BREWER AWARD

Awarded annually to a graduating senior for distinguished performance in athletics and scholarship, and for possessing a high degree of character, leadership and personality which forecast a successful career.

1951—Everett Grandelius, football
1952—Robert Carey, football-track
1953—Bert McLachlan, swimming
1954—Tom Yewcic, football-baseball
1955—John Matsock, football-baseball
1956—Earl Morrall, football-baseball
1957—Pat Wilson, football-basketball
1958—David Lean, track
1959—Sam Williams, football
1960—Crawford Kennedy, cross country-track

1961—William Steuart, swimming
1962—Stephen Johnson, gymnastics
1963—George Azar, football-baseball
1964—Sherman Lewis, track-football
1965—Douglas Roberts, hockey-football
1966—Payton Fuller, soccer, and James Curzi, gymnastics
1967—Gary Dilley, swimming
1968—John Bailey, basketball-golf
1969—Toby Towson, gymnastics
1970—Ronald Saul, football

CONFERENCE MEDAL OF HONOR

Awarded annually at each of the Big Ten institutions to the student demonstrating the greatest proficiency in scholarship and athletics.

1951—Everett Grandelius, football
1952—Orris Bender, wrestling
1953—John Wilson, football
1954—Robert Hoke, wrestling
1955—Kevan Gosper, track
1956—Carl Nystrom, football
1957—Selwyn Jones, track
1958—Robert Jasson, hockey
1959—Robert Anderegg, basketball
1960—Stan Tarshis, gymnastics
1961—William Reynolds, track-cross country

1962—Edward Ryan, football
1963—Richard Schloemer, fencing
1964—George (Pete) Gent, basketball
1965—David Price, gymnastics
1966—Steve Juday, football
1967—Eugene Washington, football-track
1968—Dale Anderson, wrestling
1969—Allen Brenner, football
1970—Richard Saul, football

SPARTAN ATHLETIC OFFICIALS

FACULTY REPRESENTATIVES

1949-1953	Lloyd C. Emmons
1953-1955	Edgar L. Harden
1955-1956	Leslie W. Scott
1956-1959	Harold B. Tukey
1959-	John A. Fuzak

ATHLETIC DIRECTORS

1899-1900	Charles O. Bemies
1901-1902	George E. Denman
1903-1910	Chester L. Brewer
1911-1915	John F. Macklin
1916	George E. Gauthier (acting)
1917	Chester L. Brewer
1918	George E. Gauthier (acting)
1919-1921	Chester L. Brewer
1922	Albert M. Barron
1923-1954	Ralph H. Young
1954-	Clarence L. (Biggie) Munn

ATHLETIC PUBLICITY DIRECTORS

1917-1924	Jim Hasselman
1924-1930	Student Directors, incl.: Keith Himebaugh, Ted Smits, Dale Stafford, Will Muller
1930-1944	George Alderton
1944-1948	Nick Kerbawy
1948-	Fred Stabley

BUSINESS MANAGERS

1922-1960	Lyman L. Frimodig
1960-	John G. Laetz

TICKET MANAGERS

1922-1951	Lyman L. Frimodig
1951-1961	Warren F. Burtt
1961-	William M. Beardsley

TRAINERS

1914-1959	John G. Heppinstall
1959-	Gayle B. Robinson

SPARTAN COACHES

BASEBALL

1883-1886	No established coach
1887-1888	Professor Carpenter
1889-1895	No established coach
1896-1898	Robert T. Gale
1899	Ferguson
1900-1901	Charles O. Bemies
1902-1903	George E. Denman
1904-1910	Chester L. Brewer
1911-1915	John E. Macklin
1916-1917	John Morrissey
1918-1920	Chester L. Brewer
1921	George "Potsy" Clark
1922	John Morrissey
1923-1924	Fred M. Walker
1925-1963	John H. Kobs
1964-	Dan Litwhiler

BASKETBALL

1899	No established coach
1900-1901	Charles O. Bemies
1902-1903	George E. Denman
1904-1910	Chester L. Brewer
1911-1916	John F. Macklin
1917-1920	George E. Gauthier
1921-1922	Lyman L. Frimodig
1923-1924	Fred M. Walker
1925-1926	John H. Kobs
1927-1949	Benjamin F. Van Alstyne
1949-1950	Alton S. Kircher
1950-1954	Peter F. Newell
1954-1965	Forrest Anderson
1965-1969	John Benington
1969-	Gus Ganakas

BOXING

1935-1941	Leon E. Burhans
1942-1943	Albert P. Kawal
1944-1945	No team
1946-1947	Louis F. Zarza
1948-1955	George Makris
1956-1958	John Brotzmann

CROSS COUNTRY

1922	Albert M. Barron
1923	Jack Heppinstall
1924	Ralph H. Young

1925-1930 Morton F. Mason
1931-1946 Lauren P. Brown
1947-1957 Karl A. Schlademan
1958-1967 Francis Dittrich
1968- James Gibbard

FENCING
1926-1929 Joseph Waffa
1930-1937 George T. Bauer
1938 Thomas L. Caniff
1939- Charles R. Schmitter

FOOTBALL
1897-1898 Henry Keep
1899-1900 Charles O. Bemies
1901-1902 George Denman
1903-1910 Chester L. Brewer
1911-1915 John F. Macklin
1916 Frank Sommers
1917 Chester L. Brewer
1918 George E. Gauthier
1919 Chester L. Brewer
1920 George "Potsy" Clark
1921-1922 Albert M. Barron
1923-1927 Ralph H. Young
1928 Harry G. Kipke
1929-1932 James H. Crowley
1933-1946 Charles W. Bachman
1947-1953 Clarence L. (Biggie) Munn
1954- Hugh Duffy Daugherty

GOLF
1929 Harry G. Kipke
1930-1931 James H. Crowley
1932-1961 Benjamin F. Van Alstyne
1962-1965 John Brotzmann
1966- Bruce Fossum

GYMNASTICS
1948- George Szypula

HOCKEY
1922-1924 No established coach
1925-1930 John H. Kobs
1931-1949 No team
1950-1951 Harold Paulsen
1952- Amo Bessone

LACROSSE
1969-1970 Robert L. Kauffman

SOCCER
1957-1969 Willard Kenney
1970- Payton Fuller

SWIMMING
1922 S. S. Flynn
1923 Richard H. Rauch
1924-1925 W. B. Jones
1926 R. D. Keifaber
1927-1928 W. Sterry Brown
1929 R. F. Hoercher
1930-1941 Russell B. Daubert
1942-1969 Charles McCaffree Jr.
1970- Richard B. Fetters

TENNIS
1921-1922 H. C. Young
1923-1946 Charles D. Ball, Jr.
1947 Gordon A. Dahlgren
1948-1951 Harris F. Beeman
1952 John Friedrich
1953-1958 Harris F. Beeman
1959- Stanley Drobac

TRACK
1897-1898 Henry Keep
1899 Max Beutner
1900-1901 Charles O. Bemies
1902-1903 George E. Denman
1904-1910 Chester L. Brewer
1911-1913 John F. Macklin
1914 Ion J. Cartright
1915-1916 George E. Gauthier
1917 Howard E. Beatty
1918-1919 George E. Gauthier
1920-1921 Arthur Smith
1922-1923 Albert M. Barron
1924-1940 Ralph H. Young
1941-1958 Karl A. Schlademan
1959- Francis Dittrich

WRESTLING
1922-1923 James H. Devers
1924-1926 Leon D. Burhans
1927-1928 Ralph G. Leonard
1929 Glenn L. Rickes
1930-1962 Fendley A. Collins
1963- Grady J. Peninger

FALL SPORTS

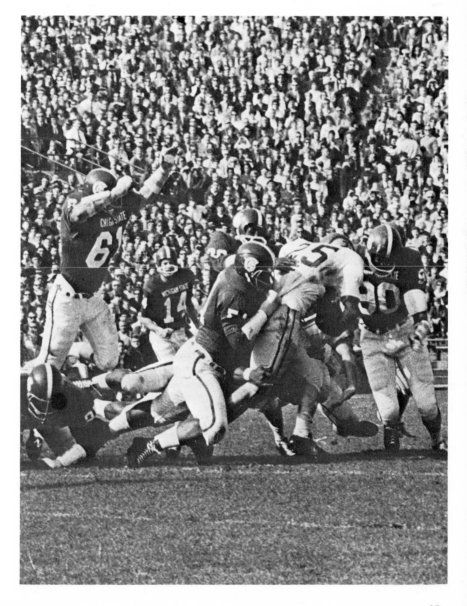

Henry Kennedy loses to Iowa's Deacon Jones in 1955 NCAA championships.

Forddy Kennedy, winner of State's first NCAA cross country individual title.

Clark Chamberlain winning the IC4A cross country title at New York City in 1930.

NCAA cross country trophies went to State in bunches in 1958, as the Spartans copped the team title and also had the individual champ in Forddy Kennedy.

CROSS COUNTRY

Cross country historically has been Michigan State's most successful varsity sport. Eight of State's 14 NCAA team titles and 12 of its 32 Big Ten team crowns have been won in the long distance gallop. Both championship figures easily lead all rival schools in the sport. Spartan units also have captured 12 prestigious IC4A crowns, again a record.

Great individuals are many, but tops have to be the Kennedy brothers, Henry and Forddy. Henry won Big Ten and IC4A titles in 1955 and 1956. Incredibly, Forddy bettered this record with an NCAA title in 1958, three straight IC4A crowns in 1957, 1958 and 1959 and a Big Ten victory in 1959.

Cross country competition at State dates to April 13, 1907, when a meet was held between two teams drawn entirely from the student body. Varsity track aces Roy Waite, the track team captain that year, and Ralph Carr drew the teams by lot. Twenty-seven men started and 25 finished, the Waite-led team winning by the score of 123-177.

The specific course is known. The runners started east from in front of the Armory, on the site of the present Music Building, to the Farm House on Farm Lane. There, they went south across the Farm Lane bridge and then followed the Red Cedar River east to Hagadorn Road. From there, they went north to Grand River Avenue, thence west along Grand River to Bogue Street. At Bogue, they cut southwest through an orchard and campus to the starting point. The course was not measured, but was estimated to be about three miles long. Waite, the winner, made it in 15:30; Carr was second.

The first intercollegiate competition came on April 9, 1910, in the first annual Hope College Invitational at Holland, Mich. A harbinger of great things to come in cross country at State was the team and individual victory scored by MAC athletes that day. Fred Tillotson of MAC won the race in a time of 21:15 for the approximate four miles. The other Aggie team members finished as follows: Charles Perkins, 4th, Arthur Warner, 9th, Robert Rosen, 11th and Horace Geib, 14th. MAC won with 39 points to 58 for Olivet, 71 for Grand Rapids YMCA, 80 for Hope and 89 for Muskegon High School.

The intramural run which started the whole thing became an annual fixture through 1947. It came to have two sections: an all-college run for men who had competed previously and a novice run for freshmen and upperclassmen who had not run in it before.

Things started happening fast after the 1910 cross country debut. Teams were entered in the Detroit YMCA meet which was run on Belle Isle each Decoration Day. In 1914, MAC sponsored the first State Intercollegiate Meet, an annual event

which continued until the 1940s. In the early 1920s, Aggie teams began competing in the annual Big Ten championships. The conference in those days invited outside schools to participate in this and other events.

The arrival in 1920 of Arthur Smith, a former coach at Tufts College, as cross country and track coach gave the sport a big boost. Schedules were enlarged during the 1920s and in the latter half of the decade, four straight Central Collegiate Conference team championships were won under Coach Morton F. Mason. This new athletic conference had just been formed by Athletic Directors Knute Rockne of Notre Dame, Conrad Jennings of Marquette and Ralph H. Young of Michigan State.

The decade of the 1930s was even richer. Lauren Brown, himself a great performer in the late 1920s, came on as head coach and guided Spartan teams to five consecutive IC4A crowns and their first NCAA victory. Karl Schlademan, who had been at State as head track coach since 1941, picked up the reins in 1947 and added six NCAA, seven Big Ten and five IC4A championships before handing the job over to his track assistant, Fran Dittrich. Dittrich and Jim Gibbard, who became head cross country coach in 1968, have continued to give State winning clubs.

The first cross country ace was Fred Tillotson, who won the Hope College Invitational Meets of 1910 and 1911. In 1917, Louis J. Geiermann won MAC's first individual title in the State Intercollegiate Championships. Lauren Brown became State's first Central Collegiate Conference champion in 1927, and Clark Chamberlain broke through for an IC4A title in 1930. Tom Ottey, who won three State Intercollegiate, two IC4A and two Central Collegiate crowns, ran on the United States Olympic team in 1932.

For many years, the course was laid out about like it had been in the first known race in 1907. Later, a course was laid out with the start and finish on Old College Field, and in the late 1950s, the newly completed Forest Akers Golf Course at Harrison and Mt. Hope roads became the site.

Perhaps the best illustration of the kind of power State has been in cross country is the fact that the first 26 NCAA meets held from 1938 through 1964 were run at Michigan State, despite an NCAA policy of moving its championships in all sports to different locales around the country.

SPARTAN CROSS COUNTRY HONOR ROLL

NCAA

Forddy Kennedy	1958	4 miles—20:07.1

IC4A

Clark S. Chamberlain	1930	6 miles—30:19.2
Tom Ottey	1933	6 miles—30:00.0
Tom Ottey	1934	6 miles—31:54.6
J. Edward Bechtold	1935	5 miles—26:23.6
Kenneth Waite	1936	5 miles—26:26.3
Henry Kennedy	1955	5 miles—24:30.3
Henry Kennedy	1956	5 miles—24:01.8
Forddy Kennedy	1957	5 miles—24:14.8
Forddy Kennedy	1958	5 miles—24:21.4
Forddy Kennedy	1959	5 miles—23:51.8

BIG TEN

Henry Kennedy	1955	4 miles—19:06.0
Henry Kennedy	1956	4 miles—20:25.3
Forddy Kennedy	1959	4 miles—20:12.3
Jerry Young	1960	4 miles—19:35.3

CENTRAL COLLEGIATE CONFERENCE CHAMPIONSHIPS

Lauren P. Brown	1927	5 miles—25:45.7
Lauren P. Brown	1929	5 miles—25:35.8
Clark S. Chamberlain	1930	5 miles—22:56.3
Clark S. Chamberlain	1931	5 miles—21:31.0
Thomas C. Ottey	1932	5 miles—25:20.2
Thomas C. Ottey	1933	5 miles—25:59.1

STATE INTERCOLLEGIATE CHAMPIONSHIPS

Louis J. Geireman	1917	3½ miles—19:29.4		Kenneth A. Waite	1936	4 Miles—20:41.2
Lloyd M. Thurston	1920	4 miles—24:25.0		Kenneth A. Waite	1937	4 miles—21:16.4
Thomas Ottey	1932	25:20.2		Richard D. Frey	1938	4 miles—21:32.9
Thomas Ottey	1933	4 miles—22:28.0		Roy B. Fehr	1939	4 miles—20:59.5
Thomas C. Ottey	1934			William J. Scott	1942	4 miles—21:40.0
Edward J. Bechtold	1935	4 miles—21:01.8		Walter C. Mack	1945	

SPARTAN TEAM RECORDS

RECORD BY SEASON

Year	W	L	T	Big Ten	IC4A	NCAA
1910	1	0	0			
1912	1	0	0			
1920	1	0	0			
1921	1	0	0			
1922	1	1	0			
1923	0	2	0			
1924	1	2	0			
1925	1	2	0			
1926	0	3	0			
1927	3	0	0			
1928	3	0	0			
1929	3	0	0		2nd	
1930	1	2	0			
1931	2	1	0			
1932	3	0	0		4th	
1933	3	0	0		1st (54 pts.)	
1934	3	0	0		1st (77 pts.)	
1935	2	1	0		1st (30 pts.)	
1936	2	1	0		1st (46 pts.)	
1937	1	1	0		1st (59 pts.)	
1938	3	0	0			4th
1939	2	1	0			1st (54 pts.)
1940	2	1	0			4th
1941	2	1	0			5th
1942	1	2	0			4th
1943						No Meet Held
1944	2	2	0			5th
1945	1	3	0			6th
1946	1	1	0			6th
1947	2	1	0			7th
1948	2	0	1		5th	1st (41 pts.)
1949	2	0	0		1st (51 pts.)	1st (59 pts.)
1950	2	1	0	2nd	3rd	2nd
1951	2	2	0	1st (49 pts.)	4th	5th
1952	1	1	0	1st (28 pts.)	4th	1st (65 pts.)
1953	1	2	0	1st (39 pts.)	1st (39 pts.)	6th
1954	1	2	0	2nd	10th	10th
1955	3	1	0	1st (36 pts.)	2nd	1st (46 pts.)

Typical scene at an NCAA cross country championship meet as hundreds of runners break with the starter's gun. State was host of the event from 1938 through 1964.

1956	4	0	0	1st (21 pts.)	1st (34 pts.)	1st (28 pts.)
1957	3	0	0	1st (43 pts.)	1st (84 pts.)	2nd
1958	1	1	0	1st (43 pts.)	1st (76 pts.)	1st (79 pts.)
1959	2	1	0	1st (17 pts.)	1st (50 pts.)	1st (44 pts.)
1960	1	1	0	1st (30 pts.)	3rd	2nd
1961	3	1	0	2nd	1st (82 pts.)	9th
1962	1	2	0	1st (39 pts.)	2nd	5th
1963	2	1	0	1st (46 pts.)	3rd	5th
1964	4	1	0	2nd	4th	16th
1965	2	3	0	2nd	6th	15th
1966	4	1	0	2nd	3rd	12th
1967	1	4	0	8th	6th	Did not compete
1968	7	0	0	1st (70 pts.)	4th	12th
1969	5	1	0	4th	Did not compete	Did not compete
	103	54	1			

RECORD BY OPPONENT

	W	L	T				
				Michigan	6	6	0
				Minnesota	2	4	0
Air Force	2	0	0	Northern Illinois	1	0	0
Alma	1	0	0	Notre Dame	22	12	0
Butler	10	0	0	Ohio State	3	3	0
Central Michigan	2	0	0	Olivet	1	0	0
Drake	2	2	0	Penn State	12	8	0
Eastern Michigan	4	0	0	Pittsburgh	5	0	0
Indiana	7	9	0	Purdue	4	0	0
Iowa	1	0	0	Wayne State	3	0	0
Marquette	4	1	0	Western Michigan	0	3	0
Miami	2	0	0	Wisconsin	9	6	1

SPARTAN COACHES' RECORD

Coach	Years	W	L	T	Pct.
Brewer, Chester L.	1910	1	0	0	1.000
Macklin, John F.	1911-1913	1	0	0	1.000
Smith, Arthur N.	1920-1921	2	0	0	1.000
Willoughby, Theodore C.	1922	1	1	0	.500
Heppinstall, John G.	1923	0	2	0	.000
Young, Ralph H.	1924	1	2	0	.333
Mason, Morton F.	1925-1930	11	7	0	.611
Brown, Lauren P.	1931-1946	30	15	0	.667
Schlademan, Karl A.	1947-1958	24	11	1	.700
Dittrich, Francis C.	1959-1967	20	15	0	.588
Gibbard, James	1968	12	1	0	.923
		103	54	1	.662

SPARTAN TOURNAMENT RECORDS

Hope Invitational Cross Country Meet

1910 First
1911 Second

Champions

		Time
1910	Tillotson, Fred H.	21:05
1911	Tillotson, Fred H.	21:05

State Intercollegiate Championships

1916 Third
1917 First
1918
1919 First
1920 First
1921 Second
1922 Fifth
1923 Did not enter
1924 Did not enter
1925 Did not enter
1926 Did not enter
1927 Did not enter
1928 Did not enter
1929 Did not enter
1930 Did not enter
1931 Did not enter
1932 Did not enter
1933 First
1934 First
1935 First
1936 First
1937 First
1938 First
1939 First
1940 First
1941 First
1942 First
1943 Not held
1944 Not held
1945 Sixth

Central Collegiate Conference Championships

1926	First	1933	First
1927	First	1934	Second
1928	First	1935	First
1929	First	1936	Third
1930	Second	1937	Second
1931	Third	1948	Fourth
1932	First	1949	Fourth

FOOTBALL

Much is made of the humble origins of great people and things—Abraham Lincoln in a cabin, the air age on a North Carolina sand dune and the atomic age under an abandoned football stands in Chicago, for a few grand examples. Add Michigan State football to the list.

Records of the sport at Michigan Agricultural College date back to 1884, just 15 years after the first collegiate contest had been staged between Rutgers and Princeton. But the sport was on such tenuous footing—frowned on by the administration, haphazardly scheduled and amateurishly, if at all, coached—that it was 1896 before it became established enough to be considered a regular sport.

The 1884 team played no games for some reason lost in time, but did have its picture taken. The coach was Prof. Rolla Carpenter, instructor in mathematics and civil engineering.

Team members, positions unknown, were: Rolla Coryell, Clarence Gillette, Edward Bartmess, William Sanson, Dorry Stryker, James Towar, George Morrice, Wilbur Power, Edward Bank, Richard Edling and Colon Lillie.

The 1886 team actually played two games as part of field day activities, but possibly wished it hadn't. Albion walloped it 79-0 and Olivet followed suit 78-0.

The first team for which personnel by positions could be found was the 1888 club. It apparently played no games and may have been organized for the express purpose of having its picture taken.

The personnel of this 1888 team was as follows: quarterback, Paul Woodworth; goal keeper, Robert Stanley; halfback, Glenn Perrigo; halfback, Frederick Stockwell; snapback, Langdon Burritt; rushers, John Stafford, Lemuel Churchill, Ernest Lodeman, Henry Thurtell, Alfred Marhoff and Paul Chapman.

There were reports of a few other games in ensuing years, most of which the Aggies lost, leading up to its first recognized season of 1896. Even then, there was no official coach, but the Aggies of 1896 played a four-game schedule. They lost to Kalamazoo College twice, tied Alma College and beat Lansing High School 10-0. It's a long way from that to the national championships of the 1950s and 1960s, Rose Bowl glory and more than 40 All-American players.

Henry Keep, a senior in mechanical engineering, was hired by the Athletic Association the following year to coach the Aggie gridders because he had done such a good job training the track team. He didn't do too badly at football, either, coaching the 1897 club to a 4-2-1 card and the 1898 club to 4-3.

Then some vigorous spadework by L. Whitney Watkins ('93) paid off. As a student, Watkins had been interested in baseball and boxing. As a member of the State Board of Agriculture, governing body of the college, to which he had been

appointed by Governor Hazen Pingree in 1895 to fill a vacancy, he campaigned for the appointment of a full-time professional coach.

He encountered much dissent, but, finally, with cooperation of President J. L. Snyder, a staunch sports fan, he carried the day. President Snyder's strategic coup was the suggestion that the Rev. Charles O. Bemies, a graduate of Western Theological Seminary, be hired to be the first head of the department of physical culture and also to assume leadership in morning chapel prior to the students' 6 a.m. breakfast. This masterstroke overcame board members' charges about the lack of respectability and possible immorality of the sport and helped Watkins slip on the mantle of "father of athletics" at Michigan State University.

The first great football era came under Chester Brewer, who racked up a formidable record of 54 wins, 10 losses and six ties in an eight-year period from 1903 to 1910. His winning percentage skidded from .814 in that span when he returned to two poor seasons in 1917 and 1919. Even so, he gets the credit for establishing the winning tradition at State.

Brewer's teams never were able to beat arch-rival Michigan, however. The best they could do was a 0-0 tie in 1908. This honor awaited John Macklin, who succeeded Brewer in 1911 and outdid Brewer's record in five brilliant seasons in which his record was 29-5. State's first All-Americans came along in Macklin's reign: Faunt Lenardson, Hugh Blacklock, Neno Jerry DaPrato and Blake Miller.

This is not to say that there weren't some outstanding men in Brewer's day. Such players as Ernest Baldwin, Ion Cortwright, Leon Exelby, James Campbell, Leon Hill, Parnell McKenna and Bert Shedd were victims of MAC's lack of prestige and the selectors' preoccupation with the Ivy League when naming All-Americans.

Other great ones of Macklin's time were Lyman Frimodig, the only 10-letterman in State's history, Gideon Smith, possibly the first Negro ever to play major college football anywhere and the first of his race in Michigan State athletics, Carp Julian, Chester Gifford, George Gauthier and Ralph Henning.

Milestone victories of the Brewer and Macklin eras included a 10-0 conquest of Marquette in 1909, a success which might be considered the first over a major team in the Aggies' brief gridiron history. The next year came an even tastier one, a 17-0 victory over Notre Dame, a team which previously had bashed the Aggies eight straight times.

Big moments during Macklin's regime were conquests of Michigan in 1913, the first ever, and 1915, plus decisions over Ohio State, Wisconsin and Penn State. The old Aggies were, indeed, putting on their go-to-town clothes.

But after Macklin, Aggie fortunes fell off abruptly. There were only three winning seasons in the next 13 years, and those were modest ones of 4-2-1 in 1916, 4-3 in 1918 and 5-3 in 1924. There were a few precious moments of glory, but mostly it was a matter of defeating the little fellows and losing to the big ones. The composite record in those 13 seasons was 43-60-6.

Major victories were scored over Notre Dame in 1918, Detroit in 1922, Centre College in 1926, when it was big time, and North Carolina State in 1929. Not much to show for 13 seasons.

Various reasons are proffered for this decline. There was a new head coach in

each of six straight seasons from 1916 through 1921, certainly indicating considerable instability. Little MAC drew no big military training programs with resultant influx of fine athletes during World War I, and the loss in program and facilities development wasn't overcome for years. The Aggies, or Spartans, which they became in 1926, had outgrown their old natural rivals from the Michigan Intercollegiate Athletic Association (MIAA), but hadn't caught up to the big powers. The truth might well be a composite of these and other reasons.

Whatever the cause, State didn't hit the victory highway again until Jim Crowley, one of the immortal Four Horsemen of Notre Dame, came on the scene in 1929. Schedules quickly became major—the MIAA schools disappeared entirely after 74-0 and 93-0 smashings of Alma in 1931 and 1932—and the Spartans found themselves capable of winning consistently against first-class foes.

Reasons advanced for this resurgence are as varied and unprovable as those for the decline after World War I. Ralph Young, who had begun his 31-year athletic directorship in 1923, had laid the groundwork well for the Spartans' great all-around program of later years, and football was one of the first to benefit. Crowley was an excellent coach and crack recruiter who benefitted greatly in the latter regard from his Notre Dame connections. State had completed its adolescence and had emerged from the awkward years as a school ready for athletic greatness. Probably all of these and other factors played a part.

Crowley's teams produced four fine winning seasons before he went to Fordham as head coach, and Charley Bachman took over. Victories were achieved over such headliners as Colgate, Syracuse, Georgetown, Detroit and Fordham. Perhaps more significant were two straight 0-0 ties with Michigan in 1930 and 1931, snapping a string of 14 straight Wolverine victories. Stars of the Crowley era included Bobby Monnett, Abe Eliowitz, Art Buss, Ed Klewicki and Roger Grove.

Bachman, like Crowley, a Notre Dame great, picked up the victory trail at once. His first six teams were winners, capped by the 1934 through 1937 clubs which compiled a 28-6-2 mark and beat Michigan four straight. An Orange Bowl bid, State's first post-season invitation, resulted. State lost 6-0 to Auburn. Guard Sid Wagner and halfback John Pingel made All-American, being the first so honored since Macklin's day. Al Agett became State's first All-Star bowl game participant with a stint in the College All-Star Game in Chicago. Most Valuable Player Award winners were Ed Klewicki, Sid Wagner, Sam Ketchman, Harry Speelman, John Pingel and Lyle Rockenbach. Bachman, himself, was honored by being elected a College All-Star Game coach. Two present-day distinguished Michigan State faculty members, Arthur Brandstatter and Dr. Howard Zindel, were top performers. Kurt Warmbein and Frank Gaines were other outstanding players.

Bachman's final seven teams, 1939-46, with 1943 out because of the war, had more modest records. State once again did not have the huge military training programs that some schools enjoyed, but there was enough manpower to escape losing seasons in all but one year. The 1944 season, in which Tom Sullivan was captain and Jack Breslin was elected most valuable player by his teammates, posted an excellent 6-1 card. Breslin, later to rise to executive vice president of the University and secretary to the Board of Trustees, played in three post-season

All-Star games: the 1946 College All-Star Game and the 1945 and 1946 East-West Shrine games. End Frank Brogger also played in the 1945 East-West Game.

Clarence (Biggie) Munn, twice All-American at the University of Minnesota and already a college assistant and head coach of 16 years experience, succeeded Bachman in 1947. He found a nucleus of fine young players awaiting him and immediately set course on the winningest football era in the school's history. Before stepping up to athletic director after the 1953 campaign, he coached seven seasons, a span in which his teams won 54, lost nine and tied two for a fabulous .857 winning percentage. His teams, individual athletes and he, himself, scaled the absolute heights of the game.

Among the more glamorous achievements were these:

The 1952 team was declared national champion. The 1951 ensemble was ranked second and the 1953 club third. These three and the 1950 club collaborated on a 28-game winning streak, one of the longest in college football annals. The 1953 club, State's first in Big Ten play, tied with Illinois for the conference title, was named to represent the conference in the Rose Bowl and went on to beat UCLA 28-20 in one of the greatest games ever played in the granddaddy of bowls.

A rare accomplishment of this period was the three-year football captaincy, 1946-48, of Bob McCurry. So far as can be determined, this is without parallel in major college football circles nationally.

One of Biggie's greatest attributes as a head coach was his ability to pick outstanding assistants. In his short tenure as head coach, he had these aides who went on to become college head grid coaches: Duffy Daugherty, Red Dawson, Dan Devine, Earle Edwards, Forest Evashevski, Al Kircher, George Makris, Steve Sebo, Kip Taylor and Lou Zarza.

Individual stars were as plentiful as ducks on the Red Cedar. Seventeen attained first-team All-American ratings. Their names comprise a Who's Who of the Munn era in Michigan State football: Lynn Chandnois, Don Mason and Ed Bagdon in 1949, Dorne Dibble and Sonny Grandelius in 1950, Bob Carey, Don Coleman, Al Dorow and Jim Ellis in 1951, Frank Kush, Don McAuliffe, Dick Tamburo, Ellis Duckett, Tom Yewcic and Jim Ellis again in 1952, and Don Dohoney, LeRoy Bolden and Larry Fowler in 1953. Bagdon won the 1949 Outland Trophy as lineman of the year. McAuliffe won the 1952 Walter Camp Trophy as back of the year. Dohoney and Bolden were All-Big Ten in 1953. Billy Wells was named outstanding player of the 1954 Rose Bowl game. More than twoscore other bowl game appearances were made by individual Spartans.

Biggie was named 1952 Coach of the Year and coached the East teams in the 1952 and 1953 East-West Shrine games. For his great career, he has subsequently received many honors, including entrance into the National Football Hall of Fame as a coach (they gave him his choice of going in as player or coach, a rare honor), Michigan Sports Hall of Fame and SPORTS ILLUSTRATED's "Silver Anniversary All-America."

Following such an act with any degree of success would seem to be a thankless, hopeless task, but Duffy Daugherty managed it.

When Munn moved up to succeed Ralph Young as athletic director, Daugherty

slid easily into the head coaching chair with Biggie's advocacy and support. There was no other candidate in the picture but the ex-Syracuse guard whom Biggie had coached while line coach there and had brought along with him to State in 1947 as his own line coach.

It took Duffy a year to get started. The personnel losses from the great 1953 team had been severe and Duffy's first team floundered to a 3-6 record. Then he put together three big ones which stamped the smiling Scotch-Irishman as a fitting successor to Munn. The 1955 team rated second nationally, finished second in the Big Ten, was named to represent the league in the Rose Bowl and beat UCLA 17-14 in another New Year's Day classic. It produced four first-team All-Americans, four All-Big Ten selections and Coach of the Year honors nationally for Duffy, himself. The four All-Big Tenners and All-Americans were Earl Morrall, Norm Masters, Buck Nystrom and Jerry Planutis.

The 1956 club might have become one of the greatest teams State ever had if it had not run afoul of a horrendous string of injuries climaxed by the loss of backfield ace Clarence Peaks in mid-season. It still wound up 7-2 and 10th nationally. The 1957 team came even closer to perpetual glory when it went 8-1 and finished second in the Big Ten and third nationally. One erroneous official's decision—not a judgment call, but a clear and later-admitted rule misapplication on a Spartan touchdown play—probably cost State the Purdue game and with it the Big Ten and national championships and Rose Bowl bid.

There followed some mediocre teams like the 3-5-1 club of 1958 and the 4-5 aggregation of 1964, as well as some strong ones like the 6-2-1 teams of 1960 and 1963 and the 7-2 club of 1961. Even the 1959 team, which finished 5-4, missed the Big Ten title by just half a game. The 1961 and 1963 teams each rated 9th nationally. And, indicative of the esteem in which Spartan teams were being held by the nation's coaches, the 1964 team was rated 20th in the land on the coaches' selection for United Press International despite its 4-5 record. It may be the only time in the era of football polls that a losing team made the nation's top 20.

This period wasn't without its great players. Eighteen received All-Big Ten recognition. Nine making major first-team All-American selections were Walt Kowalczyk and Dan Currie in 1957, Sam Williams in 1958, Dean Look in 1959, Dave Behrman in 1961, George Saimes and Ed Budde in 1962, and Sherman Lewis and Earl Lattimer in 1963.

The coaches who regarded the 1964 team so highly must have known something. Their judgment was vindicated when, in 1965, the Spartans spurted back to the pinnacle of college football with a 10-0 slate, another national championship via UPI and the Rose Bowl bid. A 14-12 upset at the hands of UCLA, a team which the Spartans had beaten rather handily 13-3 in the regular season opener, knocked off a bit of luster, but not much. Eight players made All-Big Ten and eight attained first-team All-American recognition on one or more major selections. Duffy was named Coach of the Year for the second time. All-Americans were Bob Apisa, Ron Goovert, Clinton Jones, Steve Juday, Harold Lucas, Bubba Smith, Gene Washington and George Webster.

More of the same was the order in 1966. Powered by five All-American returnees

from the previous fall, State roared almost without breathing hard through nine games. Only Ohio State died hard, losing 11-8 in a rain-drenched heart-stopper at Columbus.

Then came Armageddon! Notre Dame, also unbeaten, just as highly touted, loaded with tremendous stars, rated No. 1 nationally to State's No. 2 as a result of the Spartans' near stumble at Columbus, and eager for its first national championship since 1949, came to town. So did national television, the largest press assemblage—745 people—ever to cover a college game and an all-time Spartan Stadium record crowd of 80,011. The game ended in a 10-10 tie and will be a classic bull session subject as long as football is played. The tie kept Notre Dame No. 1 and State No. 2, although Spartan loyalists never will buy that in view of the way the Irish elected to run out the clock in the dying minutes. The confrontation started as the NCAA "Game of the Week" on television, but as its national significance mounted, so did the hyperbolas. It became successively the "Game of the Year," "Game of the Decade," "Game of the Century," "Greatest Game in History" and "Game of the Galaxy."

Once again, honors came thick and fast. Incredibly, 11 men—Bubba Smith, Clinton Jones, Gene Washington, George Webster, Bob Apisa, Jerry West, Jess Phillips, Nick Jordan, Tony Conti, Charles Thornhill and Dick Kenney—were named to the two-platoon All-Big Ten team. Six of them—Apisa, Jones, Smith, Washington, Webster and West—were named to one or more first-string All-American teams.

Virtually all top stars of the 1965 and 1966 teams completed their college play and the 1967 team suffered the consequences. It also was hit by a staggering injury toll. The result was a 3-7 season, the poorest since the 0-9 record of 1919. The 1968 team moved up to 5-5 and things appeared promising for the future. The five losses were by a total of 31 points and the team was a young one.

But there was not to be an immediate rebound. The 1969 team, hit by a horrendous injury avalanche, staggered to a 4-6 record. Twenty athletes were still on trainer Gayle Robinson's special rehabilitation list during 1970 spring drills.

One of the few happy developments of this low period was that two men achieved first-team All-America recognition: Al Brenner in 1968 and Ron Saul in 1969.

Duffy, too, proved to have the knack of picking and developing fine assistants. From 1954 through 1969, these men worked under him and went on to head jobs of their own in college and pro ranks: Lou Agase, Dan Boisture, Vince Carillot, Bob Devaney, Dan Devine, Sonny Grandelius, John McVay, Cal Stoll, Doug Weaver and Bill Yeoman.

Michigan State has played home football games on three campus sites and used at least one off-campus location prior to the development of the first on-campus athletic field. Football was one of the events at popular field days in the 1880s which brought together several Michigan colleges for day-long activity in track, gymnastics and various games. The Lansing Race Track, a horse racing oval on the south side of Michigan Avenue between Lansing and East Lansing about where the Red Cedar Golf Course is now located, was the setting for some of these early

sports carnivals. So recorded games of football in the mid-1880s probably were played there. Other Lansing area sites may have been used at times, too.

The first on-campus football field and running track were laid out in 1892. They were located in the area now encompassed by Circle Drive and occupied by the Music Building, band drill field and women's physical education field. Baseball had been played there even earlier. There were no stands for spectators.

Thirteen acres of farmland were purchased by the State Board of Agriculture in 1900 and developed into what today is Old College Field. It was first used for athletic activities in 1902. Football continued there until 1923. Wooden stands were built, including one covered section holding about 250-300 people and located approximately along the present third base line of the John Kobs baseball diamond. Permanent and knockdown bleachers were added periodically until for the Michigan game of 1914, a crowd of 4,000 could be accommodated.

Football moved to its present Spartan Stadium location in 1923. That marked the end of a nine-hole campus golf course which lay along the south bank of the Red Cedar river and occupied an area in which are now located the stadium, Men's Intramural Building, Demonstration Hall, Jenison Gymnasium and Field House, the ROTC drill field, Spartan Statue and stadium parking lot. The course had been built in 1919. Not until the Forest Akers course was opened in 1958 did the school again own and operate its own golf facility.

The original stadium stands held 14,000 people and contained the quarter-mile varsity running track. The track was removed in 1935, the field level lowered and stands added to increase its capacity to 26,000. At this stage, it was christened Macklin Field. The next enlargement came in 1948, with the seating capacity zooming to 51,000. This development involved closing the end zones with high stands and raising the sideline stands to their present 66 rows. Construction projects in 1956 and 1957 resulted in the present double-decked 76,000-capacity stadium, one of the biggest and finest in the land. It also was renamed Spartan Stadium. Overflow crowds as large as 80,011 for the 1966 Notre Dame game and 78,833 for the Michigan game the same year have been accommodated.

Although no immediate plans are afoot, additional stands construction could raise the seating capacity to about 106,000 people. This would involve double-decking all the way around the stadium.

Synthetic Tartan Turf was installed in Spartan Stadium prior to the 1969 season at a cost of approximately $250,000. Because of its durable, practically indestructible nature, all varsity football practice sessions now were held in the stadium and a variety of other activities—varsity lacrosse games, baseball practices when the varsity field was unusable due to bad weather, even girls' touch football games—moved in, too.

SPARTAN FOOTBALL HONOR ROLL

ALL-AMERICA
(List includes first, second and third team selections)
(First team selections marked by *)

1913	Faunt V. Lenardson - Guard - GR
1915	*Neno J. DaPrato - Fullback - INS, DT
	*W. Blake Miller - End - AC
1916	Hugh M. Blacklock - Tackle - CTE
1933	Arthur Buss - Tackle - AP, CM
1935	*Sidney P. Wagner - Tackle - INS, HS, LM, UP, NYS
1937	John S. Pingel - Halfback - AP
1938	*John S. Pingel - Halfback - HS, CP, NEA, LM, AP
1939	William L. Batchelor - Center - HS
1948	Donald L. Mason - Guard - AP
	Warren B. Huey - End - LkM
1949	*Lynn E. Chandnois - Halfback - NYN, UP, NEA, CP, FN, CM, CTAP, SN, LkM, RTVG
	*Donald L. Mason - Guard - PN, FN, AP, CTAP, LkM, SN
	*Edward Bagdon - Guard - LkM, UP, SN, NYN, CP, NEA, TN
1950	Robert W. Carey - End - UP
	*Everett Grandelius - Halfback - AP, INS, CTAD
	*Dorne A. Dibble - End - LkM
1951	*Robert W. Carey - End - NYN, AFCA, UP, AP, SN, NEA
	*Don E. Coleman - Tackle - AP, UP, CM, LkM, SN, NYN, FN, NEA, CP, TN, INS, CTAP, AFCA
	*Albert R. Dorow - Quarterback - INS
	*James Ellis - Halfback - CTAP
1952	*Ellis Duckett - End - NBC-TV, TN
	*Thomas Yewcic - Quarterback - NBC-TV, TN
	*Richard P. Tamburo - Center - AP, CP, NEA, INS, NYN, FD, PN, APb, SN
	*Donald F. McAuliffe - Halfback - UP, CM, FD, PN, SN
	*Frank J. Kush - Guard - UP, LkM, NYN, FM, APb, SN, CTAP, NBC-TV, TN
	*James Ellis - Halfback - CTAP
1953	*Donald C. Dohoney - End - AP, UP, CM, LkM, SN, FN, NEA, CP, NBC-TV, CTAP
	*LeRoy Bolden - Halfback - UP, CTAP, SN, NBC-TV
	*Larry D. Fowler - Guard - NBC-TV
1955	*Earl E. Morrall - Quarterback - AP, CM, LkM, INS, SN, PN, NBC-TV, CP, HS
	*Norman D. Masters - Tackle - UP, LkM, AP, NEA, INS, NBC-TV, CP, FM, NYN
	*Carl W. Nystrom - Guard - RTVG, FLN
	*Gerald R. Planutis - Fullback - JM
1956	Clarence E. Peaks - Halfback - SN
	John Matsko - Center - UP, SN, CP
1957	*Walter J. Kowalczyk - Halfback - FWA, SN, NEA, UP, CP, AFCA, NBC-TV, FD, AP
	*Daniel G. Currie - Center - FWA, AP, INS, AFCA, NBC-TV, CP, UP
	David Kaiser - End - SN, FD
1958	*Samuel F. Williams - End - UPI, AFCA, NYN, TM, CP, SN
1959	*Dean Z. Look - Quarterback - FWA, FN, UPI, FD, NEA
1961	*David W. Behrman - Guard - AP, FWA, SN
	George Saimes - Fullback - SN
1962	David W. Behrman - Guard - SN
	*George Saimes - Fullback - SN, AP, UPI, FWA, AFCA, NYN, CBC-TV
	*Edward L. Budde - Guard - TM
1963	*Sherman P. Lewis - Halfback - AP, UPI, CP, FWA, NYN, NEA
	*Earl P. Lattimer - Guard - NYN
1965	*Robert Apisa - Fullback - FN
	*Ronald E. Goovert - Linebacker - FWA
	*Clinton Jones - Halfback - FWA
	*Stephen A. Juday - Quarterback - AP
	*Harold W. Lucas - Middleguard - NEA
	*Charles A. Smith - End - NEA, UPI
	*Eugene Washington - End - CP, FN, FD
	*George Webster - Roverback - AP, UPI, AFCA, NEA, SN, FN, NYN
1966	*Robert Apisa - Fullback - FN, NYN
	*Clinton Jones - Halfback - AP, CP, NEA, SN
	*Charles A. Smith - End - AP, AFCA, UPI, FWA, NEA, SN, CP, FN, NYN
	Charles E. Thornhill - Linebacker - AP, AFCA, UPI
	*George Webster - Roverback - AP, AFCA, UPI, FWA, NEA, SN, CP, FN, NYN
	*Eugene Washington - End - UPI, AFCA, SN
	*Jerry West - Tackle - NEA
1968	Charles A. Bailey - Tackle - CP
	*Allen R. Brenner - End-Safety AFCA, NEA
	Richard R. Saul - Linebacker - CP
1969	*Ronald Saul - Offensive Guard - NEA, SN, TM

Note - Early in the century the recognized All-America selections were made by Walter Camp. Michigan State never had a player in this group. However, George "Carp" Julian showed Lyman

Frimodig a letter from Camp indicating that Julian was considered in 1914 but was passed over because at that time Michigan State allowed freshmen to play on the varsity. In 1917, Hugh Blacklock was selected by Camp on the second team All-Service All America while playing for the Great Lakes Naval Training Station team. He had completed his varsity competition at MSU in 1916.

KEY ABBREVIATIONS

		FLN	Frank Leahy (Notre Dame)
		GR	Grantland Rice
AAB	All-America Board	HS	Hearst Syndicate
AFCA	American Football Coaches Association	INS	International News Service
		JM	Jet Magazine
AP	Associated Press	LM	Liberty Magazine
APb	Athletic Publications	LkM	Look Magazine
AC	Atlanta Constitution	NBC-TV	National Broadcasting - TV
CP	Central Press	NEA	Newspapers Enterprise Association
CTE	Chicago Tribune (Eckersall)		
CTAP	Chicago Tribune All-Players	NYN	New York News
CM	Collier's Magazine	PN	Paramount News
CBS-TV	Columbia Broadcasting - TV	RTVG	Radio TV Guide
DT	Detroit Times	SN	Sporting News
FD	Football Digest	TN	Television News
FN	Football News	TM	Time Magazine
FWA	Football Writer's Association	UP	United Press
FM	Fox Movietone	UPI	United Press International

The four military teams in Michigan State's campus league pass in review in November of 1943, a year that saw all varsity activity halted because of the war.

43

ALL-WESTERN
(Name changed to All-Mid-Western in the thirties)

List includes first, second, third and honorable mention selections

1910 Leon C. Exelby - Fullback - Fielding Yost (Michigan), Chicago Tribune (Eckersall)
   Ernest W. Baldwin - Guard - Chicago Tribune (Eckersall)
   Leon J. Hill - Halfback - Chicago Tribune (Eckersall)
   James F. Campbell - Tackle - Chicago Tribune (Eckersall)
1913 W. Blake Miller - End - Chicago Record-Herald, Collier's Magazine
   Faunt V. Lenardson - Guard - Chicago Tribune (Eckersall)
   Ralph B. Henning - End - Chicago Tribune (Eckersall)
   Chester W. Gifford - Tackle - Chicago Tribune (Eckersall)
   George E. Julian - Fullback - Chicago Tribune (Eckersall), Collier's Magazine
   Gideon E. Smith - Tackle - Collier's Magazine
1914 George E. Julian - Fullback - Chicago Tribune (Eckersall), Detroit Journal
   W. Blake Miller - End - Chicago Tribune (Eckersall), Detroit Journal
1915 Gideon E. Smith - Tackle - Chicago Daily News
   Neno J. DaPrato - Fullback - International News Service
1916 Hugh M. Blacklock - Tackle - Chicago Tribune (Eckersall), Chicago Journal
1920 John H. Hammes - Fullback - Chicago Tribune (Eckersall)
1937 Frederick A. Schroeder - Guard - Newspapers Enterprise Association
   Carl W. Nelson - End - Newspapers Enterprise Association
   John S. Pingel - Halfback - Newspapers Enterprise Association
1938 John S. Pingel - Halfback - New York News
1950 Robert W. Carey - End - New York News, Chicago Tribune All-Players
   Don E. Coleman - Tackle - United Press
   Everett Grandelius - Halfback - Associated Press, United Press, Chicago Tribune All-Players
1951 Don E. Coleman - Tackle - Chicago Tribune All-Players
   James Ellis - Halfback - Chicago Tribune All-Players
   Robert W. Carey - End - Chicago Tribune All-Players
   Vincent F. Pisano - Halfback - Chicago Tribune All-Players
1952 Paul N. Dekker - End - Associated Press
   Edwin E. Luke - End - Associated Press
   Richard P. Tamburo - Center - Associated Press
   Frank J. Kush - Guard - Associated Press
   James Ellis - Halfback - Associated Press
1953 LeRoy Bolden - Halfback - New York News
1955 Earl Morrall - Quarterback - New York News
   Norman Masters - Tackle - New York News

ALL-BIG 10
List includes first, second, third and honorable mention selections
(* - First Team Selection)

1953	*Donald C. Dohoney	- End
	*LeRoy Bolden	- Back
	Ellis Duckett	- End
	Henry C. Bullough	- Guard
	Ferris E. Hallmark	- Guard
	James E. Neale	- Center
	Thomas Yewcic	- Quarterback
	Evan J. Slonac	- Fullback
	William P. Wells	- Back
1954	Randall P. Schrecengost	- Tackle
	Henry C. Bullough	- Guard
	John J. Matsock	- Back
	LeRoy Bolden	- Back
1955	*Norman D. Masters	- Tackle
	*Earl E. Morrall	- Quarterback
	*Carl W. Nystrom	- Guard
	*Gerald R. Planutis	- Fullback
	David Kaiser	- End
	John R. Lewis	- End
	Patrick F. Burke	- Tackle
	Joseph H. Badaczewski	- Center
	Walter J. Kowalczyk	- Back
	Clarence E. Peaks	- Back
1956	Joel Jones	- End
	Daniel G. Currie	- Guard
	John Matsko	- Center
	Anthony M. Kolodziej	- End
	Patrick F. Burke	- Tackle
	Dennis A. Mendyk	- Back
	Walter J. Kowalczyk	- Back
	Donald D. Gilbert	- Fullback
1957	*Samuel F. Williams	- End
	*Patrick F. Burke	- Tackle
	*Ellison L. Kelly	- Guard
	*Daniel G. Currie	- Center
	*James Ninowski	- Quarterback
	*Walter J. Kowalczyk	- Back
	David Kaiser	- End
	Francis J. O'Brien	- Guard
	Blanche Martin	- Fullback
1958	*Samuel F. Williams	- End
	*Ellison L. Kelly	- Guard
	Dean Z. Look	- Back
1959	*Dean Z. Look	- Quarterback
	Frederick V. Arbanas	- End
	William P. Pyle	- Tackle
	Donald M. Wright	- Center
	David F. Manders	- Center
	Larry L. Cundiff	- Tackle
	Herbert A. Adderley	- Back
	Gary Ballman	- Back
1960	*Herbert A. Adderley	- Back
	Frederick V. Arbanas	- End
	Frederick J. Boylen	- Guard
	David W. Behrman	- Guard
	Gary J. Ballman	- Back
1961	*David W. Behrman	- Tackle
	*George Saimes	- Fullback
	Sherman P. Lewis	- Back
	Arthur F. Brandstatter Jr.	- End
	Charles E. Brown	- Guard

	Edward L. Budde	- Guard
	Anthony L. Kumiega	- Guard
	Dewey R. Lincoln	- Back
1962	*David W. Behrman	- Center
	*George Saimes	- Fullback
	H. Matthew Snorton	- End
	Sherman P. Lewis	- Back
	Ernest R. Clark	- End
	James Bobbitt	- Tackle
	Edward L. Budde	- Guard
	Stephen T. Mellinger	- Guard
1963	*Daniel D. Underwood	- End
	*Sherman P. Lewis	- Back
	Earl B. Lattimer	- Guard
	Roger Lopes	- Fullback
	Edward D. Lothamer	- End
	H. Matthew Snorton	- End
	S. Rahn Bentley	- Tackle
	David J. Herman	- Back
	John J. Karpinski	- Guard
	Alton L. Owens	- Tackle
	Richard J. Proebstle	- Quarterback
	Dewey R. Lincoln	- Back
	Ronald R. Rubick	- Back
	Louis L. Bobich	- Back
1964	*Jerry M. Rush	- Tackle
	*Richard F. Gordon	- Back
	Charles Migyanka	- Roverback
	Donald L. Japinga	- Back
	George D. Webster	- Roverback
	Stephen A. Juday	- Quarterback
	Louis L. Bobich	- Back
1965	*Eugene Washington	- End
	*Stephen A. Juday	- Quarterback
	*Clinton C. Jones	- Back
	*Charles A. Smith	- End
	*Harold W. Lucas	- Guard
	*Ronald E. Goovert	- Linebacker
	*George D. Webster	- Roverback
	*Donald L. Japinga	- Back
	Jerry F. West	- Tackle
	John J. Karpinski	- Guard
	Boris N. Dimitroff	- Center
	Robert Apisa	- Fullback
	Robert W. Viney	- End
	Donald J. Bierowicz	- Tackle

	Alton L. Owens	- Tackle
	David G. Techlin	- Guard
	Dwight L. Lee	- Back
1966	*Eugene Washington	- Off. End
	*Jerry F. West	- Off. Tackle
	*Anthony Conti	- Off. Guard
	*Clinton C. Jones	- Off. Back
	*Robert Apisa	- Fullback
	*Charles A. Smith	- Def. End
	*J. Nicholas Jordan	- Def. Tackle
	*Charles E. Thornhill	- Def. Back
	*George D. Webster	- Def. Back
	*Jess W. Phillips	- Def. Back
	*Richard K. Kenney	- Kicker
	Phillip M. Hoag	- Def. End
	Patrick F. Gallinagh	- Def. Tackle
	Jeffrey Richardson	- Tackle
	Joseph R. Pryzbycki	- Off. Tackle
	James A. Raye	- Quarterback
	George R. Chatlos	- Def. End
	Allen R. Brenner	- Off. End
	Dwight L. Lee	- Off. Back
	Drake F. Garrett	- Def. Back
	Regis Cavender	- Fullback
1967	*George R. Chatlos	- Def. End
	Ronald A. Ranieri	- Center
	Allen R. Brenner	- Off. End
	Charles A. Bailey	- Def. Tackle
	Drake F. Garrett	- Def. Back
	Joseph R. Pryzbycki	- Off. Tackle
1968	*Allen R. Brenner	- Off. End, Safety
	*Charles A. Bailey	- Def. Tackle
	Ronald R. Saul	- Off. Guard
	Richard R. Saul	- Def. Guard
	Edward McLoud	- Center
	William Triplett	- Quarterback
	Frank Waters	- Off. Halfback
	Thomas Love	- Off. Halfback
1969	*Ronald Saul	- Off. Guard
	*Ronald Curl	- Def. Tackle
	Donald Law	- Linebacker
	Donald Highsmith	- Off. Halfback
	Eric Allen	- Off. Halfback
	Richard Saul	- Def. End & Linebacker
	Frank Foreman	- Off. End
	Tom Beard	- Off. Center

State gets its first score in 1913 victory, 12-7, against Michigan at Ann Arbor. This was first win over Wolverines for team that became Spartans' first unbeaten and untied club.

SPARTANS IN ALL-STAR ACTION

*Won or shared outstanding back or lineman award
†Team captain or cocaptain

East-West
(San Francisco)
Munn, Clarence L.,
  Head Coach, '52, '53
Daugherty, Hugh Duffy,
  Head Coach, '58, '59, '66, '68
Adderley, Herb, B, '60
Arbanas, Fred, E, '60
Bagdon, Ed, G, '50
Ballman, Gary, B, '61
Bailey, Charles, T, '68
Bobbitt, James, T, '62
Bobich, Louis, B, '65
Bolden, LeRoy, B, '55
Brenner, Allen, B, '68
Breslin, Jack, B, '45-'46
Brogger, Francis, E, '45
Budde, Ed, T, '62
Bullough, Henry, G, '55
Burke, Pat, T, '58
Chandnois, Lynn, B, '50
Coleman, Don, G, '52
Dekker, Paul, E, '53
Dibble, Dorne, E, '51
Dorow, Al, B, '52
Gilbert, Don, B, '58
Gordon, Richard, B, '65
Grandelius, Everett, B, '51
Hughes, William, G, '52
†Jones, Clinton, B, '66
Kelly, Ellison, G, '58
Kenney, Richard, K, '66
Kowalczyk, Walt, B, '58
Lewis, Sherman, B, '63
Look, Dean, B, '59
Martin, Blanche, B, '59
Mason, Don, G, '50
McAuliffe, Don, B, '53
O'Brien, Fran, T, '58
Pingel, John, B, '39
Pyle, Palmer, T, '59
Raye, James, QB, '67
Saimes, George, FB, '62
Saul, Ronald, G, '69
Tamburo, Dick, C, '53
Underwood, Dan, E, '63
Washington, Eugene, E, '66
*Webster, George, RB, '66
Wedemeyer, Charles, F, '68
*Williams, Sam, E, '58
Wilson, Tom, B, '60
Wycinsky, Craig, T, '69

North-South
(Miami)
Daugherty, Hugh Duffy,
  Head Coach, '56, '57, '61
Azar, George, G, '62
Baker, Park, B, '59
Barker, Dick, E, '58
Behrman, Dave, C, '62
Berlinski, Richard, B, '68
Carruthers, Joe, T, '57
Creamer, Jim, C, '51
Charon, Carl, B, '61
Chatlos, George, E, '67
Conti, Anthony, T, '67
Currie, Dan, C, '57
Fontes, Wayne, B, '61
Gallinagh, Pat, T, '66
Grimsley, Ike, G, '60
Herman, Dave, T, '63
Hinesly, Jim, E, '56
Horrell, Bill, T, '51

Hudas, Larry, E, '61
*Jewett, Bob, E, '57
Johnson, Herman, B, '64
Kaiser, Dave, E, '57
Kakela, Pete, T, '61
Krzemienski, Tom, G, '64
Kuh, Dick, G, '51
Kush, Frank, G, '52
LaRose, Cliff, T, '58
Lee, Dwight, B, '67
Lincoln, Dewey, B, '63
Luke, Ed, E, '52
Matsko, John, C, '56
McLoud, Eddy, C, '68
Mendyk, Dennis, B, '56
Minarik, Hank, E, '50
*Ninowski, Jim, B, '57
Richardson, Jeff, T, '66
Rody, Fred, C, '54
Rubick, Ron, B, '63
Sanders, Lonnie, E, '62
Saul, Richard, E, '69
Smith, Charles, E, '66
†Thornhill, Charles, LB, '66
Waters, Frank, B, '68
West, Jerry, T, '66
Wilson, John, B, '52
Wulff, Jim, B, '58
Zagers, Bert, B, '54
Zucco, Vic, B, '56

Blue-Gray
(Montgomery)
Benson, Bill, G, '63
Benson, Wayne, B, '52
Berger, Don, C, '57
Carey, Bill, E, '51
Cundiff, Larry, T, '59
Dotsch, Roland, T, '54
Garner, Dean, G, '51
Harness, Jason, E, '60
Heft, Kenneth, B, '68
Highsmith, Donald, B, '70
Hoag, Phil, E, '66
Kanicki, James, C, '62
Kapral, Frank, G, '51
Kauth, Don, E, '54
Kolodziej, Tony, '57
Lothamer, Ed, E, '63
McFadden, Marv, G, '51
Postula, Vic, B, '54
Pruiett, Mitch, G, '67
Przybycki, Joseph, T, '67
Rochester, Paul, T, '59
Rutledge, Les, T, '57
Ryan, Ed, B, '61
Saidock, Tom, T, '56
Serr, Gordon, G, '52
Smith, Pete, QB, '62
Summers, James, B, '66
Timmerman, Ed, C, '52
Walker, Mickey, T, '60
Wright, Don, G, '59

Senior Bowl
(Mobile)
Arbanas, Fred, E, '61
Bagdon, Ed, C, '50
Bercich, Bob, B, '60
Brandstatter, Art, E, '62
Brenner, Allen, B, '69
Budde, Ed, T, '63
Bullough, Henry, G, '55

Chandnois, Lynn, B, '50
Currie, Dan, C, '58
Dibble, Dorne, E, '51
Dohoney, Don, E, '54
Dorow, Al, B, '52
Garrett, Drake, B, '68
*Gordon, Richard, B, '65
Highsmith, Donald, B, '70
Kanicki, James, C, '63
Kowalczyk, Walt, B, '58
Kush, Frank, G, '53
Lowe, Gary, B, '56
Mason, Don, G, '50
McAuliffe, Don, B, '53
Neal, Jim, C, '54
Ninowski, Jim, B, '58
Nystrom, Carl, G, '56
†Przybycki, Joseph, T, '68
Rush, Jerry, T, '65
Ryan, Ed, B, '62
*Smith, Charles, E, '67
Tamburo, Dick, C, '53
Wells, Billy, B, '54
Zucco, Vic, B, '57

Hula Bowl
(Honolulu)
Daugherty, Hugh Duffy,
  Head Coach, '59, '68
Adderley, Herb, B, '61
Apisa, Robert, FB, '68
Ballman, Gary, B, '62
Behrman, Dave, C, '63
Bobich, Louis, B, '65
Brenner, Allen, B, '69
*Coleman, Don, T, '52
Currie, Dan, C, '58
Cundiff, Larry, T, '60
Dekker, Paul, E, '54
Foreman, Frank, E, '70
*Grandelius, Everett, B, '51
Jones, Clinton, B, '66
*Juday, Steve, QB, '66
Kelly, Ellison, G, '59
Lewis, Sherman, B, '64
Look, Dean, B, '60
Lopes, Roger, B, '64
Lucas, Harold, MG, '66
Masters, Norm, T, '56
Matsko, John, C, '57
Ninowski, Jim, B, '58
O'Brien, Fran, T, '59
Planutis, Gerald, B, '56
Raye, James, QB, '68
Saimes, George, FB, '63
Saul, Ronald, G, '70
Webster, George, B, '66
Wedemeyer, Charles, F, '69
*Williams, Sam, E, '59
Wilson, Tom, B, '61

College All-Star
Game
(Chicago)
Adderley, Herb, B, '61
Agett, Albert, B, '37
Arbanas, Fred, E, '61
Bagdon, Ed, G, '50
Behrman, Dave, C, '63
Budde, Ed, T, '63
Bullough, Henry, G, '55
Breslin, Jack, B, '46
Carey, Robert, E, '52

Chandnois, Lynn, B, '50
Coleman, Don, T, '52
Currie, Dan, C, '58
Dekker, Paul, E, '53
Dorow, Al, B, '52
Grandelius, Everett, B, '51
Guerre, George, B, '49
Huey, Warren, E, '49
Jewett, Robert, E, '58
Jones, Clinton, B, '67
Kanicki, James, C, C, '63
Kelly, Ellison, G, '59
Kowalczyk, Walt, B, '58
Kush, Frank, G, '53
Lothamer, Ed, E, '64
Matsko, John, C, '57
McAuliffe, Don, B, '53

McCurry, Robert, C, '49
Morrall, Earl, B, '56
*Ninowski, Jim, B, '58
O'Brien, Fran, T, '59
Peaks, Clarence, B, '57
Pingel, John, B, '39
Przybycki, Joseph, T, '68
Rochester, Paul, T, '60
Rush, Jerry, T, '65
Sanders, Lonnie, E, '62
*Smith, Charles, E, '67
Snorton, Matt, E, '64
Tamburo, Dick, C, '53
Washington, Eugene, E, '67
Webster, George, B, '67
Williams, Sam, E, '59

American Bowl
(Tampa)
Daugherty, Hugh Duffy,
Head Coach, 1970
Highsmith, Donald, B, '70

Coaches' All-America
(Lubbock)
Daugherty, Hugh Duffy,
Head Coach, '66
Brenner, Allen, B, '69
Goovert, Ron, LB, '66
Lewis, Sherman, B, '64
Lucas, Harold, MG, '66
Rush, Jerry, T, '65
Ryan, Ed, B, '62
Viney, Robert, E, '66
Washington, Eugene, E, '67
Webster, George, LB, '67

FOOTBALL HALL OF FAME
(Coaches)
Clarence L. Munn, 1947-53
(Players)
John S. Pingel, 1968

MICHIGAN SPORTS HALL
OF FAME
Clarence L. Munn, 1961
Ralph H. Young, 1962

UPI LINEMAN OF THE YEAR
Charles "Bubba" Smith, 1966

WALTER CAMP TROPHY
Don McAuliffe, 1962

COACH OF THE YEAR
Clarence L. Munn, 1952
Hugh Duffy Daugherty, 1955, 1965

COSIDA ACADEMIC ALL-AMERICAN
1952—John Wilson, back
1953—Donald Dohoney, end
1953—Carl Diener, end
1954—Donald Kauth, end
1955—Carl Nystrom, guard
1957—Robert Jewett, end
       Blanche Martin, back
1958—Richard Barker, end
       Ellison Kelly, guard
       Blanche Martin, back
       Blanche Martin, back
       (honorary)
1960—Ed Ryan, roverback
1965—Donald Japinga, halfback
       Donald Bierowicz, tackle
1966—Patrick Gallinagh, tackle
1968—Allen Brenner, end, safety
1969—Ronald Saul, guard
       Richard Saul, end

CLEVELAND TOUCHDOWN CLUB
PLAY-OF-THE-YEAR AWARD
Clinton Jones, 1966

SPORTS ILLUSTRATED
SILVER ANNIVERSARY
ALL-AMERICAN
Clarence L. Munn, 1956
Arthur F. Brandstatter 1961
Frank Gaines Jr., 1962

OUTLAND AWARD
Ed Bagdon, 1949

NATIONAL FOOTBALL HALL OF
FAME GRADUATE FELLOWSHIP
AWARD
Stephen Juday, 1965
Allen Brenner, 1968

NCAA POST-GRADUATE
SCHOLARSHIP
Allen Brenner, 1968

DOLLY COHEN
SCHOLARSHIP AWARD
Allen Brenner 1968

BIG TEN ALL-ACADEMIC
1959—Blanche Martin, halfback
1960—Ed Ryan, halfback
1964—Richard Gordon, halfback
       Eugene Washington, end
1965—James Proebstle, end
       Donald Japinga, halfback
       Stephen Juday, quarterback
       Donald Bierowicz, tackle
1966—Allen Brenner, end
       Patrick Gallinagh, tackle
1968—Allen Brenner, end, safety
1969—Ronald Saul, guard
       Richard Saul, end
       Dave VanElst, tackle

DANZIGER AWARD
     Trophy given annually since 1954 to the
player from the Detroit area who makes the
most outstanding contribution to the team.
Named for the late Frederick W. Danziger,
football letterman in 1926-28-29 and team
captain in 1929, and contributed by his
family.

1954—Al Fracasa, quarterback
1955—Norman Masters, tackle
1956—James Hinesly, end
1957—Jim Ninowski, quarterback
1958—Cliff LaRose, tackle
1959—Blanche Martin, fullback
1960—Mickey Walker, tackle
1961—Gary Ballman, halfback
1962—Ed Budde tackle
1963—Dewey Lincoln halfback
1964—Jerry Rush tackle
1965—Harold Lucas, middleguard
1966—Patrick Gallinagh, guard
1967—Ronald Ranieri center
1968—Kenneth Heft, halfback
1969—Craig Wycinsky, tackle

OIL CAN AWARD

This award is given annually to the player who contributes most in a humorous way to the team.

1949—Peter Fusi, tackle
1950—Jack Morgan, tackle
1951—Douglas Weaver, center
1952—Gordon Serr, guard
1953—Larry Fowler, tackle
1954—Henry Bullough, guard
1955—Embry Robinson, guard
1956—Joseph Carruthers, tackle
1957—Robert Popp, quarterback
1958—Thomas Vernon, end
1959—Edwin McLucas, guard
1960—Ronald Ike Grimsley, guard
1961—Wayne Fontes, halfback
1962—Dewey Lincoln, halfback
1963—Earl Lattimer, guard
1964—Larry Mackey, fullback
1965—Drake Garrett, halfback
1966—Drake Garrett, halfback
1967—Drake Garrett, halfback
1968—Eddy McLoud, center
1969—Clifton Hardy, halfback

DR. JOHN HANNAH AWARD

This award given annually to player for perseverance shown in efforts for the football squad.

1965—James Proebstle, end
1966—Jeffrey Richardson, guard
1967—Robert Lange, linebacker
1968—Richard Berlinski, fullback
1969—Bruce Kulesza, end

BIGGIE MUNN AWARD

This award given annually to player contributing most "extra effort" during football season.

1965—Robert Viney, end
1966—Jerry Jones, halfback
1967—Frank Waters, halfback
1968—Eddy McLoud, center
1969—Donald Highsmith, halfback

OUTSTANDING DEFENSIVE LINEMAN
(Genesee County Award)
1966—Charles "Bubba" Smith, end
1967—George Chatlos, end
1968—Charles Bailey, tackle
1969—Ronald Curl, tackle

OUTSTANDING OFFENSIVE LINEMAN
(Kent County Award)
1966—Jerry West, Tackle
1967—Mitchell Pruiett, guard
1968—Eddy McLoud, center
1969—Ronald Saul, guard

OUTSTANDING DEFENSIVE BACK
(Detroit-Oakland Award)
1966—George Webster, roverback
1967—Drake Garrett, halfback
1968—Allen Brenner, safety
1969—Thomas Kutschinski halfback

OUTSTANDING OFFENSIVE BACK
(Ingham County Award)
1966—Clinton Jones, halfback
1967—Dwight Lee, halfback
1968—Charles Wedemeyer, flanker
1969—Donald Highsmith, halfback

OUTSTANDING END
(Saginaw County Award)
1966—Eugene Washington
1967—Allen Brenner
1968—Frank Foreman
1969—Richard Saul

FRANK COWING AWARD

Presented each year to the outgoing senior team manager.

1969—Robert Beery

Col. William D. Frazer, football letterman in 1906, 07, 08, later an Olympian in pistol.

SPRING GAME OUTSTANDING PLAYER AWARD

Outstanding performers in spring football windup game have been honored since 1948.

1948—Lynn Chandnois, halfback
1949—Lynn Chandnois, halfback
1950—Everett Grandelius, halfback
1951—Wayne Benson, fullback
1952—Billy Wells, halfback
1953—James Ellis, halfback
1954—Gerald Planutis, fullback
    Howard Graves, halfback
1955—Patrick Wilson, quarterback
    James Ninowski, quarterback
1956—Clarence Peaks, halfback
1957—James Ninowski (Varsity),
    quarterback
    Gerald Planutis (Old Timers),
    fullback
1958—Blanche Martin (Varsity), fullback
    Robert Jewett (Old Timers), end
1959—Thomas Wilson (Varsity),
    quarterback
    James Ninowski (Old Timers),
    quarterback
1960—Herb Adderley (Varsity),halfback
    Thomas Yewcic (Old Timers),
    quarterback
1961—Sherman Lewis (Varsity), halfback
    Clarence Peaks (Old Timers),
    halfback

1962—George Saimes (Varsity), fullback,
    shared with Charles Migyanka
    (Varsity), quarterback
    Robert Ricucci (Old Timers), halfback
1963—Richard Proebstle, quarterback,
    outstanding back, shared with
    Stephen Juday, quarterback
    Matthew Snorton, end, outstanding
    lineman
1964—Dave McCormick, quarterback, Green
    John Walsh, guard, White
1965—Jimmy Raye, quarterback, Green
    Phil Hoag, end, White
1966—Clinton Jones, halfback, Green
    Richard Berlinski, halfback, White
1967—Jimmy Raye, quarterback, Green
    Gordon Bowdell, end, White
1968—Allen Brenner, end, Green, offense
    Wilton Martin, end, Green, defense
    Gordon Longmire, quarterback,
    White, offense
    Michael Hogan, linebacker, White,
    defense
1969—William Triplett, back, Green
    Frank Foreman, lineman, Green
    Steven Piro, back, White
    Frank Butler, lineman, White

GOVERNOR OF MICHIGAN AWARD

This award, a gold watch, given annually since 1931 to the player who is voted the most valuable on the team by the men on the football squad. Presentation made each year by the governor of Michigan.

1931—Abe Eliowitz, fullback
1932—Robert Monnett, halfback
1933—Arthur Buss, tackle
1934—Edward Klewicki, end
1935—Sid Wagner, guard
1936—Sam Ketchman, center
1937—Harry Speelman, tackle
1938—John Pingel, halfback
1939—Lyle Rockenbach, guard
1940—Jack Amon, fullback
1941—Anthony Arena, center
1942—Richard Kieppe, halfback
1943—No award
1944—Jack Breslin, fullback
1945—Steve Contos, halfback
1946—George Guerre, halfback
1947—Warren Huey, end
1948—Lynn Chandnois, halfback
1949—Eugene Glick, quarterback

1950—Everett Grandelius, halfback
1951—Donald Coleman, tackle
1952—Richard Tamburo, linebacker
1953—LeRoy Bolden, halfback
1954—John Matsock, halfback
1955—Carl Nystrom, guard
1956—James Hinesly, end
1957—Dan Currie, center
1958—Sam Williams, end
1959—Dean Look, quarterback
1960—Thomas Wilson, quarterback
1961—George Saimes, fullback
1962—George Saimes, fullback
1963—Sherman Lewis, halfback
1964—Richard Gordon, halfback
1965—Stephen Juday, quarterback
1966—George Webster, roverback
1967—Dwight Lee, halfback
1968—Allen Brenner, end-safety
1969—Ronald Saul, guard

ROSS TROPHY

Given annually since 1949 to the player who has made the best contribution to the team both athletically and scholastically. Named for the late F. Ward Ross, football letterman in 1925-26-27, and contributed by his wife, Mrs. Dorothy Ross.

1949—John Polonchek, halfback
1950—John Yocca guard
1951—Frank Kapral, guard
1952—John Wilson, halfback
1953—James Neal, center
1954—Don Kauth, end
1955—Carl Nystrom, guard
1956—Pat Wilson, quarterback
1957—Don Zysk, halfback
1958—John Middleton, guard

1959—Blanche Martin, fullback
1960—Thomas Wilson, quarterback
1961—Pete Kakela, tackle
1962—George Azar, guard
1963—Ed Youngs, center
1964—Richard Flynn, tackle
1965—Stephen Juday, quarterback
1966—Patrick Gallinagh, guard
1967—Anthony Conti, guard
1968—Allen Brenner, end-safety
1969—Donald Baird, guard

TEAM CAPTAINS

Year	Name	Position
1896	Wilfred R. Vanderhoef	Tackle
1897	Walton K. Brainard	Half
1898	J. H. Vanderstolpe	Guard
1899	Ellis W. Ranney	Quarter
1900	Charles A. McCue	End
1901	Albert H. Case	Guard
1902	Arthur D. Peters	Tackle
1903	Frank J. Kratz	Tackle
1904	Robert F. Bell	Tackle
1905	Edward B. McKenna	Half
1906	Stephen W. Doty	Full
1907	Walter H. Small	Quarter
1908	Bert Shedd	Tackle
1909	Parnell G. McKenna	Half
1910	Ion J. Cortright	Half
1911	Fred A. Stone	End
1912	William R. Riblett	Quarter
1913	Chester W. Gifford	Tackle
1914	George E. Julian	Full
1915	W. Blake Miller	Half
1916	Ralph B. Henning	End
1917	Sherman Coryell	Tackle
1918	Lawrence C. Archer	Center
1919	Harry E. Franson	Tackle
1920	Harold A. Springer	Quarter
1921	John Bos	Tackle
1922	William C. Johnson	Half
1923	Maurice R. Taylor	Guard
1924	Vivian J. Hultman	Guard
1925	Donald H. Haskins	Tackle
1926	Martin F. Rummel	Tackle
1927	Paul M. Smith	Full
1928	Lewis A. Hornbeck	End
1929	Fred W. Danziger	Half
	Vern C. Dickeson	Half
1930	Harold E. Smead	Center
1931	Milton C. Gross	Guard
1932	Abe Eliowitz	Full
	Robert C. Monnett	Half
1933	Bernard G. McNutt	Full
1934	Russell H. Reynolds	Quarter
1935	Sydney P. Wagner	Guard
1936	Gordon A. Dahlgren	Guard
	Henry S. Kutchins	End
1937	Harry E. Speelman	Tackle
1938	Allen O. Diebold	Quarter
	David D. Diehl	End
1939	Michael Kinek	End
	Lyle J. Rockenbach	Guard
1940	Jack R. Amon	Full
	Paul L. Griffeth	Guard
1941	Wilford D. Davis	Quarter
	William Rupp, Jr.	Guard
1942	Richard Mangrum	Tackle
	Walter L. Palowski	Half
1943	No football due to war.	
1944	Thomas B. Sullivan	Center
1945	Jacweir Breslin	Half
1946	Robert B. McCurry	Center
	Kenneth E. Balge	End
1947	Robert B. McCurry	Center
1948	Robert B. McCurry	Center
1949	Harold L. Vogler	Tackle
1950	LeRoy R. Crane	Full
1951	Robert Carey	End
1952	Donald McAuliffe	Half
1953	Donald Dohoney	End
1954	LeRoy Bolden	Half
	Don Kauth	End
1955	Carl Nystrom	Guard
1956	John Matsko	Center
1957	Patrick Burke	Tackle
1958	Sam Williams	End
1959	Donald Wright	Guard
1960	Fred Arbanas	End
	Fred Boylen	Guard
	Herb Adderley	Half
1961	Ed Ryan	Half
1962	George Saimes	Full
1963	Dan D. Underwood	End
	Sherman P. Lewis	Half
1964	Charles Migyanka, Jr.	Linebacker
1965	Donald Japinga	Half
	Stephen Juday	Quarter
1966	Clinton Jones	Half
	George Webster	Rover
1967	Anthony Conti	Tackle
	Drake Garrett	Half
1968	Allen Brenner	End
1969	Franklin Foreman	End
	Richard Saul	Linebacker

SPARTAN INDIVIDUAL RECORDS

Career

Yards Gained Rushing	Lynn Chandnois	'46, '47, '48, '49	2,093
Rushing Attempts	Clinton Jones	'64, '65, '66	396
Yards Gained Passing	Steve Juday	'63, '64, '65	2,576
Passes Attempted	Steve Juday	'63, '64, '65	384
Passes Completed	Steve Juday	'63, '64, '65	198
Passes Caught	Gene Washington	'64, '65, '66	102
Touchdown Passes Caught	Gene Washington	'64, '65, '66	16
Yards Gained Passes Caught	Gene Washington	'64, '65, '66	1,857
Touchdown Passes Thrown	Steve Juday	'63, '64, '65	21
Passes Had Intercepted	Steve Juday	'63, '64, '65	24
	Gene Glick	'46, '47, '48, '49	24
Pass Interceptions	Lynn Chandnois	'46, '47, '48, '49	20
Touchdowns Scored	Lynn Chandnois	'46, '47, '48, '49	31
P.A.T. Scored	George Smith	'47, '48, '49	94
Field Goals Scored	Dick Kenney	'64, '65, '66	19
Points Scored	Lynn Chandnois	'46, '47, '48, '49	186
Punting Average	Earl Morrall	'53, '54, '55	39.2

Season

Yards Gained Rushing	Everett Grandelius	'50	1,023
Rushing Attempts	Tommy Love	'68	177
Yards Gained Passing	Steve Juday	'65	1,173

Passes Attempted	Steve Juday	'65	168
Passes Completed	Steve Juday	'65	89
Passes Caught	Gene Washington	'65	40
Touchdown Passes Caught	Bob Carey	'49	8
Yards Gained Passes Caught	Gene Washington	'66	677
Touchdown Passes Thrown	Gene Glick	'48	11
Passes Had Intercepted	Steve Juday	'64	10
Pass Interceptions	Jesse Thomas	'50	8
Touchdowns Scored	Clinton Jones	'65	12
	Lynn Chandnois	'48	12
	Everett Grandelius	'50	12
P.A.T. Scored	George Smith	'48	39
Field Goals Scored	Dick Kenney	'65	11
Points Scored	Clinton Jones	'65	74
Punting Average	Earl Morrall	'55	42.9

Game

Yards Gained Rushing	Clinton Jones	Iowa, '66 (21 att.)	268
Rushing Attempts	Frank Waters	Santa Clara, '47 (119 yds.)	31
Yards Gained Passing	Earl Morrall	Marquette, '55 (14-10)	274
Passes Attempted	Steve Juday	Notre Dame, '64 (12 compl.)	26
	Earl Morrall	Purdue, '54 (10 compl.)	26
Passes Completed	Steve Juday	Indiana, '64 (20 atts.)	16
Passes Caught	Gene Washington	Notre Dame, '64	9
Touchdown Passes Caught	Gene Washington	Indiana, '65	3
Yards Gained Passes Caught	Allen Brenner	Baylor, '68	153
Touchdown Passes Thrown	Gene Glick	Iowa St., '48	4
Passes Had Intercepted	Gene Glick	Michigan, '49	4
	Al Dorow	Marquette, '51	4
	Tom Yewcic	Purdue, '53	4
Pass Interceptions	Jim Ellis	Oregon St., '51	3
	Jesse Thomas	Indiana, '50	3
	Jesse Thomas	Michigan, '50	3
	John Polonchek	Wm. & Mary, '49	3
Touchdowns Scored	Clinton Jones	Iowa, '65	4
	Bud Crane	Hawaii, '47	4
P.A.T. Scored	George Smith	Hawaii, '48	8
	George Smith	Temple, '49	8
	George Smith	Arizona, '49	8
	Evan Slonac	Marquette, '52	8
Field Goals Scored	Dick Kenney	Penn State, '65	3
Points Scored	Clinton Jones	Iowa, '65	24
	Bud Crane	Hawaii, '47	24

A spectacular play in State football history was Dick Panin's 88-yard TD run in 1951 game against Notre Dame. Spartans won, 35-0.

Play

Yards Gained Rushing	Lynn Chandnois	Arizona, '49 (TD)	90
Yards Gained Passing	Steve Juday to	So. Cal., '63 (TD)	88
	Sherman Lewis		
Yards Field Goals Kicked	Dick Kenney	So. Cal., '64	49
Yards Kickoff Return	Russ Reader	Wayne State, '46 (TD)	98
Yards Punt Return	Allen Brenner	Illinois, '66 (TD)	95
Yards Interception Return	Bob Suci	Michigan, '59 (TD-pass)	93
Yards Punted	Lou Bobich	Purdue, '63	71
	Earl Morrall	Stanford, '55	71

ALL-TIME SPARTAN TEAMS

George Webster, Gene Washington, Don Coleman, Earl Morrall—these four dominated the All-Time Michigan State Football Team which was chosen in 1970 as part of the Big Ten's 75th anniversary observance.

Webster was named the All-Time Greatest Player, Washington the top end, Coleman the best interior lineman and Morrall the supreme back.

They were the leaders on ballots which came from the 1969 Homecoming Game program, the Michigan State Alumni Magazine and the Michigan State News, the student newspaper.

The All-Time Spartan team, with senior seasons noted:

Ends   Gene Washington (1966) and Charles (Bubba) Smith (1966).
Linemen Don Coleman (1951), Dan Currie (1957), Norm Masters (1955), Dave Behrman (1962) and Ed Budde (1962).
Backs   Earl Morrall (1955), Clinton Jones (1966), George Webster (1966) and Lynn Chandnois (1949).

Nearly 100 Spartans were named on one or more ballots for all-time honors. Webster had the distinction of being named variously as a lineman, end and back.

From ballots, an all-time two-platoon team and an Old Timers' Team (pre 1940 players only) also were assembled.

The selections:

All-Time Offensive Team:

Ends   Washington and Bob Carey (1951)
Linemen Coleman, Masters, Jerry West (1966), Budde and Behrman
Backs   Morrall, Jones, John Pingel (1938) and Everett (Sonny) Grandelius (1950).

All-Time Defensive Team:

Ends   Sam Williams (1958) and Smith
Linemen Ed Bagdon (1949), Jerry Rush (1964) and Harold Lucas (1965)
Linebackers
         Currie and Frank Kush (1952)
Backs   Webster, Chandnois, Herb Adderley (1960) and George Saimes (1962)
Old-Timers' Team:

Ends   Ed Klewicki (1934) and Blake Miller (1915)
Linemen Sid Wagner (1935), Hugh Blacklock (1916), Frank Butler (1934), Gideon Smith (1915) and Lyle Rockenbach (1939)
Backs   Pingel, Bob Monnett (1932), George (Carp) Julian (1914) and Nino (Jerry) DaPrato (1915)

Other former Michigan State players who just missed making the All-Time teams on the balloting included:

Ends   Dorne Dibble (1950), Don Dohoney (1953) and Al Brenner (1968)
Linemen Carl (Buck) Nystrom (1955), Don Mason (1949), Dick Tamburo (1952), Earl Lattimer (1963), and Ron Saul (1969)
Backs   LeRoy Bolden (1954), Sherman Lewis (1963), Walt Kowalczyk (1957), Al Dorow (1951) and Bob Apisa (1967).

THREE SPARTAN NUMBERS RETIRED

Three football jersey numbers have been retired in Michigan State's gridiron history. They are No. 78, worn by Don Coleman when he was a consensus All-America tackle in 1951; No. 90, worn by George Webster, All-America roverback in the Big Ten and national championship years of 1965 and 1966, and No. 46, as a special tribute to former Michigan State University president Dr. John A. Hannah.

Coleman's 78 was pulled out of circulation by Biggie Munn, then the Spartan head coach, in honor of the young man called the

finest lineman to play for State.

The 90 belonging to Webster was set aside by Coach Duffy Daugherty in honor of the player who best symbolized the greatness of the fine Spartan teams during the two big seasons of 1965 and 1966.

Daugherty also retired the 46 jersey, presenting it to Dr. Hannah on the occasion of his leaving the university after 46 years of service to become director of the Agency for International Development in President Nixon's administration. Daugherty cited Hannah for important contributions to Spartan athletics over those years.

SPARTAN TEAM RECORDS

RECORD BY SEASON

Big Ten Year	W	L	T	Standing	AP	UPI	MIAA W	L	T
1896							0	2	0
1897							1	1	1
1898							4	1	0
1899							1	2	0
1900							1	1	0
1901							3	2	1
1902							2	2	0
1903							4	0	1
1904							4	1	0
1905							5	0	0
1906							6	1	1
							31	13	4
1950					8th	9th			
1951					2nd	2nd			
1952					1st	1st			
1953	5	1	0	1st place tie with Illinois	3rd	3rd			
1954	1	5	0	8th place tie with Northwestern	—	—			
1955	5	1	0	2nd place	2nd	2nd			
1956	4	2	0	4th place tie with Ohio State	9th	10th			
1957	5	1	0	2nd place	3rd	3rd			
1958	0	5	1	10th place	—	—			
1959	4	2	0	2nd place	—	—			
*1960	3	2	0	4th place	15th	13th			
1961	5	2	0	3rd place	8th	9th			
1962	3	3	0	5th place tie with Iowa and Purdue	—	—			
1963	4	1	1	2nd place tie with Ohio State	9th	9th			
1964	3	3	0	6th place	—	20th			
1965	7	0	0	1st place	2nd	1st			
1966	7	0	0	1st place	2nd	2nd			
1967	3	4	0	6th place tie with Illinois & Michigan	—	—			
1968	2	5	0	7th place	—	—			
1969	2	5	0	9th place	—	—			
	63	42	2						

*Michigan State University defeated Indiana University in 1960. This victory was not considered in the final Big Ten standings, because Indiana was on probation.

Michigan State, through 1969, had played in 17 Big Ten football seasons and showed a composite record of 63 victories, 42 losses and two ties. Spartan teams also had ranked in the nation's top 10 in Associated Press and United Press International polls 11 times over the past 20 years. State made the elite group for the first time in 1950 and was ranked No. 1 in both polls in 1952 and by the UPI in 1965. Four teams—1951, 1952, 1965, 1966—were recognized as national champs by the prestigious Helms Athletic Foundation.

When the Michigan Intercollegiate Athletic Association (MIAA) was formed in 1888, the membership included Albion College, Hillsdale College, Michigan State University and Olivet College. Eastern Michigan University was admitted in 1892, Kalamazoo College in 1896, Adrian College in 1900 and Alma College in 1902. Michigan State dropped out of the MIAA at the close of the 1906-07 school year after 20 years participation.

Football championships were not recognized until the 1904 season, which was won by Albion College. Michigan State won its only championship in 1905.

RECORD BY OPPONENT

Opponent	W	L	T	Opponent	W	L	T
Adrian	4	0	0	Carroll	2	0	0
Akron	2	0	0	Case	2	0	0
Albion	11	4	3	Centre	2	0	0
Alma	22	4	4	Chicago	0	1	0
Arizona	3	0	0	Chicago YMCA College	3	0	0
Armour Inst.	1	0	0	Cincinnati	1	1	0
Army	0	1	0	Colgate	1	4	0
Auburn	0	1	0	Colorado	1	0	0
Baylor	1	0	0	Cornell College	1	1	0
Boston College	0	2	1	Cornell U.	0	1	0
Butler	1	1	0	Creighton	0	2	0
California	2	0	0	Culver Military Acad.	1	0	0
Camp MacArthur	0	1	0	DePaul	1	0	1
Carnegie Tech	3	0	1	DePauw	5	1	0

	W	L	T		W	L	T
Detroit Athletic Club	3	4	1	Notre Dame	15	19	1
Detroit	7	6	1	Ohio Northern	1	0	0
Detroit YMCA	1	0	0	Ohio State	5	5	0
Eastern Michigan	3	0	0	Ohio University	1	0	0
Fordham	1	0	0	Ohio Wesleyan	2	2	0
Georgetown	1	1	0	Olivet	18	4	1
Great Lakes Naval Station	1	1	0	Oregon State	5	2	1
Grinnell	4	0	0	Penn State	8	1	1
Haskell Institute	0	1	0	Pittsburgh	4	0	1
Hawaii	2	0	0	Port Huron YMCA	2	0	0
Hillsdale	7	0	0	Purdue	11	12	1
Houston	0	1	0	Ripon	1	0	0
Illinois	5	5	0	Saginaw Naval Brigade	1	0	0
Illinois Wesleyan	5	0	0	St. Louis	0	1	1
Indiana	15	8	1	San Francisco	1	0	0
Iowa State	2	0	0	Santa Clara	1	3	2
Iowa	3	4	0	Scranton	1	0	0
Kalamazoo	9	8	0	South Dakota State	1	0	0
Kansas State	5	0	1	South Dakota	5	0	1
Kansas	4	0	0	Southern California	1	2	0
Kentucky	2	2	0	Southern Methodist	1	0	0
Lake Forest	3	1	1	Stanford	3	1	0
Lansing High School	2	0	0	Syracuse	6	3	0
Loyola (Cal.)	1	0	0	Temple	7	1	2
Manhattan	1	1	0	Texas A. & M.	2	1	0
Marietta	0	1	0	Texax Christian	1	0	0
Marquette	18	6	1	Toledo	1	0	0
Maryland	4	1	0	U.C.L.A.	3	1	0
Massachusetts State	1	0	0	Wabash	5	1	1
Miami (Fla.)	0	2	0	Washington	1	0	0
Michigan	20	37	5	Washington State	4	1	0
Michigan School—Deaf	4	0	0	Washington (St. Louis)	1	0	0
Michigan Frosh	4	0	0	Wayne State	9	0	0
Minnesota	4	8	0	Western Michigan	2	2	0
Mississippi State	2	1	1	West Virginia	4	0	0
Missouri	3	3	0	William & Mary	2	0	0
Mt. Union	4	0	0	Wisconsin	9	6	0
Nebraska	0	2	0				
North Carolina	2	1	0	Number of Teams Played			109
North Carolina State	3	1	0	Number of Games Played			622
North Central	1	0	0	Number of Games Won			385
North Dakota State	2	0	0	Number of Games Lost			202
Northwestern	11	3	0	Number of Games Tied			35
				Percentage			.647

State's football coaches since 1933 were, l. to r., Charlie Bachman, 1933-46; Duffy Daugherty, who took over in 1954, and Biggie Munn, 1947-53.

WINNING STREAKS

All Games

28—From fourth game of 1950 season through fourth game of 1953 season. Teams coached by Clarence (Biggie) Munn.

15—From third game of 1912 season through second game of 1914 season. Teams coached by John F. Macklin.

12—From third game of 1955 season through fourth game of 1956 season. Teams coached by Hugh Duffy Daugherty.

10—From first game through final game of regular 1965 season. Team coached by Hugh Duffy Daugherty.

Big Ten Games

16—From first conference game of 1965 season through second conference game of 1967 season. Teams coached by Hugh Duffy Daugherty.

SPARTAN COACHES' RECORD

Coach	Period	W	L	T	Pct.
No Established Coach	1896	1	2	1	.375
Henry Keep	1897-1898	8	5	1	.607
Charles O. Bemies	1899-1900	3	7	1	.318
George E. Denman	1901-1902	7	9	1	.441
*Chester L. Brewer	1903-1910	54	10	6	.814
John F. Macklin	1911-1915	29	5	0	.853
Frank Sommers	1916	4	2	1	.643
*Chester L. Brewer	1917	0	9	0	.000
George E. Gauthier	1918	4	3	0	.571
*Chester L. Brewer	1919	4	4	1	.500
George E. Clark	1920	4	6	0	.400
Albert M. Barron	1921-1922	6	10	2	.389
†Ralph H. Young	1923-1927	18	22	1	.451
Harry G. Kipke	1928	3	4	1	.438
James H. Crowley	1929-1932	22	8	3	.712
Charles W. Bachman	1933-1945	70	34	10	.658
†Clarence L. Munn	1947-1953	54	9	2	.846
†Hugh D. Daugherty	1954-1969	94	53	4	.637
		385	202	35	.647

*Brewer (combined record)	1903-1910				
	1917 and 1919	58	23	7	.699

1943   Intercollegiate program dropped for school year 1943-1944, World War II.

†Daugherty, Hugh D.		Coach of the Year 1955 and 1965
†Munn, Clarence L.		Coach of the Year 1952
		Michigan Sports Hall of Fame 1961
		All-American 1956
		Sports Illustrated Silver Anniversary
		Football Hall of Fame 1947-53
†Young, Ralph H.		Michigan Sports Hall of Fame 1962

Big Ten Conference

		W	L	T	Pct.
Munn, Clarence L.	1947-1953	5	1	0	.833
Daugherty, Hugh D.	1954-1969	57	36	2	.611

Michigan Intercollegiate Athletic Association (MIAA)

		W	L	T	Pct.
No Coach	1896	0	2	0	.000
Henry Keep	1897 1898	5	2	1	.686
Charles O. Bemies	1899-1900	2	3	0	.600
George E. Denman	1901-1902	5	4	1	.560
Chester L. Brewer	1903-1906	19	2	2	.869

SPARTANS IN BOWL PLAY

Michigan State football teams have appeared in four post-season bowl games. Coach Charley Bachman's squad played Auburn in the 1938 Orange Bowl game at Miami and lost 6-0. Coach Biggie Munn's eleven played UCLA in the 1954 Rose Bowl game at Pasadena and won 28-20. Coach Duffy Daugherty's unit played UCLA in the 1956 Rose Bowl encounter and won 17-14, and the same teams met again at Pasadena in 1966 with UCLA winning this time, 14-12.

1938 ORANGE BOWL GAME
January 1, 1938, Miami, Fla.

Michigan State	Lineups	Auburn
Ernest Bremer	LE	Rex McKissick
Harry Speelman (Capt.)	LT	Bo Russell
Lyle Rockenbach	LG	Happy Sivell
Tom McShannock	C	Lester Antley
Walt Lueck	RG	Hatch Howell
Howard Swartz	RT	Fred Holman
Frank Gaines	RE	Stancel Whatley
Al Diebold	QB	Osmo Smith
John Pingel	LH	Speck Kelly
Steve Szasz	RH	Jim Fenton
Usif Haney	FB	Dutch Heath

Scoring by Quarters

	1	2	3	4	Final
Michigan State	0	0	0	0	— 0
Auburn	0	6	0	0	— 6

Scoring Summary

FIRST QUARTER: No scoring. SECOND QUARTER: A—Ralph O'Gwynne caught George Kenmore's short pass and skirted three yards around left end to score, capping a 36-yard drive. Garth Thorpe's conversion attempt was wide. THIRD QUARTER: No scoring. FOURTH QUARTER: No scoring.
OFFICIAL ATTENDANCE: 18,970

1954 ROSE BOWL GAME
January 1, 1954, Pasadenca, Calif.

Michigan State	Lineups	U.C.L.A.
Bill Quinlan	LE	Rommie Loudd
Jim Jebb	LT	Jack Ellena
Ferris Hallmark	LG	Sam Boghosian
Jim Neal	C	Ira Pauly
Henry Bullough	RG	Rudy Feldman
Larry Fowler	RT	Chuck Doud
Don Dohoney (Capt.)	RE	Myron Berliner
Tom Yewcic	QB	Don Foster
LeRoy Bolden	LH	Paul Cameron
Billy Wells	RH	Bill Stits
Evan Slonac	FB	Pete Dailey

Scoring by Quarters

	1	2	3	4	Final
Michigan State	0	7	14	7	— 28
U.C.L.A.	7	7	0	6	— 20

Scoring Summary

FIRST QUARTER: U.C.L.A.—Bill Stits took 13-yard pass from Paul Cameron on goal line and scored, 11:10 (37 yards in 6 plays), John Hermann coverted. SECOND QUARTER: U.C.L.A.—Paul Cameron slanted off left tackle for two yards and scored 4:04 (18 yards in 7 plays), John Hermann converted. MS—Ellis Duckett blocked Paul Cameron's punt (scrimmage U.C.L.A. 25) and ran 6 yards for TD, 10:04. Evan Slonac converted. THIRD QUARTER: MS—LeRoy Bolden ran over guard from 1-yard line to score, 6:13 (78 yards in 14 plays), Evan Slonac converted. MS—Billy Wells runs over tackle from 2-yard line to score, 12:15 (73 yards in 11 plays), Evan Slonac converted. FOURTH QUARTER: U.C.L.A.—Rommie Loudd took 28-yard pass from Paul Cameron on goal line to score 2:24 (24 yards in 2 plays), Hermann failed to convert. MS—Billy Wells took Paul Cameron's punt on his own 38 and ran for a TD, 10:09, Evan Slonac converted.
OFFICIAL ATTENDANCE: 101,000

1956 ROSE BOWL GAME
January 2, 1956, Pasadena, Calif.

Michigan State	Lineups	U.C.L.A.
John Lewis	LE	John Hermann
Norm Masters	LT	Roger White
Dan Currie	LG	Hardiman Cureton
Joe Badaczewski	C	Steve Palmer
Buck Nystrom (Capt.)	RG	Jim Brown
Leo Haidys	RT	Gil Moreno
Dave Kaiser	RE	Rommie Loudd
Earl Morrall	QB	Bruce Ballard
Clarence Peaks	LH	Sam Brown
Walt Kowalczyk	RH	Jim Decker
Gerald Planutis	FB	Bob Davenport

Ellis Duckett blocked a Paul Cameron punt, then took ball in for TD in 1954 Rose Bowl play against UCLA. Spartans won this, their first Rose Bowl encounter, 28-20.

Scoring by Quarters

	1	2	3	4	Final
Michigan State	0	7	0	10 —	17
U.C.L.A.	7	0	0	7 —	14

Scoring Summary

FIRST QUARTER: U.C.L.A.—Bob Davenport bucked two yards for score, 3:12 (16 yards in 4 plays), Jim Decker converted. SECOND QUARTER: MS—Clarence Peaks took 13-yard pass on goal-line from Earl Morrall to score, 9:08 (80 yards in 13 plays), Gerald Planutis converted. THIRD QUARTER: No Scoring. FOURTH QUARTER: UCLA—Doug Peters bucked 1-yard for score, 8:53 (56 yards in 5 plays), Jim Decker converted. MS—Dave Kaiser kicked 41-yard field goal with 7 seconds left in game.
OFFICIAL ATTENDANCE: 100,809

1966 ROSE BOWL GAME
January 1, 1966, Pasadena, Calif

Michigan State	Lineups	UCLA
Jim Proebstle	LE	Kurt Altenberg
Jerry West	LT	Russ Banducci
Norm Jenkins	LG	Rich Deakers
Boris Dimitroff	C	Morris Freedman
John Karpinski	RG	Barry Leventhal
Joe Przybycki	RT	Larry Slagle
Gene Washington	RE	Byron Nelson
Steve Juday	QB	Gary Beban
Dwight Lee	LH	Mel Farr
Clinton Jones	RH	Dick Witcher
Eddie Cotton	FB	Paul Horgan

Scoring by Quarters

	1	2	3	4	Final
Michigan State	0	0	0	12 —	12
UCLA	0	14	0	0 —	14

Scoring Summary

FIRST QUARTER: No scoring. SECOND QUARTER: UCLA—Gary Beban sneaked one yard to score, :03 (6 yards in 2 plays), Kurt Zimmerman converted. UCLA—Gary Beban sneaked one yard for score, 3:10 (42 yards in 7 plays), Kurt Zimmerman converted. THIRD QUARTER: No scoring. FOURTH QUARTER: MS—Bob Apisa took pitchout from Jim Raye and went 38 yards for the score, 8:47 (80 yards in 2 plays), Steve Juday failed on two-point pass try. MS—Steve Juday sneaked half-a-yard for score, 14:29 (51 yards in 15 plays), Bob Apisa failed on two-point run try.
OFFICIAL ATTENDANCE: 100,087.

GRIDIRON TROPHIES

PAUL BUNYAN TROPHY

To the winner of the Michigan State-Michigan football game each year goes the "Paul Bunyan-Governor of Michigan Trophy." It was put into circulation for the first time in 1953 by Gov. G. Mennen Williams and the Spartans took initial possession with a 14-6 win. The trophy consists of a four-foot wooden statue of the legendary figure of the north woods astride an axe, mounted on a majestic five-foot stand. An "S" flag is on one side and an "M" flag on the other.

1953	MSU 14,UM 6	1961	MSU 28,UM 0
1954	UM 33,MSU 7	1962	MSU 28,UM 0
1955	UM 14,MSU 7	1963	MSU 7,UM 7
1956	MSU 9,UM 0	1964	UM 17,MSU 10
1957	MSU 35,UM 6	1965	MSU 24,UM 7
1958	MSU 12,UM12	1966	MSU 20, UM 7
1959	MSU 34,UM 8	1967	MSU 34,UM 0
1960	MSU 24,UM 17	1968	UM 28,MSU 14
		1969	MSU 23,UM 12

OLD BRASS SPITTOON

The "Old Brass Spittoon" goes to the winner each year of the Michigan State-Indiana football game. The trophy was initiated in 1950 by the junior and senior classes and the student council at Michigan State, and accepted by the Indiana U. Student Senate. The spittoon came from one of Michigan's earliest trading posts and is believed to be more than 100 years old. It was the students' thought that the spittoon was around when both institutions were founded (Indiana—1820 and MSU—1855) and mellowed along with the schools. Michigan State took first possession of the trophy with a 35-0 win in 1950.

1950	MSU 35,Ind 0	1960	MSU 35,Ind 0
1951	MSU 30, Ind 26	1961	MSU 35,Ind 0
1952	MSU 41,Ind 14	1962	MSU 26, Ind 8
1953	MSU 47,Ind 18	1963	MSU 20,Ind 3
1954	MSU 21,Ind 14	1964	Ind 27,MSU 20
1955	MSU 20,Ind 13	1965	MSU 27,Ind 13
1956	MSU 53,Ind 6	1966	MSU 37,Ind 19
1957	MSU 54,Ind 0	1967	Ind 14,MSU 13
1958	Ind 6,MSU 0	1968	Ind 24,MSU 22
1959	MSU 14,Ind 6	1969	Ind 16,MSU 0

MEGAPHONE TROPHY

To the winner of the Michigan State-Notre Dame football game each fall goes the "Megaphone Trophy," presented for the first time in 1949. The trophy is sponsored jointly by the Michigan State and Notre Dame Alumni Clubs of Detroit. The large megaphone, one half of which is blue with a gold ND monogram, and the other half white with a green MSC, has all the scores of previous games between the two schools inscribed on it. Notre Dame took initial possession with its 34-21 win in 1949.

1949	ND 34, MSU 21	1960	MSU 21, ND 0
1950	MSU 36, ND 33	1961	MSU 17, ND 7
1951	MSU 35, ND 0	1962	MSU 31, ND 7
1952	MSU 21, ND 3	1963	MSU 12, ND 7
1954	ND 20, MSU 19	1964	ND 34, MSU 7
1955	MSU 21, ND 7	1965	MSU 12, ND 3
1956	MSU 47, ND 14	1966	MSU 10, ND 10
1957	MSU 34, ND 6	1967	ND 24, MSU 12
1959	MSU 19, ND 0	1968	MSU 21, ND 17
		1969	ND 42, MSU 28

ATTENDANCE RECORDS

TOP ALL-TIME ATTENDANCES

103,234	At Michigan	1969
103,219	At Michigan	1965
103,210	At Michigan	1967
103,198	At Michigan	1961
102,785	At Michigan	1968
101,450	At Michigan	1963
101,001	At Michigan	1956
101,001	At Michigan	1957
101,000	At Rose Bowl	1954
100,809	At Rose Bowl	1956
100,087	At Rose Bowl	1966

TOP TEN SPARTAN STADIUM CROWDS

80,011	Notre Dame	1966
79,368	Michigan	1969
78,833	Michigan	1966
78,234	Michigan	1964
78,004	Purdue	1966
77,533	Indiana	1969
77,501	Michigan	1962
77,339	Notre Dame	1968
76,520	Ohio State	1960
76,490	Michigan	1960

YEAR-BY-YEAR RECORDS

EARLY UNOFFICIAL SCORES

May 5,			
1886	0	Albion	79
June 4,			
1886	0	Olivet	78
1890	0	Albion Reserves	24
1890	2	Olivet	24
April 4,			
1891	0	Olivet	72
May 2,			
1891	0	Olivet	0
Nov. 10,			
1894	6	Albion Reserves	4

1896
No Coach

Sept. 26	10	Lansing High School	0
Oct. 17	0	Kalamazoo (A)	24
Oct. 25	0	Alma	0
Nov. 14	16	Kalamazoo	18
		Lost 2 Tied 1	

1897
Henry Keep, Coach

Sept. 25	28	Lansing High School	0
Oct. 2	26	Olivet	6

Oct. 9	0	Kalamazoo	28
Oct. 16	18	Olivet (A)	18
Oct. 30	30	Alma (A)	16
Nov. 6	38	Alma	4
Nov. 25	6	Notre Dame (A)	34
		Won 4 Lost 2 Tied 1	

1898

Oct. 8	11	Eastern Michigan (A)	6
Oct. 12	0	Michigan (A)	39
Oct. 15	0	Notre Dame (A)	53
Oct. 22	62	Albion	6
Oct. 29	45	Olivet (A)	0
Nov. 19	24	Eastern Michigan	6
Nov. 24	0	Kalamazoo	17
		Won 4 Lost 3	

1899
Charles O. Bemies, Coach

Sept. 29	0	Notre Dame (A)	40
Oct. 7	6	Detroit A.C. (A)	16
Oct. 14	6	Kalamazoo	10
Oct. 21	11	Alma (A)	11
Nov. 11	18	Eastern Michigan (A)	0
Nov. 25	17	Olivet (A)	18
Nov. 30	23	DePauw	6
		Won 2 Lost 4 Tied 1	

1900

Sept. 29	0	Albion	23
Oct. 10	45	Adrian	0
Oct. 20	6	Detroit A.C. (A)	21
Oct. 27	0	Alma	23
		Won 1 Lost 3	

1901
George E. Denman, Coach

Sept. 28	5	Alma (A)	6
Oct. 5	22	Hillsdale	0
Oct. 12	11	Albion (A)	0
Oct. 19	0	Detroit A.C. (A)	33
Oct. 26	42	Kalamazoo	0
Nov. 2	17	Albion	17
Nov. 16	5	Kalamazoo (A)	15
Nov. 28	18	Olivet	23
		Won 3 Lost 4 Tied 1	

1902

Sept. 27	0	Notre Dame (A)	32
Oct. 4	11	Detroit	0
Oct. 8	0	Michigan (A)	119
Oct. 11	35	Hillsdale	0
Oct. 18	2	Michigan Freshmen	0
Oct. 25	12	DePauw	17
Nov. 1	6	Olivet (A)	11
Nov. 15	22	Albion (A)	11
Nov. 22	5	Alma	16
		Won 4 Lost 5	

1903
Chester L. Brewer, Coach

Oct. 3	0	Notre Dame (A)	12
Oct. 10	11	Alma (A)	0
Oct. 14	11	Michigan Freshmen	0
Oct. 17	11	Kalamazoo	0
Oct. 31	51	Detroit Y.M.C.A.	6
Nov. 7	43	Hillsdale (A)	0
Nov. 14	6	Albion	6
Nov. 21	45	Olivet	0
		Won 6 Lost 1 Tied 1	

1904

Oct. 1	47	Michigan Deaf School	0
Oct. 8	28	Ohio Northern	6
Oct. 15	29	Port Huron Y.M.C.A.	0
Oct. 22	0	Albion (A)	4
Oct. 29	104	Hillsdale	0
Nov. 5	39	Michigan Freshmen	0
Nov. 12	35	Olivet (A)	6
Nov. 19	40	Alma	0
Nov. 26	58	Kalamazoo	0
		Won 8 Lost 1	

1905

Sept. 30	42	Michigan Deaf School	0
Oct. 3	0	Notre Dame (A)	28
Oct. 7	43	Port Huron Y.M.C.A.	0
Oct. 14	24	Michigan Freshmen	0
Oct. 21	30	Olivet	0
Oct. 23	18	Hillsdale	0
Oct. 28	18	Armour Inst.(Chicago)	0
Nov. 4	30	Kalamazoo (A)	0
Nov. 11	46	Albion	10
Nov. 18	11	Northwestern (A)	37
Nov. 25	18	Alma (A)	0
		Won 9 Lost 2	

1906

Sept. 29	23	Olivet	0
Oct. 6	0	Alma (A)	0
Oct. 13	38	Kalamazoo	0
Oct. 20	33	DePauw	0
Oct. 27	0	Notre Dame (A)	5
Nov. 3	37	Albion	0
Nov. 10	5	Albion (A)	0

The Spartans' first football team, organized in 1884.

Nov. 12	12	Alma	0
Nov. 17	35	Hillsdale (A)	9
Nov. 24	6	Olivet (A)	8
Nov. 29	6	Detroit A.C. (A)	6
		Won 7 Lost 2 Tied 2	

1907

Oct. 3	17	Detroit coll.	0
Oct. 5	40	Michigan Deaf School	0
Oct. 12	0	Michigan (A)	46
Oct. 26	15	Wabash	6
Nov. 16	55	Olivet	4
Nov. 23	0	Alma (A)	0
Nov. 28	0	Detroit A.C. (A)	4
		Won 4 Lost 2 Tied 1	

1908

Oct. 3	51	Michigan Deaf School	0
Oct. 10	0	Michigan	0
Oct. 17	35	Kalamazoo	0
Oct. 24	0	Depauw (A)	0
Oct. 31	6	Wabash	0
Nov. 7	46	Olivet (A)	2
Nov. 21	30	Saginaw Naval Brigade	6
Nov. 26	37	Detroit A.C. (A)	14
		Won 6 Tied 2	

1909

Oct. 7	27	Detroit Coll.	0
Oct. 9	34	Alma	0
Oct. 16	28	Wabash	0
Oct. 23	0	Notre Dame	17
Oct. 30	29	Culver Military Academy (A)	0
Nov. 6	51	DePauw	0
Nov. 10	10	Marquette	0
Nov. 13	20	Olivet	0
Nov. 25	34	Detroit A.C. (A)	0
		Won 8 Lost 1	

1910

Oct. 6	35	Detroit Coll.	0
Oct. 8	11	Alma	0
Oct. 15	3	Michigan (A)	6
Oct. 22	37	Lake Forest	0
Oct. 29	17	Notre Dame	0
Nov. 5	3	Marquette (A)	2
Nov. 19	62	Olivet	0
		Won 6 Lost 1	

1911

John F. Macklin, Coach

Oct. 7	12	Alma	0
Oct. 14	3	Michigan	15
Oct. 28	29	Olivet	3
Nov. 4	6	DePauw (A)	0
Nov. 11	26	Mount Union	6
Nov. 30	17	Wabash	6
		Won 5 Lost 1	

1912

Oct. 5	14	Alma	3
Oct. 12	7	Michigan (A)	55
Oct. 19	52	Olivet	0
Oct. 26	58	DePauw	0
Nov. 2	46	Ohio Wesleyan	0
Nov. 9	61	Mount Union	20
Nov. 16	24	Wabash	0
Nov. 28	35	Ohio State (A)	20
		Won 7 Lost 1	

1913

Oct. 4	26	Olivet	0
Oct. 11	57	Alma	0
Oct. 18	12	Michigan (A)	7
Oct. 25	12	Wisconsin (A)	7
Nov. 1	41	Akron	0
Nov. 8	13	Mount Union	7
Nov. 15	19	South Dakota	7
		Won 7	

1914

Oct. 3	26	Olivet	7
Oct. 10	60	Alma	0
Oct. 17	0	Michigan	3
Oct. 24	0	Nebraska (A)	24
Oct. 31	75	Akron	6
Nov. 7	21	Mount Union	14
Nov. 13	6	Penn State (A)	3
		Won 5 Lost 2	

1915

Oct. 2	34	Olivet	0
Oct. 9	77	Alma	12
Oct. 16	56	Carroll	0
Oct. 23	24	Michigan (A)	0
Oct. 30	0	Oregon State	20
Nov. 6	68	Marquette	6
		Won 5 Lost 1	

1916

Frank Summers, Coach

Sept. 30	40	Olivet	0
Oct. 7	20	Carroll	0
Oct. 14	33	Alma	0
Oct. 21	0	Michigan (A)	9
Oct. 28	30	North Dakota State	0
Nov. 4	3	South Dakota (A)	3
Nov. 18	0	Notre Dame	14
		Won 4 Lost 2 Tied 1	

1917

Chester L. Brewer, Coach

Oct. 6	7	Alma	14
Oct. 13	3	Kalamazoo	7
Oct. 20	0	Michigan (A)	27
Oct. 27	0	Detroit	14
Nov. 3	0	Western Michigan	14
Nov. 10	6	Northwestern (A)	39
Nov. 17	0	Notre Dame (A)	23
Nov. 24	7	Syracuse	21
Nov. 29	0	Camp MacArthur (Texas)	20
		Lost 9	

1918

George E. Gauthier, Coach

Oct. 5	21	Albion	6
Oct. 12	66	Adrian	6
Nov. 2	16	Western Michigan	7
Nov. 9	6	Purdue	14
Nov. 16	13	Notre Dame	7
Nov. 23	6	Michigan (A)	21
Nov. 28	6	Wisconsin (A)	7
		Won 4 Lost 3	

1919

Chester L. Brewer, Coach

Oct. 4	14	Albion	13
Oct. 8	46	Alma	6
Oct. 11	18	Western Michigan	21
Oct. 18	0	Michigan (A)	26
Oct. 25	27	DePauw	0
Nov. 1	7	Purdue (A)	13
Nov. 8	13	South Dakota	0
Nov. 15	0	Notre Dame (A)	13
Nov. 27	7	Wabash	7
		Won 4 Lost 4 Tied 1	

1920

George E. (Potsy) Clark, Coach

Sept. 25	.2	Kalamazoo	21

Date		Opponent	
Oct. 2	16	Albion	0
Oct. 6	48	Alma	0
Oct. 9	0	Wisconsin (A)	27
Oct. 16	0	Michigan (A)	35
Oct. 23	7	Marietta	23
Oct. 30	109	Olivet	0
Nov. 13	81	Chicago Y.M.C.A. Coll.	35
Nov. 20	7	Nebraska (A)	35
Nov. 25	0	Notre Dame	25
		Won 4 Lost 6	

1921
Albert M. Barron, Coach

Date		Opponent	
Oct. 1	28	Alma	0
Oct. 8	7	Albion	24
Oct. 15	0	Michigan (A)	30
Oct. 22	17	Western Michigan	14
Oct. 27	0	Marquette (A)	7
Nov. 5	14	South Dakota	0
Nov. 12	2	Butler (A)	3
Nov. 24	0	Notre Dame (A)	48
		Won 3 Lost 5	

1922

Date		Opponent	
Sept. 30	33	Alma	0
Oct. 7	7	Albion	7
Oct. 14	0	Wabash (A)	26
Oct. 21	7	South Dakota	0
Oct. 28	6	Indiana (A)	14
Nov. 4	0	Michigan (A)	63
Nov. 11	6	Ohio Wesleyan	9
Nov. 18	0	Creighton (A)	9
Nov. 25	45	Massachusetts State	0
Nov. 30	7	St. Louis (A)	7
		Won 3 Lost 5 Tied 2	

1923
Ralph H. Young, Coach

Date		Opponent	
Sept. 29	0	Chicago (A)	34
(*)Oct. 6	21	Lake Forest	6
Oct. 13	0	Wisconsin (A)	21
Oct. 20	13	Albion	0
Oct. 27	0	Michigan (A)	37
Nov. 3	14	Ohio Wesleyan	19
Nov. 10	7	Creighton	27
Nov. 17	2	Detroit (A)	0

(*)First game to be played in new stadium
Won 3 Lost 5

1924

Date		Opponent	
Sept. 26	59	North Central	0
Oct. 4	54	Olivet	3
(*)Oct. 10	0	Michigan	7
Oct. 17	34	Chicago Y.M.C.A. Coll.	3
Oct. 25	9	Northwestern (A)	13
Nov. 1	42	Lake Forest	13
Nov. 8	3	St. Louis (A)	9
Nov. 15	9	South Dakota State	0

(*)Dedication of new stadium
Won 5 Lost 3

1925

Date		Opponent	
Sept. 26	16	Adrian	0
Oct. 3	0	Michigan (A)	39
Oct. 10	0	Lake Forest	6
Oct. 17	15	Centre	13
Oct. 24	6	Penn State (A)	13
Nov. 3	0	Colgate	14
Nov. 7	58	Toledo	0
Nov. 14	10	Wisconsin (A)	21
		Won 3 Lost 5	

1926

Date		Opponent	
Sept. 26	16	Adrian	0
Oct. 2	9	Kalamazoo	0
Oct. 9	3	Michigan (A)	55
Oct. 16	14	Cornell (A)	24
Oct. 23	0	Lake Forest	0
Oct. 30	6	Colgate (A)	38
Nov. 6	42	Centre	14
Nov. 20	7	Haskell Indians	40
		Won 3 Lost 4 Tied 1	

1927

Date		Opponent	
Sept. 24	12	Kalamazoo	6
Oct. 1	27	Ohio	0
Oct. 8	0	Michigan (A)	21
Oct. 15	13	Cornell Coll. (Iowa)	19
Oct. 29	7	Detroit	24
Nov. 5	7	Indiana (A)	33
Nov. 11	20	Albion	6
Nov. 19	25	Butler	0
Dec. 3	0	North Carolina State	19
		Won 4 Lost 5	

1928
Harry G. Kipke, Coach

Date		Opponent	
Sept. 29	103	Kalamazoo	0
Oct. 6	0	Albion	2
Oct. 13	37	Chicago Y.M.C.A. Coll.	0
Oct. 20	0	Colgate	16
Nov. 3	6	Mississippi State	6
Nov. 10	0	Detroit (A)	39
Nov. 17	0	Michigan (A)	3
Nov. 24	7	North Carolina State	0
		Won 3 Lost 4 Tied 1	

1929
James H. Crowley, Coach

Date		Opponent	
Sept. 28	59	Alma	6
Oct. 5	0	Michigan (A)	17
Oct. 12	0	Colgate (A)	31
Oct. 19	74	Adrian	0
Oct. 26	40	North Carolina State	6
Nov. 2	38	Case	0
Nov. 9	33	Mississippi State (A)	19
Nov. 16	0	Detroit	25
		Won 5 Lost 3	

1930

Date		Opponent	
Sept. 27	28	Alma	0
Oct. 4	0	Michigan (A)	0
Oct. 11	32	Cincinnati	0
Oct. 18	14	Colgate	7
Oct. 25	45	Case	0
(*)Oct. 31	13	Georgetown (A)	14
Nov. 8	19	North Dakota State	11
Nov. 22	0	Detroit	0

(*)First night game ever played by Michigan State College
Won 5 Lost 1 Tied 2

1931

Date		Opponent	
Sept. 26	74	Alma	0
Oct. 3	47	Cornell Coll. (Iowa)	0
Oct. 10	7	Army (A)	20
Oct. 17	34	Illinois Wesleyan	6
Oct. 24	6	Georgetown	0
Oct. 31	10	Syracuse	15
Nov. 7	100	Ripon	0
Nov. 14	0	Michigan (A)	0
Nov. 21	13	Detroit (A)	20
		Won 5 Lost 3 Tied 1	

1932

Date		Opponent	
Sept. 24	93	Alma	0
Oct. 1	0	Michigan (A)	26
Oct. 8	27	Grinnell	6
Oct. 15	27	Illinois Wesleyan	0
Oct. 22	19	Fordham (A)	13
Oct. 29	27	Syracuse (A)	13
Nov. 5	20	South Dakota	6
Nov. 19	7	Detroit	0
		Won 7 Lost 1	

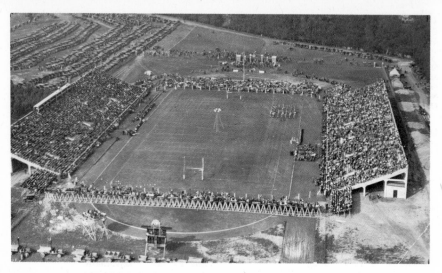

State's new football stadium as it appeared in 1924 when Michigan was the foe at dedication time.

1933
Charles W. Bachman, Coach

Sept. 30	14	Grinnell	0
Oct. 7	6	Michigan (A)	20
Oct. 14	20	Illinois Wesleyan	12
Oct. 21	6	Marquette (A)	0
Oct. 28	27	Syracuse	3
Nov. 4	0	Kansas State	0
Nov. 11	0	Carnegie Tech	0
Nov. 25	0	Detroit (A)	14

Won 4 Lost 2 Tied 2

1934

Sept. 29	33	Grinnell	20
Oct. 6	16	Michigan (A)	0
Oct. 13	13	Carnegie Tech.	0
Oct. 20	39	Manhattan (A)	0
Nov. 3	13	Marquette	7
Nov. 10	0	Syracuse (A)	10
Nov. 17	7	Detroit	6
Nov. 24	6	Kansas (A)	0
Dec. 8	26	Texas A & M (A)	13

Won 8 Lost 1

1935

Sept. 28	41	Grinnell	0
Oct. 5	25	Michigan (A)	6
Oct. 12	42	Kansas	0
Oct. 19	6	Boston (A)	18
Oct. 26	47	Washington (St. Louis)	13
Nov. 2	12	Temple (A)	7
(*)Nov. 9	7	Marquette	13
(**)Nov. 16	27	Loyola (Los Angeles) (A)	0

(*)Dedication of second addition to stadium
(**)First trip to the Western Coast
Won 6 Lost 2

1936

Sept. 26	27	Wayne State	0
Oct. 3	21	Michigan (A)	7
Oct. 10	7	Carnegie Tech. (A)	0
Oct. 17	13	Missouri	0
Oct. 24	7	Marquette	13
Oct. 31	13	Boston (A)	13
(*)Nov. 7	7	Temple	7
Nov. 14	41	Kansas (A)	0
Nov. 21	7	Arizona	0

(*)Night game
Won 6 Lost 1 Tied 2

1937

Sept. 25	19	Wayne State	0
Oct. 2	19	Michigan (A)	14
Oct. 9	0	Manhattan (A)	,3
Oct. 16	2	Missouri (A)	0
Oct. 23	21	Marquette	7
Oct. 30	16	Kansas	0
Nov. 6	13	Temple (A)	6
Nov. 13	13	Carnegie Tech.	6
Nov. 27	14	San Francisco (A)	0

ORANGE BOWL

Jan. 1			
1938	0	Auburn (A)	6

Won 8 Lost 2

1938

Sept. 24	34	Wayne State	6
Oct. 1	0	Michigan (A)	14
Oct. 8	18	Illinois Wesleyan	0
Oct. 15	26	West Virginia (A)	0
Oct. 22	19	Syracuse	12
Oct. 29	6	Santa Clara	7
Nov. 5	0	Missouri (A)	6
Nov. 12	20	Marquette (A)	14
Nov. 19	10	Temple	0

Won 6 Lost 3

1939

Sept. 30	16	Wayne State	0
Oct. 7	13	Michigan (A)	26
Oct. 14	14	Marquette	17
Oct. 21	7	Purdue (A)	20
Oct. 28	13	Illinois Wesleyan	6
Nov. 4	14	Syracuse (A)	3
Nov. 11	0	Santa Clara (A)	6
Nov. 18	7	Indiana	7
Nov. 25	18	Temple	7

Won 4 Lost 4 Tied 1

1940

Oct. 5	14	Michigan (A)	21
Oct. 12	20	Purdue	7
(*)Oct. 18	19	Temple (A)	21
Oct. 25	0	Santa Clara	0
Nov. 2	32	Kansas State	0
Nov. 9	0	Indiana (A)	20
Nov. 16	6	Marquette (A)	7
Nov. 23	17	West Virginia	0

(*) Night game

Won 3   Lost 4   Tied 1

1941

Sept. 27	7	Michigan (A)	19
Oct. 11	13	Marquette	7
Oct. 18	0	Santa Clara (A)	7
Oct. 25	39	Wayne State	6
Nov. 1	0	Missouri	19
Nov. 8	0	Purdue (A)	0
Nov. 15	46	Temple	0
Nov. 22	31	Ohio Wesleyan	7
Nov. 29	14	West Virginia (A)	12

Won 5   Lost 3   Tied 1

1942

Oct. 3	0	Michigan (A)	20
Oct. 10	46	Wayne State	6
Oct. 17	7	Marquette	28
Oct. 24	14	Great Lakes N.T.S.	0
Oct. 31	7	Temple (A)	7
Nov. 7	13	Washington State (A)	25
Nov. 14	19	Purdue	6
Nov. 21	7	West Virginia	0
Nov. 28	7	Oregon State	7

Won 4   Lost 3   Tied 2

1943

Intercollegiate athletics were dropped for the season of 1943. An intramural league of civilian and Army teams was formed. The Army Air Force cadets were not permitted to compete in this league. Neither the Army or Air Force were permitted to engage in intercollegiate competition.

1944

Sept. 30	40	Scranton	12
Oct. 7	2	Kentucky (A)	0
Oct. 14	45	Kansas State	6
(*)Oct. 20	8	Maryland	0
(*)Oct. 27	32	Wayne State (A)	0
Nov. 4	7	Missouri (A)	13
Nov. 11	33	Maryland	0

(*)Night games

Won 6   Lost 1

1945

Sept. 29	0	Michigan (A)	40
Oct. 6	7	Kentucky	6
Oct. 13	12	Pittsburgh (A)	7
Oct. 20	27	Wayne State	7
Oct. 27	13	Marquette	13
Nov. 3	14	Missouri	7
Nov. 10	7	Great Lakes N.T.S.	27
Nov. 17	33	Penn State	0
(*)Nov. 23	7	Miami (Fla.)(A)	21

(*) Night game

Won 5   Lost 3   Tied 1

1946

Sept. 28	42	Wayne State	0
Oct. 5	20	Boston	34
Oct. 12	0	Mississippi State	6
Oct. 19	19	Penn State (A)	16
Oct. 26	7	Cicinnati	18
Nov. 2	14	Kentucky (A)	39
Nov. 9	7	Michigan (A)	55
Nov. 16	20	Marquette	0
Nov. 23	26	Maryland	14
Nov. 30	26	Washington State	20

Won 5   Lost 5

1947

Clarence L. Munn, Coach

Sept. 27	0	Michigan (A)	55
Oct. 4	7	Mississippi State	0
Oct. 11	21	Washington State(A)	7
Oct. 18	20	Iowa State	0
Oct. 25	6	Kentucky	7
Nov. 1	13	Marquette	7
Nov. 8	28	Santa Clara	0
Nov. 15	14	Temple (A)	6
Nov. 29	58	Hawaii (A)	19

Won 7   Lost 2

1948

(*)Sept. 25	7	Michigan	13
Oct. 2	68	Hawaii	21
Oct. 9	7	Notre Dame (A)	26
Oct. 16	61	Arizona	7
Oct. 23	14	Penn State (A)	14
Oct. 30	46	Oregon State (A)	21
Nov. 6	47	Marquette	0
Nov. 13	48	Iowa State (A)	7
Nov. 20	40	Washington State	0
Nov. 27	21	Santa Clara (A)	21

(*)Dedicated the third enlargement of the stadium

Won 6   Lost 2   Tied 2

1949

Sept. 24	3	Michigan (A)	7
Oct. 1	48	Marquette	7
Oct. 8	14	Maryland	7
Oct. 15	42	William & Mary	13
Oct. 22	24	Penn State	0
Oct. 29	62	Temple	14
Nov. 5	21	Notre Dame	34
Nov. 12	20	Oregon State (A)	25
Nov. 19	75	Arizona (A)	0

Won 6   Lost 3

1950

Sept. 23	38	Oregon State	13
Sept. 30	14	Michigan (A)	7
Oct. 7	7	Maryland	34
Oct. 14	33	Willaim & Mary	14
Oct. 21	34	Marquette	6
Oct. 28	36	Notre Dame (A)	33
Nov. 4	35	Indiana	0
Nov. 11	27	Minnesota	0
Nov. 18	19	Pittsburgh (A)	0

Won 8   Lost 1

1951

Sept. 22	6	Oregon State	0
Sept. 29	25	Michigan (A)	0
Oct. 6	24	Ohio State (A)	20
Oct. 13	20	Marquette	14
Oct. 20	32	Penn State (A)	21
Oct. 27	53	Pittsburgh	26
Nov. 10	35	Notre Dame	0
Nov. 17	30	Indiana (A)	26
Nov. 24	45	Colorado	7

Won 9

1952

Sept. 27	27	Michigan (A)	13
Oct. 4	17	Oregon State (A)	14
Oct. 11	48	Texas A & M	6
Oct. 18	48	Syracuse	7
Oct. 25	34	Penn State	7
Nov. 1	14	Purdue (A)	7

<table>
<tr><td>Nov. 8</td><td>41</td><td>Indiana (A)</td><td>14</td></tr>
</table>

Nov. 8	41	Indiana (A)	14
Nov. 15	21	Notre Dame	3
Nov. 22	62	Marquette	14
		Won 9	

1953

Sept. 26	21	Iowa (A)	7
Oct. 3	21	Minnesota (A)	0
Oct. 10	26	Texas Christian	19
Oct. 17	47	Indiana	18
Oct. 24	0	Purdue (A)	6
Oct. 31	34	Oregon State	6
Nov. 7	28	Ohio State (A)	13
Nov. 14	14	Michigan	6
Nov. 21	21	Marquette	15
ROSE BOWL			
Jan. 1, 1954	28	U.C.L.A. (A)	20
		Won 9 Lost 1	

1954

Hugh D. Daugherty, Coach

Sept. 25	10	Iowa (A)	14
Oct. 2	0	Wisconsin	6
Oct. 9	21	Indiana (A)	14
Oct. 16	19	Notre Dame (A)	20
Oct. 23	13	Purdue	27
Oct. 30	13	Minnesota (A)	19
Nov. 6	54	Washington State	6
Nov. 13	7	Michigan (A)	33
Nov. 20	40	Marquette	10
		Won 3 Lost 6	

1955

Sept. 24	20	Indiana (A)	13
Oct. 1	7	Michigan (A)	14
Oct. 8	38	Stanford	14
Oct. 15	21	Notre Dame	7
Oct. 22	21	Illinois	7
Oct. 29	27	Wisconsin (A)	0
Nov. 5	27	Purdue (A)	0
Nov. 12	42	Minnesota	14
Nov. 19	33	Marquette	0
ROSE BOWL			
Jan. 2, 1956	17	U.C.L.A. (A)	14
		Won 9 Lost 1	

1956

Sept. 29	21	Stanford (A)	7
Oct. 6	9	Michigan (A)	0

Oct. 13	53	Indiana	6
Oct. 20	47	Notre Dame (A)	14
Oct. 27	13	Illinois (A)	20
Nov. 3	33	Wisconsin	0
Nov. 10	12	Purdue	9
Nov. 17	13	Minnesota (A)	14
Nov. 24	38	Kansas State	17
		Won 7 Lost 2	

1957

Sept. 28	54	Indiana	0
Oct. 5	19	California (A)	0
Oct. 12	35	Michigan (A)	6
Oct. 19	13	Purdue	20
Oct. 26	19	Illinois	14
Nov. 2	21	Wisconsin (A)	7
Nov. 9	34	Notre Dame	6
Nov. 16	42	Minnesota	13
Nov. 23	27	Kansas State	9
		Won 8 Lost 1	

1958

Sept. 27	32	California	12
Oct. 4	12	Michigan	12
Oct. 11	22	Pittsburgh	8
Oct. 18	6	Purdue (A)	14
Oct. 25	0	Illinois (A)	16
Nov. 1	7	Wisconsin	9
Nov. 8	0	Indiana (A)	6
Nov. 15	12	Minnesota (A)	39
Nov. 22	26	Kansas State	7
		Won 3 Lost 5 Tied 1	

1959

Sept. 28	7	Texas A & M	9
Oct. 3	34	Michigan (A)	8
Oct. 10	8	Iowa (A)	37
Oct. 17	19	Notre Dame	0
Oct. 24	14	Indiana	6
Oct. 31	24	Ohio State (A)	30
Nov. 7	15	Purdue	0
Nov. 14	15	Northwestern	10
Nov. 20	13	Miami (Fla.)(A)	18
		Won 5 Lost 4	

1960

Sept. 24	7	Pittsburgh	7
Oct. 1	24	Michigan	17
Oct. 8	15	Iowa	27
Oct. 15	21	Notre Dame (A)	0
Oct. 22	35	Indiana (A)	0

State's 1952 football team, coached by Biggie Munn, was unbeaten and untied, and was named the mythical national champion.

Date		Opponent	
Oct. 29	10	Ohio State	21
Nov. 5	17	Purdue (A)	13
Nov. 12	21	Northwestern (A)	18
Nov. 19	43	Detroit	15
		Won 6 Lost 2 Tied 1	

1961

Date		Opponent	
Sept. 30	20	Wisconsin (A)	0
Oct. 7	31	Stanford	3
Oct. 14	28	Michigan (A)	0
Oct. 21	17	Notre Dame	7
Oct. 28	35	Indiana	0
Nov. 4	0	Minnesota (A)	13
Nov. 11	6	Purdue (A)	7
Nov. 18	21	Northwestern	13
Nov. 25	34	Illinois	7
		Won 7 Lost 2	

1962

Date		Opponent	
Sept. 29	13	Stanford (A)	16
Oct. 6	38	North Carolina	6
Oct. 13	28	Michigan	0
Oct. 20	31	Notre Dame (A)	7
Oct. 27	26	Indiana (A)	8
Nov. 3	7	Minnesota	28
Nov. 10	9	Purdue	17
Nov. 17	31	Northwestern (A)	7
Nov. 24	6	Illinois (A)	7
		Won 5 Lost 4	

1963

Date		Opponent	
Sept. 28	31	North Carolina	0
(*)Oct. 4	10	Southern California (A)	13
Oct. 12	7	Michigan (A)	7
Oct. 19	20	Indiana	3
Oct. 26	15	Northwestern (A)	7
Nov. 2	30	Wisconsin	13
Nov. 9	23	Purdue (A)	0
Nov. 16	12	Notre Dame	7
Nov. 28	0	Illinois	13

(*) Night game
(**)Game originally scheduled Nov. 23, rescheduled Thanksgiving Day due to assassination of President Kennedy.
Won 6 Lost 2 Tied 1

1964

Date		Opponent	
Sept. 26	15	North Carolina (A)	21
Oct. 3	17	Southern California	7
Oct. 10	10	Michigan	17
Oct. 17	20	Indiana (A)	27
Oct. 24	24	Northwestern	6
Oct. 31	22	Wisconsin (A)	6
Nov. 7	21	Purdue	7
Nov. 14	7	Notre Dame (A)	34
Nov. 21	0	Illinois (A)	16
		Won 4 Lost 5	

1965

Date		Opponent	
Sept. 18	13	U.C.L.A.	3
Sept. 25	23	Penn State (A)	0
Oct. 2	22	Illinois	12
Oct. 9	24	Michigan (A)	7
Oct. 16	32	Ohio State	7
Oct. 23	14	Purdue (A)	10
Oct. 30	49	Northwestern	7
Nov. 6	35	Iowa (A)	0
Nov. 13	27	Indiana	13
Nov. 20	12	Notre Dame (A)	3

ROSE BOWL

Date		Opponent	
Jan. 1, 1966	12	U.C.L.A. (A)	14
		Won 10 Lost 1	

1966

Date		Opponent	
Sept. 17	28	North Carolina State	10
Sept. 24	42	Penn State	8
Oct. 1	26	Illinois (A)	10
Oct. 8	20	Michigan	7
Oct. 15	11	Ohio State (A)	8
Oct. 22	41	Purdue	20
Oct. 29	22	Northwestern (A)	0
Nov. 5	56	Iowa	7
Nov. 12	37	Indiana (A)	19
Nov. 19	10	Notre Dame	10
		Won 9 Tied 1	

1967

Date		Opponent	
Sept. 23	7	Houston	37
Sept. 30	17	Southern California	21
Oct. 7	35	Wisconsin	7
Oct. 14	34	Michigan (A)	0
Oct. 21	0	Minnesota (A)	21
Oct. 28	12	Notre Dame (A)	24
Nov. 4	7	Ohio State	21
Nov. 11	13	Indiana	14
Nov. 18	7	Purdue (A)	21
Nov. 25	41	Northwestern	27
		Won 3 Lost 7	

1968

Date		Opponent	
Sept. 21	14	Syracuse	10
Sept. 28	28	Baylor	10
Oct. 5	39	Wisconsin (A)	0
Oct. 12	14	Michigan (A)	28
Oct. 19	13	Minnesota	14
Oct. 26	21	Notre Dame	17
Nov. 2	20	Ohio State (A)	25
Nov. 9	22	Indiana	24
Nov. 16	0	Purdue	9
Nov. 23	31	Northwestern (A)	14
		Won 5 Lost 5	

1969

Date		Opponent	
Sept. 20	27	Washington	11
Sept. 27	23	Southern Methodist	15
Oct. 4	28	Notre Dame (A)	42
Oct. 11	21	Ohio State (A)	54
Oct. 18	23	Michigan	12
Oct. 25	18	Iowa (A)	19
Nov. 1	0	Indiana	16
Nov. 8	13	Purdue (A)	41
Nov. 15	10	Minnesota	14
Nov. 22	39	Northwestern (A)	7
		Won 4 Lost 6	

Reinier "Dutch" Kemeling, first-team All-American in 1961 and 1962.

Trevor Harris, first-team All-American in 1967 and 1968.

The action is lively whenever State and arch-rival St. Louis meet in soccer.

SOCCER

In the spring of 1952, a small announcement appeared in the student daily, saying that "anyone interested in soccer should attend a meeting at Jenison Gymnasium at 4:30 p.m."

A club team was formed as a result of this meeting and four years later, in the fall of 1956, soccer was elevated to varsity status on a trial basis. The following spring it was made an official varsity sport.

Soccer on a more informal basis had been played on the campus for many years. Veteran trainer Jack Heppinstall, who had played the game in his native England, coached and played the game with interested students during the 1910s and 1920s. He also taught the game in the required physical education program.

Ralph Leonard joined the athletic staff in 1927 to coach wrestling and promote interest in soccer and lacrosse, all of which he had coached at Penn State. But he remained on the staff for only two years and nothing developed in soccer and lacrosse. An influx of students from foreign countries after World War II gave impetus to the game and started the move through the club stage to varsity status.

The varsity team was greatly successful from the very beginning. The first three teams coached by Willard (Gene) Kenney, the first and only coach of the sport to this writing, were undefeated, winning a total of 19 games and tying three. Through 14 seasons, the cumulative record was 120 victories, 13 losses and 13 ties. The team was selected for eight straight NCAA championship tournaments starting in 1962, made at least the semifinals on all but two occasions, won two cochampionships and was runner-up twice.

The original soccer area was Old College Field, but when the sport went varsity in 1956, a field was laid out along Shaw Lane, due south of the varsity running track and west of the varsity football practice area.Members of the 1956 team were Al Sasanko, Jordan Tatter, Leo Vander Horst, Bill Malcolm, Ray Burdett, George Sepetys, Santiago Cabal, Al Sarria, Art Southan, Karl Snilsberg, Wally Burger, Neil Butler, Angelos Pilitsis, Morris Russ, Jocko Nevis, Al Lonigro, John Asmah, Dan Clifford and Aurelio Guzman.

Individual honors piled up along with the victories. Thirteen players have achieved first-team All-American status, headed by two-time selections Reinier Kemeling and Trevor Harris.

Only five teams have defeated State: old nemesis St. Louis nine times in 15 games and Akron, Cleveland State, Navy and Wheaton once each.

Spartan teams are second only to St. Louis in the number of games won in NCAA championship action, with 16 to the Billikens' 25.

SPARTAN SOCCER HONOR ROLL

ALL-AMERICA SELECTIONS
(Selected by the National Soccer Coaches Association)

Year	First Team		Second Team		Honorable Mention	
1956			Angelo Pilitsis	RHB		
1957			Al Sarria	IL	Angelos Pilitsis	LHB
1958	Al Sarria	IR			Bernie Cook	CF
1959	Cecil Heron	CF			Emanuel Bruce-Okine	OL
	Erich Streder	IL				
1960					Reinier Kemeling	CHB
1961	Reinier Kemeling	CF			Rubens Filizola	IR
1962	Rubens Filizola	IL				
	Reinier Kemeling	CHB				
1963					George Janes	IL
1964	Payton Fuller	OL	George Janes	IL	Louie Eckhardt	LHB
1965	Guy Busch	CF				
	Nick Krat	CHB				
1966	Peter Hens	LHB	Tony Keyes	IR	Guy Busch	CF
1967	Trevor Harris	OL	Peter Hens	LHB	Ernie Tuchscherer	OR
1968	Trevor Harris	CF				
	Tony Keyes	IR				

ALL-MIDWEST SELECTIONS
(Selected by the National Soccer Coaches Association)

First Team

Year	First Team
1956	none
1957	Al Sarria
1958	Bernie Cook
	Al Sarria
1959	Cecil Heron
	Erich Streder
1960	Ken Graham
	Reinier Kemeling
1961	Ken Graham
	Reinier Kemeling
1962	Rubens Filizola
	Reinier Kemeling
	Jean Lohri
1963	Sam Donnelly
	George Janes
	Stan Stelmashenko
1964	Louie Eckhardt
	Payton Fuller
	George Janes
1965	Guy Busch
	Nick Krat
1966	Guy Busch
	Peter Hens
	Tony Keyes
1967	Trevor Harris
	Peter Hens
	Ernie Tuchscherer
1968	Trevor Harris
	Tony Keyes
	Alex Skotarek
1969	Art Demling

Second Team or Honorable Mention

Year	Second Team or Honorable Mention
1956	Ray Burdett
	Angelos Pilitsis
	Al Sarria
1957	Ray Burdett
	Angelos Pilitsis
	Leo Vander Horst
1958	Neil Butler
	Leo Vander Horst
1959	Emanuel Bruce-Okine
	Gerhardt Grentz
	Horace Hamilton
	George Sepetys
1960	Rubens Filizola
	Cecil Heron
	Ted Saunders

Year	
	Mabricio Ventura
1961	Rubens Filizola
	Jean Lohri
	Ted Saunders
	Mabricio Ventura
1962	Sam Donnelly
1963	Louie Eckhardt
	Bill Schwarz
1964	Terry Bidiak
	Charlie Dedich
	Nick Krat
	Manny Ruscheinski
1965	Terry Bidiak
	Payton Fuller
	Peter Hens
	George Janes
	Manny Ruscheinski
1966	Gary McBrady
	Kevin O'Connell
	Barry Tiemann
1967	Tony Keyes
	Barry Tiemann
1968	Joe Baum
	Art Demling
	Tommy Kreft

SPARTAN INDIVIDUAL RECORDS

Most Goals in a Season   Tony Keyes, 28, 1968
Most Goals in a Career   Tony Keyes, 56, 1966-68
Most Assists in a Season   Tommy Kreft, 15, 1968
Most Assists in a Career   Tommy Kreft, 32, 1966-68

		G	A	TP	Year
Most Total Points in a season	Tony Keyes	28	6	34	1968
Most Total Points in a Career	Guy Busch	54	22	76	1965-67

Goalies

Most Career Shutouts   13, Joe Baum (1966-68)
Most Shutouts in a Season   8, Charlie Dedich (1964)
Lowest Career Goals Against Average   0.66, Charlie Dedich (1963-64)
Lowest Season Goals Against Average   0.46, Charlie Dedich (1964)

Game Records

Most Goals   6, Cecil Heron, vs. Earlham (1960)
     Mabricio Ventura, vs. Purdue (1960)
     Bill Schwarz, vs. Ball State (1963)
     George Janes, vs. Purdue (1964)

Most Assists   5, Bill Schwarz, vs. Purdue (1963)
     Tony Keyes, vs. Purdue (1966)

SPARTAN TEAM RECORDS

Streaks

Unbeaten Streaks	33 (1966-1968) including 29 wins and 4 ties
	25 (1956-1959) including 22 wins and 3 ties
Consecutive Wins	17 (1957-1959)
	14 (1960-1961)

Season

Most Goals Scored	77	(1968)
Most Assists Scored	68	(1968)
Most Points Scored	145	(1968)
Most Goals per Game	6.4	(1960) with 58 goals in 9 games
Fewest Goals per Game	3.1	(1957) with 25 goals in 8 games
Most Goals Allowed	16	(1959)
Most Goals Allowed per Game	2.0	(1956) with 12 goals in 6 games
Fewest Goals Allowed	6	(1961, 1966, 1969)
Fewest Goals Allowed per Game	0.5	(1966) with 6 goals in 12 games
Most Shutouts	12	(1968) including 11 wins and 1 tie
Most Wins in a Season	12	(1967)
Fewest Wins in a Season	5	(1956)
Most Losses in a Season	2	(1959, 1962, 1965, 1969)
Fewest Losses in a Season	0	(1956, 1957, 1958, 1966, 1967)
Most Ties in a Season	3	(1968)

Game

Most Goals Scored	17 vs. Purdue (1960)
Most Assists Scored	13 vs. Purdue (1968)
Most Points Scored	26 vs. Purdue (1968)
Biggest Margin of Victory	17 vs. Purdue (1960) in 17-0 game
Biggest Margin of Defeat	4 vs. St. Louis (1960) in 0-4 game

Highly successful soccer coach Gene Kenney, l., with player Guy Busch, Athletic Director Biggie Munn and 1967 NCAA cochampionship trophy.

1967 State soccer team which shared national championship with St. Louis.

RECORD BY SEASON

Year	Won	Lost	Tied	Pct.	Goals MS	Opp.	Shutouts MS	Opp.	NCAA
1956	5	0	1	.917	23	12	1	0	
1957	6	0	2	.875	25	7	4	0	
1958	8	0	0	1.000	49	9	5	0	
1959	7	2	0	.778	43	16	2	0	
1960	8	1	0	.889	58	9	5	1	
1961	8	1	0	.889	52	6	4	1	
1962	9	2	0	.818	51	10	6	1	lost in semifinals
1963	9	1	0	.900	62	9	4	1	lost in first round
1964	10	1	2	.846	67	8	8	1	second place
1965	10	2	0	.833	56	12	5	1	second place
1966	10	0	2	.917	66	6	7	0	lost in semifinals
1967	12	0	2	.929	73	11	6	1	cochampionship
1968	11	1	3	.857	77	8	12	1	cochampionship
1969	7	2	1	.750	47	6	7	2	lost in first round
	120	13	13	.866	749	129	76	10	2 cochampionships

RECORD BY OPPONENT

Team	Won	Lost	Tied	Team	Won	Lost	Tied
				Kent State	1	0	0
				Kenyon	2	0	0
Air Force	2	0	1	Long Island	1	0	1
Akron	10	1	0	Marquette	2	0	0
Army	2	0	0	Maryland	2	0	1
Ball State	7	0	0	Michigan	1	0	1
Baltimore	1	0	0	Navy	0	1	0
Brown	1	0	0	North Carolina	1	0	0
Calvin	10	0	0	Ohio	10	0	0
Cleveland State	0	1	0	Ohio State	2	0	0
Denison	3	0	0	Pittsburgh	6	0	0
Denver	2	0	0	Purdue	13	0	0
Earlham	5	0	0	Slippery Rock State	2	0	0
E. Stroudsburg St.	2	0	0	St. Louis	1	9	5
Hope	2	0	0	Temple	1	0	0
Howard	1	0	0	Toledo	2	0	0
Illinois	3	0	0	W. Chester State	0	0	1
Illinois-Chicago Circle	1	0	2	Wheaton	9	1	0
Indiana	8	0	1		120	13	13
Indiana Tech.	1	0	0				

YEAR-BY-YEAR RECORDS

1956
Willard E. Kenney, Coach

Date		Opponent	
Oct. 13	3	Michigan	1
Oct. 27	3	Kenyon (A)	2
Nov. 3	6	Illinois (A)	3
Nov. 10	4	Wheaton (A)	0
Nov. 11	2	Illinois (Chicago Circle) (A)	2
Nov. 24	5	Purdue (A)	4

Won 5   Tied 1

1957
Oct. 5	3	Michigan	3
Oct. 12	1	Illinois (Chicago Circle) (A)	1
Oct. 19	3	Purdue	2
Oct. 26	1	Illinois	0
Oct. 30	2	Wheston	1
Nov. 2	2	Ohio State (A)	0
Nov. 9	5	Kenyon	0
Nov. 16	7	Indiana (A)	0

Won 6   Tied 2

1958
Oct. 4	6	Indiana Tech.	0
Oct. 11	1	Pittsburgh	0
Oct. 18	4	Purdue (A)	0
Oct. 25	10	Illinois (A)	5
Nov. 1	8	Ohio State	1
Nov. 5	5	Weaton (A)	0
Nov. 8	4	Slippery Rock (A)	0
Nov. 15	11	Indiana (A)	3

Won 8

1959
Oct. 3	4	Indiana Tech. (A)	3
Oct. 7	9	Calvin	0
Oct. 10	4	Slippery Rock (A)	2
Oct. 17	2	St. Louis	4
Oct. 21	5	Calvin (A)	0
Oct. 24	5	Indiana	1
Oct. 31	3	Wheaton	4
Nov. 7	9	Purdue	1
Nov. 14	2	Pittsburgh (A)	1

Won 7   Lost 2

1960
Oct. 1	6	Earlham	2
Oct. 8	4	Pittsburgh	0
Oct. 15	0	St. Louis (A)	4
Oct. 22	3	Wheaton (A)	1
Oct. 26	10	Ohio	0
Oct. 29	7	Indiana Tech.	2
Nov. 2	5	Calvin	0
Nov. 5	17	Purdue (A)	0
Nov. 12	6	Indiana (A)	0

Won 8   Lost 1

1961
Sept. 30	7	Earlham (A)	0
Oct. 7	5	Wheaton	0
Oct. 14	4	Pittsburgh (A)	1
Oct. 18	4	Calvin (A)	0
Oct. 21	10	Indiana	0
Oct. 25	5	Indiana Tech. (A)	1
Oct. 28	13	Purdue	2
Nov. 4	4	Ohio (A)	1
Nov. 11	0	St. Louis	1

Won 8   Lost 1

1962
Sept. 29	3	Purdue (A)	1
Oct. 6	10	Earlham	0
Oct. 10	4	Calvin	1
Oct. 13	2	Wheaton (A)	0
Oct. 20	6	Akron	4
Oct. 25	5	Ball State	0
Oct. 27	4	Ohio	0
Nov. 3	12	Indiana (A)	0
Nov. 10	1	St. Louis (A)	2
*Nov. 19	4	Howard	0
*Nov. 29	0	St. Louis (A)	2

*National Collegiate Athletic Association Championships

Won 9   Lost 2

1963
Sept. 28	3	Earlham (A)	1
Oct. 5	6	Wheaton	0
Oct. 9	4	Calvin (A)	0
Oct. 12	14	Purdue	1
Oct. 18	3	Akron (A)	0
Oct. 23	10	Ball State (A)	1
Oct. 26	7	Indiana	0
Nov. 2	11	Ohio (A)	1
Nov. 9	4	St. Louis	3
*Nov. 21	0	St. Louis	2

*National Collegiate Athletic Association Championships

Won 9   Lost 1

1964
Sept. 26	6	Earlham	1
Oct. 3	15	Purdue (A)	0
Oct. 7	8	Calvin	0
Oct. 10	9	Wheaton (A)	0
Oct. 17	5	Akron	0
Oct. 22	8	Ball State	0
Oct. 24	3	Indiana (A)	3
Oct. 31	4	Ohio	0
Nov. 7	1	St. Louis (A)	1
**Nov. 21	1	Maryland	0
*Nov. 28	4	East Stroudsburg	0
*Dec. 3	3	U. S. Military Acad. (at Providence, R.I.)	2
*Dec. 5	0	U. S. Naval Acad. (at Providence, R.I.)	1

*National Collegiate Athletic Association Championships

Won 10   Lost 1   Tied 2

1965
Sept. 25	9	Wheaton	0
Oct. 1	4	Denison	3
Oct. 6	7	Calvin (A)	1
Oct. 9	6	Indiana	0
Oct. 15	5	Akron (A)	2
Oct. 23	9	Marquette	0
Oct. 30	2	Ohio (A)	0
Nov. 6	2	St. Louis	3
*Nov. 20	7	Baltimore	0
*Nov. 21	2	East Stroudsburg	1
*Nov. 27	3	U. S. Military Acad. (at St. Louis, Mo.)	1
*Nov. 28	0	St. Louis (at St. Louis, Mo.)	1

*National Collegiate Athletic Association Championships

Won 10   Lost 2

1966

Sept. 24	10	Purdue (A)	0
Oct. 1	6	Pittsburgh	0
Oct. 5	13	Calvin	0
Oct. 8	6	Denison (A)	1
Oct. 15	4	Akron	1
Oct. 22	7	Marquette (A)	0
Oct. 27	7	Ball State	0
Oct. 29	5	Ohio	0
Nov. 5	1	St. Louis (A)	1
*Dec. 1	2	Akron	0
		(at Berkeley, Calif.)	
*Dec. 2	3	Temple	1
		(at Berkeley, Calif.)	
*Dec. 3	2	Long Island	2
		(at Berkeley, Calif.)	

*National Collegiate Athletic Association
Championships
                    Won 10   Tied 2

1967

Sept. 23	11	Purdue	0
Sept. 26	7	Calvin	1
Sept. 30	1	Pittsburgh (A)	0
Oct. 6	3	Denver (A)	1
Oct. 8	4	Air Force (A)	0
Oct. 14	4	Akron	2
Oct. 18	11	Ball State (A)	0
Oct. 21	12	Denison	1
Oct. 30	3	St. Louis	3
Nov. 3	6	Ohio (A)	1
*Nov. 18	4	Maryland	1
*Nov. 25	3	Akron	1
*Nov. 30	4	Long Island	0
		(at St. Louis, Mo.)	
*Dec. 2	0	St. Louis	0
		(at St. Louis, Mo.)	

*National Collegiate Athletic Association
Championships
                    Won 12   Tied 2

1968

Sept. 20	13	Purdue (A)	0
Sept. 25	12	Ball State	0
Sept. 27	8	Toledo (A)	0
Oct. 4	7	Denver	0
Oct. 5	4	Illinois	0
		(Chicago Circle)	

Oct. 9	7	Hope (A)	0
Oct. 12	8	Air Force	0
Oct. 18	1	Akron (A)	4
Oct. 26	0	St. Louis (A)	0
Nov. 2	5	Ohio	0
*Nov. 18	5	North Carolina (A)	0
*Nov. 23	1	Akron (A)	0
**Nov. 30	2	West Chester (A)	2
*Dec. 5	2	Brown (Atlanta Ga.)	0
*Dec. 7	2	Maryland	2
		(Atlanta, Ga.)	

*National Collegiate Athletic
  Association Championships
**Advanced on basis or more corner kicks
            Won 11   Lost 1   Tied 3

1969

Sept. 19	8	Purdue	0
Sept. 23	6	Hope	0
Sept. 26	12	Kent State	0
Oct. 4	1	Air Force (A)	1
Oct. 8	8	Ball State (A)	0
Oct. 11	8	Toledo (A)	0
Oct. 17	1	Akron	0
Oct. 25	0	St. Louis	2
Oct. 31	3	Ohio (A)	0
*Nov. 22	0	Cleveland State	3

*National Collegiate Athletic Association
  Championships
            Won 7   Lost 2   Tied 1

Al Sarria, first State booter to make
first-team All-American, 1958.

WINTER SPORTS

Jack Quiggle, Helms All-American in 1957, star of club that reached NCAA semis.

Johnny Green, 1959 All-American, All-Big Ten and Big Ten's most valuable player.

Chet Aubuchon, 1940 varsity star and State's first All-American player.

Coach Ben VanAlstyne, l., with star basketball performer Robin Roberts.

BASKETBALL

Varsity basketball at Michigan State dates back to 1899, just eight years after it had been invented by James Naismith at the Springfield YMCA College.

Members of that first team which played and lost two games to Olivet, 7-6 and 15-6, were forwards W. J. Boone and Channing Beebe, center Samuel Kennedy, and guards Ellis Ranney and Thomas Agnew. The team had no official coach, but Walter K. Brainard, a varsity football player who captained the 1897 team, served as its manager.

Basketball has been played in four different locations, three of which remain in use today as athletic facilities. Only the first, the old Armory Building on the site of the present Music Building, is gone. The game was played there from 1899 until 1918.

The basketball scene shifted in 1918 to the then new Men's Gymnasium, now the Women's Gymnasium. In 1930, the locale again was changed to the Demonstration Hall Arena where it remained until 1940. In that year, with the completion of Jenison Gymnasium and Field House, basketball moved to its present field house home.

Each successive facility was larger and better suited to the game. The Armory held about 1,200 people. The baskets and backboards were attached flush to brick walls and the overhead girders were so low that smart Aggie shooters actually lofted long shots over them. Layups were made easier by springing up on a wooden ledge that encircled the Armory just above the heat pipes.

The gymnasium could accommodate perhaps 3,500 people on bleachers installed on both floor level and on a balcony which also held a running track with banked turns.

Demonstration Hall, dressed up for basketball with a brand new portable floor, the same one still in use in Jenison Field House, could hold about 5,500 people. Its shortcomings included restricted availability for basketball and large vertical "I" beams which could impede vision of the floor. Demonstration Hall was the last major athletic structure at State to be erected with public funds appropriated through the legislature, and was intended for joint use of the athletic department and ROTC. The arrangement which was worked out required all home basketball games to be played during the first six weeks of winter term. The portable floor then had to be removed so that ROTC could use the area for drills. Indoor polo was another complicating factor. State's ROTC program at that time featured horse cavalry, and the animals were used for polo practice and games in Demonstration Hall. This greatly compounded scheduling problems.

Jenison Field House has been a splendid site for varsity basketball games and also for the state high school basketball tournament. Its current capacity is 12,500, but an all-time record crowd of 15,384 saw the classic game with Kentucky in 1948.

Just as in football, the first fine era in Aggie basketball came under the leadership of Chester Brewer. In those days, there was one coach who handled all sports. Brewer coached seven seasons, 1904 through 1910, and produced the all-time top winning percentage, .742, on 69 victories and 24 defeats. His winningest teams were those from 1906 through 1908, which went 11-2, 14-2 and 15-5, respectively.

Early schedules contained mostly small colleges, YMCAs and an assortment of club teams, such as the Governor's Guard, Saginaw Bank Clerks, Detroit A.C., South Haven Independents, Detroit Burroughs and even some high schools.

Stronger opponents coming on the cards—Michigan, Notre Dame, Ohio State, Purdue and others—took their toll, and basketball in the Macklin era attained a more modest victory level. But there were some great players and memorable victories. Robert Goss, who won four letters from 1911 through 1914, may have been the best of them all. Other fine ones included Blake and Hiram Miller, David Peppard and Lyman Frimodig. The latter popped in 30 points on 15 field goals in 1915 against Hope College (MAC won 56-20), a single-game record which stood up for 35 years. Bill Rapchak topped it with 34 against Marquette in Jenison Field House in 1950.

From World War I days until the arrival of Ben VanAlstyne on the scene as head coach in 1926, State's cage fortunes were at a very modest level. The biggest winner was the 1920-21 team coached by Frimodig, then back at his alma mater for a stay of over 41 years. It produced a 13-8 mark, highlighted by victories over Central Michigan, Western Michigan and Notre Dame.

The preceding season of 1919-20 was a notable one in that the team played a gigantic schedule of 36 games under two coaches. The first phase was a 29-game regular schedule, in itself the biggest slate of games in State's entire basketball history, under George Gauthier. At the end of this play, early in March, Gauthier took off for a new job as director of recreation for Bay City. Frimodig, the freshman coach under Gauthier, arranged a seven-game good will barnstorming trip to the Northern Peninsula over the spring vacation break. He assumed the head coaching reigns and the team won six of the seven contests, including two over college teams: Northern Michigan and Michigan Tech.

Good players of the 1920s included Jack Foster, Ed Gilkey, Lloyd Heasley, Larry Kurtz and Hugh Robinson.

With the coming of Van Alstyne, State's basketball image acquired new lustre. His first club was a loser, but then he put together eight straight big winners that projected State into the national cage limelight like never before. The Spartans—State athletic teams had assumed that name the same year Van Alstyne came to East Lansing—played and beat the best: Marquette, Michigan, Cincinnati, Xavier, Colgate, Detroit, Cornell, Loyola of Chicago, West Virginia and many others. State's teams had some rough going in the late 1930s, but got hot again and had fine seasons right through the war years and up until Van Alstyne's retirement in 1949. Great players are almost too numerous to mention, but a few of the

standouts during the Van Alstyne era of 22 seasons were Fred DenHerder, Verne Dickeson, Carl Felt, Don Grove, Chet Aubuchon (State's first All-American), Robin Roberts, Joe Gerard, Art Haga, Bob Herrick, Martin Hutt, Milo Rouse, Arnold Van Faasen and Jim VanZylen. State's record winning streak of 16 came in the 1930-31 and 1931-32 campaigns.

State's next prosperous era came in the early years of the Forddy Anderson regime. His first five teams, 1954-55 through 1958-59, were all winners. The 1956-57 and 1958-59 clubs projected State into the national spotlight through participation in the NCAA championship tournaments. The 1956-57 team tied for the Big Ten championship and progressed all the way to the NCAA semi-final round at Kansas City before bowing out. The 1958-59 club won the Big Ten title outright and finished second in the NCAA mid-East Regional tournament. The great player of this period was 6-5 center John Green. He made All-Big Ten three straight years and, in 1959, his senior season, made All-American and was named the Big Ten's Most Valuable Player. Other outstanding players of this championship era were George Ferguson, Larry Hedden, Horace Walker, Bob Anderegg, Jack Quiggle and Lance Olson.

The most recent spurt to the top was staged under Head Coach John Benington in his first two years at State as successor to Anderson.

His initial squad (1965-1966) surprised with a 17-7 record and a second-place finish in the Big Ten at 10-4. The 1966-67 club put together a 16-7 record and shared with Indiana the Big Ten title with another 10-4 mark. Among the heroes of this surge were Stan Washington, Bill Curtis, Matthew Aitch and Lee Lafayette.

A number of outstanding players who didn't have the good fortune to be in action during championship periods also graced the modern cage era at State. High among them was Julius (Hooks) McCoy, who set State's still-standing single-game (45 points), season (600) and career (1,377) scoring marks in his 1953-54, 1954-55 and 1955-56 campaigns. McCoy was State's first first-team All-Big Ten player.

Other standouts were Al Ferrari, declared the team's Most Valuable Player for three straight seasons in the early 1950s under both Pete Newell and Forddy Anderson, and Pete Gent, who had a great career in the lean years of the early 1960s.

The Benington era came to a sudden, tragic end with the death of Benington following the second of two heart attacks he suffered in a few months time. The first struck him April 11, 1969, in the Men's Intramural Building following a paddleball game. He seemed to have recovered completely from this attack and was preparing to resume his duties as head coach for the 1969-70 season when the second brought his end. Benington died Sept. 10 at the age of 47 in the coaches' lockerroom of Jenison Gymnasium, leaving his wife and a family of nine children.

Gus Ganakas, Benington's assistant coach and former East Lansing High School mentor, was named John's successor. He led his first team to a fair 9-15 record considering the circumstances. Ralph Simpson, a sophomore from Detroit, made his varsity debut and immediately stamped himself as one of State's all-time cage greats. He set a single season Spartan scoring record of 667 points, made All-America and All-Big Ten and was the highest-scoring sophomore in the country at a 29.0 per

game average. He also made All-Big Ten and All-America academic teams.

Hopes of excellent seasons immediately ahead were dashed when Simpson signed a bonus contract with Denver of the American Basketball Association, reportedly worth in excess of $1,000,000.

SPARTAN BASKETBALL HONOR ROLL

ALL-AMERICA
Chester Aubuchon, G, 1940
Jack Quiggle, G, 1957
John Green, C, 1959
Ralph Simpson, G, 1970

ALL-BIG 10
List Contains First, Second, Third Team and
Honorary Mention Selections
(*Marks first team selections)

1953	Ferrari, Albert R.—Guard
	Stackhouse, Keith L.—Guard
1954	McCoy, Julius—Forward
	Ferrari, Albert R.—Forward
1955	Ferrari, Albert R.—Forward
	McCoy, Julius—Forward
1956	*McCoy, Julius—Forward
1957	*Quiggle, Jack E.—Guard
	*Green, John M.—Center
	Ferguson, George H.—Forward
1958	*Green, John M.—Center
	Anderegg, Robert H.—Forward
	Quiggle, Jack E.—Guard
	Hedden, Larry D.—Forward
1959	*Green, John M.—Center
	Anderegg, Robert H.—Forward
	Walker, Horace—Forward
1960	*Walker, Horace—Center
	Olson, Lance E.—Forward
	Fahs, Dave L.—Guard
1961	Fahs, Dave L.—Guard
	Hall, Richard D.—Forward
	Schwarm, Arthur V.—Guard
1962	Gent, George E.—Forward
	Schwarm, Arthur V.—Guard
	Schwarz, William R.—Guard
1963	Gent, George E.—Forward
	Sanders, Marcus L.—Forward
	Williams, Edward L.—Center
1964	Gent, George E.—Forward
1965	Washington, Stanley—Guard
	Curtis, William A.—Center
	Sanders, Marcus L.—Forward
1966	*Washington, Stanley—Forward
	Curtis, William A.—Forward
	Aitch, Matthew A.—Center
1967	Aitch, Matthew A.—Center
	Lafayette, Lee A.—Forward
	Rymal, Steven A.—Guard
1968	Lafayette, Lee A.—Center
1969	*Lafayette, Lee A.—Center
	Stepter, Harrison—Guard
	Copeland, Bernie Y.—Forward
1970	*Simpson, Ralph—Guard

BIG TEN MOST VALUABLE
1959   John Green

**MOST VALUABLE
PLAYER AWARD**
(By vote of team to receive
Chicago Tribune Award)

1951—James Snodgrass
1952—William Bower
1953—Albert Ferrari
1954—Albert Ferrari
1955—Albert Ferrari
1956—Julius McCoy
1957—George Ferguson
1958—John Green
1959—John Green*
1960—Horace Walker
1961—Arthur Schwarm
1962—George (Pete) Gent
1963—Edward (Ted) Williams
1964—Frederick Thomann
1965—Stanley Washington
1966—Stanley Washington
1967—Matthew Aitch
1968—Lee Lafayette
1969—Lee Lafayette
1970—Ralph Simpson

*Received Chicago Tribune Trophy as Most Valuable in Conference

**MOST IMPROVED
PLAYER AWARD**
Selected by Coaches to receive
Ingham County Alumni Club Trophy)

1963—William Berry
1964—Stanley Washington
1965—Edward (Ted) Crary
1966—Matthew Aitch
1967—Heywood Edwards
1968—James Gibbons
1969—Tom Lick
1970—Rudy Benjamin

SPORTSMANSHIP AWARD
(Selected by Coaches to receive
Stephen G. Scofes Award)

1963—William Schwarz
1964—Marcus Sanders
1965—John Shick
1966—Edward (Ted) Crary
1967—Edward (Ted) Crary
1968—Gerald Geistler
1969—John Holms
1970—Steve Kirkpatrick

INDIVIDUAL RECORDS

Career

Most Points Scored—1,377 by Julius McCoy, 1953-56
Most Field Goals Scored—505 by Julius McCoy, 1953-56
Most Free Throws Scored—379 by Al Ferrari, 1951-55
Most Rebounds—1,036 by John Green, 1957-59

Season

Most Points Scored—667 by Ralph Simpson, 1969-70
Best Scoring Average—29.0 by Ralph Simpson, 1969-70
Best Field Goal Average—.525 by Pat Miller, 1969-70
Best Free Throw Average—.851 by Stan Washington, 1964-65
Most Field Goals— 264 by Ralph Simpson, 1969-70
Most Free Throws—152 by Al Ferrari, 1954-55
Most Rebounds—392 by John Green, 1957-58
Best Rebound Average—17.8 by John Green, 1957-58 (G:22, Reb.: 392)

Game

Most Points Scored—45 by Julius McCoy vs. Notre Dame, 1956
Most Field Goals Scored—20 by Julius McCoy vs. Notre Dame, 1956
Most Free Throws Scored—21 by Al Ferrari vs. Indiana, 1955
Most Free Throws Attempted—25 by Al Ferrari vs. Indiana, 1955
Most Rebounds—29 by John Green vs. Washing, 1957, and by Horace Walker vs. Butler, 1959

Big Ten Game

Most Points Scored—41 by Julius McCoy vs. Michigan, 1956
Most Field Goals Scored—16 by Bill Curtis vs. Michigan, 1965
Most Free Throws Scored—21 by Al Ferrari vs. Indiana, 1955
Most Free Throws Attempted—25 by Al Ferrari vs. Indiana, 1955
Most Rebounds—28 by Horace Walker vs. Iowa, 1960

SPARTAN TEAM RECORDS

RECORD BY SEASON

Year	W	L	Pct.	Coach
1898-99	0	2	.000	No Established Coach
1899-00	2	2	.500	Charles O. Bemies
1900-01	3	0	1.000	Charles O. Bemies
1901-02	5	0	1.000	George E. Denman
1902-03	6	0	1.000	George E. Denman
1903-04	5	3	.625	Chester L. Brewer
1904-05	5	3	.625	Chester L. Brewer
1905-06	11	2	.846	Chester L. Brewer
1906-07	14	2	.875	Chester L. Brewer
1907-08	15	5	.750	Chester L. Brewer
1908-09	10	5	.667	Chester L. Brewer
1909-10	10	5	.667	Chester L. Brewer
1910-11	5	9	.357	John F. Macklin
1911-12	12	3	.800	John F. Macklin
1912-13	8	5	.615	John F. Macklin
1913-14	8	4	.667	John F. Macklin
1914-15	7	9	.438	John F. Macklin
1915-16	8	8	.500	John F. Macklin
1916-17	11	5	.688	George E. Gauthier
1917-18	6	10	.375	George E. Gauthier
1918-19	9	9	.500	George E. Gauthier
1919-20	21	15	.583	George E. Gauthier
1920-21	13	8	.619	Lyman L. Frimodig
1921-22	11	13	.458	Lyman L. Frimodig
1922-23	10	9	.526	Fred H. Walker
1923-24	10	10	.500	Fred H. Walker
1924-25	6	13	.316	John H. Kobs
1925-26	5	13	.278	John H. Kobs
1926-27	7	11	.389	Benjamin F. VanAlstyne
1927-28	11	4	.733	Benjamin F. VanAlstyne
1928-29	11	5	.688	Benjamin F. VanAlstyne
1929-30	12	4	.750	Benjamin F. VanAlstyne
1930-31	16	1	.941	Benjamin F. VanAlstyne
1931-32	12	5	.706	Benjamin F. VanAlstyne
1932-33	10	7	.588	Benjamin F. VanAlstyne
1933-34	12	5	.705	Benjamin F. VanAlstyne
1934-35	14	4	.778	Benjamin F. VanAlstyne
1935-36	8	9	.471	Benjamin F. VanAlstyne
1936-37	5	12	.294	Benjamin F. VanAlstyne

1937-38	9	8	.529	Benjamin F. VanAlstyne
1938-39	9	8	.529	Benjamin F. VanAlstyne
1939-40	14	6	.700	Benjamin F. VanAlstyne
1940-41	11	6	.647	Benjamin F. VanAlstyne
1941-42	15	6	.714	Benjamin F. VanAlstyne
1942-43	2	14	.125	Benjamin F. VanAlstyne
1943-44	No Schedule — World War II			
1944-45	10	7	.588	Benjamin F. VanAlstyne
1945-46	12	9	.571	Benjamin F. VanAlstyne
1946-47	11	10	.524	Benjamin F. VanAlstyne
1947-48	12	10	.545	Benjamin F. VanAlstyne
1948-49	9	12	.429	Benjamin F. VanAlstyne
1949-50	4	18	.182	Alton S. Kircher
1950-51	10	11	.476	Peter F. Newell
1951-52	13	9	.591	Peter F. Newell
1952-53	13	9	.591	Peter F. Newell
1953-54	9	13	.409	Peter F. Newell
1954-55	13	9	.591	Forrest A. Anderson
1955-56	13	9	.591	Forrest A. Anderson
1956-57	16	10	.615	Forrest A. Anderson
1957-58	16	6	.727	Forrest A. Anderson
1958-59	19	4	.826	Forrest A. Anderson
1959-60	10	11	.476	Forrest A. Anderson
1960-61	7	17	.292	Forrest A. Anderson
1961-62	8	14	.381	Forrest A. Anderson
1962-63	4	16	.200	Forrest A. Anderson
1963-64	14	10	.583	Forrest A. Anderson
1964-65	5	18	.217	Forrest A. Anderson
1965-66	17	7	.682	John E. Benington
1966-67	16	7	.696	John E. Benington
1967-68	12	12	.500	John E. Benington
1968-69	11	12	.478	John E. Benington
1969-70	9	15	.375	Gus G. Ganakas
All-Time	708	572	.553	

RECORD BY OPPONENT

	W	L
Adrian	12	0
Albion	10	1
Alma	15	1
Alumni	2	1
Arizona	0	1
Armour Tech	7	2
Ann Arbor YMCA	0	2
Baltimore	1	0
Battle Creek YMCA	3	0
Bay City YMCA	2	0
Bethany	2	0
Boston College	1	0
Bowling Green State	4	1
Bradley	1	0
Brigham Young	2	2
Buchtel	1	1
Buffalo	4	0
Burroughs Adding	3	0
Butler	11	10
Camp Custer Enlisted	1	1
Camp Custer Officers	1	0
Camp Grant	0	2
California	0	5
California State-Fullerton	1	0
Carleton	0	1
Carnegie Tech	4	0
Case	1	1
Central Michigan	17	0
Chicago Westside YMCA	0	1
Chicago YMCA College	3	0
Chicago	2	3
Cincinnati	5	2
Coe	1	0
Colgate	5	1
Colorado	1	1
Concordia	1	0
Cornell	3	1
Creighton	7	5
Dartmouth	1	0
Dearborn Naval AB	1	0
Defiance	2	0
Denison	0	1
Denver	1	0
Detroit	33	8
Detroit A.C.	0	3
Detroit Law College	2	0
Detroit YMCA	10	13
DePaul	3	7
DePauw	1	5
Drake	2	1
Duke	1	0
Eastern Kentucky	1	0
Eastern Michigan	17	1
Earlham	1	1
Fort Custer	1	0
Franklin	0	2
Geneva	1	0
George Washington	0	1
Georgia Tech	1	1
Governor's Guard	3	0
Grand Rapids J.C.	1	0
Grand Rapids YMCA	5	1
Great Lakes Navy	1	4
Haskell Indians	1	0
Hardin-Simmons	1	0
Harvard	2	2
Hawaiian All-Stars	1	1
Hillsdale	8	0
Hope	22	12
Illinois	13	17
Illinois A.C.	1	3
Indiana	12	24
Iowa	15	23
Iowa State	2	1
Jackson YMCA	6	0
John Carroll	1	1
Kalamazoo	18	2
Kansas	1	1
Kansas State	2	2
Kentucky	5	8

Lake Forest	6	1
Lombard	0	2
Long Island	1	2
Louisville	0	1
Loyola (La.)	1	1
Marietta	1	0
Marquette	30	23
Maryland	1	0
Meija	1	0
Memphis State	0	1
Mercer	0	1
Mercer A.C.	0	1
Mercury A.C. (Chi.)	0	1
Miami (O.)	1	0
Mich. School for Deaf	1	0
Michigan	36	53
Michigan Tech	1	0
Midland YMCA	1	0
Minnesota	15	24
Mississippi College	2	0
Missouri	1	2
Mount Union	2	0
Muskingum	1	0
Nebraska	4	3
Northern Michigan	3	1
Northwestern	20	22
Northwestern College	1	8
North Carolina	1	1
North Carolina State	0	1
Notre Dame	32	56
Oberlin	7	6
Ohio	1	0
Ohio Northern	3	0
Ohio State	15	25
Ohio Wesleyan	2	3
Oklahoma	2	0
Olivet	7	4
Oregon	0	2
Oregon State	1	2
Owosso YMCA	1	0
Pennsylvania	1	1
Pennsylvania State	4	0
Pittsburgh	2	1
Portland	1	0
Princeton	2	1
Purdue	12	22
Rayl's (Detroit)	1	0
Rochester YMCA	1	1
Rochester	0	1
Romulus Naval AB	1	0
Rose Poly	1	2
Saginaw Bank Clerks	1	0
Saginaw High	2	0
Saginaw YMCA	1	0
St. Francis	0	1
St. Ignatius College	0	2
St. John's (N.Y.)	0	1
St. John's (Ohio)	3	1
St. Joseph's (Pa.)	0	1
St. Mary's (Mich.)	2	1
St. Mary's (Ohio)	0	1
St. Viator	1	2
San Francisco	0	1
South Carolina	2	0
South Dakota	1	0
South Haven, Ind.	1	0
Southern Illinois	2	0
Southern California	2	2
Southwestern Louisiana	1	0
Spauldings (Det.)	2	1
Stanford	2	1
Syracuse	6	5
Temple	4	4
Tennessee	2	0
Toledo	1	1
Toledo Buckeyes	3	3
Tri-State	1	0
Tulane	2	0
Tulsa	1	2
UCLA	1	3
Upper Canada Law	1	0
Utah	0	3
Utah State	0	1
Valparaiso	2	1
Vanderbilt	0	1
Victoria	1	0
Villanova	0	2
Virginia	1	0
Wabash	3	6
Washington	1	1
Washington State	1	1
Washington (St. L.)	1	0
Wayne State	16	1
Western Kentucky	0	1
Western Michigan	12	8
Western Reserve	8	1
West Virginia	2	1
West Virginia Wesleyan	2	1
Wichita State	1	2
Winona	3	0
Wisconsin	21	26
Wyoming	2	0
Xavier	3	1

Al Ferrari, member of 1953, 54, 55 clubs and a star in State's early Big Ten play.

SPARTAN COACHES' RECORD

Coach	Seasons	W	L	Pct.
No Coach	1899	0	2	.000
Bemies, Charles O.	1900-1901	5	2	.714
Denham, George E.	1902-1903	11	0	1.000
Brewer, Chester L.	1904-1910	70	25	.737
Macklin, John F.	1911-1916	48	38	.559
Gauthier, George E.	1917-1920	47	39	.547
Frimodig, Lyman L.	1921-1922	24	21	.533
Walker, Fred M.	1923-1924	20	19	.513
Kobs, John H.	1925-1926	11	26	.297
VanAlstyne, Benjamin F.	1927-1949	232	163	.589
Kircher, Alton S.	1949-1950	4	18	.182
Newell, Peter F.	1950-1954	45	42	.517
Anderson, Forrest	1954-1965	126	124	.502
Benington, John E.	1965-1969	56	38	.596
*Ganakas, Gus	1969-1970	9	15	.375
All Time		708	572	.553

*Current Coach

SPARTAN TOURNAMENT RECORD

1955—Maryland Tournament, second.
1956—Big Seven Tournament, third.
1957—NCAA Championship Tournament, fourth.
1958—Dixie Classic, second.
1959—NCAA Mid-East Regional Tournament, second.
1960—Los Angeles Classic, eighth.
1961—Far West Classic, sixth.

1963—Sun Devil Classic, third.
1964—Los Angeles Classic, seventh.
1965—Rainbow Classic, third.
1966—Quaker City Tournament, seventh.
1967—Sugar Bowl Tournament, fourth.
1968—ECAC Holiday Festival, seventh.
1969—Utah Classic, second.
1969—Far West Classic, eighth

20 BIG TEN SEASONS

1950-51	5	9	7th	1961-62	3	11	9th (Tie)
1951-52	6	8	5th (Tie)	1962-63	3	11	9th
1952-53	11	7	3rd (Tie)	1963-64	8	6	4th (Tie)
1953-54	4	10	8th	1964-65	1	13	10th (Tie)
1954-55	8	6	4th	1965-66	10	4	2nd
1955-56	7	7	5th	1966-67	10	4	1st (Tie)
1956-57	10	4	1st (Tie)	1967-68	6	8	6th (Tie)
1957-58	9	5	3rd	1968-69	6	8	5th (Tie)
1958-59	12	2	1st	1969-70	5	9	6th (Tie)
1959-60	5	9	8th				
1960-61	3	11	9th	20-Year Record—Won 132, Lost 152.			

SPARTAN WINNING STREAKS

16—Last 15 games of 1930-31 season and first game of 1931-32 campaign. That 1930-31 season was the winningest in State's history, the final mark being 16 won, one lost. Ben VanAlstyne, head coach.

11—In the 1911-12 season with John Macklin as head coach. The final season won-lost mark was 12-3.

10—In the 1934-35 season, the final mark was 14-4. Ben VanAlstyne, head coach.

10—The last six games of the 1927-28 season and the first four of the 1928-29 campaign. Ben VanAlstyne, head coach.

10—In the 1956-57 season, with the final mark 16-10. Forddy Anderson, head coach.

ON THE HOME FLOOR

25—From second game of 1965-66 season through fourth game of 1967-68 season. John Benington, head coach.

YEAR-BY-YEAR RECORDS

1898-1899
No Coach
Feb. 27	6	Olivet	7
Mar. 13	6	Olivet (A)	15
		Lost 2	

1899-1900
Charles O. Bemies, Coach
Jan. 20	5	Olivet (A)	6
Feb. 3	6	Olivet	8
Mar. 3	25	Eastern Michigan (A)	8
Mar. 10	25	Governor's Guard (Lansing)	7
		Won 2 Lost 2	

1900-1901
Feb. 16	18	Olivet	10
Mar. 2	21	Eastern Michigan	6
Mar. 16	12	Eastern Michigan (A)	7
		Won 3	

1901-1902
George E. Denham, Coach
Feb. 1	102	Alma	3
Feb. 15	19	Governor's Guard (A) (Lansing)	0
Mar. 1	58	Hillsdale	20
Mar. 9	29	Alma (A)	3
Mar. 15	36	Hillsdale (A)	17
		Won 5	

1902-1903
Jan. 26	43	Detroit Y.M.C.A.	8
Jan. 29	49	Hillsdale	2
Feb. 13	23	Eastern Michigan (A)	7
Feb. 18	19	Governor's Guard (A)	7
Mar. 7	49	Eastern Michigan	5
Mar. 14	42	Grand Rapids Y.M.C.A.	7
		Won 6	

1903-1904
Chester L. Brewer, Coach
Jan. 9	13	Chicago Western Y.M.C.A.	44
Jan. 23	52	Alma	7
Feb. 6	22	Eastern Michigan (A)	2
Feb. 12	14	Grand Rapids Y.M.C.A. (A)	13
Feb. 27	14	Alma (A)	22
Mar. 5	62	Eastern Michigan	10
Mar. 12	41	Grand Rapids Y.M.C.A.	10
Mar. 25	8	Detroit A.C. (A)	33
		Won 5 Lost 3	

1904-1905
Jan. 14	62	Saginaw Y.M.C.A.	12
Jan. 21	47	Bay City Y.M.C.A.	20
Jan. 28	22	Grand Rapids Y.M.C.A. (A)	38
Jan. 31	30	Hope (A)	44
Feb. 4	47	Jackson Y.M.C.A.	12
Feb. 10	30	Detroit A.C. (A)	39
Feb. 25	94	Battle Creek Y.M.C.A.	4
Mar. 3	30	Bay City Y.M.C.A. (A)	14
		Won 5 Lost 3	

1905-1906
Jan. 18	43	Adrian	18
Jan. 26	76	Owosso Y.M.C.A.	12
Feb. 2	47	Michigan Deaf School (A)	16
Feb. 3	37	Central Michigan	12
Feb. 10	25	Grand Rapids Y.M.C.A. (A)	20
Feb. 12	20	Ann Arbor Y.M.C.A.	21
Feb. 16	21	Central Michigan (A)	18
Feb. 23	44	Albion (A)	11
Feb. 24	25	Ann Arbor Y.M.C.A. (A)	29
Mar. 2	46	Olivet	10
Mar. 3	59	Albion	8
Mar. 10	21	Adrian (A)	20
Mar. 16	52	Alma	8
		Won 11 Lost 2	

1906-1907
Jan. 5	50	Hope	30
Jan. 12	51	Armour Inst.	24
Jan. 18	35	Saginaw H.S. (A)	17
Jan. 19	29	Saginaw Bank Clerks (A)	19
Jan. 25	43	Jackson Y.M.C.A. (A)	30
Jan. 26	42	Central Michigan	18
Jan. 28	14	Detroit Y.M.C.A. (A)	31
Jan. 29	50	Eastern Michigan (A)	25
Feb. 2	41	Olivet	24
Feb. 7	54	Adrian	24
Feb. 16	33	Hope (A)	23
Feb. 19	17	Detroit Y.M.C.A.	23
Feb. 20	41	Adrian (A)	20
Feb. 22	38	Olivet (A)	24
Mar. 1	33	Central Michigan	22
Mar. 2	72	Eastern Michigan	13
		Won 14 Lost 2	

1907-1908
Jan. 4	46	Central Michigan (A)	8
Jan. 8	46	Oberlin	21
Jan. 11	67	Saginaw H.S.	23
Jan. 17	30	Adrian	14
Jan. 20	20	Detroit Y.M.C.A. (A)	33
Jan. 25	74	Grand Rapids Y.M.C.A.	16
Jan. 31	33	Notre Dame	20
Feb. 1	16	Notre Dame	23
Feb. 5	41	Central Michigan	23
Feb. 7	42	Jackson Y.M.C.A.	29
Feb. 8	40	Midland Y.M.C.A.	8
Feb. 14	27	Detroit Y.M.C.A.	29
Feb. 17	33	Haskell Indians	18
Feb. 21	37	Jackson Y.M.C.A. (A)	35
Feb. 22	42	Adrian (A)	31
Feb. 24	28	Battle Creek Y.M.C.A. (A)	14
(*)Feb. 25	20	Notre Dame (A)	39
Feb. 26	26	DePaul (A)	17
Feb. 27	26	Armour Inst. (A)	29
Feb. 28	31	South Haven Independents (A)	18

(*)1st MAC Basketball game played out of state

Won 15   Lost 5

1908-1909
(*)Jan. 9	24	Michigan (A)	16
Jan. 13	76	DePaul	7
Jan. 18	24	Detroit Burroughs	15
Jan. 22	24	Wabash (A)	39
Jan. 23	10	Notre Dame (A)	26
Jan. 25	53	Adrian	13
Feb. 8	18	Notre Dame	22
Feb. 11	18	Detroit Y.M.C.A. (A)	25
Feb. 18	32	Battle Creek Y.M.C.A.	25
Feb. 20	45	Michigan	23
Feb. 21	53	Armour Inst.	7
Feb. 22	20	Detroit Burroughs (A)	19
Mar. 2	30	Rochester Y.M.C.A. (N.Y.)	18
Mar. 3	24	Rochester Y.M.C.A. (N.Y.)	36
Mar. 11	33	Detroit Y.M.C.A.	28

(*)First basketball game with the University of Michigan

Won 10   Lost 5

Important cog of MAC cage teams around World War I was 10-letterman Lyman Frimodig, 2d from r., shown here with, l. to r., Charles Hood, Cyril Rigby, William Wood and Fred Ricker.

1909-1910

Jan. 7	51	Jackson Y.M.C.A.	18
Jan. 14	20	Detroit Spaldings	18
Jan. 25	27	Jackson Y.M.C.A. (A)	18
(*)Jan. 26	9	Purdue (A)	35
Jan. 27	28	Rose Poly (A)	31
Jan. 28	21	Wabash (A)	23
Jan. 29	28	Notre Dame (A)	21
Feb. 7	84	Bay City Y.M.C.A.	12
Feb. 11	26	Armour Inst. (A)	11
Feb. 12	14	Lake Forest (A)	13
Feb. 19	43	Notre Dame	23
Mar. 3	40	Hope	21
(*)Mar. 5	13	Ohio State (A)	31
Mar. 7	27	Detroit Y.M.C.A. (A)	24
Mar. 11	30	Hope (A)	38

(*)MAC's first competition with Purdue and Ohio State

Won 10   Lost 5

1910-1911

John F. Macklin, Head Coach

Jan. 9	9	Detroit Spaldings	21
Jan. 13	15	Wabash (A)	25
Jan. 14	20	Rose Poly (A)	26
Jan. 18	25	Detroit Spaldings (A)	18
Jan. 20	51	Alma	24
Jan. 21	51	Armour Inst.	11
Jan. 30	11	Detroit Y.M.C.A. (A)	22
Feb. 3	21	Armour Inst. (A)	36
Feb. 4	26	Lake Forest (A)	28
Feb. 10	12	Detroit A.C. (A)	54
Feb. 11	12	Ohio State (A)	42
Feb. 17	24	Hope (A)	48
Feb. 24	23	Alma (A)	21
Mar. 3	36	Hope	24

Won 5   Lost 9

1911-1912

Jan. 6	72	Central Michigan	10
Jan. 12	39	Armour Inst. (A)	30
Jan. 13	19	Northwestern Coll. (A)	25
Jan. 16	53	Alma	14
Jan. 18	37	Winona (A)	21
Jan. 19	26	Wabash (A)	32
Jan. 20	33	Rose Poly (A)	31
Jan. 23	40	Hope (A)	41
Jan. 27	51	Armour Inst.	18
Feb. 2	60	Albion	23
Feb. 10	67	Winona College (A)	4
Feb. 16	37	Alma (A)	15
Feb. 21	55	Hope	23
Feb. 24	42	Detroit Y.M.C.A.	26
Mar. 4	20	Detroit Y.M.C.A. (A)	17

Won 12   Lost 3

1912-1913

Jan. 11	75	Winona	14
Jan. 21	37	Detroit Rayls	12
Jan. 27	48	Alma	24
Jan. 29	33	Hope (A)	26
Feb. 6	21	Northwestern Coll.	23
Feb. 11	22	Detroit Y.M.C.A. (A)	23
Feb. 13	40	Notre Dame	7
Feb. 21	58	Hope	25
Feb. 26	39	St. John's (Toledo, O.) (A)	24
Feb. 27	30	Buchtel (A)	35
Feb. 28	18	Denison (A)	44
Mar. 1	26	St. Mary's (Dayton, O.) (A)	28
Mar. 8	39	Detroit Y.M.C.A.	9

Won 8   Lost 5

1913-1914

Jan. 16	40	Toledo Buckeyes	24
Jan. 22	30	Lake Forest (A)	24
Jan. 23	24	Northwestern Coll. (A)	44
Jan. 24	18	Notre Dame (A)	27
Jan. 30	29	Detroit Burroughs	22
Feb. 4	45	Notre Dame	22
Feb. 14	27	Detroit Y.M.C.A.	29
Feb. 19	38	West Virginia Wesleyan	21
Feb. 25	50	St. John's (Toledo) (A)	17
Feb. 26	26	Toledo Buckeyes (A)	25
Feb. 27	45	Akron (A)	30
Mar. 3	22	Detroit Y.M.C.A.	27

Won 8   Lost 4

1914-1915

Date		Opponent	
Jan. 9	23	Toledo Buckeyes	33
Jan. 13	56	Hope	20
Jan. 15	21	Illinois A.C. (Chicago)	22
Jan. 22	23	Detroit Y.M.C.A.	14
Jan. 23	54	Defiance	12
Jan. 28	27	Toledo Buckeyes (A)	31
Jan. 29	45	Ohio Northern (A)	16
Jan. 30	30	Defiance (A)	19
Feb. 2	14	Notre Dame	13
Feb. 6	17	Northwestern Coll.	28
Feb. 11	22	Northwestern Coll. (A)	41
Feb. 12	20	Mercury A.C. (Chicago) (A)	25
Feb. 13	19	Notre Dame (A)	24
Feb. 18	31	West Virginia Wesleyan	43
Feb. 24	46	Hope (A)	28
Mar. 2	9	Detroit Y.M.C.A. (A)	21

Won 7 Lost 9

1915-1916

Date		Opponent	
Jan. 12	51	Western Michigan	21
Jan. 14	14	Hope	20
Jan. 15	29	St. Mary's (Mich.)	19
Jan. 19	18	Notre Dame (A)	19
Jan. 20	17	Northwestern Coll. (A)	29
Jan. 22	18	Illinois A.C. (Chicago) (A)	50
Jan. 29	34	Kalamazoo	27
Feb. 2	23	Notre Dame	24
Feb. 4	21	Hope (A)	18
Feb. 9	39	Muskingum	21
Feb. 12	27	Detroit Y.M.C.A.	23
Feb. 17	30	Tri-State	13
Feb. 19	23	Toledo Buckeyes	32
Feb. 24	28	Toledo Buckeyes (A)	22
Mar. 3	21	Northwestern Coll.	28
Mar. 7	14	Detroit Y.M.C.A.	35

Won 8 Lost 8

1916-1917

George E. Gauthier, Coach

Date		Opponent	
Jan. 12	41	West Virginia Wesleyan	22
Jan. 19	34	Hope	20
Jan. 20	47	Alma	7
Jan. 26	39	Illinois A.C.	27
Jan. 27	31	Notre Dame	25
Feb. 1	36	Buffalo	17
Feb. 3	33	Detroit Y.M.C.A.	26
Feb. 8	53	Ohio Northern	9
Feb. 10	20	Wabash	19
Feb. 15	23	Illinois A.C. (A)	43
Feb. 16	16	Northwestern Coll. (A)	26
Feb. 17	19	Notre Dame (A)	33
Feb. 23	13	Hope (A)	18
Mar. 2	28	Northwestern Coll.	14
Mar. 8	30	Marietta	20
Mar. 10	15	Detroit Y.M.C.A.	30

Won 11 Lost 5

1917-1918

Date		Opponent	
Dec. 28	13	Detroit Y.M.O. (A)	31
Dec. 29	22	Detroit (A)	32
Jan. 5	21	Grand Rapids Y.M.C.A. (A)	22
Jan. 9	16	Fort Custer Enlisted Men	27
Jan. 11	13	Michigan (A)	17
Jan. 18	23	Hope (A)	33
Jan. 19	24	Fort Custer Officers	20
Jan. 25	27	St. John's (Toledo, O.) (A)	19
Jan. 26	20	Detroit Y.M.C.A. (A)	34
Feb. 1	27	Notre Dame	12
Feb. 7	23	Notre Dame (A)	25
Feb. 8	16	Northwestern U. (A)	19
Feb. 15	35	Hope	10
Feb. 23	35	Oberlin	20
(*)Mar. 2	25	Michigan	33
Mar. 9	23	Detroit Y.M.C.A.	16

(*)First game played in new gymnasium.

Won 6 Lost 10

1918-1919

Date		Opponent	
Jan. 3	15	Holland Y.M.C.A. (A)	21
Jan. 4	19	Grand Rapids Y.M.C.A. (A)	17
Jan. 8	19	Western Michigan	18
Jan. 10	16	Detroit Rayls (A)	37
Jan. 11	14	Oberlin (A)	24
Jan. 15	42	Kalamazoo	20
Jan. 17	28	Western Michigan (A)	23
Jan. 24	31	Fort Custer Officers	13
Jan. 30	19	Wabash (A)	28
Jan. 31	18	DePauw (A)	17
Feb. 1	32	Notre Dame	28
Feb. 7	37	Wabash	26
Feb. 8	18	Hope (A)	21
Feb. 12	12	DePauw	21
Feb. 15	17	Michigan	19
Feb. 22	16	Notre Dame	17
Feb. 28	33	Michigan (A)	24
Mar. 1	20	Hope	26

Won 9 Lost 9

1919-1920

Date		Opponent	
Dec. 19	11	Detroit A.C. (A)	23
Dec. 20	25	DeVilbis Coll. (Toledo) (A)	37
Dec. 19	53	Fort Custer Enlisted Men (A)	3
Dec. 20	21	Muskegon Y.M.C.A. (A)	26
Dec. 26	29	AC Spark Plug (Flint) (A)	28
Dec. 27	20	Holland Y.M.C.A. (A)	18

(The squad was divided into two teams, each playing a separate schedule during the Christmas holidays.)

Date		Opponent	
Dec. 31	25	Chicago	32
Jan. 2	36	Oberlin	8
Jan. 3	29	U. of Detroit (A)	30
Jan. 7	29	Central Michigan	15
Jan. 9	16	Hope (A)	21
Jan. 10	39	Kalamazoo (A)	21
Jan. 16	19	Indiana	20
Jan. 21	34	Kalamazoo	15
Jan. 24	23	Notre Dame	20
Jan. 28	33	Chicago Y.M.C.A. Coll.	20
Jan. 30	23	Michigan (A)	13
Feb. 6	29	Wabash	27
Feb. 9	23	Notre Dame (A)	30
Feb. 11	21	Creighton (A)	22
Feb. 12	18	Creighton (A)	15
Feb. 13	28	Nebraska (A)	43
Feb. 14	20	Nebraska (A)	29
Feb. 18	21	DePauw	33
Feb. 23	18	DePauw (A)	31
Feb. 24	16	Wabash (A)	24
Feb. 28	34	Michigan	27
Mar. 1	31	Creighton	24
Mar. 6	34	Hope	23
Mar. 20	22	Alpena Independents (A)	11
Mar. 21	17	Alger Co. Club (Munising) (A)	14
Mar. 23	43	Northern Michigan U. (A)	13
Mar. 24	24	Ishpeming American Legion (A)	37
Mar. 25	66	Gwinn Club (A)	12

Mar. 26	60	Lake Linden American Legion (A)	24
Mar. 27	28	Michigan Coll. of Mines (Houghton) (A)	26
		Won 21 Lost 15	

1920-1921
Lyman L. Frimodig, Coach

Jan. 8	26	Central Michigan	21
Jan. 11	30	Kalamazoo	18
Jan. 14	31	Hope	17
Jan. 15	22	Western Michigan	16
Jan. 18	40	Mt. Union	26
Jan. 21	19	DePauw (A)	39
Jan. 22	23	Notre Dame (A)	36
Jan. 25	29	Western Michigan (A)	19
Jan. 27	20	St. John's (Toledo) (A)	21
Jan. 28	30	Mt. Union (A)	28
Jan. 29	21	Oberlin (A)	23
Feb. 1	37	Notre Dame	25
Feb. 5	24	Michigan (A)	37
Feb. 7	23	DePauw	26
Feb. 14	26	Michigan Tech	18
Feb. 19	29	Oberlin	37
Feb. 22	10	Michigan	17
Feb. 25	27	Hope (A)	23
Feb. 26	20	Grand Rapids J.C. (A)	11
Mar. 2	41	Bethany (W.Va.)	18
Mar. 3	27	Creighton	20
		Won 13 Lost 8	

1921-1922

Dec. 10	13	Wisconsin (A)	27
Dec. 29	38	Carnegie Inst.	17
Jan. 2	33	Albion	13
Jan. 3	56	Detroit School of Law	3
Jan. 4	43	Alma	17
Jan. 6	26	Michigan (A)	27
Jan. 10	28	Western Michigan	20
Jan. 14	28	Eastern Michigan	22
Jan. 19	30	Valparaiso	21
Jan. 21	28	Kalamazoo	39
Jan. 25	27	Central Michigan	21
Jan. 28	25	Oberlin (A)	26
Jan. 29	22	Ohio Wesleyan (A)	25
Jan. 31	22	Notre Dame (A)	31
Feb. 3	30	Creighton (A)	41
Feb. 4	21	Creighton (A)	25
Feb. 6	14	Lombard (Galesburg, Ill.) (A)	26
Feb. 16	30	Notre Dame	24
Feb. 17	19	Marquette	26
Feb. 22	17	Michigan	19
Feb. 24	17	Ohio Wesleyan	29
Feb. 27	28	Creighton	34
Mar. 3	29	Hope	28
Mar. 4	25	Chicago Y.M.C.A. Coll.	21
		Won 11 Lost 13	

1922-1923
Fred M. Walker, Coach

Dec. 9	15	Notre Dame	40
Dec. 15	8	Western Michigan	17
Dec. 22	17	Valparaiso	21
Dec. 30	37	Carnegie Inst.	29
Jan. 3	11	Michigan (A)	33
Jan. 6	18	St. Ignatius (Cleveland)	27
Jan. 11	33	Victoria	10
Jan. 13	19	Eastern Michigan	17
Jan. 20	13	Michigan	29
Jan. 27	28	Central Michigan	13
Jan. 30	23	Chicago Y.M.C.A. Coll.	19

Feb. 3	22	Kalamazoo	24
Feb. 9	26	Lake Forest	18
Feb. 12	27	Armour Inst.	22
Feb. 17	27	Alma	21
Feb. 21	43	St. Mary's (Mich.)	15
Feb. 28	22	Notre Dame (A)	21
Mar. 2	17	St. Ignatius (A)	38
Mar. 3	16	Oberlin (A)	23
		Won 10 Lost 9	

1923-1924

Dec. 15	25	Adrian	12
Dec. 18	31	St. Mary's (Mich.)	26
Dec. 22	17	Chicago (A)	21
Dec. 28	25	Detroit Coll. of Law	14
Jan. 3	22	Hope	7
Jan. 5	33	Upper Canada Law School	26
Jan. 7	12	Carleton	27
Jan. 11	19	Michigan (A)	23
Jan. 18	24	John Carroll	17
Jan. 25	18	Notre Dame (A)	35
Jan. 28	14	Western Michigan (A)	29
Jan. 29	21	Central Michigan	20
Feb. 1	12	Lombard	13
Feb. 6	20	Michigan	31
Feb. 12	16	Western Michigan	25
Feb. 23	31	U. of Detroit	17
Feb. 26	25	St. Viator (Ill.)	27
Feb. 29	21	Notre Dame	23
Mar. 6	22	Valparaiso	12
Mar. 8	29	Lake Forest	19
		Won 10 Lost 10	

1924-1925
John H. Kobs, Coach

Dec. 10	42	Adrian	16
Dec. 13	10	Michigan	26
Dec. 20	29	Chicago (A)	15
Dec. 22	17	Northwestern (A)	26
Jan. 10	13	St. Mary's	21
Jan. 13	18	St. Viator	23
Jan. 16	14	Notre Dame (A)	37
Jan. 23	20	Western Michigan	21
Jan. 30	24	Earlham (A)	23
Jan. 31	14	Franklin (A)	36
Feb. 3	19	Hope	20
Feb. 11	23	U. of Detroit	22
Feb. 20	16	Franklin	28
Feb. 25	15	Western Michigan (A)	29
Feb. 28	29	Oberlin	27
Mar. 3	10	Notre Dame	42
Mar. 6	14	John Carroll (A)	30
Mar. 7	16	Oberlin (A)	25
Mar. 14	43	MAC Alumni	19
		Won 6 Lost 13	

1925-1926

Dec. 8	36	Olivet	13
Dec. 12	30	Adrian	14
Dec. 19	28	U. of Chicago (A)	21
Dec. 21	13	Northwestern (A)	42
Jan. 1	33	Mercer (Ga.)	37
Jan. 9	30	St. Viator	27
Jan. 16	15	Michigan (A)	38
Jan. 22	14	Notre Dame (A)	33
Jan. 26	10	Detroit (A)	16
Jan. 30	23	Eastern Michigan	35
Feb. 2	22	Detroit	29
Feb. 6	25	Western Michigan (A)	30
Feb. 11	25	Marquette	29
Feb. 13	21	Earlham	26
Feb. 16	25	Notre Dame	40
Feb. 19	27	Carnegie Inst.	22
Feb. 26	15	Western Michigan	38
Mar. 6	38	MSC Alumni	40
		Won 5 Lost 13	

1926-1927

Benjamin F. VanAlstyne, Coach

Dec. 8	33	Adrian	29
Dec. 11	13	Michigan (A)	34
Dec. 18	24	Chicago (A)	33
Dec. 20	22	Northwestern (A)	34
Jan. 8	35	Marquette	32
Jan. 12	31	Albion	37
Jan. 14	16	Butler (A)	53
Jan. 15	45	Concordia	25
Jan. 19	30	Detroit	23
Jan. 21	39	Lake Forest (A)	30
Jan. 22	12	Marquette (A)	24
Jan. 29	15	Notre Dame (A)	36
Jan. 31	23	Butler	29
Feb. 9	46	Hope	31
Feb. 12	27	Detroit (A)	30
Feb. 18	34	Pittsburgh	36
Feb. 23	22	Notre Dame	34
Feb. 25	36	MSC Alumni	24

Won 7   Lost 11

1927-1928

Dec. 7	30	Adrian	25
Dec. 10	23	Michigan (A)	43
Jan. 3	39	Ohio Northern	25
Jan. 7	58	Hillsdale	24
Jan. 13	27	Detroit	23
Jan. 16	35	Coe	25
Jan. 20	21	Loyola (Chicago) (A)	23
Jan. 21	18	Marquette (A)	21
Jan. 28	25	Notre Dame (A)	29
Jan. 30	36	Hope	21
Feb. 3	26	Notre Dame	16
Feb. 8	52	Albion	20
Feb. 11	36	Kalamazoo	24
Feb. 17	17	Detroit	13
Feb. 25	30	Marquette	25

Won 11   Lost 4

1928-1929

Dec. 7	31	Michigan (A)	24
Dec. 14	47	Hillsdale	15
Jan. 2	16	Penn State	14
Jan. 3	38	Cornell	24
Jan. 7	28	Ohio Wesleyan	31
Jan. 11	29	Marquette	19
Jan. 18	27	Detroit (A)	13
Jan. 23	24	Notre Dame (A)	29
Jan. 26	30	Kalamazoo	22
Feb. 1	35	Colgate (A)	36
Feb. 2	17	Syracuse (A)	24
Feb. 8	51	Hope	18
Feb. 15	40	Detroit	15
Feb. 22	27	Notre Dame	28
Mar. 1	49	Lake Forest	16
Mar. 4	26	Marquette (A)	15

Won 11   Lost 5

1929-1930

(*)Jan. 1	19	Syracuse	21
Jan. 4	30	Ohio Wesleyan	14
Jan. 9	26	Detroit	20
Jan. 16	27	Bethany (A) (W. Va.)	36
Jan. 17	35	Carnegie Inst. (A)	23
Jan. 22	28	Notre Dame (A)	21
Jan. 25	21	Detroit (A)	18
Jan. 28	55	Hope	16
Jan. 31	24	Marquette	17
Feb. 7	33	Kalamazoo	12
Feb. 11	36	Bethany	32
Feb. 14	24	Oberlin	10
Feb. 15	27	Michigan	26
Feb. 18	17	Notre Dame (A)	29
Feb. 21	34	Hillsdale	28
Mar. 1	14	Marquette (A)	21

(*)First game played on new portable floor—Demonstration Hall

Won 12   Lost 4

The 1931 varsity squad flew to Milwaukee for game with Marquette on what is believed to be first flight in U.S. for a collegiate team. Shown here are, l. to r., Dee Pinneo, Art Haga, Randall Boeskool, Coach Ben Van Alstyne, Edward Scott and Roger Grove.

1930-1931

Dec. 5	22	Cincinnati	8
Dec. 13	22	Michigan (A)	32
Dec. 29	29	Brigham Young	28
Jan. 1	25	Ohio Wesleyan	17
Jan. 9	19	Marquette	16
Jan. 13	32	Xavier (Ohio)	19
Jan. 16	41	Colgate (A)	31
Jan. 17	50	Colgate (A)	30
Jan. 23	46	Kalamazoo	10
Jan. 27	31	Central State	18
Jan. 30	25	Western Reserve (A)	24
Jan. 31	33	Oberlin (A)	22
Feb. 6	42	Alma	20
Feb. 10	34	Detroit	16
Feb. 14	24	Loyola (Chicago)	16
Feb. 21	16	Detroit (A)	11
Feb. 28	24	Marquette (A)	21

Won 16   Lost 1

1931-1932

Dec. 3	39	Alma	12
Dec. 12	5	Michigan (A)	27
Jan. 1	29	Ohio	15
Jan. 2	29	Cornell	26
Jan. 8	17	Western Reserve	15
Jan. 9	25	Notre Dame	28
Jan. 15	22	Xavier	20
Jan. 19	22	Detroit	13
Jan. 29	30	Colgate	21
Jan. 30	29	Colgate	28
Feb. 6	17	Kalamazoo	9
Feb. 13	14	Michigan	13
Feb. 15	25	Marquette	23
Feb. 17	35	Detroit (A)	34
Feb. 20	24	Xavier (A)	31
Feb. 23	20	Notre Dame (A)	28
Feb. 25	18	Marquette (A)	43

Won 12   Lost 5

1932-1933

Dec. 3	31	Albion	29
Dec. 10	20	Michigan (A)	17
Dec. 30	16	Wisconsin (A)	26
Jan. 3	23	Syracuse	16
Jan. 9	19	Notre Dame	34
Jan. 12	28	Marquette	32
Jan. 16	29	Buffalo (A)	18
Jan. 17	40	Colgate (A)	26
Jan. 21	35	Olivet	13
Jan. 27	19	Xavier	16
Jan. 28	63	Meiji U. (Japan)	15
Feb. 4	29	Kalamazoo	12
Feb. 11	16	Michigan	28
Feb. 15	30	Detroit	28
Feb. 18	16	Detroit (A)	27
Feb. 24	25	Notre Dame (A)	30
Feb. 25	21	Marquette (A)	28

Won 10   Lost 7

1933-1934

Dec. 4	23	Olivet	16
Dec. 9	26	Michigan (A)	25
Jan. 2	35	Mississippi State	25
Jan. 6	33	Notre Dame	34
Jan. 12	37	Buffalo (A)	30
Jan. 13	21	Syracuse (A)	27
Jan. 18	24	Marquette	26
Jan. 22	34	Eastern Michigan	27
Jan. 26	32	Central Michigan	27
Feb. 3	36	Loyola (Chicago)	15
Feb. 5	23	Wisconsin (A)	22
Feb. 10	33	Michigan	26
Feb. 14	27	Detroit	20
Feb. 17	28	Detroit (A)	22
Feb. 21	19	Notre Dame (A)	28

Feb. 23	16	Marquette (A)	40
Feb. 24	22	Loyola (Chicago) (A)	20

Won 12   Lost 5

1934-1935

Dec. 1	43	Central Michigan	14
Dec. 5	30	Kalamazoo	25
Dec. 15	25	Michigan (A)	31
Dec. 22	26	Northwestern (A)	39
Dec. 24	26	Loyola (Chicago) (A)	19
Dec. 27	25	Stanford	18
Dec. 31	21	Wisconsin (A)	23
Jan. 4	31	Wayne State	17
Jan. 8	35	Eastern Michigan	14
Jan. 12	34	Western Reserve (A)	33
Jan. 17	30	Marquette	29
Jan. 21	45	Hillsdale	24
Jan. 24	53	Eastern Michigan (A)	28
Jan. 26	37	Wayne State (A)	20
Feb. 4	36	Western Reserve	17
Feb. 9	30	Michigan	28
Feb. 13	32	Kentucky	26
Feb. 18	17	Marquette (A)	20

Won 14   Lost 4

1935-1936

Dec. 2	36	Albion	28
Dec. 6	21	Wisconsin (A)	26
Dec. 14	24	Michigan (A)	35
Dec. 21	25	Northwestern (A)	29
Dec. 30	25	West Virginia	24
Jan. 1	34	Syracuse (A)	38
Jan. 3	24	Temple (A)	47
Jan. 8	32	Kalamazoo	14
Jan. 10	32	Loyola	20
Jan. 17	20	Marquette	21
Jan. 18	35	Marquette	31
Jan. 21	19	Kentucky (A)	27
Jan. 25	37	Eastern Michigan (A)	24
Jan. 29	18	Eastern Michigan	15
Feb. 1	21	Butler	24
Feb. 15	23	Michigan	41
Feb. 22	29	Marquette (A)	28

Won 8   Lost 9

1936-1937

Dec. 9	32	Albion	22
Dec. 12	21	Michigan (A)	34
Jan. 2	21	Kentucky (A)	28
Jan. 6	39	Kalamazoo	18
Jan. 8	34	Case (A)	38
Jan. 9	42	Geneva (A)	41
Jan. 14	24	Kentucky	23
Jan. 16	25	Marquette	32
Jan. 19	36	Syracuse	30
Jan. 23	29	Northwestern (A)	44
Jan. 26	24	Hawaiian All Stars	25
Jan. 29	21	Hope	25
Feb. 6	17	Wisconsin (A)	22
Feb. 8	21	Butler (A)	27
Feb. 13	31	Michigan	38
Feb. 16	21	DePaul	23
Feb. 20	26	Marquette (A)	31

Won 5   Lost 12

1937-1938

Dec. 9	51	Hope	27
Dec. 11	40	Michigan (A)	43
Dec. 22	52	Iowa	37
Dec. 30	43	Missouri	33
Jan. 1	48	Case	34
Jan. 5	29	California	31
Jan. 8	43	Kentucky	38
Jan. 11	55	Hawaiian All Stars	31
Jan. 14	65	Buffalo (A)	35
Jan. 15	46	Syracuse (A)	59

Jan. 22	24	Marquette	41
Jan. 28	21	Butler	15
Feb. 5	27	Wisconsin (A)	30
Feb. 7	27	Kentucky (A)	44
Feb. 12	41	Michigan	35
Feb. 19	26	Marquette (A)	40
Feb. 21	32	Notre Dame (A)	48
		Won 9 Lost 8	

1938-1939

Dec. 7	36	Kalamazoo	26
Dec. 10	34	Michigan (A)	41
Dec. 17	58	Oberlin	23
Dec. 28	35	Penn State	21
Dec. 31	33	Indiana	37
Jan. 2	44	Loyola (Chicago) (A)	46
Jan. 7	29	Central Michigan	24
Jan. 14	36	Western Reserve	21
Jan. 21	33	Butler (A)	34
Jan. 23	35	Tennessee (A)	31
Jan. 28	39	Butler	29
Feb. 4	37	Wisconsin (A)	39
Feb. 11	25	Michigan	30
Feb. 13	35	Marquette	29
Feb. 15	29	Temple	25
Feb. 20	36	Marquette (A)	38
Feb. 24	33	Wayne State	40
		Won 9 Lost 8	

1939-1940

Dec. 4	42	Kalamazoo	22
Dec. 9	27	Michigan (A)	33
Dec. 16	52	Washington State	44
Dec. 18	32	Creighton (A)	30
Dec. 19	38	Creighton (A)	21
Dec. 22	37	California (A)	41
Dec. 27	33	Oregon State (A)	38
Dec. 28	36	Oregon State (A)	26
Jan. 1	30	Loyola (Chicago) (A)	22
(*)Jan. 6	29	Tennessee	20
Jan. 8	31	Syracuse	29
Jan. 15	48	Marquette	19
Jan. 20	27	Michigan	32
Jan. 26	25	Long Island (A)	34
Jan. 27	40	Temple (A)	42
Jan. 29	39	Baltimore (A)	28
Feb. 3	48	Wisconsin	41
Feb. 14	46	Wayne State	29
Feb. 24	21	Marquette (A)	17
Mar. 1	44	Temple	28

(*)First game played in the Jenison Field House

Won 14   Lost 6

1940-1941

Dec. 2	48	Kalamazoo	29
Dec. 7	14	Michigan (A)	42
Dec. 21	46	Ohio State	38
Dec. 23	34	Iowa	40
Dec. 30	29	Creighton	37
Dec. 31	34	Creighton	29
Jan. 4	31	Long Island (A)	26
Jan. 6	37	Temple (A)	35
Jan. 10	25	Marquette	18
Jan. 13	23	Temple	22
Jan. 18	44	West Virginia	35
Jan. 25	39	Notre Dame (A)	46
Feb. 8	40	West Virginia	40
Feb. 12	35	Michigan	32
Feb. 19	23	Long Island	24
Feb. 22	37	Marquette (A)	36
Mar. 1	44	Notre Dame	35
		Won 11 Lost 6	

1941-1942

Dec. 2	50	Fort Custer Officers	29
Dec. 8	29	Central Michigan	23
Dec. 13	20	Michigan (A)	37
Dec. 20	41	South Carolina	29
Dec. 24	39	Harvard	28
Dec. 27	33	Syracuse (A)	31
Dec. 29	27	Rochester (A)	28
Jan. 2	42	Washington State	45
Jan. 6	33	Great Lakes N.T.S.	31
Jan. 10	51	Western Reserve	22
Jan. 16	51	Marquette	40
Jan. 22	37	Cincinnati	30
Jan. 24	49	Notre Dame (A)	52
Jan. 26	40	Butler	39
Jan. 31	32	Detroit (A)	28
Feb. 6	36	Cincinnati (A)	30
Feb. 7	36	Butler (A)	38
Grn. 11	57	Michigan	34
Feb. 16	37	Detroit	39
Feb. 21	47	Marquette (A)	45
Feb. 28	46	Notre Dame	43
		Won 15 Lost 6	

1942-1943

Dec. 7	31	Michigan (A)	36
Dec. 29	29	Oregon State	33
Jan. 1	28	Harvard	31
Jan. 4	26	Michigan	29
Jan. 9	34	Great Lakes N.T.S.(A)	38
Jan. 11	32	Marquette (A)	41
Jan. 13	32	Minnesota (A)	46
Jan. 19	55	Dearborn Naval Station	24
Jan. 23	37	DePaul (A)	45
Jan. 29	31	Camp Grant (III.)	39
Feb. 4	69	Romulus Army Air Base	27
Feb. 6	34	Notre Dame (A)	45
Feb. 11	39	Great Lakes N.T.S.	56
Feb. 15	36	Marquette	47
Feb. 20	31	Camp Grant (A)	43
Feb. 27	42	Notre Dame	45
		Won 2 Lost 14	

1943-1944

Intercollegiate Athletics was suspended during the school year 1943-1944.

1944-1945

Dec. 2	44	Drake	36
Dec. 9	31	Ohio State (A)	58
Dec. 28	31	Ohio State	67
Dec. 30	29	Iowa (A)	66
Jan. 6	37	Cincinnati	39
Jan. 8	72	Albion (A)	36
Jan. 12	50	Cincinnati (A)	54
Jan. 13	35	Kentucky (A)	66
Jan. 18	75	Eastern Michigan (A)	31
Jan. 20	47	Wayne State	38
Jan. 22	58	Albion	38
Jan. 27	47	Temple (at Buffalo, N.Y.)	64
Feb. 5	66	Kentucky (A)	50
Feb. 14	53	Detroit	29
Feb. 19	81	Kalamazoo	26
Feb. 24	62	Detroit (A)	38
		Won 10 Lost 7	

1945-1946

Dec. 1	39	Michigan (A)	47
Dec. 5	49	Great Lakes N.T.S.	53
Dec. 24	50	Minnesota	48
Dec. 27	42	Ohio State (A)	62
Jan. 2	76	Syracuse	48
Jan. 5	69	Cincinnati	38

The new portable floor at Demonstration Hall saw first use as State hosted Notre Dame in basketball in January of 1930.

Jan. 7	49	Michigan	36
Jan. 12	44	Kentucky	55
Jan. 15	43	Wayne State (A)	37
Jan. 18	52	DePaul (A)	58
Jan. 23	40	Detroit	38
Jan. 31	57	Notre Dame (A)	62
Feb. 2	51	Kentucky	59
Feb. 4	69	Cincinnati (A)	39
Feb. 7	46	Wayne State	45
Feb. 9	58	Detroit	46
Feb. 11	58	Great Lakes N.T.S.(A)	59
Feb. 16	64	Ohio State	41
Feb. 20	54	Notre Dame	56
Feb. 23	59	Wisconsin (A)	48
Mar. 1	56	Wisconsin	52
		Won 12 Lost 9	

1946-1947

Dec. 7	29	Michigan (A)	51
Dec. 20	57	Stanford University	45
Dec. 28	52	Wayne State (A)	25
Dec. 31	61	Syracuse (A)	57
Jan. 2	43	Arizona	45
Jan. 4	62	Georgia Tech	52
Jan. 6	53	Marquette	51
Jan. 11	52	Detroit (A)	44
Jan. 14	56	Notre Dame	74
Jan. 18	59	Minnesota	73
Jan. 20	48	Wisconsin	58
Jan. 25	45	DePaul (A)	52
Jan. 27	36	Kentucky (A)	86
Feb. 1	49	Wayne State	36
Feb. 3	56	Marquette (A)	55
Feb. 8	54	Notre Dame (A)	70
Feb. 11	51	Virginia	46
Feb. 15	46	Ohio State	58
Feb. 19	55	Detroit	48
Feb. 22	70	Boston Coll.	49
Mar. 1	47	Michigan	59
		Won 11 Lost 10	

1947-1948

Dec. 18	43	Michigan	38
Dec. 20	48	Purdue (A)	50
Dec. 23	64	Indiana	60

Dec. 27	57	Wayne State (A)	55
Dec. 29	53	Harvard	47
Jan. 3	46	Washington (St. Louis) (A)	
Jan. 5	44	Missouri (A)	46
Jan. 10	45	Kentucky	47
Jan. 13	57	Marquette	54
Jan. 17	65	Western Reserve (A)	57
Jan. 20	52	Detroit (A)	34
Jan. 24	42	DePaul (A)	52
Jan. 26	66	Detroit	31
Jan. 31	63	Minnesota (A)	69
Feb. 3	49	DePaul	63
Feb. 9	39	Wisconsin (A)	51
Feb. 14	53	Marquette (A)	48
Feb. 17	44	Notre Dame	51
Feb. 21	50	Ohio State	72
Feb. 24	54	Notre Dame (A)	50
Feb. 28	63	Wayne State	49
Mar. 6	28	Michigan (A)	69
		Won 12 Lost 10	

1948-1949

Nov. 27	46	Alma	33
Nov. 27	53	Hillsdale	43
Dec. 4	33	Michigan (A)	66
Dec. 6	36	Indiana (A)	48
Dec. 18	49	Iowa	43
Dec. 20	45	Cornell	56
Dec. 29	74	Mississippi State	28
Jan. 7	48	Marquette	68
Jan. 10	66	Detroit	49
Jan. 14	44	Western Reserve	43
Jan. 17	34	Detroit (A)	35
Jan. 22	37	Wayne State (A)	35
Jan. 27	63	Wayne State	48
Jan. 31	38	Michigan	49
Feb. 3	47	Notre Dame (A)	63
Feb. 5	42	Marquette (A)	59
Feb. 12	48	Purdue	66
Feb. 19	62	Virginia	43
Feb. 21	47	Minnesota	57
Feb. 23	41	Notre Dame	43
Feb. 28	51	Ohio State (A)	70
		Won 9 Lost 12	

1949-1950
Alton S. Kircher, Coach

Dec. 1	49	Michigan	52
Dec. 5	53	Iowa (A)	73
Dec. 10	58	Indiana	73
Dec. 17	54	Missouri	73
Dec. 22	60	Georgia Tech	68
Dec. 23	46	Northwestern (A)	68
(*)Dec. 28	57	Harvard	68
(*)Dec. 29	61	Cornell	54
Jan. 2	50	Indiana (A)	60
Jan. 7	65	Notre Dame	76
Jan. 9	55	Detroit (A)	66
Jan. 13	81	Marquette	64
Jan. 18	65	Notre Dame (A)	71
Jan. 23	56	Minnesota	73
Jan. 28	54	Western Reserve	57
Feb. 4	53	Purdue (A)	69
Feb. 6	47	Wisconsin	66
Feb. 11	43	Ohio State (A)	87
Feb. 14	57	Detroit	54
Feb. 17	68	Wayne State	44
Feb. 20	53	Michigan (A)	70
Feb. 25	58	Marquette (A)	75

(*)Holiday Tournament at East Lansing
Won 4   Lost 18

1950-1951
Peter Newell, Coach

Dec. 2	51	Wayne State (A)	50
Dec. 5	45	Detroit	31
Dec. 19	74	Marquette	42
(*)Dec. 29	51	Penn State	44
(*)Dec. 30	46	Princeton	52
Jan. 6	67	Northwestern (A)	62
Jan. 8	52	Wisconsin	53
Jan. 13	37	Indiana	47
Jan. 15	42	Iowa (A)	46
Jan. 20	49	Michigan (A)	36
Jan. 25	60	Notre Dame	43
Jan. 27	49	Ohio State (A)	58
Jan. 29	55	Purdue (A)	59
Feb. 5	50	Minnesota	44
Feb. 12	52	Northwestern	48
Feb. 17	43	Michigan	32
Feb. 19	46	Notre Dame (A)	56
Feb. 24	29	Wisconsin (A)	35
Feb. 26	39	Minnesota (A)	46
Mar. 3	52	Iowa	65
Mar. 5	43	Illinois	49

(*)Holiday Tournament at East Lansing
Won 10   Lost 11

1951-1952

Dec. 1	52	Wayne State	43
Dec. 13	50	Denver	48
Dec. 15	53	Marquette (A)	47
Dec. 18	52	Detroit (A)	47
(*)Dec. 28	47	Dartmouth	42
(*)Dec. 29	52	Princeton	46
Jan. 2	66	Notre Dame (A)	52
Jan. 5	60	Iowa	61
Jan. 7	82	Northwestern	49
Jan. 12	49	Minnesota (A)	55
Jan. 15	48	Notre Dame	56
Jan. 19	36	Michigan (A)	50
Jan. 21	50	Wisconsin	39
Jan. 26	56	Purdue	47
Feb. 2	76	Northwestern (A)	86
Feb. 9	70	Ohio State	52
Feb. 11	62	Illinois (A)	84
Feb. 16	57	Wisconsin (A)	55
Feb. 18	58	Minnesota	60
Feb. 25	64	Iowa (A)	64
Mar. 1	80	Michigan	59
Mar. 3	67	Indiana (A)	70

(*)Holiday Tournament at East Lansing
Won 13   Lost 9

1952-1953

Dec. 6	62	Marquette	51
(*)Dec. 19	55	California	60
(*)Dec. 20	80	Kansas State	63
Dec. 27	52	Northwestern (A)	47
Dec. 30	47	Minnesota (A)	64
Jan. 3	68	Ohio State	57
Jan. 5	62	Indiana	69
Jan. 10	68	Iowa	61
Jan. 17	66	Michigan (A)	64
Jan. 19	64	Illinois	76
Jan. 24	76	Northwestern	63
Jan. 31	64	Minnesota	60
Feb. 7	62	Ohio State (A)	73
Feb. 9	60	Iowa (A)	48
Feb. 14	50	Indiana (A)	65
Feb. 16	64	Notre Dame (A)	72
Feb. 21	68	Purdue	57
Feb. 23	53	Wisconsin	45
Feb. 28	77	Purdue (A)	72
Mar. 2	53	Illinois (A)	66
Mar. 7	55	Michigan	52
Mar. 9	51	Wisconsin (A)	58

(*)Holiday Tournament at East Lansing
Won 13   Lost 9

1953-1954

Dec. 5	88	Creighton	51
Dec. 17	65	Marquette	60
Dec. 19	81	Southern California	63
Dec. 22	83	Pittsburgh	51
Dec. 30	73	Southern California (A)	75
Dec. 31	57	U.C.L.A. (A)	67
Jan. 4	63	Iowa (A)	73
Jan. 5	78	Kansas State (A)	63
Jan. 9	60	Illinois	59
Jan. 16	62	Michigan (A)	64
Jan. 18	53	Wisconsin	57
Jan. 23	83	Ohio State	76
Jan. 30	71	Minnesota (A)	79
Feb. 1	65	Northwestern	62
Feb. 6	74	Indiana (A)	79
Feb. 9	71	Notre Dame	74
Feb. 13	50	Purdue (A)	64
Feb. 20	61	Indiana	63
Feb. 22	71	Northwestern (A)	80
Feb. 27	48	Iowa	60
Mar. 1	56	Wisconsin (A)	79
Mar. 6	76	Michigan	61

Won 9   Lost 13

1954-1955
Forrest Anderson, Coach

Dec. 1	91	Marquette	72
Dec. 4	78	Detroit	84
Dec. 17	79	Princeton (A)	67
Dec. 18	67	Pennsylvania (A)	73
Dec. 22	75	DePaul	76
Dec. 30	85	Penn State	74
Jan. 3	76	Ohio State (A)	83
Jan. 8	94	Wisconsin	77
Jan. 10	81	Iowa (A)	94
Jan. 15	84	Michigan	82
Jan. 17	79	Indiana 9A)	88
Jan. 22	87	Minnesota	75
Jan. 29	88	DePaul (A)	72
Jan. 31	79	Purdue	72
Feb. 5	73	Wisconsin (A)	70
Feb. 7	93	Notre Dame (A)	79
Feb. 12	54	Northwestern (A)	56
Feb. 14	72	Illinois (A)	90
Feb. 19	69	Iowa	78
Feb. 21	71	Northwestern	69
Feb. 28	93	Indiana	77
Mar. 5	83	Michigan (A)	68

Won 13   Lost 9

1955-1956

Date		Score	Opponent	Opp.
Dec. 13		97	Southern Illinois	71
Dec. 17		82	Pittsburgh (A)	81
Dec. 21		84	Notre Dame (A)	78
Dec. 23		72	Wyoming	62
(*)Dec. 29		95	Maryland (A)	75
(*)Dec. 30		62	George Washington (A)	65
Jan. 2		65	Illinois (A)	73
Jan. 7		65	Iowa (A)	64
Jan. 14		62	Purdue	66
Jan. 16		70	Indiana (A)	79
Jan. 21		80	Minnesota	69
Jan. 28		94	Ohio State	91
Feb. 1		85	Detroit (A)	78
Feb. 6		86	Michigan	76
Feb. 8		81	Marquette (A)	90
Feb. 13		73	Minnesota (A)	77
Feb. 18		76	Illinois	96
Feb. 20		96	Northwestern	93
Feb. 25		56	Purdue (A)	63
Feb. 27		89	Wisconsin	82
Mar. 3		84	Ohio State (A)	96
Mar. 5		76	Michigan (A)	75

(*)Holiday Tournament at College Park, Md.

Won 13 Lost 9

1956-1957

Date		Score	Opponent	Opp.
Dec. 1		53	Iowa State	60
Dec. 8		79	Brigham Young	61
Dec. 17		79	Butler (A)	83
Dec. 22		92	Marquette	65
(*)Dec. 27		79	Nebraska (A)	65
(*)Dec. 28		87	Colorado (A)	90
(*)Dec. 29		76	Oklahoma (A)	74
Jan. 5		71	Purdue	72
Jan. 7		69	Michigan	70
Jan. 15		76	Notre Dame (A)	86
Jan. 19		51	Ohio State (A)	70
Jan. 26		72	Minnesota (A)	59
Jan. 28		73	Ohio State	64
Feb. 2		77	Northwestern (A)	63
Feb. 9		70	Illinois	64
Feb. 11		68	Purdue (A)	66
Feb. 16		77	Iowa	67
Feb. 18		89	Illinois (A)	83
Feb. 23		70	Minnesota	65
Feb. 25		78	Wisconsin (A)	62
Mar. 2		76	Indiana	61
Mar. 4		72	Michigan (A)	81
(**)Mar. 15		85	Notre Dame (A)	83
(**)Mar. 16		80	Kentucky (A)	68
(***)Mar. 22		70	North Carolina (A)	74
(***)Mar. 23		60	San Francisco (A)	67

(*)Holiday Tournament at Kansas City, Mo. (Big Seven)

(**)National Collegiate Athletic Association Midwest Regional at Lexington, Ky.

(***)National Collegiate Athletic Association Championships at Kansas City, Mo.

Won 16 Lost 10

1957-1958

Date		Score	Opponent	Opp.
Dec. 2		74	Butler	55
Dec. 6		71	Detroit (A)	59
Dec. 14		84	Colorado	44
Dec. 21		79	Notre Dame	72
Dec. 23		57	Iowa State (A)	51
(*)Dec. 27		63	Southern California (A)	61
(*)Dec. 28		77	U.C.L.A. (A)	67
Dec. 30		69	Washington (A)	71
Jan. 4		56	Ohio State (A)	70
Jan. 11		84	Purdue	75
Jan. 18		83	Northwestern (A)	78
Jan. 20		52	Wisconsin (A)	66
Jan. 25		74	Northwestern	60
Feb. 1		88	Minnesota	64
Feb. 8		79	Indiana (A)	82
Feb. 10		90	Iowa	84
Feb. 15		69	Illinois	56
Feb. 17		79	Michigan (A)	69
Feb. 22		93	Wisconsin	59
Feb. 24		70	Purdue (A)	72
Mar. 1		83	Iowa (A)	65
Mar. 8		72	Indiana	75

(*)Holiday Tournament at Los Angeles Calif.

Won 16 Lost 6

1958-1959

Date		Score	Opponent	Opp.
Dec. 6		88	Detroit	51
Dec. 8		72	Butler	46
Dec. 17		74	Notre Dame (A)	56
Dec. 20		80	Nebraska	55
(*)Dec. 29		82	Duke (A)	57
(*)Dec. 30		75	North Carolina (A)	58
(*)Dec. 31		61	North Carolina State (A)	70
Jan. 3		79	Indiana	77
Jan. 5		68	Iowa (A)	80
Jan. 10		97	Illinois (A)	96
Jan. 17		63	Michigan State Alumni	56
Jan. 19		92	Ohio State	77
Jan. 24		82	Minnesota	76
Jan. 31		81	Northwestern	72
Feb. 2		88	Wisconsin (A)	57
Feb. 7		81	Purdue (A)	85
Feb. 14		103	Michigan	91
Feb. 16		71	Northwestern (A)	68
Feb. 21		94	Purdue	87
Feb. 28		86	Indiana (A)	82
Mar. 2		93	Wisconsin	73
Mar. 7		84	Iowa	74
(**)Mar. 13		74	Marquette	69
(**)Mar. 14		81	Louisville (A)	88

(*)Holiday Tournament at Raleigh, N.C. (Dixie Classic)

(**)National Collegiate Athletic Association Mideast Regional at Raleigh, N.C.

Won 20 Lost 4

1959-1960

Date		Score	Opponent	Opp.
Dec. 3		96	Bowling Green	67
Dec. 5		61	Notre Dame	56
Dec. 17		82	Nebraska	80
Dec. 19		82	Wyoming (A)	72
Dec. 21		75	Brigham Young (A)	79
Dec. 23		60	California (A)	71
Dec. 28		85	Butler (A)	80
Jan. 2		91	Wisconsin (A)	79
Jan. 9		89	Michigan	58
Jan. 11		79	Iowa (A)	92
Jan. 16		88	Illinois (A)	96
Jan. 23		90	Iowa	80
Jan. 30		79	Ohio State (A)	111
Feb. 1		84	Minnesota	63
Feb. 6		65	Purdue	68
Feb. 8		78	Illinois	77
Feb. 13		73	Minnesota (A)	82
Feb. 20		83	Ohio State	84
Feb. 22		69	Northwestern (A)	71
Feb. 27		65	Michigan (A)	72
Mar. 5		80	Indiana	86

Won 10 Lost 11

1960-1961

Date		Score	Opponent	Opp.
Dec. 3		77	Butler	71
Dec. 5		70	Bowling Green (A)	67
Dec. 16		69	Kansas (A)	93
Dec. 17		82	Kansas State (A)	104
Dec. 22		92	Iowa State	81

		Left	
(*)Dec. 28	61	U.C.L.A. (A)	98
(*)Dec. 29	80	Stanford (A)	81
(*)Dec. 30	77	Minnesota (A)	83
Jan. 7	71	Wisconsin	74
Jan. 9	55	Indiana (A)	79
Jan. 14	72	Iowa (A)	86
Jan. 16	81	Michigan	69
Jan. 21	62	Northwestern	77
Jan. 23	70	Minnesota (A)	89
Jan. 30	92	Illinois (A)	93
Feb. 4	71	Northern Michigan (A)	79
Feb. 6	89	Notre Dame	74
Feb. 11	68	Ohio State	83
Feb. 13	67	Michigan (A)	78
Feb. 18	72	Minnesota	75
Feb. 20	90	Illinois	80
Feb. 25	74	Purdue (A)	85
Mar. 4	83	Ohio State (A)	91
Mar. 6	74	Iowa	64

(*)Holiday Tournament at Los Angeles, Calif.

Won 7 Lost 17

1961-1962

Dec. 2	75	Northern Michigan	59
Dec. 9	90	Tulsa	70
Dec. 16	72	Notre Dame	73
Dec. 18	99	South Carolina	91
Dec. 23	77	Butler (A)	72
(*)Dec. 28	59	Oregon (A)	71
(*)Dec. 29	74	Portland (A)	60
(*)Dec. 30	72	California (A)	85
Jan. 6	71	Indiana (A)	76
Jan. 8	78	Wisconsin	83
Jan. 13	65	Illinois	66
Jan. 15	74	Purdue	89
Jan. 20	80	Michigan (A)	74
Jan. 22	84	Minnesota	79
Jan. 27	70	Northwestern	71
Feb. 3	64	Purdue (A)	86
Feb. 10	72	Wisconsin (A)	77
Feb. 17	72	Ohio State	80
Feb. 19	51	Iowa (A)	59
Feb. 24	97	Indiana	85
Feb. 26	64	Northwestern (A)	71
Mar. 3	91	Minnesota (A)	98

(*)Holiday Tournament at Portland, Ore.

Won 8 Lost 14

1962-1963

Dec. 1	56	Kansas State	66
Dec. 4	85	Notre Dame (A)	92
Dec. 8	81	Kansas	62
Dec. 19	69	Wichita (A)	80
Dec. 21	79	Utah (A)	88
Dec. 22	87	Utah State (A)	102
Jan. 5	84	Indiana	96
Jan. 12	75	Wisconsin (A)	68
Jan. 19	80	Northwestern	68
Jan. 21	59	Iowa	60
Jan. 26	61	Minnesota (A)	59
Feb. 2	71	Michigan	72
Feb. 4	81	Purdue (A)	103
Feb. 9	86	Illinois (A)	91
Feb. 16	70	Minnesota	75
Feb. 18	77	Ohio State (A)	87
Feb. 23	94	Indiana (A)	113
Mar. 2	89	Wisconsin	92
Mar. 4	93	Purdue	94
Mar. 9	83	Northwestern	100

Won 4 Lost 16

1963-1964

Nov. 30	109	Northern Michigan	86
Dec. 4	101	Western Michigan	100
Dec. 7	104	Bowling Green	81

Dec. 14	87	Pennsylvania (A)	75
Dec. 18	88	Tulsa (A)	89
(*)Dec. 20	68	California (A)	78
(*)Dec. 21	118	Oklahoma (A)	100
Dec. 23	90	Brigham Young (A)	95
Dec. 28	76	Butler (A)	65
Jan. 4	66	Illinois (A)	87
Jan. 6	106	Wisconsin	90
Jan. 11	107	Indiana	103
Jan. 14	82	Minnesota (A)	103
Jan. 18	80	Notre Dame	95
Jan. 25	77	Michigan	91
Jan. 27	102	Ohio State	99
Feb. 1	79	Michigan (A)	95
Feb. 3	98	Purdue (A)	101
Feb. 8	86	Northwestern (A)	93
Feb. 15	107	Iowa	82
Feb. 17	85	Illinois	82
Feb. 22	107	Iowa (A)	89
Feb. 29	107	Northwestern	97
Mar. 7	81	Ohio State	80

(*)Holiday Tournament at Tempe, Ariz.

Won 14 Lost 10

1964-1965

Dec. 3	82	Northern Michigan	76
Dec. 5	89	Western Michigan	80
Dec. 8	93	Notre Dame (A)	100
Dec. 12	75	Drake	91
Dec. 19	89	Butler (A)	90
Dec. 22	94	Loyola (La.)	70
(*)Dec. 28	96	Utah (A)	98
(*)Dec. 29	69	Southern California (A)	100
(*)Dec. 30	93	Washington (A)	92
Jan. 9	78	Iowa	85
Jan. 16	68	Iowa (A)	111
Jan. 23	75	Northwestern	76
Jan. 26	98	Michigan	103
Jan. 30	75	Northwestern (A)	77

Julius McCoy, All-Big Ten for State in 1956 when he scored 600 points.

A full house of better than 12,500 watches the Spartans in action at Jenison Field House, since 1940 the site of home basketball games.

Feb. 6	79	Minnesota	88
Feb. 8	94	Indiana	112
Feb. 13	83	Michigan (A)	98
Feb. 20	94	Illinois	113
Feb. 22	90	Ohio State (A)	101
Feb. 27	89	Wisconsin (A)	99
Mar. 1	110	Purdue	92
Mar. 6	75	Ohio State	97
Mar. 9	89	Illinois (A)	121

(*)Holiday Tournament at Los Angeles, Calif.

Won 5 Lost 18

1965-1966
John E. Benington, Coach

Dec. 4	82	Western Michigan	85
Dec. 7	84	Bowling Green (A)	59
Dec. 9	75	Butler	56
Dec. 11	93	Notre Dame (A)	69
Dec. 18	65	St. Joseph (Pa.)	82
Dec. 20	80	Tulane	61
Dec. 22	61	Drake (A)	50
(*)Dec. 27	84	Hawaiian Marines (A)	53
(*)Dec. 28	67	Tulsa (A)	78
(*)Dec. 30	97	Hawaiian Army (A)	69
Jan. 8	85	Minnesota	65
Jan. 10	89	Purdue (A)	78
Jan. 15	80	Ohio State	64
Jan. 22	76	Iowa (A)	90
Jan. 24	92	Purdue	74
Jan. 29	77	Northwestern (A)	68
Feb. 5	79	Wisconsin	65
Feb. 12	71	Minnesota (A)	81
Feb. 19	77	Wisconsin (A)	78
Feb. 22	68	Illinois	66
Feb. 26	69	Indiana	63
Feb. 28	98	Ohio State (A)	79
Mar. 5	76	Indiana (A)	86

Mar. 7	86	Michigan	77

(*)Holiday Tournament held at Honolulu, Hawaii

Won 17 Lost 7

1966-1967

Dec. 1	77	Western Michigan	55
Dec. 3	63	Miami (Ohio)	51
Dec. 5	81	South Dakota	54
Dec. 10	103	Wichita State	68
(*)Dec. 20	70	Loyola (La.) (A)	74
(*)Dec. 21	76	Tulane (A)	66
(*)Dec. 27	63	Villanova (A)	66
Dec. 28	67	Bowling Green (A)	75
Jan. 7	76	Illinois (A)	74
Jan. 14	79	Iowa	70
Jan. 21	59	Michigan (A)	81
Jan. 28	68	Wisconsin	61
Feb. 1	85	Notre Dame (A)	80
Feb. 6	77	Indiana (A)	82
Feb. 11	79	Purdue (A)	77
Feb. 13	86	Indiana	77
Feb. 18	67	Minnesota	66
Feb. 20	64	Ohio State (A)	80
Feb. 25	64	Wisconsin (A)	68
Feb. 27	74	Ohio State	63
Mar. 4	75	Purdue	71
Mar. 6	67	Minnesota (A)	59
Mar. 11	79	Northwestern	66

(*)Tournament at New Orleans, La.

Won 16 Lost 7

1967-1968

Dec. 1	80	California State (Fullerton)	49
Dec. 12	78	Western Michigan (A)	67
Dec. 14	55	Butler (A)	65
Dec. 16	95	Hardin-Simmons	76

Dec. 20	74	Hebraska	70
Dec. 23	80	Wichita (A)	90
(*)Dec. 29	63	Vanderbilt (A)	73
(*)Dec. 30	57	Memphis State (A)	73
Jan. 6	56	Illinois (A)	66
Jan. 13	86	Michigan (A)	81
Jan. 16	68	Wisconsin (A)	70
Jan. 20	75	Northwestern	62
Jan. 23	71	Iowa	76
Jan. 27	68	Southern Illinois (A)	56
Jan. 30	89	Notre Dame	68
Feb. 3	82	Michigan	77
Feb. 10	62	Ohio State (A)	90
Feb. 17	61	Northwestern (A)	69
Feb. 20	75	Indiana	70
Feb. 24	87	Wisconsin	77
Feb. 27	58	Iowa (A)	76
Mar. 2	68	Minnesota	75
Mar. 5	75	Purdue (A)	93
Mar. 9	62	Illinois	59

(*)Sugar Bowl Tournament held in New Orleans, La.

Won 12   Lost 12

1968-1969

Dec. 3	90	Southwestern Louisiana	84
Dec. 6	86	Western Michigan	71
Dec. 7	81	Toledo (A)	80
Dec. 13	70	Butler	60
(*)Dec. 14	63	Western Kentucky (at Chicago)	67
Dec. 16	59	Nebraska (A)	73
(**)Dec. 27	51	St. John's (A)	61
(**)Dec. 28	66	Villanova (A)	75
Jan. 4	71	Northwestern	85
Jan. 7	77	Wisconsin	67
Jan. 14	76	Iowa (A)	77
Jan. 18	89	Northwestern (A)	75
Jan. 25	70	Michigan	75
Feb. 1	76	Indiana (A)	79
Feb. 8	86	Michigan (A)	82
Feb. 11	71	Notre Dame (A)	59
Feb. 15	75	Illinois	70
Feb. 18	78	Iowa	60
Feb. 22	64	Wisconsin (A)	76
Feb. 25	72	Purdue	74
Mar. 1	85	Ohio State	72
Mar. 4	57	Illinois (A)	71
Mar. 8	65	Minnesota (A)	78

(*)Second game of Chicago Stadium doubleheader
(**)ECAC Holiday Festival Tournament, New York

Won 11   Lost 12

1969-1970

Gus Ganakas, Coach

Dec. 1	89	Eastern Kentucky	85
Dec. 6	80	Toledo	82
Dec. 13	86	Western Michigan (A)	71
Dec. 17	60	Butler (A)	81
(*)Dec. 19	89	Bradley (A)	87
(*)Dec. 20	85	Utah (A)	105
(**)Dec. 27	82	Oregon (A)	87
(**)Dec. 29	77	Illinois (A)	86
(**)Dec. 30	51	Temple (A)	90
Jan. 3	85	Indiana (A)	84
Jan. 10	98	Northwestern	93
Jan. 17	78	Minnesota (A)	85
Jan. 20	85	Notre Dame	82
Jan. 24	88	Michigan	91
Jan. 31	87	Minnesota	92
Feb. 3	86	Purdue (A)	105
Feb. 7	79	Wisconsin (A)	89
Feb. 10	66	Ohio State	89
Feb. 14	77	Iowa (A)	103

Feb. 21	78	Indiana	66
Feb. 24	67	Illinois	74
Feb. 28	82	Ohio State (A)	80
Mar. 3	98	Purdue	101
Mar. 7	81	Illinois (A)	76

(*)Utah Classic at Salt Lake City, Utah.
(**)Far West Classic at Portland, Ore.

Won 9   Lost 15

Ralph Simpson, All-American and All-Big Ten as soph in 1970, scored 667 points.

Chuck Davey, all-time Spartan great, won four NCAA titles, was on Olympic Team.

Chuck Spieser, two-time NCAA 178-pound champ and Olympic team member.

The remarkable John Horne, who won three straight NCAA 178-pound crowns, the last two coming when Spartans did not have a team.

BOXING

Boxing at Michigan State had its roots in the popular Field Days of the late 1800s. There is a record of it as one of the events at an informal field day involving only MAC students in the 1880s. It surfaced as an intercollegiate sport at a field day with Albion College at Albion on June 4-5, 1886.

When the Michigan Intercollegiate Athletic Association (MIAA) was formed in 1888, boxing was included in the program. It was dropped by the conference, however, in 1892.

The first boxer to represent the college in outside competition was Bailey B. Smith, class of 1886, in the lightweight division.

After this brief experience, boxing at MAC dwindled until the advent of the new Men's Gymnasium, now the Women's Gymnasium, after World War I. It then appeared on the intramural program and became one of its most popular activities for years.

In 1935, the winners of the all-college boxing tournament represented Michigan State College in a dual match with the University of Wisconsin at Madison. It was the beginning of modern intercollegiate boxing at State, although the sport did not achieve regular varsity status until 1938.

Members of that first Spartan boxing team which met Wisconsin at Madison were: 115, Wendell E. Genson; 125, Roosevelt Barnes; 135, Loren G. Farrell; 145, William A. Frutig; 155, Frederick H. Lindenfeld; 165, Louis F. Zarza; 175, Mario J. Ceverelli, and heavyweight, Frank Gaines Jr. The first major boxing award was given in 1938 to Donald A. Rossi.

The first boxing coach of record was James H. Devers, a former professional fighter and referee, who joined the athletic staff in 1921. The sport then was on the physical education program and in intramurals. Leon Burhans took over in 1935 and became the first varsity coach. Assistant football coaches Albert Kawal and Louis Zarza each did two-year stints separated by a two-year break in the war years of 1944 and 1945. Then came George Makris in 1948 and the sport quickly boomed into its brief, but spectacular, glory phase.

Makris-coached teams won two NCAA championships, finished second three times and third twice in eight seasons. Produced were nine individual NCAA titlists and three U.S. Olympic team members.

The individual star was Charles P. (Chuck) Davey, the only four-time NCAA boxing champion in the sport's history, as well as an Olympic team member in 1948. He also was a three-time winner of the La Rowe trophy given annually to the outstanding boxer of the NCAA tournament. Davey is generally considered to be the greatest college boxer ever to climb into the ring. Two-time NCAA winners Charles (Chuck) Spieser and Herb Odom also rank with the greatest in the college game.

John Brotzmann succeeded Makris and coached the final three Spartan teams before the sport was abandoned at State after the 1958 season. He had a national titlist and La Rowe winner in 1956 in Choken Maekawa, a Hawaiian, who also made the 1956 U.S. Olympic team.

But the last Spartan boxing champion, John Horne, was one of the greatest of all. He won three straight NCAA titles at 178 pounds in 1958-59-60. The last two came after there no longer was a Spartan team in competition. Horne had no boxing schedule to sharpen him, no regular coach, no regular sparring partners. He often worked alone in Jenison gymnasium and accomplished what Athletic Director "Biggie" Munn called one of the greatest athletic feats of his experience.

Boxing was dropped from the Spartan sports program because schedules became very difficult and costly to arrange. The only other team left in the Midwest when State abandoned the sport was Wisconsin. Today, the sport is dead except for a few schools on the Pacific Coast.

Boxing in the MIAA days was staged in the armory. Later, the events took place in the Men's Gymnasium and finally in Jenison Field House.

SPARTAN BOXING HONOR ROLL

U. S. OLYMPIC TEAM MEMBERS

1948	Charles Davey
1948-52	Charles Spieser
1956	Choken Maekawa

Choken Maekawa, NCAA 119-pound champ and Olympic team member.

NCAA CHAMPIONS

1943	Bill Zurakowski	120
1943	Charles Davey	127
1947	Charles Davey	135
1948	Ernie Charboneau	112
1948	Charles Davey	136
1949	Charles Davey	145
1951	Gerald Black	145
1951	Charles Spieser	175
1952	Charles Spieser	178
1953	Tom Hickey	165
1954	Herb Odom	147
1955	Herb Odom	147
1956	Choken Maekawa	119
1958	John Horne	178
1959	John Horne	178
1960	John Horne	178

LA ROWE TROPHY WINNERS
(NCAA outstanding boxer award)

1947	Charles Davey
1948	Charles Davey
1949	Charles Davey
1956	Choken Maekawa

MICHIGAN INTERCOLLEGIATE ATHLETIC ASSOCIATION CHAMPIONS

1888
| Ronald J. Cleland | Featherweight |

1890
Edwin W. Devendorf	Featherweight
Nelson S. Mayo	Lightweight
Edward H. Polhemus	Middleweight
Edward H. Polhemus	Heavyweight

1891
| Jonathan E. Tracey | Featherweight |
| Edward H. Polhemus | Heavyweight |

1892
O. H. Pagelson	Lightweight
Edward H. Polhemus	Middleweight
Edward H. Polhemus	Heavyweight

SPARTAN TEAM RECORDS

RECORD BY SEASON

	W	L	T	NCAA	COACH
1935	0	1	0		Leon Burhans
1936	0	1	0		Leon Burhans
1937	2	0	1		Leon Burhans
1938	0	3	0		Leon Burhans
1939	2	1	1	12th	Leon Burhans
1940	0	3	3		Leon Burhans
1941	4	2	0		Leon Burhans
1942	3	3	0	7th	Al Kawal
1943	2	3	1	2nd	Al Kawal
1944	No Team				
1945	No Team				
1946	0	3	1		Lou Zarza
1947	4	2	0	3rd	Lou Zarza
1948	1	5	1	2nd	George Makris
1949	4	3	1	2nd	George Makris
1950	6	0	0	3rd	George Makris
1951	2	3	2	1st	George Makris
1952	7	1	2	2nd	George Makris
1953	5	2	0	4th	George Makris
1954	4	1	2	6th	George Makris
1955	5	1	1	1st	George Makris
1956	0	4	1	4th	John Brotzmann
1957	2	3	0	8th	John Brotzmann
1958	0	2	2	6th	John Brotzmann
	53	47	19		

RECORD BY OPPONENT

	W	L	T
Army	3	2	0
Bolling A.F.B.	1	0	0
Bucknell	1	1	1
Catholic U.	0	1	0
DePaul	2	0	0
Florida	1	1	0
Fort Custer	2	0	0
Gonzaga	1	1	0
Georgetown	1	0	0
Idaho State	1	2	1
John Carroll	1	0	0
Louisiana State	0	2	0
Maryland	5	3	1
Miami	1	0	0
Minnesota	7	1	1
Ottumwa Navy	0	1	1
Penn State	5	4	2
Purdue	1	0	0
Quantico Marines	5	1	3
San Jose State	0	2	2
St. Norbert	0	1	1
Syracuse	0	4	1
Temple	1	0	1
Toledo	2	0	0
Virginia	0	3	0
Virginia Poly	1	0	0
Washington State	0	1	0
West Virginia	5	1	0
Wisconsin	4	15	4
Wisconsin State	2	0	0
	53	47	19

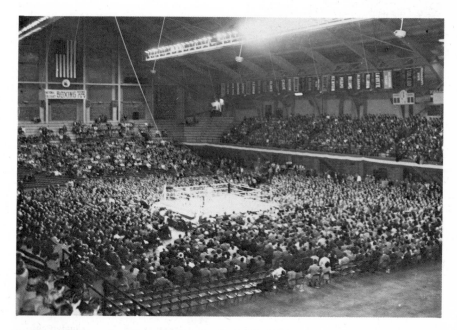

Jenison Field House drew fine crowds as the site of NCAA championship tournaments in 1949 (shown here) and 1951.

1935
Leon D. Burhans, Coach

March	MSC	2	Wisconsin (A)	6

Lost 1

1936

April	MSC	1	Wisconsin (A)	7

Lost 1

1937

Feb. 26	MSC	6½	Toledo	1½
Mar. 8	MSC	5	Toledo (A)	3
Mar. 11	MSC	4	St. Norberts (Wisc.)	4

Won 2   Tied 1

1938

Feb. 28	MSC	3½	Florida	4½
Mar. 10	MSC	3	St. Norberts (Wisc.) (A)	5
Apr. 5	MSC	3	Washington State	5

Lost 3

1939

Feb. 25	MSC	3	Syracuse (A)	5
Mar. 3	MSC	7	W. Virginia	1
Mar. 14	MSC	6	Miami (Fla.)	2
Mar. 18	MSC	4	Penn State	4

Won 2   Lost 1   Tied 1

1940

Feb. 10	MSC	4	Syracuse	4
Feb. 16	MSC	1	Wisconsin (A)	7
Feb. 24	MSC	1½	Penn State (A)	6½
Feb. 26	MSC	4	Bucknell (A)	4
Mar. 4	MSC	4	Temple	4
Mar. 9	MSC	6	W. Virginia (A)	2

Won 1   Lost 2   Tied 3

1941

Feb. 8	MSC	4½	W. Virginia (A)	3½
Feb. 10	MSC	6½	Temple (A)	1½
Feb. 22	MSC	5	Bucknell	3
Feb. 26	MSC	5	W. Virginia	3
Mar. 7	MSC	0	Wisconsin (A)	8
Mar. 15	MSC	3½	Penn State	4½

Won 4   Lost 2

1942
Albert P. Kawal, Coach

Jan. 30	MSC	6	Purdue	2
Feb. 11	MSC	4½	Florida	3½
Feb. 23	MSC	5½	W. Virginia	2½
Feb. 28	MSC	1	Penn State (A)	7
Mar. 2	MSC	1½	Bucknell (A)	6½
Mar. 6	MSC	0	Wisconsin (A)	8

Won 3   Lost 3

1943

Jan. 30	MSC	4	Penn State	4
Feb. 4	MSC	5	Virginia Poly at Blacksburg, Pa.	3
Feb. 6	MSC	3½	Virginia (A)	4½
Feb. 9	MSC	3½	Catholic U. (A)	4½
Feb. 19	MSC	1½	Wisconsin (A)	6½
Mar. 6	MSC	5	W. Virginia (A)	3

Won 2   Lost 3   Tied 1

1944

Intercollegiate competition dropped
World War II

1945

Did not sponsor a team

1946
Louis F. Zarza, Coach

Feb. 9	MSC	1	Ottumwa N.T.S. (A)	7
Feb. 16	MSC	3½	Syracuse	4½
Feb. 22	MSC	2	Wisconsin (A)	6
Mar. 2	MSC	4	Ottumwa N.T.S.	4

Lost 3   Tied 1

1947

Feb. 9	MSC	2	Syracuse (A)	6
Feb. 11	MSC	3½	Virginia	4½
Feb. 17	MSC	7	Georgetown	1
Feb. 24	MSC	6½	Minnesota (A)	1½
Mar. 1	MSC	5	Penn State	3
Mar. 14	MSC	5½	Wisconsin	2½

Won 4   Lost 2

1947-48
George Makris, Coach

Dec. 29	MSC	3½	Maryland at New Orleans (Sugar Bowl)	4½
Jan. 30	MSC	6	Minnesota	2
Feb. 9	MSC	4	Maryland	4
Feb. 16	MSC	5½	W. Michigan	2½
Feb. 21	MSC	2½	Virginia (A)	5½
Feb. 28	MSC	3½	Penn State (A)	4½
Mar. 2	MSC	4	W. Michigan (A)	4
Mar. 5	MSC	3½	LSU (A)	4½

Won 2   Lost 4   Tied 2

1948-49

Dec. 28	MSC	2½	LSU at New Orleans (Sugar Bowl)	5½
Jan. 22	MSC	3	Army (A)	5
Jan. 25	MSC	6	DePaul	2
Feb. 18	MSC	2½	Maryland (A)	5½
Feb. 26	MSC	5	Penn State	3
Mar. 5	MSC	4½	Minnesota (A)	3½
Mar. 12	MSC	4	Wisconsin	4
Apr. 1	MSC	7	John Carroll	1

Won 4   Lost 3   Tied 1

1950

Jan. 28	MSC	5	Penn State (A)	3
Feb. 13	MSC	5½	Maryland	2½
Feb. 17	MSC	5½	DePaul (A)	2½
Feb. 25	MSC	6½	Army	1½
Mar. 3	MSC	5	Minnesota	3
Mar. 10	MSC	4½	Wisconsin (A)	3½

Won 6

1951

Jan. 6	MSC	6	Quantico Marines	2
Jan. 27	MSC	3½	Army (A)	4½
Feb. 2	MSC	4	Minnesota (A)	4
Feb. 19	MSC	4½	Gonzaga	3½
Mar. 3	MSC	3½	Maryland (A)	4½
Mar. 10	MSC	3½	San Jose State	4½
Mar. 31	MSC	4	Wisconsin	4

Won 2   Lost 3   Tied 2

1952

Jan. 19	MSC	7	Army	1
Jan. 26	MSC	4½	San Jose St. (A)	4½
Jan. 28	MSC	3	Gonzaga (A)	6
Feb. 8	MSC	8	Fort Custer	0
Feb. 16	MSC	6½	Minnesota (A)	2½
Feb. 26	MSC	7	Minnesota	2
Feb. 29	MSC	7	Maryland	1
Mar. 8	MSC	7	Fort Custer (A)	1
Mar. 14	MSC	7	Quantico Marines	1
Mar. 28	MSC	4	Wisconsin (A)	4

Won 7   Lost 1   Tied 2

Two-time NCAA 147-pound champ Herb Odom hammers Arnold Perry of the always-tough Quantico Marines in dual meet at State.

1953
Jan. 6	MSC	4½	Minnesota	3½
Jan. 24	MSC	5½	Army (A)	2½
Feb. 7	MSC	5½	Penn State	2½
Feb. 20	MSC	3	Minnesota (A)	5
Mar. 28	MSC	5	Maryland	3
Apr. 4	MSC	5	Quantico Marines	3

Won 5 Lost 1

1954
Jan. 22	MSC	4½	Quantico Marines	3½
Jan. 30	MSC	5	Penn State (A)	3
Feb. 13	MSC	4	Idaho State (A)	4
Feb. 26	MSC	4½	Maryland	3½
Mar. 13	MSC	4	Quantico Marines (A)	4
Mar. 20	MSC	2½	Wisconsin (A)	5½

Won 3 Lost 1 Tied 2

1955
Jan. 29	MSC	6½	Maryland	1½
Feb. 5	MSC	8	Wisconsin St.	0
Feb. 12	MSC	4	Quantico Marines (A)	4
Feb. 26	MSC	6	Wisconsin	2

Mar. 5	MSC	2	Wisconsin St. (A)	1
Mar. 12	MSC	5½	Quantico Marines	2½
Mar. 26	MSC	3	Wisconsin (A)	5

Won 5 Lost 1 Tied 1

1956
John Brotzmann, Coach
Jan. 27	MSU	3	Quantico Marines	5
Feb. 11	MSU	3½	Syracuse (A)	4½
Feb. 18	MSU	5	Quantico Marines	5
Mar. 10	MSU	3½	Wisconsin	4½
Mar. 29	MSU	1½	Wisconsin (A)	6½

Lost 4 Tied 1

1957
Feb. 15	MSU	5	Bolling A.F.B.	3
Mar. 2	MSU	1	Idaho State (A)	7
Mar. 4	MSU	2½	San Jose St. (A)	5½
Mar. 11	MSU	5	Wisconsin	3
Mar. 23	MSU	3½	Wisconsin	4½

Won 2 Lost 3

1958
Feb. 14	MSU	4	Wisconsin	4
Feb. 24	MSU	4	San Jose State	4
Mar. 5	MSU	3	Wisconsin (A)	5
Mar. 10	MSU	3	Idaho State	4

Lost 2 Tied 2

Spartan fencers hold their home meets on the mats at the Men's IM Sports Arena. In epee competition, shown here, fencers are literally "wired for sound" to record each touch.

George Thomas, winner of Big Ten titles in sabre in 1955 and 1957.

Dick Berry, winner of Big Ten crowns in epee in 1952 and foil in 1953.

FENCING

The earliest recorded intercollegiate fencing match involving Michigan State occurred in 1895 at a Michigan Intercollegiate Athletic Association Field Day. An MAC senior named Stoichi Yebena defeated a Mr. Swift of Michigan Normal College, now Eastern Michigan, in a match probably fought with the foil.

This was the only known fencing activity at State until after World War I when Athletic Director Chester L. Brewer activated the sport.

Joseph Waffa, an Egyptian student, and Omar M. Lebel, an instructor in the Department of Foreign Languages, organized the first MAC fencing club in the early 1920s. At first, it performed exhibitions only, with Waffa and Lebel themselves participating. The sport went intercollegiate in 1926 in a bout with Michigan that the Aggies won, 10-6. Fencing became a minor sport and remained that way until 1931 when the distinction between major and minor sports at State was abolished.

State's fencers in the first meet with Michigan were Waffa, who led the way with a 4-0 mark in bouts, Max Goodwin with 3-1, Gordon Jarman with 2-2 and Theodore Carbine with 1-3.

The 1930 and 1931 teams were coached by an undergraduate and participating team member, George T. Bauer. In 1931, the coach had the distinction of winning the first major award for fencing given in the school's history. He continued coaching the team until he completed work on an advanced degree in 1937. Thomas L. Caniff, an instructor in the chemistry department and himself a former State fencer, coached the 1938 team. He was succeeded in 1939 by Charles Schmitter, who has been the head coach ever since.

Schmitter was an outstanding collegiate fencer as an undergraduate at the University of Detroit and served as unofficial coach of the Titan swordsmen from 1930 to 1935. He was appointed the Titans' first official fencing coach in 1935 and served in that capacity until 1939, when he took over as Spartan coach.

Schmitter's career has spanned 32 years to date. In that stretch, his teams won 161 dual matches, lost 148 and tied two. He has coached 10 individual Big Ten champions and a team champion in 1963. He also has coached two Olympians: Allan Kwartler, who fenced foil and sabre in the 1952, 1956 and 1960 games, and Judy Goodrich on the 1956 and 1960 teams.

Fencing matches originally were held in the Men's Gymnasium and moved in 1940 to the newly completed Jenison Gymnasium. In 1959, they were shifted to the Men's Intramural Sports Arena.

State has hosted Big Ten meets in 1952, 1963 and 1969. These and the 1955 NCAA championships were all held in Jenison Field House.

ALL-AMERICA

1941	Francis Thalken
1947	Ed Popper
1948	Chandler Washburn
1950	William H. Lacey
1952	Richard N. Berry
	Fred E. Freiheit
1966	Mark L. Haskell

OLYMPIC PARTICIPANTS

1952	Allan S. Kwartler
1956	Allan S. Kwartler
1956	Judy Goodrich
1960	Allan S. Kwartler
1960	Judy Goodrich

PAN-AMERICAN PARTICIPANTS

1959	Richard N. Berry
	Allan S. Kartler
	Judy Goodrich

BIG TEN CHAMPIONS

1952	Dick Berry	Epee
1952	Fred Freiheit	Sabre
1953	Dick Berry	Foil
1955	George Thomas	Sabre
1957	George Thomas	Sabre
1961	Don Johnson	Sabre
1962	Bob Brooks	Epee
1963	Dick Schloemer	Foil

1963	Lou Salamone	Sabre
1966	Mark Haskel	Sabre

CLARENCE L. MUNN AWARD (GOLD WATCH)

To the team member who won the most bouts during the year.

1963	Richard L. Schloemer
1964	Nels V. Marin
1965	Mark L. Haskell
1966	Melvin E. Laska

CHARLES SCHMITTER

To the team member who won the most bouts during the year.

1967	Charles H. Baer
1968	Charles H. Baer
1969	Glenn Williams
1970	Ira Schwartz

MOST VALUABLE

1961	Charles R. Schmitter Jr.
1962	Robert A. Brooks
1963	Richard L. Schloemer
1964	Nels V. Marin
1965	Mark L. Haskell
1966	Melvin E. Laska
1967	Charles H. Baer
1968	Charles H. Baer
1969	Glenn Williams
1970	Paul Herring

SPARTAN TEAM RECORDS

RECORD BY SEASON

	W	L	T	Big Ten		NCAA	
1926	1	0	0				
1927	2	2	0				
1928	1	3	0				
1929	4	3	0				
1930	2	3	0				
1931	1	3	0				
1932	5	4	0				
1933	4	3	0				
1934	5	1	0				
1935	6	2	0				
1936	7	4	0				
1937	2	7	0				
1938	5	2	2				
1939	8	4	0				
1940	14	1	0				
1941	2	7	0				
1942	4	3	1				
1943	2	4	0				
1944	No Schedule—World War II						
1945	1	1	0				
1946	3	5	0				
1947	5	3	0				
1948	6	3	0				
1949	3	5	0				
1950	7	1	1				
1951	7	3	0	5th	14 points	7th	47 points
1952	8	1	0	2nd	33	5th	62
1953	5	5	0	3rd	29	15th	55
1954	2	9	0	6th	15	25th	24
1955	3	9	0	3rd	25	14th	31
1956	3	5	0	5th	20	13th	60
1957	7	3	0	4th	23	14th	34 (3-way tie)
1958	5	5	0	4th	16	14th	15 (2-way tie)
1959	3	8	0	3rd	17	12th	40

Year	W	L	T					
1960	1	7	0	4th	15 (2-way tie)		20th	23 (2-way tie)
1961	4	5	0	4th	20		17th	40 (2-way tie)
1962	6	6	0	2nd	27		13th	53 (2-way tie)
1963	7	3	0	1st	33		17th	18 (2-way tie)
1964	7	2	0	2nd	27 (2-way tie)		37th	12
1965	7	5	0	6th	15		43rd	23 (2-way tie)
1966	9	4	0	3rd	22		4th	87
1967	4	8	0	3rd	25		26th	25
1968	6	8	0	5th	23		27th	39 (2-way tie)
1969	6	8	0	4th	14 (2-way tie)		36th	3 (3-way tie)
1970	6	7	0	4th	22		8th	46 (2-way tie)
	206	185	4					

RECORD BY OPPONENT

	W	L	T
Buffalo	6	4	0
Cadillac Athletic Club	0	2	0
Case Tech	4	1	0
Chanute Air Force Base	2	1	0
Chicago	22	11	1
Cincinnati	4	0	1
Cranbrook School	1	0	0
Dartmouth	1	0	0
Detroit Fencing Club	1	1	0
Detroit Turnverein	4	0	0
Detroit, Univ. of	17	14	0
Duke	1	0	0
Fenn	1	0	0
Illinois	4	24	1
Illinois (Chicago)	4	1	0
Indiana Tech	1	0	0
Indiana	12	0	0
Iowa State	3	0	0
Iowa	12	8	0
Kalamazoo Fencing Club	2	0	0
Kansas	3	0	0
Lake Superior State	1	0	0
Lawrence Tech	10	3	0
Marquette	1	1	0
Oakland	1	0	0
Michigan	2	8	0
Milwaukee Tech	19	8	0
Minnesota	2	0	0
Northwestern	8	6	0
Notre Dame	11	23	0
Oberlin	2	0	0
Ohio Northern	1	0	0
Ohio State	14	28	0
Ohio Wesleyan	4	0	0
Purdue	3	0	0
St. Thomas	1	0	0
Salle de Tuscan Club	1	0	0
Air Force	0	7	0
Wayne State	15	25	1
Western Reserve	3	1	0
Wisconsin	15	15	0
Wisconsin Parkside	0	0	0
Wittenberg	3	0	0
	206	185	4

State's 1963 fencing team which won school's first Big Ten title included, kneeling, l. to r., Dick Schloemer and Lou Salamone, and standing, l. to r., Nels Marin, Bob Brooks, John Pelletier and Phil Slayton.

SPARTAN COACHES' RECORDS

Coach	Years	W	L	T	Pct.
Joseph Waffa	1926-1929	8	8	0	.500
George T. Bauer	1930-1937	32	27	0	.542
Thomas L. Caniff	1938	5	2	2	.667
Charles R. Schmitter	1939-	161	148	2	.522
		206	185	4	

YEAR-BY-YEAR RECORDS

1926
Joseph Waffa, Coach
	10	Michigan	6

1927
Jan. 29	1	Ohio State (A)	8
Feb. 12	7	Ohio Wesleyan	2
Mar. 5	0	Michigan (A)	9
Mar. 19	5	Michigan	4

Won 2 Lost 2

1928
Jan. 28	4	Ohio State	13
Feb. 11	15	Ohio Wesleyan (A)	0
Feb. 18	5	Detroit Fencing Club (A)	12
Mar. 3	6	Michigan (A)	9

Won 1 Lost 3

1929
Feb. 9	8	Kalamazoo Fencing Club	1
Feb. 23	6	Michigan	11
Feb. 26	6	Detroit (A)	3
Mar. 1	8	Ohio State	9
Mar. 9	9	Kalamazoo Fencing Club (A)	0
Mar. 15	6	Wisconsin	8
Mar. 16	9	Detroit	2

Won 4 Lost 3

1930
George T. Bauer, Coach
Jan. 22	4	Michigan (A)	8
Feb. 1	12	Ohio Wesleyan (A)	3
Feb. 1	4	Ohio State (A)	13
Mar. 1	10	Ohio Wesleyan	7
Mar. 8	5	Chicago	7

Won 2 Lost 3

1931
Feb. 18	5½	Michigan	11½
Feb. 20	6	Northwestern (A)	11
Feb. 21	10	Chicago (A)	11
Mar. 6	9	Northwestern	8

Won 1 Lost 3

1932
Jan. 16	5	Michigan (A)	12
Jan. 22	11	Wittenberg (A)	6
Jan. 23	5	Ohio State (A)	12
Feb. 6	7	Cadillac A.C.	10
Feb. 12	10	Detroit (A)	7
Feb. 12	9	Detroit Turnverein (A)	8
Feb. 20	11	Detroit	6
Feb. 27	8	Cadillac A.C.	9
Mar. 5	12	Detroit Turnverein	5

Won 5 Lost 4

1933
Jan. 17	7	Michigan	10
Feb. 17	10	Detroit Turnverein (A)	7
Feb. 18	8	Detroit (A)	9
Mar. 1	13	Detroit Fencing Club	6
Mar. 3	7	Michigan (A)	10
Mar. 4	9	Detroit Turnverein	8
Mar. 18	11	Detroit	4

Won 4 Lost 3

1934
Feb. 2	7	Ohio State (A)	10
Feb. 3	11	Wittenberg (A)	5
Feb. 3	15	Ohio Northern (A)	2
Feb. 9	11	Notre Dame (A)	6
Feb. 10	11	Purdue (A)	5
Feb. 22	11	Notre Dame	6

Won 5 Lost 1

1935
Jan. 19	12	Lawrence Tech (A)	5
Jan. 26	12	Ohio State	5
Feb. 2	9	Wayne State	8
Feb. 8	9½	Salle De Tuscan Club	7½
Feb. 16	9½	Wayne State (A)	7½
Feb. 21	7	Illinois (A)	10
Feb. 22	10	Northwestern (A)	7
Feb. 23	5	Chicago (A)	12

Won 6 Lost 2

1936
Jan. 18	14	Lawrence Tech	3
Feb. 1	5	Chicago	12
Feb. 8	6	Notre Dame	12
Feb. 14	10	Wayne State (A)	6
Feb. 15	10	Lawrence Tech (A)	7
Feb. 21	10	Wayne State	7
Feb. 28	4	Ohio State (A)	13
Feb. 29	10	Wittenberg (A)	7
Mar. 16	12	Detroit (A)	5
Mar. 18	13	Detroit	4
Mar. 21	5	Notre Dame (A)	12

Won 7 Lost 4

1937
Jan. 8	6	Wayne State	11
Jan. 20	8	Chanute A.F.B. (A)	9
Jan. 20	7	Illinois (A)	10
Jan. 22	6	Northwestern	11
Jan. 23	4	Chicago	13
Feb. 19	4	Ohio State	13
Feb. 27	11	Lawrence Tech (A)	6
Mar. 6	11	Lawrence Tech	6
Mar. 13	6	Wayne State (A)	11

Won 2 Lost 7

1938
Thomas L. Caniff, Coach
Jan. 15	7½	Wayne State	9½
Jan. 27	8	Western Reserve (A)	9
Jan. 28	10	Ohio State (A)	7
Jan. 29	11	Cincinnati (A)	6
Feb. 5	10½	Lawrence Tech	6½
Feb. 12	16	Cranbrook School	11
Feb. 19	8½	Wayne State (A)	8½
Feb. 26	9½	Lawrence Tech	7½
Mar. 5	8½	Chicago (A)	8½

Won 5 Lost 2 Tied 2

In sabre competition, as shown here, the target is the body above the hips. The sabre is a descendent of the cut-and-thrust rapier through the cavalry sabre.

1939
Charles R. Schmitter, Coach

Jan. 13	11	Wayne State (A)	6
Jan. 20	7	Wayne State	9
Jan.	7	Lawrence Tech	10
Feb. 10	13	Marquette at Madison, Wis.	4
Feb. 11	11	Wisconsin (A)	6
Feb. 11	12	Purdue at Madison, Wis.	5
Feb. 18	11	Chanute A.F.B.	5
Feb. 23	6	Lawrence Tech (A)	11
Feb. 25	13	Buffalo	4
Mar. 4	8	Ohio State at Detroit, Mich.	9
Mar. 10	9	Western Reserve	8
April 6	11	Dartmouth	6

Won 8   Lost 4

1940

Jan. 13	8	Lawrence Tech	9
Jan. 26	9	Wayne State (A)	8
Jan. 27	12	Lawrence Tech (A)	5
Feb. 2	14	Western Reserve	3
Feb. 3	10	Notre Dame	7
Feb. 8	11	Buffalo (A)	6
Feb. 9	13	Western Reserve (A)	4
Feb. 16	16	Case Tech (A)	11
Feb. 17	14	Case Tech at Detroit, Mich.	12
Feb. 22	12	Northwestern (A)	4
Feb. 23	19	Chanute A.F.B. (A)	8
Feb. 23	18	Illinois (A)	9
Feb. 24	10	Notre Dame (A)	7

| Mar. 8 | 10 | Wayne State | 7 |
| Mar. 29 | 9 | Lawrence Tech (A) | 8 |

Won 14   Lost 1

1941

Jan. 31	8	Northwestern (A)	19
Jan. 31	10	Chicago (A)	17
Feb. 1	9	Illinois (A)	18
Feb. 14	11	Ohio State (A)	16
Feb. 15	17	Case Tech (A)	10
Feb. 28	13	Wisconsin	14
Mar. 1	13	Notre Dame	14
Mar. 8	6	Wayne State (A)	11
Mar. 8	9	Lawrence Tech (A)	8

Won 2   Lost 7

1942

Jan. 23	10	Purdue (A)	7
Jan. 24	13	Notre Dame (A)	14
Jan. 30	15	Oberlin	12
Feb. 13	12½	Marquette (A)	14½
Feb. 14	15	Wisconsin (A)	12
Feb. 21	13	Cincinnati (A)	13
Feb. 28	5½	Illinois	6½
Mar. 7	10	Ohio State	7

Won 4   Lost 3   Tied 1

1943

Feb. 13	14	Notre Dame	13
Feb. 19	6½	Ohio State (A)	10½
Feb. 20	11½	Case Tech at Oberlin, Ohio	15½
Feb. 20	14½	Oberlin (A)	12½

Feb. 27	13	Wisconsin at Chicago, Ill.	14
Feb. 27	13	Chicago (A)	14
		Won 2 Lost 4	

1944
Intercollegiate athletics dropped—World War II

1945
Feb. 17	14½	Ohio State	12½
Mar. 3	13	Ohio State	14
		Won 1 Lost 1	

1946
Jan. 15	9½	Wayne State	17½
Jan. 26	13	Chicago (A)	14
Feb. 2	16	Wisconsin at Chicago, Ill.	12
Feb. 9	14	Chicago at Detroit, Mich.	13
Feb. 9	10½	Wayne State (A)	16½
Feb. 16	13	Ohio State (A)	14
Mar. 2	9½	Ohio State	17½
Mar. 9	20½	Cincinnati	6½
		Won 3 Lost 5	

1947
Jan. 25	10½	Wayne State	16½
Feb. 1	17	Notre Dame	10
Feb. 7	18	Northwestern (A)	9
Feb. 8	12	Illinois (A)	15
Feb. 14	16½	Ohio State (A)	10½
Feb. 15	15½	Cincinnati (A)	6½
Mar. 1	7½	Chicago at Detroit, Mich.	19½
Mar. 7	15	Wisconsin	12
		Won 5 Lost 3	

1948
Jan. 24	11½	Northwestern	15½
Jan. 31	14	Ohio State	13
Feb. 7	12	Notre Dame (A)	15
Feb. 13	18	Wisconsin (A)	9
Feb. 14	11	Chicago (A)	12
Feb. 21	16	Illinois	11
Feb. 28	20	Cincinnati	7[
Mar. 6	15	Wayne State (A)	12
Mar. 6	16	Detroit (A)	11
		Won 6 Lost 3	

1949
Jan. 22	10½	Ohio State (A)	16½
Jan. 29	12	Notre Dame	15
Feb. 5	12	Chicago	15
Feb. 18	17	Wisconsin	10
Feb. 26	18	Detroit	9
Mar. 3	9	Illinois (A)	18
Mar. 4	17	Northwestern (A)	10
Mar. 12	9	Wayne State	18
		Won 3 Lost 5	

1950
Jan. 21	7	Notre Dame (A)	20
Jan. 28	21	Ohio State	6
Feb. 3	22½	Buffalo	4½
Feb. 4	16	Northwestern	11
Feb. 13	13½	Illinois	13½
Feb. 17	18	Chicago (A)	9
Feb. 18	18	Wisconsin (A)	7
Feb. 25	14	Wayne State (A)	13
Feb. 25	20	Detroit (A)	7
		Won 7 Lost 1 Tied 1	

1951
Jan. 20	16	Detroit	11
Jan. 26	17	Buffalo (A)	10
Jan. 27	15	Ohio State (A)	12
Feb. 10	15	Chicago	12
Feb. 16	8	Illinois (A)	19
Feb. 17	19	Iowa at Evanston, Ill.	8
Feb. 17	14	Northwestern (A)	13
Mar. 2	12	Notre Dame	15
Mar. 10	13	Wisconsin	14
Mar. 10	16	Wayne State	11
		Won 7 Lost 3	

1952
Jan. 26	18	Detroit (A)	9
Jan. 26	15	Wayne State (A)	12
Feb. 2	14	Notre Dame (A)	13
Feb. 8	18	Ohio State	9
Feb. 23	18	Northwestern	9
Feb. 29	16	Chicago (A)	11
Mar. 1	15	Wisconsin at Iowa City, Iowa	12
Mar. 1	20	Iowa (A)	7
Mar. 8	11	Illinois	16
		Won 8 Lost 1	

1953
Jan. 24	19	Detroit	8
Jan. 24	12	Wayne State	15
Feb. 7	10	Wisconsin (A)	17
Feb. 7	20	Iowa at Madison, Wis.	7
Feb. 13	10	Notre Dame	17
Feb. 14	9	Ohio State (A)	18
Feb. 14	16	Indiana at Columbus, Ohio	11
Feb. 27	10	Illinois (A)	17
Feb. 28	17	Northwestern (A)	10
Feb. 28	14	Chicago at Evanston, Ill.	13
		Won 5 Lost 5	

1954
Jan. 16	13	Detroit (A)	14
Jan. 16	11	Wayne State (A)	16
Jan. 23	10	Northwestern	17
Feb. 5	6	Illinois	21
Feb. 13	7	Ohio State	20
Feb. 13	9	Buffalo	18
Feb. 20	10	Wisconsin	17
Feb. 20	14	Iowa	13
Feb. 26	10	Notre Dame (A)	17
Feb. 27	18	Chicago (A)	9
Feb. 27	12	Iowa (A)	15
		Won 2 Lost 9	

1955
Jan. 15	9	Notre Dame at Iowa City, Iowa	18
Jan. 15	14	Iowa (A)	13
Jan. 22	12	Ohio State (A)	15
Jan. 29	10	Detroit	17
Jan. 29	15	Chicago	12
Feb. 5	12	Wayne State	15
Feb. 11	11	Ohio State	16
Feb. 11	13	Buffalo	14
Feb. 25	13	Northwestern (A)	14
Feb. 25	10	Illinois at Evanston, Ill.	17
Feb. 26	11	Iowa at Madison, Wis.	16
Feb. 26	14	Wisconsin (A)	13
		Won 3 Lost 9	

1956

Jan. 21	12	Detroit (A)	15
Feb. 4	8	Illinois (A)	19
Feb. 4	19	Chicago at Champaign, Ill.	8
Feb. 11	7	Wisconsin at Iowa City, Iowa	20
Feb. 11	9	Iowa (A)	18
Feb. 18	13	Notre Dame (A)	14
Feb. 24	19	Buffalo	8
Feb. 25	16	Wayne State	11
		Won 3 Lost 5	

1957

Jan. 19	14	Detroit	13
Feb. 1	14	Buffalo	13
Feb. 2	17	Wayne State (A)	10
Feb. 9	15	Illinois at Chicago, Ill.	12
Feb. 9	16	Chicago (A)	11
Feb. 16	11	Wisconsin (A)	16
Feb. 16	16	Iowa at Madison, Wis.	11
Feb. 23	12	Notre Dame	15
Feb. 23	10	Ohio State	17
Mar. 2	15	Indiana (A)	12
		Won 7 Lost 3	

1958

Jan. 11	14	Indiana	7
Jan. 18	12	Wayne State	15
Jan. 25	14	Detroit (A)	13
Feb. 1	15	Illinois	12
Feb. 1	18	Chicago	9
Feb. 15	21	Iowa	6
Feb. 15	9	Wisconsin	18
Feb. 20	13	Buffalo (A)	14
Feb. 22	11	Notre Dame at Columbus, Ohio	16
Feb. 22	13	Ohio State (A)	14
		Won 5 Lost 5	

1959

Jan. 23	12	Detroit	15
Jan. 30	12	Buffalo	15
Feb. 7	16	Chicago at Champaign, Ill.	11
Feb. 7	7	Illinois (A)	20
Feb. 14	13	Iowa (A)	14
Feb. 14	11	Wisconsin at Iowa City, Iowa	16
Feb. 21	9	Ohio State at Notre Dame	18
Feb. 21	7	Notre Dame (A)	20
Feb. 28	14	Case Tech at Detroit, Mich.	13
Feb. 28	17	Indiana at Detroit, Mich.	10
Feb. 28	10	Wayne State (A)	17
		Won 3 Lost 8	

1960

Jan. 23	13	Detroit (A)	14
Jan. 30	8	Notre Dame (A)	19
Jan. 30	8	Air Force at South Bend	19
Feb. 6	12	Illinois at Chicago	15

A father-and-son team represented the Spartans in 1959-61. Here, Coach Charles Schmitter works with son, Chuck, a three-year member of the fencing varsity.

Date	Score	Opponent	Opp
Feb. 6	19	Chicago (A)	8
Feb. 20	11	Notre Dame	16
Feb. 20	13	Ohio State	14
Feb. 27	11	Wayne State	16
		Won 1 Lost 7	

1961

Date	Score	Opponent	Opp
Jan. 21	13	Detroit	14
Feb. 4	6	Illinois	21
Feb. 4	17	Chicago	10
Feb. 11	17	Iowa	10
Feb. 11	12	Wisconsin	15
Feb. 18	14	Notre Dame at Columbus, Ohio	13
Feb. 18	12	Ohio State (A)	15
Feb. 25	12	Wayne State at Bloomington, Ind.	15
Feb. 25	18	Indiana (A)	9
		Won 4 Lost 5	

1962

Date	Score	Opponent	Opp
Jan. 13	10	Wayne State (A)	17
Jan. 13	4	Air Force at Detroit, Mich.	23
Feb. 3	9	Illinois (A)	18
Feb. 3	17	Chicago at Champaign, Ill.	10
Feb. 3	18	Iowa State at Champaign, Ill.	9
Feb. 10	16	Iowa (A)	11
Feb. 10	14	Wisconsin at Iowa City, Iowa	13
Feb. 17	14	Ohio State at Notre Dame, Ind.	13
Feb. 17	10	Notre Dame (A)	17
Feb. 24	18	Indiana	9
Feb. 24	11	Detroit	16
Feb. 24	12	Wayne State	15
		Won 6 Lost 6	

1963

Date	Score	Opponent	Opp
Feb. 2	10	Illinois at Chicago, Ill.	17
Feb. 2	19	Chiago (A)	8
Feb. 9	15	Iowa at Madison, Wis.	12
Feb. 9	20	Wisconsin (A)	7
Feb. 16	15	Ohio State	12
Feb. 16	8	Air Force	19
Feb. 16	17	Notre Dame	10
Feb. 23	19	Indiana at Detroit, Mich.	8
Feb. 23	14	Wayne State (A)	13
Feb. 23	13	Detroit (A)	14
		Won 7 Lost 3	

1964

Date	Score	Opponent	Opp
Feb. 8	15	Chicago	12
Feb. 8	18	Wayne State	9
Feb. 8	13	Illinois	14
Feb. 15	15	Iowa	12
Feb. 15	18	Wisconsin	9
Feb. 22	16	Ohio State (A)	11
Feb. 22	9	Notre Dame at Columbus, Ohio	18
Feb. 29	14	Detroit at Bloomington, Ind.	13
Feb. 29	16	Indiana (A)	11
		Won 7 Lost 2	

1965

Date	Score	Opponent	Opp
Jan. 30	16	Wayne State (A)	11
Jan. 30	19	Fenn at Detroit, Mich.	8
Feb. 6	4	Illinois (A)	23
Feb. 6	17	Chicago at Champaign, Ill.	10
Feb. 12	17	Kansas at Iowa City, Iowa	10
Feb. 12	5	Air Force at Iowa City, Iowa	22
Feb. 13	13	Iowa (A)	14
Feb. 13	18	Wisconsin at Iowa City, Iowa	9
Feb. 20	11	Notre Dame (A)	16
Feb. 20	14	Ohio State at Notre Dame, Ind.	13
Feb. 27	19	Indiana	8
Feb. 27	13	Detroit	14
		Won 7 Lost 5	

1966

Date	Score	Opponent	Opp
Jan. 20	12	Wayne State	15
Jan. 22	16	Illinois (Chicago Circle) (A)	11
Feb. 5	11	Illinois at Chicago, Ill.	16
Feb. 5	7	Air Force at Chicago, Ill.	20
Feb. 5	17	Chicago (A)	10
Feb. 12	15	Iowa at Madison, Wis.	11
Feb. 12	19	Kansas at Madison, Wis.	8
Feb. 12	15	Wisconsin (A)	12
Feb. 17	11	Wayne State (A)	16
Feb. 19	14	Ohio State	13
Feb. 19	14	Notre Dame	13
Feb. 26	24	Indiana at Detroit, Mich.	3
Feb. 26	16	Detroit (A)	11
		Won 9 Lost 4	

1967

Date	Score	Opponent	Opp
Jan. 14	14	Illinois (Chicago Circle) (A)	13
Jan. 19	19	Iowa State at Detroit, Mich.	8
Feb. 4	12	Illinois	15
Feb. 10	10	Wayne State	17
Feb. 10	16	Chicago	11
Feb. 11	13	Iowa	14
Feb. 11	10	Wisconsin	17
Feb. 11	8	Air Force	19
Feb. 18	7	Ohio State (A)	20
Feb. 18	6	Notre Dame at Columbus, Ohio	21
Feb. 25	17	Indiana (A)	10
Feb. 25	10	Detroit at Bloomington, Ind.	17
		Won 4 Lost 8	

1968

Date	Score	Opponent	Opp
Jan. 20	20	Oakland	7
Jan. 27	6	Air Force at Denver, Colo.	21
Feb. 3	10	Illinois (A)	17
Feb. 3	18	Chicago at Champaign, Ill.	9
Feb. 9	12	Iowa (A)	15
Feb. 9	14	Wisconsin at Iowa City, Iowa	13
Feb. 9	17	Kansas at Iowa City, Iowa	10
Feb. 17	6	Notre Dame (A)	21
Feb. 17	14	Duke at Notre Dame, Ind.	13
Feb. 17	9	Ohio State at Notre Dame, Ind.	18
Feb. 22	11	Wayne State (A)	16
Feb. 24	12	Detroit at Chicago, Ill.	15
Feb. 24	15	Illinois (Chicago) (A)	12

Feb. 29	9	Wayne State	18
		Won 6 Lost 8	

1969

Jan. 24	18	Minnesota (A)	9
Jan. 25	16	Iowa State at Minneapolis, Minn.	11
Jan. 25	21	St. Thomas at Minneapolis, Minn.	6
Jan. 31	15	Chicago (A)	12
Feb. 1	10	Illinois at Chicago, Ill.	17
Feb. 1	9	Air Force at Chicago, Ill.	18
Feb. 5	10	Wayne State	17
Feb. 8	12	Iowa at Madison, Wis.	15
Feb. 8	10	Wisconsin (A)	16
Feb. 8	19	Indiana Tech at Madison, Wis.	8
Feb. 15	9	Ohio State	18
Feb. 15	4	Notre Dame	23
Feb. 22	12	Detroit (A)	15

Feb. 22	21	Illinois (Chicago) at Detroit, Mich.	6
		Won 6 Lost 8	

1970

Jan. 31	18	Indiana	9
Feb. 7	8	Illinois	19
Feb. 7	15	Chicago	12
Feb. 7	24	Lake Superior State	3
Feb. 14	21	Minnesota	5
Feb. 14	12	Wisconsin	15
Feb. 18	9	Wayne State (A)	18
Feb. 21	8	Notre Dame at Columbus, O.	19
Feb. 21	10	Ohio State (A)	17
Feb. 28	10	Chicago Circle (A)	17
Feb. 28	13	Detroit at Chicago Circle	14
Feb. 28	19	Milwaukee Tech at Chicago Circle	8
Feb. 28	14	Wisconsin Parkside at Chicago Circle	13
		Won 6 Lost 7	

Dale Cooper, NCAA still rings titlist in 1962 and 1963.

Dave Thor, first Olympic gymnast, three-time Big Ten champ and NCAA winner.

Carlton Rintz, winner of nine Big Ten and four NCAA titles in varsity career.

State's 1958 gymnastics team shared the NCAA championship with Illinois in competition at Jenison Field House. Dual meet record that year was 7-3.

GYMNASTICS

Gymnastics is one of Michigan State's newest varsity sports, but it has traditions almost as long as the University itself. MAC's entire athletic plant in the 1860s was a natural gymnasium consisting of one trapeze and some swinging rings suspended from campus trees. The first gym was located in the field just north of the present Women's Gymnasium.

Such events as tumbling and horizontal bar are mentioned in early records as part of field days which were so popular in the 1880s and '90s. When the school's first real gymnasium was outfitted in 1890 with $250 appropriated by the State Board of Agriculture, the equipment included parallel and horizontal bars, dumb bells, Indian clubs, parallel and vertical bars, a trapeze, rings and knotted ropes. The gym was located in the drill room of the old Armory on the site of the present Music Building. A student publication, THE SPECULUM, reported that Lt. Wendell Lee Simpson, a West Point graduate assigned to the ROTC department at MAC, had consented to give instruction on the apparatus to interested students.

But gymnastics remained a recreational activity until after World War II. Then, in 1948, George Szypula, a former Temple University great, became State's first varsity gymnastics coach and began a program which has been quite successful through the years. By the end of the 1970 season, his teams had garnered 126 victories in 189 dual meets.

Letter-winning members of State's first varsity team in 1948 were Capt. Louis Beechnau, Rene Carnahan, Arnold Nelson, Jack Parker, Gordon Thomas and Ivan Towns.

In Big Ten action, Spartan gymnasts won a conference team cochampionship in 1968, finished second five times and never placed lower than fourth. State reached the summit of national competition as host to the 1958 NCAA meet in which it took a cochampionship with Illinois after finishing third in the Big Ten meet.

Early meets were held in Jenison Field House. But competitors in the ring and horizontal bar events worked upstairs in the gymnasium during the first four years of Spartan varsity gymnastics until equipment for these events could be installed in the field house. Since 1960, the sports arena of the Men's Intramural Building has been the scene of gymnastics competition. It has a capacity of 2,000 spectators and provides an ideal setting for gymnastics performances and viewing.

Michigan State has produced some of the finest individual performers in the nation. Szypula-coached athletes have captured 43 Big Ten and 18 NCAA individual titles.

The Spartans had an early hero in Mel Stout, a two-time national champion. Stout tied for the national crown on the parallel bars in 1949 and won the flying rings in 1951. That same year, Stout swept through the Spartans' first Big Ten

tournament, winning five individual titles: all-around, flying rings, floor exercise, parallel bars and horizontal bar.

The Spartans received their greatest individual performances in national competition from Carlton Rintz. Winner of nine Big Ten championships from 1953 to 1955, Rintz took the 1953 NCAA side horse crown and in 1955 won three NCAA titles: horizontal bar, parallel bars and side horse.

Other great competitors on the national scene included Stan Tarshis, the Big Ten horizontal bar czar from 1958 to 1960 and two-time NCAA bar champion, and Dale Cooper, a conference triple winner on the still rings from 1962 to 1964 and also a double national titlist in this event.

During the last half of the 1960s, Jim Curzi, Dave Thor and Toby Towson kept the Spartan name in the center of gymnastics circles. Curzi was the first winner of the Nissen Award in 1966, given annually since then to the nation's top senior gymnast. He won five conference titles in three different events between 1964 and 1966 and also won two national titles. Thor, who took the third annual Nissen Award in 1968, won the Big Ten all-around event three straight years, 1966-68, and was the highest-placed American gymnast in the 1968 Olympic Games and the first Spartan gymnast to make the Olympic team. Towson won three straight Big Ten and National AAU titles in floor exercise between 1967 and 1969 and NCAA titles in 1968 and 1969.

SPARTAN GYMNASTICS HONOR ROLL

NISSEN AWARD WINNERS
(Awarded annually to the outstanding senior gymnast in the country)

1966	Jim Curzi	Michigan State
1968	Dave Thor	Michigan State

BIG TEN CHAMPIONS / NCAA Champions

Year	Big Ten Champion	Event	NCAA Champion	Event
1949			Mel Stout	PB(tie)
1951	Mel Stout	AA-FR-FX-HB-PB	Mel Stout	FR
1953	Carlton Rintz	FX-HB-SH	Carlton Rintz	SH
1954	Carlton Rintz	AA-FR-HB		
1955	Carlton Rintz	AA-FR-SH	Carlton Rintz	HB-PB-SH
1956	Roland Brown	FX		
	Don Leas	FR		
1958	Stan Tarshis	HB	Ted Muzyczko	PB
1959	Stan Tarshis	HB	Stan Tarshis	HB
1960	Stan Tarshis	HB	Stan Tarshis	HB
1961	Larry Bassett	PB(tie)		
1962	Gani Browsh	FX	Dale Cooper	SR
	Dale Cooper	SR	Steve Johnson	T
	Steve Johnson	T		
1963	Dale Cooper	SR	Dale Cooper	SR
1964	Dale Cooper	SR		
	Jim Curzi	AA-HB		
1965	Jim Curzi	PB	Jim Curzi	HB(tie)-PB
	Tom Hurt	V		
1966	Dave Croft	SR	Ed Gunny	SR
	Jim Curzi	HB-PB		
	Dave Thor	AA-FX-SH		
1967	Dave Croft	SR		
	Dave Thor	AA		
	Toby Towson	FX		
1968	Dave Thor	AA-V	Dave Thor	AA(Optionals)
	Toby Towson	FX	Toby Towson	FX(tie)
1969	Toby Towson	FX	Toby Towson	FX
	Norm Haynie	HB		

AA—All-Around, FR—Flying Rings, FX—Floor Exercise, HB—Horizontal Bar, PB—Parallel Bars, SH—Side Horse, SR—Still Rings, T—Trampoline, V—Vault

SPARTAN TEAM RECORDS

RECORD BY SEASON

Dual Meets				Big Ten		NCAA	
Year	W	L	T				
1948	1	5	1				
1949	1	5	1			6th	15
1950	4	4	0			5th	17.5
1951	5	3	0	2nd	49	7th	13.5
1952	6	0	0	2nd	85.5	6th	26
1953	2	6	0	3rd	72	7th	38
1954	3	4	0	4th	71	5th	37
1955	5	1	0	2nd	91.5	5th	55
1956	3	3	1	3rd	66.5	6th	21.5
1957	7	1	0	3rd	68.5	12th	11
1958	7	3	0	3rd	63.5	1st (tie)	79
1959	7	2	0	3rd	72	4th	39
1960	10	0	1	3rd	104	5th	37.5
1961	8	2	0	2nd	106.5	5th	38.5
1962	8	4	0	3rd	91	5th	52.5
1963	7	3	0	4th	51	11th (tie)	11
1964	5	3	1	3rd	93	8th	23.5
1965	6	4	0	3rd	(5-2)		
1966	8	0	0	2nd	21	3rd	184.75
1967	5	3	0	3rd	11		
1968	6	3	0	1st (tie)	13		
1969	7	3	0	4th	172.35		
1970	4	7	0	3rd	152		
	125	69	5	1 cochampionship		1 cochampionship	

RECORD BY OPPONENT

	W	L	T
Ball State	1	0	0
Central Michigan	5	0	1
Chicago	1	0	0
Illinois	8	15	0
Illinois-Chicago Circle	14	3	1
Indiana	16	2	0
Indiana State	1	1	0
Iowa	7	10	1
Kent State	1	0	0
Michigan	8	16	1
Minnesota	18	8	0
New Mexico	1	0	0
Northwestern	1	0	0
Notre Dame	1	0	0
Ohio State	19	2	1
Penn State	0	4	0
Southern Illinois	3	8	0
Wisconsin	20	0	0
	125	69	5

YEAR-BY-YEAR RECORDS

1948
George Szypula, Head Coach

Jan. 10	42	Central Michigan	42
Jan. 19	23	Minnesota	73
Jan. 24	28½	Illinois (A)	67½
Jan. 30	30	Michigan (A)	66
Feb. 17	32½	Michigan	62½
Feb. 21	38	Central Michigan	26
Apr. 3	34½	Illinois (Chicago) (A)	60½
	Won 1	Lost 5 Tied 1	

1949
Jan. 22	48	Ohio State (A)	48
Feb. 7	51	Penn State	61
Feb. 11	65½	Wisconsin (A)	29½
Feb. 12	38	Minnesota (A)	58

Toby Towson, winner of two NCAA (1968, 69) and three Big Ten championships (1967, 68, 69) in floor exercise.

Feb. 19	46	Illinois	50
Feb. 25	45½	Illinois (Chicago) (A)	50½
Mar. 7	41½	Michigan	54½

Won 1 Lost 5 Tied 1

1950

Jan. 18	51½	Kent State (A)	44½
Jan. 28	52½	Penn State (A)	59½
Feb. 6	62½	Wisconsin	33½
Feb. 13	47	Minnesota	49
Feb. 18	44	Illinois (A)	52
	59	Wisconsin (A)	35
Mar. 2	60	Ohio State	35
Mar. 10	45	Michigan (A)	51

Won 4 Lost 4

1951

Jan. 20	48	Kent State	(Forfeit)
Feb. 3	43½	Ohio State (A)	52½
Feb. 17	64	Wisconsin	32
	67	Chicago	29
Feb. 19	45	Minnesota (A)	51
Feb. 24	77	Notre Dame	19
	62	Indiana	34
Mar. 2	42	Illinois	54
Mar. 5	56	Michigan	40

Won 6 Lost 3

1952

Jan. 11	56	Illinois (Chicago) (A)	40
Jan. 19	61	Ohio State	35
Feb. 9	60	Indiana	36
Feb. 16	53	Illinois (A)	43
Feb. 23	55½	Minnesota	40½
Mar. 1	57	Michigan (A)	39

Won 6 Lost 0

1953

Jan. 10	52	Wisconsin	44
Jan. 17	41½	Indiana (A)	54½
Jan. 24	46	Ohio State	50
	40	Iowa	56
Jan. 30	42	Penn State	70
Feb. 7	40	Minnesota (A)	56
Feb. 13	43½	Illinois	52½
Feb. 28	48½	Michigan	47½

Won 2 Lost 6

1954

Jan. 23	41	University of Iowa (A)	55
Jan. 30	40	Penn State (A)	72
Feb. 6	49	Ohio State	47
Feb. 11	49	Minnesota	47
Feb. 20	38	Illinois (A)	58
Feb. 27	59	Wisconsin (A)	37
Mar. 3	40	Michigan (A)	56

Won 3 Lost 4

1955

Jan. 15	59	Michigan	37
Jan. 22	51½	Iowa	44½
Feb. 5	54	Ohio State (A)	42
Feb. 18	69	Indiana	26
Feb. 19	43	Illinois	53
Feb. 25	55	Minnesota (A)	41

Won 5 Lost 1

1956

Jan. 7	56	Illinois (Chicago) (A)	56
Jan. 9	47	Michigan (A)	65
Jan. 20	49	Minnesota	63
Feb. 4	70	Ohio State	42
Feb. 17	44	Illinois (A)	68
Feb. 25	60	Iowa	52
	67	Illinois (Chicago)	45

Won 3 Lost 3 Tied 1

1957

Jan. 11	70½	Illinois (Chicago)	41½
Jan. 19	69	Ohio State	43
Jan. 26	78	Minnesota	33
Feb. 9	47	Illinois	65
Feb. 16	66½	Iowa	42½
Feb. 18	58½	Michigan	53½
Feb. 23	74	Wisconsin	36
Mar. 2	62½	Indiana (A)	49½

Won 7 Lost 1

1958

Jan. 10	56½	Minnesota	55½
Jan. 18	71	Ohio State (A)	41
Jan. 25	52	Illinois (A)	60
Feb. 1	72	Indiana	40
Feb. 15	77	Wisconsin (A)	35
	65	Illinois (Chicago) (A)	47
Feb. 22	81	Northwestern	30
Feb. 28	50½	Michigan (A)	61½
Mar. 8	43½	Iowa (A)	68½
Mar. 11	88	Central Michigan (A)	40

Won 7 Lost 3

1959

Jan. 10	79	Wisconsin	33
	84½	Central Michigan	27½
Jan. 17	64	Southern Illinois	48
Jan. 31	63	Ohio State (A)	49
Feb. 7	60	Indiana (A)	52
Feb. 16	38½	Michigan	73½
Feb. 21	73	Illinois (Chicago)	39
	59	Minnesota	53
Feb. 28	48	Illinois	64

Won 7 Lost 2

1960

Jan. 9	87	Central Michigan (A)	25
Jan. 16	85	Ohio State	27
Jan. 23	65	Minnesota	46½
Jan. 29	80	Illinois (Chicago) (A)	32
Jan. 30	90½	Wisconsin (A)	21½
Feb. 5	60	Southern Illinois (A)	52
	72	Minnesota	40
Feb. 6	65½	Illinois (A)	46½
Feb. 12	56	Iowa	56
Feb. 20	85	Indiana	27
Feb. 26	60	Michigan (A)	52

Won 10 Tied 1

1961

Jan. 14	77	Iowa (A)	35
Jan. 14	78	Minnesota (A)	34
Jan. 21	73	Ohio State (A)	38
Jan. 28	73½	Indiana (A)	38½
Feb. 4	69	Wisconsin (A)	41
Feb. 10	49	Illinois	63
Feb. 14	57½	Southern Illinois	54½
Feb. 18	72½	Minnesota	39½
Feb. 21	54½	Michigan	57½
Feb. 25	74	Illinois (Chicago)	38

Won 8 Lost 2

1962

Jan. 12	72	Ball State (A)	39
Jan. 13	64½	Indiana (A)	47½

Stan Tarshis, winner of two NCAA crowns (1959,60) and three Big Ten titles (1958, 59, 60) in the high bar.

Jan. 20	49	Michigan	63
	72½	Iowa	38½
Jan. 27	84	Wisconsin	27
Feb. 3	71	Minnesota (A)	41
Feb. 10	71	Illinois	40
		(Chicago) (A)	
Feb. 16	43	Southern Illinois (A)	69
Feb. 17	38	Illinois	73
	62	Iowa	44
Feb. 23	50½	Michigan (A)	61½
Feb. 24	79	Ohio State	32
		Won 8 Lost 4	

1963

Jan. 19	73½	Ohio State (A)	38½
Jan. 26	78	Central Michigan	32
	73½	Indiana	37½
Feb. 2	46	Iowa (A)	66
Feb. 9	57	Wisconsin (A)	55
Feb. 15	79	Illinois	21
Feb. 20	39	Michigan	70
Feb. 23	63	Minnesota	48
Feb. 25	43	Southern Illinois	69
Mar. 2	66½	Illinois (Chicago)	45½
		Won 7 Lost 3	

1964

Jan. 11	62	Wisconsin	50
	54	Iowa	58
Jan. 18	60½	Ohio State	51½
Feb. 1	55½	Minneosta (A)	56½
Feb. 9	64	Illinois (Chicago)	47
Feb. 15	75	Indiana (A)	37
Feb. 22	56	Michigan (A)	56
Feb. 28	47	Southern Illinois (A)	65
Feb. 29	64½	Illinois (A)	46½
		Won 5 Lost 3 Tied 1	

1965

Jan. 16	54	Iowa (A)	64
Jan. 23	75	Minnesota (A)	45
	42½	Iowa (A)	74½
Jan. 30	75	Ohio State	37
Feb. 6	80½	Indiana	31½
Feb. 12	52	Michigan (A)	66
Feb. 15	47	Southern Illinois	73
Feb. 20	63	Wisconsin	57
Feb. 26	66	Illinois	54
		(Chicago) (A)	
Feb. 27	71	Illinois (A)	49
		Won 6 Lost 4	

1966

Jan. 8	187.60	Illinois(Chicago)	156.05
Jan. 15	181.85	Ohio State (A)	134.40
Jan. 22	188.10	Iowa	177.20
Jan. 29	153.45	Indiana (A)	137.60
Feb. 12	188.25	Wisconsin (A)	174.60
Feb. 18	178.55	Minnesota	165.00
Feb. 19	192.45	Illinois	184.00
Feb. 26	190.45	Michigan	188.35
		Won 8	

1967

Dec. 3	178.83	Minnesota (A)	169.93
Jan. 14	178.475	Ohio State	138.635
Jan. 20	190.25	Southern Illinois	
		(A)	190.90
Jan. 28	178.075	Indiana	171.80
Feb. 4	180.50	Wisconsin	163.85
Feb. 11	184.525	Illinois (A)	189.175
Feb. 15	190.80	Michigan (A)	190.425
Feb. 18	186.70	Iowa	189.25
		Won 5 Lost 3	

1968

Jan. 6	186.10	Ohio State (A)	165.75
Jan. 13	181.65	Indiana (A)	160.25
Jan. 19	187.45	Southern Illinois (A)	188.90
Jan. 27	188.30	Illinois	183.50
Feb. 2	185.40	Minnesota	177.20
Feb. 8	187.05	Michigan	188.60
Feb. 10	182.95	Wisconsin (A)	168.50
Feb. 17	176.35	Illinois (Chicago)	164.85
Feb. 24	187.25	Iowa	188.75

Won 6   Lost 3

1969

Jan. 17	153.350	Southern Illinois	157.075
Jan. 25	180.075	Minnesota	173.825
	154.575	Indiana State (A)	153.800
Feb. 1	179.975	Illinois (A)	179.750
Feb. 8	181.375	Iowa (A)	184.750
Feb. 15	184.875	Michigan	190.825

	182.225	Indiana (A)	167.000
Feb. 22	181.450	Ohio State	173.675
	178.750	Wisconsin	162.350
Mar. 1	154.850	Illinois (Chicago)	150.375

Won 7   Lost 3

1970

Jan. 10	155.25	Illinois - Chicago Circle (A)	156.55
Jan. 24	150.40	Michigan	161.90
Jan. 28	155.85	New Mexico	155.45
Jan. 30	157.05	Minnesota	146.35
Jan. 31	157.45	Illinois	158.30
Feb. 7	157.05	Iowa	157.20
Feb. 14	152.60	Southern Illinois (A)	159.15
Feb. 16	157.95	Wisconsin (A)	148.50
Feb. 21	155.95	Ohio State (A)	147.40
Feb. 27	151.85	Indiana State (A)	158.25
Feb. 28	151.85	Indiana (A)	153.60

Won 4   Lost 7

Mel Stout, winner of five indiviudal titles in the Spartans' first Big Ten gymnastics championship meet in 1951. He also won two NCAA crowns.

Jim Curzi, winner of five Big Ten titles and one NCAA crown. He also was voted the nation's outstanding senior gymnast in 1966.

State's 1965-66 Cinderella hockey team which finished sixth in the WCHA and second in the Big Ten, but went on to win the NCAA team title.

Joe Selinger, first Spartan All-American in hockey. He made it in 1959.

Doug Roberts, All-American for State in 1965, later a NHL performer.

HOCKEY

Ice hockey at Michigan State dates back to 1906 when a team was organized and played two games with Lansing High School on Piatt's Dam in Lansing. The Aggies lost the first game 2-1, but won the second a week later 3-1.

This early interest in hockey was sparked mainly by students from the Upper Peninsula, where it had been imported from Canada. The Upper Peninsula, in fact, is credited by some veteran sports followers with introducing the sport to the United States. A point cited is that the first professional hockey league consisted of teams from the Copper Country area of the Northern Peninsula, the American and Canadian Sault Ste. Marie communities and Pittsburgh, Pa.

The lineup for the Aggie team of 1906 was as follows: Goal tender, Richard J. Edwards; point, William D. Frazer; cover point, Francis O'Gara; center, Charles Edwards; rover, Alward M. Boxx; right wing, Glenn W. Hughes, and left wing, Walter Hopson. Hockey fans will note at once that teams in those days used seven men rather than the six employed today, and that position designations were different. Frazer also was a football and track letterwinner at MAC and in 1924, popped up in another athletic connection. He was a member of the U.S. pistol team in the 1924 Olympic games while serving in the U.S. Army as a career officer. Col. Frazer thus became the school's first Olympian.

Hockey was played intermittently at State through the early years of this century, usually on the Red Cedar River. In 1922, an area on the tennis courts located on Grand River avenue north and east of Morrill Hall was flooded to make the first special arena. The 1922 team had no coach, but played a three-game schedule. John Kobs became the first ice hockey coach at State in 1923 and continued in this capacity, in addition to baseball and football coaching and other chores, until the sport was discontinued in 1931. The rink by this time had been moved to the new varsity tennis courts on the site of the present Men's Intramural Building. Hockey was completely at the mercy of the elements and in the winter of 1931, the entire schedule was wiped out by adverse conditions.

That schedule debacle eliminated hockey from the formal sports scene until an artificial ice arena was built in Demonstration Hall in 1949 and State returned to hockey with the season of 1950. Demonstration Hall, where once varsity basketball had been played, became available for this purpose when the ROTC horse cavalry gave way to mechanized cavalry and the tanbark arena no longer was needed for cavalry drill and polo.

Harold Paulsen became State's first modern-day coach and was succeeded after two seasons by Amo Bessone. Bessone has held the reins ever since, producing two Big Ten, one NCAA and three Michigan champions, the latter in competition with

Michigan and Michigan Tech.

In 1952, MSU joined with other midwest and western colleges and universities in forming the Western Intercollegiate Hockey League. After the 1957-58 season, State, Michigan and Minnesota withdrew from the WIHL to develop hockey in the Big Ten. The next year, 1958-59, State enjoyed a great hockey campaign, posting a 17-6-1 record, finishing runner-up to North Dakota in the NCAA championships and placing goalie Joe Selinger and wing Bill MacKenzie on the first-team NCAA tournament All-Star squad and defenseman Ed Pollosel and wing Tom Mustonen on the second team. Selinger also made All-American first-team honors.

Michigan State, Michigan and Minnesota renewed their membership in the Western Hockey League (now called the Western Collegiate Hockey Association or WCHA) for the 1959-60 campaign and thereafter. The WCHA is now composed of Michigan Tech, North Dakota, Colorado College, Denver, Minnesota-Duluth, Minnesota, Michigan, Wisconsin and Michigan State.

Probably the most colorful of all Michigan State hockey units was the 1965-66 team. It finished the WCHA season in sixth place with a 9-11-0 record and then, in storybook fashion, topped Michigan, Michigan Tech, Boston University and, finally, Clarkson for the NCAA crown at Minneapolis. It was a Cinderella year for Coach Amo Bessone's Spartans, who stood 4-9 near mid-season before catching fire to win 12 of their last 16 games.

The 1966-67 Spartans almost did a repeat, but lost to Boston University, 4-2, in the NCAA semifinals at Syracuse, N.Y. State rebounded to win the consolation game over North Dakota, 6-1, to finish with a 16-15-1 mark.

Three Spartan stars became members of United States Olympic teams: Weldon Olson in 1956 and 1960, Eugene Grazia in 1960 and Doug Volmar in 1968. The 1956 U.S. team was second in the games and the 1960 club won the championship. Several have become successful professionals, including Doug Roberts and Doug Volmar.

Five Spartans have achieved recognition on the annual All-WCHA team selected by the Denver Post, 11 have been named to NCAA tournament All-Star teams selected by press people at the event and six have made the annual All-America teams selected by the American Hockey Coaches Association

SPARTAN HOCKEY HONOR ROLL

ALL-AMERICA SELECTIONS
(Selected by American Hockey Coaches Association)

1959 Goalie Joe Selinger
1962 Goalie John Chandik
1964 Defenseman Carl Lackey
1965 Forward Doug Roberts
1966 Forward Doug Volmar
1969 Goalie Rick Duffett

NCAA ALL-TOURNAMENT SELECTIONS

1959 Goalie Joe Selinger (first)
      Forward Bill MacKenzie (first)
      Defenseman Ed Pollesel (second)
      Forward Tom Mustonen (second)
1966 Goalie Gaye Cooley (first)
      (Also named Most Valuable Player)
      Defenseman Don Heaphy (first)

Forward Mike Coppo (first)
Forward Brian McAndrew (first)
Defenseman Bob Brawley (second)
Defenseman Tom Mikkola (second)
1967 Forward Tom Mikkola (first)

WESTERN COLLEGIATE HOCKEY ASSOCIATION ALL-STAR SELECTIONS
(Picked by Denver Post)

First Team
Forward Doug Volmar, 1966
Forward Tom Mikkola, 1967

Second Team
Goalie Joe Selinger, 1958
Defense Carl Lackey, 1964
Forward Doug Roberts, 1965

Sophomore of the Year
Forward Don Thompson, 1970

Career Scoring Leader

	G	A	TP	Yrs.
*Tom Mikkola	52	79	131	1964-67

Career Assist Leader

	A	Yrs.
*Tom Mikkola	79	1964-67

*Includes 7 games in 1967-68 season

Single Season Goal Leader

	G	Yr.
Mike Jacobson	29	1964-65

Career Goal Leader

	G	Yrs.
Doug Volmar	74	1964-67

Single Season Scoring Leader

	G	A	TP	Yr.
Doug Roberts	28	33	61	1964-65

Single Season Assist Leader

	A	Yr.
Doug Roberts	33	1964-65

MICHIGAN PRESS TROPHY

Originating in 1950, the Michigan Press Trophy is presented each year to either Michigan, MSU or Michigan Tech, according to the team with the highest standing among games between the schools. It is a 32-inch-high gold cup with a hockey player mounted on top. It is donated by the three newspapers serving the three schools: The Lansing State Journal, Ann Arbor News and Houghton Daily Mining Gazette.

Michigan (11)—50, 51, 52, 53, 54, 55, 56, 57, 61, 62, 64
Michigan State (3)—58, 59, 67
Michigan Tech (6)—60, 63, 65, 66, 68, 69, 70

SPARTAN TEAM RECORDS

Year	W	L	T	WCHA Place	League Record	BIG TEN Place	League Record	Champion
1922	0	3	0					
1923	2	4	0					
1925	0	1	0					
1926	0	4	0					
1927	1	3	0					
1928	3	3	0					
1929	3	3	1					
1930	1	4	0					
(Games prior to 1950 played outside.)								
1950	0	14	0					
1950-51	6	11	0					
1951-52	7	13	0					
1952-53	5	16	1	6th	2-16-0	(Note: Big Ten started league		
1953-54	8	14	1	6th	4-13-1	hockey play in '58-'59.)		
1954-55	9	17	1	7th	5-14-1			
1955-56	5	18	0	7th	1-17-0			
1956-57	7	15	0	7th	5-15-0			
1957-58	12	11	0	5th	9-11-0			
1958-59	17	6	1	League Disbanded		1st	5-2-1	Michigan State
1959-60	4	18	2	7th	4-18-2	3rd	3-5-0	Minnesota
1960-61	11	16	0	6th	5-15-0	3rd	1-7-0	Michigan
1961-62	13	11	1	4th	6-9-1	2nd	3-4-1	Michigan
1962-63	11	12	0	5th (tie) 6-10-0		2nd	5-3-0	Minnesota
1963-64	8	17	1	7th	1-12-1	3rd	0-8-0	Michigan
1964-65	17	12	0	4th	7-7-0	2nd	4-4-0	Minnesota
1965-66	16	13	0	6th	9-11-0	2nd	4-4-0	Minnesota
1966-67	16	15	1	5th	8-11-1	1st	5-3-0	Michigan State
1967-68	11	16	2	6th	6-13-1	3rd	2-6-0	Michigan
1968-69	11	16	1	6th	7-10-1	2nd	5-4-1	Michigan
1969-70	13	16	0	7th	10-12-0	4th	5-7-0	Minnesota
	217	321	13		95-214-9		42-57-3	

RECORD BY OPPONENT

	W	L	T	Pct.
Battle Creek Civic Club	1	1	0	.500
Battle Creek Fisher Body	0	1	0	.500
Battle Creek Independents	3	0	0	1.000
Battle Creek Ralph's Sport Shop	0	1	1	.500
Boston College	3	0	0	1.000
Boston University	2	1	0	.667
Brown	1	1	0	.500
Clarkson	4	7	1	.375
Colorado College	19	28	1	.406
Cornell	0	1	0	.000
Denver	6	32	0	.162
Detroit	3	1	0	.750
Harvard	1	0	0	1.000
Lansing Independents	1	0	0	1.000
Marquette	0	1	0	.000
Michigan	30	69	1	.305
Michigan Tech	23	46	2	.338
Middlebury	1	0	0	1.000
Minnesota	22	61	4	.287
Minnesota-Duluth	13	9	0	.590
New Hampshire	0	2	0	.000
North Dakota	16	38	2	.303
Northeastern	3	0	0	1.000
Notre Dame	0	4	0	.000
Ohio State	4	0	0	1.000
Ohio University	10	0	0	1.000
Ontario Agriculture College	15	0	0	1.000
Princeton	2	0	0	1.000
Providence	0	1	0	.000
Queen's College	1	0	0	1.000
Rensselaer	1	1	0	.500
St. Lawrence	16	6	0	.714
Toronto	0	0	1	.000
Western Ontario	2	3	0	.400
Wisconsin	14	6	0	.736
	217	321	13	.422

ALL-TIME RECORDS

Team

	Season
Best Pct.—.729,	1958-59 (17-6-1)
Worse Pct.—.000,	1950 (0-14)

Most Wins—17,	1958-59, 1964-65
Most Losses—18,	1955-56, 1959-60
Most Goals Scored—165,	1964-65
Highest Average Goals Scored Per Game—5.6,	1964-65
Most Assists—203,	1964-65
Most Total Points—368,	1964-65
Most Shutouts—4,	1958-59
Most Times Shutout—4,	1959-60
Most No. of Penalties—201,	1966-67
Most Penalty Minutes—469,	1966-67

Opponents

Most Goals Scored—157,	1950
Highest Average Goals Per Game—11.2,	1950
Fewest Goals—64,	1958-59 (Modern Record)
Lowest Average Goals Per Game—2.7,	1958-59
Most Assists—173,	1963-64
Most Total Points—307,	1963-64

Miscellaneous Individual Marks

Most Penalty Minutes—94, Doug Volmar, 1966-67

Most Number Shutouts by Goalie—4, Joe Selinger, 1958-59

Most Goals In Game—5, Don Thompson, 1969-70, vs. Michigan

Team In Game

Most Goals — 18, Ohio State, 12-7-57 (MS 18-0)

Biggest Victory Margin—18, Ohio State, 12-7-57 (MS 18-0)

Opponent

Most Goals—17, Michigan, 3-10-50 (UM 17-1)

Biggest Victory Margin—16, Michigan, 3-10-50 (UM 17-1)

Hockey Win-Loss Streaks

Longest winning streak 8, in 1961-62 season.

Longest losing streak 15, included the final game of the 1930 season and all games in the 1950 season when the sport was re-activated.

SPARTAN COACHES' RECORDS

Coach	Years	W	L	T	Pct.
No Coach	1922-23	2	7	0	.222
John H. Kobs	1925-30	8	18	1	.315
Harold Paulsen	1950-51	6	25	0	.194
Amo Bessone	1951-70	201	271	12	.426
		217	321	13	.422

YEAR-BY-YEAR RECORDS

1922
No Coach

Jan. 11	1	Michigan (A)	5
Jan. 18	1	Notre Dame	3
Jan. 23	0	Michigan	9
		Lost 3	

1923
No Coach

Jan. 11	1	Michigan	5
Jan. 18	1	Notre Dame	3
Jan. 26	0	Notre Dame (A)	11
Feb. 11	6	Lansing Independents	1
Feb. 17	0	Michigan (A)	9
Feb. 25	9	Lansing Independents	1
		Won 2 Lost 4	

1924
No Team Organized

1925
John H. Kobs, Coach

Jan. 24	3	Michigan	6
		Lost 1	

1926

Jan. 23	0	Michigan (A)	4
Feb. 5	1	Michigan	4
Feb. 10	4	Fisher Body	5
		((Battle Creek)	
Feb. 19	0	Minnesota	2
		Lost 4	

1927

Jan. 15	1	Notre Dame	3
Feb. 5	5	Michigan (A)	2
Feb. 12	0	Michigan	2
Feb. 14	1	Michigan (A)	2
		Won 1 Lost 3	

1928

Jan. 25	1	Battle Creek Independents	0
Jan. 28	1	Battle Creek Independents	0
Feb. 1	2	Michigan	1
Feb. 2	1	Marquette	5
Feb. 7	1	Michigan (A)	3
Feb. 15	0	Michigan Tech.	5
		Won 3 Lost 3	

1929

Jan. 12	0	Battle Creek Civic Club (A)	1
Jan. 14	1	Michigan (A)	9
Feb. 2	8	Detroit	0
Feb. 5	4	Battle Creek Civic Club	1
Feb. 8	2	Michigan	8
Feb. 15	8	Detroit	0
Feb. 26	0	Ralph's Sport Shop (Battle Creek) (A)	0
		Won 3 Lost 3 Tied 1	

1930

Jan. 23	1	Detroit (A)	2
Jan. 25	0	Michigan	7
Feb. 1	1	Ralph's Sport Shop (Battle Creek)	2
Feb. 6	2	Detroit	0
Feb. 17	1	Michigan (A)	7
		Won 1 Lost 4	

1950
Harold W. Paulson, Coach

*Jan. 12	2	Michigan Tech.	6
Jan. 13	2	Michigan Tech.	15
Jan. 20	2	Minnesota	8
Jan. 21	1	Minnesota	11
Feb. 3	3	Michigan Tech. (A)	11
Feb. 4	0	Michigan Tech. (A)	10
Feb. 10	1	North Dakota	14
Feb. 11	3	North Dakota	13
Feb. 17	1	Minnesota (A)	12
Feb. 18	0	Minnesota (A)	8
Feb. 22	4	Michigan	10
Feb. 28	5	Western Ontario	9
Mar. 2	2	Western Ontario (A)	12
Mar. 9	1	Michigan (A)	17
		Lost 14	

*First game at Demonstration Hall Ice Arena

1950-51

Dec. 1	9	Ontario Aggies	5
Dec. 2	12	Ontario Aggies	3
Jan. 4	4	North Dakota (A)	5
Jan. 5	3	North Dakota (A)	7
Jan. 12	3	Ontario Aggies	1
Jan. 26	3	Minnesota (A)	9
Jan. 27	2	Minnesota (A)	6
Feb. 2	4	Michigan Tech. (A)	3
Feb. 3	2	Michigan Tech. (A)	4
Feb. 9	3	Minnesota	7
Feb. 10	1	Minnesota	7
Feb. 15	3	Michigan Tech.	2
Feb. 16	5	Michigan Tech.	3
Feb. 21	1	Michigan	10
Feb. 27	2	Denver	7
Feb. 28	2	Denver	7
Mar. 3	6	Michigan (A)	9
		Won 6 Lost 11	

1951-52
Amo Bessone, Coach

Nov. 29	8	Ontario Aggies	2
Nov. 30	7	Ontario Aggies	4
Dec. 5	1	Michigan	11
Jan. 7	2	Denver (A)	8
Jan. 8	4	Denver (A)	7
Jan. 11	2	North Dakota	7
Jan. 12	4	North Dakota	3
Jan. 16	1	Michigan (A)	7
Jan. 25	9	Michigan Tech.	4
Jan. 26	6	Michigan Tech.	4
Feb. 8	2	Minnesota (A)	9
Feb. 9	4	Minnesota (A)	6
Feb. 12	0	Colorado Coll.	3
Feb. 13	3	Colorado Coll.	6
Feb. 15	5	Michigan Tech. (A)	3
Feb. 16	3	Michigan Tech. (A)	2
Feb. 22	4	Minnesota	5
Feb. 23	3	Minnesota	5
Feb. 29	2	Michigan	8
Mar. 1	2	Michigan (A)	6
		Won 7 Lost 13	

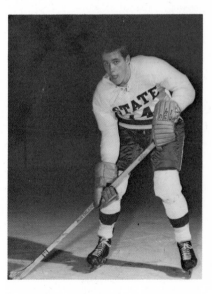

Doug Volmar, All-American in 1966 and Olympic team member in 1968.

1952-53

Dec. 5	3	Lawrence Coll.	2
Dec. 12	6	Toronto	6
Dec. 26	4	North Dakota (A)	5
Dec. 27	4	North Dakota (A)	5
Dec. 30	1	Denver (A)	2
Dec. 31	4	Denver (A)	5
Jan. 2	4	Colorado Coll. (A)	6
Jan. 3	3	Colorado Coll. (A)	5
Jan. 7	0	Michigan	6
Jan. 9	1	Minnesota (A)	3
Jan. 10	0	Minnesota (A)	5
Jan. 14	2	Michigan (A)	10
Jan. 22	13	Ontario Aggies	1
Jan. 23	7	Ontario Aggies	1
Feb. 6	2	Michigan Tech. (A)	1
Feb. 7	2	Michigan Tech. (A)	5
Feb. 11	0	Michigan (A)	4
Feb. 20	6	Michigan Tech.	5
Feb. 21	3	Michigan Tech.	5
Mar. 4	4	Michigan	8
Mar. 5	3	Minnesota	7
Mar. 6	2	Minnesota	7

Won 5   Lost 16   Tied 1

1953-54

Nov. 27	3	St. Lawrence (A)	5
Nov. 28	9	Clarkson Tech. (A)	1
Nov. 30	5	St. Lawrence (A)	1
Dec. 4	13	Ontario Aggies	4
Dec. 5	6	Ontario Aggies	1
Jan. 8	4	Michigan	7
Jan. 9	1	Michigan (A)	3
Jan. 22	4	Minnesota (A)	5
Jan. 23	3	Minnesota (A)	8
Jan. 29	2	Minnesota	7
Jan. 30	3	Minnesota	5
Feb. 5	2	Denver	3
Feb. 6	4	Denver	5
Feb. 9	2	Colorado Coll.	3
Feb. 10	8	Colorado Coll.	4
Feb. 19	0	Michigan	0
Feb. 20	2	Michigan (A)	3
Feb. 26	4	Michigan Tech. (A)	1
Feb. 27	1	Michigan Tech. (A)	2
Mar. 5	5	North Dakota	6
Mar. 6	2	North Dakota	1
Mar. 8	3	Michigan Tech.	5
Mar. 9	6	Michigan Tech.	1

Won 8   Lost 14   Tied 1

1954-55

Nov. 26	0	Rensselaer (A)	3
Nov. 27	5	Clarkson Tech. (A)	10
Nov. 29	5	St. Lawrence (A)	4
Dec. 3	6	North Dakota	2
Dec. 4	3	North Dakota	4
Dec. 17	3	Denver (A)	8
Dec. 18	5	Denver (A)	4
Dec. 21	4	Colorado Coll. (A)	5
Dec. 22	4	Colorado Coll. (A)	2
Dec. 31	1	Michigan Tech.	5
Jan. 1	5	Michigan Tech.	3
Jan. 7	0	Michigan	7
Jan. 8	1	Michigan (A)	3
Jan. 21	4	Michigan Tech. (A)	9
Jan. 22	2	Michigan Tech. (A)	5
Jan. 28	1	Western Ontario	8
Jan. 29	4	Western Ontario	2
Feb. 4	0	Minnesota	7
Feb. 5	2	Minnesota (A)	3
Feb. 11	4	Michigan	7
Feb. 12	3	Michigan (A)	4
Feb. 18	2	North Dakota (A)	3
Feb. 19	2	North Dakota (A)	1

Feb. 25	5	Minnesota	5
Feb. 26	6	Minnesota	7
Mar. 4	9	Ontario Aggies	2
Mar. 5	3	Ontario Aggies	2

Won 9   Lost 17   Tied 1

1955-56

Nov. 24	2	St. Lawrence (A)	0
Nov. 25	1	Clarkson Tech. (A)	6
Nov. 26	6	Middlebury Coll. (A)	2
Dec. 2	1	North Dakota (A)	3
Dec. 3	4	North Dakota (A)	5
Dec. 16	1	Denver	7
Dec. 17	4	Denver	3
Dec. 22	1	Minnesota (A)	7
Dec. 23	3	Minnesota (A)	4
Jan. 6	2	Michigan	5
Jan. 7	1	Michigan (A)	3
Jan. 20	2	Michigan	3
Jan. 21	1	Michigan (A)	7
Jan. 27	1	Michigan Tech. (A)	8
Jan. 28	5	Michigan Tech. (A)	6
Feb. 3	2	Colorado Coll.	4
Feb. 4	1	Colorado Coll.	6
Feb. 13	1	Minnesota	2
Feb. 14	1	Minnesota	2
Feb. 24	3	Michigan Tech.	4
Feb. 25	1	Michigan Tech.	3
Mar. 2	4	Ontario Aggies	2
Mar. 3	7	Ontario Aggies	4

Won 5   Lost 18

1956-57

Nov. 30	1	North Dakota (A)	4
Dec. 1	0	North Dakota (A)	1
Dec. 18	3	Denver (A)	2
Dec. 19	1	Denver (A)	3
Dec. 22	2	Colorado Coll. (A)	8
Dec. 23	1	Colorado Coll. (A)	7
Jan. 8	3	Michigan	4
Jan. 11	14	Ontario Aggies	2
Jan. 12	6	Ontario Aggies	1
Jan. 15	2	Michigan (A)	3
Jan. 25	1	Michigan Tech.	3
Jan. 26	2	Michigan Tech.	4
Feb. 1	2	Minnesota	1
Feb. 2	4	Minnesota	0
Feb. 8	3	Michigan Tech. (A)	5
Feb. 9	2	Michigan Tech. (A)	6
Feb. 22	4	Michigan	5
Feb. 23	1	Michigan (A)	2
Mar. 1	4	Minnesota (A)	2
Mar. 2	2	Minnesota (A)	3
Mar. 8	4	North Dakota	2
Mar. 9	0	North Dakota	3

Won 7   Lost 15

1957-58

Dec. 7	19	Ohio State (A)	0
Dec. 17	2	Colorado Coll.	7
Dec. 18	6	Colorado Coll.	4
Dec. 20	2	Denver	5
Dec. 21	2	Denver	4
Jan. 4	6	Harvard	2
Jan. 8	4	Michigan	2
Jan. 10	2	Minnesota (A)	3
Jan. 11	4	Minnesota (A)	2
Jan. 15	2	Michigan (A)	4
Jan. 17	4	Michigan Tech.	3
Jan. 18	6	Michigan Tech.	1
Jan. 24	2	North Dakota (A)	5
Jan. 25	3	North Dakota (A)	6
Jan. 31	17	Ohio State	3
Feb. 7	5	Michigan Tech. (A)	2
Feb. 8	1	Michigan Tech. (A)	3
Feb. 14	3	Michigan	1

Date		Opponent	
Feb. 15	2	Michigan (A)	1
Feb. 21	1	North Dakota	3
Feb. 22	2	North Dakota	3
Feb. 28	4	Minnesota	3
Mar. 1	1	Minnesota	5

Won 12   Lost 11

1958-59

Date		Opponent	
Dec. 5	6	North Dakota	0
Dec. 6	4	North Dakota	5
Dec. 26	7	Northeastern U. (A)	1
Dec. 27	6	Boston Coll. (A)	0
Dec. 28	3	Boston U. (A)	2
Jan. 1	11	Brown (A)	3
Jan. 2	7	Princeton (A)	4
Jan. 3	10	Rensselaer (A)	3
Jan. 9	3	Minnesota (A)	7
Jan. 10	3	Minnesota (A)	3
Jan. 23	5	Minnesota	4
Jan. 24	5	Minnesota	4
Jan. 30	7	Michigan Tech. (A)	0
Jan. 31	4	Michigan Tech. (A)	5
Feb. 6	3	Michigan	1
Feb. 7	5	Michigan (A)	2
Feb. 13	3	North Dakota (A)	2
Feb. 14	2	North Dakota (A)	4
Feb. 27	3	Michigan Tech.	0
Feb. 28	5	Michigan Tech.	2
Mar. 6	2	Michigan Tech.	4
Mar. 7	4	Michigan (A)	1
*Mar. 13	4	Boston Coll. (A)	3
*Mar. 14	3	North Dakota (at Troy, N.Y.)	4

Won 17   Lost 6   Tied 1
*National Collegiate Athletic Association (NCAA) Championships

1959-60

Date		Opponent	
Nov. 27	2	North Dakota (A)	2
Nov. 28	1	North Dakota (A)	5
Dec. 7	3	Colorado Coll.	4
Dec. 8	1	Colorado Coll.	5
Dec. 18	3	Colorado Coll. (A)	5
Dec. 19	3	Colorado Coll. (A)	6
Dec. 21	1	Denver (A)	10
Dec. 22	0	Denver (A)	11
Jan. 8	5	North Dakota	6
Jan. 9	4	North Dakota	3
Jan. 15	1	Michigan (A)	6
Jan. 16	4	Michigan	2
Jan. 22	3	Michigan Tech. (A)	3
Jan. 23	1	Michigan Tech. (A)	9
Feb. 5	3	Michigan Tech.	5
Feb. 6	0	Michigan Tech.	7
Feb. 9	4	Michigan	3
Feb. 16	3	Michigan (A)	5
Feb. 19	0	Minnesota (A)	5
Feb. 20	2	Minnesota (A)	10
Feb. 26	0	Denver	5
Feb. 27	1	Denver	5
Mar. 4	4	Minnesota	5
Mar. 5	4	Minnesota	3

Won 4   Lost 18   Tied 2

1960-61

Date		Opponent	
Nov. 24	8	St. Lawrence (A)	5
Nov. 25	8	Clarkson (A)	4
Nov. 26	2	St. Lawrence (A)	6
Dec. 2	3	Minnesota	6
Dec. 3	5	Minnesota	6
Dec. 16	5	Colorado Coll. (A)	2
Dec. 17	5	Colorado Coll. (A)	6
Dec. 19	2	Denver (A)	10
Dec. 20	0	Denver (A)	9
Jan. 6	12	Ohio U.	0
Jan. 7	8	Ohio U.	1
*Jan. 13	1	Michigan Tech. (A)	0
Jan. 14	1	Michigan Tech. (A)	3
Jan. 20	4	Michigan Tech.	3
Jan. 21	1	Michigan Tech.	3
Jan. 27	2	Minnesota (A)	5
Jan. 28	3	Minnesota (A)	7
Feb. 3	3	Michigan	2
Feb. 4	2	Michigan (A)	3
Feb. 10	3	North Dakota (A)	6
Feb. 11	3	North Dakota (A)	4
Feb. 17	14	Ohio U. (at Columbus, Ohio)	4
Feb. 18	12	Ohio U. (at Columbus, Ohio)	4
Feb. 24	2	North Dakota	4
Feb. 25	6	North Dakota	1
Mar. 3	1	Michigan	6
Mar. 4	3	Michigan (A)	4

*Won by forfeit
Won 11   Lost 16

1961-62

Date		Opponent	
Nov. 23	3	St. Lawrence (A)	2
Nov. 24	0	Clarkson (A)	3
Nov. 25	3	St. Lawrence (A)	2
Dec. 1	5	North Dakota (A)	3
Dec. 1	4	North Dakota (A)	6
Dec. 22	5	Minnesota	2
Dec. 23	6	Minnesota	1
Dec. 26	13	Northeastern U. (A)	4
Dec. 28	6	Queens Theology Coll. (A)	1
Jan. 5	5	Minnesota	3
Jan. 6	5	Minnesota	2
Jan. 11	5	Colorado Coll.	4
Jan. 12	8	Colorado Coll.	2
Jan. 26	1	Minnesota (A)	1
Jan. 27	5	Minnesota (A)	3
Feb. 2	3	Michigan	5
Feb. 3	1	Michigan (A)	5
Feb. 9	2	Michigan Tech. (A)	8
Feb. 10	2	Michigan Tech. (A)	3
Feb. 15	4	Denver	6
Feb. 16	3	Denver	6
Feb. 23	2	Michigan	4
Feb. 24	2	Michigan (A)	10
*Mar. 1	1	Michigan Tech. (at Ann Arbor)	5
*Mar. 2	4	Denver (at Ann Arbor)	3

Won 13   Lost 11   Tied 1
*Western College Hockey Association (WCHA) Playoffs

1962-63

Date		Opponent	
Nov. 22	7	St. Lawrence (A)	3
Nov. 23	2	Clarkson (A)	1
Nov. 24	2	St. Lawrence (A)	5
Nov. 30	2	Michigan (A)	1
Dec. 1	4	Michigan (A)	3
Dec. 7	4	North Dakota	11
Dec. 8	6	North Dakota	5
Jan. 4	2	Denver (A)	6
Jan. 5	7	Colorado Coll. (A)	8
Jan. 7	4	Denver (A)	6
Jan. 8	7	Colorado Coll. (A)	8
Jan. 11	5	Minnesota (Duluth)	4
Jan. 12	3	Minnesota (Duluth)	4
Jan. 25	2	Michigan Tech.	6
Jan. 26	2	Michigan Tech.	6
Feb. 1	5	Minnesota (Duluth) (A)	4
Feb. 2	4	Minnesota (Duluth) (A)	1
Feb. 15	4	Minnesota (A)	7
Feb. 16	1	Minnesota (A)	6

Feb. 22	6	Michigan	2
Feb. 23	2	Michigan	1
Mar. 1	1	Minnesota	7
Mar. 2	6	Minnesota	3

Won 11 Lost 12

1963-64

Nov. 28	5	St. Lawrence (A)	1
Nov. 29	1	Clarkson (A)	7
Nov. 30	3	St. Lawrence (A)	5
Dec. 13	6	Ohio	4
Dec. 14	7	Ohio	1
Dec. 20	2	Colorado Coll. (A)	6
Dec. 21	5	Colorado Coll. (A)	4
Jan. 10	2	Minnesota (Duluth) (A)	5
Jan. 11	1	Minnesota (Duluth) (A)	6
Jan. 16	10	Ohio State (A)	2
Jan. 17	11	Ohio (A)	1
Jan. 18	7	Ohio (A)	4
Jan. 24	2	Minnesota (A)	6
Jan. 25	2	Minnesota (A)	4
Jan. 31	6	Minnesota	7
Feb. 1	2	Minnesota	4
Feb. 7	1	Minnesota (Duluth)	6
Feb. 8	4	Minnesota (Duluth)	2
Feb. 14	0	Michigan	2
Feb. 15	2	Michigan (A)	7
Feb. 21	3	Michigan Tech. (A)	7
Feb. 22	1	Michigan Tech. (A)	11
Feb. 28	4	Colorado Coll.	5
Feb. 29	5	Colorado Coll.	5
Mar. 6	4	Michigan	9
Mar. 7	4	Michigan (A)	13

Won 8 Lost 17 Tied 1

1964-65

Nov. 26	6	St. Lawrence (A)	5
Nov. 27	2	Clarkson (A)	3
Nov. 28	8	St. Lawrence (A)	5
Dec. 4	12	Ohio	0
Dec. 5	13	Ohio	1
Dec. 11	9	Wisconsin	2
Dec. 12	9	Wisconsin	0
Jan. 1	2	Brown (A)	6
Jan. 2	5	Providence (A)	6
Jan. 8	4	Minnesota (A)	3
Jan. 9	2	Minnesota (A)	5
Jan. 15	1	Colorado Coll. (A)	3
Jan. 16	10	Colorado Coll. (A)	3
Jan. 22	7	Minnesota	5
Jan. 23	5	Minnesota	5
Jan. 27	3	Michigan	6
Jan. 29	5	Minnesota (Duluth) (A)	4
Jan. 30	1	Minnesota (Duluth) (A)	7
Feb. 5	7	Michigan (A)	4
Feb. 6	6	Michigan	2
Feb. 12	8	Wisconsin (A)	4
Feb. 13	9	Wisconsin (A)	3
Feb. 17	2	Michigan (A)	7
Feb. 19	3	Michigan Tech.	4
Feb. 20	4	Michigan Tech.	5
Feb. 26	8	Colorado Coll.	2
Feb. 27	7	Colorado Coll.	6
Mar. 5	1	North Dakota (A)	7
Mar. 6	6	North Dakota (A)	4

Won 17 Lost 12

1965-66

Nov. 19	0	Colorado Coll. (A)	4
Nov. 20	3	Colorado Coll. (A)	4
Nov. 25	3	St. Lawrence (A)	5
Nov. 26	3	Clarkson (A)	6
Nov. 27	6	St. Lawrence (A)	4
Dec. 3	11	North Dakota	5
Dec. 4	3	North Dakota	5
Dec. 10	6	Denver	8
Dec. 11	4	Denver	1
Jan. 7	4	Colorado Coll.	5
Jan. 8	6	Colorado Coll.	2
Jan. 14	5	Minnesota	7
Jan. 15	1	Minnesota	5
Jan. 21	6	Minnesota (Duluth)	5
Jan. 22	5	Minnesota (Duluth)	2
Jan. 28	5	Minnesota (A)	6
Jan. 29	4	Minnesota (A)	3
Feb. 4	8	Michigan	7
Feb. 5	5	Michigan (A)	2
Feb. 11	3	Wisconsin (A)	1
Feb. 12	5	Wisconsin (A)	3
Feb. 18	4	Michigan Tech. (A)	8
Feb. 19	2	Michigan Tech. (A)	4
Feb. 25	7	Michigan	1
Feb. 26	0	Michigan (A)	1
*Mar. 4	3	Michigan	2
*Mar. 5	4	Michigan Tech.	3
Mar. 17	2	Boston U. (at Minneapolis, Minn.)	1
Mar. 19	6	Clarkson (at Minneapolis, Minn.)	1

*WCHA Playoffs
**National Collegiate Athletic Association (NCAA) Championships

Won 16 Lost 13

1966-67

Dec. 2	4	Minnesota (A)	5
Dec. 3	3	Minnesota (A)	2
Dec. 9	4	Michigan	10
Dec. 10	2	Michigan (A)	3
Dec. 16	5	Boston Coll. (At Boston, Mass.)	3
Dec. 17	2	Cornell (at Boston, Mass.)	3
Dec. 22	5	Western Ontario (at Detroit)	4
Dec. 23	3	Michigan (at Detroit)	5
Dec. 27	4	North Dakota (at St. Paul, Minn.)	2
Dec. 28	3	Minnesota (at St. Paul, Minn.)	9
Jan. 6	6	Colorado Coll.	0
Jan. 7	7	Colorado Coll.	5
Jan. 13	2	Denver (A)	8
Jan. 14	2	Colorado Coll. (A)	1
Jan. 16	3	Colorado Coll. (A)	4
Jan. 17	2	Denver (A)	4
Jan. 20	4	Michigan Tech.	3
Jan. 21	2	Michigan Tech.	3
Jan. 27	5	Minnesota (Duluth) (A)	6
Jan. 28	3	Minnesota (Duluth) (A)	7
Feb. 3	6	Minnesota	4
Feb. 4	6	Minnesota	3
Feb. 10	4	Michigan (A)	3
Feb. 11	5	Michigan	1
Feb. 17	3	North Dakota (A)	4
Feb. 18	1	North Dakota (A)	5
Mar. 3	7	Wisconsin	3
Mar. 4	4	Wisconsin	3
*Mar. 9	4	Michigan (A)	2
*Mar. 10	2	Michigan Tech.	1
Mar. 16	2	Boston U. (at Syracuse, N.Y.)	4
Mar. 18	6	North Dakota (at Syracuse, N.Y.)	1

*WCHA Play-offs
**NCAA Championships

Won 16 Lost 15 Tied 1

1967-68

Date		Opponent	
Nov. 23	7	St. Lawrence (A)	4
Nov. 24	3	Clarkson (A)	3
Nov. 25	3	St. Lawrence (A)	2
Dec. 1	3	Minnesota (Duluth)	5
Dec. 2	6	Minnesota (Duluth)	2
Dec. 8	2	North Dakota	2
Dec. 9	2	North Dakota	6
Dec. 28	3	Minnesota (A)	6
Dec. 29	7	Ohio State	0
Dec. 30	4	Wisconsin (at	3
		Minneapolis, Minn.)	
Jan. 5	1	Michigan	7
Jan. 6	4	Michigan (A)	3
Jan. 12	2	Denver	3
Jan. 13	1	Denver	3
Jan. 19	2	Minnesota (A)	3
Jan. 20	3	Minnesota (A)	8
Feb. 2	1	Michigan Tech. (A)	4
Feb. 3	2	Michigan Tech. (A)	6
Feb. 9	3	Michigan	4
Feb. 10	0	Michigan (A)	9
Feb. 16	7	Colorado Coll. (A)	3
Feb. 17	3	Colorado Coll. (A)	0
Feb. 23	5	Minnesota	2
Feb. 24	2	Minnesota	6
Feb. 27	6	Colorado Coll.	2
Feb. 28	2	Colorado Coll.	4
Mar. 1	3	Wisconsin (A)	5
Mar. 2	3	Wisconsin (A)	1
*Mar. 5	2	North Dakota (A)	5

*WCHA Play-off
Won 11   Lost 16   Tied 2

1968-69

Date		Opponent	
Nov. 22	3	North Dakota (A)	4
Nov. 23	4	North Dakota (A)	7
Nov. 28	5	St. Lawrence (A)	1
Nov. 29	1	Clarkson (A)	3
Nov. 30	0	St. Lawrence (A)	3
Dec. 6	1	Michigan (A)	2
Dec. 7	1	Michigan	2
Dec. 20	4	Wisconsin (at	6
		Detroit)	
Dec. 21	4	Michigan (at	2
		Detroit)	
Dec. 26	3	Wisconsin (at	2
		Madison, Wis.)	
Dec. 28	3	Michigan (at	8
		Madison, Wis.)	
Jan. 10	2	Colorado Coll.	3
Jan. 11	5	Colorado Coll.	1
Jan. 17	2	Minnesota (A)	2
Jan. 18	2	Minnesota (A)	1
Jan. 24	7	Michigan	3

1967-68 (continued)

Date		Opponent	
Jan. 25	5	Michigan (A)	1
Jan. 31	6	Minnesota (Duluth) (A)	3
Feb. 1	1	Minnesota (Duluth) (A)	6
Feb. 7.	1	Wisconsin	2
Feb. 8	4	Wisconsin	3
Feb. 14	4	Denver (A)	9
Feb. 15	2	Denver (A)	1
Feb. 21	2	Minnesota	1
Feb. 22	0	Minnesota	1
Feb. 28	3	Michigan Tech.	4
Mar. 1	1	Michigan Tech.	6
*Mar. 7	2	Michigan Tech. (at Ann Arbor)	4

*WCHA Play-offs
Won 11   Lost 16   Tied 1

1969-70

Date		Opponent	
Nov. 28	8	North Dakota	3
Nov. 29	2	North Dakota	4
Dec. 5	3	Michigan (A)	2
Dec. 6	6	Michigan	8
Dec. 19	2	Princeton (at Detroit)	1
Dec. 20	3	New Hampshire (at Detroit)	4
Dec. 22	5	Michigan (A)	4
Dec. 23	3	Wisconsin (at Ann Arbor)	6
Dec. 29	5	New Hampshire (at Boston, Mass.)	6
Dec. 30	6	Northeastern (at Boston, Mass.)	5
Jan. 2	4	Wisconsin	3
Jan. 3	6	Wisconsin	4
Jan. 16	2	Minnesota	3
Jan. 17	4	Minnesota	1
Jan. 23	6	Colorado Coll. (A)	2
Jan. 24	6	Colorado Coll. (A)	4
Jan. 30	4	Denver	6
Jan. 31	4	Denver	5
Feb. 6	1	Michigan Tech. (A)	8
Feb. 7	4	Michigan Tech. (A)	5
Feb. 13	0	Minnesota (A)	8
Feb. 14	2	Minnesota (A)	4
Feb. 20	3	Michigan	6
Feb. 21	7	Michigan (A)	1
Feb. 27	8	Minnesota (Duluth)	5
Feb. 28	3	Minnesota (Duluth)	1
Mar. 6	0	Wisconsin (A)	5
Mar. 7	3	Wisconsin (A)	4
*Mar. 12	2	Denver (A)	6

*WCHA Play-offs
Won 13   Lost 16

State on the offense against arch-rival Michigan before a packed house at the MSU Ice Arena. The Wolverines hold a 25-19 edge over the Spartans in games played in the past decade.

Billy Steuart, winner of four NCAA titles
and South African Olympic team member.

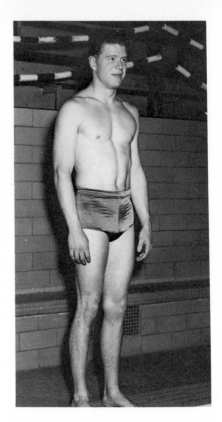

Clark Scholes, great sprinter who won Big
Ten, NCAA and Olympic championships.

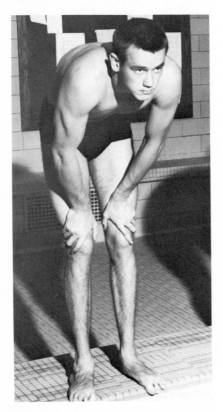

Freestyler George Hoogerhyde, member of
U.S. Olympic team in 1948.

Gary Dilley, l., and Ken Walsh were Olympic
team members and NCAA titlists.

SWIMMING

The first swimming pool on the campus was installed in 1902 in the so-called bath house, a wing of the Armory which stood on the site of the present Music Building. It was quite a structure for those days. The bath house was 77 by 66 feet and the pool was 17 by 35. The area also contained locker and rubbing rooms, showers, private bathrooms, a barber shop and an office for the athletic director. The pool was surrounded by eight white Grecian columns to give it an "antique air," according to a report of the day.

Somehow, this $18,000 beauty of a natatorium failed to excite the competitive urge and there are no records of swimming meets being held there. Varsity swimming didn't arrive on the athletic scene until several years after the Men's Gymnasium, now the Women's Gymnasium, had been opened in 1918.

The first varsity team of record appeared in 1922 under Coach Southard F. Flynn. It lost its opener to Detroit Junior College, but swimming was on its way. Members of that team were John Bos, Murray W. Jacklin, John S. Bailey, Frank B. Neiderstadt, Arne H. Johnson, Leonard M. Van Noppen, Edwin J. Brown, Maurice R. Taylor and Bertrand L. Gilbert.

Fortunes were low in the 1920s, but better teams began to appear in the 1930s under Coach Russell Daubert. His 1937 and 1940 teams, for example, had 7-2 records against good competition.

But the advent of the fine new swimming pool in Jenison Gymnasium in 1940 and Charles McCaffree Jr. as head coach in 1942 heralded the major era of Spartan swimming which still continues. Spartan teams hit the heights right after World War II, winning one NAAU team title in 1945, finishing as high as second (1951) in the NCAA, winning eight straight Central Collegiate Conference crowns and establishing itself as one of the Big Ten powers. One of McCaffree's teams won the Big Ten crown (1957) and three others (1951, 1952, 1958) finished second. Only one slumped out of the first division.

Star performers came thick and fast. State's first individual national crowns were acquired in the 1945 NAAU meet when Dave Seibold won the 300-meter individual medley and the 200-meter breaststroke and teamed with Howard Patterson and James Quigley to take the 300-meter medley relay. The first NCAA title was claimed the following year when a team composed of Zigmund Indyke, John DeMond, James Quigley and Robert Allwardt beat the field in the 400-yard freestyle relay.

From 1946 through 1970, Spartan splashers won 22 NCAA, seven NAAU and 34 Big Ten titles. Eight won the honor of representing their native lands in Olympic games. Two acquired gold medals in record-setting performances: Clark Scholes

in the 100-meter freestyle at the 1952 games and Ken Walsh anchoring the 400-meter freestyle relay combination in the 1968 games.

Swimming has known four homes on the campus, starting with the bath house in 1902. The Men's Gymnasium followed with its odd-distance 30-yard pool in 1922. The scene changed to the Jenison Pool with the Ohio State meet of 1941 and finally to the present Men's Intramural Building pool with its seating of 2,000 spectators in 1959.

State, today, probably has the finest swimming facilities in the country. There are five pools in the athletic complex. There are two in the Women's Gymnasium, the old 30-yard pool and a fine new one, the Jenison gym pool and two at the Men's Intramural Building. One of the Intramural Building pools is the regular varsity indoor pool and the other an Olympic-size outdoor pool in which the U.S. trials for the 1959 Pan American games were held. This pool is a summertime recreational mecca for the campus and also is used for the training of swimmers and divers for international competition.

McCaffree was succeeded in 1970 by Richard Fetters, his assistant for seven years. Fetters served immediate notice that swimming fortunes weren't going to sag when his first team cracked eight varsity records in winning 10 of 11 dual meets and finished third in the Big Ten.

SPARTAN SWIMMING HONOR ROLL

NCAA CHAMPIONS

1946	400 Yard Freestyle Relay	(Zigmund Indyke, John DeMond, James Quigley, Robert Allwardt)	3:37.2
1947	George Hoogerhyde	1,500 meters	19:44.2
1948	400 Yard Freestyle Relay	(Abel Gilbert, George Hoogerhyde, Robert Allwardt, James Duke)	3:31.0
1950	Clarke Scholes	100 yard freestyle	:50.9
1951	Clarke Scholes	100 yard freestyle	:51.0
	Clarke Scholes	50 yard freestyle	:22.9
	400 Yard Freestyle Relay	(David Hoffman, James Quigley, Clarke Scholes, George Hoogerhyde)	3:26.7
1952	Clarke Scholes	100 yard freestyle	:49.9
1957	400 Yard Medley Relay	(Donald Nichols, Paul Reinke, Roger Harmon, Frank Parrish)—tie	3:50.0
1958	Billy Steuart	1,500 meters	18:45.8
	Billy Steuart	440 yard freestyle	4:34.3
	Frank Modine	100 yard breaststroke	1:05.2
	Frank Modine	200 yard breaststroke	2:25.4
	Don Patterson	100 yard freestyle	:49.5
1959	Billy Steuart	1,500 yard freestyle	18:26.2
	Billy Steuart	440 yard freestyle	4:31.9
1962	400 Yard Freestyle Relay	(Jeff Mattson, Doug Rowe, Bill Wood, Mike Wood)—tie (NCAA Meet Record)	3:15.8
1965	Gary Dilley	100 yard backstroke	:52.6
	Gary Dilley	200 yard backstroke	1:56.2
1966	Gary Dilley	100 yard backstroke (American Record)	:52.3
	Gary Dilley	200 yard backstroke	1:56.2
1967	Kenneth Walsh	100 yard freestyle	:45.67

NAAU OUTDOOR CHAMPIONS

1945	300 Meter Medley Relay	(Howard Paterson, David Seibold, James Quigley)	3:32.4
	David Seibold	300 meter individual medley	4:18.5
	David Seibold	200 meter breaststroke	2:55.5
1953	John Dudeck	100 meter butterfly	1:08.4
1967	Peter Williams	400 meter individual medley	4:50.8

NAAU INDOOR CHAMPIONS

1950	Clarke Scholes	100 yard freestyle	:51.3
1952	Clarke Scholes	100 yard freestyle	:50.3

BIG TEN CHAMPIONS

Year		Event	Time
1951	Bert McLachlan	220 yard freestyle	2:10.9
	Bert McLachlan	440 yard freestyle	4:41.8
	Clarke Scholes	50 yard freestyle	:23.0
	Clarke Scholes	100 yard freestyle	:50.7
1952	Clarke Scholes	100 yard freestyle	:49.8
1953	Bert McLachlan	440 yard freestyle	4:43.9
	John Dudeck	100 yard breaststroke-butterfly	:61.1
1954	John Dudeck	100 yard breaststroke-butterfly	:59.7
1957	Paul Reinke	100 yard breaststroke	:63.8
	400 Yard Medley Relay	(Donald Nichols, Paul Reinke, Roger Harmon, Frank Parrish)	3:51.4
	400 Yard Freestyle Relay	(Donald Patterson, Jim Clemens, Gordy Fornell, Frank Parrish)	3:25.0
1958	Billy Steuart	1,500 meters	18:40.5
	Billy Steuart	440 yard freestyle	4:37.5
1959	Billy Steuart	1,500 meters	18:36.6
	Billy Steuart	440 yard freestyle	4:30.9
	Billy Steuart	220 yard freestyle	2:04.2
	Frank Modine	100 yard breaststroke	1:04.8
1962	Mike Wood	220 yard freestyle (Big Ten Record)	2:01.3
	400 Yard Freestyle Relay	(Jeff Mattson, Doug Rowe, Bill Wood, Mike Wood) (Big Ten record with no-hand touch)	3:14.5
1963	Jeff Mattson	100 yard backstroke	:54.0
1964	400 Yard Freestyle Relay	(Bob Sherwood, Dick Gretzinger, Darryle Kifer, Jim MacMillan)	3:13.9
1965	Gary Dilley	100 yard backstroke	:53.15
	Gary Dilley	200 yard backstroke	1:56.28
	Ken Walsh	100 yard freestyle	:47.51
	400 Yard Freestyle Relay	(Darryle Kifer, Dick Gretzinger, Gary Dilley, Jim MacMillan)	3:11.54
1966	Gary Dilley	100 yard backstroke	:54.2
	Gary Dilley	200 yard backstroke	1:57.4
1967	Ken Walsh	200 yard freestyle	1:43.45
	Ken Walsh	100 yard freestyle	:46.17
	Gary Dilley	100 yard backstroke	:53.10
	Gary Dilley	200 yard backstroke	1:56.23
	400 Yard Freestyle Relay	(Ken Walsh, Gary Langley, Don Rauch, Gary Dilley)	3:08.68
1969	Bruce Richards	400 yard individual medley	4:16.09
	400 Yard Freestyle Relay	(Mike Kalmbach, Mark Holdridge, Dick Crittenden, Don Rauch)	3:10.99
1970	Dick Crittenden	50 yard freestyle	:21.496

VARSITY SWIMMING RECORDS
SHORT COURSE (25-YARD POOL)

Event	Time	Record Holder	Year
50 Yard Freestyle	:21.438	Michael Kalmbach	1970
100 Yard Freestyle	:45.6	Kenneth M. Walsh	1967
200 Yard Freestyle	1:43.39	Kenneth M. Walsh	1967
220 Yard Freestyle	2:01.3	Michael J. Wood	1962
440 Yard Freestyle	4:28.4	William Steuart	1961
500 Yard Freestyle	4:42.5	Kenneth M. Walsh	1967
1000 Yard Freestyle	10:04.0	John Thuerer	1970
1650 Yard Freestyle	16:47.23	John Thuerer	1970
1500 Meter Freestyle	18:26.2	William Steuart	1959
100 Yard Backstroke	:52.3	Gary J. Dilley	1966
200 Yard Backstroke	1:56.2	Gary J. Dilley	1965
100 Yard Breaststroke	1:00.88	Jeff Lanini	1970
200 Yard Breaststroke	2:14.09	Bruce Richards	1968
100 Yard Butterfly	:51.07	Kenneth Winfield	1970
200 Yard Butterfly	1:52.34	Kenneth Winfield	1970
200 Yard Individual Medley	1:57.97	Bruce Richards	1970
400 Yard Individual Medley	4:13.7	Peter E. Williams	1967
400 Yard Medley Relay	3:30.83	Alan Dilley	1970
		Jeff Lanini	
		Kenneth Winfield	
		Michael Kalmbach	
400 Yard Freestyle Relay	3:07.7	Darryle L. Kifer	1965
		James A. MacMillan	
		Kenneth M. Walsh	
		Gary J. Dilley	

RECORD BY SEASON

	W	L	T	NCAA		NAAU		Big Ten		Central Collegiate	
1922	0	5									
1923	1	3									
1924	3	4									
1925	2	4									
1926	2	4									
1927	4	3									
1928	No meets, pool under repair										
1929	3	3									
1930	4	3									
1931	4	1									
1932	1	3									
1933	3	4									
1934	1	4									
1935	4	3	1								
1936	5	2									
1937	7	2									
1938	6	3									
1939	3	5									
1940	7	2									
1941	6	3									
1942	2	3	2							1st	80
1943	4	2		12th	4					1st	100
1944	No meets—World War II										
1945	0	1		4th	12	1st	26			1st	83
1946	4	3		3rd	18	9th	3			1st	77
1947	8	2		4th	18	5th	12			1st	102
1948	8	2		4th	21	5th	17			1st	91
1949	8	1		7th	10	10th	4			1st	105
1950	10	1		5th	17	5th	17			1st	147
1951	9	1		2nd	60	3rd	23	2nd	68		
1952	8	2		4th	20	4th	20	2nd	66		
1953	7	1		5th	14			3rd	48		
1954	6	2		8th	9			3rd	45		
1955	7	3						5th	27½	BIG TEN RELAYS	
1956	4	3						6th	32	1st	76
1957	7	2		3rd	52			1st	87	Not Scored	
1958	8	1		3rd	62			2nd	76	Not Scored	
1959	5	3		5th	35			4th	53½	Not Scored	
1960	7	3		16th(tie)	3			5th	35	Not Scored	
1961	8	2		5th	24			4th	100	2nd	59
1962	5	4		6th	20			4th	96¾	2nd	74
1963	9	4		8th	15			5th	84	3rd	59.5
1964	6	2						5th	88¼	1st	92
1965	11	1		6th	90			3rd	273	3rd	57.5
1966	10	2		4th	173			3rd	325	3rd	133
1967	9	1		8th	115			3rd	308	3rd	69
1968	8	3		13th	38			3rd	248	3rd	74
1969	12	2		12th	38			3rd	304	3rd	89
1970	10	1		13th	43			3rd	311	3rd	97
	266	119	3								

RECORD BY OPPONENT

	W	L	T		W	L	T
Armour Tech	1	0	0	Great Lakes NTS	0	1	0
Ball State	1	0	0	Grinnell	1	0	0
Bowling Green	15	0	0	Illinois	17	0	0
Butler	1	0	0	Illinois Wesleyan	2	0	0
Case	3	0	0	Indiana	12	14	0
Chicago YMCA	1	0	0	Indianapolis	1	0	0
Cincinnati	9	5	0	Iowa	17	2	0
DePauw	4	0	0	Iowa State	26	2	0
Detroit J.C.	0	2	0	Kentucky	1	0	0
Eastern Michigan	6	1	0	Kenyon	2	0	0
Grand Rapids J.C.	6	0	0	LaSalle	1	0	0
Grand Rapids YMCA	3	5	0	Loyola	0	2	0

Miami (O.)	2	0	0	Pittsburgh	3	0	1
Michigan	4	43	0	Purdue	28	3	0
Minnesota	14	3	0	Toronto	1	0	0
Nebraska	1	0	0	Toronto YMCA	1	0	0
N. C. State	1	0	0	Wayne State	15	4	0
Northwestern	11	3	1	Western Reserve	3	2	1
Notre Dame	0	3	0	Wooster	3	1	0
Oakland	2	0	0	Western Michigan	2	0	0
Ohio State	10	20	0	Wisconsin	22	3	0
Ohio	5	0	0				
Ohio Weslevan	8	0	0		266	119	3

SPARTAN COACHES' RECORDS

Coach	Year	W	L	T	Pct.
Southard E. Flynn	1922	0	5	0	.000
Richard H. Rauch	1923	1	3	0	.250
Wright B. Jones	1924-25	5	8	0	.385
Rollin D. Keifaber	1926	2	4	0	.333
W. Sterry Brown	1927	4	3	0	.571
Frank R. Hoercher	1929	3	3	0	.500
Russell B. Daubert	1930-41	51	35	1	.593
Charles McCaffree, Jr.	1942-69	190	57	2	.769
Richard B. Fetters	1970	10	1	0	.909
		266	119	3	.689

SPARTAN TOURNAMENT RECORD

Triangular Meets

Feb. 8, 1930	Michigan State	45	Feb. 10, 1933	Crane, J.C.	39
	Case	36		Loyola	38
	Western Reserve	21		Michigan State	25
	(at East Lansing, Mich.)			(at Chicago, III.)	
Feb. 7, 1931	Michigan State	54	Feb. 3, 1945	Indiana	47
	Case	32		Michigan State	44
	Western Reserve	16		Detroit Tech	13
	(at Cleveland, Ohio)			(at East Lansing, Mich.)	
Feb. 20, 1932	Western Reserve	43	Jan. 29, 1966	Michigan	209
	Michigan State	40		Michigan State	159
	Case	19		Ohio State	104
	(at Cleveland, Ohio)			(at Ann Arbor, Mich.)	

Spartan home swimming meets are held in the spacious Men's IM Building Pool, site of the 1967 NCAA championship meet shown here.

Central Collegiate Conference Championships

1942 Michigan State
1943 Michigan State
1944 No Meet
1945 Michigan State
1946 Michigan State
1947 Michigan State
1948 Michigan State
1949 Michigan State
1950 Michigan State

CCC Individual Champions

1942
Frederick T. Himmelein—220 yard freestyle
Harold J. Heffernan—50 yard freestyle
Warren McNicol—One-meter diving
Huntley Johnson—100 yard freestyle
Herbert E. Gluski—440 yard freestyle
(Huntley Johnson, Harold Heffernan, Donald Farmer, Ralph Newton—400 relay)

1943
Robert K. Allwardt—220 yard freestyle
James M. Richards—50 yard freestyle
Lawrence Luoto—One-meter diving
Ralph J. Newton—100 yard backstroke
Robert D. Knox—200 yard breststroke
John W. Nichols—440 yard freestyle
Robert Allwardt, Harold Heffernan, James P. Thomas, Ralph Newton—400 relay)

1945
Ralph E. Mercer—220 yard freestyle
Frederick Stillman—50 and 100 yard freestyle
Thomas K. Barber—One-meter diving
Jack Kasten—440 yard freestyle
(Ralph Mueller, William Steven, Robert Byerly, Ralph Mercer—400 relay)

1946
(Zigmund Indyke, John DeMond, James Quigley, Robert Allwardt—400 relay)

1947
George Hoogerhyde—1500 meters and 220 yard freestyle
James R. Duke—50 and 100 yard freestyle
Raymond P. Williams—One-meter diving
Donald H. Korten—150 yard backstroke

David H. Seibold—200 yard breststroke
Roger B. Miller—440 yard freestyle
(Willard Cooley, Paul Seibold, Orlin Johnston—300 yard medley relay)
(Edwin Dzioba, Orlin Johnston, George Hoogerhyde, James Duke—400 yard freestyle relay)

1948
Abel O. Gilbert—220 yard freestyle
Henry D. Paton—50 yard freestyle
Donald H. Korten—150 yard backstroke
David H. Seibold—200 yard breaststroke
George A. Hoogerhyde—440 yard freestyle
(Donald Korten, Paul Seibold, Robert Allwardt—300 yard medley relay)
(Abel Gilbert, William Clemons, Robert Allwardt, James Duke—400 yard freestyle relay)

1949
David L. Hoffman—1500 meter freestyle
George A. Hoogerhyde—220 and 100 and 440 yard freestyle
Henry D. Paton—50 yard freestyle
Howard F. Patterson—150 yard breaststroke
(Howard Patterson, Glen Omans, James Quigley—300 yard medley relay)
(Donald Miller, Gordon Verity, David Hoffman, James Quigley—400 yard freestyle relay)

1950
David L. Hoffman—1500 meter and 220 yard freestyle
Henry D. Paton—50 yard freestyle
Donald E. Miller—150 yard individual medley
Raymond P. Williams—1 and 3 meter diving
Howard F. Patterson—100 and 150 yard backstroke
Glen A. Omans—100 yard breaststroke
David H. Seibold—200 yard breaststroke
(Howard Patterson, Glen Omans, Gordon Verity—300 yard medley relay)
(Donald Miller, Gordon Verity, Clarke Scholes, James Quigley—400 yard freestyle relay)

Michigan Amateur Athletic Union (MAAU) Carnival
Reinhold Thomas—150 yard backstroke

YEAR-BY-YEAR RECORDS

1922
Southard F. Flynn, Coach

Jan. 29	23	Detroit J.C.	45
Feb. 3	22	Grand Rapids YMCA	46
Feb. 18	16	Michigan	52
Feb. 18	16	Grand Rapids YMCA (A)	52
Feb. 18	22	Detroit J.C. (A)	46
		Lost 5	

1923
Richard H. Rauch, Coach

Jan. 19	44	Grand Rapids J.C.	24
Jan. 26	20	Michigan	48
Feb. 2	18	Indiana (A)	50
Mar. 3	20	Michigan (A)	48
		Won 1 Lost 3	

1924
Wright B. Jones, Coach

Jan. 12	18	Indiana	50

Feb. 2	39	Grand Rapids J.C.	29
Feb. 13	38	Eastern Michigan	30
Feb. 23	25	Grand Rapids YMCA (A)	42
Mar. 4	18	Michigan	50
Mar. 10	36	Grand Rapids YMCA	32
Mar. 14	31	Wayne State (A)	37
		Won 3 Lost 4	

1925

Jan. 24	49	Eastern Michigan	19
Jan. 31	19	Indiana (A)	49
Feb. 7	46	Ohio Wesleyan	22
Feb. 26	30	Wayne State	38
Feb. 28	19	Notre Dame	49
Mar. 5	15	Michigan	53
		Won 2 Lost 4	

1926
Rollin D. Keifaber, Coach

Jan. 16	34	Grand Rapids J.C.	25

Feb. 5	23	Wooster Coll. (A)	37
Feb. 6	36	Ohio Wesleyan (A)	24
Feb. 12	19	Cincinnati	50
Feb. 17	11	Michigan (A)	58
Feb. 27	22	Notre Dame	47
		Won 2 Lost 4	

1927
W. Sterry Brown, Coach

Jan. 22	43	Grand Rapids J.C.	17
Feb. 11	31	Cincinnati	38
Feb. 19	51	Eastern Michigan	18
Feb. 21	13	Michigan (A)	56
Feb. 25	31	Notre Dame (A)	38
Feb. 26	38	DePauw (A)	31
Mar. 4	45	Wooster Coll.	24
		Won 4 Lost 3	

1928
No schedule—Repairs to pool

1929
Frank R. Hoercher, Coach

Feb. 2	38	Grand Rapids YMCA	20
Feb. 9	51	Eastern Michigan	16
Feb. 27	13	Michigan (A)	58
Mar. 2	50	DePauw	17
Mar. 6	34	Grand Rapids YMCA (A)	37
Mar. 9	15	Northwestern	52
		Won 3 Lost 3	

1929-30
Russell B. Daubert, Coach

Dec. 13	22	Northwestern (A)	54
Feb. 1	38	Grand Rapids YMCA	37
Feb. 15	44	Eastern Michigan (A)	31
Feb. 19	18	Michigan	57
Feb. 21	52	DePauw (A)	23
Feb. 22	44	Purdue (A)	31
Feb. 26	27	Grand Rapids YMCA (A)	48
		Won 4 Lost 3	

1931

Jan. 31	55	Grand Rapid J.C.	20
Feb. 6	55	Wooster Coll. (A)	20
Feb. 8	13	Michigan (A)	62
Feb. 20	57	Wooster Coll.	18
Feb. 27	59	Chicago YMCA	16
		Won 4 Lost 1	

1932

Jan. 23	50	Grand Rapids J.C.	25
Feb. 19	27	Ohio State (A)	57
Feb. 23	17	Michigan	67
Feb. 27	31	Cincinnati	44
		Won 1 Lost 3	

1933

Jan. 28	44	Eastern Michigan	31
Feb. 4	54	Illinois Wesleyan	21
Feb. 11	45	Armour Tech. (A)	30
Feb. 18	36	Eastern Michigan (A)	39
Feb. 23	17	Michigan (A)	58
Feb. 24	27	Cincinnati (A)	50
Mar. 4	22	Northwestern	53
		Won 3 Lost 4	

1934

Jan. 24	23½	Michigan	60½
Feb. 9	37	Loyola (Chicago)(A)	47
Feb. 10	57	Illinois Wesleyan(A)	18

Feb. 17	33	Ohio State	51
Feb. 24	17	Iowa	67
		Won 1 Lost 4	

1935

Jan. 23	22	Michigan (A)	62
Feb. 2	57	Wayne State	27
Feb. 9	42	Western Reserve	42
Feb. 15	61	Butler	22
Feb. 18	54	Grinnell (A)	30
Feb. 19	30	Iowa State (A)	54
Feb. 23	41	Loyola (Chicago)	43
Mar. 2	53	Wayne State (A)	31
		Won 4 Lost 3 Tied 1	

1936

Jan. 24	26	Michigan	58
Feb. 8	62	Cincinnati	21
Feb. 12	63	Wayne State	21
Feb. 21	44	Case Tech. (A)	40
Feb. 22	38	Western Reserve (A)	46
Feb. 26	54	Wayne State (A)	30
Mar. 6	53	Wisconsin (A)	31
		Won 5 Lost 2	

1937

Jan. 27	22	Michigan (A)	58
Feb. 10	58	Wayne State (A)	26
Feb. 17	58	Cincinnati (A)	16
Feb. 20	57	Case Tech. (A)	27
Feb. 27	41½	Western Reserve	33½
Mar. 1	39	Wisconsin	42
Mar. 6	68	Ohio Wesleyan	16
Mar. 9	60	Wayne State (A)	24
Mar. 12	70	DePauw	14
		Won 7 Lost 2	

1938

Jan. 26	17	Michigan	67
Feb. 5	49	Purdue	35
Feb. 12	64	Cincinnati	10
Feb. 18	52	Case Tech.	23
Feb. 19	31	Western Reserve (A)	44
Feb. 21	44	Ohio Wesleyan (A)	31
Mar. 2	56	Wayne State	25
Mar. 5	22	Wisconsin (A)	62
Mar. 9	52	Wayne State (A)	32
		Won 6 Lost 3	

1939

Jan. 25	17	Michigan (A)	67
Jan. 27	55	Kenyon (A)	40
Jan. 28	32	Cincinnati (A)	43
Feb. 11	37	Ohio Wesleyan	23
Feb. 18	52	Western Reserve	28
Feb. 23	19	Wayne State	56
Mar. 3	36	Purdue (A)	48
Mar. 4	18	Indiana (A)	57
		Won 3 Lost 5	

1940

Feb. 3	52	Ohio Wesleyan	23
Feb. 10	53	Purdue	22
Feb. 15	19	Wayne State	56
Feb. 17	55	Toronto (A)	20
Feb. 20	14	Michigan	70
Feb. 24	44	Indiana	31
Mar. 2	52	Western Reserve (A)	23
Mar. 6	45	Kenyon	30
Mar. 9	58	Cincinnati	15
		Won 7 Lost 2	

1941

Jan. 25	33	Ohio State	42
Feb. 1	36	Purdue	39
Feb. 8	58	Ohio Wesleyan	16

The first indoor swimming pool for the then Michigan Agricultural College was opened for student use in 1902.

Feb. 21	54	Cincinnati (A)	20
Feb. 22	58	Kentucky (A)	17
Feb. 28	47	Wisconsin	28
Mar. 10	34	Michigan (A)	50
Mar. 14	49	Indiana (A)	35
Mar. 15	47	Ball State (A)	26
		Won 6 Lost 3	

1942
Charles McCaffree, Jr., Coach

Jan. 24	42	Northwestern (A)	42
Jan. 31	36	Purdue (A)	48
Feb. 7	62	Ohio Wesleyan	18
Feb. 9	51	Illinois	33
Feb. 20	27	Ohio State (A)	43
Mar. 2	25	Michigan	59
Mar. 7	42	Pittsburgh (A)	42
		Won 2 Lost 3 Tied 2	

1943

Jan. 25	19	Ohio State	62
Feb. 10	21	Michigan (A)	63
Feb. 19	62	Iowa State (A)	21
Feb. 20	57	Iowa State (A)	27
Mar. 1	48	Illinois (A)	36
Mar. 6	62	Bowling Green	22
		Won 4 Lost 2	

1944
Intercollegiate program dropped—World War II

1945

Mar. 3	24	Ohio State (A)	60
		Lost 1	

1946

Jan. 5	51	Northwestern (A)	33
Jan. 19	48	Illinois	36
Jan. 25	57	Purdue	27
Feb. 2	36	Michigan	48
Feb. 9	64	Wisconsin (A)	20
Feb. 21	21	Ohio State (A)	63
Mar. 2	39	Great Lakes N.T.S.	45
		Won 4 Lost 3	

1947

Jan. 6	60	Univ. of Cincinnati	24
Jan. 10	39	Michigan (A)	45
Jan. 17	54	Purdue (A)	30
Jan. 18	61	Indiana (A)	23
Jan. 25	55	Illinois (A)	29
Jan. 31	62	Wisconsin	22
Feb. 7	68	Wayne State	16
Feb. 14	56	Iowa State	28
Feb. 22	37	Ohio State	47
Feb. 28	64	Bowling Green	20
		Won 8 Lost 2	

1948

Jan. 10	55	Purdue	29
Jan. 14	60	Bowling Green (A)	24
Jan. 30	55	Wayne State	28
Feb. 6	58	Iowa State (A)	26
Feb. 7	57	Nebraska (A)	26
Feb. 14	63	Indiana	21
Feb. 20	53	Cincinnati (A)	30
Feb. 21	41	Ohio State (A)	43
Feb. 27	53	Wisconsin (A)	31
Mar. 5	31	Michigan	53
		Won 8 Lost 2	

1949

Jan. 8	68	Wisconsin	16
Jan. 15	57	Toronto YMCA	17
Jan. 29	60	Cincinnati	24
Feb. 7	56	LaSalle	19
Feb. 12	33	Michigan (A)	51
Feb. 19	53	Iowa State	28
Feb. 19	68	Bowling Green	16
Feb. 26	44	Purdue (A)	40
Mar. 3	50	Wayne State	32
		Won 8 Lost 1	

1950

Jan. 14	68	Minnesota (A)	25
Jan. 16	57	Indiana (A)	27
Jan. 21	60	Bowling Green (A)	24
Jan. 28	38	Ohio State	42
Feb. 8	46	Michigan	38

Feb. 11	54	Purdue	30
Feb. 20	57	Iowa	27
Feb. 24	48	Iowa State (A)	36
Feb. 25	74	Iowa State (A)	37
Mar. 3	55	Wayne State (A)	29
Mar. 4	62	Cincinnati (A)	30
		Won 10 Lost 1	

1951

Jan. 6	35	Northwestern	29
Jan. 15	55	Michigan	29
Jan. 20	35	Ohio State (A)	49
Jan. 27	60	Iowa State	24
Jan. 27	55	Bowling Green	19
Feb. 5	48	Purdue (A)	36
Feb. 10	54	Minnesota	26
Feb. 17	59	Iowa (A)	33
Feb. 24	56	Indiana	37
Feb. 28	66	Wayne State	18
		Won 9 Lost 1	

1952

Jan. 5	66	Bowling Green	27
Jan. 12	54	Iowa State (A)	39
Jan. 19	61	Indiana (A)	32
Feb. 1	66	Purdue	27
Feb. 9	40	Ohio State	53
Feb. 16	41	Michigan (A)	52
Feb. 20	68	Wayne State (A)	25
Feb. 22	68	Minnesota (A)	25
Feb. 26	56	Northwestern (A)	37
Mar. 1	70	Pittsburgh	23
		Won 8 Lost 2	

1953

Jan. 10	75	Bowling Green	18
Jan. 17	66	Indiana	27
Jan. 31	51	Ohio State (A)	39
Feb. 2	65	Illinois	28
Feb. 7	58	Purdue (A)	35
Feb. 14	38	Michigan	55
Feb. 21	69	Minnesota	24
Feb. 23	59	Iowa State	34
		Won 7 Lost 1	

1954

Jan. 9	61	Illinois (A)	32
Jan. 16	66	Wisconsin	27
Jan. 22	53	Iowa State (A)	40
Jan. 23	53	Iowa (A)	40
Feb. 5	58	Purdue	35
Feb. 13	24	Michigan (A)	69
Feb. 20	38	Ohio State	55
Feb. 27	57	Indiana (A)	36
		Won 6 Lost 2	

1955

Jan. 8	48	Iowa State	45
Jan. 12	63	Bowling Green	30
Jan. 15	55	Wisconsin (A)	37
Jan. 22	39	Iowa State (A)	54
Jan. 29	28	Ohio State (A)	65
Feb. 3	54	Illinois	39
Feb. 5	59	Purdue (A)	34
Feb. 11	25	Michigan	68
Feb. 18	48	Iowa	44
Feb. 26	49	Indiana	44
		Won 7 Lost 3	

1956

Jan. 7	71	Wisconsin	22
Jan. 21	48	Michigan (A)	45
Jan. 28	42	Ohio State	51
Feb. 4	66	Purdue	27
Feb. 11	46	Indiana (A)	47
Feb. 18	46	Iowa (A)	47
Feb. 19	50	Iowa State	43
		Won 4 Lost 3	

1957

Jan. 3	54	North Carolina State	30
Jan. 12	77	Bowling Green	19
Jan. 19	71	Indianapolis A.C.	34
Jan. 26	42	Ohio State (A)	59
Feb. 2	72	Purdue (A)	33
Feb. 9	63	Indiana (A)	42
Feb. 23	73	Northwestern (A)	31
Feb. 25	47	Michigan	58
Mar. 2	70	Wisconsin (A)	35
		Won 7 Lost 2	

1958

Jan. 6	76	Iowa State (A)	29
Jan. 18	62	Iowa	43
Jan. 25	68	Ohio State	37
Feb. 1	59½	Purdue	33½
Feb. 8	59	Indiana	42
Feb. 14	69	Northwestern	35
Feb. 15	67	Minnesota (A)	38
Feb. 22	30	Michigan (A)	67
Mar. 1	62	Wisconsin	43
		Won 8 Lost 1	

1959

Jan. 8	73	Iowa State	23
Jan. 17	63	Iowa (A)	42
Jan. 24	70	Minnesota	31
Jan. 31	76	Purdue (A)	29
Feb. 7	46½	Indiana	58½
Feb. 14	38	Ohio State (A)	67
Feb. 20	41	Michigan	64
Feb. 28	59	Wisconsin (A)	46
		Won 5 Lost 3	

1960

Jan. 7	77	Iowa State	28
Jan. 16	70	Iowa	31
Jan. 23	72	Minnesota (A)	33
Jan. 29	71	Wisconsin	22
Jan. 30	74	Northwestern (A)	31
Feb. 2	73	Purdue	32
Feb. 6	33	Indiana (A)	72
Feb. 13	43	Michigan (A)	62
Feb. 20	48	Ohio State	57
Feb. 27	74	Illinois	31
		Won 7 Lost 3	

1961

Jan. 13	74	Iowa State (A)	27
Jan. 14	71	Iowa (A)	34
Jan. 20	72	Minnesota	33
Jan. 21	47	Indiana	58
Jan. 28	80	Purdue (A)	21
Feb. 4	68	Illinois (A)	37
Feb. 10	46	Michigan	59
Feb. 11	77	Northwestern	28
Feb. 18	56½	Ohio State (A)	48½
Feb. 25	68	Wisconsin (A)	37
		Won 8 Lost 2	

1962

Jan. 13	75	Illinois	30
Jan. 13	75	Iowa	30
Jan. 20	40½	Indiana (A)	64½
Jan. 27	77	Purdue	28
Feb. 3	50	Minnesota	55
Feb. 3	71	Iowa State	34
Feb. 10	46	Ohio State	59
Feb. 16	46	Michigan (A)	59
Feb. 24	81	Wisconsin	24
		Won 5 Lost 4	

1963

Jan. 12	73	Iowa (A)	32
Jan. 19	44	Indiana	61

Date	Score	Opponent	Opp
Jan. 26	64	Purdue (A)	40
Jan. 29	74	Wisconsin	31
Jan. 29	75½	Bowling Green	29½
Jan. 29	84	Wayne State	20
Feb. 2	52	Minnesota	53
Feb. 2	73	Iowa State	32
Feb. 9	68	Northwestern	36
Feb. 9	69	Bowling Green	36
Feb. 16	42	Ohio State (A)	63
Feb. 23	63	Illinois (A)	42
Mar. 2	50	Michigan	55
		Won 9 Lost 4	

1964

Date	Score	Opponent	Opp
Jan. 11	79	Iowa	26
Jan. 18	66	Iowa State (A)	39
Jan. 24	76	Purdue	29
Feb. 1	49	Minnesota (A)	56
Feb. 8	44	Michigan (A)	61
Feb. 15	61	Ohio State	44
Feb. 21	74	Wisconsin (A)	31
Feb. 22	66	Illinois	39
		Won 6 Lost 2	

1965

Date	Score	Opponent	Opp
Jan. 6	78	Bowling Green	27
Jan. 15	63	Iowa State (A)	42
Jan. 16	62	Iowa (A)	43
Jan. 23	41½	Michigan	63½
Jan. 29	66	Purdue (A)	38
Jan. 30	66	Illinois (A)	38
Feb. 5	68	Minnesota	36
Feb. 6	77	Ohio	28
Feb. 13	60	Ohio State (A)	45
Feb. 20	73	Northwestern	31
Feb. 27	70	Wisconsin	34
Feb. 27	82	Pittsburgh	21
		Won 11 Lost 1	

1965-66

Date	Score	Opponent	Opp
Dec. 3	72	Ohio (A)	33
Dec. 4	90	Pittsburgh (A)	33
Jan. 15	63	Northwestern	42
Jan. 15	89	Iowa State	34
Jan. 21	53	Michigan (A)	70
Jan. 22	86	Iowa	37
Jan. 28	73	Illinois	38
Jan. 28	81	Purdue	30
Feb. 5	53	Indiana	70
Feb. 12	75	Ohio State	48
Feb. 18	73	Wisconsin (A)	50
Feb. 19	77	Minnesota (A)	46
		Won 10 Lost 2	

1966-67

Date	Score	Opponent	Opp
Dec. 10	144½	Bowling Green	54½
Jan. 13	70	Iowa State (A)	44
Jan. 14	88	Iowa (A)	35
Jan. 21	63	Michigan	60
Jan. 26	79	Wisconsin	44
Jan. 26	102	Ohio	17
Jan. 28	82	Purdue (A)	37
Feb. 4	45	Indiana (A)	78
Feb. 11	71	Ohio State (A)	52
Feb. 18	86	Minnesota	37
		Won 9 Lost 1	

1968

Date	Score	Opponent	Opp
Jan. 13	70	Iowa State	42
Jan. 13	90	Bowling Green	33
Jan. 19	50	Michigan	69
Jan. 20	75	Iowa	43
Jan. 26	76	Purdue	47
Jan. 27	79	Illinois	35
Jan. 27	78	Ohio	45
Feb. 3	43	Indiana	80
Feb. 10	87	Ohio State	40
Feb. 16	55	Wisconsin	68
Feb. 17	72	Minnesota	50
		Won 8 Lost 3	

1969

Date	Score	Opponent	Opp
Jan. 4	78	Western Michigan	45

State's 1957 swimming team captured the school's first Big Ten team championship. The squad posted a 7-2 conference record and placed third in the NCAA championships.

Jan. 4	77	Oakland	46
Jan. 6	79	Illinois	35
Jan. 13	84	Minnesota	39
Jan. 17	83	Iowa State	30
Jan. 18	82	Iowa	40
Jan. 24	83	Miami	30
Jan. 25	87	Purdue	36
Feb. 1	57	Michigan	66
Feb. 7	44	Indiana	79
Feb. 8	77	Northwestern	42
Feb. 8	85	Ohio	38
Feb. 15	64	Ohio State	59
Feb. 22	92	Wisconsin	31
		Won 12 Lost 2	

1970
Richard B. Fetters, Coach

Jan. 3	83	Western Michigan	40
Jan. 3	77	Oakland	45
Jan. 9	86	Iowa	37
Jan. 9	66	Illinois	48
Jan. 17	83	Iowa State	28
Jan. 17	71	Miami (Ohio)	42
Jan. 23	100	Purdue	23
Jan. 31	53	Michigan	70
Feb. 14	71	Ohio State	52
Feb. 20	77	Wisconsin	51
Feb. 21	72	Minnesota	51
		Won 10 Lost 1	

One of the gems in State's modern athletic plant is the Men's Intramural Building outdoor Olympic-size pool, site of the Pan American Games trials in 1959.

Gale Mikles, NCAA and National AAU
winner in 1947 and 1945, respectively.

Burl, I., and Merle Jennings, twin brothers
who each won two straight NCAA titles.

Walter Jacob, State's first NCAA wrestling
champion, won 160-pound title in 1936.

Site of varsity wrestling matches at State is the Men's Intramural Building Sports Arena which
seats 2,000.

WRESTLING

Wrestling probably made its debut on the campus of Michigan Agricultural College in 1884. It was listed as one of many activities at an informal field day for MAC students. The first competition with other institutions probably took place at a triangular field day with Albion and Olivet colleges at East Lansing on May 14 and 15, 1886.

The styles of wrestling were quite different from those used today. The most popular were the "sidehold" and "collar and elbow" types. Later, Greco-Roman and Japanese styles were introduced. Early matches had five weight divisions: featherweight, lightweight, welterweight, middleweight and heavyweight.

MAC had three winners in the 1886 triangular. They were William T. Welch ('86) in the lightweight class sidehold, Bailey B. Smith ('86) in the lightweight collar and elbow and William Needham ('89) in the heavyweight collar and elbow.

That meet was a forerunner of the Michigan Intercollegiate Athletic Association (MIAA). Wrestling was a conference sport from the first MIAA field day in 1888 until 1906 when the sport was dropped.

Interest in wrestling at MAC waned until the completion of the new Men's Gymnasium after World War I. By this time, the style of wrestling had become standardized as "free style," and more weight classes were added. During Olympic years, there would be as many as 10 weight classes to conform to the Olympic format.

The first modern-era team, formed in 1921, participated in four meets and won one. Team members were Everett R. Bristol, Ivan P. Galpin, Homer G. Hansen, F. T. Neller, Zera C. Foster, Elton G. Neller, Harold Koopman, Ellsworth Holden, Leonard Vear and John Schwei.

State's wrestling fortunes continued at a very modest level until the era of Fendley Collins, the head coach from 1930 through 1962. He produced some powerful teams, including a Big Ten champion in 1961 and NCAA runners-up in 1941, 1942 and 1948. He coached individuals to 13 NCAA and 14 Big Ten titles.

Grady Peninger succeeded Collins and, after three fair seasons, put together a succession of powerhouses that won an unprecedented five straight Big Ten team titles (1966-67-68-69-70) and the only official NCAA title (1967) ever won by a Big Ten wrestling team. Another of his teams (1970) was second in the NCAA, and two—1968 and 1969—finished fourth. Individual Spartans accumulated 24 Big Ten and five NCAA crowns in his first eight years.

State's first NCAA titlist, Walter Jacob in 1936, also won three straight NAAU crowns in 1937-38-39. The Walter Jacob award, given annually to the Spartan grappler scoring the most points, was established in his honor.

Michigan State wrestlers who made the U. S. Olympic team are Leland Merrill in 1940, Bob Maldegan in 1948 and Don Behm in 1968.

Other exceptional Spartans included Gale Mikles, winner of an unmatched four straight Jacob awards (1945-48), one NCAA and one NAAU championship; the Jennings twins, Merle and Burl, each of whom won two NCAA titles (1941-42); Dale Anderson, who won two NCAA crowns (1967-68) and three Big Ten titles (1966-67-68); Jim Ferguson, winner of one Big Ten, two NAAU and one Pan-American Games championships; Mike Bradley, winner of three straight Big Ten crowns (1966-67-68); George (Tim) Woodin, who copped two Big Ten titles (1958-59) and an NAAU crown in 1958, and Bob Hoke, winner of two Big Ten crowns (1953-54), an NCAA title (1954) and an NAAU championship (1951).

Early wrestling meets were held in the Armory, located on the site of the present Music Building. In 1918, the meets were transferred to the Men's Gymnasium, now the Women's Gymnasium. The site shifted to Jenison Field House in 1940 and to the Men's Intramural Building in 1959.

SPARTAN WRESTLING HONOR ROLL

Year	BIG TEN		NCAA		NAAU SENIOR	
1936			Walter Jacob	160		
1937					Walter Jacob	160
1938					Walter Jacob	160
1939					Walter Jacob	160
1940						
1941			Merle Jennings	121		
			Burl Jennings	128		
1942			Merle Jennings	121		
			Burl Jennings	128		
			J. William Maxwell	136		
1943					Merle Jennings	134
					J. William Maxwell	145
1944	No Schedule—World War II					
1945					Gale Nikles	145
1946						
1947			Gale Mikles	155		
1948			Richard Dickenson	136	Leland Maxwell	160
1949					Robert Maldegan	Hvy
1950						
1951	George Bender	167	Eugene Gibbons	167	Bob Hoke	145
	Eugene Gibbons	177				
1952	Orris Bender	167				
1953	Bob Hoke	157			James Sinadinos	136
	Vito Perrone	167				
1954	Bob Hoke	157	Bob Hoke	157	Norman Gill	147*
1955						
1956	Donald Stroud	123	James Sinadinos	137	Ken Maidlow	191*
	James Sinadinos	137				
1957					George Woodin	191
1958	George Woodin	177	Ken Maidlow	191		
1959	Norman Young	130			James Ferguson	174#
	James Ferguson	167				
	George Woodin	Hvy				
1960					James Ferguson	174
1961	Okla Johnson	115	Norman Young	137		
	Norman Young	137				
1962						
1963						
1964						
1965	Don Behm	130				
	Jeff Richardson	Hvy				
1966	Dale Anderson	137	Dick Cook	152		
	Dale Carr	145				
	Mike Bradley	177				

1967	Don Behm	130	Dale Anderson	137
	Dale Anderson	137	George Radman	167
	Dale Carr	145		
	George Radman	167		
	Mike Bradley	177		
1968	Dale Anderson	137	Dale Anderson	137
	Mike Bradley	177		
	Jeff Smith	Hvy		
1969	Gary Bissell	115		
	Keith Lowrance	137		
	John Abajace	152		
	Tom Muir	160		
	Jack Zindel	177		
	Jeff Smith	Hvy		
1970	Greg Johnson	118	Greg Johnson	118
	Tom Milkovich	134		
	Keith Lowrance	142		
	Jack Zindel	190		
	Vic Mittelberg	Hvy		

*Greco-Roman: #Pan American champion
also at 174

WALTER C. JACOB WRESTLING AWARD

Awarded annually to the Spartan wrestler with the highest point total.

1940 Leland G. Merrill
1941 John W. Maxwell
     Leland G. Merrill
1942 Merle Jennings
1943 Merle Jennings
1944 No Award
1945 Gale E. Mikles
1946 Gale E. Mikles
1947 Gale E. Mikles
1948 Gale E. Mikles
1949 Robert G. Maldegen
1950 Eugene V. Gibbons
1951 Eugene V. Gibbons
1952 Orris H. Bender

1954 Bob Hoke
1955 James P. Sinadinos
1956 James P. Sinadinos
     Donald E. Stroud
1957 LeRoy A. Fladseth
1958 Kenneth A. Maidlow
1959 George B. Woodin
1960 John D. Baum
1961 George W. Hobbs
1962 John D. Baum
1963 Alexander A. Valcanoff
1964 Homer R. McClure
1965 Donald R. Behm
1966 Richard Cook
1967 Dale Anderson
1968 Jeff Smith
1969 Jeff Smith
1970 Keith Lowrance

SPARTAN TEAM RECORDS

Year	W	L	D	BIG TEN	NCAA		Captains
1922	1	3	0				Leonard Vear
1923	1	3	0				Ellsworth Holden
1924	0	3	0				Zera Foster
1925	2	4	0				Homer Hansen
1926	0	5	0				Howard Houghton
1927	4	3	0				Allerd Berquist
1928	4	2	0				George Landsburg
1929	1	3	0				Harry Kurrle
1930	3	3	0		14th (tie)	1	Mariond Joslin
1931	3	1	0				Richard Tompkins
1932	4	1	0		13th (tie)	2	Norman Stoner
1933	3	2	0				Stanley Ball
1934	2	4	0				Floyd Austin
1935	4	4	0				Gordon Reavely
1936	0	6	0		5th	5	Walter Jacob
1937	1	6	0				Samuel Aldrich
1938	5	4	0				Gordon Purdy
1939	5	3	0				Stanislow Slezak
1940	5	2	1		15th (tie)	1	Charles Hutson
							Benjamin Riggs
1941	8	1	0		2nd	26	Charles Hutson
							Benjamin Riggs
1942	7	1	0		2nd	26	Leland Merrill
1943	5	2	0				Burl Jennings
							Merle Jennings
1944	No Schedule—World War II						
1945	5	0	0				Donald Anderson
1946	5	2	0		8th	5	Iggy Konrad
1947	7	3	0		4th	11	Donald Johnson
1948	9	0	0		2nd	28	Gale Mikles
1949	6	1	1		4th	13	Robert Maldegan

Year	W	L	D	Finish	Pts	Conf	Pts	Names
1950	5	5	0			12th (tie)	2	Robert Gang / Eugene Gibbons
1951	6	3	0	3rd	19	6th (tie)	7	George Bender / Eugene Gibbons
1952	5	2	2	3rd	19	12th (tie)	5	Orris Bender
1953	7	2	0	2nd	22	8th (tie)	7	Ralph Gill / Vito Perrone
1954	6	2	0	3rd	20	6th	11	Bob Hoke
1955	2	7	0	6th	15	15th	9	Jim Sinadinos
1956	4	4	1	4th	39	8th (tie)	20	Jim Sinadinos
1957	7	2	0	6th (tie)	18	21st (tie)	5	Norman Gill
1958	3	5	0	3rd	44	4th	35	Don Stroud
1959	5	3	1	3rd	45	9th	17	Jim Ferguson
1960	7	1	1	3rd	37	18th (tie)	9	Bob Moser
1961	8	1	0	1st	69	8th (tie)	19	Norm Young
1962	6	1	2	5th	27	9th (tie)	18	John Baum
1963	7	3	0	8th	16	21st (tie)	10	Alex Valcanoff
1964	5	5	1	10th	1			Monty Byington
1965	7	3	1	2nd	38	15th (tie)	11	Gary Smith
1966	10	2	0	1st	71	6th	32	Dick Cook
1967	9	1	1	1st	92	1st	74	Don Behm
1968	9	4	0	1st	74	4th	55	Dale Anderson
1969	9	2	0	1st	93	4th	57	Jeff Smith
1970	16	1	0	1st	96	2nd	84	Keith Lowrance
	243	131	14	6 championships		1 championship		

RECORD BY OPPONENT

Team	W	L	D
Air Force Academy	4	0	0
Alfred	1	0	0
Arizona State	3	0	0
Bowling Green	3	0	0
Brown	1	0	0
California Poly	1	0	0
Case	7	0	0
Chicago	3	2	0
Chicago YMCA	1	0	0
Cincinnati	1	0	0
Colorado State College	2	1	0
Cornell College	4	7	0
Dearborn B.C.	0	2	0
Detroit Tech	2	0	0
Eastern Michigan	1	0	0
Franklin & Marshall	0	1	0
Illinois	18	2	4
Indiana	18	14	2
Iowa	12	6	0
Iowa State	2	4	0
Kansas State	4	0	0
Kent State	3	5	0
Lawrence	1	0	0
Mankato State	3	1	0
Maryland	2	0	0
Massachusetts Tech	1	0	0
Mechanics Institute	2	0	0
Michigan	17	31	2
Minnesota	12	5	0
Nebraska	5	0	0
Northern Iowa	15	8	3
Northwestern	9	2	0
Notre Dame	1	0	0
Ohio	4	1	0
Ohio State	24	15	2
Oklahoma	2	5	0
Oklahoma State	0	5	1
Pittsburgh	3	8	0
Purdue	23	5	0
Syracuse	2	0	0
Southern Illinois	4	0	0
Toronto	1	0	0
Washington & Lee	0	1	0
West Virginia	2	0	0
Western Reserve	2	0	0
Wheaton	10	0	0
Wisconsin	7	0	0
	243	131	14

State's outstanding 1967 varsity squad, coached by Grady Peninger, went 9-1-1 for the season and went on to win the Big Ten and NCAA team titles.

SPARTAN COACHES' RECORD

Coach	Year	W	L	T	Pct.
(No coach)	1886-1905	8	1	0	.889
James H. Devers	1922-1923	2	6	0	.250
Leon D. Burhans	1924-1926	2	12	0	.133
Ralph G. Leonard	1927-1928	8	5	0	.615
Glenn L. Riches	1928-1929	1	3	0	.250
Fendley A. Collins	1930-1962	158	84	11	.653
Grady Peninger	1963-1970	72	21	3	.765
		251	132	14	.648

SPARTAN TOURNAMENT RECORD

Inter-state Tournament

1938	Freiberger, Clifford H.	145
	Pletz, David J.	155
1939	Martin, William P.	145
1940	Martin, William P.	145
1941	Jennings, Merle	121
	Maxwell, John W.	136
	Merrill, Leland G.	145
1942	Jennings, Merle	121
	Maxwell, John W.	136
	Merrill, Leland G.	155
	Spalink, John	175
1947	Gang, Robert	136
	Anderson, Donald E.	155
	Dowell, John K.	165
	Maldegen, Robert G.	Heavy
1948	Anderson, Donald E.	145
	Mikles, Gale A.	165
	Maldegen, Robert G.	Heavy
1949	Dickenson, Richard C.	136
	Anderson, Donald E.	145
	Bender, George A.	165
	Gibbons, Eugene V.	175
	Maldegen, Robert G.	Heavy
1950	DiBello, Joseph V.	136
	Gang, Robert W.	145
	Gibbons, Eugene V.	175

Quadrangular Meet

Michigan State University—Hillsdale College—Olivet College—Albion College; June 3 & 4, 1887 at East Lansing, Michigan.
Michigan State won, Hillsdale, Albion & Olivet tied for third.

Quadrangular Meets

Michigan State University, University of Minnesota, Purdue University, Northwestern University—held annually at Evanston, Ill.

1954 Michigan State and Minnesota tied for first, Purdue and Northwestern tied for third.
1955 Michigan State won, Purdue, Northwestern, Minnesota
1956 Purdue won, Minnesota, Michigan State, Northwestern
1957 Michigan State won, Minnesota, Purdue, Northwestern
1958 Minnesota won, Purdue, Michigan State, Northwestern

1959 Michigan State won, Northwestern, Minnesota, Purdue
1960 Michigan State won, Purdue, Minnesota, Northwestern
1961 Michigan State won, Purdue, Minnesota, Northwestern
1962 Minnesota won, Michigan State, Purdue and Northwestern tied for third
1963 Northwestern won, Michigan State, Minnesota, Purdue
1964 Northwestern won, Minnesota, Purdue, Michigan State
1965 Michigan State won, Minnesota, Northwestern, Purdue
1966 Minnesota won, Michigan State, Northwestern, Purdue
1967 Michigan State won, Northwestern, Minnesota, Purdue

MSU Quadrangular

1968 Michigan State, Miami (0), Eastern Michigan, Central Michigan
1969 Michigan State, Central Michigan, Miami (O), Eastern Michigan
1970 Michigan State, Central Michigan, Miami (O), Eastern Michigan

Midlands Tournament

1964
2nd, 50 pts.
    Dick Cook (147)

1965
6th, 39 pts.
    Don Behm (130)

1966
1st, 92 pts.
    Dale Anderson (137), George Radman (167)

1967
2nd, 69 pts.
    Dale Carr (145), Mike Bradley (177), Jeff Smith (Hvt.)

1968
1st, 102 pts.
    John Abajace (152), John Schneider (191), Jeff Smith (Hvt.)

1969
1st, 79 pts.
    Mike Ellis (134), Ron Ouellet (150), Pat Karslake (167)

1886
No Coach

May 15	2½	Olivet	½
June 5	2	Albion (A)	0
		Won 2	

1898

Jan. 29	3	Lansing High School	1
		Won 1	

1902

May 26	5	Olivet (A)	1
May 31	4	Albion	1
		Won 2	

1904

Mar. 12	4	Alma (A)	2
May 13	2	Alma	3
		Won 1 Lost 1	

1905

Mar. 4	5	Olivet	0
Mar. 17	5	Albion	2
		Won 2	

1922
James H. Devers, Coach

Jan. 14	6	Indiana	42
Feb. 17	0	Iowa State (A)	50
Feb. 25	24	Michigan (A)	20
Mar. 7	18	Michigan	20
		Won 1 Lost 3	

1923

Feb. 2	18	Chicago YMCA	13
Feb. 15	0	Iowa State (A)	27
Feb. 17	11	Cornell Coll. (A)	17
Mar. 2	5	Ohio State (A)	28
		Won 1 Lost 3	

1924
Leon D. Burhans, Coach

Jan. 12	2	Indiana (A)	24
Jan. 19	2	Ohio State	18
Mar. 1	10	Iowa State	22
Mar. 4	9	Michigan (A)	11
		Lost 4	

1925

Jan. 17	20	Michigan	6
Jan. 24	15	Northwestern (A)	2
Jan. 31	0	Indiana	29
Feb. 7	7	Ohio State (A)	13
Feb. 21	3	Iowa State (A)	17
Mar. 7	9	Purdue	11
		Won 2 Lost 4	

1926

Jan. 16	5	Indiana (A)	18
Jan. 23	2	Purdue (A)	12
Feb. 6	0	Cornell Coll.	17
Feb. 20	2	Ohio State	15
Feb. 27	0	Michigan	14
		Lost 5	

1927
Ralph G. Leonard, Coach

Jan. 8	16	Cincinnati	4
Jan. 15	14	Chicago	11
Jan. 22	8	Michigan (A)	15
Jan. 29	6	Ohio State (A)	19
Feb. 5	9	Northwestern	18
Feb. 11	36	Notre Dame	0
Feb. 26	17	Ohio U.	10
		Won 4 Lost 3	

1928

Jan. 14	36	Lawrence Tech.	0
Jan. 20	18	Chicago (A)	11
Jan. 28	3	Ohio State	22
Feb. 4	5	Michigan (A)	22
Feb. 14	30	Eastern Michigan	8
Feb. 18	16	Ohio U. (A)	11
		Won 4 Lost 2	

1929
Glenn L. Rickes, Coach

Jan. 12	9	Chicago	21
Jan. 25	0	Michigan (A)	26
Feb. 16	16	Ohio U. (A)	18
Mar. 2	27	Western Reserve	3
		Won 1 Lost 3	

1930
Fendley A. Collins, Coach

Jan. 17	11	Chicago (A)	23
Jan. 18	25	Northwestern (A)	3
Jan. 25	6	Michigan	24
Feb. 8	12	Ohio U.	18
Feb. 21	28	Case Tech. (A)	8
Feb. 22	26	Western Reserve	8
		Won 3 Lost 3	

1931

Jan. 24	5	Michigan (A)	23
Feb. 7	24	Ohio U.	8
Feb. 27	22	Mechanics Inst. (Rochester, N.Y.) (A)	10
Feb. 28	25	Alfred (A)	5
		Won 3 Lost 1	

1932

Jan. 11	36	Toronto	0
Jan. 15	14½	Michigan	13½
Jan. 23	28	Mechanics Inst. (N.Y.)	0
Feb. 12	20	Syracuse	6
Feb. 27	5	Indiana (A)	25
		Won 4 Lost 1	

1933

Jan. 21	14	Michigan (A)	18
Feb. 1	4½	Indiana	19½
Feb. 4	15½	Ohio State	12½
Feb. 11	25½	Cornell Coll.	4½
Feb. 25	25½	Syracuse (A)	6½
		Won 3 Lost 2	

1934

Jan. 20	11½	Michigan (A)	16½
Jan. 27	8	Ohio State (A)	22
Feb. 16	14	Cornell Coll.	16
Feb. 24	17½	Chicago	10½
Mar. 3	11	Michigan	15
Mar. 10	18	Kent State	14
		Won 2 Lost 4	

1935

Jan. 12	20	Michigan	14
Jan. 19	36	Detroit Tech. (A)	0
Jan. 26	10	Ohio State	20
Feb. 2	13	Kent State (A)	17
Feb. 7	13	Cornell Coll.	17
Feb. 9	18	Michigan (A)	12
Feb. 22	10	Indiana	22
Mar. 1	28	Detroit Tech.	8
		Won 4 Lost 4	

The first Spartan wrestling team to win a Big Ten championship was the 1961 varsity squad coached by Fendley Collins.

1936

Jan. 25	10½	Michigan (A)	15½
Feb. 1	3	Ohio State (A)	27
Feb. 8	10	Indiana (A)	20
Feb. 15	13	Michigan	21
Feb. 22	8	Washington & Lee	20
Mar. 6	3	Cornell Coll.	23
		Lost 6	

1937

Jan. 16	13	Dearborn Boys Club	19
Jan. 23	10	Northwestern (A)	26
Jan. 30	8	Ohio State	20
Feb. 6	10½	Kent State	15½
Feb. 19	17	Wheaton	9
Feb. 27	13	Dearborn Boys Club (A)	17
Mar. 5	0	Michigan	24
		Won 1 Lost 6	

1938

Jan. 15	25	Wheaton (A)	5
Jan. 17	0	Michigan (A)	32
Jan. 29	6	Ohio State	26
Feb. 12	23	Northwestern	5
Feb. 18	20	Case Tech. (A)	6
Feb. 19	6	Kent State (A)	24
Feb. 25	1½	Franklin & Marshall (A)	26½
Feb. 26	15½	Brown (A)	14½
Feb. 28	38	Massachusetts Tech. (A)	0
		Won 5 Lost 4	

1939

Jan. 14	22	Wheaton	8
Jan. 21	9	Kent State	19
Jan. 28	8	Ohio State (A)	24
Feb. 4	20	Case Tech.	6
Feb. 10	20	Wisconsin (A)	8
Feb. 11	22	Northwestern (A)	8
Feb. 18	3	Michigan (A)	29
Mar. 4	20	West Virginia (A)	8
		Won 5 Lost 3	

1940

Jan. 13	30	Wheaton (A)	6
Jan. 22	23	Northwestern	11
Jan. 27	14	Ohio State (A)	14
Feb. 8	22	Nebraska	6
Feb. 10	8	Michigan	26
Feb. 17	25	West Virginia	5
Feb. 23	26	Case Tech. (A)	6
Feb. 24	6	Kent State (A)	24
		Won 5 Lost 2 Tied 1	

1941

Jan. 11	33	Wheaton	5
Jan. 25	21	Ohio State	3
Jan. 29	16	Michigan	14
Feb. 3	31	Case Tech.	5
Feb. 8	27	Wisconsin	3
Feb. 14	27	Nebraska (A)	3
Feb. 15	28	Kansas State (A)	8
Feb. 18	5	Oklahoma State (A)	25
Feb. 22	20	Kent State	8
		Won 8 Lost 1	

1942

Jan. 10	24	Wheaton (A)	10
Jan. 13	17	Kansas State	11
Jan. 17	17	Michigan (A)	13
Jan. 24	19	Ohio State (A)	11
Feb. 14	15	Oklahoma A & M	19
Feb. 17	21	Nebraska	10
Feb. 20	20	Case Tech. (A)	8
Feb. 21	19	Kent State (A)	11
		Won 7 Lost 1	

1943

Date		Opponent	
Jan. 18	16	Michigan	14
Jan. 23	28	Case Tech.	0
Feb. 10	14	Michigan (A)	16
Feb. 13	22	Ohio State	6
Feb. 19	24	Iowa State (A)	8
Feb. 20	14	Iowa State Teachers (A)	14
Feb. 26	23	Purdue (A)	11
Feb. 27	11	Indiana (A)	15
		Won 5 Lost 2 Tied 1	

1944

Intercollegiate athletics dropped because of World War II

1945

Jan. 13	22	Wheaton (A)	8
Jan. 20	23	Ohio State (A)	11
Feb. 2	14	Indiana	12
Feb. 3	18	Ohio State	13
Feb. 17	24	Wheaton	6
		Won 5	

1946

Jan. 12	33	Wheaton	3
Jan. 19	15	Illinois (A)	11
Jan. 25	11	Purdue	19
Feb. 2	28	Northwestern (A)	0
Feb. 2	23	Minnesota at Evanston, Ill.	8
Feb. 16	17	Ohio State	11
Feb. 25	9	Michigan (A)	15
Mar. 1	12	Iowa State Teachers	12
		Won 5 Lost 2 Tied 1	

1947

Jan. 18	20	Purdue	6
Jan. 25	9	Indiana (A)	15
Feb. 1	17	Ohio State (A)	9
Feb. 8	14	Purdue (A)	12
Feb. 14	14	Illinois	12
Feb. 15	24	Wheaton (A)	6
Feb. 21	6	Cornell Coll. (A)	24
Feb. 22	9	Iowa State Teachers (A)	15
Feb. 28	18	Michigan	8
Mar. 10	25	Nebraska (A)	3
		Won 7 Lost 3	

1948

Jan. 16	14	Iowa State Teachers	13
Jan. 24	24	Ohio State (A)	0
Feb. 4	27	Kansas State	2
Feb. 7	17	Illinois (A)	11
Feb. 9	19	Indiana	8
Feb. 14	18	Purdue	12
Feb. 21	25	Cornell Coll.	3
Feb. 23	19	Michigan (A)	8
Feb. 28	17	Nebraska	8
		Won 9	

1949

Jan. 7	13	Illinois	13
Jan. 14	32	Kansas State (A)	0
Jan. 22	28	Ohio State (A)	0
Jan. 24	20	Purdue	6
Jan. 29	9	Iowa State Teachers (A)	15
Feb. 7	15	Cornell Coll.	13
Feb. 12	15	Purdue (A)	9
Feb. 21	24	Indiana	5
		Won 6 Lost 1 Tied 1	

1950

Jan. 7	28	Bowling Green (A)	0
Jan. 14	19	Indiana (A)	9
Jan. 16	6	Iowa State Teachers	18
Jan. 21	12	Illinois (A)	16
Jan. 28	6	Ohio State	18
Jan. 30	16	Purdue (A)	11
Feb. 7	18	Michigan	6
Feb. 11	13	Purdue	14
Feb. 18	12	Cornell Coll. (A)	14
Feb. 25	21	Bowling Green	9
		Won 5 Lost 5	

1951

Jan. 5	18	Pittsburgh	11
Jan. 15	25	Indiana	8
Jan. 19	10	Iowa State Teachers (A)	21
Jan. 27	8	Ohio State (A)	19
Feb. 1	17	Wisconsin	8
Feb. 3	18	Purdue (A)	11
Feb. 9	15	Illinois	9
Feb. 17	8	Michigan (A)	17
Feb. 24	20	Northwestern (A)	5
		Won 6 Lost 3	

1952

Jan. 12	16	Pittsburgh (A)	14
Jan. 18	8	Iowa State Teachers	21
Jan. 26	16	Ohio State	11
Feb. 1	19	Purdue	8
Feb. 9	15	Illinois (A)	15
Feb. 15	26	Northwestern	5
Feb. 16	16	Wisconsin (A)	11
Feb. 23	13	Michigan	13
Mar. 1	12	Indiana (A)	14
		Won 5 Lost 2 Tied 2	

1953

Jan. 3	9	Pittsburgh	17
Jan. 10	17	Indiana	8
Jan. 17	20	Ohio State (A)	5
Jan. 24	22	Iowa	5
Jan. 31	23	Purdue (A)	3
Feb. 7	13	Michigan (A)	17
Feb. 13	18	Illinois	6
Feb. 21	15	Northwestern (A)	9
Feb. 28	16	Iowa State Teachers (A)	13
		Won 7 Lost 2	

1954

Jan. 16	9	Pittsburgh (A)	21
Jan. 18	15	Iowa (A)	14
Jan. 30	20	Ohio State	6
Feb. 5	18	Purdue	10
Feb. 6	24	Iowa State Teachers	4
Feb. 13	20	Illinois (A)	10
Feb. 20	9	Michigan	15
Feb. 27	26	Indiana (A)	5
		Won 6 Lost 2	

1955

Jan. 8	5	Pittsburgh	24
Jan. 14	12	Indiana	14
Jan. 29	14	Ohio State (A)	16
Feb. 5	14	Purdue (A)	15
Feb. 8	10	Illinois	16
Feb. 11	21	Minnesota	8
Feb. 19	14	Iowa	11
Feb. 21	7	Michigan (A)	19
Feb. 26	11	Iowa State Teachers (A)	16
		Won 2 Lost 7	

1956

Jan. 16	11	Iowa State Teachers	15
Jan. 21	14	Iowa (A)	16
Jan. 28	29	Ohio State	9

Feb. 2	20	Wisconsin	5
Feb. 4	20	Purdue	19
Feb. 6	12	Michigan	14
Feb. 11	17	Illinois (A)	17
Feb. 18	12	Minnesota (A)	24
Feb. 25	20	Indiana (A)	12
		Won 4 Lost 4 Tied 1	

1957

Jan. 12	17	Indiana	9
Jan. 19	9	Iowa	15
Jan. 26	24	Ohio State (A)	5
Feb. 2	19	Purdue (A)	11
Feb. 4	26	Illinois	5
Feb. 9	16	Iowa State	14
		Teachers (A)	
Feb. 16	16	Michigan (A)	15
Feb. 23	24	Wisconsin (A)	5
Mar. 1	13	Minnesota (A)	14
		Won 7 Lost 2	

1958

Jan. 11	9	Iowa (A)	17
Jan. 18	11	Iowa State Teachers	17
Jan. 25	22	Ohio State	6
Feb. 1	27	Purdue	3
Feb. 8	11	Indiana (A)	17
Feb. 15	19	Illinois (A)	9
Feb. 22	13	Michigan	14
Mar. 1	12	Minnesota (A)	21
		Won 3 Lost 5	

1959

Jan. 10	7	Indiana	20
Jan. 17	9	Iowa	17
Jan. 24	16	Iowa State Teachers	10
Jan. 31	10	Purdue (A)	12
Feb. 6	24	Illinois	5
Feb. 9	11	Pittsburgh (A)	15
Feb. 14	22	Ohio State (A)	6
Feb. 20	16	Minnesota	14
Feb. 27	14	Michigan (A)	14
		Won 5 Lost 3 Tied 1	

1960

Jan. 16	22	Illinois (A)	5
Jan. 23	26	Ohio State	6
Jan. 30	18	Minnesota (A)	6
Feb. 2	24	Purdue	6
Feb. 6	24	Indiana (A)	6
Feb. 12	15	Iowa State	15
		Teachers (A)	
Feb. 15	11	Pittsburgh	13
Feb. 20	18	Iowa (A)	9
Feb. 27	14	Michigan	11
		Won 7 Lost 1 Tied 1	

1961

Jan. 9	24	Indiana	11
Jan. 14	30	Ohio State (A)	5
Jan. 21	20	Iowa State Teachers	12
Jan. 28	22	Purdue (A)	13
Jan. 28	30	Bowling Green (A)	7
Feb. 2	8	Pittsburgh (A)	19
Feb. 18	31	Iowa	3
Feb. 20	20	Michigan (A)	16
Feb. 25	40	Minnesota	0
		Won 8 Lost 1	

1962

Jan. 13	14	Indiana (A)	14
Jan. 19	19	Iowa State	8
		Teachers (A)	
Jan. 20	15	Iowa (A)	13
Jan. 27	22	Purdue	12
Feb. 2	20	Southern Illinois	6

Feb. 3	22	Illinois	8
Feb. 10	14	Ohio State	14
Feb. 17	11	Michigan	14
Feb. 23	14	Minnesota	12
		Won 6 Lost 1 Tied 2	

1963

Grady Peninger, Coach

Jan. 11	19	Purdue (A)	8
Jan. 19	19	Ohio State (A)	8
Jan. 26	11	Oklahoma	14
Feb. 2	10	Pittsburgh	16
Feb. 4	20	Iowa State	5
Feb. 9	14	Illinois (A)	11
Feb. 15	17	Indiana	8
Feb. 16	14	Iowa	11
Feb. 23	8	Michigan (A)	19
Mar. 2	15	Minnesota (A)	9
		Won 7 Lost 3	

1964

Jan. 11	20	Mankato State	5
Jan. 18	8	Oklahoma (A)	19
Jan. 24	22	Purdue	5
Jan. 25	12	Illinois	5
Jan. 31	21	Iowa State (A)	7
Feb. 8	5	Pittsburgh (A)	22
Feb. 13	13	Iowa (A)	15
Feb. 15	14	Indiana (A)	11
Feb. 22	28	Michigan	20
Feb. 24	14	Ohio State	11
Feb. 28	9	Minnesota	15
		Won 6 Lost 4 Tied 1	

1964-65

Dec. 5	27	Air Force	3
Dec. 11	14	Indiana	14
Jan. 9	18	Iowa	10
Jan. 16	20	Illinois (A)	8
Jan. 23	21	Pittsburgh	8
Jan. 30	18	Purdue (A)	6
Feb. 6	11	Minnesota (A)	14
Feb. 6	14	Makato State	15
Feb. 13	23	Ohio State	3
Feb. 20	20	Iowa State	6
Feb. 27	8	Michigan (A)	17
		Won 7 Lost 3 Tied 1	

1965-66

Dec. 4	16	Colorado State	14
		(at Air Force)	
Dec. 4	36	Air Force (A)	3
Dec. 11	15	Indiana (A)	9
Jan. 15	15	Ohio State (A)	11
Jan. 22	20	Minnesota	8
Jan. 28	25	Purdue	3
Jan. 29	5	Oklahoma	27
Feb. 5	25	Illinois	3
Feb. 12	27	Cornell Coll. (A)	5
Feb. 18	21	Iowa (A)	8
Feb. 19	24	Iowa State (A)	10
Feb. 26	11	Michigan	16
		Won 10 Lost 2	

1966-67

Dec. 3	40	Air Force	0
Dec. 9	25	Iowa State	5
Dec. 10	25	Indiana	5
Jan. 14	37	Ohio State	0
Jan. 20	14	Oklahoma A & M	14
		(A)	
Jan. 21	15	Oklahoma (A)	12
Feb. 4	17	Minnesota (A)	12
Feb. 11	24	Iowa	8
Feb. 18	32	Illinois (A)	3
Feb. 25	14	Michigan (A)	16
		Won 8 Lost 1 Tied 1	

1967-68

Dec. 1	19	Colorado State (A)	20
Dec. 2	25	Air Force (A)	8
Dec. 12	20	Indiana (A)	9
Jan. 13	16	Arizona State (A)	13
Jan. 20	15	Oklahoma	16
Jan. 26	35	Purdue	0
Jan. 27	6	Oklahoma State	21
Feb. 3	30	Illinois	2
Feb. 9	21	Northern Iowa (A)	6
Feb. 10	12	Iowa (A)	15
Feb. 17	17	Michigan	12
Feb. 24	28	Minnesota (A)	3
Feb. 24	20	Mankato State	9
		at Minneapolis	

Won 9   Lost 4

1968-69

Dec. 5	24	Maryland (A)	11
Jan. 6	31	Indiana	0
Jan. 18	35	Southern Illinois	4
Jan. 24	3	Oklahoma (A)	24
Jan. 25	14	Oklahoma State (A)	15
Jan. 29	30	Arizona State	2
Feb. 1	32	Illinois (A)	3

Feb. 7	23	Northern Iowa	5
Feb. 8	18	Iowa	9
Feb. 15	20	Michigan (A)	9
Feb. 22	27	Minnesota	5

Won 9   Lost 2

1969-70

Dec. 6	32	Maryland	0
Jan. 7	30	Colorado State	6
Jan. 9	28	Arizona State (A)	5
Jan. 10	18	Cal Poly (A)	12
Jan. 17	24	Southern Illinois (A)	15
Jan. 23	35	Purdue	2
Jan. 24	16	Oklahoma State	17
Jan. 27	36	Indiana (A)	0
Jan. 31	40	Illinois	0
Feb. 6	31	Northern Iowa (A)	3
Feb. 7	20	Iowa (A)	13
Feb. 7	28	Wisconsin (A)	6
Feb. 7	26	Southern Illinois (A)	5
Feb. 14	26	Oklahoma	6
Feb. 21	25	Michigan	8
Feb. 28	30	Minnesota (A)	5
Feb. 28	27	Mankato State (A)	3

Won 16   Lost 1

SPRING SPORTS

Ron Perranoski, Spartan pitcher who later became top relief performer in the majors.

Robin Roberts, Spartan pitching great who later earned stardom in the major leagues.

Dick Billings lettered in 1957, 58, 59 and eventually moved up to the major leagues.

John H. Kobs Field, home of the Spartan baseball team, is one of the finest and most beautiful diamonds to be found anywhere.

BASEBALL

The first organized athletic activity at Michigan Agricultural College probably was baseball.

There is a record of a Star Baseball Club at the College in 1865 and 1866 which played a five-game series with the Capital Club of Lansing and also made the first road trip of any Aggie team. It traveled 16 miles on the newly opened Jackson, Lansing and Saginaw Railroad to Mason in 1866 to play a game, accompanied by its own rooting section of four fans. The game result is not known.

There may have been even earlier teams. President Frank S. Kedzie (class of 1877) once recalled that there had been a team in the early 1860s for which Joseph W. Gunnison was the catcher and William W. Daniels was the pitcher. Both were of the class of 1864.

There are records of another team in 1871 which even traveled to Detroit to play one of that city's top sand-lot teams. The game was rained out and with the cancellation went the game receipts which Aggie players figured on to pay their return trip to Lansing, probably by train. They hitch-hiked back on horse-drawn buggies. Members of that team included: Peter Felker, second base; Byron Halstead, pitcher; F. A. Sessions, left field; Edward Shelton, third base, and Daniel Strange, center field.

The best organized and most renowned of the early baseball clubs at MAC was the Nine Spots of 1877 and 1878. This team played 11 games, winning eight, and barnstormed to such places as Jackson, Charlotte, Hastings, Grand Rapids, Owosso and Flint. The organizer and sponsor of the team was a well-heeled sophomore named Walter K. Prudden who, in later life, became a prominent Lansing financier and philanthropist. The complete lineup of this team was:

James Lewis, third base; Charles Shilling, second base; F. E. Skeels, left field; Alpheus Kerr, center field; J. R. Monroe, pitcher; H. V. Clark, right field; B. Trowbridge, first base; Ed Rawson, shortstop, and W. K. Prudden, catcher.

The 1884 team is credited with playing the first intercollegiate schedule. There were two games with college teams: one at Olivet as part of a field day and the other at East Lansing with Michigan. The Aggies beat Olivet, 20-9, and lost to Michigan, 13-3.

The student publication, *The Speculum,* carried in its August, 1884, issue a full box of the game with Michigan which looks very much like a modern-day newspaper box score.

This is how *The Speculum* ran it:

Box Score

University of Michigan	POS.	AB	R	H	TB	PO	A	E
Walker	3rd	5	4	4	5	4	2	2
Weatherwax	2nd	5	1	2	3	1	2	2
McMillan	SS	5	1	0	0	1	1	0
Condon	LF	5	1	1	1	0	0	0
Hibbard	P	5	1	0	0	2	8	2
Payne	RF	5	0	1	1	0	0	0
Palmer	1st	5	0	0	0	14	1	1
Bast	CF	4	2	1	1	0	1	0
Smith	C	5	3	2	2	4	6	1
		44	13	11	13	*26	21	8

*Welch (MAC) Hit By Batted Ball

Michigan Agricultural College								
Vance	P	5	0	0	0	1	15	2
Welch	1st	5	0	0	0	13	0	4
Hinebauch	3rd	4	0	1	1	4	0	4
Sage	C	4	1	1	1	9	3	2
Lawson	CF	4	2	3	3	0	0	1
Ross	SS	4	0	0	0	0	4	0
Gammon	2nd	3	0	1	1	0	1	0
Mathews	RF	4	0	0	0	0	0	1
McCullough	LF	4	0	0	0	0	0	0
		37	3	6	6	27	23	14

Earned Runs: Michigan 2, MAC 1. First on Errors: Michigan 9, MAC 6. First on Balls: Michigan 2, MAC 1. Total Called Balls: Michigan 44, MAC 83. Struck out: Michigan 9, MAC 5. Total Strikes: Michigan 36, MAC 56. Left on Bases: Michigan 4, MAC 6. Two Base Hits: Michigan 2, MAC 0. Double Plays: Michigan 1, MAC 1. Passed Balls: Michigan 1, MAC 0. Wild Pitches: Michigan 1, MAC 2. Flies Caught: Michigan 2, MAC 1. Fouls Caught: Michigan 2, MAC 1. Time of Game: 2 hours and 15 minutes.

Baseball, as a bona fide intercollegiate sport, thus dates from 1884 at MAC, but it was 1897 before a professional coach came on the scene. He was Bobby Gale, a member of the Detroit Tigers, who came to campus for three weeks in early spring to tutor the Aggies before reporting to the Bengals. For this, he received $50.

Since that first game in 1884 with Olivet, State has played 1,690 games, more than in any other sport. It has won 996, lost 670 and tied 24 for a winning percentage of .588.

State's early teams were largely mediocre, with a few bright exceptions—11-4 both in 1904 and 1905 and five straight winners under John Macklin, for example.

But it remained for the John Kobs era which began in 1925 to bring the national pastime to a consistently excellent level at State. Kobs coached State's baseball teams 38 seasons and had winners in 34 of them. He retired after the 1963 season and Danny Litwhiler came from Florida State to take the Spartan helm. Litwhiler has kept the winning tradition going—all but one of his seven teams at this writing were solid winners.

Eighteen Spartans have achieved All-America honors and more than 60 have been named to All-Big Ten teams. Many have done well in professional baseball, including such major leaguers as Robin Roberts, Ron Perranoski, Dick Radatz, Milt Lehnhardt, Hobie Landrith, Ed Hobaugh, Al Luplow, Dick Billings, Bruce Look and Steve Garvey.

Baseball has been played at just two sites at State, on the present-day band practice field just west of the music building and president's home and at its current Old College Field location. The baseball field portion of Old College Field was renamed John Kobs Field in 1969.

Spartan teams have won one Big Ten title, finished second three times and generally have been in the first division of the league.

SPARTAN BASEBALL HONOR ROLL

ALL-AMERICA SELECTIONS
(Selected by American Association of College Baseball Coaches)

First Team
Tom Yewcic, c, 1954

Second Team
Jack Kinney, of, 1949
Albert Cummins, 2b, 1950
Jack Risch, of, 1954
Bob Powell, of, 1955
Jim Sack, of, 1956
Dick Radatz, p, 1959
Tom Riley, of, 1961
John Biedenbach, 3b, 1965
Steve Garvey, 3b, 1968

Third Team
George Rutenbar, of, 1949
Darrell Lindley, of, 1951
George Smith, 2b, 1955
Jerry Sutton, 1b, 1963

ALL-NCAA
DISTRICT 4

First Team
Steve Garvey, 3b, 1968
Mel Behney, p, 1968
Harry Kendrick, c, 1969
Rick Miller, of, 1969

ALL-AMERICA SELECTIONS
(The Sporting News)
Steve Garvey, 3b, 1968
Harry Kendrick, c, 1969
Rick Miller, of, 1969

ALL-BIG TEN SELECTIONS

First Team
Darrell Lindley, of, 1951
Jack Risch, of, 1954

Tom Yewcic, c, 1954
Charley Mathews, 1b, 1954, 1955
Bob Powell, of, 1955
Dick Idzkowski, p, 1955
Jim Sack, of, 1956
Roscoe Davis, 1b, 1957
Alan Luce, c, 1957
Frank Palamara, 2b, 1958
Ron Perranoski, p, 1958
Dean Look, of, 1958
John Fleser, of, 1959
Dick Radatz, p, 1959
Tom Riley, of, 1961
Joe Porrevecchio, of,
    1962, 1963, 1964
Jerry Sutton, 1b, 1963
Jerry Walker, 2b, 1965
John Biedenbach, 3b, 1965, 1966
Bob Speer, of, 1966
Bill Steckley, 3b, 1967
Steve Garvey, 3b, 1968
Mel Behney, p, 1968
Harry Kendrick, c, 1968, 1969
Rick Miller, of, 1969
Dick Vary, 3b, 1970

Second Team
Bob Cioleck, 1b, 1951
Charley Mathews, 1b, 1953
John Matsock, ss, 1954
Ernest Erickson, p, 1954
George Smith, 2b, 1955
Frank Palamara, 2b, 1957
Ron Perranoski, p, 1957
Don Gilbert, c, 1958
Dick Radatz, p, 1958
Dean Look, of, 1959
Malcolm Chiljean, ss, 1963
Dick Billings, of, 1964
Bob Maniere, of, 1965
Tom Binkowski, 1b, 1968
Steve Rymal, 2b, 1968
Dan Bielski, p, 1968

Third Team

George Smith, 2b, 1954
Bob Powell, of, 1954
Ed Hobaugh, p, 1954
Alan Luce, c, 1956
John Fleser, of, 1958
William Schudlich, 1b, 1960
Mickey Sinks, p, 1960
Sam Calderone, 3b, 1961
Dennis Ketcham, 2b, 1962
Jerry Sutton, 1b, 1964
Mal Chiljean, ss, 1964
Dick Billings of, 1965
Jim Goodrich, p, 1966
Dick Kenney, p, 1966
Tom Hummel, of, 1968
Dan Bielski, p, 1969
Rob Ellis, 2b, 1970
Phil Fulton, p, 1970
Gary Boyce, of, 1970

ANNUAL TEAM AWARDS

Most Valuable Offensive Player

1953 Wayne Lawrie, 3b
1954 John Matsock, ss
1955 Jim Sack, of
1956 Jim Sack, of
1957 Frank Palamara, 2b
1958 Dean Look, of
1959 Dean Look, 2b
1960 John Hendee, of
1961 Bill Schudlich, 1b
1962 Joe Porrevecchio, of
1963 Jerry Sutton, 1b
1964 Joe Porrevecchio, of
1965 John Biedenbach, 3b
1966 Tom Binkowski 1b
1967 Tom Hummel, of
1968 Harry Kendrick, c
1969 Rick Miller, of
1970 Gary Boyce, of

Most Improved Player

1953 Jack Risch, of
1954 Dick Idzkowski, p
1955 Bob Powell of
1956 Frank Palamara, 2b
1957 Bill Mansfield, p
1958 Dick Schiesel, 3b
1959 Bob Ross, p
1960 Mickey Sinks, p
1961 Tom Riley, of

1962 Jerry Sutton, 1b
1963 John Hines, 3b
1964 Dick Billings, of
1965 Jerry Walker, 2b
1966 Dennis Maedo, 2b
1967 Mickey Knight, p
1968 Steve Rymal 2b
1969 Richie Jordan, of
1970 Dick Vary, 3b

Leading Pitcher

1953 Ernest Erickson
1954 Ed Hobaugh
1955 Dick Idzkowski
1956 Walt Godfrey
1957 Ron Perranoski
1958 Ron Perranoski
1959 Dick Radatz
1960 Mickey Sinks
1961 Robert Ross
1962 Gary Ronberg
1963 Jack Nutter
1964 John Krasnan
1965 Doug Dobrei
1966 Dick Kenney
1967 Zana Easton
1968 Mickey Knight
1969 Dan Bielski
1970 Phil Fulton

Most Valuable Frosh Performer

1953 Ray Collard
1954 Barry Fullerton
1955 Robert Bird
1957 Dennis Martin
1958 Pat Sartorius
1959 Gordon Hjortaas
1960 Sam Calderone
1961 Malcolm Chiljean
1962 Dick Billings
1963 John Krasnan
1964 John Claney
1965 Jim Blight
1966 Mel Behney
1967 Richard Miller
1968 Tim Bograkos
1969 John Dace
1970 Larry Ike

Captain

1968 Tom Binkowski, 1b
1969 Harry Kendrick, c
1970 Phil Fulton, p

Old College Field in 1907, as a large crowd watched MAC host Michigan, with Forest Akers on the mound for the home team that day.

SPARTAN BATTING CHAMPIONS

Year	Name	Pos.	AB	H	R	Avg.
1925	Don Fleser	OF	56	33	18	.589
1926	Don Fleser	OF	81	54	32	.667
1927	D Zimmerman	OF	79	43	30	.545
1928	Gerald Bryne	P-OF	66	27	13	.409
1929	Forest Rinehart	OF	85	32	19	.376
1930	Ed Gibbs	OF	99	45	32	.454
1931	H. Cuthbertson	2B	81	29	14	.361
1932	John Madona	SS	97	34	19	.349
1933	Alton Kircher	OF	86	37	20	.430
1934	William McCann	2B	80	30	12	.375
1935	Steve Sebo	C	76	26	12	.342
1936	Steve Sebo	C	87	35	17	.402
1937	Milt Lenhardt	OF	95	31	23	.326
1938	John Kuk	OF	96	34	17	.354
1939	Norman Duncan	SS	88	30	16	.341
1940	Norman Duncan	SS	88	35	18	.398
1941	Howard Ladue	OF	65	27	20	.415
1942	Peter Fornari	C	66	20	18	.303
1943	Arthur Maichoss	3B	60	20	8	.333
1944	(No varsity team—war year)					
1945	Ben Hudenko	C	54	20	9	.370
1946	Jacweir Breslin	1B	77	26	19	.338
1947	Edward Barbarito	2B	75	26	17	.347
1948	Dan Urbanik	3B	94	32	15	.340
1949	George Rutenbar	OF	106	40	29	.377
1950	Al Cummins	2B	117	43	30	.367
1951	Darrell Lindley	OF	103	43	28	.413
1952	Robert Ciolek	1B	55	20	9	.364
1953	Charles Mathews	1B	89	29	18	.326
1954	Charles Mathews	1B	105	37	25	.352
1955	George Smith	2B	103	42	29	.408
1956	Jim Sack	LF	117	42	25	.393
1957	Frank Palamara	2B	106	38	23	.358
1958	Ted Kearly	RF	61	23	13	.377
1959	John Fleser	OF	95	33	15	.347
1960	Robert Monczka	C	53	15	6	.283
1961	Tom Riley	LF	103	37	9	.359
1962	Jerry Sutton	1B	63	25	22	.397
1963	John Hines	3B	59	22	18	.373
1964	Jerry Sutton	1B	115	44	30	.383
1965	John Biedenbach	3B	146	57	29	.390
1966	Steve Polisar	SS	136	45	27	.331
1967	Bill Steckley	3B	157	51	34	.325
1968	Harry Kendrick	C	143	56	25	.392
1969	Richard Miller	OF	118	42	24	.356
1970	Robert Ellis	LF	158	60	26	.380

CAREER MARKS

Batting

Highest Batting Average
Ed Gibbs, '30, '31   .398

Most Hits
John Biedenbach, '64, '65, '66   132

Most Runs
Chuck Mathews, '52, '53, '54   87

Most Runs Batted In
Jerry Sutton, '62, '63, '64   89

Most Doubles
John Biedenbach, '64, '65, '66   27

Most Triples
Ray Collard, '54, '55, '56   11
Chuck Mathews, '52, '53, '54, '55   11

Most Home Runs
Jerry Sutton, '62, '63, '64   18

Pitching

Most Wins
Ron Perranoski, '56, '57, '58   21

Most Losses
Richard Kenney, '65, '66, '67   11

High Winning Percentage
Keith Steffe, '45, '46, '47   .889 (16-2)

Most Innings Pitched
Ron Perranoski, '56, '57, '58   213 2/3

Most Strikeouts
Ron Perranoski, '56, '57, '58   223

Most Bases On Balls
Ron Perranoski, '56, '57, '58   115

SEASON

Batting

Highest Batting Average
Don Fleser, '26   .667

Most Hits
Rob Ellis, '70   60

Most Runs Scored
Chuck Matthews, '55   40

Most Runs Batted In
Steve Garvey, '68   38

Most Doubles
Rob Ellis, '70   13
Bob Speer, '66   13

Most Triples
Abe Eliowitz, '31   6

Most Home Runs
Steve Garvey, '68   9

Most Total Bases
Rob Ellis, '70   98

Most Stolen Bases
Joe Gavel, '69   21

Pitching

Most Games Worked
Phil Fulton, '70   22

Most Wins
Dick Radatz, '59   10

Most Losses
Richard Kenney, '67   7

Most Innings Pitched
Dick Radatz, '59   96

Most Strikeouts
Mel Behney, '68   107

Most Bases On Balls
Ron Perranoski, '57, '58   45

**Lowest Earned Run Average
(30 or more innings)**
Dick Holmes, '65   0.47

SPARTAN TEAM RECORDS

RECORD BY SEASON

Year	W	L	T	Pct.	Coach	Big Ten W	L	Pct.	Place
1884	1	1	0	.666					
1886	3	1	0	.750					
1887	5	1	0	.833	Prof. Carpenter				
1888	2	1	0	.667	Prof. Carpenter				
1889	3	2	0	.600					
1890	2	2	0	.500					
1891	2	2	0	.500					
1892	2	0	0	1.000					
1893	3	1	0	.750					
1894	3	1	1	.750					
1895	4	3	0	.571					
1896	2	9	0	.182					
1897	3	6	0	.333	Robert T. Gale				
1898	6	5	1	.545	Robert T. Gale				
1899	5	4	0	.555	Charles Ferguson				
1900	3	6	0	.333	Charles O. Bemies				
1901	1	5	0	.167	Charles O. Bemies				
1902	1	9	1	.100	George E. Denman				
1903	8	6	0	.571	George E. Denman				
1904	11	4	0	.733	Chester L. Brewer				
1905	11	4	0	.734	Chester L. Brewer				
1906	11	9	0	.550	Chester L. Brewer				
1907	4	8	0	.334	Chester L. Brewer				
1908	7	5	1	.584	Chester L. Brewer				
1909	9	3	0	.750	Chester L. Brewer				
1910	8	6	0	.572	Chester L. Brewer				
1911	11	5	0	.688	John F. Macklin				
1912	11	3	0	.786	John F. Macklin				
1913	11	7	0	.612	John F. Macklin				
1914	12	6	0	.667	John F. Macklin				
1915	8	6	0	.572	John F. Macklin				
1916	11	4	0	.734	John Morrissey				
1917	6	5	0	.546	John Morrissey				
1918	7	5	0	.584	Chester L. Brewer				
1919	4	9	0	.308	Chester L. Brewer				
1920	6	9	0	.400	Chester L. Brewer				
1921	6	8	0	.429	Geo. "Potsy" Clark				
1922	7	10	0	.412	John Morrissey				
1923	14	4	0	.778	Fred M. Walker				
1924	6	7	0	.462	Fred M. Walker				
1925	9	5	1	.643	John H. Kobs				
1926	13	7	0	.650	John H. Kobs				
1927	13	8	0	.619	John H. Kobs				

Mobile press box, located back of home plate at Kobs Field, affords an excellent working spot for media people covering the Spartans.

1928	11	7	0	.611	John H. Kobs				
1929	12	11	1	.522	John H. Kobs				
1930	18	6	0	.750	John H. Kobs				
1931	13	9	1	.591	John H. Kobs				
1932	10	12	2	.455	John H. Kobs				
1933	13	7	0	.650	John H. Kobs				
1934	10	11	1	.477	John H. Kobs				
1935	11	9	1	.550	John H. Kobs				
1936	13	7	0	.650	John H. Kobs				
1937	16	11	0	.593	John H. Kobs				
1938	15	9	0	.615	John H. Kobs				
1939	13	10	0	.566	John H. Kobs				
1940	12	8	2	.600	John H. Kobs				
1941	13	10	0	.566	John H. Kobs				
1942	13	11	1	.542	John H. Kobs				
1943	9	7	0	.563	John H. Kobs				
1944	(No varsity team, war year)								
1945	12	4	0	.750	John H. Kobs				
1946	21	5	0	.808	John H. Kobs				
1947	16	8	0	.667	John H. Kobs				
1948	10	14	1	.416	John H. Kobs				
1949	19	8	1	.696	John H. Kobs				
1950	19	9	0	.679	John H. Kobs				
1951	17	9	0	.653	John H. Kobs	4	6	.400	7th
1952	18	14	0	.563	John H. Kobs	7	6	.538	5th
1953	11	17	0	.393	John H. Kobs	6	7	.462	7th
1954	25	10	1	.708	John H. Kobs	11	2	.846	1st
1955	21	11	0	.656	John H. Kobs	10	5	.667	2nd(Tie)
1956	16	13	0	.551	John H. Kobs	4	7	.364	8th
1957	18	13	1	.580	John H. Kobs	5	6	.455	7th
1958	22	12	0	.647	John H. Kobs	10	5	.667	2nd
1959	21	14	0	.600	John H. Kobs	8	7	.533	4th(Tie)
1960	17	13	0	.567	John H. Kobs	4	7	.364	8th
1961	21	11	1	.656	John H. Kobs	6	8	.429	5th
1962	17	13	0	.567	John H. Kobs	6	8	.429	5th(Tie)
1963	18	14	1	.560	John H. Kobs	5	9	.357	8th
1964	22	12	0	.647	Daniel W. Litwhiler	8	7	.533	5th(Tie)
1965	28	11	0	.718	Daniel W. Litwhiler	9	6	.600	3rd
1966	24	13	1	.644	Daniel W. Litwhiler	8	5	.615	4th
1967	22	23	1	.489	Daniel W. Litwhiler	8	10	.444	6th
1968	32	10	1	.734	Daniel W. Litwhiler	13	4	.765	2nd
1969	24	17	0	.585	Daniel W. Litwhiler	8	8	.500	5th(Tie)
1970	28	15	2	.651	Daniel W. Litwhiler	9	7	.562	3rd
	996	670	24	.588		149	130	.534	

RECORD BY OPPONENT

	W	L	T	1st Game
Adrian	3	0	0	1927
Akron	1	0	0	1914
Alabama	1	1	0	1957
Albion	50	21	1	1886
Alma	24	2	0	1900
Amherst	0	1	0	1957
Arizona	1	0	0	1954
Armour Tech	9	1	0	1906
Army	2	0	1	1967
Auburn	0	2	0	1926
Ball State	7	2	0	1966
Beloit	1	1	0	1902
Bethany	2	2	0	1914
Bradley	6	1	0	1926
Buchtel	1	0	0	1913
Buffalo	1	0	0	1916
Butler	2	1	0	1924
California	1	2	0	1938
Cp. Lajeune	0	1	0	1953
Case	1	1	0	1913
Central Michigan	16	6	0	1911
Cherry Pt.	0	2	0	1953
Chicago	4	3	0	1923
Cincinnati	6	1	0	1929
Clemson	9	3	1	1935
Coe	1	0	0	1934
Colgate	1	2	0	1929
Georgia	10	7	0	1913
Ga. South	1	0	0	1964
Ga. Tech	2	0	1	1932
Great Lakes	2	1	0	1942
Hillsdale	24	5	0	1896
Hope	8	1	0	1923
Hosei	0	2	0	1931
Hunter AFB	1	0	0	1958
Illinois	17	15	0	1952
Ill. Wesleyan	0	1	0	1940
Indiana	23	19	0	1919
Iowa	30	20	1	1921
Iowa St. Col.	1	1	0	1930
Ithaca	0	1	0	1963
Kalamazoo	19	12	0	1895
Kentucky	1	0	0	1913
Lake Forest	6	1	0	1908
Marshall	2	2	0	1915
Maryville	2	4	0	1927
Massachusetts	2	1	0	1954
Mercer	1	1	0	1926
Miami (Fla.)	7	8	2	1965
Michigan	56	97	1	1882
Minnesota	11	21	0	1925
Miami (O.)	1	1	0	1930
Mississippi	0	2	0	1931
Miss. A & M	1	0	0	1931
Missouri	0	1	0	1954
Nebraska	1	0	0	1937
Connecticut	1	0	0	1970
Cornell	1	0	0	1936
Cumberland	2	0	1	1928
Davidson	1	1	0	1934
Defiance	1	0	0	1929
DePaul	6	1	0	1908
DePauw	2	2	0	1903
Detroit	45	10	0	1915
Det. Bus.	1	0	0	1905
Det. College	3	2	0	1902
Det. U. School	2	0	1	1907
Duke	10	14	0	1933
E. Kentucky	2	0	0	1937
East. Michigan	46	21	1	1896
Elon	2	1	0	1933
Fairleigh Dickinson	1	0	1	1961
Florida	1	1	0	1965
Florida A & M	1	0	0	1969
Florida St.	5	7	0	1957
Ft. Belvoir	2	0	0	1962
Ft. Benning	6	7	1	1926
Ft. Custer	0	2	0	1942
Ft. Eustis	1	2	0	1954
Ft. Jackson	2	1	0	1946
Ft. Knox	3	0	0	1959
Ft. Lee	7	2	0	1953
Furman	2	0	0	1935
Geo. Washington	1	0	0	1963
Newberry	5	1	1	1935
Newport News	1	0	0	1961
New York	2	0	0	1966
Niagara	2	0	0	1916
N. Carolina	6	13	1	1933
N. Car. St.	9	2	0	1936
Northwestern	26	9	1	1931
Notre Dame	54	50	0	1907
Oberlin	7	3	0	1914
Ogelthorpe	1	0	0	1926
Ohio	8	6	0	1932
Ohio Northern	1	1	0	1913
Ohio State	31	42	1	1911
Ohio Wesleyan	4	2	0	1910
Olivet	39	16	1	1884
Parris Island	2	4	0	1956
Penn State	1	1	0	1920
Pensacola Navy	2	1	0	1942
Pittsburgh	2	1	0	1969
Presbyterian	2	0	0	1940
Pressman Tech	1	0	0	1928
Purdue	20	10	0	1949
Rhode Island	1	0	0	1961
Richmond	1	0	1	1950
Rochester	2	0	0	1916
Rollins	2	3	0	1954
Rutgers	3	1	0	1966
St. John's (O.)	1	0	0	1911
St. Mary's (Mich.)	6	1	0	1917
St. Viator	5	1	2	1909
Selfridge AFB	2	0	0	1943
S. Carolina	16	5	0	1935
Springfield	0	1	0	1960
Spring Arbor	2	0	0	1965
Syracuse	8	4	0	1908
Tennessee	1	0	0	1949
Toledo	5	1	0	1936
Toronto	1	0	0	1904
Valparaiso	2	4	0	1920
Vanderbilt	2	6	0	1929
Virginia	2	0	0	1963
Vir. Tech	2	1	0	1951
VMI	1	0	0	1956
Wabash	8	5	0	1908
Wake Forest	5	11	0	1933
Wash. & Jeff.	1	0	0	1903
Wayne State	28	1	0	1942
Wesleyan	1	0	0	1967
West. Kentucky	0	1	0	1927
West. Michigan	36	49	0	1916
West. Res.	10	0	0	1910
Wilm. J.C.	1	1	0	1961
Wisconsin	32	25	2	1904
Yale	4	1	0	1952
Xavier	5	1	0	1927

SPARTAN COACHES' RECORDS

Coach	Years	G	W	L	T	Pct.
No Established Coach	1883-1886	6	4	2	0	.667
Prof. Carpenter	1887-1888	9	7	2	0	.778
No Established Coach	1889-1895	42	21	20	1	.501
Robert T. Gale	1896-1898	20	9	1	0	.450
Coach Ferguson	1899	9	5	4	0	.556
Charles O. Bemies	1900-1901	15	4	11	0	.267
George E. Denman	1902-1903	25	9	15	1	.368
Chester L. Brewer	1904-1910	101	61	39	1	.604
John F. Macklin	1911-1915	80	53	27	0	.663
John Morrissey	1916-1917	26	17	9	0	.654
Chester L. Brewer	1918-1920	40	17	23	0	.425
George Clark	1921	14	6	8	0	.429
John Morrissey	1922	17	7	10	0	.412
Fred M. Walker	1923-1924	31	20	11	0	.645
John H. Kobs	1925-1963	969	576	377	16	.605
Daniel W. Litwhiler	1964-	286	180	101	5	.638
All Time Record		1690	996	670	24	.588

YEAR-BY-YEAR RECORDS

1884
No Coach

May 19	20	Olivet	9
June 14	3	Michigan	13

Won 1 Lost 1

1886

May 14	11	Olivet	3
May 15	16	Albion	1
May 15	12	Olivet	1
June 5	8	Albion	9

Won 3 Lost 1

1887
Prof. Carpenter, Coach

Apr. 29	10	Michigan	8
May 14	8	Olivet (A)	2
May 27	7	Albion (A)	9
June 3	8	Olivet	0
June 4	21	Albion	8
June 11	11	Michigan (A)	9

Won 5 Lost 1

1888

June 1	12	Olivet	2
June 2	10	Albion	8
June 23	5	Michigan	13

Won 2 Lost 1

One of State's earliest baseball teams—the varsity outfit of 1897.

1889
No Coach

Apr. 20	17	Olivet	6
June 6	8	Albion	6
June 11	12	Michigan	10
June 11	5	Michigan	17
Spet. 14	4	Albion	5

Won 3   Lost 2

1890

June 5	5	Michigan	19
June 5	5	Albion	6
July 4	11	Albion	3
July 4	11	Albion	3

Won 2   Lost 2

1891

Apr. 18	0	Michigan	10
Apr. 25	4	Michigan	26
June 5	11	Albion	8
June 6	10	Olivet	9

Won 2   Lost 2

1892

| June 2 | 16 | Albion | 5 |
| June 4 | 2 | Olivet | 1 |

Won 2

1893

Apr. 15	14	Albion	13
Apr. 29	10	Olivet	9
June 2	15	Albion	8
June 3	3	Olivet	14

Won 3   Lost 1

1894

Apr. 14	15	Albion	10
Apr. 20	6	Albion	6
Apr. 30	4	Olivet	3
May 14	9	Olivet	1
June 3	3	Albion	6

Won 3   Lost 1   Tied 1

1895

Apr. 20	12	Albion	8
Apr. 27	7	Kalamazoo Coll.	21
Apr. 29	6	Olivet	21
May 25	12	Kalamazoo Coll.	11
June 1	21	Olivet	13
June 6	18	Olivet	15
June 7	0	Albion	3

Won 4   Lost 3

1896

Apr. 4	6	Michigan (A)	20
Apr. 11	1	Hillsdale (A)	4
Apr. 18	5	Albion	31
Apr. 25	10	Mich. Military Academy	15
Apr. 27	15	Olivet	8
May 2	16	Kalamazoo Coll.	18
May 9	9	Kalamazoo Coll.	10
May 16	1	Albion (A)	12
May 18	16	Olivet (A)	13
May 20	7	Mich. Military Academy (A)	9
June 5	11	Eastern Michigan (A)	12

Won 2   Lost 9

1897
Robert T. Gale, Coach

Apr. 17	2	Albion (A)	5
Apr. 24	7	Albion	2
May 1	5	Kalamazoo Coll. (A)	19
May 3	37	Hillsdale	5
May 8	7	Olivet (A)	10
May 15	5	Kalamazoo Coll.	9

May 22	11	Hillsdale (A)	4
May 31	12	Olivet	13
June 4	0	Albion (A)	2

Won 3   Lost 6

1898

Apr. 16	13	Kalamazoo Coll. (A)	26
Apr. 18	13	Hillsdale (A)	9
Apr. 23	6	Olivet (A)	7
Apr. 30	10	Eastern Michigan	6
May 3	1	Michigan (A)	20
May 7	23	Albion (A)	14
May 13	5	Michigan	5
May 14	20	Eastern Michigan (A)	8
May 16	5	Hillsdale	10
May 20	14	Albion	12
May 23	3	Olivet	8
May 28	9	Kalamazoo Coll.	4

Won 6   Lost 5   Tied 1

1899
Charles Ferguson, Coach

Apr. 29	19	Eastern Michigan	6
May 1	10	Albion	6
May 5	13	Eastern Michigan (A)	6
May 6	2	Olivet (A)	6
May 8	11	Hillsdale (A)	6
May 13	7	Olivet	6
May 15	5	Hillsdale	10
May 20	11	Kalamazoo Coll.	16
June 2	1	Eastern Michigan	2

Won 5   Lost 4

1900
Charles O. Bemies, Coach

Apr. 21	6	Hillsdale (A)	5
Apr. 28	9	Detroit A.C.	21
Apr. 30	11	Olivet	17
May 5	5	Eastern Michigan	9
May 12	11	Alma	6
May 14	0	Kalamazoo Coll. (A)	4
May 19	1	Eastern Michigan (A)	8
May 21	34	Hillsdale	7
May 26	7	Kalamazoo Coll.	8

Won 3   Lost 6

1901

Apr. 27	3	Albion	19
May 4	11	Eastern Michigan (A)	14
May 11	8	Alma	10
May 13	7	Olivet (A)	14
May 18	8	Eastern Michigan	10
May 27	9	Albion (A)	6

Won 1   Lost 5

1902
George E. Denman, Coach

Apr. 12	20	Lansing High School	23
Apr. 18	2	Michigan	20
Apr. 25	3	Beloit	11
Apr. 28	10	Eastern Michigan	12
May 3	22	Olivet	6
May 14	5	Albion (A)	15
May 17	4	Eastern Michigan (A)	8
May 22	8	Detroit Coll.	11
May 24	3	Olivet (A)	3
May 31	0	Albion	2
May 31	3	Alma	5

Won 1   Lost 9   Tied 1

1903

Apr. 8	26	Lansing High School	4
Apr. 18	10	Michigan	9
Apr. 23	7	Albion	8
Apr. 25	27	Eastern Michigan	22
May 2	5	Alma (A)	0
May 7	3	DePauw	4
May 12	7	Olivet	3

Date		Opponent	
May 14	2	Hillsdale (A)	5
May 16	11	Alma	10
May 20	4	Hillsdale	5
May 23	5	Kalamazoo Coll.	6
May 27	0	Albion	15
May 28	19	Detroit Coll.	1
May 30	10	Walpole Indians	4
		Won 8 Lost 6	

1904
Chester L. Brewer, Coach

Date		Opponent	
Apr. 14	12	Detroit Coll. (A)	2
Apr. 22	3	Michigan (A)	7
Apr. 26	1	Albion (A)	3
Apr. 27	5	Kalamazoo Coll. (A)	8
Apr. 30	4	Detroit Coll.	5
May 4	11	Hillsdale	1
May 7	10	Alma	2
May 9	16	Olivet (A)	7
May 14	3	Kalamazoo Coll.	0
May 20	3	Wisconsin	2
May 21	14	Olivet	6
May 28	11	Alma	0
May 30	3	Lansing Oldsmobile (A)	2
June 4	2	Albion	1
June 8	8	Univ. of Toronto	7
		Won 11 Lost 4	

1905
Date		Opponent	
Apr. 15	13	Michigan Deaf School	1
Apr. 21	6	Michigan	9
Spr. 22	2	Michigan	11
Apr. 26	14	Hillsdale	5
Apr. 29	2	Alma	1
May 8	7	Olivet	1
May 13	20	Kalamazoo Coll. (A)	4
May 18	6	Albion	2
May 20	5	Hillsdale (A)	2
May 26	11	Detroit (A)	10
May 27	3	Kalamazoo Coll.	2
May 30	2	Detroit Business Univ.	1
May 31	0	Albion (A)	1
June 2	6	Hillsdale	2
June 3	2	Albion	12
		Won 11 Lost 4	

1906
Date		Opponent	
Apr. 11	11	Lansing High School	2
Apr. 14	5	Olivet	2
Apr. 14	4	Olivet	7
Apr. 20	4	Albion (A)	0
Apr. 21	5	Olivet	0
Apr. 28	2	Mich. Military Academy	7
May 1	3	DePauw	1
May 1	2	DePauw	5
May 2	5	Hillsdale (A)	2
May 5	19	Alma (A)	1
May 7	9	Kalamazoo Coll. (A)	8
May 12	1	Hillsdale	0
May 18	0	Eastern Michigan	7
May 19	1	Michigan (A)	8
May 24	1	Albion	4
May 26	3	Olivet (A)	4
May 28	8	Hillsdale	1
May 30	4	Armour Tech.	9
June 1	3	Olivet	0
June 2	0	Albion	2
		Won 11 Lost 9	

1907
Date		Opponent	
Apr. 18	2	Michigan	7
Apr. 19	0	Michigan	8
Apr. 20	2	Michigan	7
Apr. 27	13	Univ. of Detroit	5

Date		Opponent	
May 7	0	Notre Dame (A)	1
May 8	16	Kalamazoo Coll. (A)	10
May 11	2	Alma	3
May 15	15	Hillsdale	0
May 17	2	Eastern Michigan (A)	5
May 18	13	Kalamazoo Coll.	1
May 29	0	Michigan (A)	2
June 7	2	Albion	4
		Won 4 Lost 8	

1908
Date		Opponent	
Apr. 20	5	Olivet	0
Apr. 23	6	DePaul (A)	5
Apr. 24	2	Culver Military Academy (A)	3
Apr. 25	2	Notre Dame (A)	4
May 2	4	Alma	0
May 9	1	Univ. of Detroit	1
May 15	0	Wabash	5
May 20	5	Lake Forest	1
May 21	6	Lake Forest	3
May 23	10	Eastern Michigan	2
May 29	2	Syracuse	4
June 3	4	Olivet (A)	2
June 5	2	Detroit A.C.	4
		Won 7 Lost 5 Tied 1	

1909
Date		Opponent	
Apr. 17	1	Olivet	0
Apr. 20	8	Culver Military Academy (A)	3
Apr. 24	3	Michigan	8
May 5	3	Michigan (A)	9
May 8	8	Univ. of Detroit	2
May 19	5	Wabash (A)	4
May 20	10	Wabash (A)	4
May 22	0	St. Viator's Coll. (A)	7
May 26	5	DePaul	4
May 27	10	DePaul	1
May 29	7	Olivet (A)	5
May 31	4	DePaul (at Lansing, Mich.)	2
		Won 9 Lost 3	

Chester Brewer was coach of MAC baseball team in 1904.

1910

Apr. 16	1	Olivet	5
Apr. 21	9	Culver Military Academy	1
Apr. 23	1	Notre Dame (A)	3
Apr. 29	12	Ohio Wesleyan	1
Apr. 30	4	Western Reserve Univ.	0
May 7	2	Michigan (A)	4
May 11	4	Alma (A)	5
May 13	12	Western Michigan	7
May 14	1	Syracuse	5
May 21	3	Alma	1
May 28	6	Wabash	0
May 30	4	Wabash	1
June 4	5	Eastern Michigan	1
June 11	2	Olivet (A)	11

Won 8 Lost 6

1911

John F. Macklin, Coach

Apr. 15	2	Olivet	6
Apr. 18	14	DePauw	1
Apr. 22	1	Michigan	3
Apr. 28	5	Western Reserve Univ.	0
May 5	6	Ohio State	1
May 6	2	Eastern Michigan (A)	1
May 11	3	Wabash	2
May 12	6	Syracuse	4
May 13	6	Alma	2
May 18	7	Culver Military Academy (A)	3
May 19	0	Wabash (A)	4
May 25	2	Lake Forest	1
May 27	15	St. John's Univ. (Toledo)	2
May 30	2	Michigan (A)	8
June 3	5	Central Michigan	0
June 10	2	Olivet (A)	3

Won 11 Lost 5

1912

Apr. 13	3	Olivet	0
Apr. 20	7	Lansing Senators (Mich. League)	1
Apr. 22	8	Ohio State	11
Apr. 26	5	Western Reserve Univ.	1
May 1	1	Ohio Wesleyan	2
May 4	7	Michigan	6
May 10	2	Syracuse	1
May 17	8	Wabash	4
May 18	5	Michigan (A)	1
May 22	5	Ohio Wesleyan (A)	2
May 23	2	Western Reserve Univ. (A)	1
May 30	8	Michigan (A)	3
June 1	0	Olivet	2
June 8	8	Eastern Michigan	0

Won 11 Lost 3

1913

Apr. 18	3	Western Reserve Univ.	2
Apr. 19	8	Olivet (A)	2
Apr. 24	3	Georgia	9
Apr. 25	0	Georgia	4
Apr. 26	7	Alma	6
Apr. 30	8	Kentucky	1
May 2	4	Case Tech.	11
May 7	7	Washington & Jefferson	5
May 9	5	Syracuse	1
May 14	9	Olivet	8
May 17	2	Michigan	9
May 22	1	Western Reserve (A)	0
May 23	2	Ohio Northern (A)	3
May 24	6	Buchtel Coll. (A)	3
May 30	4	Michigan (A)	5

May 31	2	Michigan (A)	7
June 5	4	Lake Forest	3
June 6	5	Ohio State	4

Won 11 Lost 7

1914

Apr. 18	14	Olivet	12
Apr. 23	5	Ohio Wesleyan	4
Apr. 24	7	Western Reserve Univ.	1
Apr. 25	8	Bethany Coll. (W. Va.)	3
May 1	2	Case Tech.	1
May 2	3	Notre Dame (A)	6
May 5	4	Alma	1
May 6	7	Akron	6
May 8	5	Syracuse	4
May 16	0	Michigan (at Lansing, Mich.)	6
May 19	4	Oberlin (A)	2
May 20	13	Western Reserve Univ. (A)	3
May 21	5	Ohio State (A)	3
May 27	3	Lake Forest	8
May 29	3	Michigan (A)	10
May 30	8	Michigan (A)	1
June 4	4	Notre Dame	12
June 5	2	MSU Alumni	3

Won 12 Lost 6

1915

Apr. 14	19	Albion	5
Apr. 19	9	Olivet	3
Apr. 23	6	Western Reserve Univ.	1
Apr. 24	4	Bethany Coll. (W. Va.)	3
Apr. 29	3	Univ. of Detroit	1
May 1	2	Notre Dame (A)	3
May 7	3	Syracuse	4
May 12	3	Michigan (A)	1
May 15	7	Alma	1
May 18	1	Ohio Wesleyan (A)	2
May 19	2	Marshall Coll. (A)	3
May 28	1	Michigan	8
May 29	4	Michigan	2
June 3	2	Notre Dame	4

Won 8 Lost 6

1916

John Morrissey, Coach

Apr. 16	13	Olivet	1
Apr. 21	8	Marshall Coll. (W. Va.)	2
Apr. 26	1	Western Michigan	2
Apr. 29	0	Notre Dame (A)	2
May 3	5	Kalamazoo Coll.	1
May 5	3	Syracuse	0
May 12	4	Wabash	1
May 13	6	Wabash	1
May 18	4	Buffalo (A)	0
May 19	6	Rochester (A)	5
May 20	2	Syracuse (A)	3
May 23	4	Niagara Univ.	3
May 27	3	Michigan	5
June 1	4	Notre Dame	1
June 3	9	Eastern Michigan	1

Won 11 Lost 4

1917

Apr. 14	19	Olivet	2
Apr. 20	6	Marshall Coll. (W. Va.)	2
Apr. 21	1	Marshall Coll.	2
Apr. 27	3	Western Michigan	5
Apr. 28	9	Western Reserve Univ.	1
May 5	12	Alma	1
May 12	0	Notre Dame (A)	12

May 18	5	Niagara Univ.	4
May 19	8	St. Mary's Coll.	
		(Mich.)	9
May 31	5	Notre Dame	2
June 1	2	Notre Dame	4
		Won 6 Lost 5	

1918
Chester L. Brewer, Coach

Apr. 13	16	Alma	7
Apr. 19	9	Olivet	3
Apr. 20	6	Kalamazoo Coll.	4
Apr. 24	2	Michigan	12
Apr. 26	11	St. Mary's Coll.	
		(Mich.)	9
Apr. 27	1	Eastern Michigan (A)	4
May 4	8	Notre Dame	11
May 7	3	Indiana	8
May 9	10	Kalamazoo Coll. (A)	6
May 10	10	Western Michigan (A)	3
May 11	4	Notre Dame (A)	0
May 15	2	Michigan (A)	5
		Won 7 Lost 5	

1919

Apr. 19	11	Alma	3
Apr. 23	3	Kalamazoo Coll.	6
Apr. 28	0	Indiana	6
Apr. 30	2	Notre Dame (A)	1
May 2	0	Indiana (A)	1
May 10	20	Western Michigan	12
May 14	0	Michigan (A)	4
May 15	2	Eastern Michigan	10
May 22	2	Michigan	5
May 31	5	Notre Dame	12
June 7	2	Western Michigan (A)	0
June 11	2	Wabash	5
June 12	4	Wabash	20
		Won 4 Lost 9	

1920

Apr. 12	7	Rochester (A)	0
Apr. 14	5	Penn State (A)	14
Apr. 24	12	Albion	2
May 1	5	Eastern Michigan	1
May 3	13	Armour Tech.	4
May 5	3	Michigan	5
May 6	6	Armour Tech. (A)	4
May 7	1	Valparaiso (A)	3
May 8	10	Notre Dame (A)	11
May 12	8	Michigan (A)	9
May 14	2	Oberlin	7
May 20	2	Valparaiso	6
May 25	8	Notre Dame	10
May 26	1	Oberlin (A)	0
May 29	4	Univ. of Detroit (A)	5
		Won 6 Lost 9	

1921
George E. Clark, Coach

Apr. 20	11	Albion	1
Apr. 27	12	Western Michigan	6
May 5	5	Valparaiso	6
May 6	12	St. Mary's Coll.	
		(Mich.) (A)	9
May 7	9	Oberlin (A)	6
May 11	6	Michigan	7
May 13	3	Iowa	5
May 19	4	Notre Dame	7
May 20	10	Oberlin	2
May 21	1	Oberlin	3
May 25	3	Western Michigan (A)	2
May 26	4	Notre Dame (A)	8
May 27	3	Valparaiso	6
June 1	5	Michigan	8
		Won 6 Lost 8	

1922
John Morrissey, Coach

Apr. 22	3	Western Michigan	4
Apr. 25	9	Albion	5
Apr. 26	8	Kalamazoo Coll. (A)	4
Apr. 27	2	Wabash (A)	3
Apr. 28	3	Armour Tech. (A)	7
Apr. 29	6	Notre Dame (A)	12
May 6	1	Notre Dame	3
May 9	4	DePauw	10
May 10	2	DePauw	1
May 13	5	Eastern Michigan	4
May 20	10	Western Michigan (A)	11
May 27	1	Wisconsin	10
May 30	15	Chicago Y.M.C.A.	
		Coll.	1
June 15	3	Bethany Coll. (A)	6
June 16	7	Bethany Coll. (A)	8
June 17	10	Oberlin (A)	8
June 19	6	Kalamazoo Coll.	2
		Won 7 Lost 10	

1923
Fred M. Walker, Coach

Apr. 6	7	St. Mary's Coll.	
		(Mich.)	6
Apr. 13	6	Eastern Michigan	5
Apr. 16	5	Valparaiso (A)	6
Apr. 17	9	Chicago (A)	0
Apr. 18	9	Notre Dame (A)	16
Apr. 19	8	Kalamazoo Coll. (A)	0
Apr. 24	0	Michigan	21
Apr. 28	13	Albion	1
May 2	2	Michigan (A)	16
May 4	6	Notre Dame	5
May 11	7	DePaul	6
May 12	10	Valparaiso	5
May 15	10	Beloit	2
May 19	3	Hope Coll.	1
May 22	14	Kalamazoo Coll.	1
May 24	5	St. Viator's Coll.	3
May 30	12	Eastern Michigan (A)	8
June 7	8	Alma	1
		Won 14 Lost 4	

1924

Apr. 11	8	Hope Coll.	2
Apr. 18	1	Western Michigan	6
Apr. 23	0	Michigan (A)	1
Apr. 29	8	St. Mary's Coll.	
		(Mich.)	0
May 3	4	Chicago	8
May 9	1	Western Michigan (A)	2
May 16	4	Lake Forest	2
May 21	1	Michigan	3
May 26	10	St. Viator's Coll.	7
May 30	7	Wisconsin	4
May 31	8	Butler	4
June 6	3	Notre Dame	4
June 7	2	Notre Dame (A)	8
		Won 6 Lost 7	

1925
John H. Kobs, Coach

Arp. 16	9	Armour Tech. (A)	0
Apr. 17	5	St. Viator's	
		Coll. (A)	5
Apr. 18	4	Wisconsin (A)	13
Apr. 21	17	Olivet	4
Apr. 25	2	Western Michigan (A)	3
Apr. 29	4	Michigan (A)	10
May 4	7	St. Mary's Coll.	
		(Mich.)	5
May 9	13	Hope Coll.	1
May 14	6	Minnesota	2
May 20	6	Michigan	13

May 23	7	Notre Dame (A)	11
May 28	5	St. Viator's Coll.	4
May 30	8	Butler	6
June 6	5	Notre Dame	4
June 20	5	MSU Alumni	4
		Won 9 Lost 5 Tied 1	

1926

Apr. 1	5	Ft. Benning (A)	7
Apr. 2	4	Ft. Benning (A)	1
Apr. 3	1	Mercer Univ. (A)	0
Apr. 5	5	Alabama Inst. (A)	8
Apr. 6	8	Oglethorpe Univ. (A)	6
Apr. 14	7	Albion	2
Apr. 17	18	Bradley	3
Apr. 21	1	Michigan (A)	6
Apr. 29	4	Syracuse	3
May 1	27	Lake Forest	5
May 4	11	Olivet	0
May 8	4	Butler	7
May 13	6	Hope Coll.	2
May 15	2	St. Viator's Coll.	3
May 24	8	Michigan	5
May 27	7	Western Michigan	4
May 29	9	Armour Tech.	1
June 2	0	Western Michigan (A)	7
June 5	5	Notre Dame	3
June 12	0	Notre Dame (A)	6
		Won 13 Lost 7	

1927

Mar. 26	3	Western Kentucky (A)	4
Mar. 28	11	Ft. Benning (A)	19
Mar. 29	12	Ft. Benning (A)	8
Mar. 30	3	Ft. Benning (A)	5
Mar. 31	0	Mercer Univ. (A)	7
Apr. 1	4	Marysville Coll. (A)	7
Apr. 2	0	Marysville Coll. (A)	17
Apr. 3	1	Xavier (A)	0
Apr. 13	17	Albion	0
Apr. 22	13	Adrian	2
Apr. 23	16	Olivet	0
Apr. 26	4	Michigan (A)	6
Apr. 28	9	West Virginia	3
May 5	7	Hope Coll.	5
May 7	4	Notre Dame (A)	1
May 13	9	Bradley	5
May 20	5	St. Viator's Coll.	1
May 25	0	Notre Dame	5
May 28	7	Armour Tech.	3
June 1	4	Michigan	1
June 11	11	Xavier	7
		Won 13 Lost 8	

1928

Mar. 24	5	Cumberland Coll. (A)	3
Mar 26.	0	Ft. Benning (A)	5
Mar. 27	2	Ft. Benning (A)	21
Mar. 28	9	Ft. Benning (A)	7
Mar. 29	0	Marysville Coll. (A)	7
Mar. 31	7	Pressman's Technical Trade School (A)	4
Apr. 11	12	Adrian	0
Apr. 14	10	Kalamazoo Coll.	4
Apr. 26	2	Syracuse	1
May 1	5	Ohio State (A)	12
May 4	5	Armour Tech.	2
May 9	1	West Virginia	21
May 15	8	Bradley	7
May 30	5	Chicago Y.M.C.A.	2
June 2	0	Notre Dame (A)	8
June 6	11	Hope Coll.	0
June 15	6	Michigan (A)	7
June 16	9	Michigan	4
		Won 11 Lost 7	

1929

Apr. 1	5	Cumberland Coll. (A)	2
Apr. 2	4	Cumberland Coll. (A)	4
Apr. 3	2	Vanderbilt (A)	7
Apr. 4	1	Vanderbilt (A)	12
Apr. 6	2	Xavier (A)	14
Apr. 8	13	Xavier (A)	4
Apr. 18	20	Kalamazoo Coll.	2
Apr. 23	4	Adrian	1
Apr. 27	2	Luther	17
May 4	0	Colgate	4
May 7	8	Hope Coll.	1
May 10	1	Notre Dame	9
May 13	9	Albion	1
May 16	5	Notre Dame (A)	12
May 17	4	Coe Coll.	3
May 21	4	Michigan	3
May 23	4	Defiance	3
May 25	10	St. Mary's Coll. (Mich.)	5
May 29	1	Oberlin (A)	5
May 31	2	Ohio State	5
June 6	3	Hillsdale	2
June 14	2	Michigan (A)	6
June 15	6	Michigan (A)	15
June 22	6	Auto Owners Insurance (Lansing)	5
		Won 12 Lost 11 Tied 1	

1930

Mar. 31	2	Marysville Coll. (A)	11
Apr. 1	3	Marysville Coll. (A)	0
Apr. 3	4	Vanderbilt (A)	5
Apr. 5	9	Xavier (A)	2
Apr. 7	13	Cincinnati (A)	3
Apr. 8	3	Miami (Ohio) (A)	5
Apr. 12	12	Chicago	4
Apr. 19	4	Eastern Michigan (A)	1
Apr. 24	4	Syracuse	3
Apr. 26	11	Central Michigan	1
Apr. 30	4	Iowa State Teachers Coll.	5
May 3	3	Notre Dame	2
May 10	7	Western Michigan	4
May 13	13	Hope Coll.	5
May 17	7	Western Michigan (A)	4
May 19	3	Chicago (A)	4
May 22	11	Miami (Ohio)	3
May 24	3	Oberlin	0
May 26	5	Notre Dame (A)	3
May 27	5	Cincinnati	3
May 30	3	Michigan	1
June 7	9	Eastern Michigan	3
June 20	3	Michigan (A)	6
June 21	8	Michigan	4
		Won 18 Lost 6	

1931

Mar. 30	4	Mississippi State (A)	3
Apr. 1	4	Mississippi (A)	5
Apr. 2	1	Mississippi (A)	10
Apr. 3	3	Vanderbilt (A)	2
Apr. 4	3	Vanderbilt (A)	5
Apr. 6	8	Xavier (A)	4
Apr. 18	3	Eastern Michigan	2
Apr. 23	10	Hope Coll.	2
Apr. 25	6	Central Michigan	0
May 2	2	Western Michigan	1
May 8	17	Iowa State Teachers Coll.	2
May 11	3	Hosei Univ. (Japan)	5
May 13	1	Hosei Univ. (Japan)	4
May 14	16	Central Michigan (A)	5
May 23	8	Michigan	4
May 26	9	Chicago (A)	10
May 27	4	Northwestern (A)	5

June 1	10	Indiana	9
June 2	3	Indiana	6
June 10	5	Western Michigan	3
June 13	5	Eastern Michigan	5
June 19	2	Michigan (A)	3
June 20	5	Michigan	0
		Won 13 Lost 9 Tied 1	

1932

Mar. 28	6	Ft. Benning (A)	8
Mar. 29	4	Ft. Benning (A)	5
Mar. 30	6	Ft. Benning (A)	3
Mar. 31	4	Georgia Tech. (A)	4
Apr. 1	1	Vanderbilt (A)	2
Apr. 2	8	Vanderbilt (A)	4
Apr. 7	7	Xavier (A)	6
Apr. 16	6	St. Viator's Coll. (A)	1
Apr 21	16	Central Michigan	2
Apr. 25	1	Luther	3
Apr. 29	12	Iowa	4
Apr. 30	4	Iowa	3
May 3	3	Michigan (A)	3
May 7	3	Eastern Michigan	7
May 11	8	Hillsdale	5
May 14	5	Notre Dame	2
May 19	8	Ohio	10
May 25	3	Michigan	4
May 27	5	Central Michigan (A)	6
May 28	2	Western Michigan	5
May 30	7	Chicago	6
June 2	0	Eastern Michigan (A)	1
June 4	3	Notre Dame (A)	6
June 8	4	Western Michigan (A)	6
		Won 10 Lost 12 Tied 2	

1933

Mar. 28	6	Elon Coll. (A)	5
Mar. 29	6	Wake Forest (A)	8
Mar. 30	6	North Carolina (A)	5
Mar. 31	5	North Carolina (A)	3
Apr. 1	7	Duke (A)	8
Apr. 13	4	Iowa	0
Apr. 15	5	Northwestern	4
Apr. 20	12	Hillsdale	0
Apr. 22	7	Northwestern (A)	3
Apr. 29	5	Michigan (A)	1
May 3	5	Notre Dame	3
May 13	0	Western Michigan (A)	1
May 18	14	Oberlin	3
May 20	1	Eastern Michigan (A)	5
May 24	3	Michigan	4
May 27	3	Indiana	10
May 30	9	Chicago	2
June 3	14	Notre Dame (A)	5
June 7	5	Western Michigan	8
June 10	8	Eastern Michigan	3
		Won 13 Lost 7	

1934

Mar. 26	16	Davidson (A)	6
Mar. 27	4	Duke (A)	14
Mar. 28	11	Elon Coll. (A)	10
Mar. 29	4	Wake Forest (A)	9
Mar. 30	4	North Carolina (A)	5
Mar. 31	8	Rocky Mound Amateurs (A)	8
Apr. 18	3	Hillsdale	2
Apr. 21	5	Eastern Michigan	2
Apr. 24	9	Northwestern	3
May 1	3	Michigan (A)	13
May 5	1	Western Michigan (A)	4
May 9	8	Notre Dame	1
May 12	4	Western Michigan	9
May 18	4	Ohio State	6
May 19	13	Ohio State	4
May 22	0	Eastern Michigan (A)	3

May 25	2	Indiana	5
May 30	1	Michigan	5
June 2	13	Notre Dame (A)	9
June 4	4	Cleveland Indians (American League)	14
June 8	6	Iowa	0
June 9	6	Iowa	1
		Won 10 Lost 11 Tied 1	

1935

Mar. 25	0	Clemson (A)	5
Mar. 26	17	Furman (A)	1
Mar. 27	7	Newberry Coll. (A)	7
Mar. 28	5	South Carolina (A)	1
Mar. 29	1	Davidson (A)	3
Mar. 30	3	Wake Forest (A)	4
Apr. 13	10	Hillsdale	9
Apr. 20	8	Northwestern	7
Apr. 25	4	Wisconsin	3
Apr. 26	7	Wisconsin	6
May 4	4	Western Michigan (A)	6
May 10	4	Eastern Michigan	3
May 12	5	Notre Dame	4
May 17	7	Ohio State (A)	8
May 18	2	Ohio State (A)	5
May 21	5	Eastern Michigan (A)	4
May 25	2	Western Michigan	5
May 30	4	Michigan	1
June 1	1	Notre Dame (A)	2
June 7	2	Iowa	5
June 8	5	Iowa	4
		Won 11 Lost 9 Tied 1	

John Kobs, highly successful coach, 1925-1963, for whom varsity field is named.

1936			
Mar. 30	18	Clemson (A)	0
Mar. 31	5	Newberry Coll. (A)	0
Apr. 3	13	North Carolina State (A)	5
Apr. 4	4	Wake Forest (A)	1
Apr. 18	7	Toledo	0
Apr. 23	5	Wisconsin	7
Apr. 24	6	Wisconsin	5
Apr. 30	3	Notre Dame	12
May 7	19	Eastern Michigan	0
May 9	11	Western Michigan (A)	0
May 14	7	Cornell (A)	2
May 16	19	Eastern Michigan (A)	5
May 22	6	Ohio State	5
May 23	6	Ohio State	9
May 29	1	Michigan (A)	2
May 30	2	Michigan	5
June 4	4	Iowa	3
June 5	3	Iowa	0
June 6	4	Notre Dame (A)	6
June 13	1	Western Michigan	11

Won 13   Lost 7

1937			
Mar. 27	12	Eastern Kentucky State (A)	8
Mar. 29	8	Newberry Coll. (A)	2
Mar. 30	8	Oakridge Military Academy (A)	6
Mar. 31	5	Duke (A)	12
Apr. 1	5	North Carolina (A)	8
Apr. 2	4	Elon Coll. (A)	6
Apr. 3	1	Wake Forest (A)	6
Apr. 5	4	Ohio Univ. (A)	3
Apr. 22	3	Wisconsin	5
Apr. 23	3	Wisconsin	5
Apr. 29	2	Western Michigan (A)	11
May 1	7	Notre Dame	1
May 6	1	Western Michigan	3
May 8	6	Indiana	5
May 12	4	Northwestern	1
May 13	8	Univ. of Toledo (A)	3
May 14	0	Ohio State (A)	9
May 15	12	Ohio State (A)	2
May 19	4	Univ. of Toledo	3
May 26	10	Notre Dame (A)	3
May 29	4	Michigan	1
May 31	0	Michigan (A)	1
June 5	18	Eastern Michigan	0
June 6	6	Eastern Michigan	4
June 7	3	Iowa	1
June 8	5	Iowa	7
June 12	6	Nwbraska	0

Won 16   Lost 11

1938			
Mar. 26	2	Eastern Kentucky State (A)	1
Mar. 28	8	Georgia (A)	5
Mar. 29	12	Georgia (A)	6
Mar. 30	6	Newberry Coll. (A)	4
Mar. 31	10	South Carolina (A)	4
Apr. 4	4	West Virginia (A)	2
Apr. 5	4	Ohio Univ. (A)	1
Apr. 20	1	Wisconsin	2
Apr. 21	0	Wisconsin	1
Apr. 23	5	Eastern Michigan	3
Apr. 26	9	Michigan	3
Apr. 29	5	Iowa (A)	2
Apr. 30	3	Iowa (A)	5
May 6	7	Indiana	4
May 7	5	Notre Dame	4
May 14	5	Armour Tech.	4
May 21	7	Eastern Michigan (A)	10
May 24	1	Notre Dame (A)	9
May 26	2	California	6
May 28	1	Univ. of Toledo	2
May 30	0	Michigan	3
June 3	2	Ohio State (A)	0
June 4	2	Ohio State (A)	7
June 7	5	Western Michigan (A)	1

Won 15   Lost 9

1939			
Mar. 27	2	Georgia (A)	3
Mar. 28	5	Georgia (A)	4
Mar. 29	10	South Carolina (A)	5
Mar. 31	0	Duke (A)	3
Apr. 1	0	Wake Forest (A)	1
Apr. 3	7	West Virginia (A)	5
Apr. 4	6	West Virginia (A)	4
Apr. 22	11	Eastern Michigan	13
Apr. 28	6	Michigan (A)	3
May 5	17	Ohio Wesleyan	7
May 6	14	Notre Dame	9
May 11	0	Indiana	7
May 13	7	Ohio Univ.	8
May 18	7	Hillsdale	4
May 20	8	Minnesota	3
May 24	5	Univ. of Toledo	0
May 26	5	Wisconsin (A)	7
May 27	5	Armour Tech. (A)	2
May 30	5	Michigan	13
June 1	1	Eastern Michigan (A)	7
June 4	4	Notre Dame (A)	3
June 6	1	Western Michigan (A)	2
June 10	1	Western Michigan	0

Won 13   Lost 10

1940			
Mar. 22	3	Georgia (A)	2
Mar. 23	4	Georgia (A)	5
Mar. 25	3	Clemson (A)	3
Mar. 26	11	Presbyterian Coll. (A)	5
Mar. 27	14	South Carolina (A)	12
Apr. 17	6	Wisconsin	6
Apr. 18	7	Wisconsin	6
Apr. 27	6	Western Michigan	19
Apr. 30	5	Michigan (A)	4
May 4	2	Notre Dame	1
May 11	7	Western Michigan (A)	5
May 17	4	Iowa (A)	8
May 18	0	Iowa (A)	4
May 22	8	Univ. of Toledo	3
May 24	7	Eastern Michigan	1
May 25	16	Hillsdale (A)	2
May 28	17	Hillsdale	4
May 30	4	Michigan	5
June 1	4	Notre Dame (A)	2
June 4	8	Illinois Wesleyan	10
June 7	3	Ohio State	4
June 8	3	Ohio State	7

Won 12   Lost 8   Tied 2

1941			
Mar. 24	14	South Carolina (A)	4
Mar. 25	5	Clemson (A)	4
Mar. 26	6	Georgia (A)	4
Mar. 28	12	Ft. Benning (A)	9
Mar. 29	10	Ft. Benning (A)	7
Mar. 31	8	Alabama Inst. (A)	9
Apr. 2	10	Vanderbilt (A)	11
Apr. 11	4	Ohio State (A)	5
Apr. 12	5	Ohio State (A)	3
Apr. 26	10	Eastern Michigan	3
Apr. 29	3	Michigan (A)	4
May 2	2	Wisconsin (A)	1
May 3	2	Wisconsin (A)	3
May 7	5	Notre Dame (A)	14
May 10	10	Notre Dame	2
May 15	4	Indiana	3

May 17	4	Eastern Michigan (A)	0
May 23	3	Western Michigan	2
May 31	4	Michigan	6
June 2	2	Iowa	3
June 3	2	Iowa	6
June 6	7	California	0
June 7	5	California	8

Won 13 Lost 10

1942

Mar. 23	2	Pensacola N.A.B. (A)	5
Mar. 24	4	Pensacola N.A.B. (A)	1
Mar. 25	6	Pensacola N.A.B. (A)	3
Mar. 28	6	Ft. Benning (A)	6
Mar. 30	4	Georgia (A)	18
Mar. 31	9	Georgia (A)	20
Apr. 1	11	Clemson (A)	5
Apr. 15	2	Wayne State (A)	1
Apr. 17	3	Ohio State	5
Apr. 18	2	Ohio State	3
Apr. 22	5	Univ. of Detroit (A)	3
Apr. 24	9	Wisconsin	6
Apr. 25	8	Wisconsin	7
Apr. 28	1	Michigan (A)	2
May 1	14	Wayne State	7
May 4	2	Iowa (A)	9
May 9	2	Ft. Custer Enlisted Men	4
May 14	8	Univ. of Detroit	7
May 20	1	Western Michigan (A)	3
May 23	4	Eastern Michigan (A)	2
May 25	3	Great Lakes N.T.S.	4
May 28	12	Michigan	1
May 30	2	Ft. Custer Enlisted Men	8
June 3	3	Western Michigan	1
June 6	10	Eastern Michigan	5

Won 13 Lost 11 Tied 1

1943

Apr. 17	1	Michigan (A)	7
Apr. 23	0	Ohio State (A)	3
Apr. 24	10	Ohio State (A)	6
Apr. 27	2	Notre Dame (A)	12
Apr. 29	0	Notre Dame	8
May 1	9	Univ. of Detroit	3
May 10	6	Wisconsin (A)	7
May 11	5	Wisconsin (A)	9
May 15	12	Hillsdale	2
May 20	10	Univ. of Detroit (A)	1
May 22	7	Eastern Michigan (A)	1
May 25	0	Western Michigan (A)	5
May 28	6	Eastern Michigan	4
June 5	2	Western Michigan	1
June 8	4	Selfridge A.B. (A)	2
June 10	10	Selfridge A.B.	1

Won 9 Lost 7

1944

Intercollegiate athletics dropped because of World War II.

1945

Apr. 6	3	Indiana (A)	15
Apr. 7	5	Indiana (A)	7
Apr. 25	4	Michigan State Reformatory at Ionia, Mich.	3
Apr. 28	7	Michigan State Reformatory at Jackson, Mich.	0
May 2	6	Wayne State (A)	2
May 9	7	Eastern Michigan (A)	4
May 11	1	Ohio State	2
May 12	3	Ohio State	0
May 19	4	Ohio Univ. at Lansing, Mich.	11

May 19	8	Ohio Univ. at Lansing, Mich.	7
May 23	10	Wayne State	6
May 24	2	Univ. of Detroit (A)	0
May 25	6	Univ. of Detroit (A)	5
May 29	9	Univ. of Detroit	2
May 30	15	Univ. of Detroit	3
June 7	3	Percy Jones Hospital (Battle Creek)	2

Won 12 Lost 4

1946

Mar. 20	6	Georgia (A)	4
Mar. 21	16	Georgia (A)	1
Mar. 22	9	South Carolina (A)	4
Mar. 23	9	South Carolina (A)	6
Mar. 24	9	Ft. Jackson (A)	6
Mar. 25	5	North Carolina (A)	3
Mar. 26	3	North Carolina (A)	2
Mar. 27	5	Duke (A)	3
Mar. 28	3	North Carolina State (A)	1
Apr. 19	11	Wisconsin	3
Apr. 20	12	Wisconsin	2
Apr. 23	2	Michigan (A)	4
Apr. 24	7	Wayne State (A)	8
Apr. 27	1	Western Michigan (A)	9
May 10	10	Eastern Michigan (A)	3
May 11	4	Notre Dame	5
May 13	3	Univ. of Detroit (A)	1
May 15	3	Wayne State	0
May 21	7	Univ. of Detroit	2
May 24	11	Eastern Michigan	0
May 26	8	Great Lakes N.T.S. (A)	0
May 30	4	Ohio State	3
May 30	7	Ohio State	3
June 1	7	Western Michigan	0
June 5	0	Michigan	2
June 6	6	Great Lakes N.T.S.	3

Won 21 Lost 5

1947

Mar. 22	10	Maryville Coll. (A)	1
Mar. 24	18	Georgia (A)	7
Mar. 25	8	Georgia (A)	4
Mar. 27	9	Newberry Coll. (A)	0
Mar. 28	12	South Carolina (A)	2
Mar. 29	13	South Carolina (A)	7
Mar. 31	3	North Carolina (A)	4
Apr. 1	4	Duke (A)	2
Apr. 12	9	Northwestern (A)	0
Apr. 12	0	Northwestern (A)	4
Apr. 19	9	Univ. of Detroit	0
Apr. 26	7	Notre Dame	,4
Apr. 30	1	Western Michigan (A)	9
May 3	12	Eastern Michigan	0
May 6	2	Michigan (A)	1
May 10	1	Western Michigan	4
May 12	8	Wisconsin (A)	9
May 13	8	Wisconsin (A)	5
May 19	6	Wayne State	0
May 23	2	Notre Dame (A)	10
May 27	8	Michigan	1
May 30	8	Wisconsin	5
May 31	4	Wisconsin	14
June 6	1	Ohio State	,2

Won 16 Lost 8

1948

Mar. 22	3	South Carolina (A)	4
Mar. 24	14	Newberry Coll. (A)	15
Mar. 25	6	Newberry Coll. (A)	1
Mar. 26	5	Presbyterian Coll. (A)	3
Mar. 29	2	North Carolina (A)	5
Mar. 30	3	Wake Forest (A)	2

Apr. 9	11	Ohio State (A)	12
Apr. 10	3	Ohio State (A)	4
Apr. 16	9	Northwestern (A)	9
Apr. 17	5	Northwestern (A)	7
Apr. 21	11	Wisconsin	9
Apr. 22	6	Wisconsin	5
Apr. 30	3	Ohio Univ. (A)	5
May 1	4	Ohio Univ. (A)	5
May 4	7	Univ. of Detroit (A)	5
May 8	3	Eastern Michigan	1
May 12	7	Michigan (A)	3
May 15	3	Western Michigan (A)	4
May 18	4	Univ. of Detroit	2
May 22	4	Notre Dame	5
May 26	2	Michigan	9
May 29	1	Notre Dame	10
June 1	5	Western Michigan	6
June 4	3	Ohio Univ.	6
June 5	5	Ohio Univ.	4

Won 10   Lost 14   Tied 1

1949

Mar. 24	5	Tennessee (A)	0
Mar. 25	9	Georgia Tech. (A)	5
Mar. 26	7	Georgia Tech. (A)	2
Mar. 28	3	South Carolina (A)	7
Mar. 29	5	South Carolina (A)	3
Mar. 30	5	North Carolina (A)	5
Mar. 31	2	North Carolina (A)	4
Apr. 1	13	North Carolina State (A)	10
Apr. 22	5	Northwestern	1
Apr. 23	6	Northwestern	4
Apr. 26	0	Michigan	5
Apr. 28	22	Wayne State	2
Apr. 30	6	Western Michigan (A)	7
May 4	7	Notre Dame	5
May 6	5	Ohio State	4
May 7	14	Ohio State	0
May 11	13	Eastern Michigan (A)	10
May 13	3	Purdue (A)	6
May 14	7	Purdue (A)	3
May 16	6	Wisconsin (A)	5
May 17	10	Wisconsin (A)	5
May 21	9	Michigan	10
May 28	10	Notre Dame (A)	8
May 30	8	Univ. of Detroit	3
May 31	11	Wayne State	1
June 3	9	Bradley	11
June 4	11	Bradley	3
June 6	0	Western Michigan	5

Won 19   Lost 8   Tied 1

1950

Mar. 24	12	Clemson Coll. (A)	14
Mar. 25	18	Clemson Coll. (A)	5
Mar. 27	6	South Carolina (A)	3
Mar. 28	5	South Carolina (A)	6
Mar. 29	8	Wake Forest at Kannapolis, N.C.	11
Mar. 30	1	North Carolina (A)	8
Mar. 31	6	North Carolina (A)	7
Apr. 1	7	Univ. of Richmond(A)	2
Apr. 18	6	Michigan (A)	5
Apr. 21	8	Purdue	5
Apr. 22	9	Purdue	3
Apr. 28	1	Ohio State (A)	4
Apr. 29	6	Ohio State (A)	3
May 4	11	Notre Dame (A)	10
May 5	3	Iowa (A)	5
May 6	7	Iowa (A)	6
May 10	7	Michigan	6
May 13	11	Wayne State	7
May 16	15	Wayne State (A)	7
May 18	11	Eastern Michigan	3
May 20	5	Univ. of Detroit	0
May 24	7	Notre Dame	1

May 26	3	Western Michigan	7
May 27	5	Western Michigan (A)	1
May 29	4	Univ. of Detroit (A)	3
June 3	6	Bradley	3
June 3	4	Bradley	3
June 8	6	Wisconsin	13

(*)Fourth District National Collegiate Athletic Association Playoff

Won 19   Lost 9

1951

Mar. 23	6	Duke (A)	7
Mar. 24	8	Duke (A)	5
Mar. 26	8	Clemson Coll. (A)	7
Mar. 27	16	Clemson Coll. (A)	6
Mar. 28	4	South Carolina (A)	3
Mar. 30	6	North Carolina (A)	7
Mar. 31	17	Virginia Tech. (A)	4
Apr. 21	25	Wayne State	1
Apr. 25	9	Notre Dame (A)	1
Apr. 28	3	Wayne State (A)	0
May 2	5	Western Michigan	12
May 4	8	Iowa	5
May 5	12	Iowa	9
May 9	3	Notre Dame	2
May 12	1	Michigan	15
May 15	12	Western Michigan (A)	2
May 16	3	Eastern Michigan	1
May 18	7	Indiana (A)	5
May 19	1	Indiana (A)	6
May 23	15	Univ. of Detroit (A)	3
May 25	2	Minnesota (A)	9
May 26	4	Minnesota (A)	5
May 29	10	Michigan (A)	5
May 30	13	Univ. of Detroit (A)	4
June 1	0	Ohio State	8
June 2	8	Ohio State	9

Won 17   Lost 9

1952

Mar. 24	13	Clemson Coll. (A)	3
Mar. 25	5	Clemson Coll. (A)	1
Mar. 26	2	Camp Gordon	8
Mar. 27	4	South Carolina (A)	1
Mar. 28	1	South Carolina (A)	4
Mar. 29	3	North Carolina (A)	0
Mar. 31	6	Yale at Chapel Hill, N.C.	3
Apr. 1	6	Yale at Chapel Hill, N.C.	0
Apr. 1	6	North Carolina (A)	3
Apr. 2	5	North Carolina (A)	9
Apr. 3	7	North Carolina State (A)	3
Apr. 4	9	Duke (A)	10
Apr. 25	1	Ohio State	4
Apr. 26	1	Illinois	12
Apr. 26	1	Illinois	0
May 2	7	Minnesota (A)	4
May 3	1	Iowa (A)	4
May 3	1	Iowa (A)	0
May 7	2	Notre Dame	4
May 9	6	Michigan	5
May 10	2	Michigan (A)	10
May 10	4	Michigan (A)	0
May 16	5	Purdue	7
May 17	5	Indiana	3
May 17	8	Indiana	2
May 19	4	Univ. of Detroit (A)	5
May 23	4	Wisconsin (A)	5
May 28	4	Notre Dame (A)	5
May 30	2	Univ. of Detroit	1
May 31	10	Wayne State	3
June 6	1	Western Michigan (A)	8
June 7	11	Western Michigan	2

Won 18   Lost 14

1953

Date		Opponent	
Mar. 27	4	North Carolina at Camp LeJeune, N.C.	11
Mar. 28	3	Camp LeJeune (A)	6
Mar. 28	9	North Carolina at Camp LeJeune, N.C.	11
Mar. 30	2	Cherry Point Marines (A)	16
Mar. 31	7	Cherry Point Marines (A)	8
Apr. 1	8	North Carolina State (A)	7
Apr. 2	0	Duke (A)	1
Apr. 3	3	Duke (A)	7
Apr. 4	1	Ft. Lee (A)	5
Apr. 18	15	Wayne State	0
Apr. 24	1	Illinois (A)	2
Apr. 25	1	Ohio State (A)	4
Apr. 25	1	Ohio State (A)	2
May 1	3	Iowa	2
May 2	1	Minnesota	4
May 2	3	Minnesota	2
May 6	8	Notre Dame	5
May 8	1	Michigan (A)	9
May 9	6	Michigan	5
May 9	2	Michigan	20
May 15	6	Indiana (A)	1
May 22	2	Northwestern	0
May 23	3	Wisconsin	10
May 23	5	Wisconsin	1
May 27	4	Notre Dame (A)	2
May 30	8	Univ. of Detroit	0
June 3	5	Western Michigan (A)	8
June 6	3	Western Michigan	9

Won 11   Lost 17

1954

Date		Opponent	
Mar. 26	3	Duke (A)	6
Mar. 27	8	Duke (A)	2
Mar. 29	2	North Carolina (A)	6
Mar. 30	5	North Carolina State (A)	3
Apr. 2	4	Ft. Eustis (A)	12
Apr. 3	4	Ft. Eustis (A)	5
Apr. 3	4	Ft. Eustis (A)	0
Apr. 17	4	Wayne State	2
Apr. 21	9	Univ. of Detroit	3
Apr. 23	4	Northwestern (A)	0
Apr. 24	3	Wisconsin (A)	3
Apr. 30	17	Illinois	3
May 1	12	Purdue	0
May 1	2	Purdue	5
May 5	8	Notre Dame	1
May 7	6	Iowa (A)	3
May 8	5	Minnesota (A)	5
May 8	6	Minnesota (A)	2
May 14	6	Michigan	4
May 15	8	Michigan (A)	4
May 15	8	Michigan (A)	9
May 19	6	Wayne State (A)	2
May 21	5	Indiana	2
May 22	6	Ohio State	4
May 22	6	Ohio State	5
May 26	6	Notre Dame (A)	4
May 29	6	Univ. of Detroit (A)	3
(*)May 31	14	Ohio Univ.	10
(*)May 31	0	Ohio Univ.	7
June 1	5	Ohio Univ.	3
June 5	4	Western Michigan	5
(**)June 10	16	Massachusetts at Omaha, Nebr.	5
(**)June 11	2	Arizona at Omaha, Nebr.	1
(**)June 12	4	Rollins Coll. at Omaha, Nebr.	5
(**)June 13	3	Rollins Coll. at Omaha, Nebr.	2
(**)June 14	3	Missouri at Omaha, Nebr.	4

(*)Fourth District National Collegiate Athletic Association Playoff
(**)Final National Collegiate Athletic Association Playoff

Won 25   Lost 10   Tied 1

1955

Date		Opponent	
Mar. 25	6	South Carolina (A)	3
Mar. 26	19	South Carolina (A)	11
Mar. 28	5	Ft. Jackson (A)	9
Mar. 28	11	Ft. Jackson (A)	1
Mar. 29	11	Ft. Jackson (A)	5
Mar. 30	11	North Carolina State (A)	9
Mar. 31	4	Wake Forest (A)	5
Apr. 1	5	Camp LeJeune (A)	7
Apr. 1	9	Camp LeJeune (A)	18
Apr. 2	1	North Carolina (A)	4
Apr. 16	16	Univ. of Detroit	6
Apr. 22	14	Wisconsin	8
Apr. 23	6	Northwestern	17
Apr. 23	6	Northwestern	1
Apr. 29	22	Purdue (A)	8
Apr. 30	1	Illinois (A)	7
Apr. 30	5	Illinois (A)	9
May 4	14	Western Michigan (A)	1
May 6	0	Minnesota	3
May 7	9	Iowa	6
May 7	2	Iowa	1
May 10	8	Univ. of Detroit (A)	9
May 13	3	Michigan (A)	0
May 14	8	Michigan	5
May 14	4	Michigan	3
May 18	5	Notre Dame	4
May 20	1	Ohio State (A)	5
May 21	7	Indiana (A)	3
May 21	7	Indiana (A)	2
May 23	4	Notre Dame (A)	3
June 1	13	Wayne State (A)	5
June 4	13	Wayne State	1

Won 21   Lost 11

1956

Date		Opponent	
Mar. 24	5	South Carolina (A)	7
Mar. 26	2	Parris Island Marines (A)	11
Mar. 26	6	Virginia Military Inst. at Parris Island, S.C.	3
Mar. 27	5	Parris Island Marines (A)	6
Mar. 28	4	Camp LeJeune (A)	0
Mar. 30	10	North Carolina State (A)	15
Mar. 31	5	Wake Forest (A)	6
Apr. 3	4	Duke (A)	3
Apr. 4	2	North Carolina (A)	1
Apr. 11	19	Univ. of Detroit	3
Apr. 21	17	Wayne State	3
Apr. 21	8	Wayne State	2
Apr. 27	7	Ohio State	8
May 1	4	Western Michigan (A)	2
May 4	11	Wisconsin (A)	6
May 11	3	Purdue at Battle Creek, Mich.	4
May 12	2	Illinois at Battle Creek, Mich.	0
May 12	2	Illinois at Battle Creek, Mich.	1
May 14	7	Univ. of Detroit	3
May 16	2	Notre Dame (A)	8
May 18	3	Minnesota (A)	7
May 19	3	Iowa (A)	5
May 19	3	Iowa (A)	8

May 23	5	Notre Dame	4
May 25	10	Michigan	4
May 26	3	Michigan (A)	7
May 26	1	Michigan (A)	2
May 29	9	Wayne State (A)	1
June 2	12	Western Michigan	9
		Won 16 Lost 13	

1957

Mar. 25	8	Florida State (A)	3
Mar. 26	5	Duke at Talla-hassee, Fla.	21
Mar. 27	19	Yale at Talla-hassee, Fla.	9
Mar. 28	4	Florida State (A)	7
Mar. 29	3	Duke at Talla-hassee, Fla.	2
Mar. 30	17	Yale at Talla-hassee, Fla.	8
Apr. 1	6	Alabama at Winter Park, Fla.	12
Apr. 2	9	Alabama at Winter Park, Fla.	4
Apr. 3	3	Rollins Coll. at Winter Park, Fla.	7
Apr. 4	3	Rollins Coll. at Winter Park, Fla.	9
Apr. 5	8	Rollins Coll. at Winter Park, Fla.	3
Apr. 6	2	Rollins Coll. at Winter Park, Fla.	3
Apr. 13	8	Univ. of Detroit	2
Apr. 18	21	Wayne State	2
Apr. 20	8	Albion	3
Apr. 20	7	Albion	0
Apr. 26	4	Indiana (A)	2

Apr. 27	2	Ohio State (A)	6
Apr. 27	1	Ohio State (A)	2
Apr. 30	4	Notre Dame (A)	3
May 3	2	Northwestern	7
May 4	6	Wisconsin	7
May 4	11	Wisconsin	4
May 7	8	Wayne State (A)	0
May 8	12	Western Michigan	6
May 10	8	Illinois (A)	7
May 13	1	Notre Dame	3
May 17	6	Iowa	5
May 18	2	Minnesota	4
May 18	2	Minnesota	3
May 21	3	Univ. of Detroit (A)	4
May 24	3	Michigan (A)	0
		Won 18 Lost 13 Tied 1	

1958

Mar. 24	5	Clemson (A)	7
Mar. 26	5	Parris Island Marines (A)	3
Mar. 27	3	Parris Island Marines (A)	5
Mar. 28	0	Parris Island Marines (A)	8
Mar. 29	2	Parris Island Marines (A)	0
Mar. 30	7	Hunter A.F.B. (A)	0
Mar. 31	12	South Carolina (A)	0
Arp. 1	8	Georgia (A)	9
Apr. 2	5	Georgia (A)	2
Apr. 3	3	Clemson (A)	2
Apr. 19	16	Albion	0
Apr. 19	14	Albion	1
Apr. 25	4	Michigan	2
Apr. 26	1	Michigan (A)	10
Apr. 26	1	Michigan (A)	2
Apr. 30	5	Western Michigan (A)	7
May 2	10	Indiana	3
May 3	14	Ohio State	0
May 3	7	Ohio State	1
May 6	13	Wayne State (A)	2
May 7	0	Notre Dame	7
May 9	9	Northwestern (A)	6
May 10	8	Wisconsin (A)	3
May 10	5	Wisconsin (A)	9
May 13	4	Univ. of Detroit (A)	2
May 16	3	Illinois	0
May 17	8	Purdue	5
May 17	3	Purdue	1
May 21	8	Wayne State	0
May 23	5	Iowa	2
May 24	2	Minnesota (A)	3
May 24	1	Minnesota (A)	2
May 30	11	Univ. of Detroit	5
June 7	4	Western Michigan	5
		Won 22 Lost 12	

1959

Mar. 26	10	Ft. Knox (A)	0
Mar. 27	2	Ft. Knox (A)	0
Mar. 28	8	Ft. Knox (A)	0
Mar. 30	2	Florida State (A)	5
Mar. 31	3	Illinois at Talla-hassee, Fla.	8
Apr. 1	1	Western Michigan at Tallahassee, Fla.	9
Apr. 2	7	Duke at Talla-hassee, Fla.	2
Apr. 2	8	Duke at Talla-hassee, Fla.	13
Apr. 3	1	Michigan at Talla-hassee, Fla.	0
Apr. 4	8	Florida State (A)	0
Apr. 11	1	Albion	0
Apr. 11	11	Albion	5

Dick Radatz, Spartan star who later achieved fame as major league reliefer.

174

		Left	
Apr. 15	26	Wayne State	6
Apr. 18	5	Univ. of Detroit	7
Apr. 21	1	Western Michigan	6
Apr. 24	3	Michigan (A)	2
Apr. 25	17	Michigan	12
Apr. 25	1	Michigan	2
May 1	5	Ohio State (A)	3
May 2	1	Indiana	6
May 2	3	Indiana	4
May 5	1	Notre Dame (A)	3
May 8	5	Wisconsin	3
May 9	8	Northwestern	6
May 9	3	Northwestern	8
May 12	6	Wayne State (A)	1
May 13	5	Notre Dame	4
May 15	6	Purdue (A)	3
May 16	2	Illinois (A)	8
May 16	4	Illinois (A)	1
May 20	8	Univ. of Detroit (A)	0
May 22	6	Minnesota	4
May 23	0	Iowa	2
May 23	1	Iowa	4
June 6	8	Western Michigan	0

Won 21   Lost 14

1960

Mar. 25	17	Virginia Tech. (A)	2
Mar. 26	1	Springfield Coll. at Camp LeJeune, N.C.	2
Mar. 27	5	Yale at Camp LeJeune, N.C.	7
Mar. 27	4	Camp LeJeune (A)	9
Mar. 28	10	Camp LeJeune (A)	9
Mar. 28	5	Camp LeJeune (A)	1
Mar. 29	2	North Carolina State (A)	1
Mar. 31	1	Wake Forest (A)	4
Apr. 2	10	Ohio Univ. (A)	7
Apr. 18	6	Albion	0
Apr. 19	5	Alma	1
Apr. 19	7	Alma	0
Apr. 22	9	Purdue	2
Apr. 23	1	Illinois	2
Apr. 23	1	Illinois	15
Apr. 29	6	Minnesota (A)	13
May 3	6	Western Michigan (A)	1
May 7	2	Michigan (A)	1
May 7	5	Michigan (A)	6
May 10	5	Notre Dame (A)	3
May 13	4	Ohio State	2
May 14	0	Indiana	3
May 14	2	Indiana	0
May 18	1	Notre Dame	8
May 20	0	Wisconsin	1
May 21	2	Northwestern (A)	3
May 23	5	Univ. of Detroit (A)	14
May 25	3	Central Michigan	2
May 28	4	Univ. of Detroit	2
June 6	6	Western Michigan	5

Won 17   Lost 13

1961

Mar. 23	6	Wilmington J.C. at Camp LeJeune, N.C.	8
Mar. 24	8	Camp LeJeune (A)	2
Mar. 25	0	Camp LeJeune (A)	7
Mar. 25	5	Wilmington J.C. at Camp LeJeune, N.C.	2
Mar. 26	5	Camp LeJeune (A)	4
Mar. 26	4	Fairleigh Dickinson at Camp LeJeune, N.C.	4
Mar. 27	8	Fairleigh Dickinson at Camp LeJeune, N.C.	2
Mar. 28	10	Newports News Tech. at Ft. Lee, Va.	2
Mar. 29	7	Ft. Lee (A)	2

Mar. 30	3	Rhode Island at Ft. Lee, Va.	2
Mar. 30	4	Ft. Lee (A)	0
Apr. 8	7	Alma	1
Apr. 8	7	Alma	2
Apr. 15	16	Albion	1
Apr. 15	1	Albion	0
Apr. 21	3	Iowa	2
Apr. 22	3	Minnesota	5
Apr. 22	0	Minnesota	3
Apr. 29	1	Michigan	5
Apr. 29	4	Michigan	6
Apr. 29	3	Michigan	4
May 4	6	Notre Dame (A)	3
May 6	6	Ohio State (A)	7
May 6	9	Ohio State (A)	3
May 12	11	Northwestern	8
May 13	4	Wisconsin	6
May 13	8	Wisconsin	4
May 17	11	Central Michigan	0
May 19	3	Illinois (A)	6
May 20	4	Purdue (A)	0
May 20	4	Purdue (A)	1
May 24	5	Notre Dame	4
May 27	11	Univ. of Detroit	13

Won 21   Lost 11   Tied 1

1962

Mar. 22	4	Camp LeJeune (A)	0
Mar. 23	9	Camp LeJeune (A)	5
Mar. 24	3	Camp LeJeune (A)	8
Mar. 25	2	Camp LeJeune (A)	6
Mar. 27	7	Ft. Lee (A)	3
Mar. 28	13	Ft. Lee (A)	0
Mar. 28	0	Ft. Lee (A)	4
Mar. 29	0	Massachusetts at Ft. Lee, Va.	6
Mar. 30	13	Ft. Belvoir (A)	9
Mar. 31	6	Ft. Belvoir (A)	4
Apr. 20	11	Purdue	5
Apr. 21	3	Illinois	11
Apr. 21	4	Illinois	5
Apr. 25	23	Alma	5
Apr. 25	14	Alma	2
Apr. 28	10	Iowa (A)	13
Apr. 28	7	Iowa (A)	5
May 4	13	Michigan	16
May 5	0	Michigan (A)	4
May 5	1	Michigan (A)	14
May 8	7	Univ. of Detroit (A)	3
May 11	3	Ohio State	6
May 12	4	Indiana	3
May 12	7	Indiana	4
May 14	16	Central Michigan (A)	,4
May 16	4	Notre Dame	0
May 18	0	Wisconsin (A)	4
May 19	12	Northwestern (A)	4
May 19	20	Northwestern (A)	3
May 23	11	Univ. of Detroit	16

Won 17   Lost 13

1963

Mar. 22	2	Camp LeJeune (A)	0
Mar. 23	9	Camp LeJeune (A)	2
Mar. 24	1	Camp LeJeune (A)	5
Mar. 25	5	Ithaca Coll. (N.Y.) at Camp LeJeune, N.C.	10
Mar. 26	25	Ft. Lee (A)	4
Mar. 26	5	Ft. Lee (A)	4
Mar. 27	16	Ft. Lee (A)	5
Mar. 28	9	Virginia (A)	5
Mar. 29	6	Richmond (A)	6
Mar. 30	10	George Washington Univ. (A)	2
Apr. 13	9	Albion	1
Apr. 13	2	Albion	1

Apr. 20	13	Wayne State	1
Apr. 20	10	Wayne State	3
Apr. 24	2	Central Michigan	1
Apr. 26	3	Purdue (A)	11
Apr. 27	4	Illinois (A)	8
Apr. 27	6	Illinois (A)	4
May 3	2	Minnesota	3
May 4	16	Iowa	8
May 6	3	Univ. of Detroit (A)	4
May 7	5	Western Michigan	9
May 10	3	Michigan (A)	4
May 11	3	Michigan	1
May 11	2	Michigan	4
May 15	6	Univ. of Detroit	0
May 17	2	Ohio State (A)	5
May 18	8	Indiana (A)	5
May 18	3	Indiana (A)	4
May 21	3	Western Michigan (A)	13
May 24	7	Wisconsin	12
May 25	3	Northwestern	5
May 25	7	Northwestern	3

Won 18   Lost 14   Tied 1

1964

Mar. 22	4	Virginia (A)	3
Mar. 25	10	Virginia Tech. (A)	6
Mar. 26	9	North Carolina State (A)	2
Mar. 27	6	Camp LeJeune (A)	3
Mar. 27	22	Camp LeJeune (A)	1
Mar. 28	12	Massachusetts at Camp LeJeune, N.C.	2
Mar. 30	9	Georgia Southern (A)	0
Mar. 31	5	Florida State (A)	10
Apr. 1	6	Florida State (A)	7
Apr. 2	10	Wake Forest at Tallahassee, Fla.	16
Apr. 8	11	Albion	3
Apr. 11	22	Hillsdale	5
Apr. 11	5	Hillsdale	4
Apr. 18	1	Central Michigan	0
Apr. 18	5	Central Michigan	1
Apr. 24	13	Northwestern (A)	7
Apr. 25	8	Wisconsin (A)	9
Apr. 25	2	Wisconsin (A)	1
Apr. 28	5	Univ. of Detroit	4
May 1	5	Illinois	2
May 2	5	purdue	4
May 2	3	Purdue	0
May 5	8	Notre Dame (A)	9
May 8	4	Iowa	5
May 9	1	Minnesota (A)	4
May 9	4	Minnesota (A)	7
May 16	3	Michigan (A)	6
May 16	1	Michigan (A)	4
May 18	3	Michigan	2
May 22	14	Indiana	6
May 23	7	Ohio State	8
May 23	3	Ohio State	1
May 26	8	Western Michigan (A)	7
May 26	2	Western Michigan (A)	6

Won 22   Lost 12

1965

Mar. 23	2	Miami at Coral Gables, Fla.	1
Mar. 23	1	Miami at Coral Gables, Fla.	2
Mar. 24	13	Miami at Coral Gables, Fla.	3
Mar. 25	8	Florida at Coral Gables, Fla.	3
Mar. 26	12	U.S. Military Academy at Coral Gables, Fla.	5
Mar. 27	2	Florida at Coral Gables, Fla.	7

Mar. 29	8	Florida State (A)	11
Mar. 30	2	Wake Forest at Tallahassee, Fla.	0
Mar. 30	11	Baltimore Orioles (Recruits) at Thomasville, Fla.	3
Apr. 1	4	Duke at Tallahasse, Fla.	0
Apr. 2	4	Duke at Tallahasse, Fla. (A)	2
Apr. 2	4	Wake Forest (A)	2
Apr. 3	6	Wake Forest at Tallahassee, Fla.	0
Apr. 10	7	Central Michigan	2
Apr. 10	3	Central Michigan	5
Apr. 17	12	Spring Arbor J.C.	0
Apr. 17	5	Spring Arbor J.C.	4
Apr. 20	8	Univ. of Detroit (A)	2
Apr. 23	10	Northwestern	1
Apr. 24	4	Wisconsin	5
Apr. 24	5	Wisconsin	1
Apr. 27	1	Univ. of Detroit	0
Apr. 30	4	Illinois (A)	5
May 1	8	Purdue (A)	4
May 1	0	Purdue (A)	1
May 7	4	Iowa	3
May 8	7	Minnesota	2
May 8	3	Minnesota	2
May 10	3	Notre Dame	0
May 11	20	Albion	1
May 14	6	Michigan (A)	3
May 15	1	Michigan	6
May 15	5	Michigan	4
May 17	8	Notre Dame (A)	6
May 18	3	Western Michigan at Lansing, Mich.	2
May 21	6	Indiana (A)	1
May 22	10	Ohio State (A)	13
May 22	0	Ohio State (A)	2
May 25	1	Western Michigan (A)	3

Won 28   Lost 11

1966

Mar. 21	3	Ohio State at Coral Gables, Fla.	0
Mar. 22	3	Ohio State at Coral Gables, Fla.	7
Mar. 23	2	Miami at Coral Gables, Fla.	6
Mar. 24	6	Miami at Coral Gables, Fla.	6
Mar. 24	4	U.S. Military Academy at Coral Gables, Fla.	7
Mar. 25	4	New York Univ. at Coral Gables, Fla.	3
Mar. 26	7	New York Univ. at Coral Gables, Fla.	2
Mar. 28	3	Wake Forest at Tallahassee, Fla.	7
Mar. 28	0	Florida State (A)	5
Mar. 29	1	Wake Forest at Tallahassee, Fla.	7
Mar. 29	7	Florida State (A)	6
Mar. 30	7	Rutgers at Tallahassee, Fla.	6
Mar. 30	4	Florida State (A)	5
Mar. 31	9	Wake Forest at Tallahassee, Fla.	8
Apr. 8	15	Ball State	4
Apr. 9	5	Ball State	9
Apr. 9	5	Ball State	1
Apr. 16	12	Univ. of Detroit	8
Apr. 16	7	Univ. of Detroit	1
Apr. 19	8	Albion	4
Apr. 22	0	Ohio State	2

176

Date		Opponent	
Apr. 23	1	Indiana	2
Apr. 29	4	Wisconsin (A)	2
Apr. 30	20	Northwestern (A)	4
Apr. 30	4	Northwestern (A)	6
May 3	10	Central Michigan (A)	4
May 3	4	Central Michigan (A)	0
May 6	5	Purdue	0
May 7	15	Illinois	6
May 7	6	Illinois	5
May 9	5	Notre Dame	0
May 14	4	Iowa (A)	2
May 14	1	Iowa (A)	0
May 16	7	Notre Dame	3
May 20	6	Michigan	5
May 21	1	Michigan (A)	2
May 21	3	Michigan (A)	5
May 24	3	Western Michigan (A)	0
	Won 24	Lost 13 Tied 1	

1967

Date		Opponent	
Mar. 20	5	Rutgers at Coral Gables, Fla.	8
Mar. 20	11	Miami at Coral Gables, Fla.	3
Mar. 21	5	Rutgers at Coral Gables, Fla.	2
Mar. 22	1	Miami at Coral Gables, Fla.	5
Mar. 23	9	U.S. Military Academy at Coral Gables, Fla.	4
Mar. 24	8	Italian National Champions at Coral Gables, Fla.	0
Mar. 25	1	Miami at Coral Gables, Fla.	2
Mar. 26	3	U.S. Military Academy at Coral Gables, Fla.	3
Mar. 27	10	Duke at Coral Gables, Fla.	1
Mar. 28	3	Duke at Coral Gables, Fla.	5
Mar. 29	8	Furman at Coral Gables, Fla.	0
Mar. 30	3	Duke at Coral Gables, Fla.	4
Mar. 31	4	Duke at Coral Gables, Fla.	12
Apr. 1	6	Wesleyan Univ. at Coral Gables, Fla.	0
Apr. 1	1	Miami at Coral Gables, Fla.	4
Apr. 8	4	Ball State (A)	6
Apr. 8	3	Ball State (A)	1
Apr. 11	1	Eastern Michigan	5
Apr. 11	2	Eastern Michigan	0
Apr. 14	9	Ohio State (A)	10
Apr. 14	2	Ohio State (A)	3
Apr. 15	6	Indiana (A)	10
Apr. 15	8	Indiana (A)	6
Apr. 18	7	Albion	0
Apr. 18	7	Albion	2
Apr. 25	4	Univ. of Detroit (A)	1
Apr. 25	0	Univ. of Detroit (A)	1
Apr. 28	0	Wisconsin	1
Apr. 28	10	Wisconsin	0
Apr. 29	11	Northwestern	0
Apr. 29	8	Northwestern	4
May 1	4	Univ. of Detroit	5
May 5	2	Purdue (A)	0
May 5	1	Purdue (A)	2
May 7	7	Illinois (A)	2
May 7	5	Illinois (A)	4
May 8	4	Central Michigan	3
May 8	2	Central Michigan	6
May 9	4	Notre Dame (A)	5

Date		Opponent	
May 12	0	Minnesota	7
May 12	4	Minnesota	2
May 13	0	Iowa	3
May 13	3	Iowa	4
May 16	7	Western Michigan	1
May 19	4	Michigan (A)	5
May 20	4	Michigan	6
	Won 22	Lost 23 Tied 1	

1968

Date		Opponent	
Mar. 18	9	Ohio State at Coral Gables, Fla.	4
Mar. 19	1	Miami at Coral Gables, Fla.	5
Mar. 20	17	Rutgers at Coral Gables, Fla.	3
Mar. 21	6	Ohio State at Coral Gables, Fla.	2
Mar. 22	11	U.S. Military Academy at Coral Gables, Fla.	3
Mar. 23	4	Miami at Coral Gables, Fla.	7
Mar. 25	9	Ohio State at Coral Gables, Fla.	7
Mar. 26	1	Western Michigan at Coral Gables, Fla.	2
Mar. 26	3	Miami at Coral Gables, Fla.	4
Mar. 27	5	Western Michigan at Coral Gables, Fla.	1

Coach Danny Litwhiler, former State player Ed Ciolek and scoreboard donated by ex-Spartan star Bruce Look.

Date	Score	Opponent	Score
Mar. 28	12	Wesleyan Univ. at Coral Gables, Fla.	1
Mar. 29	6	Western Michigan at Coral Gables, Fla.	0
Mar. 30	1	Miami at Coral Gables, Fla.	2
Apr. 6	2	Ball State (A)	1
Apr. 6	6	Ball State (A)	1
Apr. 13	5	Univ. of Detroit	1
Apr. 13	13	Univ. of Detroit	1
Apr. 17	6	Albion	2
Apr. 17	3	Albion	1
Apr. 23	15	Notre Dame (A)	2
Apr. 26	2	Michigan (A)	4
Apr. 26	1	Michigan (A)	4
Apr. 30	5	Eastern Michigan	1
Apr. 30	5	Eastern Michigan	0
May 3	4	Indiana	1
May 3	2	Indiana	1
May 4	4	Ohio State	0
May 4	8	Ohio State	2
May 7	6	Notre Dame	2
May 10	6	Northwestern (A)	0
May 10	12	Northwestern (A)	0
May 11	3	Wisconsin (A)	1
May 11	7	Wisconsin (A)	3
May 17	9	Illinois	0
May 17	3	Illinois	2
May 18	9	Purdue	0
May 18	1	Purdue	0
May 21	9	Western Michigan	11
May 24	5	Iowa (A)	2
May 24	4	Iowa (A)	4
May 25	2	Minnesota (A)	3
May 25	4	Minnesota (A)	10
May 28	7	Western Michigan (A)	4

Won 32   Lost 10   Tied 1

1969

Date	Score	Opponent	Score
Mar. 17	0	Miamia at Coral Gables, Fla.	11
Mar. 18	7	Miami at Coral Gables, Fla.	8
Mar. 19	10	Cincinnati at Coral Gables, Fla.	5
Mar. 20	9	Cincinnati at Coral Gables, Fla.	7
Mar. 21	1	Army at Coral Gables, Fla.	0
Mar. 22	0	Miami at Coral Gables, Fla.	3
Mar. 23	6	Cincinnati at Coral Gables, Fla.	2
Mar. 24	13	Pittsburgh at Coral Gables, Fla.	2
Mar. 25	6	Cincinnati at Coral Gables, Fla.	9
Mar. 27	16	Florida A&M at Coral Gables, Fla.	1
Mar. 28	5	Pittsburgh at Coral Gables, Fla.	7
Mar. 28	4	Miami at Coral Gables, Fla.	3
Mar. 29	5	Pittsburgh at Coral Gables, Fla.	3
Apr. 12	10	Detroit (A)	2
Apr. 12	2	Detroit (A)	1
Apr. 16	6	Albion	0
Apr. 16	4	Albion	0
Apr. 18	5	Michigan	4
Apr. 19	18	Michigan (A)	3
Apr. 24	2	Eastern Michigan	3
Apr. 26	7	Eastern Michigan (A)	5
Apr. 26	8	Eastern Michigan (A)	1
Apr. 29	5	Western Michigan	6

State's fine 1954 baseball team, coached by John Kobs, was winner of the school's first Big Ten team title.

May 2	1	Indiana (A)	5
May 2	2	Indiana (A)	3
May 3	1	Ohio State (A)	2
May 3	6	Ohio State (A)	7
May 6	17	Notre Dame (A)	12
May 10	1	Wisconsin	0
May 10	5	Wisconsin	2
May 13	0	Central Michigan	11
May 13	7	Central Michigan	5
May 16	0	Illinois (A)	1
May 16	0	Illinois (A)	1
May 17	2	Purdue (A)	6
May 17	6	Purdue (A)	1
May 20	3	Western Michigan (A)	4
May 23	5	Iowa	0
May 23	14	Iowa	5
May 24	5	Minnesota	2
May 24	0	Minnesota	9

Won 24   Lost 17

Tyler (Ty) Caplin, runner-up, National
Public Links Golf Tournament.

Gene Hunt, NCAA semi-finalist and loser
to Jack Nicklaus in 1961.

State's Forest Akers Golf Course looking towards northeast corner, with clubhouse and parking
area to right of center.

GOLF

Michigan State had its own golf course on the campus eight years before it sent a team into regular intercollegiate competition.

A nine-hole course was laid out in 1920 in the area just south of the Red Cedar river now occupied by Spartan Stadium, the Men's Intramural Building, Demonstration Hall, Jenison Field House and the huge parking lot between the stadium and Intramural Building and the river.

Varsity golf evolved, as did many other sports, through intramural activity. The first team to play a regular intercollegiate schedule was the 1928 aggregation. It did very well, considering it had no coach and tradition as a team, winning six meets and losing two. Members of that team which played its home matches at Lansing Country Club were Capt. William Connellan, H. G. Minier, L. M. Cook, G. H. Campbell, Jack DeLair and L. B. Haigh.

Golf was placed on a minor sport basis in 1930 and in 1931 the first major award was given in the sport to Minier. The team continued to play its matches at one or another of three local courses: Groesbeck, a Lansing public course, Lansing Country Club and Walnut Hills Country Club, until the University's Forest Akers Golf Course was completed in 1958. This splendid 18-hole layout and the adjoining nine-hole course which came along later were given to Michigan State by Forest Akers, a distinguished alumnus and long-time member of the University's Board of Trustees and automotive executive.

State's first golf coach was Harry Kipke, better known as a football mentor. Another head football coach, Jim Crowley, succeeded him in 1930 and Ben VanAlstyne came on in 1932. VanAlstyne held the post along with basketball for many years. He relinquished his basketball duties after the 1949 season, but kept going with golf until his retirement in 1961. John Brotzmann picked up the reins then and held them until the current coach, Bruce Fossum, took over in 1966.

State's golf experience has been solidly successful. There have been only a dozen losing seasons in 42, as well as some really big ones, such as the unbeaten one, 12-0-1, of 1962 and an 11-1 in 1959.

The form of intercollegiate golf has changed drastically in the last decade. Schedules of dual meets and occasional triangulars or quadrangulars were transformed in only a few years to a series of weekend tournaments involving as many as 25 college teams at one time. One of the biggest and most prestigious of these is the annual Spartan Invitational which started in 1966 with eight teams and grew to 25 teams in 1969 and 1970. There were no dual meets at all on the 1969 and 1970 schedules.

State has won one Big Ten team title, in 1969, and has finished second twice and third three times. In five seasons, 1966-1970, it won 10 of the popular regular season tournaments.

Perhaps as good a barometer as any of the quality of golf played by Spartan athletes through the years is the fact that they have won 11 Michigan amateur golf titles. They are: Denny Vass, 1970; Lynn Janson, 1968; Robert Meyer, 1966; Dennis Hankey, 1964; Don Stevens, 1960; Glenn Johnson, 1954, 1955, 1956, 1958, and 1961; and Reggie Myles Jr., 1946.

SPARTAN TEAM RECORDS

RECORD BY SEASON
Dual Meets

	W	L	T
1927-28	6	2	0
1928-29	4	1	0
1929-30	7	2	0
1930-31	6	4	0
1931-32	5	4	0
1932-33	5	4	1
1933-34	2	8	0
1934-35	4	4	1
1935-36	7	3	0
1936-37	5	4	0
1937-38	7	1	0
1938-39	5	3	0
1939-40	5	3	1
1940-41	5	3	0
1941-42	3	4	1
1942-43	3	4	1
1943-44	No schedule—		
	World War II		
1944-45	0	6	0
1945-46	7	5	0
1946-47	4	6	0
1947-48	6	6	0
1948-49	3	5	0
1949-50	4	6	0
1950-51	10	3	0
1951-52	5	5	0
1952-53	5	5	1
1953-54	7	4	0
1954-55	4	7	0
1955-56	4	5	0
1956-57	8	6	0
1957-58	6	2	1
1958-59	11	1	0
1959-60	9	1	0
1960-61	10	3	1
1961-62	12	0	1
1962-63	7	4	1
1963-64	7	12	0
1964-65	5	12	0
1965-66	0	1	0
1966-67	4	1	0
1967-68	2	0	0
	219	160	10

RECORD BY OPPONENT

	W	L	T
Aquinas College	1	0	0
Central Michigan	1	0	0
Detroit City Coll.	7	1	0
Detroit Coll. of Law	2	0	0
Detroit J.C.	0	1	0
University of Detroit	42	13	2
Eastern Michigan	10	1	1
Flint J.C.	2	0	0
Grand Rapids J.C.	12	4	0
Hillsdale	4	0	0
Illinois State	1	0	0
Illinois	9	2	1
Indiana	3	9	0
Iowa	5	1	0
Marquette	9	0	0
Mars Hill College	1	0	0
Michigan	15	47	3
Minnesota	3	0	0
New Haven College	1	0	0
Northern Illinois	2	1	0
Northwestern	13	11	2
Notre Dame	11	25	0
Ohio State	6	16	0
Ohio	0	1	0
Purdue	3	13	0
St. Johns	2	0	0
Southern Illinois	2	0	0
Tri State	1	0	0
U. of Toledo	2	1	0
Wayne State	17	5	0
Western Illinois	0	1	0
Western Michigan	15	1	0
Wisconsin	15	7	1
Wofford College	1	0	0
Western Reserve	1	0	0
	219	160	10

SPARTAN COACHES' RECORDS

Coach	Years	W	L	T	Pct.
(No Coach)	1928	6	2	0	.750
Harry G. Kipke	1929	4	1	0	.800
James H. Crowley	1930-1931	13	6	0	.684
Benjamin F. VanAlstyne	1932-1959	140	117	7	.581
John Brotzmann	1960-1965	50	32	3	.606
Bruce Fossum	1966-1968	6	2	0	.750
		219	160	10	.576

IN-SEASON TOURNAMENTS

Indiana University Invitational at Bloomington, Indiana

Apr. 13, 1963	5th	10 teams
Apr. 13, 1968	2nd	3 teams
Apr. 24-25, 1970	1st	12 teams
	(Lee Edmundson—co-medalist)	

Michigan State University Invitational at East Lansing, Michigan

Apr. 30, 1966	1st	4 teams
	(Kenneth C. Benson—medalist)	
Apr. 27, 1968	2nd	4 teams

Northern Intercollegiate Invitational

May 6-7, 1966 at Bloomington, Ind.	4th	13 teams
May 5-6, 1967 at Ann Arbor, Mich.	5th	15 teams
May 3-4, 1968 at East Lansing, Mich.	3rd	13 teams
May 2-3, 1969 at Columbus, Ohio	3rd	15 teams
May 1-2, 1970 at Champaign, Ill.	4th	15 teams

Ohio State (Robert Kepler) University Invitational

Apr. 16, 1966	4th	4 teams
Apr. 15, 1967	4th	6 teams
Apr. 20, 1968	4th	6 teams
	(Steve R. Benson—medalist)	
Apr. 11-12, 1969	4th	14 teams

Purdue University Invitational at Lafayette, Indiana

Apr. 16, 1966	4th	4 teams
Apr. 13, 1967	2nd	5 teams
Apr. 20, 1968	5th	6 teams
Apr. 26, 1969	1st	6 teams

Red Fox Country Club Invitational at Tryon, North Carolina

Mar. 22-23, 1967	1st	7 teams
	(Larry Murphy—medalist)	
Mar. 22-24, 1968	8th (tie)	13 teams
Mar. 19-21, 1969	5th	12 teams
Mar. 25-27, 1970	6th	12 teams

Spartan Invitational at East Lansing, Mich.

May 3, 1966	1st	8 teams
	(Albert A. Thiess—medalist)	
May 12-13, 1967	1st	11 teams
	(Steve R. Benson—medalist)	
May 10-11, 1968	2nd	10 teams
May 9-10-, 1969	4th	25 teams
May 8-9, 1970	1st	25 teams

University of Iowa Invitational at Iowa City, Iowa

Apr. 23, 1967	3rd	4 teams

University of Miami Invitational at Coral Gables, Florida

1964	8th	
Mar. 23-26, 1966	9th	35 teams

University of Notre Dame Invitational at Notre Dame

May 9, 1966	2nd	4 teams

University of Wisconsin Invitational at Madison, Wisconsin

May 1, 1967	1st (tie)	3 teams
Apr. 21, 1969	1st	4 teams

Palmetto Invitational at Greenville, S.C.

Mar. 27-29, 1969	6th	17 teams

Illinois Invitational at Champaign, Ill.

Apr. 19, 1969	4th	13 teams

THE FOREST AKERS GOLF COURSE

NAMED IN HONOR OF AN ALUMNUS, GREAT FRIEND, AND GENEROUS BENEFACTOR OF MICHIGAN STATE UNIVERSITY, WHO WAS A MEMBER OF ITS GOVERNING BOARD FOR 18 YEARS, AND CONTRIBUTED BEYOND ESTIMATION TO ITS GROWTH AND DEVELOPMENT AS A WORLD CENTER OF LEARNING WHERE PHYSICAL FITNESS AND KEEN ATHLETIC COMPETITION HAVE THEIR PROPER PLACES IN THE TOTAL EDUCATION OF YOUNG AMERICANS.

A commemorative plaque, located near the clubhouse, honors the late Forest Akers, class of 1909, who donated the course.

Apr. 17-18, 1970   1st   15 teams
(Lynn Janson and
Rick Woulfe—
were two of three
co-medalists)

Cape Coral Invitational at Ft. Myers, Fla.
Apr. 1-3, 1970   8th   40 teams

Miami (Ohio) Invitational at Oxford, Ohio
Apr. 20, 1970   2nd   12 teams

POST-SEASON TOURNAMENTS

Big Ten Championship Results

Year	Place	Strokes
1951	6th	1,567
1952	10th	1,661
1953	10th	1,586
1954	8th	1,576
1955	7th	1,204
1956	6th (tie)	1,549
1957	7th	1,564
1958	6th	1,572
1959	7th	1,615
1960	2nd	1,520
1961	3rd	1,539
1962	7th	1,541
1963	7th (tie)	1,562
1964	7th	1,534
1965	7th	1,540
1966	4th (tie)	1,519
1967	3rd	1,583
1968	2nd	1,523
1969	1st	1,501
1970	3rd	1,561

Top Spartan Finishers (Big Ten)

1951	Carl Mosack	10th (Tie)-304
1956	Ken Rodewald	4th (Tie)-297
1960	C. A. Smith	3rd-296
	Ty Caplin	9th (Tie)-305
1961	C. A. Smith	6th-305
1964	Phil Marston	6th (Tie)-298
1967	Larry Murphy	6th (Tie)-310
	John Bailey	10th (Tie)-314
1968	Steve Benson	4th-297
	Lynn Janson	7th-200
1969	Lynn Janson	3rd-298
	Rick Woulfe	6th-301
	Lee Edmundson	7th (Tie)-302
1970	Lynn Janson	4th (Tie)-306

NCAA Championship Results

1939	21st	657
1940	9th	620
1941	7th (Tie)	615
1942	11th	625
1943	(No tournament)	
1944	5th	344
1946	10th	644
1956	17th	623
1960	19th (Tie)	631
1961	6th	603
1967	6th (Tie)	598
1968	9th	1,175
1969	13th	1,260

Top Spartan Finishers (NCAA)

1961
Gene Hunt lost to Jack Nicklaus (Ohio State), 2 and 1, in semifinals.

Al Badger lost to Mike Podolski (Ohio State), 1 up (19 holes), in third round.

YEAR-BY-YEAR RECORDS

1928
No Coach

May 9	3	Flint J.C. (A)	0
May 11	3	Grand Rapids J.C. (A)	1
May 12	2½	Detroit (A)	12½
May 17	13	Detroit Law (A)	5
May 21	16½	Grand Rapids J.C.	1½
May 22	9	Flint J.C.	0
May 25	½	Detroit	14½
May 29	8	Detroit Law	4
		Won 6 Lost 2	

1929
Harry G. Kipke, Coach

May 8	9	Grand Rapids J.C. (A)	6
May 16	10½	Detroit City Coll. (A)	4½
May 17	3	Detroit (A)	12
May 22	12	Grand Rapids J.C.	3
May 29	7	Detroit City Coll.	5
		Won 4 Lost 1	

1930
James H. Crowley, Coach

May 2	9½	Grand Rapids J.C.	8½
May 3	13½	St. Johns (Toledo)	4½
May 7	1	Michigan (A)	17
May 8	8	Detroit (A)	10
May 9	12	St. Johns (A)	6
May 17	11½	Detroit City Coll. (A)	6½
May 24	15	Grand Rapids J.C. (A)	3
May 29	12	Detroit	9
May 31	9½	Detroit City Coll.	8½
		Won 7 Lost 2	

1931

Apr. 17	½	Notre Dame	17½
Apr. 25	,3	Michigan	15
May 1	12	Grand Rapids J.C.	6
May 2	14	Detroit City Coll.	4
May 8	15½	Detroit	2½
May 9	3½	Notre Dame (A)	17½
May 15	15½	Grand Rapids J.C. (A)	2½
May 29	10	Detroit City Coll. (A)	8
May 30	6½	Detroit (A)	11½
June 3	12	Eastern Michigan	6
		Won 6 Lost 4	

1932
Benjamin F. Van Alstyne, Coach

Apr. 23	2½	Michigan (A)	24½
Apr. 30	5	Notre Dame	13
May 7	3½	Grand Rapids J.C. (A)	14½
May 14	7½	Detroit City Coll.	10½
May 16	11½	Detroit	6½
May 20	11	Grand Rapids J.C.	10
May 27	9½	Detroit City Coll. (A)	8½
May 28	9½	Detroit (A)	8½
June 4	11	Eastern Michigan (A)	7
		Won 5 Lost 4	

1933

Apr. 29	,3	Michigan (A)	24
May 5	9	Detroit	9
May 6	1	Notre Dame (A)	17
May 12	12	Grand Rapids J.C. (A)	0
May 16	2	Michigan	25

May 19	9½	Eastern Michigan (A)	8½
May 20	13½	Detroit (A)	4½
May 25	10	Eastern Michigan	8
May 26	12½	Grand Rapids J.C.	5½
June 2	6½	Detroit J.C.	11½
		Won 5 Lost 4 Tied 1	

1934
Apr. 21	0	Michigan (A)	27
Apr. 24	3	Grand Rapids J.C.	15
May 5	14½	Detroit	3½
May 12	4½	Wayne State	13½
May 18	3½	Detroit (A)	11½
May 19	1	Wayne State (A)	17
May 22	7½	Grand Rapids J.C. (A)	10½
May 26	½	Michigan	26½
May 29	8½	Eastern Michigan (A)	9½
June 4	13½	Eastern Michigan	4½
		Won 2 Lost 8	

1935
Apr. 20	3½	Michigan	32½
May 4	12½	Wayne State (A)	5½
May 6	9½	Grand Rapids J.C.	8½
May 10	7	Grands Rapids J.C. (A)	11
May 17	4½	Notre Dame	7½
May 18	1	Michigan (A)	26
May 22	12	Eastern Michigan	6
May 25	11½	Wayne State	6½
June 1	9	Eastern Michigan (A)	9
		Won 4 Lost 4 Tied 1	

1936
Apr. 25	5	Michigan (A)	19
May 2	8	Western State (A)	4
May 8	10½	Western Michigan	1½
May 9	14	Wayne State	4
May 16	12½	Eastern Michigan	5½
May 18	3½	Notre Dame (A)	8½
May 23	9	Ohio State (A)	3
May 29	10	Michigan	10½
June 5	14	Eastern Michigan (A)	4
June 6	11	Wayne State (A)	7
		Won 7 Lost 3	

1937
Apr. 30	18	Marquette (A)	0
May 1	8	Northwestern (A)	10
May 5	6	Michigan (A)	12
May 7	9½	Wayne State (A)	8½
May 8	15½	Toledo (A)	2½
May 15	12½	Marquette	5½
May 17	4	Notre Dame (A)	14
May 24	7½	Michigan	10½
May 29	16½	Wayne State	1½
		Won 5 Lost 4	

1938
Apr. 23	11½	Michigan (A)	6½
Apr. 30	13½	Wayne State (A)	4½
May 2	16½	Western Reserve (A)	1½
May 7	9½	Northwestern	8½
May 13	18	Wayne State	0
May 14	14½	Michigan	3½
May 21	11	Notre Dame	7
May 30	8½	Ohio State (A)	9½
		Won 7 Lost 1	

1939
Apr. 24	6½	Northwestern (A)	11½
Apr. 28	4½	Toledo (A)	13½
Apr. 29	14½	Wayne State (A)	3½
May 3	10	Michigan (A)	8
May 5	8	Ohio State	10
May 12	18	Toledo	0
May 13	10	Wayne State	8
May 22	11½	Michigan	6½
		Won 5 Lost 3	

1940
Apr. 20	3	Michigan (A)	15
Apr. 27	12½	Ohio State (A)	5½
Apr. 29	16½	Wayne State (A)	1½
May 4	16½	Northwestern	1½
May 10	8½	Indiana (A)	9½
May 11	14	Purdue (A)	4
May 13	7½	Notre Dame	10½
May 17	9	Michigan	9
May 20	18	Wayne State	0
		Won 5 Lost 3 Tied 1	

1941
Apr. 19	5	Ohio State (A)	13
Apr. 26	6	Michigan (A)	12
May 3	26	Detroit	1
May 9	10½	Notre Dame (A)	16½
May 10	15½	Northwestern (A)	11½
May 12	14½	Marquette (A)	12½
May 17	24	Detroit (A)	3
May 23	19	Michigan	8
		Won 5 Lost 3	

1942
Apr. 25	7	Michigan	17
May 5	13	Detroit	8
May 9	13½	Ohio State	22½
May 13	7½	Michigan (A)	7½
May 16	5½	Northwestern at Ann Arbor, Mich.	15½
May 16	13	Indiana at Ann Arbor, Mich.	5
May 23	13½	Detroit (A)	7½
June 5	12	Notre Dame	15
		Won 3 Lost 4 Tied 1	

The 14th hole at Forest Akers, known to Spartan golfers as "Cardiac Hill."

1943

Date		Opponent	
Apr. 24	2½	Michigan (A)	12½
Apr. 24	7	Notre Dame at Ann Arbor, Mich.	8
May 1	3	Notre Dame (A)	18
May 10	4½	Northwestern (A)	13½
May 15	10½	Detroit (A)	7½
May 22	9	Detroit	9
May 29	17	Eastern Michigan	1
June 5	12	Eastern Michigan (A)	6
		Won 3 Lost 4 Tied 1	

1944

Intercollegiate sports dropped because of World War II.

1945

Date		Opponent	
May 4	5	Wayne State (A)	16
May 5	6½	Detroit (A)	11½
May 12	0	Ohio State (A)	12
May 12	5½	Detroit at Columbus, Ohio	6½
May 16	6½	Wayne State	11½
May 19	6	Detroit	12
		Lost 6	

1946

Date		Opponent	
Apr. 20	3	Michigan (A)	24
Apr. 27	23½	Detroit	3½
Apr. 29	20	Marquette	4
May 6	6	Northwestern	21
May 8	20	Michigan	7
May 10	21	Detroit (A)	6
May 13	15	Wayne State (A)	12
May 18	2	Ohio State	25
May 27	14½	Detroit at Lafayette, Ind.	½
May 27	9	Purdue (A)	18
May 31	8	Notre Dame	10
May 31	10	Wayne State	8
		Won 7 Lost 5	

1947

Date		Opponent	
Apr. 19	8	Ohio State (A)	22
Apr. 25	21	Wayne State (A)	15
Apr. 30	13	Michigan (A)	23
May 3	6½	Notre Dame (A)	20½
May 5	12½	Northwestern (A)	14½
May 10	8	Purdue	19
May 10	15	Detroit	3
May 14	10½	Michigan	16½
May 17	22½	Detroit (A)	10½
May 28	19	Wayne State	8
		Won 4 Lost 6	

1948

Date		Opponent	
Apr. 26	18½	Western Michigan	26½
May 1	23½	Detroit	3½
May 3	7	Michigan (A)	23
May 5	23½	Western Michigan (A)	21½
May 8	14	Ohio State	13
May 15	20½	Marquette (A)	6½
May 17	7	Wisconsin (A)	11
May 20	14	Michigan	16
May 22	25	Detroit (A)	2
May 24	10½	Notre Dame	19½
May 26	7½	Wayne State (A)	19½
May 28	22½	Wayne State	4½
		Won 6 Lost 6	

1949

Date		Opponent	
Apr. 16	4	Ohio State (A)	32
Apr. 19	18	Wisconsin	15
Apr. 30	4	Detroit (A)	23
May 2	5½	Michigan	19½
May 7	16	Detroit	11
May 13	14½	Illinois	12½
May 16	5	Notre Dame (A)	22
May 24	0	Michigan (A)	18
		Won 3 Lost 5	

1950

Date		Opponent	
Apr. 22	35½	Western Michigan (A)	32
Apr. 24	36½	Western Michigan	2½
Apr. 26	10	Detroit (A)	17
Apr. 29	9½	Illinois (A)	20½
May 3	11½	Michigan (A)	15½
May 5	20	Wisconsin (A)	7
May 13	9	Purdue	18
May 18	11½	Michigan	15½
May 22	11	Notre Dame	16
May 27	18½	Detroit	8½
		Won 4 Lost 6	

1951

Date		Opponent	
Apr. 21	35	Western Michigan (A)	4
Apr. 21	21	Marquette at Kalamazoo, Mich.	6
Apr. 28	37	Western Michigan	2
May 1	15	Detroit (A)	12
May 5	11½	Michigan	24½
May 5	26	Illinois	10
May 7	17	Detroit	10
May 12	6½	Michigan (A)	29½
May 12	5½	Ohio State at Ann Arbor, Mich.	30½
May 14	19	Wisconsin	8
May 18	15	Notre Dame (A)	12
May 19	462	Northwestern (A)	465
May 19	462	Minnesota at Evanston, III	470
		Won 10 Lost 3	

1952

Date		Opponent	
Apr. 19	23½	Western Michigan	3½
Apr. 26	14½	Western Michigan (A)	12½
May 3	17	Detroit (A)	10
May 5	17	Detroit	10
May 7	11	Michigan	16
May 16	11	Illinois (A)	16
May 16	12½	Wisconsin (A)	14½
May 17	21½	Marquette (A)	5½
May 24	2	Michigan (A)	16½
May 26	13½	Notre Dame	16½
		Won 5 Lost 5	

1953

Date		Opponent	
Apr. 18	23	Western Michigan	13
Apr. 25	12½	Detroit (A)	14½
Apr. 27	19	Detroit	8
May 2	13½	Northwestern (A)	13½
May 4	14	Notre Dame (A)	13
May 9	32½	Marquette	3½
May 9	16½	Michigan	19½
May 16	6	Purdue at Ann Arbor, Mich.	30
May 16	3½	Ohio State at Ann Arbor, Mich.	32½
May 16	6½	Michigan (A)	29½
May 18	15½	Wisconsin (A)	11½
		Won 5 Lost 5 Tied 1	

1954

Date		Opponent	
Apr. 16	17½	Western Michigan (A)	9½
Apr. 19	15½	Detroit	11½
May 3	15½	Notre Dame	11½
May 7	16	Wisconsin (A)	11
May 8	25	Marquette (A)	2
May 10	12½	Northwestern	14½
May 13	20½	Western Michigan	6½
May 15	5½	Ohio State at Ann Arbor, Mich.	30½

Late, Great golf pro Horton Smith gets driving instructions from Biggie Munn on site of what is now Forest Akers Golf Course. MSU course planners watch.

May 15	15	Michigan (A)	21
May 17	17	Michigan	19
May 22	16	Detroit (A)	11
		Won 7 Lost 4	

1955

Apr. 16	7½	Purdue (A)	28½
Apr. 16	10½	Wisconsin at Lafayette, Ind.	25½
Apr. 16	15½	Detroit at Lafayette, Ind.	20½
Apr. 20	10	Michigan (A)	26
Apr. 26	14½	Michigan	21½
Apr. 30	15½	Detroit	2½
May 2	21½	Detroit	5½
May 9	20	Wisconsin	16
May 14	5	Northwestern	31
May 14	17½	Illinois	18½
May 16	20½	Notre Dame (A)	15½
		Won 4 Lost 7	

1956

Apr. 14	12	Purdue (A)	24
Apr. 14	22½	Illinois at Lafayette, Ind.	13½
Apr. 14	27½	Detroit at Lafayette, Ind.	8½
Apr. 21	12	Michigan (A)	24
Apr. 28	17½	Detroit	9½
May 7	20	Wisconsin (A)	7
May 14	13½	Northwestern	14
May 19	8½	Michigan (A)	20½
May 21	9½	Notre Dame	13
		Won 4 Lost 5	

1957

Apr. 26	13½	Wisconsin	22½
Apr. 26	26½	Detroit	9½
May 4	16	Notre Dame at Bloomington, Ind.	20
May 4	22½	Iowa at Bloomington, Ind.	13½
May 4	26	Detroit at Bloomington, Ind.	10
May 6	16½	Notre Dame at Evanston, Ill.	19½
May 6	18½	Iowa at Evanston, Ill.	17½

May 6	21½	Northestern (A)	14½
May 11	9	Ohio State at Ann Arbor, Mich.	27
May 11	9½	Purdue at Ann Arbor, Mich.	26½
May 11	11½	Michigan (A)	24½
May 13	26½	Michigan	9½
May 18	30	Detroit	6
May 18	19½	Michigan	16½
		Won 8 Lost 6	

1958

Apr. 26	18	Northwestern	6
May 3	31	Detroit	5
May 3	23	Notre Dame	13
May 10	18	Illinois at Bloomington, Ind.	18
May 10	6	Indiana (A)	30
May 12	25	Northwestern at Madison, Wis.	10
May 12	15½	Wisconsin (A)	20½
May 17	32	Detroit (A)	4
May 17	28½	Michigan at Detroit, Mich.	7½
		Won 6 Lost 2 Tied 1	

1959

Apr. 25	12	Western Michigan	9
Apr. 25	14	Central Michigan	4
May 2	21	Northwestern (A)	15
May 2	18½	Wisconsin at Evanston, Ill.	17½
May 2	20	Notre Dame at Evanston, Ill.	16
May 4	39	Notre Dame (A)	18
May 4	27½	Iowa at Notre Dame	8½
May 9	15½	Indiana	20½
May 9	27	Detroit	9
May 16	19½	Michigan at Detroit, Mich.	16½
May 16	23	Wisconsin at Detroit, Mich.	13
May 16	32	Detroit (A)	4
		Won 11 Lost 1	

1960
John Brotzmann, Coach

Apr. 15	18½	Western Michigan (A)	5½
Apr. 23	16½	Detroit	4½
Apr. 30	15	Hillsdale	3
May 2	26½	Northestern	9½
May 2	27	Wisconsin	15
May 7	26½	Illinois	9½
May 7	14	Purdue	22
May 14	29½	Michigan	12½
May 14	22	Iowa	14
May 16	18½	Notre Dame	17½

Won 9   Lost 1

1961

Apr. 8	16	Detroit	2
Apr. 22	13	Hillsdale Coll.	5
Apr. 29	904	Northwestern (A)	904
Apr. 29	904	Wisconsin at at Evanston, Ill.	953
May 1	962	Notre Dame at Madison, Wis	974
May 1	962	Wisconsin (A)	979
May 1	920	Northwestern at Madison, Wis.	988
May 6	920	Purdue (A)	912
May 6	920	Ohio State at Lafayette, Ind.	946
May 6	920	Indiana at Lafayette, Ind.	960
May 8	925	Northern Illinois	994
May 13	949	Michigan (A)	925
May 13	949	Ohio State at Ann Arbor, Mich.	927
May 15	928	Illinois	982

Won 10   Lost 3   Tied 1

1962

Apr. 14	23½	Illinois (A)	12½
Apr. 14	29	Illinois State at Champaign, Ill.	7
Apr. 21	30	Hillsdale Coll.	6
Apr. 21	22	Aquinas Coll. (Grand Rapids)	14
Apr. 21	18	Detroit	0
Apr. 30	21½	Notre Dame (A)	14½
Apr. 30	17	Tri-State Coll. at Notre Dame	1
Apr. 30	27½	Southern Illinois at Notre Dame	8½
May 5	30	Wisconsin	24
May 7	22½	Northwestern	13½
May 12	21	Ohio State at Ann Arbor, Mich.	15
May 12	24	Purdue at Ann Arbor, Mich.	12
May 12	11½	Michigan (A)	11½

Won 12   Tied 1

1963

Apr. 20	45	Hillsdale Coll.	3
Apr. 27	15½	Ohio State	20½
Apr. 27	16	Northern Illinois	14
Apr. 27	20½	Notre Dame	15½
May 4	14½	Michigan	17½
May 10	15	Wisconsin (A)	15
May 10	14	Indiana at Madison, Wis.	16
May 10	16	Purdue at Madison, Wis.	14
May 11	770	Illinois at Evanston, Ill.	804
May 11	770	Indiana at Evanston, Ill.	775
May 11	770	Northwestern (A)	779
May 14	6	Michigan (A)	21

Won 7   Lost 4   Tied 1

First Spartan golf team to win a Big Ten title was 1969 squad which included, l. to r., Larry Murphy, Graham Cooke, Rick Woulfe, Lynn Janson, Denny Vass, Lee Edmondson and Coach Bruce Fossum.

1964

Date		Opponent	
Apr. 11	20	Ohio State (A)	16
Apr. 11	16	Ohio at Columbus, Ohio	20
Apr. 13	31½	Western Michigan at Notre Dame	5½
Apr. 13	11½	Notre Dame (A)	24½
Apr. 13	12½	Western Illinois at Notre Dame	23½
Apr. 25	16	Purdue (A)	32
May 2	912	Northwestern	926
May 2	1072	Indiana	1067
May 2	1390	Michigan	1407
May 2	912	Wisconsin	950
May 9	807	Notre Dame at Iowa City, Ia.	779
May 9	807	Indiana at Iowa City, Ia.	784
May 9	807	Northwestern at Iowa City, Ia.	791
May 9	807	Iowa (A)	793
May 9	807	Wisconsin at Iowa City, Ia.	802
May 9	807	Illinois at Iowa City, Ia.	812
May 9	807	Minnesota at Iowa City, Ia.	815
May 16	17½	Northern Illinois	18½
May 18	711	Michigan (A)	706

Won 7   Lost 12

1965

Date		Opponent	
Apr. 17	10½	Indiana at Columbus, Ohio	25
Apr. 17	11½	Purdue at Columbus, Ohio	24½
Apr. 17	10½	Ohio State (A)	25½
Apr. 26	20	Southern Illinois at Madison, Wis.	16
Apr. 26	17½	Wisconsin (A)	18½
May 8	775	Purdue	763
May 8	775	Ohio State	756
May 8	775	Michigan	772
May 8	775	Notre Dame	762
May 8	775	Indiana	762
May 15	771	Wisconsin at Lafayette, Ind.	783
May 15	771	Minnesota at Lafayette, Ind.	804
May 15	771	Indiana at Lafayette, Ind.	752
May 15	771	Illinois at Lafayette, Ind.	804
May 15	771	Purdue (A)	738
May 15	771	Northerwestern at Lafayette, Ind.	784
May 17	557	Michigan (A)	530

Won 5   Lost 12

1966

Bruce Fossum, Coach

Date		Opponent	
May 12	623	Michigan (A)	620

Lost 1

1967

Date		Opponent	
Mar. 24	12½	Wofford College (A)	11½
Mar. 24	15	New Haven Coll. (Conn.) at Spartanburg, S.C.	9
Mar. 24	15	Mars Hill Coll. at Spartanburg, S.C.	3
May 3	654	Michigan (A)	627
May 10	620	Michigan	627

Won 4   Lost 1

1968

Date		Opponent	
Apr. 24	719	Michigan (A)	730
May 8	618	Michigan	638

Won 2

1969

No dual meets

1970

No dual meets

Aerial view from the east of Forest Akers Golf Course, with nine-hole East course in foreground and 18-hole West layout beyond.

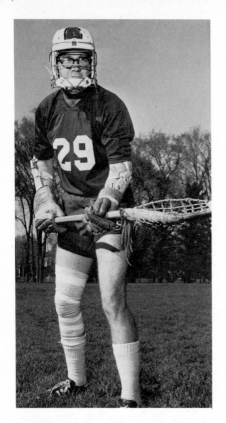

Rick Bays, midfieldman and second leading scorer in 1970.

Doug Kalvelage, attackman, top scorer in State's first varsity season.

The Spartans on the attack against Wittenberg in 1970 game action.

LACROSSE

Lacrosse is Michigan State's first new varsity sport since soccer came on the scene in 1956. The old American Indian game was graduated to varsity sports status in 1970 after a successful run of seven years as a club activity associated with the men's intramural sports program.

Robert Kauffman, a 1966 Michigan State graduate, coached the club team in 1968 and 1969 and then became the sport's first varsity coach.

A 10-game schedule was played in the spring of 1970 and the results were as might have been expected. The new, inexperienced team was walloped nine times, frequently by top-heavy scores. It scored its lone victory over Notre Dame, the first varsity lacrosse win in State's history, a 9-8 triumph. It also played strong games against Michigan and Chicago.

The former varsity football practice field on Shaw Lane, just south of the varsity tennis courts, became the lacrosse practice area. The team played three of its five home games on the new artificial turf of Spartan Stadium and the other two on its practice field. The practice field became available for lacrosse because, with the installation of artificial turf in Spartan Stadium in 1969, all varsity football practices were conducted in the stadium.

The first Spartan to show star potential was Doug Kalvelage, a 5-8, 150-pound sophomore from Grosse Pointe Woods. He led State scorers in 1970 with 15 points on nine goals and six assists.

Lacrosse at State may prove to be an historic precedent in the annals of sport here and at other schools. It was elevated to varsity status at a time of such economic stress nationally that many schools were eliminating sports, not adding new ones. The key was that lacrosse was made varsity on a low-budget basis, with no grants-in-aid, limited travel funds and other economies. It could set a pattern that other sports will follow.

FIRST LACROSSE LETTERWINNERS

Letterwinners on Michigan State's first varsity lacrosse team were: Richard Bays, midfieldman; John Beach, midfieldman; Thomas Bowman, midfieldman; Thomas Condit, midfieldman; Daniel Denov, attackman; Emery Freeman, midfieldman; John Herrmann, goalie; Andrew Homa, midfieldman; Douglas Kalvelage, attackman; Jon Keene, defenseman; John Kelley, attackman; Charles Kronk, defenseman; Stephen Lee, attackman; Joseph McClain, midfieldman; Michael Moody, midfieldman; Kenneth Richardson, attackman; Paul Safran, defenseman; Robert Stevenson, midfieldman; Frank Stobinski, defenseman, James Venia, midfieldman.

FIRST-YEAR RECORD

1970

Robert Kauffman, Coach

Date		Opponent	
Apr. 4	8	Michigan L.C.	18
Apr. 8	2	Kenyon (A)	10
Apr. 11	0	Ohio State (A)	13
Apr. 15	5	Michigan L.C. (A)	13
Apr. 17	2	Denison (A)	25
Apr. 21	7	Oberlin	14
Apr. 25	9	Notre Dame L.C. (A)	8
Apr. 29	0	Bowling Green	12
May 9	5	Chicago L.C.	6
May 23	5	Wittenberg	12

Won 1   Lost 9

The late Rex Norris, who won letters in 1933 and 1934, was one of Midwest's top players.

Tom Belton, l., and Stan Drobac won Big Ten No. 1 doubles title in 1952 and 1953.

John Sahratian, l., and Len Brose won 1951 Big Ten No. 1 doubles. Brose took singles.

State's tennis matches are held on the varsity courts located just south of Spartan Stadium. Spartans hosted 1964 NCAA championships here.

TENNIS

Tennis is one of the oldest sports activities at Michigan State. There are records of it being played in the 1880s as part of the then-popular field days involving several colleges in a wide range of athletic competition.

The first permanent courts were built in 1900. There were two of them, clay-surfaced, located just north of Morrill Hall, where today there is a large parking lot and the east-bound section of Grand River Avenue. In those days, campus property extended through the present boulevard median. Within a few years, four more courts were constructed in this area. Prior to 1900, tennis was played on temporary courts laid out on campus lawns.

Tennis was a part of the Michigan Intercollegiate Athletic Association (MIAA) program from its organization in 1888. State won its only MIAA team title in 1907. Harry G. Taft was the individual star, winning the singles and teaming with Fletcher A. Gould to take the doubles. Women's singles and doubles and mixed doubles were included in tennis meets in those days, but MAC coeds won no MIAA titles.

A new battery of courts was constructed on the site of the present Men's Intramural Building when Grand River Avenue was made into a boulevard in the early 1930s. This new group consisted of six clay and nine hard-surface courts. The present-day group of 40 hard-surface courts just south of Spartan Stadium was constructed in 1957 to make way for the new Men's Intramural Building at the old site.

Charles D. Ball, a professor of chemistry who played tennis at Penn State, was the first tennis coach of record. He directed the team from 1921 through 1946, with the exception of 1922, when he was on military duty.

During the 1920s and 1930s, there were two annual tournaments in which State participated with great success: the State Intercollegiate and the State Invitational. State won seven of the Intercollegiates from 1921 to 1934 and two of the Invitationals. Stars of that era included Rex Norris, C. R. Coe, John Croll, Stanley Weitz, Ted Hendershott, Merwyn Farleman, Burwell Cummings and Dean Lawrence.

Tennis has the distinction of being the first sport in which State won a Big Ten team championship. This occurred in 1951, State's first year in conference competition. Leonard Brose won the No. 1 singles and teamed with John Sahratian to win the No. 1 doubles.

Spartan teams continued strong, placing second five times and third four times in league action. In 1967, another Big Ten team crown was won, along with two singles and all three doubles titles. Through 1970, State had won 14 singles and nine doubles championships. Two of the singles titles were at No. 1, by Brose in

1951 and Stan Drobac, later to become head coach, in 1953. Four of the doubles crowns were at No. 1, by Brose and Sahratian in 1951, Drobac and Tom Belton in 1952 and 1953, and Rich Monan and Chuck Brainard in 1967.

State hosted the NCAA championships in 1964 and the conference meet in 1959, 1961, 1966 and 1970.

SPARTAN TENNIS HONOR ROLL

BIG TEN CHAMPIONS

Singles

1951	Leonard Brose	No. 1
	Dick Rieger	No. 6
1953	Stan Drobac	No. 1
	Jim Pore	No. 5
1955	Dana Squire	No. 6
1960	Ron Mescall	No. 5
1961	Dick Hall	No. 2
	Jack Damson	No. 4
1966	Mickey Szilagyi	No. 2
	Vic Dhooge	No. 5
1967	John Good	No. 4
	Jim Phillips	No. 6
1968	Rich Monan	No. 2
	Steve Schafer	No. 5

Doubles

1951	Leonard Brose/John Sahratian	No. 1
1952	Stan Drobac/Tom Belton	No. 1
	Dick Roberts/Jim Pore	No. 3
1953	Stan Drobac/Tom Belton	No. 1
	Dick Roberts/John Sahratian	No. 2
1966	Jim Phillips/Vic Dhooge	No. 2
1967	Rich Monan/Chuck Brainard	No. 1
	John Good/Mickey Szilagyi	No. 2
	Jim Phillips/Vic Dhooge	No. 3

SPARTAN TEAM RECORDS

RECORD BY SEASON

CHAMPIONSHIP RESULTS

Year	W	L	T	Pct.	Big Ten	Points
1913	1	1	1	.500		
1914	1	1	1	.500		
1915	5	0	0	1.000		
1916	8	2	1	.772		
1917	—	—	—			
1918	1	0	1	.525		
1919	3	2	1	.583		
1920	4	1	0	.800		
1921	3	4	0	.428		
1922	3	2	2	.642		
1923	2	6	1	.277		
1924	1	2	0	.333		
1925	4	3	0	.571		
1926	9	5	0	.650		
1927	2	7	1	.250		
1928	5	2	0	.714		
1929	3	3	0	.500		
1930	2	9	0	.181		
1931	2	6	1	.222		
1932	9	2	0	.818		
1933	11	1	0	.916		
1934	12	0	0	1.000		
1935	4	5	1	.450		
1936	12	2	0	.857		
1937	11	1	0	.916		
1938	7	4	0	.636		
1939	10	5	0	.666		
1940	6	6	1	.500		
1941	7	7	0	.500		
1942	10	5	0	.666		
1943	7	1	0	.875		
1944	—	—	—			
1945	3	1	0	.750		
1946	4	10	0	.285		

Year	W	L	T	Pct.	Finish	Pts
1947	11	6	0	.647		
1948	13	4	0	.770		
1949	11	6	0	.647		
1950	8	10	0	.444		
1951	12	4	0	.750	1st	17
1952	12	4	0	.750	2nd	56
1953	12	4	0	.750	2nd	58½
1954	9	7	0	.562	3rd	34½
1955	8	7	0	.533	6th	18½
1956	12	5	0	.705	6th	17
1957	7	10	0	.411	6th	10½
1958	6	8	0	.428	6th	14½
1959	9	7	0	.562	5th	19½
1960	17	3	0	.850	3rd	27
1961	16	4	0	.800	2nd	55
1962	11	5	0	.688	3rd	29
1963	17	4	0	.809	4th	30½
1964	14	6	0	.700	4th	25½
1965	11	6	0	.647	4th	82
1966	12	6	0	.666	2nd	113
1967	15	4	0	.789	1st	134½
1968	11	10	0	.523	2nd	100½
1969	6	12	0	.333	8th	42
1970	11	8	0	.584	3rd	74
	443	256	12	.631		

RECORD BY OPPONENT

Team	W	L	T	Pct.
Alabama Poly Technical	1	0	0	1.000
Alabama State Teachers	1	0	0	1.000
Albion College	8	1	0	.888
Alleghaney College	0	0	1	.500
Alma College	4	0	0	1.000
Andrews Air Force Base	1	0	0	1.000
Arkansas	1	1	0	.500
Armour Institute	1	3	0	.250
Ball State	1	0	0	1.000
Baylor	1	1	0	.500
Central Michigan	5	1	2	.750
Chicago	3	2	0	.600
Cincinnati	3	2	0	.600
Citadel, The	1	0	0	1.000
Clemson	0	1	0	.000
Corpus Christi	0	1	0	.000
Dartmouth	2	0	0	1.000
Davidson	7	2	0	.777
Detroit	22	5	1	.803
Detroit J.C.	1	0	0	1.000
Detroit School of Law	2	0	1	.833
Duke	2	7	0	.222
East Carolina	4	0	0	1.000
Eastern Michigan	19	3	2	.854
Florida	1	1	0	.500
Florida Southern	1	0	0	1.000
Florida State	3	5	0	.375
Fort Belvoir	1	0	0	1.000
Fort Eustis	0	1	0	.000
Fort Lee	1	0	0	1.000
Georgetown	4	0	0	1.000
George Washington	6	1	0	.857
Georgia	2	1	0	.666
Georgia Tech	1	0	0	1.000
Grand Rapids J.C.	0	1	0	.000
Hillsdale	0	1	2	.333
Houston	1	0	0	1.000
Howard	1	0	0	1.000
Illinois	19	12	0	.612
Indiana	15	12	0	.555
Iowa	10	4	0	.714
Kalamazoo College	11	5	0	.687
Kentucky	7	1	0	.875
Kenyon (Ohio)	1	0	0	1.000
Louisiana State	0	2	0	.000
Loyola (Ill.)	1	0	0	1.000
Lynchburg	1	0	0	1.000
Marquette	5	0	0	1.000
Marshall	1	1	0	.500
Maryland	0	1	0	.000
Miami (Fla.)	0	4	0	.000
Michigan State Alumni	1	0	0	1.000
Michigan	16	45	1	.250
Michigan All-Fresh	1	0	0	1.000
Milsaps College	1	0	0	1.000
Minnesota	12	3	0	.800
Mississippi College	1	0	0	1.000
Mississippi State	0	1	0	.000
North Carolina	3	19	0	.104
North Carolina State	9	2	0	.818
Northwestern	12	8	0	.600
Notre Dame	23	16	0	.589
Oberlin	7	5	0	.583
Ohio State	26	6	0	.812
Ohio Wesleyan	1	0	0	1.000
Oklahoma	0	5	0	.000
Oklahoma City	1	0	0	1.000
Oklahoma State	1	0	0	1.000
Olivet	7	1	1	.833
Pan American	0	1	0	.000
Penn State	0	3	0	.000
Pensacola Naval Station	1	1	0	.500
Pittsburgh	0	1	0	.000
Purdue	19	2	0	.904
Pontiac Tennis Club	2	2	0	.500
Presbyterian College	1	3	0	.250
Rice	0	1	0	.000
Richmond	1	0	0	1.000
Rollins College	0	2	0	.000
Sedgefield Inn	1	0	0	1.000
South Carolina	1	0	0	1.000
Tennessee	2	0	0	1.000
Texas	0	1	0	.000
Texas A & M	1	1	0	.500

Texas Christian	1	0	0	1.000	Western Michigan	31	13	0	.720
Toledo	2	0	0	1.000	Western Reserve	2	0	0	1.000
Trinity	0	2	0	.000	West Virginia	1	0	0	1.000
Tulane	0	2	0	.000	West Virginia				
Tulsa	0	1	0	.000	Wesleyan	1	0	0	1.000
Valparaiso	1	0	0	1.000	William & Mary	1	4	0	.200
Vanderbilt	1	0	0	1.000	Williams College	1	0	0	1.000
Virginia	4	7	0	.363	Wisconsin	20	2	0	.909
Virginia Military	1	0	0	1.000	Xavier	0	1	0	.000
Wake Forest	4	0	0	1.000	Yale	0	1	0	.000
Wayne State	38	10	0	.791		443	256	12	.631

SPARTAN COACHES' RECORD

Coach	Seasons	W	L	T
(No Coach)	1913-20	23	7	5
Ball, Charles D.	1921	3	4	0
Young, Harry C.	1922	3	2	2
Ball, Charles D.	1923-46	143	93	5
Dahlgren, Gordon A.	1947	11	6	0
Beeman, Harris F.	1948-50	32	20	0
Martin, Thomas	1951	12	4	0
Friedrich, John A.	1952	12	4	0
Beeman, Harris F.	1953-57	48	33	0
Drobac, Stanley	1958-	156	83	0
		443	256	12

SPARTAN TOURNAMENT RECORD

State Intercollegiate Tennis Tournament
(Team winners and Michigan State finishes)

1919 No team title
1920 Kalamazoo won. Michigan State third
1921 Michigan State won
1922 Michigan State won
1923 Michigan State won. C. R. Coe and J. T. Croll won doubles.
1924 Michigan State and Western tied for first. J. T. Croll won singles.
1925 Michigan State and Western tied for first.
1926 Grand Rapids J.C. won. Michigan State third
1927 No team standing listed. Theodore Hendershott and Merwyn Farleman won doubles.
1928 Western won, State second.
1929 Western won. State second.
1930 Western won. State tied for third with Eastern.
1931 Western won. State tied for third with Eastern.
1932 Western won. State third.
1933 Michigan State won. S. E. Weitz won

singles. Weitz and Rex Norris won doubles.
1934 Michigan State won. Rex Norris won singles over teammate S. E. Weitz and Norris and Weitz won doubles.

State Invitational Tennis Tournament
(Team winner and State finishes.)

1922 Michigan State won championship and singles and doubles titles, but no names available.
1923 Michigan State and Western tied. Burwell Cummings won singles and unnamed Spartan doubles team also won.
1924 Western won. Michigan State second. J. T. Croll won singles. Croll and Dean Lawrence won doubles.
1925 Western won. State was 5th.
1926 No record available.
1927 Hillsdale won. State third.
1928 Western won. State and Hillsdale tied for second.
1929 Western won. State third.

YEAR-BY-YEAR RECORDS

1913
No Coach
0	Eastern Michigan	6
6	Olivet	0
3	Olivet	3
Won 1 Lost 1 Tied 1

1914
5	Olivet	1
3	Eastern Michigan	3
2	Olivet	4
Won 1 Lost 1 Tied 1

1915

Date		Opponent	
May 14	5	Olivet (A)	1
May 15	5	Alma	1
May 21	7	Eastern Michigan (A)	2
May 29	6	Detroit Law	0
June 17	5	Michigan All-Fresh	1

Won 5

1916

Date		Opponent	
May 11	6	Olivet	1
May 12	3	Detroit Law	0
May 13	3	Albion (A)	5
May 16	6	Alma	0
May 17	3	Hillsdale (A)	3
May 19	6	Albion	3
May 20	6	Eastern Michigan	3
May 26	9	Alma (A)	0
May 27	3	Hillsdale	4
May 31	5	Olivet (A)	1
June 3	7	Eastern Michigan (A)	2

Won 8   Lost 2   Tied 1

1918

Date		Opponent	
May 14	5	Eastern Michigan	1
May 21	3	Eastern Michigan (A)	3

Won 1   Tied 1

1919

Date		Opponent	
May 15	0	Michigan (A)	3
May 16	3	Eastern Michigan (A)	0
May 17	3	Central Michigan	3
May 23	3	Alma	2
May 30	2	Central Michigan (A)	4
June 3	3	Eastern Michigan	0

Won 3   Lost 2   Tied 1

1920

Date		Opponent	
May 15	3	Kalamazoo Coll.	1
May 20	6	Albion	0
May 22	4	Eastern Michigan	0
June 5	1	Kalamazoo Coll. (A)	3
June 6	6	Central Michigan	0

Won 4   Lost 1

1921

Charles D. Ball, Coach

Date		Opponent	
Apr. 30	4	Pontiac Tennis Club (A)	5
May 7	1	Kalamazoo Coll.	5
May 11	5	Albion (A)	1
May 20	3	Eastern Michigan	0
May 21	1	Oberlin	2
May 30	7	Pontiac Tennis Club	2
May 31	0	Michigan (A)	6

Won 3   Lost 4

1922

Harry C. Young, Coach

Date		Opponent	
Apr. 22	4	Pontiac Tennis Club (A)	5
May 5	4	Oberlin	2
May 6	0	Oklahoma	4
May 10	6	Kalamazoo Coll.	0
May 30	8	Pontiac Tennis Club	1
June 3	3	Detroit Law	3
June 10	3	Central Michigan (A)	3

Won 3   Lost 2   Tied 2

1923

Charles D. Ball, Coach

Date		Opponent	
Apr. 27	0	Michigan	6
May 2	0	Michigan (A)	6
May 11	1	Kalamazoo Coll. (A)	5
May 12	4	Valparaiso (A)	2
May 29	4	Detroit J. C. (A)	0
May 30	1	Oberlin (A)	3
June 1	1	Penn State (A)	3
June 2	1	Pittsburgh (A)	3
June 4	2	Alleghany Coll. (A)	2

Won 2   Lost 6   Tied 1

1924

Date		Opponent	
May 3	0	Michigan (A)	6
May 10	3	Wayne State	1
May 20	2	Penn State	8

Won 1   Lost 2

1925

Date		Opponent	
Apr. 25	0	Michigan	7
May 9	6	Central Michigan	0
May 14	1	Oberlin	6
May 15	2	U. of Detroit	5
May 16	4	Wayne State	1
May 30	4	Western Michigan	3
June 3	5	U. of Detroit	2

Won 4   Lost 3

1926

Date		Opponent	
Apr. 23	4	U. of Detroit (A)	2
Apr. 24	0	Michigan (A)	7
Apr. 30	6	Wayne State	2
May 1	7	Central Michigan	0
May 4	4	Notre Dame	3
May 8	4	Western Michigan	3
May 12	7	Albion	0
May 14	4	Wayne State (A)	5
May 15	5	Eastern Michigan	1
May 17	6	West Va. Wesleyan (A)	1
May 19	3	Penn State	4
May 21	0	U. of Cincinnati (A)	7
May 22	2	Xavier (A)	5
May 29	5	U. of Detroit	2

Won 9   Lost 5

1927

Date		Opponent	
Apr. 29	4	Kalamazoo Coll.	3
Apr. 30	3	Grand Rapids J.C.	4
May 5	0	Michigan (A)	7
May 6	2	Wayne State (A)	5
May 7	3	Hillsdale	3
May 11	0	Michigan	8
May 13	1	Armour	6
May 26	1	Armour (A)	6
May 27	5	Marquette (A)	2
May 28	1	Notre Dame (A)	6

Won 2   Lost 7   Tied 1

1928

Date		Opponent	
Apr. 27	5	Wayne State	1
Apr. 28	7	Albion	0
May 3	0	Michigan (A)	9
May 12	4	Notre Dame	3
May 15	1	Marquette	3
May 21	3	Armour	4
May 31	5	Wayne State (A)	2

Won 5   Lost 2

1929

Date		Opponent	
Apr. 20	5	Wayne State	2
Apr. 27	7	Albion	0
May 11	1	Western Michigan	6
May 13	0	Notre Dame (A)	7
May 15	4	Armour (A)	3
May 16	0	Chicago (A)	7

Won 3   Lost 3

1930

Date		Opponent	
Apr. 25	6	Albion	1
Apr. 26	5	Eastern Michigan	2
May 2	0	Northwestern	9
May 3	2	U. of Detroit	7
May 6	0	Michigan	9
May 10	2	Oberlin	4
May 14	0	Western Michigan (A)	7
May 20	1	Notre Dame	8
May 22	3	Oberlin (A)	4
May 23	1	Wayne State (A)	4
May 24	1	U. of Detroit (A)	8

Won 2   Lost 9

1931

Apr. 25	2	Kalamazoo Coll.	7
May 1	0	Michigan (A)	9
May 3	3	Eastern Michigan (A)	6
May 12	5	Wayne State (A)	2
May 18	4	U. of Detroit	4
May 22	1	U. of Detroit	8
May 26	2	Western Michigan	5
May 28	3	Eastern Michigan	6

Won 2   Lost 6   Tied 1

1932

Apr. 23	9	Kalamazoo Coll.	0
Apr. 29	8	U. of Detroit	1
May 3	3	Michigan	6
May 7	6	Ohio Wesleyan	1
May 11	7	Loyola (Ill.)	0
May 14	6	Oberlin	1
May 16	6	Eastern Michigan (A)	3
May 20	7	Wayne State (A)	2
May 21	7	Notre Dame	2
May 27	4	Western Michigan (A)	5
May 28	8	Notre Dame (A)	1

Won 9   Lost 2

1933

Apr. 22	9	Kalamazoo Coll.	0
Apr. 28	7	Eastern Michigan	2
Apr. 29	8	Notre Dame	1
May 6	8	Notre Dame (A)	1
May 12	5	Ohio State	0
May 13	7	Oberlin	0
May 18	6	Western Michigan	3
May 19	4	Michigan (A)	5
May 23	7	Michigan	2
May 26	6	U. of Detroit	1
May 27	6	Wayne State	1
May 30	7	U. of Detroit	0

Won 11   Lost 1

1934

Apr. 27	5	Michigan (A)	4
Apr. 28	9	Kalamazoo Coll.	0
May 3	8	Oberlin (A)	1
May 4	10	Ohio State (A)	0
May 10	5	Eastern Michigan	4
May 11	9	Oberlin	0
May 12	7	Notre Dame	2
May 18	5	Western Michigan (A)	4
May 19	6	Notre Dame (A)	3
May 25	7	Michigan	2
May 26	5	Ohio State	1
May 28	5	Chicago	1

Won 12

1935

Apr. 26	1	Michigan	8
Apr. 29	1	Chicago	5
May 8	7	Albion	0
May 10	9	Wayne State	1
May 11	5	Notre Dame (A)	3
May 17	1	Michigan (A)	8
May 24	9	Eastern Michigan	0
May 25	3	Western Michigan	6
May 31	5	Toledo Tennis Club (A)	5
June 1	2	Ohio State (A)	8

Won 4   Lost 5   Tied 1

1936

Apr. 18	12	Kalamazoo Coll.	3
Apr. 21	6	Michigan	3
Apr. 24	9	Wayne State (A)	0
Apr. 25	6	Eastern Michigan	1
Apr. 30	9	Oberlin	0
May 1	4	Western Michigan (A)	5
May 8	8	Toledo Tennis Club (A)	1
May 9	3	Ohio State (A)	6
May 14	5	Kentucky	4
May 15	8	Michigan (A)	1
May 22	9	Oberlin (A)	0
May 23	6	Western Reserve (A)	3
May 29	8	Notre Dame	1
May 30	6	Western Michigan	3

Won 12   Lost 2

1937

Apr. 16	4	Wisconsin	2
Apr. 23	7	Ohio State	3
Apr. 30	2	Northwestern (A)	7
May 1	9	Marquette	0
May 6	8	Indiana (A)	1
May 7	8	Kentucky (A)	1
May 8	9	Cincinnati (A)	0
May 15	8	Notre Dame (A)	1
May 29	8	Western Reserve	1
May 31	5	Wayne State	4
June 2	9	Kalamazoo Coll.	0
June 12	6	Michigan State Coll. Alumni	3

Won 11   Lost 1

1938

Apr. 16	5	Kalamazoo Coll.	4
Apr. 22	9	Toledo (A)	0
Apr. 23	5	Ohio State (A)	4
Apr. 30	4	Michigan (A)	5
May 6	6	Indiana	3
May 7	2	Kentucky	7
May 10	6	Michigan	3
May 12	6	Notre Dame	3
May 21	6	Marquette	1
May 26	1	Wayne State (A)	8
June 1	0	Wayne State	9

Won 7   Lost 4

1939

Apr. 3	5	Richmond (A)	1
Apr. 4	0	Virginia (A)	9
Apr. 6	5	Kentucky (A)	1
Apr. 21	8	Cincinnati	1
Apr. 22	9	Toledo	0
Apr. 29	6	Notre Dame (A)	3
May 4	8	Indiana	1
May 6	6	Kalamazoo Coll.	3
May 12	3	Michigan (A)	6
May 13	9	Eastern Michigan	0
May 19	3	Illinois	6
May 20	5	Ohio State	4
May 24	3	Illinois	6
May 26	5	Western Michigan	4
June 2	3	Wayne State (A)	6

Won 10   Lost 5

1940

Mar. 21	1	Davidson (A)	6
Mar. 22	1	Duke (A)	8
Mar. 23	8	North Carolina State (A)	1
Mar. 25	6	Wake Forest (A)	1
Apr. 20	9	Kentucky	0
May 2	2	Illinois (A)	7
May 3	3	Purdue (A)	1
May 4	3	Ohio State (A)	6
May 11	9	Indiana	0
May 18	3	Michigan (A)	6
May 20	3	Michigan	3
May 25	4	Western Michigan (A)	5
May 30	6	Wayne State	3

Won 6   Lost 6   Tied 1

1941

Mar. 26	4	Arkansas (A)	5
Mar. 27	2	Tulsa (A)	5

Mar. 28 6 Oklahoma State (A) 3
Apr. 26 4 Ohio State 5
May 1 2 Michigan 7
May 2 8 Illinois 1
May 15 3 Notre Dame (A) 6
May 16 9 Ball State (A) 0
May 17 6 Kentucky (A) 3
May 23 8 Eastern Michigan 1
May 24 4 Michigan (A) 5
May 28 8 Wayne State (A) 1
May 30 6 Western Michigan 3
Won 7 Lost 7

1942
Mar. 25 7 Arkansas (A) 1
Mar. 27 3 Oklahoma (A) 6
Mar. 28 4 Oklahoma (A) 5
Apr. 16 2 Michigan (A) 7
Apr. 17 3 Notre Dame 6
Apr. 24 7 Kentucky 2
Apr. 25 9 Ohio State (A) 0
Apr. 29 1 Michigan 8
May 2 9 Indiana 0
May 7 5 Illinois (A) 4
May 8 7 Purdue (A) 0
May 16 8 Eastern Michigan 1
May 22 9 Wayne State 0
May 23 8 U. of Detroit 1
May 30 5 Western Michigan (A) 4
Won 10 Lost 5

1943
Apr. 26 6 Michigan 3
Apr. 30 6 Notre Dame 3
May 10 3 Mcihigan (A) 6
May 20 8 U. of Detroit (A) 0
May 21 7 Eastern Michigan 0
May 22 7 Western Michigan (A) 2
May 28 5 Central Michigan 1
June 4 4 Central Michigan (A) 2
Won 7 Lost 1

1944
Intercollegiate Athletic program dropped—World War II

1945
May 19 5 U. of Detroit 1
May 23 3 Wayne State (A) 6
May 24 4 U. of Detroit (A) 2
May 28 5 Wayne State 4
Won 3 Lost 1

1946
Apr. 20 4 Northwestern (A) 5
Apr. 24 2 Michigan (A) 7
Apr. 25 2 Ohio State (A) 7
Apr. 26 1 Cincinnati (A) 8
Apr. 27 6 Kentucky (A) 3
May 3 5 Western Michigan (A) 4
May 4 9 Indiana (A) 0
May 10 4 Illinois (A) 5
May 11 5 Purdue (A) 4
May 18 4 Notre Dame 5
May 23 4 Michigan 5
May 27 4 Wayne State 5
May 29 4 Wayne State 5
May 31 3 Western Michigan 6
Won 4 Lost 10

1947
Gordon A. Dahlgren, Coach
Mar. 22 5 Virginia (A) 4
Mar. 24 5 Virginia (A) 4
Mar. 25 1 William & Mary (A) 8
Mar. 26 9 Georgetown U. (A) 0
Apr. 14 7 Cincinnati 2
Apr. 19 8 Chicago 1
Apr. 21 8 Wayne State 1
Apr. 25 6 Purdue 1
Apr. 26 3 Notre Dame (A) 6
Apr. 30 3 Michigan (A) 6
May 2 7 Western Michigan (A) 2
May 3 3 Kalamazoo Coll. (A) 6
May 12 5 Wayne State (A) 4
May 19 4 Illinois (A) 5
May 22 4 Michigan 5
May 23 8 Ohio State 1
May 27 7 Western Michigan 2
Won 11 Lost 6

Tennis during the early days at State was played on grass. This pause in the action was taken sometime during the late 1800s or early 1900s.

1948
Harris F. Beeman, Coach

Date		Opponent	
Mar. 23	9	Lynchburg (A)	0
Mar. 24	1	William & Mary (A)	8
Mar. 25	7	William & Mary (A)	9
Mar. 29	0	North Carolina (A)	9
Apr. 23	9	Ohio State (A)	0
Apr. 28	6	Michigan	3
Apr. 30	9	Purdue (A)	0
May 1	9	Chicago (A)	0
May 7	6	Illinois	2
May 8	7	Kalamazoo Coll.	2
May 15	9	Wayne State	0
May 19	9	Western Michigan	0
May 21	4	Michigan (A)	5
May 22	8	U. of Detroit	1
May 28	8	Wayne State (A)	1
May 29	9	U. of Detroit (A)	0
June 1	9	Western Michigan (A)	0

Won 13   Lost 4

1949

Date		Opponent	
Mar. 25	1	North Carolina (A)	8
Mar. 26	0	North Carolina (A)	9
Mar. 28	9	East Carolina Coll. (A)	0
Mar. 30	1	Virginia (A)	8
Apr. 25	8	U. of Detroit	0
Apr. 26	9	Wayne State (A)	0
Apr. 28	2	Michigan	7
May 5	5	Illinois (A)	4
May 6	5	Wisconsin (A)	4
May 7	8	Marquette (A)	0
May 11	8	Western Michigan (A)	1
May 14	7	Notre Dame (A)	2
May 16	1	Michigan (A)	8
May 18	5	Purdue (A)	2
May 20	4	Ohio State	5
May 21	8	Western Michigan	1
May 23	9	Wayne State	0

Won 11   Lost 6

1950

Date		Opponent	
Mar. 23	1	Duke (A)	8
Mar. 24	1	Duke (A)	8
Mar. 25	9	North Carolina State (A)	0
Mar. 27	0	North Carolina (A)	10
Mar. 28	1	North Carolina (A)	9
Mar. 30	2	Virginia (A)	8
Mar. 31	1	William & Mary (A)	9
Apr. 26	9	U. of Detroit	0
Apr. 28	6	Wisconsin	3
May 2	5	Notre Dame	4
May 12	1	Illinois	8
May 13	7	Purdue	2
May 15	1	Michigan (A)	7
May 19	9	Ohio State (A)	0
May 20	3	Indiana (A)	6
May 24	5	Wayne State (A)	0
May 27	4	Michigan	5
May 29	8	Western Michigan	1

Won 8   Lost 10

1951
Thomas F. Martin, Coach

Date		Opponent	
Mar. 22	4	Duke (A)	5
Mar. 23	2	Duke (A)	7
Mar. 24	9	North Carolina State (A)	0
Mar. 26	3	Virginia (A)	6
Mar. 27	5	William & Mary (A)	4
Mar. 29	4	North Carolina (A)	5
Mar. 30	5	North Carolina (A)	4
Apr. 23	9	Wayne State	0
Apr. 27	9	Wisconsin	0

Date		Opponent	
Apr. 28	9	Minnesota (A)	0
May 4	9	Purdue (A)	0
May 5	9	Notre Dame (A)	0
May 12	7	Indiana	2
May 14	8	Illinois (A)	1
May 17	8	Michigan	1
May 18	9	Ohio State	0

Won 12   Lost 4

1952
John A. Friedrich, Coach

Date		Opponent	
Mar. 25	4	North Carolina (A)	5
Mar. 26	4	North Carolina (A)	5
Mar. 27	9	North Carolina State (A)	0
Mar. 29	6	Davidson (A)	3
Mar. 30	8	Sedgefield Inn (A)	1
Mar. 31	4	Duke (A)	3
Apr. 1	1	Virginia (A)	6
Apr. 26	8	Western Michigan	1
Apr. 29	9	Wayne State	0
May 3	4	Indiana (A)	5
May 6	9	U. of Detroit (A)	0
May 9	5	Illinois	2
May 10	9	Wisconsin	0
May 13	9	Michigan	0
May 17	9	Ohio State (A)	0
May 19	7	Notre Dame	1

Won 12   Lost 4

1953
Harris F. Beeman, Coach

Date		Opponent	
Mar. 27	4	Presbyterian Coll. (A)	5
Mar. 28	3	Presbyterian Coll. (A)	6
Mar. 30	8	Davidson (A)	1
Mar. 31	1	Duke (A)	8
Apr. 1	9	North Carolina State (A)	0
Apr. 4	3	North Carolina (A)	6
Apr. 25	9	Illinois (A)	0
May 7	9	Northwestern	0
May 8	8	Notre Dame	1
May 11	9	Western Michigan	0
May 13	7	Michigan (A)	2
May 15	8	Ohio State	1
May 16	6	Indiana	3
May 18	7	Michigan	2
May 22	9	Iowa (A)	0
May 23	8	Wisconsin (A)	1

Won 12   Lost 4

1954

Date		Opponent	
Mar. 27	9	Marshall (A)	0
Mar. 29	3	Davidson (A)	6
Mar. 30	9	North Carolina State (A)	0
Mar. 31	0	North Carolina (A)	6
Apr. 1	3	Virginia (A)	7
Apr. 2	10	West Virginia (A)	0
Apr. 27	8	Wayne State	1
Apr. 30	6	Northwestern (A)	3
May 1	5	Notre Dame (A)	4
May 6	2	Western Michigan (A)	7
May 8	3	Indiana (A)	6
May 11	8	Michigan	1
May 14	9	U. of Detroit	0
May 15	7	Wisconsin	2
May 19	3	Michigan	6
May 21	4	Illinois	5

Won 9   Lost 7

1955

Date		Opponent	
Mar. 26	2	Marshall (A)	7
Mar. 28	9	Davidson (A)	0
Mar. 29	9	North Carolina (A)	0

Date		Opponent	
Mar. 30	0	North Carolina State (A)	9
Apr. 22	0	U. of Detroit (A)	9
Apr. 23	2	Wayne State (A)	7
Apr. 30	9	Indiana	0
May 2	6	Illinois (A)	3
May 5	7	Northwestern	2
May 7	3	Purdue	6
May 9	7	Western Michigan	2
May 14	4	Notre Dame	5
May 16	9	Michigan	0
May 20	9	Minnesota (A)	0
May 21	2	Wisconsin (A)	7
		Won 8 Lost 7	

1956

Date		Opponent	
Mar. 26	8	Davidson (A)	1
Mar. 27	7	Kenyon (A)	2
Mar. 28	7	Wake Forest (A)	2
Mar. 30	8	Fort Belvoir (A)	1
Mar. 31	9	Andrews Air Force Base (A)	0
Apr. 2	5	George Washington (A)	4
Apr. 3	9	Fort Lee (A)	0
Apr. 5	9	North Carolina State (A)	0
Apr. 27	4	Purdue (A)	5
Apr. 28	1	Indiana (A)	8
Apr. 30	9	Wayne State	0
May 4	1	Western Michigan (A)	8
May 5	8	Wisconsin	1
May 8	5	Notre Dame (A)	4
May 12	5	Illinois	4
May 14	0	Michigan (A)	9
May 18	2	Northwestern (A)	7
		Won 12 Lost 5	

1957

Date		Opponent	
Mar. 25	0	Naval Air Base (A)	11
Mar. 26	6	Florida State (A)	3
Mar. 27	1	Florida (A)	8
Mar. 28	4	Rollins Coll. (A)	5
Mar. 30	8	Florida Southern (A)	1
Apr. 1	0	Miami (A)	9
Apr. 5	2	Presbyterian Coll. (A)	7
Apr. 20	8	Ohio State (A)	1
Apr. 27	9	U. of Detroit (A)	0
Apr. 29	9	Wayne State (A)	0
May 2	3	Northwestern	6
May 4	0	Illinois (A)	9
May 7	6	Western Michigan	3
May 11	1	Notre Dame	5
May 13	0	Michigan	9
May 17	0	Iowa (A)	9
May 18	5	Wisconsin (A)	4
		Won 7 Lost 10	

1958

Stanley Drobac, Coach

Date		Opponent	
Mar. 25	5	Naval Air Base (A)	1
Mar. 27	4	Florida State (A)	5
Mar. 28	5	Florida (A)	4
Mar. 29	2	Rollins Coll. (A)	7
Mar. 31	0	Miami (A)	9
Apr. 3	7	Tennessee (A)	2
Apr. 30	9	U. of Detroit (A)	0
May 2	1	Notre Dame (A)	8
May 3	3	Indiana (A)	6
May 6	7	Wayne State	2
May 7	2	Western Michigan (A)	7
May 9	7	Wisconsin	2
May 10	0	Illinois	9
May 13	0	Michigan (A)	9
		Won 6 Lost 8	

1959

Date		Opponent	
Mar. 28	1	Florida State (A)	8
Mar. 30	9	Alabama State Teachers Coll. (A)	0
Mar. 31	9	Alabama Polytechnical Inst. (A)	0
Apr. 2	2	Georgia (A)	7
Apr. 25	5	Ohio State (A)	4
May 2	2	Illinois (A)	7
May 4	9	U. of Detroit	0
May 6	1	Notre Dame	8
May 7	7	Northwestern	2
May 9	8	Purdue	1
May 12	2	Michigan	7
May 13	6	Western Michigan	3
May 15	8	Wisconsin (A)	1
May 16	3	Minnesota (at Madison, Wis.)	6
May 16	3	Iowa (at Madison, Wis.)	6
May 19	6	Indiana	3
		Won 9 Lost 7	

1960

Date		Opponent	
Mar. 24	7	Vanderbilt (A)	2
Mar. 26	8	Howard (A)	1
Mar. 28	5	Florida State (A)	4
Mar. 29	5	Florida State (A)	4
Mar. 31	5	Georgia Tech. (A)	4
Apr. 1	6	Georgia (A)	3
Apr. 2	6	Tennessee (A)	3
Apr. 19	9	U. of Detroit (A)	0
Apr. 22	9	Purdue (A)	0
Apr. 23	5	Illinois (at Bloomington, Ind.)	4
Apr. 23	5	Indiana (at Bloomington, Ind.)	4
Apr. 26	9	Wayne State	0
Apr. 29	5	Northwestern (A)	4
Apr. 30	7	Iowa (at Minneapolis, Minn.)	2
Apr. 30	6	Minnesota (at Minneapolis, Minn.)	1
May 7	8	Illinois	1
May 10	2	Michigan (A)	7
May 12	4	Western Michigan (A)	5
May 14	4	Notre Dame (A)	5
May 18	8	Ohio State (A)	1
		Won 17 Lost 3	

1961

Date		Opponent	
Mar. 23	8	George Washington (A)	1
Mar. 24	7	Georgetown U. (A)	2
Mar. 25	3	Virginia (A)	6
Mar. 27	4	North Carolina (A)	5
Mar. 28	5	North Carolina (A)	4
Mar. 29	7	North Carolina State (A)	1
Mar. 30	9	Davidson (A)	0
Apr. 15	8	Ohio State (A)	0
Apr. 21	6	Notre Dame	3
Apr. 22	9	U. of Detroit	0
May 1	9	Wayne State (A)	0
May 3	9	Western Michigan	0
May 5	7	Northwestern	2
May 6	8	Iowa (at Evanston, Ill.)	1
May 6	8	Minnesota (at Evanston, Ill.)	1
May 9	4	Michigan	6
May 12	9	Wisconsin (A)	0
May 12	9	Purdue (at Madison, Wis.)	0
May 12	8	Illinois (at Madison, Wis.)	1
May 17	4	Indiana	6
		Won 16 Lost 4	

1962

Date		Opponent	
Mar. 22	5	Davidson (A)	2
Mar. 23	3	Duke (A)	6
Mar. 24	9	North Carolina State (A)	0
Mar. 26	2	North Carolina State (A)	7
Mar. 27	9	East Carolina Coll. (A)	0
Apr. 20	1	Northwestern	8
Apr. 24	9	U. of Detroit	0
Apr. 27	9	Minnesota (at Iowa City, Ia.)	0
Apr. 28	6	Wisconsin (at Iowa City, Ia.)	3
Apr. 28	4	Iowa (A)	5
May 2	9	Notre Dame (A)	0
May 4	8	Indiana	1
May 5	8	Illinois	1
May 8	2	Michigan (A)	7
May 12	8	Ohio State (at Ann Arbor, Mich.)	1
May 14	8	Western Michigan	1

Won 11   Lost 5

1963

Date		Opponent	
Mar. 22	9	Davidson (A)	0
Mar. 23	9	Wake Forest (A)	0
Mar. 25	4	Fort Eustis (A)	5
Mar. 26	5	East Carolina (A)	2
Mar. 27	0	North Carolina (A)	9
Mar. 28	7	Virginia (A)	2
Mar. 29	5	George Washington (A)	4
Mar. 30	7	Dartmouth (A)	2
Mar. 30	5	Georgetown U. (A)	4
Apr. 19	5	Wisconsin (at Champaign, Ill.)	4
Apr. 20	0	Illinois (A)	9
Apr. 23	0	Northwestern (A)	9
Apr. 26	7	Purdue (at Bloomington, Ind.)	0
Apr. 26	4	Indiana (A)	5
Apr. 26	9	Minnesota (at Bloomington, Ind.)	0
May 3	5	Notre Dame	4
May 7	5	Michigan	4
May 8	6	Western Michigan (A)	3
May 10	9	Iowa	0
May 11	9	Minnesota	0
May 11	9	Ohio State	0

Won 17   Lost 4

1964

Date		Opponent	
Mar. 24	6	Duke (A)	3
Mar. 26	1	North Carolina (A)	7
Mar. 27	1	North Carolina (A)	8
Mar. 28	7	Williams Coll. (A)	2
Mar. 30	5	George Washington (A)	4
Mar. 31	9	Georgtown U. (A)	0
Apr. 1	5	The Citadel (A)	1
Apr. 4	9	Virginia (A)	0
Apr. 10	7	Ohio State (A)	2
Apr. 11	8	Purdue (A)	1
Apr. 18	4	Notre Dame (A)	5
Apr. 22	9	Wayne State (A)	0
Apr. 28	7	Western Michigan (A)	0
May 5	1	Michigan (A)	8
May 8	7	Iowa	2
May 9	9	Illinois	0
May 12	1	Northwestern	7
May 15-16	8	Minnesota (A)	1
May 15-16	2	Indiana (at Minneapolis, Minn.)	5
May 15-16	6	Wisconsin (at Minneapolis, Minn.)	3

Won 14   Lost 6

1965

Date		Opponent	
Mar. 23	9	Wake Forest (A)	0
Mar. 26	1	North Carolina (A)	8
Mar. 27	3	North Carolina (A)	6
Mar. 29	5	Prebyterian Coll. (A)	4
Mar. 30	9	Virginia Military Inst. (A)	0
Apr. 20	9	Wayne state	0
Apr. 23	5	Illinois (at Bloomington, Ind.)	4
Apr. 23	2	Indiana (A)	7
Apr. 24	3	Northwestern (at Bloomington, Ind.)	6
Apr. 29	2	Notre Dame	7
May 1	8	Iowa (A)	1
May 5	5	Western Michigan (A)	4
May 7	9	Ohio State	0
May 8	8	Purdue	1
May 11	1	Michigan	8
May 14	5	Minnesota (A)	2
May 15	8	Wisconsin (A)	1

Won 11   Lost 6

1966

Date		Opponent	
Mar. 22	4	Houston (A)	2
Mar. 23	2	Rice Inst. (A)	5
Mar. 28	1	Trinity (A)	8
Mar. 29	3	Texas A & M (A)	6
Mar. 30	3	Baylor (A)	4
Mar. 31	4	Texas Christian (A)	3
Apr. 15	1	Michigan (A)	8
Apr. 16	8	Minnesota (A)	1
Apr. 27	9	Wayne State	0
Apr. 29	6	Wisconsin	3
Apr. 30	9	Northwestern	0
May 3	2	Notre Dame (A)	7
May 6	8	Ohio State (A)	1
May 7	7	Illinois (A)	2
May 10	9	Western Michigan	0
May 13	5	Indiana (at Lafayette, Ind.)	4
May 13	9	Iowa (at Lafayette, Ind.)	0
May 14	9	Purdue (at Lafayette, Ind.)	0

Won 12   Lost 6

1967

Date		Opponent	
Mar. 22	3	Florida State (A)	6
Mar. 23	5	Georgia (A)	4
Mar. 24	4	Clemson (A)	5
Mar. 25	7	South Carolina (A)	2
Mar. 27	9	East Carolina (A)	0
Ma.r 29	2	North Carolina (A)	7
Mar. 29	1	North Carolina (A)	8
Mar. 31	8	George Washington (A)	1
Apr. 18	9	Wayne State (A)	0
Apr. 21	7	Northwestern	2
Apr. 22	8	Wisconsin	1
Apr. 28	8	Iowa (A)	1
Apr. 29	8	Minnesota (A)	1
May 3	7	Western Michigan (A)	2
May 5	9	Ohio State	0
May 7	7	Indiana	2
May 9	5	Michigan	4
May 12	9	Illinois	0
May 13	9	Purdue (A)	0

Won 15   Lost 4

1968

Date		Opponent	
Mar. 20	1	Tulane (at New Orleans, La.)	8
Mar. 21	0	Tulane (at New Orleans, La.)	5
Mar. 22	4	Louisiana State (A)	5
Mar. 23	3	Louisiana State (A)	6

First State tennis team to win Big Ten championship was 1951 varsity, which included, l. to r., Coach Frank Beeman, Dave Mills, Keith Kimble, Ken Kimble, Len Brose, John Sahratian, Dick Rieger, Wally Kau and Coach Tom Martin.

Mar. 25	6	Millsaps Coll. (A)	0
Mar. 26	9	Mississippi Coll. (A)	0
Mar. 27	0	Mississippi State (at Starkville, Miss.)	9
Mar. 28	2	Florida State (at Starkville, Miss.)	7
Mar. 29	2	Oklahoma (at Starkville, Miss.)	5
Apr. 12	5	Illinois	4
Apr. 13	9	Purdue	0
Apr. 19	8	Iowa	1
Apr. 20	4	Minnesota	5
Apr. 26	9	Indiana (A)	0
Apr. 27	8	Ohio State (A)	1
Apr. 30	7	Wayne State (A)	0
May 3	8	Wisconsin (A)	1
May 4	7	Northwestern (A)	1
May 7	7	Western Michigan	2
May 11	0	Michigan (A)	9
May 13	0	Miami	9

Won 11 Lost 10

1969

Mar. 18	2	Yale (at Miami, Fla.)	7
Mar. 19	0	Miami (A)	9
Mar. 21	1	Florida State (A)	8
Mar. 24	5	Dartmouth (A)	4
Mar. 25	2	George Washington (A)	6
Mar. 26	3	Maryland (A)	6
Mar. 28	0	North Carolina (A)	9
Apr. 11	0	Illinois (A)	9
Apr. 12	6	Purdue (A)	3

Apr. 18	5	Northwestern	4
Apr. 19	2	Wisconsin	7
Apr. 22	7	Wayne State (A)	2
Apr. 29	6	Western Michigan (A)	3
May 2	1	Minnesota (A)	8
May 3	2	Iowa (A)	7
May 6	0	Michigan	9
May 9	7	Ohio State	2
May 10	2	Indiana	7

Won 6 Lost 12

1970

Mar. 25	2	Oklahoma City (A)	6
Mar. 27	7	Baylor (A)	2
Mar. 30	4	Pan American (A)	5
Mar. 31	1	Corpus Christi (A)	8
Apr. 1	0	Trinity (A)	9
Apr. 2	2	Texas (A)	7
Apr. 3	5	Texas A & M (A)	4
Apr. 10	9	Ohio State (A)	0
Apr. 11	3	Indiana (A)	6
Apr. 17	5	Northwestern (A)	4
Apr. 18	7	Wisconsin (A)	2
Apr. 22	3	Notre Dame (A)	6
Apr. 28	9	Wayne State	0
May 1	9	Iowa	0
May 2	6	Minnesota	0
May 5	3	Michigan (A)	6
May 6	9	Western Michigan	0
May 8	3	Purdue	1
May 9	6	Illinois	3

Won 11 Lost 8

Ralph Young Field, the home of Spartans' outdoor track events, was the site of the 1960 Big Ten championship meet.

Fred Johnson won the NCAA and IC4A long jump titles in 1949.

Leander Burnett, an early State track great, won five letters, 1888-1892.

TRACK

Track was the first organized athletic activity to achieve a degree of acceptance from Michigan Agricultural College fathers. But they didn't extend it willingly. The faculty of the 1880s considered any vigorous sport to be rowdy and frivolous and a poor substitute for farm work as a healthy form of exercise.

But the students felt otherwise and kept pressure on their elders through columns in the campus newspaper, THE SPECULUM, and repeated urgings of sports-oriented campus groups. Finally, the faculty relented and permitted, first, intramural field days and, later, intercollegiate field days, with heavy emphasis on track events.

The first of the intercollegiate field days for which there is a detailed record available was a triangular affair involving Olivet, Albion and MAC at East Lansing on May 14-15, 1886. On June 4-5, 1886, MAC competed with Albion at Albion in MAC's first dual track meet. It ended in a 25-25 tie. (Summaries of these meets are contained in the records section of this chapter.)

These field days were the forerunners of the Michigan Intercollegiate Athletic Association (MIAA). It was formed in 1888, with MAC, Olivet, Albion and Hillsdale the charter members. The first annual MIAA field day was held at MAC on May 31, 1888. MAC was a mighty power in field days, taking 15 team championships in 20 years of competition prior to dropping out of the conference in 1907 because of this very domination. It also produced the school's first major athletic hero in Leander Burnett, a full-blooded Indian. Burnett participated in five MIAA field days for MAC, 1888 through 1892, and won three all-around championships and an incredible 37 individual events. He also was an excellent baseball player who, in one game of record, had six hits in six times at bat.

The first track coach was Henry Keep, an engineering student who also served as sports coach in 1898. Prior to that, Aggie trackmen had trained on their own. Among the outstanding runners of the era were Harry Moon and Ralph Carr. Moon was one of the first athletes to achieve a :10.0 clocking in the 100-yard dash and was an Olympic trials participant in 1904. In 1908, MAC entered the Big Ten track championships for the first time. In those days, outside teams could compete in certain Big Ten meets. Carr won the two-mile run in the then excellent time of 9:56.2. For this performance, Carr was chosen to be a member of the 1908 U. S. Olympic team at London in the three-mile and five-mile races, but for some reason turned down the invitation.

The Michigan State intercollegiate meet was started in 1916. Meets were held annually through 1945 and State won 17 team titles and 151 individual championships. A great track star of the early 1920s was DeGay Ernst, who

established a world record in the 40-yard dash, the first such accomplishment by an MAC athlete.

The opening of the new Men's Gymnasium, now the Women's Gymnasium, in 1920, ushered in a new track era. The MAC Track Carnival, later renamed the Michigan State Relays, was inaugurated on March 11, 1921, in the new gym. MAC won the meet, with Michigan second and Western State Normal, now Western Michigan, third. In those days, only colleges from Michigan participated. After that first meet, the keeping of team scores was abolished and only individual event winners since have been recognized. MAC sent its first team to the Penn Relays in 1909 and to the Drake Relays in 1922. The first Penn Relays winner was an 880-yard relay team in 1927 composed of Forrest Lang, Henry Henson, Bohn Grim and Fred Alderman. This same quartet tied the world record in the 440-yard relay that year. The first Drake winner was DeGay Ernst in the 440-yard hurdles in 1922 in the meet record time of :54.5.

The late Ralph H. Young, athletic director at State for 31 years, as well as football, track and cross country coach in his early period, was a pivotal figure in track at State. He built its track program to national importance for the first time. In his years at the helm (1923-1940), he developed three Olympic team members and 20 All-American trackmen. The Olympians were Fred Alderman, who was a member of the Olympic champion U.S. 1,600-meter relay team in 1928, distance runner Tom Ottey in 1932 and walker Ernest Crosbie in 1932, 1936 and 1948. One of his most significant contributions to track and other sports at State was his participation with Notre Dame's Knute Rockne and Marquette's Conrad Jennings in forming, in 1926, the Central Intercollegiate Conference, later renamed the Central Collegiate Conference (CCC). State, which has participated only sporadically in CCC championships since joining the Big Ten in 1949, won six CCC outdoor and four indoor team crowns. Young also was the prime mover in State's joining the IC4A in 1927, a largely Eastern athletic organization of many colleges and various sports. State was a track power in the IC4A until joining the Big Ten, winning three team titles and 20 individual crowns.

The years 1940 and 1941 are important in State's track history. Jenison Field House became the home of Spartan indoor track action in 1940 and Karl Schlademan arrived on the scene as head track coach in 1941. One of Schlademan's first and most important actions was to expand the Michigan State Relays beyond state borders, building it into a major annual national indoor event. This began in 1942. The war years were dull, but immediately thereafter the golden period of Spartan track was enjoyed. There came the three IC4A titles, an epic dual meet tie with Southern California, a world-record two-mile relay team (Dave Peppard, Don Makielski, Warren Druetzler and Bill Mack) at 7:31.8 and wholesale Big Ten, IC4A, Drake Relays and NCAA individual and relay titles. Olympians of the Schlademan era included miler Warren Druetzler in 1952, walker Adolph Weinacker in 1948, 1952 and 1956, middle-distance aces David Lean in 1956 and Kevan Gosper in 1956 and 1960. The first two represented the U.S.; the latter two, Australia.

Francis Dittrich, assistant coach and Spartan broad jumper of the 1930s, succeeded his old boss as head track coach in 1959 and maintained a successful

pace through the 1960s. The highlights were State's first Big Ten team championships in track: the outdoor title in 1965 and 1966 and the indoor crown in 1966.

Indoor track has had three sites on campus and outdoor track four. Indoor activities began in the old Armory on the site of the present Music Building. From there, it went to the present Women's Gymnasium in 1920 and thence to Jenison Field House in 1940. Outdoor competition started on the band drill field north of the Women's Gym, went from there to Old College Field in 1902, to Macklin Field Stadium in 1926 and to its present home on Ralph H. Young Field in 1937.

SPARTAN TRACK HONOR ROLL

NCAA INDIVIDUAL CHAMPIONS

1927	Fred Alderman	100-yard dash	:09.9
1927	Fred Alderman	220-yard dash	:21.1
1931	Clark Chamberlain	Two-mile run	9:23
1940	Roy Fehr	Two-mile run	9:18.9
1949	Fred Johnson	Broad Jump	25-2½
1951	Warren Druetzler	Mile Run	4:08
1956	Selwyn Jones	10,000-meter run	31:15.3
1956	Henry Kennedy	3,000-meter steeplechase	9:16.5
1965*	Eugene Washington	60-yard high hurdles	:07.2
1966	Robert Steele	440-yard hurdles	:50.4
1967	Robert Steele	440-yard hurdles	:50.2
1969*	Bill Wehrwein	600-yard run	1:09.8
1970*	Herb Washington	60-yard dash	:05.9

*Indoors

BEST NCAA OUTDOOR CHAMPIONSHIP FINISH

1949	Michigan State	Fourth	26

BEST NCAA INDOOR CHAMPIONSHIP FINISH

1965	Michigan State	Fourth (2-way tie)	10

BIG TEN INDIVIDUAL CHAMPIONS

1951	Jesse Thomas	100-yard dash	:10.0
1951	Jesse Thomas	220-yard low hurdles	:23.8
1951	Don Makielski	880-yard run	1:56
1951	Robert Carey	Shot Put	53-0
1953*	James Vrooman	High Jump	6-4½
1953	James Kepford	Mile Run	4:18.4
1954*	John Cook	880-yard run	1:54.9
1954	John Cook	Mile Run	4:14.1
1955*	Kevan Gosper	440-yard dash	:48.2
1955*	Kevan Gosper	600-yard run	1:11.3
1955	Kevan Gosper	440-yard run	:47.8
1955*	Ed Brabham	60-yard dash	:06.2
1955	Ed Brabham	Long Jump	23-8
1956*	Ed Brabham	60-yard dash	:06.3
1956	Ed Brabham	100-yard dash	:09.7
1956	Ed Brabham	220-yard dash	:21.2
1956*	Joe Savoldi	70-yard high hurdles	:08.5
1956	Henry Kennedy	Two-mile run	9:19.1
1957*	Dave Lean	440-yard run	:49.4
1957	Dave Lean	880-yard run	1:52.9
1958*	Dave Lean	600-yard run	1:10.2
1958	Dave Lean	880-yard run	1:50.3
1959*	Bob Lake	Mile Run	4:10.9
1959	Bob Lake	Mile Run	4:09
1959	Forddy Kennedy	Two-mile run	9:15.1
1960*	Willie Atterberry	1000-yard run	2:11.7
1960	Mike Kleinhans	Pole Vault (2-way tie)	14-3 5/8
1961*	Gerald Young	Two-Mile Run	9:08.1
1962*	Sherman Lewis	300-yard dash	:31.2
1962*	Sherman Lewis	Long Jump	24-6
1962	Gerald Young	Two-mile run	9:12
1963*	Sherman Lewis	Long Jump	23-8½

Year	Name	Event	Time/Mark
1963*	Robert Moreland	60-yard dash	:06.1
1963	Jan Bowen	Mile Run	4:14.3
1964*	Robert Moreland	60-yard dash	:06.1
1964*	Mike Martens	1000-yard run	2:10.3
1964*	Jim Garrett	Long Jump	24-7
1965*	Jim Garrett	Long Jump	24-11
1965*	Gene Washington	70-yard low hurdles	:07.7
1965*	Das Campbell	300-yard dash	:30.9
1965*	Keith Coates	Mile Run	4:09.5
1965	Jim Garrett	Long Jump	24-5½
1965	Jim Garrett	220-yard dash	:21.6
1965	Gene Washington	120-yard high hurdles	:14.2
1965	Keith Coates	Mile Run	4:08.2
1965	Mike Bowers	High Jump	6-7
1966	John Spain	880-yard run	1:48.0
1966	Gene Washington	120-yard high hurdles	13.8
1966	Bob Steele	440-yard intermediate hurdles	:50.7
1966*	Jim Garrett	Long Jump	24-1½
1966*	Gene Washington	70-yard high hurdles	:08.3
1966*	Gene Washington	70-yard low hurdles	:07.8
1966*	Dick Sharkey	Two-mile run	9:01.4
1966	Mike Martens, Rick Dunn, Das Campbell, John Spain	Mile Relay	3:10.9
1967*	Patrick Wilson	600-yard run	1:11.3
1967*	Richard Sharkey	Two-mile run	9:03.8
1967*	Mike Bowers	High Jump	6-9
1967*	Roland Carter	Pole Vault	15-0
1967	Gene Washington	120-yard high hurdles	:13.7
1967	Roland Carter	Pole Vault	16-0¾
1967	John Spain	660-yard run	1:16.7
1968*	Don Crawford, Rich Stevens, Pat Wilson, Bill Wehrwein	Mile Relay	3:14.4
1969*	Bill Wehrwein	600-yard run	1:09.4
1969*	James Bastian, Roger Merchant, Pat Wilson, Bill Wehrwein	Mile Relay	3:13.4
1969	Bill Wehrwein	440-yard run	:46.2
1970*	Bill Wehrwein	600-yard run	1:09.3
1970*	Herb Washington	60-yard dash	:06.0
1970*	Al Henderson, Mike Murphy, John Mock, Bill Wehrwein	Mile Relay	3:15.5
1970	Herb Washington	100-yard dash	:09.5

BIG TEN OUTDOOR CHAMPIONS

1965	Michigan State	56
1966	Michigan State	52½

BIG TEN INDOOR CHAMPIONS

1966	Michigan State	50

IC4A INDIVIDUAL CHAMPIONS

Year	Name	Event	Time/Mark
1927	Fred Alderman	440-yard dash	:48.3
1938	Wilbur Greer	100-yard dash	:09.9
1938	Harvey Woodstra	220-yard low hurdles	:23.8
1939	Walt Arrington	High Jump (3-way tie)	6-4
1942	Ted Wonch	Pole Vault (3-way tie)	13-0
1946	Ted Wonch	Pole Vault	13-0
1947	Fred Johnson	Broad Jump	24-7 3/8
1947	Fred Johnson	220-yard low hurdles	:23.7
1948	Fred Johnson	Broad Jump	24-1 5/8
1948	Jack Dianetti	880-yard run	1:53.2
1948	Paige Christiansen	120-yard high hurdles	:14.9
1949	Horace Smith	120-yard high hurdles	14:3
1949	Horace Smith	220-yard low hurdles	:22.9
1949	Fred Johnson	Broad Jump	24-2
1949*	Horace Smith	60-yard high hurdles	:07.2
1949*	Fred Johnson	Broad Jump	24-6¼
1949*	Don Makielski, Dave Peppard, Bill Mack, Jack Dianetti	Two-mile relay	7:49.5
1950*	Bill Mack	Mile	4:11
1950*	Fred Johnson	Broad Jump	24-8¾

*Indoors

208

IC4A OUTDOOR CHAMPIONS

1949	Michigan State	43

IC4A INDOOR CHAMPIONS

1949	Michigan State	35 2/5
1950	Michigan State	21

DRAKE RELAYS WINNERS

1922	DeGay Ernst	440-yard hurdles	:54.4
1931	Clark Chamberlain	Two-mile run	9:23.1
1938	Robert Adcock, William Carpenter, Harvey Woodstra, Wilbur Greer	880-yard relay	1:27.1
1946	Alfred LaGrou, Jim Fraser, Kinsey Tanner, Walter Mack	Sprint Medley Relay	3:32.2
1946	Richard Zobel, Jim Gibbard, Alfred LaGrou, Walter Mack	Two-Mile relay	7:57.3
1947	Jim Fraser, Harold Mayhew, Bob Schepers, Jack Dianetti	Sprint Medley Relay	3:25.7
1949	Jack Dianetti, Warren Druetzler, Tom Irmen, Bill Mack	Four-mile relay	17:32.3
1949	Paige Christiansen	120-yard high hurdles	:14.6
1949	Horace Smith, George Watson, Jesse Thomas, Paige Christiansen	480-yard shuttle hurdle relay	:60.0
1951	Jim Kepford, John Walter, Don Makielski, Warren Druetzler	Four-mile relay	17:21.2
1952	Bob Carey	Shot Put	51-4½
1954	Harlan Benjamin, Ray Eggleston, Bill Brendel, John Corbelli	480-yard shuttle hurdle relay	1:01.0
1956	Joe Savoldi	120-yard high hurdles	:14.2
1961	Solomon Akpata	Triple jump	47-0
1965	Clint Jones, Bob Steele, Fred McKoy, Gene Washington	480-yard shuttle hurdle relay	:57.9
1966	Clint Jones, Bob Steele, Fred McKoy, Gene Washington	480-yard shuttle hurdle relay	:57.4
1967	Robert Steele, Charles Pollard, Stephen Derby, Gene Washington	480-yard shuttle hurdle relay	:57.3
1967	Gene Washington, Daswell Campbell, Richard Dunn, John Spain	Sprint medley	3:19.5

Site of Spartan track meets in the early 1920s was Old College Field. The action here is a dual meet between State and Ohio State, May 21, 1922.

PENN RELAYS WINNERS

1927	Forrest Lang, Henry Henson, Bohn Grim,		
	Fred Alderman	880-yard relay	1:28.4
1934	Alvin F. Jackson	Triple jump	45-0 7/8
1935	Dee Weaver, James Wright, Tom Ottey,		
	Wesley Hurd	Distance medley relay	10:18.4
1935	Charles Dennis, John Gardner, Tom Ottey,		
	Wesley Hurd	Four-mile relay	17:49.8
1940	Ray Fehr	Two-mile run	9:25.9
1958	Brian Castle, Bob Lake, Dave Lean, Willie		
	Atterberry	Two-mile relay	7:30.1
1960	Willie Atterberry	400-meter hurdles	:51.5
1963	Bob Moreland	100-yard dash	:09.8
1963	John Parker, Walker Beverly, Sherman		
	Lewis, Bobby Moreland	440-yard relay	:41.5
1963	John Parker, Walker Beverly, Sherman		
	Lewis, Bobby Moreland	880-yard relay	1:25.1

MICHIGAN INTERCOLLEGIATE ATHLETIC ASSOCIATION CHAMPIONSHIPS (MIAA)

Team Standings

1888	2nd	1893	2nd	1898	1st	1903	1st
1889	1st	1894	2nd	1899	1st	1904	1st
1890	1st	1895	1st	1900	1st	1905	1st
1891	2nd	1896	5th	1901	1st	1906	1st
1892	1st	1897	1st	1902	1st	1907	1st

Individual Champions

1888	Harris F. Hall	Running Bases	16.5
	Leander L. Burnett	Standing Broad Jump	12'7"
	Leander L. Burnett	Running Hop, Step and Jump	41'4½"
	Leander L. Burnett	Backward Broad Jump	9'8"
	John W. Toan	High Handspring Jump	4'6"
	Leander L. Burnett	High Kick (Both Feet)	6'2"
	George L. Chase	Baseball Throw	338'3½"
	James H. Hooper	Hammer Throw (16 lb.)	68'10½"
	James H. Hooper	Shot Put	32'2"

The conference introduced an all-around award in 1889. Competitors had to qualify in 10 different events.

Qualifications for All-Around

Hammer Throw	70'	440 Yds.	:60.0
Running High Jump	4'8"	Running Broad Jump	18'6"
Running Hop, Step and Jump	35'	Pole Vault	7'6"
Standing Broad Jump	9'4"	100 Yds	:11.5
Shot Put	25'	120 Yd. High Hurdles	:20.0

1889	Leander L. Burnett	All-Around Award	
	George L. Chase	Baseball Throw	339'9"
	Leander L. Burnett	Hammer Throw (16 lbs.)	76'10"
	Leander L. Burnett	Shot Put (17 lb.)	33'5"
	Leander L. Burnett	Standing Broad Jump	12'3¾"
	Leander L. Burnett	Running Broad Jump	18'6½"
	Leander L. Burnett	Backward Broad Jump	8'11¾"
	Leander L. Burnett	Standing Hop, Step and Jump	32'1"
	Leander L. Burnett	Running Hop, Step and Jump	40'1½"
	Leander L. Burnett	Standing High Jump	4'3½"
	Leander L. Burnett	High Kick (Both Feet)	6'2"
	Samuel K. Boyd	Standing High Kick	7'4"
	Y.S. Hillyer	High Handspring Jump	4'2½"
	Samuel K. Boyd	Backward Kick	7'2½"
	Daniel W. Bradford	Pole Vault	8'3"
1890	Leander L. Burnett	All-Around Award	
	Lewis C. Gibbs	Baseball Throw	307'
	Leander L. Burnett	Hammer Throw (16 lb.)	65'7"
	Leander L. Burnett	Shot Put (16 lb.)	31'2"
	Leander L. Burnett	Standing Hop, Step and Jump	29'6"
	Leander L. Burnett	Running Hop, Step and Jump	39'3"
	Leander L. Burnett	Standing High Jump	4'8"
	Leander L. Burnett	Standing Broad Jump	11'11½"
	Leander L. Burnett	Running Broad Jump	16'9¾"
	Leander L. Burnett	Backward Broad Jump	8'3¾"
	Leander L. Burnett	Standing Three Jumps	34'5"
	Leander L. Burnett	Hitch and Kick	8'½"

1891	Leander L. Burnett	Hammer Throw (16 lb.)	80'10"
	Leander L. Burnett	Shot Put (16 lb.)	33'
	Guy Mitchell	880 Yd. Bicycle Race	1:41.6
	George C. Monroe	Broad Handspring Jump	16'3"
	Edward H. Polhamus	50 Yd. Backward Run	:08.2
	Leander L. Burnett	Standing Hop, Step and Jump	29'1"
	Leander L. Burnett	Running Hop, Step and Jump	41'1½"
	Daniel W. Bradford	Pole Vault	8'7"
	William F. Bernart	Standing High Kick	19"
	Leander L. Burnett	High Kick (Both Feet)	6'9½"
	Leander L. Burnett	Standing Broad Jump	10'4"
	Leander L. Burnett	Running Broad Jump	17'11½"
	Leander L. Burnett	Standing Three Jumps	31'4½"
	Guy Mitchell	440 Yd. Bicycle Race	:43.8
	Leander L. Burnett	Standing High Jump	4'6"
	George C. Monroe	Running High Jump	5'
	Guy Mitchell	Mile Bicycle Race	3:28.0
	Louis C. Gibbs	Baseball Throw	346'1"

NOTE: Although Leander Burnett scored the most points, he lost the all-around medal. He did not qualify in the required number of events.

1892	Leander L. Burnett	All-Around Award	
	Arthur J. Beese	Mile	5:42.0
	William K. Sagendort	Broad Handspring Jump	17'1"
	Hugh M. Mulheron	Running High Jump	5'1"
	Leander L. Burnett	Baseball Throw	298'4"
	Leander L. Burnett	Hammer Throw (16 lb.)	94'
	Hugh M. Mulheron	Running Broad Jump	20'3"
	Leander L. Burnett	Standing Broad Jump	10'3¾"
	Leander L. Burnett	Standing High Jump	4'5"
	William F. Bernart	220 Yd. Low Hurdles	:28.5
	Frank R. Poss	Running High Kick	8'3"
	William F. Bernart	120 Yd. High Hurdles	:17.2
	Ralph Haskins	440 Yds.	:57.4
	Ralph Haskins	100 Yds.	:10.5
	Leander L. Burnett	Standing Hop, Step and Jump	30'4"
	George L. Chase	Mile Bicycle Race	3:31.0
	Roscoe Kedzie	440 Yd. Bicycle Race	:44.2
	William Bernart, Ralph Haskins, Hugh Mulheron, Charles Rittenger	Mile Relay	
1893	Paton	Shot Put	31'8½"
	Frank R. Poss	Running High Kick	8'6"
	Arthur J. Beese	100 Yds.	:11.0
	Frank R. Poss	120 Yd. High Hurdles	:18.6
	Frank R. Poss	Running Broad Jump	
	Arthur J. Beese	220 Yds.	:25.0
	Arthur J. Beese	440 Yds.	:56.6
	James R. Petley	880 Yds.	
	Arthur J. Beese	220 Yd. Low Hurdles	
	Frank R. Poss	Pole Vault	7'6"
1894	Frank R. Poss	All-Around Award	
	John E. Tracy	Mile Run	5:02.0
	Charles R. Tock	Mile Bicycle Race	2:54.5
	James R. Petley	440 Yds.	:55.7
	James R. Petley	220 Yd Low Hurdles	:29.6
	Frank R. Poss	Standing Broad Jump	10'1"
	John E. Tracy	880 Yds.	2:13.0
	James R. Petley	220 Yds.	:23.5
	William F. Bernart	120 Yd High Hurdles	:17.6
1895	Otis R. Cole	All-Around Award	
	Almus R. Speare	100 Yds.	:10.4
	Charles E. Rork	5-Mile Bicycle Race	14:32.4
	Otis R. Cole	Running Broad Jump	19'6"
	Royal S. Fisher	Shot Put	32'3½"
	E. D. Partridge	440 Yds.	:54.6
	E. D. Partridge	880 Yds.	2:08.4
	Almus R. Speare	220 Yds.	:24.8
	Otis R. Cole	Standing Broad Jump	9'8¾"
	Otis R. Cole	Running Hop, Step and Jump	41'2"
	Charles E. Rork	440 Yd. Bicycle Race	:36.2
	Otis R. Cole	120 Yd. High Hurdles	:18.0
1896	Charles B. Laitner	220 Yds.	:29.0
1897	George B. Wells	All-Around Award	
	George B. Wells	Pole Vault	8'7"
	Fred T. Williams	Hammer Throw (16 lb.)	83'7"

	George B. Wells	120 Yd. High Hurdles	:18.8
	Alexander C. Krentel	Standing Broad Jump	9'8¼"
	Charles B. Laitner	220 Yd. Low Hurdles	:28.0
	Byron H. Holdsworth	880 Yds.	2:10.6
	George B. Wells	Running Hop, Step and Jump	41'10"
	Byron H. Holdsworth	Mile	5:00.0
1898	George B. Wells	All-Around Award	
	Roy L. Brown	440 Yd. Bicycle Race	:37.0
	Byron H. Holdsworth	Mile	4:49.6
	Chandler Z. Tompkins	Running Hop, Step and Jump	44'4"
	Roy L. Brown	Mile Bicycle Race	2:28.4
	George B. Wells	440 Yds.	:51.4
	Chandler Z. Tompkins	Standing Broad Jump	9'9 7/8"
	Chandler Z. Tompkins	Shot Put	35'4¼"
	George B. Wells	Pole Vault	10'
	William E. Russell	220 Yds.	:23.2
	George B. Wells	120 Yd. High Hurdles	:17.6
	Chandler Tompkins and Hickok	Mile Tandem Bicycle	2:39.2
1899	William E. Russell	All-Around Award	
	William E. Russell	100 Yds.	:10.6
	Roy L. Brown	440 Yd. Bicycle Race	:35.8
	Harry P. Weydemeyer	Running Hop, Step and Jump	44'11½"
	Roy L. Brown	Mile Bicycle Race	3:15.0
	Harry P. Weydemeyer	Standing Broad Jump	10'
	Clarence W. Christopher	Pole Vault	9'9"
	William E. Russell	220 Yds.	:23.2
	Roy L. Brown	5-Mile Bicycle Race	14:07.4
	Harry P. Weydemeyer	Running Broad Jump	19'10"
	Roy Brown and Purcell	Mile Tandem Bicycle Race	2:26.0
	F. E. Olson	220 Yd. Low Hurdles	:28.0
1900	Harry P. Weydemeyer	All-Around Award	
	Harry P. Weydemeyer	Running Hop, Step and Jump	41'11"
	Harry P. Weydemeyer	Standing Broad Jump	10'1"
	Harry P. Weydemeyer	Running High Jump	5'3"
	A. C. Miller	440 Yd. Bicycle Race	:40.0
	John B. Stewart	Mile Walk	9:15.0
	Albert H. Case	5-Mile Bicycle Race	18:57.0
	Frank G. Carpenter	Shot Put	33'10" (tie)
	Eugene S. Brewer	Shot Put	33'10" (tie)
	Harry G. Driskel	880 Yds.	2:18.6
	Harry P. Weydemeyer	Pole Vault	9'6"
	Harry W. Schultz	Running Broad Jump	21'4¾"
1901	Harry W. Schultz	All-Around Award	
	Harry W. Schultz	100 Yds.	:10.6
	Harry W. Schultz	220 Yds.	:23.8
	Lyman Carrier	Mile Walk	8:24.2
	Conyne	440 Bicycle Race	:37.4
	Conyne	Mile Bicycle Race	2:43.4
	Frank G. Carpenter	Standing Broad Jump	10'1½"
	Harry W. Schultz	Running Broad Jump	20'5¾"
	Harry W. Schultz	Running Hop, Step and Jump	43'6½"
	Harry W. Schultz	Pole Vault	9'8"
	Harry W. Schultz	Running High Jump	5'2¾"
1902	George A. Rae	5-Mile Bicycle Race	14:51.0
	Frank G. Carpenter	Standing Broad Jump	10'4"
	Phillip H. Holdsworth	880 Yds.	2:06.0
	Frank Phillips, Phillip Holdsworth, William Kastner, Matt Crosby	Mile Relay	3:42.4
1903	Harry E. Moon	100 Yds.	:10.4
	Gray K. Burrington	Running Broad Jump	21'9½"
	Wilson F. Millar	Pole Vault	10'4"
	Frank G. Phillips	Mile	4:48.4
	Harry C. Meek	880 Yds.	2:05.4
	Harry E. Moon	220 Yds.	:22.2
	Frank J. Kratz	Discus Throw	99'0"
	Garfield Verran, Frank Phillips, Harry Meek, Harry Moon	Mile Relay	3:45.0
1904	Harry E. Moon	100 Yds.	:10.2
	Wilson F. Millar	Pole Vault	10'6"
	Frank J. Kratz	Discus Throw	101'6"
	Harry E. Moon	220 Yds.	:21.4
	Harry E. Moon	440 Yds.	:54.0
	Harry E. Moon	Running Broad Jump	22'0"
	Ralph Graham, Ropha Pearsall, Orange Burrell, Harry Moon	Mile Relay	3:42.5
1905	Harry E. Moon	100 Yds.	:10.2
	Elmer Nichoson	Running High Jump	5'7¼"

State's outstanding hurdling corps of 1949 with Coach Karl Schlademan. They are, l. to r., Jesse Thomas, Fred Johnson, Paige Christiansen and Horace Smith.

	J. Verne Gongwer	Pole Vault	10'2'' (Tie)
	Frank J. Kratz	Discus Throw	102'4''
	Harry E. Moon	220 Yds.	:22.4
	Roy H. Waite	Two Mile	10:41.0
	Harry E. Moon	440 Yds.	:53.2
	Elmer Nicholson	Running Broad Jump	21'1½''
	Harry Moon, Orange Burrell,		
	James Tryon, Ralph Graham	Mile Relay	3:34.3
1906	Roy H. Gilbert	Pole Vault	10'0''
	Walter Small	120 Yd. High Hurdles	:17.0
	Gerald H. Allen	880 Yds.	2:06.8
	Ropha V. Pearsall	220 Yd. Low Hurdles	:28.6
	Ropha Pearsall, George Bignell,		
	Walter Hough, Gerald Allen	Mile Relay	3:40.0
1907	Walter H. Small	120 Yd. High Hurdles	:16.8
	Walter H. Small	Running Broad Jump	21'1½''
	J. Verne Gongwer	Pole Vault	10' (Tie)
	Chester A. Griffin	220 Yds.	:24.4
	Roy H. Gilbert	Pole Vault	10' (Tie)
	Ropha V. Pearsall	220 Yd. Low Hurdles	:27.8
	Charles Burroughs	Shot Put	38'6''
	Roy S. Wheeler	Hammer Throw	112'9¼''
	Chester Griffin, Gerald Allen,		
	Charles Ouiatt, George Bignell	Mile Relay	3:38.6

MICHIGAN STATE UNIVERSITY INTERCOLLEGIATE TRACK MEET

Team Standing

1916	1st	1920	3rd	1925	4th
1917	1st	1921	1st	1926	3rd
1918	1st	1922	1st	1927	1st
1919	1st	1923	3rd	1928	1st
		1924	3rd	1929	1st

1930	2nd	1935	1st	1940	2nd
1931	2nd	1936	3rd	1941	1st
1932	2nd	1937	1st	1942	1st
1933	2nd	1938	1st	1943	1st
1934	1st	1939	1st	1944	World War II
				1945	2nd

Individual Champions

Year	Name	Event	Result
1916	Earl B. Sheldon	800 Yds.	2:05.6
	Earl B. Sheldon	Mile	4:52.8
	Howard E. Beatty	120 High Hurdles	:16.6
	Howard E. Beatty	220 Low Hurdles	:27.4
	Frank T. Warner	Broad Jump	20'2"
1917	Ernest F. Carlson	100 Yds.	:10.4
	Ernest F. Carlson	220 Yds.	:23.6
	David L. Peppard	440 Yds.	:53.8
	Carl L. Warren	Two Mile	10:52.0
	Clark L. Barrell	120 Yd. High Hurdles	:17.2
	Earle G. Baxter	220 Yd. Low Hurdles	:30.0
	Frank T. Warner	Broad Jump	20'3"
	Arthur W. Atkin	Discus Throw	113'8"
1918	Louis J. Geiermann	Mile	4:54.8
	Arthur W. Atkin	Broad Jump	19'11½"
	Arthur W. Atkin	Shot Put	37'10¾" (Tie)
1919	Walter H. Simmons	100 Yds.	:10.1
	William H. Harvie	220 Yds.	:23.8
	Anthony J. Brendel	Mile	4:40.6
	Fred C. Spiedel	Pole Vault	11'0"
	Arthur W. Atkin	Shot Put	38'6"
	Walter Simmons, Howard Hoffman, Ray Schench, Lawrence Kurtz	Mile Relay	3:38.6
1920	Hazen S. Atkins	High Jump	5'8"
	Lester L. Beltz	Discus Throw	114'2½"
1921	DeGay Ernst	440 Yds.	:50.4
	Anthony J. Brendel	880 Yds.	2:01.8
	Frederick P. Adolph	Mile	4:33.2
	DeGay Ernst	120 Yd. High Hurdles	:15.8
	DeGay Ernst	220 Yd. Low Hurdles	24.6
	Hazen S. Atkins	High Jump	5'9" (Tie)
	Clarence W. Fessenden	Discus Throw	131'1½"
	John J. Schwei	Javelin	157'2"
		Mile Relay	3:32.2
1922	Mark C. Herdell	100 Yds.	:10.2
	Mark C. Herdell	220 Yds.	:22.4
	DeGay Ernst	440 Yds.	:50.2
	Anthony J. Brendel	880 Yds.	1:59.8
	DeGay Ernst	120 Yd. High Hurdles	:15.6
	DeGay Ernst	220 Yd. Low Hurdles	:26.0
	Hazen S. Atkins	High Jump	5'10½"
	Clarence W. Fessenden	Discus Throw	121'1"
	John J. Schwei	Javelin Throw	158'6"
1923	Leonard S. Klasse	880 Yds.	2:02.9
	Hazen S. Atkins	High Jump	5'8"
	Clarence W. Fessenden	Discus Throw	123'5"
1924	Mark C. Herdell	100 Yds.	:10.0
	Paul J. Hartsuch	880 Yds.	2:03.9
	Mark C. Herdell	220 Yd. Low Hurdles	:25.1
	Lloyd B. Kurtz	High Jump	5'8½"
1925	Frederick P. Alderman	100 Yds.	:09.7
	Frederick P. Alderman	220 Yds.	:21.2
	Frederick P. Alderman	Broad Jump	23'3/8"
1926	Frederick P. Alderman	100 Yds.	:10.2
	Frederick P. Alderman	220 Yds.	:22.7
	Bohn W. Grim	440 Yds.	51.1
	Henry E. Wylie	Mile	4:30.0
	Floyd A. Harper	Two Mile	10:40.0
	Frederick P. Alderman	Broad Jump	22'6½"
1927	Frederick P. Alderman	100 Yds.	:09.6
	Frederick P. Alderman	220 Yds.	:20.5
	Bohn W. Grim	440 Yds.	:48.9
	Harold L. McAtee	Pole Vault	12'4" (Tie)
	Bohn Grim, Henry Henson, William Kroll, Frederick Alderman	Mile Relay	3:26.0
1928	H. Lyle Henson	100 Yds.	:10.0
	H. Lyle Henson	220 Yds.	:22.2

	Lauren P. Brown	Two Mile	9:45.2
	Harold L. McAtee	Pole Vault	12' (Tie)
	Paul M. Smith	Shot Put	43'6¼"
1929	Lauren P. Brown	Two Mile	9:41.3
	Harold L. McAtee	Pole Vault	12'9¾"
1930	Lauren P. Brown	Two Mile	9:34.8
	Kenneth W. Yarger	120 Yd. High Hurdles	:15.6
	Walter F. Russow	220 Yd. Low Hurdles	:25.0
	Robert C. Olson	Pole Vault	12'6½" (Tie)
1931	Clark S. Chamberlain	Mile	4:16.8
	Clark S. Chamberlain	Two Mile	9:54.4
	Robert C. Olson	Pole Vault	13' (Tie)
	Kenneth W. Yarger	120 Yd. High Hurdles	:14.9
	Robert K. Russell	220 Yd. Low Hurdles	:24.8
1932	Roger Keast	440 Yds.	:49.3
	Otto W. Pongrace	880 Yds.	1:56.5
	Ralph E. Small	Two Mile	9:47.5
1933	Otto W. Pongrace	880 Yds.	1:56.6
	Wesley V. Hurd	Mile	4:28.3
	Edwin G. Bath	120 Yd. High Hurdles	:15.4
	Otto Pongrace, Frank Hoff, Charles Warren, Roger Keast	Mile Relay	3:21.4
1934	Otto W. Pongrace	880 Yds.	1:56.4
	William W. Hart	100 Yds.	:10.0
	Wesley V. Hurd	Mile	4:23.7
	Francis C. Dittrich	Broad Jump	22'6½"
	Cleo E. Beaumont	Javelin	184'9¾"
1935	Carl T. Mueller	220 Yds.	:22.5
	William H. Smith	75 Yds. (Shot Putters)	:08.4
	James H. Wright	880 Yds.	1:56.5
	Francis Dittrich	Broad Jump	23'2¼"
1936	Harold L. Sparks	Two Mile	9:44.0
1937	Gerald H. Boss	Two Mile	9:37.2
1938	Richard D. Frey	Mile	4:22.4
	Ernest W. Greer	100 Yds.	:09.8
	Harvey P. Woodstra	120 High Hurdles	:14.3
	Ernest W. Greer	220 Yds.	:21.2
	Kenneth A. Waite	Two Mile	9:40.3
	Harvey P. Woodstra	220 Yd. Low Hurdles	:23.1
	Lodo A. Habrle	Pole Vault	12'8"
	Clare A. Graft	Broad Jump	23'2"
	Ernest K. Bremer	Javelin	192'8¾"
	Robert Adcock, Willard Fager, Francis Caluory, Robert Hills	Mile Relay	3:24.0
1939	Roy B. Fehr	Mile	4:18.7
	Rudolph (Urick) Yovonovitz	120 Yd. High Hurdles	:15.2
	Edmund H. Lautenschlager	880 Yd.	1:57.1
	Edward W. VanAuken	Two Mile	9:26.4
	Rudolph (Urick) Yovonovitz	220 Yd. Low Hurdles	:24.1
	Walter A. Arrington	High Jump	6'2 3/8" (Tie)
	Walter A. Arrington	Broad Jump	23'4 3/8"
	Ernest K. Bremer	Shot Put	44'5 5/8"
	Ernest K. Bremer	Javelin	190'7¼"
1940	Roy B. Fehr	Mile	4:14.4
	Walter A. Arrington	High Jump	6'2 7/8"
	Walter A. Arrington	Broad Jump	23'3"
	Leslie C. Bruckner	Shot Put	45'7/8"
	Leslie C. Bruckner	Discus Throw	132'2 5/8"
1941	Theodore N. Wonch	Pole Vault	13'2" (Tie)
	Lynn H. Harris	Pole Vault	13'2" (Tie)
	Walter A. Arrington	High Jump	6'½" (Tie)
	James A. Milne	High Jump	6'½" (Tie)
	Walter A. Arrington	Broad Jump	22'5 7/8"
	Walter A. Arrington	Shot Put	44'6½"
	Walter A. Arrington	Discus Throw	134' 8 7/8"
1942	William J. Scott	Mile	4:49.4
	Robert J. McCarthy	100 Yds.	:10.4
	John A. Liggett	880 Yds.	2:00.8
	Theodore N. Wonch	Pole Vault	12'6"
	James A. Milne	High Jump	6'4½"
1943	William J. Scott	Mile	4:22.0
	Robert J. McCarthy	100 Yds.	:10.4
	Melvin C. Buschmann	120 Yd. High Hurdles	:15.7
	John A. Liggett	880 Yds.	1:57.0
	Robert J. McCarthy	220 Yds.	:23.2
	Jerry M. Page	Two Mile	9:44.9
	Melvin C. Buschmann	220 Yd. Low Hurdles	:26.0

	James A. Milne	High Jump	6'2¼"
	August Sunnen	Discus Throw	122'7 5/8"
	Leonard G. Naab	Javelin Throw	180'1½"
	John VonEberstein, Joseph Kennedy,		
	John Liggett, Dale Kaulitz	Mile Relay	3:27.4
1944	World War II		
1945	Robert J. O'Leary	440 Yds.	:51.3
	William R. Maskill	880 Yds.	2:04.3
	Robert E. Price	Two Mile	10:55.8
	Jack McClain	Shot Put	42'3¾"
	Harold Pickering, Wayne Finkbeiner,		
	William Maskill, Robert O'Leary	Mile Relay	3:30.7

CENTRAL COLLEGIATE CONFERENCE INDOOR WINNERS

1927	Fred Alderman	Broad Jump	22-5 3/8
	Ivan Tillotson	Shot Put	45-1¼
1928	Harold McAtee	Pole Vault	12-6
1929	Harold McAtee	Pole Vault	12-10 3/8
1930	Robert Olsen (tie)	Pole Vault	12-7
1931	Clark Chamberlain	Two-Mile Run	9:42.2
1932	Edwin Bath	60-Yard High Hurdles	:07.6
1933	Kennith Warren, Roger Keast,		
	Andrew Cobb, Donald Hovey	One-Mile Relay	3:26.9
1934	Otto Pongrace	880-Yard Run	1:58.2
	Alvin Jackson	65-Yard Low Hurdles	:07.3
	Alvin Jackson	60-Yard High Hurdles	:08.0
	Tom Ottey	Two-Mile Run	9:28.7
1938	Ernest Greer	60-Yard Dash	:06.2
	Harvey Woodstra	60-Yard High Hurdles	:07.5
1939	Ernest Greer	60-Yard Dash	:06.3
1940	Richard Frey	Two-Mile Run	9:31.9
	Walter Arrington	High Jump	6-2
1945	Harold Pickering, Wayne Finkbeiner,		
	Ray Beckord, Herb Speerstra	One-Mile Relay	3:23.3
1946	Mason Kelley	75-Yard Dash	:07.8
1947	Jack Dianetti	440-Yard Run	:50.3
	Jack Dianetti	880-Yard Run	1:56.1
	Robert Vosburg (tie)		
	Francis Bowerman (tie)	Pole Vault	12-6
1948	Fred Johnson	75-Yard Dash	:07.6
	Tom Irmen	One-Mile Run	4:21.9
	Jack Dianetti	880-Yard Run	1:59.1
	Bob Kritzer	300-Yard Run	:31.7
	Fred Johnson	75-Yard Low Hurdles	:08.3
	Fred Johnson	Broad Jump	25-4¾
1949	Fred Johnson	Broad Jump	24-8 7/8
	Bill Mack	One-Mile Run	4:15.5
	Horace Smith	75-Yard High Hurdles	:09.0
	Tom Irmen	Two-Mile Run	9:31.2
	Warren Druetzler	880-Yard Run	1:55.6
1950	Fred Johnson	Broad Jump	23-1¾
	Bill Mack (tie)		
	Warren Druetzler (tie)	One-Mile Run	4:19.3
	Fred Johnson	75-Yard Dash	:07.5
	Fred Johnson	75-Yard Low Hurdles	:08.3
	Don Makielski	880-Yard Run	1:53.4

CENTRAL COLLEGIATE CONFERENCE INDOOR CHAMPIONS

1934	Michigan State	—
1947	Michigan State	54
1948	Michigan State	—
1949	Michigan State	60½

CENTRAL COLLEGIATE CONFERENCE OUTDOOR WINNERS

1926	Frederick Alderman	100-Yard Dash	:10.2
	Frederick Alderman	220-Yard Dash	:22.4
	Frederick Alderman	Broad Jump	22-9¼
	Ivan Tillotson	Discus Throw	133-7¾
1927	Frederick Alderman	100-Yard Dash	:10.3
	Frederick Alderman	220-Yard Dash	:22.6
	Henry Wylie	One-Mile Run	4:29.9
	Clarence Passink (tie)	120-Yard High Hurdles	:16.5
	Forrest Lang, Russell Lord,		

	Henry Henson, Frederick Alderman	880-Yard Relay	1:30.0
	Harold McAtee	Pole Vault	13-3 5/8
	Frederick Alderman	Broad Jump	22-7
	Paul Smith	Shot Put	43-10 3/8
	Albert McCabe	Discus Throw	120½
	Earl Wareham (tie)	High Jump	5-9 5/8
1928	Lewis Hackney	880-Yard Run	2:00.0
	Henry Wylie	One-Mile Run	4:22.2
	Harold McAtee	Pole Vault	13-0
	Paul Smith	Shot Put	42-2
	Ivan Tillotson	Discus Throw	128-4½
1929	Lewis Hackney	880-Yard Run	1:58.1
	Harold McAtee (tie)	Pole Vault	12-6
1930	Clark Chamberlain	Two-Mile Run	9:32.0
	Kenneth Yarger	120-Yard High Hurdles	:15.5
1931	Clark Chamberlain	Two-Mile Run	9:18.7
	Kenneth Yarger	120-Yard High Hurdles	:15.2
	Robert Olsen (tie)		
	Arthur Arbogast (tie)		
	Monte Holcomb (tie)	Pole Vault	12-0
1932	Otto Pongrace	880-Yard Run	1:56.3
	Otto Pongrace, Donald Hovey,		
	Roger Keast, Charles Warren	One-Mile Relay	3:20.6
1933	Clifford Liberty	220-Yard Low Hurdles	:24.5
1934	Wesley Hurd	One-Mile Run	4:20.4
1938	Ernest Greer	100-Yard Dash	:09.7
1939	Ernest Bremer	Javelin Throw	187-0
1941	James Milne	High Jump	6-2 1/8
1942	James Milne	High Jump	6-4
1943	Leonard Naab	Javelin Throw	202½
1947	Robert Schepers	220-Yard Dash	:22.5
	James Frazer, Robert Frazer,		
	James Gibbard, Robert Schepers	One-Mile Relay	3:27.6
	Robert Frazer, William Frazer,		
	Robert Schepers, Harold Mayhew	440-Yard Relay	:43.2
1948	Jack Dianetti	880-Yard Run	1:53.3
1949	Jack Dianetti	880-Yard Run	1:52.8
	Fred Johnson	220-Yard Low Hurdles	:23.7
	Fred Johnson	Broad Jump	24-8½
1950	Warren Druetzler	Two-Mile Run	9:12.3
	Richard Henson, Paul Shek,		
	Jack Dianetti, Donald Makielski	One-Mile Relay	3:19.3
1953	James Kepford	One-Mile Run	4:14.2
1954	Edgar Brabham	220-Yard Dash	:21.9
	Kevan Gosper	440-Yard Run	:47.8
	Edgar Brabham, Kevan Gosper,		
	Richard Stutsman, John Corbelli	One-Mile Relay	3:17.8
1955	Kevan Gosper	440-Yard Run	:47.5
	Charles Coykendall	Pole Vault	13-4
1956	Selwyn Jones	Two-Mile Run	9:08.4

Fred Alderman, State's first NCAA track champion, winning the 100-yard dash title at the 1927 meet at Chicago's Soldier Field.

1960	Solomon Akpata	Broad Jump	23-9¼
1965	Jim Garrett	Long Jump	24-5¼
	Gene Washington, Clint Jones,		
	Daswell Campbell, James Summers	440-Yard Relay	:41.1
	Gene Washington	120-Yard High Hurdles	:14.3
1966	Robert Steele	440-Yard Low Hurdles	:50.8
	John Spain	880-Yard Run	1:50.3
	Gene Washington	120-Yard High Hurdles	:14.1
	Roland Carter (tie)	Pole Vault	14-6
	Robert Steele, Daswell Campbell,		
	Richard Dunn, John Spain	One-Mile Relay	3:12.7
1967	John Spain	880-Yard Run	1:49.7
1968	Roland Carter (tie)	Pole Vault	15-6
1969	Roger Merchant	880-Yard Run	1:48.9
	Bill Wehrwein, John Mock,		
	Pat Wilson, Roger Merchant	One-Mile Relay	3:08.3
1970	Herb Washington	100-Yard Dash	:09.4

CENTRAL COLLEGIATE CONFERENCE OUTDOOR CHAMPIONS

1927	Michigan State	73½
1947	Michigan State	41
1949	Michigan State	50
1950	Michigan State (co-champion)	31
1954	Michigan State	32
1966	Michigan State	49½

VARSITY TRACK RECORDS — INDOOR
(As of April 1970)

50 Yard Dash	5.1	Herb Washington	1970
60 Yard Dash	5.9	Herb Washington	1970
300 Yard Dash	30.8	Bill Wehrwein	1968
440 Yard Dash	48.2	Kevin Gosper	1955
600 Yard Dash	1:08.6	Bill Wehrwein	1969
60 Yard Low Hurdles	6.8	Fred Johnson	1950
		Gene Washington	1967
60 Yard High Hurdles	7.1	Gene Washington	1967
65 Yard Low Hurdles	7.3	Alvin Jackson	1934
65 Yard High Hurdles	7.9	Gene Washington	1965
70 Yard Low Hurdles	7.7	Gene Washington	1965
70 Yard High Hurdles	8.2	Gene Washington	1967
		Charles Pollard	1967
880 Yard Run	1:50.6	John Spain	1967
		John Mock	1970
1000 Yard Run	2:10.3	Mike Martens	1964
One Mile Run	4:04.4	Ken Popejoy	1970
Two Mile Run	8:51.2	Dick Sharkey	1967
Long Jump	25'4¾"	Fred Johnson	1948
Pole Vault	16'4"	Roland Carter	1968
Shot Put	53'4¾"	Dave Mutchler	1964
High Jump	6'9"	Mike Bowers	1967
One Mile Relay	3:13.4	Jim Bastian, Roger Merchant,	1969
		Pat Wilson, Bill Wehrwein	
Two Mile Relay	7:38.5	James Carr, Brian Castle,	1960
		Willie Atterberry, Bob Lake	
Sprint Medley Relay	3:24.2	Rick Dunn, Bob Steele,	1967
		Don Crawford, John Spain	
Distance Medley Relay	10:03.8	Pat Wilson, Roger Merchant,	1967
(440-880-¾ Mile)		Art Link, Dean Rosenberg	
240 Yard Shuttle Hurdle Relay	28.5	Howard Doughty, Wayne Hartwick,	1970
		John Morrison, Charles Pollard	
220 Yard Shuttle Hurdle Relay	24.3	Bob Steele, Clint Jones,	1966
		Fred McKoy, Gene Washington	
Triple Jump	48'5½"	Eric Allen	1970

VARSITY TRACK RECORDS — OUTDOOR
(As of June 1970)

100 Yard Dash	9.2	Herb Washington	1970
220 Yard Dash	20.7	Robert Moreland	1963
440 Yard Dash	45.7	Bill Wehrwein	1969
660 Yard Dash	1:16.7	John Spain	1967
880 Yard Run	1:48.0	John Spain	1966
Mile Run	4:04.9	Robert Lake	1959
Two Mile Run	8:56.2	Dick Sharkey	1967
Three Mile Run	13:55.7	Ken Leonowicz	1969

3000 Meter Steeplechase	8:59.5	Dick Sharkey	1967
5000 Meter Run	14:52.2	Selwyn Jones	1956
Six Mile Run	28:37.8	Dick Sharkey	1966
10,000 Meter Run	31:15.3	Selwyn Jones	1956
120 Yard High Hurdles	13.7	Gene Washington	1967
440 Yard Hurdles	50.1	Bob Steele	1966
400 Meter Hurdles	50.8	Bob Steele	1966
Long Jump	25-4 3/8	Fred Johnson	1948
High Jump	7-0	Mike Bowers	1967
Hop-Step-Jump	48-9½	Jim Garrett	1965
Shot Put	53-11¾	Robert Carey	1952
Discus	163-4	Tom Herbert	1965
Javelin	213-10	Tony Kumiega	1961
Pole Vault	16-3	Roland Carter	1968
440 Yard Relay	41.1	Das Campbell, Jim Summers, Clint Jones, Gene Washington	1965
		LaRue Butchee, Mike Holt Al Henderson, Herb Washington	1970
480 Yard Shuttle Hurdle Relay	57.3	Charles Pollard, Bob Steele, Steve Derby, Gene Washington	1967
880 Yard Relay	1:25.1	Walker Beverly, John Parker, Sherm Lewis, Robert Moreland	1963
Mile Relay	3:08.3	Pat Wilson, John Mock, Roger Merchant, Bill Wehrwein	1969
Spring Medley Relay (440-220-220-880)	3:19.5	Das Campbell, Gene Washington, Rick Dunn, John Spain	1967
Two Mile Relay	7:21.4	Brian Castle, Robert Lake David Lean, Willie Atterberry	1958
Distance Medley Relay	9:49.6	John Mock, Pat Wilson, Roger Merchant, Kim Hartman	1969
Four Mile Relay	16:59.4	Roger Humbarger, Michael Kaines, Donald Castle, Jan Bowen	1963

JENISON FIELD HOUSE RECORDS
(As of April 1970)

Long Jump	25'4¾"	Fred Johnson (Michigan State)	1948
Pole Vault	16'4"	Roland Carter (Michigan State)	1968
Shot Put	62'7"	Steve Wilhelm (Kansas)	1969
High Jump	7'0"	Pat Matzdorf (Wisconsin)	1970
60 Yard Dash	6.0	Herb Washington (Michigan State)	1970
300 Yard Run	30.0	Mel Barnwell (Pittsburgh)	1959
440 Yard Run	47.8	Dave Mills (Purdue)	1962
600 Yard Run	1:08.6	Bill Wehrwein (Michigan State)	1969
70 Yard High Hurdles	8.2	Gene Washington (Michigan State)	1967
		Charles Pollard (Michigan State)	1967
70 Yard Low Hurdles	7.7	Gene Washington (Michigan State)	1967
		Mike Butler (Wisconsin)	1967
880 Yard Run	1:49.8	Mark Winzenreid (Wisconsin)	1970
1000 Yard Run	2:10.4	Roger Kathol (Kansas)	1969
One Mile Run	4:03.4	Jim Ryun (Kansas)	1968
Two Mile Run	8:51.8	John Jones (Air Force)	1970
240 Yard Shuttle Hurdle Relay	28.5	(Michigan State) Howard Doughty, John Morrison, Wayne Hartwick, Charlie Pollard)	1970
Sprint Medley Relay	3:24.2	Rick Dunn, Bob Steele, Don Crawford, John Spain (Michigan State)	1967
Distance Medley Relay	9:49.8	Jim Neihouse, Jim Hatcher, Thorn Bigley, Doug Smith (Kansas)	1969
Two Mile Relay	7:26.1	J. Jetcalf, J. Perry, T. Von Ruden, D. Perry (Oklahoma State)	1965
College One Mile Relay	3:17.7	(Loyola) G. Crosby, B. O'Connor, J. Drozd, B. Brown	1965
University One Mile Relay	3:15.5	(Michigan State) Al Henderson, John Mock, Mike Murphy, Bill Wehrwein	1970
Triple Jump	48'5½"	Eric Allen (Michigan State) Mike Bond (Wisconsin)	1970

RALPH H. YOUNG FIELD RECORDS
(As of May 1970)

Pole Vault	16-1¾	Roland Carter (MSU)	1968
High Jump	7-0	Mike Bowers (MSU)	1967
Long Jump	24-6½	Paul Warfield (Ohio State)	1962
Triple Jump	48-6	Mike Bond (Wisconsin)	1968
Shot Put	57-2¾	Bob Winchell (Indiana)	1970

Discus Throw	163-11½	Bob Hawke (Wisconsin)	1968
Javelin	213-10	Tony Kumiega (MSU)	1961
100 Yard Dash	9.6	Herb Washington (MSU)	1970
		Bill Hurd (Notre Dame)	1968
220 Yard Dash	21.4	Mike Goodrich (Indiana)	1970
		Tom Robinson (Michigan)	1960
		Bill Jacobs (Chicago)	1957
440 Yard Dash	46.1	George Kerr (Illinois)	1960
660 Yard Run	1:17.7	John Spain (MSU)	1967
880 Yard Run	1:49.1	John Spain (MSU)	1966
One Mile Run	4:07.0	Ken Popejoy (MSU)	1970
Two Mile Run	8:59.6	Bill Clark (Notre Dame)	1965
Three Mile Run	13:54.7	Scott Hiles (Indiana)	1970
3000 Meter Steeplechase	8:53.8	Steve Kelley (Indiana)	1970
120 Yard High Hurdles	13.8	Mike Butler (Wisconsin)	1968
440 Yard Intermediate Hurdles	52.6	Bob Steele (MSU)	1967
One Mile Relay	3:15.3	MSU—Wilson, Dunn, Wehrwein, Crawford	1968
440 Yard Relay	41.2	Indiana—Goodrich, Miller, Lundgren, Highbaugh	1970
880 Yard Relay	1:27.8	Michigan—Hessler, Carroll, Coates, LaRue	1953
Two Mile Relay	7:36.2	MSU—Walter, Kepford, Coor, Jarrett	1953
Four Mile Relay	17:29.9	MSU—Jones, Wheeler, Denslow, Kennedy	1956

SPARTAN TEAM RECORDS

RECORD BY SEASON

Year	W	L	T	BIG TEN Indoors Points	Outdoors Points
1886	0	0	1		
1898	2	0	1		
1902	2	0	0		
1903	1	0	0		
1904	2	0	0		
1905	5	0	0		
1906	2	0	0		
1907	2	1	0		
1908	3	0	0		
1909	1	1	0		
1910	1	0	0		
1911	No Dual Meets				
1912	0	1	0		
1913	1	3	0		
1914	1	1	0		
1915	1	1	0		
1916	1	1	0		
1917	0	1	0		
1918	0	1	0		
1919	1	1	0		
1920	2	4	0		
1921	3	1	0		
1922	4	1	0		
1923	1	3	0		
1924	2	3	0		
1925	1	3	0		
1926	2	3	0		
1927	4	0	0		
1928	2	2	0		
1929	2	2	0		
1930	2	3	0		
1931	5	0	0		
1932	4	1	0		
1933	3	0	0		
1934	1	2	0		
1935	0	2	0		
1936	1	1	0		
1937	5	1	0		
1938	5	3	0		
1939	2	5	0		
1940	0	5	0		
1941	0	6	0		
1942	3	4	0		

Year	W	L	T					
1943	3	2	0					
1944	No Meets — World War II							
1945	2	2	0					
1946	4	2	0					
1947	6	1	0					
1948	2	2	1					
1949	5	0	1					
1950	3	0	0					
1951	2	4	0	3rd	28	2nd	49	
1952	4	1	0	5th	11 3/5	5th	10	17/20
1953	4	1	0	5th	15 5/12	3rd	25	
1954	1	2	0	5th	19 1/4	3rd	37	9/14
1955	2	1	0	2nd	46 1/2	5th	19	4/9
1956	2	2	0	4th	33 2/5	4th	28	1/2
1957	3	2	0	3rd	30 3/5	5th (2-way tie)	16	
1958	3	3	0	5th	19	4th	23	1/2
1959	1	4	0	7th	13 3/4	8th	11	
1960	2	1	0	3rd	31 9/10	4th	22	
1961	2	2	0	6th	20	6th	16	
1962	2	0	0	3rd	28	3rd	34	2/5
1963	2	0	0	4th	30	4th	31	
1964	4	1	0	3rd	32	4th	22	
1965	4	0	0	2nd	45 1/2	1st	56	
1966	4	0	0	1st	50	1st	52	1/2
1967	4	0	0	2nd	53	2nd	49	
1968	0	1	0	4th	49	7th	21	
1969	1	3	0	4th	26	4th	27	
1970	1	3	0	3rd	43	3rd	68	
	153	107	4					

State's indoor track meets are conducted in spacious Jenison Field House.

RECORD BY OPPONENT

School	W	L	T
Albion	3	0	1
Alma	5	0	0
Armour Tech	3	0	0
Central Michigan	2	0	0
Chicago Track Club	2	0	0
Chicago	2	1	0
Chicago Y.M.C.A.	1	0	0
DePaul	1	0	0
DePauw	2	1	0
Detroit City Coll.	8	1	0
Detroit J.C.	2	0	0
Detroit	3	0	0
Detroit Y.M.C.A.	0	2	0
Eastern Michigan	7	2	0
Great Lakes N.T.S.	Triangular Meet Only		
Hillsdale	Quadrangular Meet Only		
Illinois	1	6	0
Indiana	4	4	0
Iowa State	0	2	0
Iowa	2	1	0
Kalamazoo	1	0	0
Kansas	0	2	0
Kentucky	Triangular Meet Only		
Lansing H.S.	1	0	1
Marquette	14	13	0
Maryland	1	0	0
Michigan	1	13	1
Miami (Ohio)	2	0	0
Minnesota	0	1	0
Missouri	Triangular Meet Only		
Murray State	Triangular Meet Only		
Nebraska	0	1	0
Notre Dame	23	30	0
Northwestern	1	0	0
Oberlin	2	0	0
Oklahoma	Triangular Meet Only		
Olivet	5	0	0
Ohio	1	0	0
Ohio State	15	11	0
Ohio Wesleyan	5	1	0
Penn State	8	6	0
Purdue	4	2	0
Southern California	0	0	1
Syracuse	1	0	0
Wabash	Triangular Meet Only		
Wayne State	2	0	0
Western Michigan	8	3	0
Western Reserve	2	0	0
Wisconsin	6	2	0
Yale	Triangular Meet Only		

SPARTAN COACHES' RECORDS

Coach		W	L	T
None		0	0	1
Henry Keep	(1898)	2	0	1
George E. Denman	(1902-03)	3	0	0
Chester L. Brewer	(1904-10)	16	2	0
John F. Macklin	(1912-13)	1	4	0
Ion J. Cortright	(1914)	1	1	0
George Gauthier	(1915-19)	3	5	0
Arthur N. Smith	(1920-21)	5	5	0
Albert M. Barron	(1922-23)	5	4	0
Ralph H. Young	(1924-40)	41	36	0
Karl A. Schlademan	(1941-58)	49	35	2
Francis C. Dittrich	(1959-)	27	15	0
		153	107	4

SPARTAN TOURNAMENT RECORD

MIAA FIELD DAYS

The MIAA originated with Field Days which lasted two grueling days. The competitors must have been gluttons for punishment. To win the all-around championships, they had to qualify in 10 events. They also might compete in several other activities.

The following 51 events were in the program some time or other during State's 20-year membership in the conference.

Running Events
100 Yds.
220 Yds.
880 Yds.

Mile Run
Two Mile Run
Mile Relay
Mile Walk
120 Yd. High Hurdles
220 Yds. Low Hurdles
50 Yd. Backward Run
100 Yd. Three-Legged Race
Running Bases

Special Events
Boxing   Fencing
Wrestling   Tug of War

Jumps
Standing Broad Jump
Running Broad Jump
Standing Hop, Step and Jump
Running Hop, Step and Jump
Standing High Jump
Running High Jump
Backward Jump
Standing Three Jumps
Pole Vault
High Handspring Jump
Broad Handspring Jump

Team Sports
Baseball
Football
Tennis (Men & Women)

Kicks
Standing High Kick
Running High Kick
High Kick
(Both Feet)
Backward Kick
Hitch and Kick
Drop-Kick (Rugby)

Gymnastics
Parallel Bars
Horizontal Bars
Indian Club
Tumbling

Throws
Shot Put
Hammer
Discus

Baseball
Pass-Rugby

Bicycle Races
440 Yds.
880 Yds.
Mile
Five Mile
Fancy
Tandem

The first Field Day in 1888, held at East Lansing, listed the 34 following events: 100 Yds., 220 Yds., 880 Yds., 50 Yd. Backward Run, Running Bases, Three-Legged Race, Mile Relay, Standing Broad Jump, Running Broad Jump, Standing Hop, Step and Jump, Running Hop, Step and Jump, Standing High Jump, Running High Jump, Backward Jump, High Handspring Jump, Broad Handspring Jump, Hammer Throw, Shot Put, Baseball Throw, Pass (Rugby), 880 Yd. Bicycle Race, Standing High Kick, Running High Kick, High Kick (both feet), Backward Kick, Hitch and Kick, Drop-Kick (Rugby), Parallel Bars, Horizontal Bars, Indian Club Swinging, Tennis (Doubles & Singles), Baseball, Boxing, and Wrestling.

First Recorded Track Meets

Triangular Meet - Olivet, Albion, MAC

Called Field Day

May 14-15, 1886, At East Lansing, Mich.

Weather conditions resulted in the cancellation of many of the events. Only the winners were given recognition. Wrestling, baseball, football, tumbling, gymnastics, boxing, sack race, tug-of-war and the relay race were called off.

Track Events Completed
Standing Broad Jump—Donald Yerkes (MAC) Won
Running Broad Jump—Van Loo (Albion) Won
Running Hop, Step and Jump—Van Loo (Albion) Won
Running High Kick—William Kinnan (MAC) Won
(*)Standing High Kick—Henry Avery (MAC) Won
   100 Yd. Dash—Van Loo (Albion) and Hemphill (MAC Tied)
      Times and distance are not available
      (*) The standing high kick must have been a very popular event at that time. Henry Avery never lost in competition. The previous summer, he competed against Henry Zimmerman, the Canadian champion at Sarnia, Ontario, Canada, and defeated him. Avery's record was 21 inches above his head. He competed in 90 contests.

Field Day

Albion College - Michigan Agricultural College
   June 4-5, 1886, at Albion, Mich.

Shot Put (21 lbs.)—Donald Yerkes (MAC) 24'9"
Sledge Throw (14 lbs.)—Sanson (MAC) 31'6"
100 Yd. Dash—Van Loo (Albion) Won
Half Mile—Snell (Albion) Won
Hitch and Kick—William Kinnan (MAC) 8'2½"
Running Broad Jump—Van Loo (Albion)
Running Hop, Step and Jump—Van Loo (Albion)
Standing Broad Jump—Donald Yerkes (MAC) 12'3¾"
Running High Jump—Waldo (Albion)
Standing High Kick—Henry Avery (MAC)

Quadrangular Meets

June 2, 1887 - East Lansing, Mich.
         MSU 55   Albion 35   Hillsdale 20   Olivet Coll. 10

May 16, 1911 - Detroit, Mich.
         Detroit Y.M.C.A. 43   MSU 21   Adrian Y.M.C.A. 13   Ann Arbor Y.M.C.A. 3

April 20, 1946 - Columbus, Ohio
         Ohio State 74   Purdue 45½   MSU 35¾   Miami (Ohio) 25¾

February 12, 1965 - East Lansing, Mich.
         Missouri 54   Penn State 45½   MSU 37   Ohio State 30½

May 4, 1968 - Des Moines, Iowa
         Indiana 68   Illinois 53   MSU 52   Iowa 47

Meets 5   First 1   Second 1   Third 3

Triangular Meets

May 14-15, 1886 - East Lansing, Mich.
         MSU 19   Albion 14   Alma 0

May 26, 1906 - East Lansing, Mich.
         MSU 77   Kalamazoo Coll. 49   Central Michigan 9

June 1, 1907 - East Lansing, Mich.
         MSU 54   Olivet Coll. 39   Alma 15

May 23, 1908 - Chicago, Ill.
Wabash 53   MSU 36   Armour Inst. 19

June 5, 1909 - East Lansing, Mich.
Notre Dame 65   MSU 38   Armour Inst. 32

May 21, 1910 - East Lansing, Mich.
MSU 77   Olivet Coll. 42   Alma 7

May 28, 1910 - At Notre Dame, Ind.
Notre Dame 72   MSU 43   Armour Inst. 11

May 20, 1911 - At East Lansing, Mich.
MSU 58   Olivet Coll. 42   Alma 26

May 25, 1912 - At East Lansing, Mich.
MSU 61   Olivet Coll. 39   Alma 35

May 9, 1914 - At East Lansing, Mich.
MSU 87   Alma 25   Olivet Coll. 19

May 1, 1915 - At East Lansing, Mich.
MSU 90   Alma 27   Olivet Coll. 14

Feb. 27, 1930 - At Ann Arbor, Mich.
Michigan 63½   Eastern Michigan 38½   MSU 17

Feb. 24, 1934 - At Ann Arbor, Mich.
Michigan 60   MSU 30½   Eastern Michigan 28½

Feb. 22, 1935 - At Ann Arbor, Mich.
Michigan 72½   Eastern Michigan 24 1/3   MSU 22 1/6

Feb. 13, 1940 - At Ann Arbor, Mich.
Michigan 79   MSU 29½   Eastern Michigan 21½

Feb. 23, 1941 - At East Lansing, Mich.
Michigan 75 1/5   Eastern Michigan 39 7/10   MSU 15 1/10

Feb. 14, 1942 - At East Lansing, Mich.
Michigan 64½   MSU 35½   Eastern Michigan 30

May 7, 1943 - At Ann Arbor, Mich.
Michigan 82   Ohio State 41½   MSU 28½

May 5, 1945 - At Columbus, Ohio
Great Lakes N.T.S. 74½   Ohio State 64   MSU 12½

Feb. 16, 1946 - At Notre Dame, Ind.
Notre Dame 78 2/3   MSU 44 1/3   Marquette 6

March 2, 1946 - At Ann Arbor, Mich.
Michigan 70 1/3   Notre Dame 33 1/6   MSU 25½

Feb. 24, 1947 - At East Lansing, Mich.
MSU 106   Marquette 24   Wayne State 22

April 19, 1947 - At Columbus, Ohio
Ohio State 77 1/3   MSU 50 2/3   Purdue 29

April 17, 1948 - At Columbus, Ohio
Ohio State 94   Purdue 34½   MSU 32½

April 22, 1950 - At Columbus, Ohio
MSU 65½   Ohio State 57½   Penn State 38

April 29, 1950 - At Los Angeles, Calif.
Southern California 96   MSU 34   Yale 32

Feb. 10, 1951 - At East Lansing, Mich.
MSU 66 2/3   Penn State 47½   Northwestern 26 5/6

Feb. 15, 1954 - At East Lansing, Mich.
Illinois 48½   MSU 42   Kansas 39½

Feb. 26, 1955 - At East Lansing, Mich.
MSU 92 5/6   Western Michigan 49 5/6   Northwestern 31 1/3

May 11, 1957 - At East Lansing, Mich.
Ohio State 66½   MSU 47½   Penn State 47

Feb. 21, 1959 - At Kalamazoo, Mich.
Western Michigan 92   MSU 45   Marquette 35

Feb. 20, 1960 - At Iowa City, Iowa
MSU 71½   Iowa 65½   Northwestern 35

May 7, 1960 - At Lafayette, Ind.
Illinois 84   MSU 40   Purdue 33

May 6, 1961 - At East Lansing, Mich.
Penn State 65 1/3   MSU 49 2/3   Ohio State 46

Jan. 27, 1962 - At East Lansing, Mich.
MSU 90½   Ohio State 60½   Northwestern 22

Feb. 24, 1962 - At Bloomington, Ind.
MSU 58½   Oklahoma 54½   Indiana 45

May 5, 1962 - At East Lansing, Mich.
MSU 75½   Michigan 65¼   Ohio State 31¼

Feb. 16, 1963 - At Mt. Pleasant, Mich
MSU 72½   Central Michigan 55   Bowling Green 24½

Feb. 23, 1963 - At East Lansing, Mich.
Wisconsin 80   MSU 79   Indiana 13

Feb. 22, 1964 - At Madison, Wis.
Wisconsin 86   MSU 50   Indiana 35

Feb. 20, 1965 - At Bloomington, Ind.
Wisconsin 77   Indiana 51½   MSU 47½

May 8, 1965 - At Kalamazoo, Mich.
Western Michigan 70   MSU 69   Miami (Ohio) 34

Jan. 29, 1966 - At Columbus, Ohio
MSU 101   Ohio State 53   Kentucky 17

Feb. 24, 1968 - At Lafayette, Ind.
MSU 77   Purdue 57   Murray State College 37

April 13, 1968 - At Champaign, Ill.
MSU 93   Illinois 74   Northwestern 44

May 11, 1968 - At East Lansing, Mich.
Wisconsin 87   Notre Dame 68   MSU 56

April 12, 1969 - At Champaign, Ill.
Wisconsin 104   Illinois 64   MSU 40

April 11, 1970 - At Lafayette, Ind.
Purdue 86   MSU 84   Bradley 21

May 2, 1970 - At East Lansing, Mich.
Indiana 84   Wisconsin 66   MSU 41

Number of Triangular Meets; 49:   First 20   Second 18   Third 11

Track action at State in pre-1935 days took place on the running oval located inside Spartan Stadium.

1886
No Coach
June 4   25   Albion (A)   25
                  Tied 1

1898
Henry Keep, Coach
Feb. 5   10   Lansing H.S. (A)   10
Mar. 12   11   Lansing H.S.   5
May 13   120   Olivet at Charlotte   29
                  Mich.
                  Won 2   Tied 1

1902
George E. Denman, Coach
May 24   114   Alma at Ithaca,   62
                  Mich.
May 31   74   Albion   47
                  Won 2

1903
May 23   80   Albion   31
                  Won 1

1904
Chester L. Brewer, Coach
Mar. 12   50   Alma (A)   38
May 21   56½   Alma   28½
                  Won 2

1905
Feb. 25   21   Alma (A)   3
Mar. 4   38½   Olivet   31½
Mar. 17   49½   Albion   22½
(*)May 6   75   Notre Dame (A)   56
May 27   93   Armour Inst.   38
(*) First track outside of Michigan.
                  Won 5

1906
Feb. 20   23   Olivet   22
May 12   66   Armour Inst. (A)   47
                  Won 2

1907
Feb. 2   37½   Olivet   15½
Feb. 16   42   Notre Dame (A)   71
May 25   81   Armour Inst.   36
                  Won 2   Lost 1

1908
Mar. 2   43 2/3   Eastern Michigan 33 1/3
May 2   88   Alma   38
May 16   65 5/6   Notre Dame   60 1/6
                  Won 3

1909
May 13   39   Notre Dame (A)   87
May 29   82   Olivet   48
                  Won 1   Lost 1

1910
Feb. 25   43½   Eastern Michigan   28½
                  Won 1

1912
John F. Macklin, Coach
Feb. 15   37   Detroit Y.M.C.A. (A)40
                  Lost 1

1913
Feb. 27   46   Detroit Y.M.C.A.   49
Mar. 15   19   Michigan Fresh-   63
                   men (A)
May 5   78   Western Reserve   52
May 10   44   Michigan Freshmen 87
                  Won 1   Lost 3

1914
Ion J. Cortright, Coach
May 2   81   Western Reserve   50
May 30   49   Michigan   82
                  Won 1   Lost 1

1915
George E. Gauthier, Coach
May 22   51½   Notre Dame   78½
May 29   70½   Michigan Freshmen 59½
                  Won 1   Lost 1

1916
May 3   41   Notre Dame (A)   90
May 27   90   Michigan Freshmen 41
                  Won 1   Lost 1

1917
May 19   42 1/3   Notre Dame   83 2/3
                  Lost 1

1918
May 11   35   Notre Dame (A)   85
                  Lost 1

1919
May 10   101   Detroit J.C.   29
May 17   31   Notre Dame   95
                  Won 1   Lost 1

1920
Arthur N. Smith, Coach
(*)Feb. 25 40   Western Michigan 46
Mar. 5   79   Kalamazoo   25
Mar. 13   27   Notre Dame   50
May 8   80   Detroit J.C.   46
May 19   31 5/6 Notre Dame (A) 85 1/6
May 22   30   DePauw   96
(*)First meet in new gymnasium (present
Women's Gymnasium)
                  Won 2   Lost 4

1921
Mar. 5   54   Western Michigan   32
May 7   81   Western Michi-   49
                    gan (A)
May 14   40   Notre Dame   77
May 21   73   DePauw (A)   53
                  Won 3   Lost 1

1922
Albert M. Barron, Coach
Feb. 4   50½   Western Michigan   34½
Feb. 18   64½   DePauw   30½
May 6   104   DePaul   22
May 13   78½   Oberlin   47½
May 20   58   Ohio State   68
                  Won 4   Lost 1

1923
Feb. 10   32½   Eastern Michigan   53½
May 5   34½   Ohio State (A)   91½
May 12   66   Oberlin (A)   65
May 19   32½   Notre Dame (A)   93½
                  Won 1   Lost 3

1924
Ralph H. Young, Coach

Feb. 9	68½	Chicago Y.M.C.A.	26½
Feb. 23	30	Western Michigan	56
May 3	67	Detroit City College	64
May 10	29	Iowa State (A)	102
May 17	34 1/6	Notre Dame	91 5/6

Won 2   Lost 3

1925

Feb. 21	48	Western Michigan	38
Mar. 13	31	Eastern Michigan	73
May 2	61	Detroit City Coll.	70
May 8	50	Western Michigan	81

Won 1   Lost 3

1926

Feb. 13	34½	Marquette	74½
Feb. 20	47½	Western Michigan	38½
(*)May 1	74½	Detroit City Coll.	56½
May 8	64	Iowa State Coll.	67
May 15	48	Notre Dame	78

(*)First meet on stadium track
Won 2   Lost 3

1927

Feb. 11	67½	Western Michigan (A)	41½
Mar. 12	75	Marquette	34
May 7	86 2/3	Detroit City Coll.	44 1/3
May 13	68	Notre Dame (A)	58

Won 4

1928

Feb. 18	70 1/6	Ohio Wesleyan	38 5/6
Mar. 10	52½	Marquette (A)	56½
May 5	85	Detroit City Coll.	46
May 12	62	Notre Dame	64

Won 2   Lost 2

1929

Feb. 16	44	Ohio Wesleyan (A)	65
Feb. 23	67 1/3	Marquette	41 2/3
Apr. 20	85	Detroit City Coll.	46
May 11	40 2/3	Notre Dame (A)	85 1/3

Won 2   Lost 2

1930

Feb. 15	36½	Marquette (A)	72½
Feb. 22	66	Ohio Wesleyan	43
Mar. 22	39½	Chicago (A)	46½
Apr. 19	78 2/3	Detroit City Coll.	52 1/3
May 10	37	Notre Dame	89

Won 2   Lost 3

1931

Feb. 7	58 2/3	Chicago	36 1/3
Feb. 18	58½	Marquette	50½
Feb. 21	55	Ohio Wesleyan	54
Apr. 18	78	Detroit City Coll.	53
May 9	80	Detroit	51

Won 5

1932

Feb. 19	73½	Ohio Wesleyan	35½
Mar. 1	44½	Marquette (A)	64½
Apr. 23	110	Detroit City Coll.	21
May 7	65¾	Notre Dame	65¼
May 14	96½	Detroit (A)	34½

Won 4   Lost 1

1933

Feb. 25	83¾	Ohio Wesleyan	25¼
Mar. 3	61 3/5	Marquette	47 2/5
May 6	67	Notre Dame (A)	64

Won 3

1934

Mar. 2	37	Marquette (A)	72
May 5	95	Detroit	34
May 12	50 2/3	Notre Dame (A)	80 1/3

Won 1   Lost 2

1935

Mar. 2	47¾	Marquette	61¼
May 11	38½	Notre Dame	92½

Lost 2

1936

Feb. 21	36	Michigan (A)	59
Feb. 29	55½	Marquette (A)	53½

Won 1   Lost 1

1937

Feb. 17	63	Eastern Michigan	32
Feb. 20	28	Michigan (A)	67
Mar. 1	84	Marquette	20
(*)Apr. 17	88	Chicago	43
May 1	84	Marquette (A)	47
May 21	66½	Notre Dame	64½

(*)New track dedication
Won 5   Lost 1

1938

Feb. 12	73	Eastern Michigan at Ann Arbor, Mich.	22
Feb. 17	26½	Michigan (A)	68½
Feb. 26	52½	Marquette (A)	56½
Mar. 30	83½	Maryland (A)	47½
Apr. 1	75	Penn State (A)	51
Apr. 16	87	Purdue	44
May 7	82 1/6	Marquette	53 5/6
May 14	45 1/3	Notre Dame (A)	85 2/3

Won 5   Lost 3

1939

Feb. 11	30	Notre Dame (A)	65
Feb. 14	18	Michigan (A)	77
Feb. 25	31	Marquette	78
Apr. 15	76 1/6	Purdue	54 5/6
May 6	45	Marquette	91
May 8	57	Penn State	74
May 15	70	Notre Dame	61

Won 2   Lost 5

1940

Feb. 5	37 1/3	Notre Dame	57 2/3
Feb. 23	32	Marquette	86
Apr. 13	53	Purdue	69
May 4	35½	Marquette (A)	101½
May 11	52	Notre Dame (A)	79

Lost 5

1941
Karl A. Schlademan, Coach

Feb. 7	20	Notre Dame (A)	84
Feb. 21	49½	Marquette	68½
Apr. 12	62	Purdue	69
May 3	53	Marquette (A)	83
May 10	40½	Notre Dame	90½
May 24	44	Penn State (A)	87

Lost 6

1942

Jan. 31	34	Ohio State	75
Feb. 7	37	Illinois (A)	67
Feb. 21	65½	Marquette	45½
Apr. 11	67 2/3	Purdue	54 1/3
May 2	58	Penn State	73
May 9	48	Notre Dame (A)	83
May 23	69	Marquette (A)	62

Won 3   Lost 4

1943
Jan. 29	36	Ohio State	73
Feb. 9	39	Michigan (A)	65
Feb. 20	62	Illinois	42
Apr. 17	81	Purdue	41
May 1	77	Marquette	59

Won 3 Lost 2

1944
Dropped Intercollegiate schedules for one year—World War II.

1945
Jan. 27	31	Ohio State	73
Feb. 7	66 2/3	Wayne State	37 1/3
Feb. 24	37 1/3	Indiana	66 2/3
May 19	61½	Indiana (A)	60½

Won 2 Lost 2

1946
Jan. 26	50	Ohio State	68
Feb. 23	86 2/3	Wayne State	17 1/3
May 4	51	Ohio State (A)	71
May 11	92	Marquette (A)	44
May 18	87	Notre Dame	44
June 1	96½	Penn State	34½

Won 4 Lost 2

1947
Jan. 25	74 2/3	Ohio State	45 1/3
Feb. 15	53 14/15	Michigan (A)	60 1/15
Mar. 1	61 1/3	Notre Dame (A)	52 2/3
May 3	76	Notre Dame	65
May 10	71 3/5	Penn State (A)	59 2/5
May 17	99 2/3	Marquette (A)	50 1/3
May 23	68 1/3	Michigan	63 2/3

Won 6 Lost 1

1948
Jan. 24	57 1/6	Ohio State	56 5/6
Feb. 27	57	Michigan (A)	57
May 8	54	Penn State	77
May 15	77	Notre Dame (A)	54
May 22	46	Illinois	86

Won 2 Lost 2 Tied 1

1949
Feb. 17	79½	Ohio State	34½
Apr. 16	61	Southern California (A)	61
Apr. 23	86	Notre Dame	56
May 7	79½	Ohio State	52½
May 14	83½	Penn State (A)	47½
May 21	105	Marquette	36

Won 5 Tied 1

1950
Feb. 18	67	Ohio State	47
May 6	82	Penn State	59
May 17	78	Notre Dame	53

Won 3

1951
Feb. 17	68	Iowa (A)	40
Feb. 24	56 1/6	Wisconsin (A)	57 5/6
Apr. 21	55	Indiana (A)	77
May 5	74	Ohio State	58
May 12	47½	Michigan (A)	84½
May 19	59½	Illinois	72½

Won 2 Lost 4

1952
Feb. 2	62 2/3	Notre Dame	51 1/3
Feb. 23	39 2/3	Michigan	74 1/3
May 3	91	Penn State (A)	40
May 10	84	Wisconsin	48
May 17	100	Syracuse	36

Won 4 Lost 1

1953
Feb. 20	77 2/3	Eastern Michigan	36 1/3
Feb. 24	73 1/3	Notre Dame (A)	40 2/3
May 2	43	Illinois (A)	89
May 9	89	Penn State	47
May 16	84 1/3	Wisconsin (A)	47 2/3

Won 4 Lost 1

1954
Feb. 27	56	Indiana (A)	75
May 1	79	Notre Dame	62
May 15	61	Penn State (A)	70

Won 1 Lost 2

1955
Feb. 5	79	Eastern Michigan	48
May 6	71½	Indiana	60½
May 19	63 2/3	Illinois (A)	68 1/3

Won 2 Lost 1

1956
Feb. 17	95 1/3	Eastern Michigan (A)	45 2/3
May 5	54	Notre Dame	86
May 12	72	Wisconsin (A)	60
May 18	63	Michigan	84

Won 2 Lost 2

1957
Feb. 11	53	Kansas	88
Feb. 18	74½	Ohio State (A)	66½
Feb. 22	108	Western Michigan	33
May 7	88½	Chicago Track Club	51½
May 18	67	Notre Dame (A)	74

Won 3 Lost 2

1958
Feb. 14	36	Kansas (A)	68
Feb. 21	78	Western Michigan	63
Mar. 1	74	Iowa	49
May 3	75	Notre Dame	66
May 10	55	Nebraska (A)	72
May 17	51½	Ohio State	80½

Won 3 Lost 3

1959
Francis C. Dittrich, Coach
Feb. 14	49	Ohio State (A)	65
Feb. 28	60 1/3	Iowa (A)	79 2/3
May 2	72½	Wisconsin	59½
May 9	39¼	Penn State (A)	91¾
May 15	57	Notre Dame (A)	74

Won 1 Lost 4

1960
Feb. 6	62 2/3	Ohio State (A)	51 1/3
Feb. 27	54	Michigan	87
May 14	72	Notre Dame	69

Won 2 Lost 1

1961
Jan. 28	64 1/3	Ohio State (A)	61 2/3
Feb. 17	44 1/3	Michigan (A)	96 2/3
Feb. 25	71½	Central Michigan	69½
May 13	51	Notre Dame (A)	80

Won 2 Lost 2

1962
| Feb. 15 | 97 | Central Michigan (A) | 44 |
| May 15 | 73 | Penn State | 63 |

Won 2

1963
| Jan. 26 | 82 | Ohio State (A) | 59 |
| May 11 | 72 | Notre Dame | 67 |

Won 2

State's 1965 varsity track team, coached by Fran Dittrich, captured the school's first Big Ten outdoor title.

1964

Jan. 25	63	Ohio State (A)	78
Feb. 29	66	Miami (Ohio)	47
May 2	81	Ohio State	51
May 9	67	Notre Dame (A)	55
May 16	84	Chicago Track Club	53

Won 4   Lost 1

1965

Jan. 30	87	Ohio State (A)	54
Feb. 27	87	Miami (Ohio)	54
May 1	97½	Ohio State	43½
May 15	98	Notre Dame	43

Won 4

1966

Feb. 19	98	Indiana	43
Feb. 29	73	Wisconsin (A)	68
May 7	104	Ohio State	37
May 14	87	Notre Dame	54

Won 4

1967

Feb. 18	94	Indiana (A)	47
Feb. 25	76	Wisconsin	64
May 6	115	Ohio State	58
May 10	97½	Notre Dame (A)	47½

Won 4

1968

Feb. 17	67	Ohio State	83

Lost 1

1969

Feb. 15	63	Wisconsin (A)	86
Feb. 19	65	Indiana (A)	84
Feb. 22	80	Ohio	69
May 3	82	Minnesota (A)	91

Won 1   Lost 3

1970

Feb. 21	59	Illinois (A)	81
Feb. 28	51	Michigan (A)	89
Apr. 18	91	Northwestern	62
May 9	65	Notre Dame (A)	80

Won 1   Lost 3

Rob Ellis, All-American outfielder, collegiate "player of the year," 1971.

Ken Popejoy, 1970 cross country All-American performer

Bill Mathers, Big Ten champion fencer in epee, 1971.

Don Thompson, All-American hockey center, 1971, and State's leading scorer.

Greg Johnson, NCAA and Big Ten 118-pound wrestling champion, 1970 and 1971.

1971: A BIG YEAR FOR SPARTANS

Paced by five Big Ten championship teams, Michigan State had one of its finest athletic years in 1970-71, topping it off by winning unofficial all-around sports honors in the conference.

The cross country, fencing, hockey, wrestling and baseball teams took league crowns. All the other clubs, except basketball which tied for seventh, finished in the first division.

The all-sports championship was State's sixth in the 21 years it has competed in the Big Ten. There also have been 11 second-place finishes, three thirds and one fifth. There never has been a second-division finish, attesting to the consistent quality performance of Spartan athletes and teams in all sports.

Compilation of the all-sports standings was begun in the Michigan State Sports Information Office with the 1950-51 school year, the first in which Spartan teams competed in the Big Ten. The annual press release on the final all-sports standings receives wide publicity. Unlike some other conferences, however, the Big Ten has never established an official all-sports award because of the opposition of some schools whose all-around programs are chronically weak.

State's excellent records year after year are a testimonial to the philosophy of seeking excellence in all areas espoused by former Athletic Director Ralph H. Young (1923-54) and continued by current Athletic Director Biggie Munn.

Track and cross country runner Kim Hartman won the Chester L. Brewer Award and wrestler Tom Muir was awarded the Big Ten Conference Medal of Honor.

Summary of team performances in 1970-71:

CROSS COUNTRY — Team record in dual meets was 3-3. Won the Big Ten team championship for the 13th time in 21 years, and placed seventh in the NCAA championship run. Ken Popejoy was MSU's high finisher in the Big Ten at fourth.

FOOTBALL — Team record was 4-6-0 overall, and 3-4-0 in the Big Ten, good for a two-way tie for fifth in loop standings. Eric Allen had a fine season, leading the team in ground gaining with 811 yards and in scoring with 60 points. He and Gordon Bowdell, the team's leading pass receiver, made the All-Big Ten second team of UPI. Quarterback Mike Rasmussen set records for passes attempted and completed and for total yards gained passing.

SOCCER — Record for the season was 5-1-3. John Houska, Art Demling and Jerry Murray were named to the All-Midwest team and Demling made All-America first team and Houska All-America second team.

BASKETBALL — Team record was 10-14 and in the Big Ten 4-10, good for a three-way tie for seventh place. Rudy Benjamin wound up as leading scorer with 520 points, third best single season in Spartan history. Bill Kilgore was

Big Ten's No. 2 rebounder and team's MVP award winner. High note of the season was the winning of the Lobo Invitational Tournament title at New Mexico in December.

FENCING — Team record in dual meets was 9-6, and squad went on to win the Big Ten team championship. Bill Mathers captured first-place honors in epee.

GYMNASTICS — Record in dual meets was 5-5, and the Spartans finished fifth in the Big Ten championships.

HOCKEY — Spartans posted an overall mark of 19-12, most wins ever in school's history, and record in WCHA was 12-10, good for fourth place in regular season standings. Don Thompson was named to All-America squad and to Denver Post All-WCHA first team.

TRACK (INDOOR) — Team won two dual meets and lost one, and finished second in the Big Ten championships with 46 points. Big Ten titles were won by Herb Washington in the 60-yard dash, Bob Cassleman in the 600-yard run, and the mile relay team of Mike Holt, Mike Murphy, John Mock and Cassleman in Big Ten and American record time of 3:12.9. Washington won the 60 at the MSU Relays in world-record-tying time of :05.9.

SWIMMING — Record in dual meets was 9-3, and team placed fourth in the Big Ten meet with 207 points. Jeff Lanini won the 100-yard breaststroke at the Big Ten meet, and set a Big Ten mark of :59.5 in a preliminary heat of the event.

WRESTLING — State's record in dual meets was 7-3-2, and the Spartans captured the team honors in the Big Ten meet for the sixth straight year with 101 points. Spartans had five Big Ten champions: Greg Johnson (118), Tom Milkovich (134), Gerald Malecek (167), Dave Ciolek (190) and Ben Lewis (hwt). State won NCAA District 4 regional and qualified seven to nationals, with winners in Johnson and Milkovich. At the NCAA meet, MSU finished third with 44 points, and Johnson repeated as 118-pound king. Johnson also wrestled in East-West All-Star Classic.

BASEBALL — Record was 36-10, the best mark of any Spartan team in history. Won the Big Ten title, but lost in the NCAA District Four tournament played on John Kobs Field. Outfielder Rob Ellis was named the team's Most Valuable Player and won All-Big Ten and All-America recognition. He was team batting champion at .407. He set all-time Spartan marks in home runs (14), runs batted in (44) and total bases (128) and tied the team mark in triples (6). Left-handed pitcher Rob Clancy made All-Big Ten with a 10-1 record and a 2.01 earned run average.

TENNIS — Team posted a 7-5 dual meet record and finished fourth in the Big Ten meet. Mike Madura won the No. 3 singles championship in the Big Ten. DeArmond Briggs at No. 2 singles had the best regular season record at 11-1.

GOLF — Team won two tournaments—the Western Michigan Tournament and Spartan Invitational—and finished second in the Big Ten. Rick Woulfe posted the best average of 73.95 strokes per 18 holes. He and John VanderMeiden were named to the All-Big Ten team.

TRACK (OUTDOOR) — Team won two of three dual meets and finished fourth in the Big Ten. Herb Washington tied Jesse Owens' Big Ten record of :09.4 in winning the 100. Bob Cassleman won the 660 in 1:18.3. The mile relay team of Tom Spuller, Mike Murphy, John Mock and Bob Cassleman won in 3:11.5. Eric Allen was credited with a Big Ten meet record in the triple jump of 50-5¼, even though placing second to Pat Onyango of Wisconsin. The reason was that Onyango made his big effort while wind-aided, so his distance was unacceptable as a record. The Spartan shuttle hurdle relay team of Wayne Hartwick, Rich Jacques, Dave Martin and John Morrison won two major championships in the Florida and Kentucky Relays. They tied the national collegiate record (and best on the books anywhere) of :56.7 in beating Tennessee at Florida.

LACROSSE — In its second varsity year, the team improved its record to 4-7. It was 1-9 in 1970. Doug Kalvelage established himself as State's first lacrosse star by winning the individual scoring title for the second straight year with 32 points. Last year he scored 15.

BIG TEN ALL-SPORTS STANDINGS
(Fall, Winter, Spring, 1970-71)

School	FB	CC	BB	FEN	GYM	HOC	SW	TR-I	WR	BASE	GO	TEN	TR-O	TOTAL PTS.	QUALITY PTS.**
Michigan State	5.5	10	3	10	6	10	7	9	10	10	9	7	7	103.5	7.96
Michigan	8.5	x	9	x	10	7	9	3	8	8.5	4	10	6	83.0	7.54
Indiana	1.5	8	7	6	7	x	10	8	3	2.5	6.5	9	10	78.5	6.54
Wisconsin	5.5	6	3	8	3	9	5	10	6	5	2	5	9	76.5	5.88
Illinois	1.5	7	5.5	7	8	x	4	4	2	7	6.5	6	8	66.5	5.54
Ohio State	10	5	10	9	4	x	8	5	1	2.5	8	1	3	66.5	5.54
Minnesota	4	9	5.5	4	5	8	6	6	5	8.5	3	3	5	72.0	5.53
Iowa	7	4	3	x	9	x	2	1	9	6	5	8	1	55.5	5.04
Purdue	3	3	8	5	x	x	3	2	4	4	10	2	2	45.5	4.13
Northwestern	8.5	2	1	x	x	x	1	7	7	1	1	4	4	36.5	3.65

** Quality points are obtained by dividing the number of points accumulated on the basis of 10 for a first, 9 for a second, etc., by the number of sports in which each school entered a team

Key to abbreviations of sports: FB-football;   CC-cross country;   BB-basketball; FEN-fencing; GYM-gymnastics; HOC-ice hockey; SW-swimming; TR-I-indoor track; WR-wrestling; BASE-baseball; GO-golf; TEN-tennis; TR-O-outdoor track.

SPARTAN OFFICIALS

Biggie Munn
Athletic Director

Dr. John Fuzak
Faculty Representative

Burt Smith
Assistant
Athletic Director

John Laetz
Business Manager

Fred Stabley
Sports Information
Director

Nick Vista
Assistant Sports
Information Director

Dr. James Feurig
Team Physician

Bill Beardsley
Ticket Manager

Gayle Robinson
Trainer

Ken Earley
Equipment Manager

SPARTAN COACHES

 As of June 30, 1969

Dan Litwhiler
Baseball

Gus Ganakas
Basketball

James Gibbard
Cross Country

Charles Schmitter
Fencing

Duffy Daugherty
Football

Bruce Fossum
Golf

George Szypula
Gymnastics

Amo Bessone
Hockey

Robert Kauffman
Lacrosse

Willard Kenney
Soccer

Richard Fetters
Swimming

Stanley Drobac
Tennis

Francis Dittrich
Track

Grady Peninger
Wrestling

ALL-TIME LETTERWINNERS

10 LETTERS

Frimodig, Lyman L. Baseball—14,15,16,17
Basketball—14,15,16,17
Football—15,16

9 LETTERS

Burnett, Leander L. Baseball—89,90,91,92
Track—88,89,90,91,92

Carey, Robert W. Track—50,51,52
Basketball—50,51,52
Football—49,50,51

Cortright, Ion J. Baseball—10,11
Football—07,08,09,10
Track—08,09,10

McKenna, Parnell G. Basketball—06,07,08,09,10
Football—06,07,08,09

Millar, Wilson F. Baseball—02,03,04
Football—03
Track—02,03,04
Basketball—03,04

Miller, William B. Baseball—13,14,15
Football—12,13,14,15
Basketball—13,15

Small, Walter H. Football—03,04,05,06,07
Track—04,05,06,08

Ziegel, Frederick K. Baseball—34,35,36
Football—34,35,36
Swimming—34,35,36

8 LETTERS

Campbell, Arthur L. Basketball—09,10
Football—06,07,08,09
Track—09,10

Hammes, John H. Baseball—17,18,19
Basketball—18,20
Football—17,19,20

Dianetti, Jack Cross Country—46,47,48,49
Track—47,48,49,50

Sewell, Robert A. Cross Country—46,47,48,49
Track—47,48,49,50

Snider, Irving J. Baseball—18,19,20
Basketball—18,19
Football—17,18,19

7 LETTERS

Atcheson, Walter C. Cross Country—47,48,49
Track—47,48,49,50

Bremer, Ernest K. Track—37,38,39
Baseball—37
Football—36,37,38

Kratz, Frank J. Football—01,02,03,04
Track—03,04,05

MacMillan, Roy A. Baseball—21,23,24
Basketball—23,25
Football—20,22

McKenna, Edward B. Baseball—05
Football—03,04,05
Track—02,04,05

Mills, Herbert Baseball—07,08,09,10
Basketball—07,08,09

Ranney, Ellis W. Baseball—97,98,99,00
Football—97,98,99

Smith, Horace Football—46,47,48,49
Track—48,49,50

DIRECTORY

ALUMNI VARSITY LETTERMEN

This directory contains the names of the major letterwinners at Michigan State from 1886 through 1970, along with the sports and years in which they were so honored. Also included are those who received varsity letters for manager. No minor or service awards presented after World War I are listed.

Any additions or corrections to this directory should be sent to the Editor for inclusion in the next edition.

Key Abbreviations

BS	Baseball		LA	Lacrosse
BK	Basketball		SO	Soccer
BX	Boxing		SW	Swimming
CC	Cross Country		TN	Tennis
FC	Fencing		TR	Track
FB	Football		WR	Wrestling
GO	Golf		C	Captain
GY	Gymnastics		CoC	CoCaptain
HO	Hockey		M	Manager

A

		Albright, Joseph W.	GO 52,53,54C
		Alcorn, William P.	TR 61
Abajace, John	WR 69	Alderman, A. LeRoy	TR 13,14
Abbott, A. O.	TR 02	Alderman, Fred P.	TR 25,26,27C
Abdo, Edward S.	FB 38,39,40	Aldrich, Bruce D.	SW 52,53,54
Abraham, Richard J.	WR 54,55	Aldrich, Samuel R.	WR 37
Abrecht, Jeffery L.	FB 61,62	Alexanderson, Earl M.	CC 51M
	BS 62,63	Alfsen, Albert H.	FB 99
Ackerman, Holt	BX 48M	Allen, Eric	TR 70
Acosta, Arthur	FB 58		FB 69
Adams, A. Gordon Jr.	FB 41M	Allen, Gerald H.	FB 07,08
Adams, Charles H.	BS 96C,97,98		TR 06,07,08,09M
Adams, Howard J.	FB 52	Allen, Henry R.	TR 92
Adcock, Robert L.	TR 36,37,38	Allen, Wade W.	TR 35,36
Adderley, Herbert A.	FB 58,59,60C	Allen, William C.	WR 58
Adler, Orville	TR 32,33	Alling, Ronald V.	FB 37,38,39
Adolph, Bryce E.	FB 67M	Allmann, Robert M.	FB 34,35
Adolph, Fred P. Sr.	TR 20,21,22	Allwardt, Robert K.	SW 43,46,47,48C
Aenis, James E.	SW 60	Alozie, Sydney O.	SO 64
Agett, Albert H.	FB 34,35,36	Alsup, John M.	WR 67,68
	TR 34,36	Altobelli, Aldo	HO 57,58
Agnew, Thomas G.	FB 02	Alward, George	SW 69
Ahlgren, Robert	SW 66	Amie, Jack M.	CC 64
Aitch, Matthew	BK 66,67	Ammon, Harry R. Jr.	FB 63,64
Akers, Forrest H.	BS 06,07	Amon, Jack R.	FB 39,40C
Akpata, Solomon S.	TR 60,61	Amos, Henry C.	BX 50,51C
	WR 61	Anderegg, Robert H.	BK 57,58,59C

Andersen, Roger W.	GY 61M
Anderson, Dale	WR 66,67,68
Anderson, Don E.	WR 45C,47,48,49
Anderson, Earl	FB 68
Anderson, Felix A.	TR 32M
Anderson, John H.	FB 26,27,28
Anderson, Paul J.	FB 24
Anderson, Valda R.	BK 29M
Anderson, Warren J.	CC 39
	TR 40
Andreoli, Robert L.	BS 42,43
Andrews, C. Ward	BS 18,19,20
	FB 19
Andrews, Earl	GY 65
Andrews, Herbert J.	BS 19
Andrews, Vernon J.	FC 50
Andrews, W. Earl	GY 65
Andrie, Norman E.	BX 52,54
Angel, Anthony J.	FB 65
Annesi, Genero M.	WR 58
Ansorge, William A.	BS 93,94,95C
Anstey, Kenneth W.	HO 67,68,69CoC
Antonetti, Joseph	FC 62
Apisa, Robert	FB 65,66,67
Aquino, John	BS 62,63
Arbanas, Frederick V.	FB 58,59,60C
Arbogast, Arthur	TR 31
Arbury, James	FB 60M,61M
Archbold, Harold K.	FB 21
Archer, Lawrence C.	FB 17,18C,19
Archer, Nick	SO 67,68,69
Archer, Robert L.	WR 63
Arena, Anthony G.	FB 39,41
	TR 42
Arend, Donald R.	FB 56,58
Armstrong, Andrew	BS 03,04,05C,06C
Armstrong, George W.	SW 37
Armstrong, Robert E.	FB 32,33,34
Armstrong, Robert P.	HO 58,59
Armstrong, Sterling	FB 65,66,67
Armstrong, Theodore R.	BK 53,54,55
Armstrong, William C.	BS 99,00
Arndt, Mayo L.	TR 47,48,49,50
Arnest, Stephen R.	FC 59C,60
Arnold, David	GY 65
Arnold, James F.	CC 51
Arnott, Scobie I.	SW 53M
Arnson, Don	FB 44,45,46,47
Arntz, Arthur B.	FB 44
Aronson, Fred	FB 44
	TR 45
Arrington, Walter A.	TR 39,40,41C
Arteaga, Manuel R.	FC 38,39C
Ashley, Amos H.	FB 03,04
Aslin, Richard	CC 68
Asmah, John H.	SO 57,58
Atack, James	HO 59,60,61
Atcheson, Walter C.	CC 47,48,49
	TR 47,48,49,50
Atkin, Arthur W.	TR 16,17,19C,20
Atkins, Hazen S.	TR 21,22,23C
Atterberry, Willie J.	TR 58,60
Atwood, Michael D.	SW 63
Aubuchon, Chester J.	BK 39,40,42C
Auffrey, Joe J.	TR 69
Auge, Robert L.	FC 50
Aurand, Rex H.	TR 32,33
Aure, Ronald	GY 65,66,67
Austin, Charles O.	FB 49M
Austin, Floyd E.	WR 34C
Avellano, Anthony F.	WR 57
Avery, Henry	TR 86,87
Avery, Kenneth	BS 60,61
Ayala, Reginald P.	BK 52,53
Azar, George	BS 61,62,63
	FB 60,61,62
Azikiwe, Ayo	TR 63,64

B

Bach, Jay D.	BS 62,63,64
Badaczewski, Joseph H.	FB 53,54,55
Badger, Albert E.	GO 60,61,62
Baer, Charles	FC 66,67,68C
Bagdon, Ed	FB 46,47,48,49
Bagdon, Frank A.	BS 47,48,49
Baguley, Keith	TR 22,23,24C
Bailey, Charlie	FB 66,67,68
Bailey, John	BK 66,67,68
	GO 66,67,68
Bailey, Philip F.	FB 17
Baird, Donald G.	FB 67,68
Baker, Albert H.	FB 34
Baker, Dennis K.	SW 57,59,60
Baker, Harry D.	TR 43
Baker, Harry L.	BS 08,09,10C,11
	TR 08
Baker, Hugh P.	FB 97,98,99
Baker, J. Fred	BS 00
Baker, Park F.	FB 58,59
Balai, Joseph T.	HO 56
Balbach, Edward	BK 02,03,04C
	TR 04
Baldwin, Charles C.	SW 52,53,54
Baldwin, Ernest W.	FB 10
Baldwin, Irving	TR 50M
Baldwin, Patrick K.	HO 61,62,63
Baldwin, Russell H.	TR 02
Baldwin, Tim L.	GO 58,59,60
Baldwin, William W.	FB 46
Balge, Kenneth E.	FB 42,46C,47
Balhorn, Randall	GY 70
Ball, B. Dale	WR 39
Ball, Elton E.	FB 20
Ball, Stanley	WR 32,33C
Ball, Walter J.	FB 40
Ballard, Clint V.	FB 11
Ballman, Gary	FB 59,60,61
Balogh, Eugene M.	FC 50
Balthrop, George	TR 65,66,67
Bancroft, H. Lee	FB 11M
Barbarito, Edward R.	BS 47,48
Barbas, Constino J.	FB 45
	TR 46
Barber, Thomas K.	SW 45
Barbour, James M.	TR 43,46
Barcroft, Glenn A.	TR 10
Barcroft, John E.	TR 09,10
Barker, Arthur W.	HO 56
Barker, Richard	FB 57,58
Barley, Kenneth L.	CC 53
	TR 53,54
Barnard, John A.	BS 29,30,31
	BK 32
Barnett, Clayton F.	TR 14,15,16
Barnett, Michael D.	BS 63
Barnett, William D.	BK 10
	FB 09
Barr, Doug	FB 69
Barr, John H.	BK 21
Barr, Ronald W.	CC 51,53
Barrell, Clark L.	TR 17
Barrett, Fred W.	BS 27
	FB 26
Barrett, Gary D.	GO 59,61,62
Barrie, Joseph H.	FB 34,35
Barrington, Gordon L.	BS 36
Barry, Joseph Robert	HO 52
Barta, Joseph W.	BS 48,49,50
Bartling, Irving H.	BS 34,35,36C
Bartmess, Edward A.	BS 86
Basich, Peter P.	BK 40,41
Bass, Julian R.	BX 53
Bassett, Charles F.	FB 17,19,20

Bassett, Donald B.	WR 51
Bassett, Larry A.	GY 60,61,62
Bastian, James J.	TR 68,69
Batchelor, William	FB 39,40
Bates, Erving B.	BS 86,87
Bates, Roy E.	TR 56
Bateson, George F.	BS 94,95
	TR 95
Bateson, Rueben E.	BS 94,95
Bath, Edwin G.	TR 31,32,33C
Bathrop, George	CC 66
Bauer, George T.	FC 31C
Baum, Joe	SO 66,67,68
Baum, John D.	WR 58,60,62C
Bauman, Paul L.	BK 45
Bayless, Paul A.	TR 30
Baylor, Art	BK 66,67
Baynes, Carl D.	BS 24,26,27
Bays, Richard P.	LA 70
Beach, John	LA 70
Beachum, James C.	TN 54,55,56
Beale, John	FB 39M
Beam, John P.	FC 65,66
Bean, Stephen Michael	TN 60M,61M,62M
Beard, Thomas L., Jr.	FB 69
Beardslee, Walter E.	CC 41
Beardsley, William	FB 42
Beattie, Jack R.	SW 54,55,56
Beatty, Charles	WR 67M,68M
Beatty, Howard E.	FB 15
	TR 12,13,14,15C,16
Beaubien, Paul J.	FB 36
Beaudet, Albert	GY 70
Beaumont, C. E.	TR 33,34
Beauvais, Joseph W.	BS 93
Bechard, Joseph E.	BS 48,49,50
Bechtold, J. Edward	CC 33,34,35C
Becker, Henry L.	FB 96,97
Becker, John	GO 65
Becker, John T.	SW 41,42C
Becker, Richard J.	GY 58,60
Beckley, Arthur K.	BS 23,24
	FB 22,23,24
Beckord, Raymond	TR 45,46
Beebe, Channing D.	BS 99C,00C
Beechnau, Louis H.	GY 48C
Beeman, Harris Frank	TN 41,42C,43C
Beery, Robert L.	FB 69
Beese, Arthur J.	TR 92,93
Begeny, Joseph	FB 62,63
Beggs, Wallace J.	BS 49
Behm, Donald	WR 65,66,67
Behney, Melvin	BS 67,68
Behrman, David	FB 60,61,62
Belknap, Leon V.	BK 09
	BS 09
Belknap, Leslie H.	BS 09
Bell, Preston C.	SW 37
Bell, Robert Floyd	FB 02,03,04C
Bell, William D.	SW 36,37,38C
Belloli, Thomas	SO 65,66,67
Belt, Thomas A.	TR 26
Belton, Thomas W.	TN 52,53
Beltz, Lester L.	TR 20
Bencie, Charles J.	BK 56,57,58
Bender, George A.	WR 49,50,51
Bender, Orris H.	WR 50,51,52C
Benedict, Richard R.	FB 67,68
Benjamin, Harlan L.	TR 52,53,54
Benjamin, Sylvester	BK 69,70
Bennett, Byron D.	BK 32M
Bennett, Ralph E.	FB 38,39
Bennett, Wilfred P.	TR 42,43
Benson, Hubert E.	FB 63
Benson, Ken C.	GO 64,65,66
Benson, Steve	GO 66,67,68
Benson, Wayne E.	FB 50,51,52

Bentley, Rahn S.	FB 62,63,64
Benton, Chandler	FC 54
Benus, John A.	SO 61
Berby, Ronald F.	CC 61,62,63
	TR 63
Bercich, Robert E.	FB 57,58,59
Berg, John C.	BS 34,35
Berger, Donald	FB 57,58,59
Bergin, Gerald P.	HO 52,53
Bergquist, Allerd W.	WR 27C
Bergstrom, Wayne R.	GY 61,62
Berlinski, Richard A.	FB 66,67,68
Berman, Edward	TR 51
Bernard, Lacey	FB 56
Bernart, William F.	TR 91,92,93
	BS 94
Bernitt, Richard O.	BS 42,43
Berry, Richard N.	FC 52,53C
Berry, Richard O.	BS 42,43
Berry, William E.	BK 62,63,64
	TR 62,63
Best, George R.	TR 55,56,57
Beuter, John H.	BX 55,56M
Beverly, Walker	TR 63,64
Beyer, George J.	BK 45
Beyer, Howard	FB 42
Bibbins, Arthur Leal	BS 12,13,14,15C
Bidiak, Terry	SO 65,66,67M
Biedenbach, John C.	BS 64,65,66
Bielat, Lawrence J.	FB 57,58,59
Bielski, Daniel N.	BS 68,69
Bierowicz, Donald J.	FB 64,65
Bigelow, Charles A.	SW 41,42
Bigelow, Rolla L.	FB 98
Bignell, George A.	TR 06,07,08,09
Bilkey, Robert B.	BK 24
Billig, Robert F.	GO 47C,48
Billings, Richard A.	BS 63,64,65C
Binge, Ronald E.	BK 70
Binkowski, Thomas E.	BS 66,67,68
Biondo, Michael H.	FB 60
Bird, John C.	SO 58
Bird, Ralph C.	BS 06
Birnbaum, Herman A.	TR 42M
Bisard, William	TN 56,57,58C
Bisgeier, Benjamin	FC 40
Bishop, Judson E.	FB 96
Bishop, Richard T.	GO 52
Bissell, Gary	WR 67,69,70
Bissell, Warren	SW 36
Black, Allan R.	SW 36,37,38
Black, Donald D.	FB 45
Black, Gerald D.	BX 51,52
Blackburn, Bruce	FB 38,39,40
Blacklock, Hugh M.	FB 13,14,15,16
	TR 15
Blackman, Mark S.	FB 45,46,47,48
Blair, William B.	HO 50,51C
Blanchard, Charles M.	BK 02,01C
	FB 00,01
	TR 02,03C
Blanchard, Richard D.	BS 50,51
Blazejewski, Richard J.	SW 60,61,62
Blenkhorn, James	FB 46,47,48,49
Blight, James	BS 66
Bloch, Louis P.	BS 48,49,50
Block, Terrance J.	CC 54,55,56
	TR 55
Blood, Douglas K.	WR 62M
Blount, Dale M.	FC 55
Blount, Harry M.	FC 54,55
Blue, William W.	TR 10,11,15
Bobbitt, James	FB 60,61,62
Bobich, Louis L.	FB 62,63,64
Bobo, Douglas M.	FB 51,52
Bodary, Charles E.	BS 53
Bodoh, Robert B.	TR 43

Boehringer, Rudolph E.	FB 25,26
Boeskool, Randall D.	BK 31,32
Bograkos, Timothy G.	BK 69,70
	BS 69,70
Bohn, Ted	FB 67
Bois, Richard	HO 66,67,68
Bolden, LeRoy	FB 51,52,53,54C
Boles, Denis	SO 67,68,69
Boles, Emerson E.	WR 64,65
Boles, Kevin	SO 68
Bologlu, Ali	SO 60
Bolster, Maurice W.	BS 41
Bolton, George L.	HO 53,56
Bonacci, Anthony O.	HO 57
Bond, Robert C.	TR 62M
Boomsliter, George P.	FB 04,05
Borgman, Paul G.	BS 19M
Boring, Burl J.	WR 46,47
Borton, Thomas E.	WR 58
Bos, John	FB 18,19,20,21C
Boss, Gerard H.	CC 35,36,37
	TR 35,36,37
Boucher, Thomas	HO 58,60,61
Boudreaux, Robert	BX 55
Bouma, Robert	BK 67,68
	FB 67
Boutell, William H.	FB 57M
Bowdell, Gordon	FB 68,69
Bowditch, John J.	BS 03,04
Bowen, Jan A.	CC 62,63
	TR 63,64,65
Bowen, Robert C.	GO 43
Bower, William R.	BS 50,51,52C
	BK 50,51,52
Bowerman, Francis E.	TR 47,48,49,50
Bowers, Charles P.	FB 51,52
Bowers, John E.	TR 65,66,67
Bowers, Michael J.	TR 65,66,67
Bowman, Gary R.	HO 58
Bowman, Thomas Y.	LA 70
Boyce, Gary C.	FB 68,69
	BS 69,70
Boyd, Leo J.	FB 51,52
Boyd, Samuel K.	TR 88,89
Boyle, Jesse G.	BS 05,06
	FB 05,06
Boyle, Michael	SW 69,70
Boylen, Fred J.	FB 58,59,60C
Brabham, Edger C.	TR 54,55,56
Brackett, Richard H.	SW 66
Braden, Ralph L.	TN 55
Bradford, Daniel W.	TR 88,91
Bradley, Charles T.	BS 12
Bradley, Leon H.	TR 33
Bradley, Michael	FB 66
	WR 66,67,68
Bradow, Richard A.	GO 70
Brady, Jacob O.	BS 22,23
	FB 20,21,22
	TR 21
Brainard, Charles	TN 67,68
Brainard, Walter K.	BS 99M
	FB 97C, 01
Brakeman, James R.	FB 34
Brand, Louis J.	FB 42
Brand, Thomas H.	GO 36,38
Brandstatter, Arthur F.	FB 34,35,36
Brandstatter, Arthur F.Jr.	FB 59,60,61
Brannum, Robert W.	BK 48C
Braun, Norwin W.	BK 49M
Brawley, Robert L.	FB 65,66
	HO 65,66,67
Brecher, Sidney R.	TR 41,42,43
Breck, Samuel L.	HO 51M
Breen, Gerald	FB 29,30
Breen, Gerald M.	FC 55,56

Bremer, Ernest K.	TR 37,38,39
	BS 37
	FB 36,37,38
Bremer, Robert K.	BS 27
Bremer, William M.	TN 63
Brendel, Anthony J.	TR 19,21,22
Brendel, William J.	TR 52,53,54
Breniff, Robert G.	FB 52
Brenner, Allen	FB 66,67,68
Brentar, Jerome A.	WR 47,48
Breslin, Jacweir	BS 45,46
	FB 44,45C
Breslin, Jacweir, Jr.	FB 69
Brevitz, Robert B.	TN 49
Brewer, Eugene S.	TR 00
Breza, James	GY 55,56,57
Brezsny, Robert M.	FC 48
Bridges, Lloyd	TR 70
Briggs, DeArmond	TN 70
Brigham, G. Hobart	BK 18
Brightman, Alan H.	SW 37,38C
Brinn, David	SO 69M
Bristol, Cornelius G.	HO 50,51
Bristol, Ralph W.	FC 34
Bristol, Robert W.	FC 52,53
Britton, Dean R.	TN 54
Brogan, David H.	TN 54,55,56C
Brogan, John C.	TN 54,55C
Brogger, Robert H.	FB 44
Bronson, Arthur A.	GY 54
Brookens, Harold A.	BK 59,61
Brooks, Raynard E.	HO 51,52
Brooks, Robert A.	FC 62,63C
Brose, Alfred E.	BS 32
Brose, Leonard D.	TN 50,51C
Brown, Arthur Lynn	BS 15,16,21,22C
	FB 16
	BK 22
Brown, Charles E.	FB 61,62,63
Brown, Charles M.	BS 34
	FB 33
Brown, C. Dean	TR 36M
Brown, Daniel R.	BS 53,54
Brown, Gavin A.	BS 26M
Brown, Gregory B.	SW 67,68,69
Brown, Haxen N.	BS 96
Brown, Lauren H.	BS 30M
Brown, Lauren P.	CC 27,28C,29
	TR 28,29,30C
Brown, Neil P.	FB 62
Brown, Ray L.	TR 98,99
Brown, Robert A.	TR 13C,14
Brown, Robert F.	TR 55
Brown, Roland M.	GY 57
Browsh, Gani	GY 60,61,62
Bruce-Okine, Emanuel	SO 58.59
Bruckner, Leslie C.	FB 37,38,39
	TR 39,40
Brumm, Lynn S.	BS 12M
Brundage, Joseph E.	CC 37M
Brunette, Ralph H.	FB 30,31,32
Bryan, Paul S.	CC 65
Buck, Charles W.	TR 43M
Buck, Conrad F.	HO 51,52C
Buckingham, William J.	WR 49,50,51
Buckridge, Francis P.	FB 00
Budde, Donald J.	BS 49M
Budde, Edward	FB 60,61,62
Budinski, John	FB 38
Bufe, Noel C.	FB 55,56
Buggs, Travis	FB 54
	TR 54,55
Bullach, Melville E.	BS 28,29,30
Bullough, Henry	FB 52,53,54
Bulson, Albert E.	BS 86,87,88
Bunn, William K.	WR 64
Burchill, Kenneth Q.	BK 51M

Name	Codes
Burde, John	BS 67M,68M
Burdett, Raymond A.	SO 57
Burge, Frederick L.	FB 38M
Burgess, William G.	TR 33
Burgett, Glenn E.	TR 57,58
Burk, William R.	BK 41,42
Burke, Oliver W.	BS 03,04,05C
Burke, Patrick	SW 70
Burke, Patrick F.	FB 55,56,57C
Burke, Robert	SW 68,69,70
Burke, Tom	FB 69M
Burlingame, Mark V.	BS 25M
Burnett, Leander L.	BS 89,90,91C,92
	TR 88,89,90,91,92
Burrell, Orange B.	TR 04,05
Burrington, Gray K.	BS 03
	FB 02
Burroughs, Charles G.	FB 05,06,08
	TR 05,06,07
Burtch, James E.	CC 55M
Busch, Fred	BS 09,10,11
Busch, George A.,Jr	GO 42
Busch, Guy	SO 65,66,67CoC
Buschman, Melvin	TR 41,42,43
Buse, John	TN 67,68,69
Bushnell, Elwood P.	TR 09
Buss, Arthur	FB 31,32,33
	TR 32,33,34
Butchee, LaRue	TR 70
Buth, George	GO 67,68
Butler, Charles O.	FB 15,16
Butler, Frank J.	FB 32,33
Butler, Harry L.	TR 37
	CC 36,37
Butler, John H.	BX 55,56,57
Butler, Neil H.	SO 57,58
Buys, Joe D.	SW 65
Buysse, Maurice J.	BK 34,36
Buzenberg, Robert J.	BS 38M
Byam, Harry S.	WR 31
Byington, Walter M.	WR 62,63,64C
Byram, Jack L.	WR 58
Byrne, Keith M.	BS 30,31
Byrum, Robert G.	WR 68

C

Name	Codes
Cady, Earl C.	TR 41
Calderone, Sam	BS 61,62,63
Calhoun, George H.	SW 37
Calkins, Charles F.	BX 43
Callahan, Leo A.	BK 37,38,39C
Callinicos, James D.	FB 61M
Caluory, Francis D.	TR 36,38
Calvert, William W.	HO 50
Campanini, Henry P.	HO 53,55
Campbell, Arthur L.	BK 09,10M
	FB 06,07,08,09
	TR 09,10
Campbell, Daswell	TR 65,66,67
Campbell, David J.	WR 66,67
Campbell, James F.	FB 08,09,10
Campbell, Leroy W.	FB 11,12
Campbell, Thomas R.	GY 68,69
Campbell, Troy	GO 66,67,68
Canfield, Birkley K.	BS 86,87,89C
Canfield, Russell S.	BS 04,05,06,07C
Cantrell, Harmon W.	TR 36,37
Caplin, T. Tyler	GO 60
Cappaert, Carl W.	FB 46,47,48,49
Cappaert, Francis J.	TR 46
Carey, Charles L.	FB 40
Carey, Owen	FB 09
Carey, Robert W.	TR 50,51,52
	BK 50,51,52
	FB 49,50,51C

Name	Codes
Carey, William R.	BK 51,52
	FB 49,50,51
Carleton, Monroe P.	TR 08,10
Carlson, Arnold O.	CC 27M
Carlson, Charles R.	BS 50,51,52
Carlson, Ernest F.	TR 17
Carlson, Gustaf F.	BS 51,52,53
	HO 51
Carlson, Leif M.	BK 50,51,52
Carlson, Sherman F.	BK 27M
Carlstrom, Emil H.	TR 48
Carmen, Robert E.	GY 61,63
Carnahan, Rene P.	GY 48,49
Carpenter, Frank G.	TR 00,01,02
Carpenter, William E.	BK 37,38
	TR 37,38,39
Carr, Dale	WR 66,67,68
Carr, George L.	FC 52
Carr, Harry F.	SW 37,38
Carr, James M.	TR 58,59,60
Carr, Nels R.	BS 19,20,21
Carr, Ralph J.	TR 06,07,08C
Carrier, Lyman	TR 01
Carrier, Robert D.	TR 43
Carrigan, Cornelius R.	FB 47
Carruthers, Joseph D.	FB 55,56,57
Carruthers, Robert H.	BK 31M
Carter, Amien A.	TR 46
Carter, Fred L.	FB 39,40,41
Carter, John M.	BS 58,59
Carter, Roland	TR 65,66,67,68
Cartwright, Wade R.	BS 59,60,61
Caruso, John I.	BS 27,28
Carver, Francis T.	TR 20,22
Casalicchio, Eddie	WR 52,53,54
Casavola, John J.	TR 37,39
Case, Albert H.	FB 99,00,01C
Case, Athol A.	FB 03
Case, Ralph W.	BS 99,01,02
	FB 99
Castellani, Rudolph J.	BS 45
Castle, Brian F.	TR 58,59,60
Castle, Donnard L.	CC 60,61,62C
	TR 62,63
Caukin, Elmer A.	FB 12
Cavender, Regis	FB 66,67,68
Cawood, John F.	BK 43,47
Cerez, Steve	BS 70
Ceskowski, Joseph A.	BX 40
Cessna, S. Roger	TN 45,46,47C
Chaddock, Frank G.	FB 12,14
Chadwick, Jerry H.	SW 58,59,60
Chamberlain, Clark S.	CC 29,30C,31C
	TR 30,31C,32
Chamberlain, Ralph G.	BK 10,11,12CM,13
	FB 12M
	TR 10
Chandik, John	HO 61,62,63
Chandler, Stanley L.	BK 62
Chandnois, Lynn E.	BK 47
	FB 46,47,48,49
Chapman, Clayton W.	BS 04
Chappie, Clarence	FC 65
Charboneau, Ernest R.	BX 47,48,49,50
Charon, Carl H.	FB 59,60,61
	BS 61
Charter, Brien	GO 47
Chartos, William	FB 39
Chase, Albert B.	BS 91,93
Chase, David W.	FC 53
Chase, George L.	BS 86,87,89
	TR 87,88,89
Chastain, James W.	FB 58,59
Chatlos, George	FB 65,66,67
Chaurest, Michel	HO 70
Checco, Albert	HO 60,61
Checkett, Chester M.	SO 62,63,64

Name	Reference
Chesney, Marion J.	FB 60
Childs, Donald M.	FB 02
Childs, Harold A.	TR 02
	FB 02
Chiljean, Malcolm	BS 62,63,64C
Chilton, Elmer	BS 14
Chilton, Leslie	BS 14
Chlopan, Roy	BS 41,42,43
Christensen, Kowster L.	FB 26,27,28
Christiansen, Paige W.	TR 47,48,49,50
Christiansen, Paul	BK 70M
Christie, David	SO 59,60,61
Christofferson, Keith A.	HO 57,58
Christofferson, Melvin	HO 58,59,60
Christoff, Larry	SO 63,64,65
Christopher, Clarence W.	TR 99
Chuck, Robert T.	TN 47,48
Ciolek, David	WR 70
Ciolek, Edwin W.	BS 42,43
Ciolek, Eugene S.	BS 37,38,39
	FB 37,38
Ciolek, Robert W.	BS 50,51,52
	FB 49,51
Clabbers, Reinier P.	SO 62
Clancy, Robert	BS 70
Clark, Alvah B.	BS 96,97,98
Clark, Ernest	FB 60,61,62
Clark, Harold A.	BS 15,16
Clark, Howard C.	TR 35,37
Clark, Howard K.	SW 31
Clark, Kenneth	BS 48M
Clark, Meredith G.	TR 27,28,29
Clary, James R.	FC 59
Cleland, Roland J.	BS 89
Clemens, C. James	SW 55,56,57
Clemons, William G.	SW 48,49
Click, David C.	FN 63,64
Clifford, James V.	SO 57
Climer, Joseph H.	TN 41M
Clise, Burton B.	TR 07M
Clupper, Steve	FB 68M
Coates, Keith	TR 65,66
	CC 65
Cobb, Andrew W.	TR 32,33,34
Cobb, Clifton A.	TR 31
Cobb, Leslie A.	FB 14
Cochran, Donald D.	GO 60,61
Coco, Michael	GY 56,59
Cohrs, William	BK 70
Colby, Richard H.	TN 62
Cole, Clarence L.	BK 26
Cole, Otis R.	TR 95
Cole, William L.	TR 62
Coleman, Don E.	FB 49,50,51
Colina, Richard W.	FB 33,34,35
	TR 34,35
Collard, Raymond D.	BS 54,55,56
Collins, Dennis J.	SW 62,63
Collins, Franklyn M.	TR 47,48
Collins, Robert W.	TR 51M
Collins, William M.	BS 63,64,65
Collinson, William R.	BS 18
Colvin, John C.	BK 27,28
Colwell, Fred E. Jr.	FB 40M
Condit, Thomas	LA 70
Conigilio, Chris P.	WR 56
Conley, James M.	WR 58,60
Conlin, James L.	BS 58,59,60
Connell, John M.	FC 47C
Conner, Alger V.	FB 42,46
Conover, Frank W.	BS 31M
Conti, Dominic F.	FB 45
Conti, Anthony N.	FB 66,67
Contos, Steve G.	FB 45
Convertini, Fred E.	FB 65
Convis, Danny	SW 60
Conway, Lynn V.	FB 46
Cook, Albert B. Jr.	TR 23M
Cook, Bernard K.	SO 58,59,60
Cook, Edward F.	SW 27,30C
Cook, Harvey J.	BS 39,40
Cook, Herbert R.	CC 50
Cook, John F.	CC 52,53
	TR 52,53,54
Cook, Kenneth C.	GY 51,54
Cook, Richard A.	WR 65,66
Cook, R. James	GY 57,58
Cooke, Graham	GO 69,70M
Cooke, Paul	TR 70
Cooley, Charles W.	TR 39,40
Cooley, Gaye	HO 66,67
Cooley, Harry R.	SW 43
Cooley, Willard D.	SW 46,47C
Coolidge, John K.	FB 36,37
Coombs, David L.	CC 59M,61M
	TR 59M
Cooney, Edward G.	BS 87
Cooper, Dale L.	GY 62,63,64
Cooper, James A.	BK 02CM
Cooper, John K.	TR 63,65
Cooper, Larry S.	HO 54
Copeland, Bernard	BK 68,69
Coppo, Michael	HO 65,66CoC
Corbelli, John P.	TR 52,53,54
Corbelli, Joseph J.	TR 50,51
Corbitt, Donald R.	BK 54
Cordaro, Robert	GY 66
Cordley, Arthur B.	BS 86,87,89C,90
Corgiat, James	FB 59,61
Corless, Rex E.	FB 51,52
Corrigan, Michael E.	SW 61,62,63
Cortright, Ion J.	BS 10,11C
	FB 07,08,09,10C
	TR 08,09,10
Cortright, Wesley H.	FB 02
Coryell, Sherman	FB 16,17C,19
Costanzo, Louis P.	BS 55
	FB 54
Costello, Daniel W.	BS 62,63
Cotton, Eddie	FB 64,65
Couey, Darrell R.	BS 45
Coward, David	SW 70
Cowden, David G.	TR 40
Cox, Don	WR 67,68
Coxon, Alfred G. Jr.	SW 56,58,59
Coykendall, Charles E.	TR 53,54,55
Coyne, Kenneth G.	SW 51,52,53
Crabill, Charles J.	FB 26,27,28
Craig, Douglass A. Jr.	TR 33
Craig, Horace S.	SW 29,30,31C
Craig, Robert C.	TR 41
Crall, Max B.	BS 28,29,30
	FB 29
Cramer, Thomas	SW 69,70
Crane, Alexander, A.	SW 47
Crane, Bud C.	FB 47,48,49
Crane, Leroy R.	FB 48,49,50C
Crary, Edward M. Jr.	BS 65,66,67
Crary, John R.	FB 35M
Crawford, Donald	TR 67,68
Creager, Basil J.	FB 33M
Creamer, James E.	FB 50,51
Creamer, Norman R.	BS 57
Crissey, Chase	BS 07,08,09
Crissman, William I.	CC 39M
Cristofoli, Nino	HO 66,67,68
Criswell, Elmont E.	TR 31,33
Crittenden, Richard	SW 69,70
Croft, Dave	GY 66,67,68
Crosby, Dick J.	BS 93,95,96
Crosby, Matt A.	FB 98,99,00,01
	TR 02
Croll, John T.	TN 24C
Crosthwaite, Duane T.	FB 39

Crow, Irvin S. CC 27
Crowell, Jack L. TR 60
Culver, Edward G. FB 10,11
Cummins, Albert B. BS 49,50
Cundiff, Larry L. FB 57,58,59
Curl, Ron FB 68,69
Curley, Douglas G. TN 50,52
Currie, Daniel G. FB 56,57,58
Currie, Michael J. FB 61,63
Curtis, Fred S. FB 98,99
Curtis, William BK 65,66C
Curzi, James J. GY 64,65,66
Custer, George A. FC 48,49C
Cuthbertson, Harold G. BS 30,31,32
Cutler, Donald E. FB 52

D

Dace, John BS 70
Dafoe, Kenneth F. CC 56,57
Daggett, Dean FC 68
Dahlgren, Gordon FB 34,35,36C
Dahlstrom, John D. BS 09
Dahlstrom, John R. BS 38,39
Dales, Herbert P. SW 38
Dales, Oliver O. BS 02M
Daley, Daniel HO 61,62,63
Daley, William B. BS 22,23
Dalponte, Peter L. BS 38,39
Dalrymple, Max E. BK 38,39,40C
Damson, Jack E. TN 61,62,63C
Dancer, Paul C. BS 12,13
Dancui, George W. FB 40,41
Dangl, Robert W. BS 51,52,53
Daniels, John F. GY 59,60,61
Dann, Roscoe J. GY 63M,64M
Danziger, Frederick W. FB 26,28,29C
Daprato, Neno J. BK 15
 FB 12,14,15
Darby, Keith A. FB 53M
Dare, Charles W. TN 56
Dargush, Bennie J. BK 37,38
Davenport, Charles S. GO 52
Davey, Berten E. BX 49
Davey, Charles P. BX 43,47C,48C,49C
Davey, James FC 68
Davis, Benjamin BS 94
Davis, Charles E. BK 39M
Davis, Deland H. TR 27,29
Davis, Frank R. FB 11
Davis, Hugh G. FB 42,43
Davis, J. Francis BS 15
Davis, Jon C. BS 56
Davis, Rondle L. CC 54
Davis, Roscoe W. BS 56,57
Davis, Russell J. BS 27,28
Davis, Wilford D. BS 40,41,42
 FB 39,40,41C
Davis, Wyman Dale BS 40,41,42
 FB 39,40,41
Dawson, Hugh A. Jr. BK 47,48,49
 TR 47,51
Dawson, John B. BS 11,1213
Dawson, William Jr. FB 68
Day, Arthur E. TR 11,12
Deacon, Frederick E. FB 26,27
Deal, Wade H. BS 62,63,64
Dean, Paul BK 69,70
Dear, Rawdon E. TR 54M
DeBenedet, Flavio Nelson HO 67,68,69
Debergh, John SO 62
Deboer, Clarence L. SO 63,64
Debrine, Thomas R. FB 64M
Decker, Arthur J. BS 99,00
Decker, John W. FB 02,03
Dedich, Charles SO 63,64

Dedich, Peter SO 64
Dehenau, Gerald TR 60,61,62
Dehn, Arthur J. TR 42
Deibert, Glenn E. FB 41,42
Deihl, Roy H. BK 42,43
Dekker, James BK 33,34
Dekker, Paul N. FB 51,52
Delgrosso, Daniel J. FB 58
Dell, Arlin L. GO 56,57,58
DeMarco, Frank HO 70
DeMarco, Gerald HO 69,70
DeMarco, Michael HO 69,70
DeMarco, Robert J. HO 67,68,69C
Demarest, Benjamin H. FB 33,34
Demling, Art SO 68,69
Demond, John E. SW 46,49,51
Demond, Raymond J. BS 16,17,18C
Demos, Constantine S. FB 64M
Dendal, Charles T. FB 12
Dendrinos, Peter C. FB 44
Dendy, Robert F. GY 60,61
Denherder, Fred J. BK 28,29,30
Dennis, Charles B. CC 34
 TR 34,35,36C
Denov, Daniel LA 70
Densley, Theodore BK 69M
Denslow, Gaylord E. CC 54,55,56
 TR 55,56,57
Derby, Steven G. TN 67,68,69
Derrickson, Paul W. BS 39,40,41
 FB 38,39
Dersnah, Vernard E. FB 06
Desmond, Robert G. SW 64,65
Devenny, Robert H. BK 53,54,55
Devereaux, Fred A. BS 65,66
DeVuono, Alfred J. HO 57,58,59
Dewell, Ernest P. SW 59
Dhooge, Vic TN 65,66,67
Diane, Jean P. SO 64
Dianetti, Jack CC 46,47,48,49
 TR 47,48,49C,50
Dibble, Dorne A. FB 49,50
Dibello, Joseph V. WR 49,50,51
Dickenson, Richard C. WR 47,48,49
Dickeson, Verne C. FB 27,28,29
 BK 27,28C,29
Dickson, Robert M. BK 06,07,08,09
Diebold, Allen O. BS 37,38,39C
 FB 36,37,38C
Diedrich, William B. GO 54
Diehl, Clifford C. GY 67,68
Diehl, David D. FB 36,37,38C
Diener, Carl A. FB 53,54
Dieters, Dick I. BS 47,48
Dietz, William FB 98
Diget, David K. SW 59,60,61
Diggins, William GY 67
Dilday, Bobbie D. BS 52,53
Dill, Rueben E. FB 28,29,31
 TR 29,30,32
Diller, Burgoyne A. TR 27
Dilley, Alan SW 70
Dilley, Gary SW 65,66,67
Dillon, John H. BS 43,46,48,49
Dimitroff, Boris N. FB 64,65
Dimitrou, Van SO 63,64
Dimmick, Guerdon L. TR 11M
Dinan, Ralph E. TR 14
Dittrich, Francis C. Jr. TR 34,35,36C
Divjak, Ronald BK 62,63
Dixon, Kenneth K. TN 58M
Dobler, Wally SW 57,59C
Dobrei, Douglas M. BS 63,64,65C
Dodge, Glenn W. BK 05
Dodge, Harland P. SW 46
Dodge, Ralph J. BS 11,12,14
 BK 12,13

Doerr, Maxwell H.	BK 30M
Dohoney, Donald C.	FB 51,52,53C
Dominguez, Cesar A.	SO 60,62
Donnahoo, Roger J.	FB 57,58
Donnelly, Paul E.	BS 18,19,20
Donnelly, Samuel	SO 61,62,63C
Dooley, James D.	FC 56
Doolittle, Steward I.	BS 00
Doran, George E.	TR 40,41
Dorow, Albert R.	FB 49,50,51
Doscher, Herman C.	BS 18,19
Dotsch, Allan J.	TR 48
Dotsch, Roland D.	FB 53,54
Doty, Stephen W.	BS 07M
	FB 03,04,05,06C
Dougherty, Patrick F.	BS 47,49,50
Doughty, Howard	TR 70
Douglas, Thomas H.	BK 63,64
Dowd, Arthur B. Jr.	FC 59,60
Dowd, Charles E.	TR 31M
Dowd, Leonard R.	CC 28
Dowell, John K.	WR 46,47,48,49
Doyle, James W.	HO 50C,51C
Doyle, Robert	HO 61,62,63
Drago, Noel	SO 57,58,59
Drake, Gerald A.	FB 38,39
Drew, Franklin F.	FB 02
Drew, Kenneth L.	BK 26,27
	FB 25,26,27
Drilling, Frederick M.	TN 41
Driskel, Harry G.	TR 00
Driver, Lee P.	SW 64,66
Driver, William F.	SW 62,63
Drobac, Stanley	TN 52,53
Druetzler, Warren O.	CC 48,49,50C
	TR 49,50,51C
Drynan, Bruce W.	TR 40,41,42C,46
Dubois, Stanley	HO 54,56
Dubpernell, James E.	TN 55M
Duckett, Ellis	FB 52,53,54
Dudeck, John E.	SW 53,54,55,56
Dudley, Darwin C.	FB 36,37
	TR 37
Duffett, Richard	HO 68,69,70
Duffett, Wayne	HO 66,67,68
Duffield, Arnold W.	BK 32
Duke, James R.	SW 47,48,50C
Dukes, Harold C.	FB 56,57
Dunbar, Donald H.	SW 46
Duncan, Harold A.	CC 61
Duncan, Norman J.	BS 39,40,41C
Dunford, Charles S.	BS 34M
Dunford, John A.	TR 02
Dunlap, Charles W.	FB 06
Dunn, Ernest C.	BX 39
Dunn, Richard G.	TR 66,67,68
Dunphy, Herbert G.	FB 18
Dunsmore, Robert S.	SO 59,60M
Durkee, James L.	GY 60,61,62C
Dust, Robert C.	SW 54
	TR 53
Duthie, Herbert I.	BK 10,11
Dworken, Arthur M.	SO 61M, 62,63
Dysert, Walter J.	TR 33

E

Early, Thomas W.	GO 62
Easton, Zana E.	BS 67,68,69
Eaton, James P.	FB 60
Ebey, Warren W.	FB 59M
Eckel, Clifford B.	FB 41
Eckerman, Harold	FB 22,23,24
Eckert, Edward C.	FB 22,23,24
Eckhardt, Ludwig, Jr.	SO 62,63,64
Eckstrom, William R.	BK 51,52

Eddy, Howard J.	FB 20
Edgar, Oliver W.	TR 98
Edgerton, Robert E.	TR 34
Edin, Richard J.	BS 52,53
Edington, D. W.	SW 57,58
Edmunds, Allen T.	FB 23
Edmundson, Lee	GO 68,69,70
Edwards, Heywood	BK 67,68
Edwards, Hulett N.	TR 63
Edwards, Richard A.	FB 34,35
	TR 37
Egeler, Charles C.	SW 52,53
Eggert, Marvin A.	BS 27,29,29C
Eggleston, Raymond C.	TR 54,55,56
Eisner, Brian W.	TN 60,61,62C
Eissler, Walter G.	TN 36
Ejups, Gunars	FC 54
Ekstrom, Lee K.	TR 59
Ekstrom, William R.	BK 51,52
Eldred, Robert R.	BK 27
Elias, John	BS 61,62
Eliowitz, Abe	BS 31,32,33
	FB 30,31,32C
Eliowitz, Samuel	TR 57,58
Elis, Milton	BS 50M
Ellias, Howard S.	TR 52M
Ellinger, Alvin G.	SW 27
Elliott, Gordon B.	TN 47
Elliott, James E.	FB 96
Elliott, Maurice F.	TR 25
Elliott, Robert C.	TR 57
Elliott, Robert H.	CC 32
	TR 32,33
Elliott, Tony A.	HO 62,63,64
Ellis, Ben C.	BS 06,07,08C
Ellis, Larry A.	SW 56,57
Ellis, Michael	WR 69
Ellis, Robert	BS 70
Ellis, Thomas	BS 67,68
Ellsworth, Bert B.	BS 04
Ellward, John E.	BS 64
Elsasser, Richard L.	TR 68,69
English, Ronald J.	GO 70
Enrico, William	HO 67,68,69
Enustun, Orhan	SO 65,67,68
	TN 68
Enustun, Turgud	SO 63,64,65
Epperson, Robert N.	BX 58
Erickson, Dennis J.	BS 63
Erickson, Edward M.	BS 47,48C
Erickson, Ernest B., Jr.	BS 53,54
Ernst, DeGay	TR 20,21C,22C
Esbaugh, Ernest Kent	FB 45,48,49
Eva, Wesley L.	BK 23,24C
Evans, James D.	BX 52
Exelby, Leon C.	FB 07,08,09,10
Exo, Lester W.	FB 29,30

F

Fager, Theron C.	BS 33,34,35
Fager, Willard J.	TR 38
Fahs, David	BK 59,60,61C
Fairbanks, Charles L.	FB 54
Fairman, Robert P.	GO 49
Fales, Thomas	HO 70M
Fall, George	BK 38,39
Fallat, Robert	HO 66,67,68
Fanning, Lawrence E.	BK 60
Farleman, Arthur W.	TR 03
Farley, Horace B.	TR 26
Farmer, Donald I.	SW 40,41C
Fase, Jacob P.	FB 29,30,31
Faughn, John H.	TR 47
Faulman, Duane L.	BS 43
	FB 40

Name	Code
Faunt, William N.	HO 65,66,67
Faust, Ralph	HO 66M,67M
Fawcett, Charles E.	BS 31,32,33
Fayerweather, Bruce L.	BS 29M
Fedorchik, Joseph	GY 68,70
Fehr, Roy B.	CC 38,39
	TR 38,39,40C
Feldmeier, Robert J.	GY 50,51,52C
Felt, Carl R.	BK 27,29,29C
Fenton, Jack W.	FB 40,41,42
Ferguson, Alan G.	BK 61
Ferguson, George H.	BK 56,57C
Ferguson, James T.	WR 57,58,59
Ferman, Richard D.	TN 70
Ferrar, George D.	FB 27,28,29
Feraco, William A.	FB 67,68,69
Ferrar, Joseph C.	FB 32
Ferrari, Albert R.	BK 53,54,55C
Ferrari, George D.	FB 27,28,29
Ferris, Dean V.	FB 18
Ferris, Henry M.	FB 47
Fertig, Norman	FB 36
Fessenden, Clarence W.	BK 21,22,23C
	TR 21,22,23C
Festa, Angelo R.	GY 58,59,60C
Fick, Hilmar A.	BS 14,15,16,17C
	FB 15,16
Fiedler, Edward	BS 33,34,35
Fiegelson, Arthur R.	FB 46M
Field, Howard W.	TR 30
Fifield, William	HO 70
Filizola, Rubens	SO 60,61,62
Finegan, Daniel	HO 69,70
Finkbeiner, Wayne	TR 45,46
Finn, John B.	BK 50
Finneran, William J.	HO 50,51,52
Fischer, Robert H.	FB 47
Fishbeck, Kenneth B.	BS 27M
Fisher, Carleton W.	BS 25
Fisher, Duncan	GO 46,47,48,49
Fisher, Gerald	HO 65,66,67
Fisher, Royal S.	BS 93,94,95,97
	TR 95
Fisk, James E.	FB 04,05
Fitzsimmons, James W.	BS 41,42C
Fladseth, LeRoy A.	WR 56,57,58
Flake, Rudolf G.	TR 39
Flanders, Walter B.	HO 50
Fleischmann, Donald W.	BS 41,42
Fleischmann, Robert C.	TN 48,49
Fleser, Don W.	BS 25,26,27C
	TR 25
Fleser, John P.	BS 58,59,60
Fletcher, Clifford H.	WR 45,46
Flowers, Edward L.	GO 37,38
Flynn, John J.	BX 49
Flynn, Richard O.	FB 62,63,64
Flynn, Thomas R.	TR 55,56
Flynn, Walter H.	FB 98M
Foerch, Craig M.	GY 69M
Foerch, Richard L.	GY 49,50C
Fogg, Cecil C.	FB 28,29,30
Follis, Daniel	FB 58
Foltz, Dale E.	FB 54
Fomenko, Joseph	FB 57
Fontes, Wayne	BS 61
	FB 59,60,61
Foote, Jack B.	HO 60
Ford, John A.	HO 63,64,65
Ford, Zachary, III	TR 60,61,62
Fordyce, James	FC 65
Foreman, Franklin S.	FB 67,68,69CoC
Forman, Walter H.	FB 65
Fornari, Peter A.	BS 42,46
	FB 41,42
Fornell, Gordon E.	SW 56,57,58C
Fortino, M. Samuel	BK 45,46

Name	Code
Foster, Joseph F.	BS 90
Foster, Larry L.	BS 58
Foster, Walter J.	BK 19,20,21C,22
Fournel, Claude A.	HO 60,62
Fouts, Leslie J.	FB 25
Fowler, Larry D.	FB 51,52,53
	WR 52,53,54
Fox, Calvin J.	FB 68,69
Fracassa, Albert	FB 54
Fraleigh, Royden G.	FB 41,42
Franchi, Frank	BS 56
Francis, Milton J.	FB 25M
Francisco, George D.	BS 00
Frank, Charles W.	FB 51,52,53
Frankel, Charles M.	BK 45
Franson, Harry E.	FB 17,18,19C
Fraser, Albert M.	BS 02,03
Fraser, James M.	TR 43,46,47C
Fraser, John A.	BS 00,02
Fraser, Robert A.	TR 47,48,49
Fraser, William B.	TR 47,48,49
Fratcher, Charles W.	BS 42M
Frazer, William D.	FB 06,07,08
	TR 06M
Frazier, Walter E.	TR 17
Frederick, Charles C.	BK 25,26
Freeland, P. F.	SW 29
Freeman, Emery	LA 70
Freiberger, Clifford H.	WR 38
Freiheit, Fred E.	FC 51,52
Fremont, Perry J.	BS 24,25,26
	FB 24
French, Douglas	HO 66,67,68
Frey, Richard D.	CC 37,38,39C
	TR 37,38,39
Friar, Edward J.	TR 10,11
Friedlund, Robert M.	FB 39,40,41
	TR 40
Friedman, Allan	HO 60M,61M,62M
Friedrich, Michael H.	CC 62M
Frimodig, Lyman L.	BS 14,15,16,17
	BK 14,15,16C,17
	FB 15,16
Frizzo, Leo V.	BK 35
Fruit, Kenneth R.	TR 69
Fry, Clement C.	BS 17M
Fry, Robert G.	WR 62,63
Frye, John	BS 66
Fryman, George R.	BS 04M
Fulcher, Robert S.	CC 61,62,63C
	TR 62,63,64
Fullen, Noel V.	BS 21,22
Fuller, Merrill S.	BS 13,14,15,16C
	FB 15M
Fuller, Payton	SO 63,64,65
Fullerton, Barry A.	BS 56,57
Fullerton, Loring V.	CC 32
	TR 30,33
Fulton, Philip N.	BS 69,69,70
Funston, James E.	GO 41,46C
Furry, John A.	GY 53,54C
Furseth, Erik O.	BK 51,52,53C
Fusi, Peter	FB 46,47,48,49

G

Name	Code
Gach, Ronald E.	BX 58M
Gaddini, Rudolph	FB 55,56
Gaffrey, Norman M.	HO 69,70
Gafner, John	BS 31,32,33
Gage, Ronald W.	SW 60
Gagnon, Giles	HO 70
Gaines, Frank Jr.	FB 35,36,37
Gale, Robert S.	BK 68,69,70
Gallinagh, Patrick F.	FB 65,66
Gang, Robert W.	WR 47,49,50,51

Ganz, Joseph G.	WR 64,65	Girard, Calvin J.	GY 57,58,59C
Garbe, Lyle E.	CC 51,52,53C	Givens, Terry	FC 65,66,67
	TR 52,53,54	Glass, Morris W.	FC 34C
Garbus, Jerome J.	SW 58	Glaza, Stephen M.	BS 36
Gardner, John Nelson	CC 34,35,36C	Glick, Edgar	SW 65,66,67CoC
	TR 35,36,37	Glick, Gene R.	FB 46,47,48,49
Gardner, Robert D.	BS 89,90	Glimn, Terrance C.	FC 59
Gardner, Robert M.	CC 34	Goble, Gary D.	HO 63,64,65
Gargett, George G.	FB 38,39	Godfrey, Robert B.	TR 35,39
Garlock, Ronald B.	BK 35,36,37C	Godfrey, Robert E.	FB 44,45
Garratt, George A.	BK 18,19,20C	Godfrey, Walter G.	BS 54,55,56
Garrett, Drake	FB 65,66,67		BK 55,56C
Garrett, James T.	TR 64,65,66	Golden, Richard J.	BS 58,59,60C
	FB 65	Goldberg, Larry	GY 66,67,68
Garver, John E.	FB 24,25,26	Golis, William	BK 60
Garvey, C. Ross	TR 09	Gongwer, J. Verne	TR 05,07
Garvey, Phillip L.	SW 37M	Gonzalez, George	SW 69,70
Garvey, Steven	FB 67	Gonzenbach, Max A.	BK 56,58
	BS 68	Good, John P.	TN 67,68,69
Gasser, Harold F.	FB 47,48,49	Goode, Benjamin L.	FB 24
Gasser, Harold H.	BS 23	Goodell, David L.	TR 54,55
Gates, Todd M.	GY 63,64	Goodenough, Walter J.	BS 94,95
Gauthier, George	BK 11,12,13,14CM	Goodison, Nigel	SO 69
	FB 12,13	Goodrich, James	BS 65,66
Gavel, Joseph A.	BS 68,69	Goodrow, Richard A.	SW 51M
Geahan, Robert R.	BK 47,48,49C	Goodwin, Marshall B.	TN 34
Geggie, Charles W.	SW 67,68,69	Goovert, Ronald E.	FB 63,64,65
Gehan, John C.	BX 57,58	Gordon, Richard F.	FB 63,64
Geib, Horace V.	TR 09,10,11,12C	Gorenflo, Elmer F.	BS 11,12,13C
Geiermann, Louis J.	TR 18		FB 11,12
Geiger, Jay	SW 69M	Gorenflo, Oscar W.	BS 94,95
Geistler, Gerald	BK 66,67,68	Gorman, Charles D.	BS 51,53,54
Gelmisi, John	SO 60	Gorman, John	BK 66
Gemmell, James S.	BX 49,50	Gorman, Robert J.	HO 50,51
Genova, Kenneth E.	SW 65,66	Gorman, Thomas P.	GO 62
Genson, Wendell E.	WR 35	Gortat, Thomas A.	FB 35,36,37
Gent, George D.	BK 62,63,64C	Gosper, Richard Kevan	TR 54,55
George, Gerald W.	GY 62	Goss, Robert W.	BK 11,12,13CM,14
Gerard, Joe E.	BK 40,41,42	Gough, Geoffrey S.	SW 39
Gerhard, Gerald M.	TR 60	Gould, George N.	BS 96,97,98,99
Gest, Kenneth W.	SW 56,57	Gowens, Arthur L.	BK 59
Getz, Colin W.	BS 42,43	Graft, Clare A.	TR 37,38,39
Gezelius, Roy A.	TR 28M	Graham, Ernest R.	TR 04
Ghise, Cornell	BS 51,52	Graham, Kenneth J.	SO 60,61
Gibbard, James R.	CC 46,48	Graham, Ralph C.	BK 05M,06M
	TR 46,47,48,49		TR 04,05,06G
Gibbons, Eugene V.	WR 49,50,51	Grams, James P.	WR 45
Gibbons, James	BK 68,69,70	Grams, Milton H.	BK 28M
Gibbs, Charles V.	TR 39C	Granack, John W.	BK 46,49
Gibbs, Edward H.	BS 29,30,31C	Grandelius, Everett J.	FB 48,49,50
Gibbs, Frank J.	WR 27	Grant, Alexander W.	BS 41M
Gibbs, Louis C.	BS 90,91	Grant, Howard B.	BS 37M
Gibson, Arthur K.	TR 50	Grant, James	BS 45,46
Gibson, Charles C.	BS 98	Grantham, George R.	CC 36
Giddings, Rupert J.	TR 10		TR 36,37,38
Gieche, Adelbert E.	HO 50	Grau, James A.	TR 55M
Gifford, Chester W.	FB 11,12,13C	Graves, Harry C.	FB 18,21,22
Gilbert, Abel O.	SW 46,47,48	Gray, Tom	TN 69,70
Gilbert, Donald D.	BS 58	Graydon, Edward B.	CC 59
	FB 56,57	Grazia, Eugene W.	HO 55,56,57
Gilbert, George D.	TR 12	Green, Arthur L.	CC 35,36,37
Gilbert, Gregory	TR 70		TR 36,37,38
Gilbert, Roy H.	TR 06,07,08	Green, Duane E.	SW 67,69,69CoC
Gildemeister, Gerald L.	GY 53,54,55	Green, Harry A.	BK 43M
Giliberto, Richard A.	GY 62,63,64C	Green, John J.	TN 58
Gilkey, Edward A.	BK 20,21,22	Green, John M.	BK 57,58,59C
Gill, Norman R.	WR 55,56,57C	Green, William R.	TR 61
Gill, Ralph A.	WR 50,53C	Greene, David G.	HO 57M,58M
Gilliland, William O.	FB 33	Greenway, William E.	BX 53,54,55
Gillis, Henry L.	TR 52,53,54	Greer, Ernest W.	TR 37,38,39C
Gilman, John L.	FB 47,48,49	Gregg, James M.	GY 63
Gilpin, Russell L.	FB 42,46,47	Gregory, J. Nicholas	BS 45,46
Gilson, Kenneth B.	SO 60,62	Grentz, Gerhard	SO 58,59,60
Gingrass, Morgan J.	FB 41,42	Grenzke, George R.	FC 40
Gingrich, Wayne A.	BS 22M	Gretzinger, Richard E.	SW 63,64,65C
	FB 20,21	Griffeth, Paul L.	FB 38,39,40
Gipp, John M.	HO 53,54,55	Griffin, Chester A.	TR 07

Griffin, Charles W.	BS 30,31,32
Griffin, Richard L.	BS 57
Griggs, Mark K.	BS 11,12,13,14
Grim, Bohn W.	FB 25,26
	TR 25,26C,27
Grimes, Ogden E.	FB 26,27
Grimm, Robert A.	TR 68
Grimsley, Ike R.	FB 59,60
Grommes, George H.	SW 63
Grondzak, Donald	FB 44
Groseth, Rolf	SW 66,67,68
Gross, Carl E.	FC 64,65,66
Gross, Milton C.	FB 29,30,31
Grove, Donald B.	BK 28,29,30
Grove, Roger R.	BK 29,30,31C
	FB 29,29,30
Groves, Robert W.	BS 46
Gucciardo, Biagio Jr.	WR 59,60,62
Guerre, George T.	FB 46,47,48
Guest, James F.	BS 46
Gunderson, Leroy E.	FB 45
	TR 45
Gunesch, Mike	WR 66M
Gunn, Frank S.	BS 97
Gunner, Richard J.	WR 52,53,56
Gunner, Robert W.	WR 52,53,55
Gunning, Benjamin N.	GY 54,55
Gunnison, E. J.	BS 02,03,05
Gunny, Edmund R. III	GY 66,67,68
Guthard, Theordore	FB 62
Gutkowski, Ronald J.	BK 70
Gyde, Richard J.	CC 61

H

Habrle, Lodo A.	TR 36,37,38
Hach, Charles A.	TR 03
Hackel, Melvin A.	SW 61
Hackett, Paul M.	BK 25,26C
	FB 23,24,25
Hackney, Lewis H.	TR 27,28,29
Haftencamp, Joseph P.	BS 03M
	BK 02,03C,04
	FB 03M,04M
Haga, Arthur J.	BK 29,30,31C
Hagan, Terry A.	SW 65
Hahn, Harvey D.	FB 04
Hahn, Oscar Charles	FB 58,59,60
Haidys, Leo T.	FB 55
Halbert, Charles J.	FB 36,37
Hale, Elmer B.	BS 93
Hall, Clifford C.	BK 26M
Hall, Harris F.	BS 89,90
	TR 88
Hall, Marion E.	TR 06
Hall, Richard D.	BK 61
	TN 61
Hall, Robert E.	BS 39,40
Halliday, Douglas G.	FB 69
Hallmark, Ferris E.	FB 52,53,54
Hamann, Kenneth	SO 67,68,69
Hamilton, Geoffrey	BK 61M,62M,63M
Hamilton, Horace F.	SO 58,59
Hamilton, Leon G.	BX 51,52
Hamilton, Richard C.	HO 57,58,59
Hammer, John M.	CC 32,33,34
	TR 33,34,35
Hammes, John H.	BS 17,18,19C
	BK 18,20
	FB 17,19,20
Hammond, William J.	FC 40
Hancock, Jack M.	WR 48
Hancock, John	HO 68M,69M,70M
Handler, George W.	TR 39,40
Handloser, Robert A.	FB 56,58

Handy George B.	FB 30,31,32
Hanes, William N.	GO 49
Haney, Usif	FB 36,37,38
Hannas, Allan E.	GY 50,51,52
Hanish, Claude C.	BK 06,07,08,09,
	10C,11
Hankey, Dennis	GO 67
Hankey, Douglas	GO 65
Hansen, Dale W.	SW 40
Hansen, Martin W.	BS 45,46,47C
Hansen, Robert	HO 51,53
Hansen, Robert L.	WR 65
Hanson, T.	TR 07
Harding, Larry R.	FB 56,57
	TR 56M
Hardy, Clifton	FB 68,69
Hargreaves, Richard	HO 63,64,65
Harlow, Peter C.	TR 39,40
Harlow, Richard	BS 66,67,68
Harmon, Glen R.	TR 64M
Harmon, Roger N.	SW 57,58
Harner, F. Daniel	SW 65,66
Harness, Jason E.	FB 58,59,60
	TR 59
Harper, Floyd A.	TR 26
Harris, Chester	TR 63
Harris, Donald R.	BS 47
Harris, James P.	BK 55
Harris, Lynn H.	TR 41
Harris, Michael H.	FB 62M
Harris, Robert B.	TR 41,42
Harris, Trevor	SO 67,68,69
Harrison, Howard H.	BS 07,08,09
Harrison, Richard	SW 66M,67M,68M
Harryman, James E.	SW 35,36,37C
Hart, Edward W.	TR 34M
Hart, William W.	TR 34
Hartman, Frank	TN 61M
Hartman, Kim	CC 68
	TR 69
Hartman, Leonard Deneal	BK 52,53,54
Hartsig, Lawrence J.	TR 46
Hartsuch, Paul J.	TR 22,23,24
Hartwick, Norman R.	TR 52
Hartwick, Wayne	TR 69,70
Hartwig, Herbert B.	BS 19,20
Harvey, Burwell	BS 10,11,12C,13
Harvie, William H.	TR 19
Hashu, Nicholas	BK 42,43,45C
Haskell, Mark L.	FC 65,66
Haskin, Ralph	TR 91,92
Haskins, Donald R.	BS 26
	FB 23,24,25C
Hatcher, Ronald	FB 64
Hatfield, Glen J.	FB 44
Hathaway, Leland	HO 67,68
Hatland, Clarence M.	TR 19
Haun, Harold E.	BK 30
	FB 29
Hauptli, Clifford H.	FB 26M
Hauser, Fred	TR 40
Haven, Frank S.	TR 25
Havens, Glyn D.	TR 51
Hawrylciw, Peter C.	TR 39,40
Hayden, James G.	BS 28,30
	FB 29
	TR 28,29
Hayes, George R.	BS 18
Haynes, A. Maurice	FB 66,67
Haynes, Sherald E.	BX 57,58
Haynie, Norman	GY 67,68,69
Headen, John W.	BK 67M
Heaphy, Donald	HO 65,66CoC
Heasley, Lloyd E.	BK 20,21,22C
Hecker, Paul Gene	FB 57
Hedden, Larry	BK 56,57,58
Heffernan, Harold J.	SW 41,43C

Heft, Kenneth	FB 67,68
Hegre, Arthur B.	TR 43
Hellwege, John A.	SW 52,53,54
Hemphill, Charles M.	TR 86
Hendee, John C.	BS 59,60
Hendershott, Karl J.	BS 20
Henderson, Alwin	TR 70
Henderson, Harry	BS 02
Henderson, James	SW 68,69,70
Henderson, Ronald G.	BS 61
Hendricks, Donald R.	FB 45
Hendrickson, David J.	HO 54,55,56
Hendrickson, Gustav	HO 60,61,62
Hendrie, Leland J.	FB 58M
Henkel, Blaine M.	BS 36,37
Henn, Phillip L.	SW 37M
Henning, Ralph B.	FB 13,14,15,16C
Henry, Charles A.	BK 38,39
Henry, Ronald L.	TN 60,61
Hens, Peter	SO 65,66,67C
Henson, H. L.	TR 27,28,29C
Henson, Richard L.	TR 50,51,52
Herbert, Fred W.	FB 95M
Herbert, Thomas A.	TR 64,65,66
Herdell, Mark C.	TR 22,23,24
Herman, Charles F.	BS 96M
Herman, David J.	FB 61,62,63
Herner, Arthur R.	SW 35
Heron, Cecil B.	SO 59,60
Heron, Gerald W.	SO 60,61,62
Herr, Charles R.	TR 13,14
Herrick, Robert C.	BK 33,34,35C
Herrick, William M.	TR 43M
Herring, Paul	FC 70
Herrman, John W.	LA 70
Hertzler, Walter L.	CC 33
Hervey, H. William	TR 50,52
Hess, Leon J.	BK 48
Hesse, Robin R.	SW 54
Hickey, Daniel H.	BX 47
Hickey, Thomas E.	BX 52,53,54
Hicks, Lon G.	WR 70
Higbie, Charles C.	BS 22
	BK 18,20,21
Higgins, Kevin P.	CC 46,47
Higgins, Sheldon J.	BS 23
Highsmith, Donald C.	FB 68,69
Hilarides, Robert M.	TR 48
Hildebrant, Edgar V.	FC 57,58
Hill, Dennis D.	SW 65,66C
Hill, Douglas W. Jr.	GO 52
Hill, George R.	BS 35,36,37
Hill, Leon J.	FB 09,10,11
	TR 10,11
Hill, Richard B.	GO 67
Hillmer, Donald	TR 54,55,56
Hills, Arthur W.	GO 50,51,53
Hills, Robert W.	TR 36,38,39C
	CC 35,37
Himmelein, Fred T.	SW 40,41
Hindman, Oren M.	BK 39,40,41
Hines, John	BS 63
Hinsely, James	FB 54,55,56
Hinkin, Paul E.	BK 54
Hinkle, Olin N.	BS 17
Hippler, Ralph	FC 58
Hitchcock, Lytton B.	FB 05M
Hitchings, Glenn E.	FB 26,27,28
Hjortars, Gordon	BS 61,62
Hoag, Philip M.	FB 64,66
Hobaugh, Edward R.	BS 54,55,56C
Hobbs, George W.	WR 60,61,62
Hoddy, George R.	WR 68,69
Hodges, Karl P.	BS 00
Hodgson, Arthur D.	SO 59,61
Hoff, Frank W.	TR 33,34
Hoff, Guy F.	BK 11
Hoffman, Arnold G.	TN 54
Hoffman, Howard V.	TR 19,20C
Hoffman, Lee S.	BK 50M
Hoffman, Robert F.	TN 57,58,59C
Hoffman, Robert L.	BX 53
Hoffmann, David	SW 49,50,51
Hofstetter, John N.	BS 51
Hogan, Michael P.	FB 68,69
Hoisington, Clark D.	BS 27,28
Hoke, Bob	WR 52,53,54C
Hoke, David	TR 54,55,56
	CC 54
Hoke, Dick P.	WR 55
Hoke, Jerry	WR 56,57,61
Holcomb, Monte S.	BK 31
	TR 31,32,33
Holdridge, Mark	SW 68,69,70
Holdsworth, Byron H.	TR 97,98
Holdsworth, Phillips H.	TR 02C,03,04
Holdsworth, Wilbur G.	FB 04,05
Hollern, Dale F.	FB 53,54,55
Holly, Irvin R.	FC 63
Holmes, Cecil C.	WR 63,65
Holmes, Richard	BS 65,66
Holmes, Ronald M.	BS 60
Holms, D. John	BK 67,68,69
Holms Richard	BK 65,66
Holt, Michael E.	TR 70
Homa, Andrew	LA 70
Hood, Charles C.	BS 14,15,17
	BK 15,16
Hood, Oliver Z.	BK 26,27
Hood, Robert L.	FB 62M
Hoogerhyde, George A.	SW 47,48,49,51
Hooper, James H.	TR 88
Hooth, Douglas W.	BX 47
Hoover, Herbert D.	TN 42,46
Hopely, George J.	GY 57,58
Hopkins, F. George	BS 34,35
Hopping, William	BS 53,54
Horan, James J.	CC 58
	TR 58,59
Horn, William G.	SO 63M
Hornbeck, Lewis A.	FB 26,27,28C
Horne, John M.	BX 58,59
Horning, Donald L.	TR 62,63,64C
Horrell, William G.	FB 49,50,51
Horski, Maurice L.	CC 41
	TR 42
Hotchkiss, H. N.	HO 50
Hotchkiss, William G.	TN 58,59,60
Hough, Walter K.	TR 06
Houston, Robert E.	TR 21,22
Houska, John	SO 68,69
Houtteman, Richard	HO 69
Hovanesian, Dan	BS 50
Hovey, Donald D.	TR 32,33,34
Howard, Carroll I.	SW 53
Howard, Roger E.	BS 51,52
Howell, Carl	HO 65
Howell, Charles O.	BS 60M
Howell, Franklin J.	TR 29M
Howell, Richard P.	WR 48
Howitt, Shaun	BS 70
Hoxie, Herbert E.	WR 47M
Hruby, Paul F.	HO 57,59
Huckins, Alan R.	WR 64
Hudas, Larry J.	FB 60,61
Hudenko, Benjamin J.	BS 45,46C
Huebel, Robert	BS 16
	FB 15,16
Huey, Warren B.	FB 45,46,47,48
Hughes, Harrison W. Jr.	BS 46,47
Hughes, Hugh E.	TR 46
Hughes, James M.	TN 36M
Hughes, Leslie W.	BS 38
Hughes, Robert B.	TR 57,58,59

Hughes, William L.	FB 50,51	Jobo, Edwin L.	SW 47,48,49,50
Hughlett, Charles A.	BX 47,48,49	Johengen, George A.	BS 49
Hultman, V. Joseph	BX 23	Johns, J. Edmund	FB 18
	FB 22,23,24C	Johns, Lawrence A.	CC 48M
Humbarger, Roger H.	CC 60,61,62C	Johnson, Arthur L.	FB 56,57,58
	TR 61	Johnson, Carl V.	FB 57M
Hume, George J.	TR 87	Johnson, Chauncey J.	SW 60
Hummel, Thomas	BS 67,68	Johnson, David B.	FB 36M
Hunt, Gene A.	GO 61	Johnson, Donald E.	FC 61C
Hunt, Gilbert A.	CC 48	Johnson, Donald F.	WR 47C
Hunt, Mark W.	SW 65	Johnson, Fred D.	TR 47,48,49,50
Hunter, John R.	GO 63	Johnson, Glenn H.	FB 41,45
Hurd, Martin A.	GO 55	Johnson, Gordon C.	WR 60
Hurd, Wesley V.	TR 33,34,35C	Johnson, Greg	WR 70
Hurley, Albert E.	BS 94	Johnson, Harold C.	FB 44
Hurt, Paul Thomas	GY 64,65	Johnson, Herman	FB 61,62,64
Hutson, Charles T.	WR 39,40C,41C		TR 62
Hutt, Martin, C.	BK 38,39,40C	Johnson, Huntley A.	SW 40
Hutton, Kenneth W.	FB 12	Johnson, Lanny L.	GO 55
Hyatt, George Jr.	TN 36,37		SW 52,53,54,55
Hyde, Carl W.	BS 04	Johnson Leo G.	BS 11M
Hynes, Robert W.	SW 52,53		FB 09M
		Johnson, Marvin K.	SW 43
I		Johnson, Mike	WR 66
		Johnson, Okla	WR 61,62,63
Ichesco, Wesley R.	TN 69	Johnson, Paul C.	SW 62,63
Idzkowski, Richard J.	BS 53,54,55	Johnson, Robert	HO 68,69
Ike, Larry	BS 70	Johnson, Robert B.	BK 53
Indyke, Zigmund J.	SW 46	Johnson, Stephen C.	GY 60,61,62
Ingram, Arthur L.	TR 51,54	Johnson, Thomas A.	FB 40,41
Irmen, Thomas L.	CC 47,48	Johnson, Vernon	BK 67,68
	TR 48,49C	Johnson, Warner A.	FC 57
		Johnson, William C.	BS 21,22,23
J			FB 20,21,22C
		Johnson, William M.	FB 44
Jackard, Jerald W.	WR 58,59	Johnson, Wilmer L.	TR 62,63
Jacks, Fred H.	FB 16	Johnston, Orlin T.	SW 47
Jackson, Alvin F.	FB 33	Johnston, Rae	BK 50
	TR 33,34	Johnston, Stanley	BS 18,19,20C
Jackson, Karl F.	HO 54,55,56	Johnstone, Walter D.	HO 61,62,63C
Jacob, Walter C.	WR 34,35,36C	Jolin, Norman B.	GY 68,69
Jacobs, Allan J.	FC 50	Jones, Albert E. III	BS 41,42
Jacobsen, Bert	SO 65,66,67		TR 42
Jacobson, Charles M.	HO 65,66,67	Jones, Allen Jr.	FB 51
Jacobson, James A.	HO 62,63,64	Jones, Bernard L. Jr.	TR 50,51,52
Jakubiec, Jim	TN 66	Jones, Bruce M.	BS 53
Jakubowski, Stephen A.	BS 40,41	Jones, Clinton	FB 64,65,66CoC
James, David	WR 60,61,63		TR 65,66
James, Kenneth A.	HO 56,57	Jones, Don F.	TR 14
Jamieson, Daniel K.	SW 61,62	Jones, Dudley P.	BK 41,42,46
Jamieson, Thomas K.	TN 62,63,64C	Jones, George L.	SW 59,60,61
Janes, George	SO 63,64,65	Jones, Gerald R.	FB 31,32
Janson, Lynn	GO 68,69,70	Jones, Jerald L.	FB 64,65,66
Janson, Ronald J.	FB 62M	Jones, Joel	FB 55,56
Japinga, Donald	FB 63,64,65CoC	Jones, Milford H.	FB 45
Jarrard, Donald S.	GO 48C		TR 46
Jarrett, Richard S.	CC 51,52	Jones, Robert M.	SW 69,70
	TR 52,53,54	Jones, Selwyn	CC 55C,56
Jasson, Robert W.	HO 56,57,58C		TR 56,57C
Jebb, James R.	FB 53		WR 57
Jefferson, Thomas G.	TR 60,61	Jordan, J. Nicholas	FB 66,67,68
Jeffrey, LeRoy	BX 52	Jordan, Richard C.	BK 67
Jemilo, Robert F.	BX 56,57		BS 67,68,69
Jenkins, Arthur G.	TR 36,37,38	Jordan, Thomas W.	FB 62
Jenkins, Norman F.	FB 65	Joseph, Ronald J.	FB 68,69
Jenkins, Robert N.	BS 63M,64M,65M	Joslin, M. L.	FB 27,28,29
Jenkins, William R.	FB 60M		WR 30C
Jennings, Burl	WR 41,42,43C	Joyce, Donn	BK 49
Jennings, Merle	WR 41,42,43C	Joyce, Douglas O.	GY 50M
Jewell, Douglas F.	FC 59	Jozwiak, Max W.	BK 53
Jewett, Robert G.	FB 55,56,57	Juday, James	FB 67
Jiron, Roger K.	FC 58	Juday, Stephen A.	FB 63,64,65CoC
Joachim, Joseph L.	TR 27		BS 65,66
Joblonski, Charles F.	BS 50,51	Juengel, Allen V.	BS 50M
		Julian, George E.	FB 11,12,13,14C
			TR 13,14C
		Junker, Herman J.	GY 55,56

Juntikka, John   HO 68
Justice, Morgan A.   FB 69

K

Kaae, William K.   FB 55
Kage, Lowell M.   WR 51
Kahl, Harris A.   BS 29,30,31
Kaines, Michael A.   CC 62,63,64
    TR 62,63,64C
Kaiser, David M.   FB 55,56,57
Kakela, Peter J.   FB 59,60,61
Kalman, Kazmer C.   FB 57M
Kalmar, H. Ralph   FC 52
Kalmbach, Michael   SW 68,69,70
Kalmbach, Walter A. Jr.   CC 44
    TR 45,47,48
Kalvelage, Douglas   LA 70
Kaman, Roman J.   FB 39
Kamrath, Robert M.   BS 40,41
Kane, Paul L.   TN 30C
Kanicki, James H.   FB 60,61,62
Kanitz, Hugo F.   FB 26,27
Kapral, Frank S.   FB 50,51
    WR 50,51
Karpinski, John J.   FB 63,64,65
Karr, Robert F.   TR 70
Karslake, Pat   WR 68,69,70
Kasten, Jack   SW 45
Kastner, William R.   TR 02
Kathrein, John A.   BK 52M
Kau, Wallace Y.   TN 51
Kaufmann, Anton J.   SW 59
Kaulitz, Dale E.   TR 41,42,43
Kauppi, D. K.   HO 50
Kauth, Don F.   FB 52,53,54C
Kaye, George E.   WR 64M
Kearly, Ted H.   BS 57,58
Keast, Roger   BK 32
    FB 32
    TR 32,33,34
Kebschull, Herbert W.   CC 46
Keeler, David   BK 66,67
Keene, Jon   LA 70
Keesler, Starr H.   TR 39,40,41
Keir, Gerald J.   BK 64M
Keller, George C.   CC 38,39
    TR 40
Keller, Wayne M.   BX 53
Kelley, John   LA 70
Kelley, Mason J.   TR 46
Kellogg, Orson T.   BS 18
    FB 17
Kelly, Ellison L.   FB 56,57,58
Kelly, Martin J.   FB 48
Kelly, Russell W.   FB 57
Kemeling, Reiner   SO 60,61,62C
Kemler, John   BK 65,66
Kempf, Robert   HO 60,61,62
Kendall, Gerald G.   BX 56
Kendrick, Harry E.   BS 67,68,69
Kennedy, Crawford E.   CC 57,58,59C
    TR 57,58,59
Kennedy, Henry   CC 55,56,57C
    TR 56,57,58
Kennedy, Joseph K.   TR 43
Kennedy, Samuel J.   BS 98,99,00
Kennedy, William J.   FB 39,40,41
Kenney, Richard K.   BS 65,66,67
    FB 64,65,66
Kent, Bryan D.   CC 69
Kent, William R.   GO 46
Kenyon, Pierre M.   TR 28
Kepford, James R.   CC 50,51C,52C
    TR 51,52,53

Kepple, Ted   FB 54
Kern, Sidney A.   BK 45M
Kerner, William   FC 68
Ketcham, Donald D.   BS 62,63,64
Ketchman, Sam   FB 36
Ketchum, James P.   FB 50M
Ketzko, Alexander G.   FB 38,39
Keyes, Tony   SO 66,67,68C
Kiczenski, Edward L.   CC 46
Kidder, Charles A.   CC 29M
Kidman, James L.   BK 24
Kiebler, Harold C.   BS 24,25,26C
Kieppe, Richard N.   FB 40,41,42
Kifer, L. Darryle   SW 65,66
Kilbourn, Richard   BS 65,66
Kilbride, Duane R.   BK 61
Kiljan, John J.   TR 39
Killoran, John L.   TR 24
Kilpatrick, Randall J.   CC 69
Kimble, Keith D.   TN 50,51,52
Kimble, Kenneth G.   TN 51
Kinek, Michael K.   FB 37,39C
King, Gary   WR 61
King, Gordon A.   HO 52,53,54,55
King, James M.   FB 50
King, LeRoy B.   BS 95
King, Thomas V.   BS 43
King, Tom   GY 68M
Kinkel, Ted   GY 65,66
Kinnan, William A.   TR 86
Kinney, Charles E.   GY 60M
Kinney, John R.   BS 49,50C
Kinsey, Craig, M.   GY 68,69
Kinsey, Daniel B.   GY 67,68,69
Kipke, Ray L.   FB 23,24
    BS 31,32,33
    BK 32,33C
    FB 32
Kircher, Alton S.   GY 69
Kirchoff, John   BK 70
Kirkpatrick, Steve   BK 24
Kitto, Clyde A.   TR 23
Klaase, Leonard S.   FB 49,51,52
Klein, Joseph A.   TR 59,60
Kleinhans, Michael L.   TR 31,32,33
Kleinheksel, John   GO 61
Kleva, Marty L.   BS 39,40,41
Klewicki, Casmer J.   BS 33,34
Klewicki, Edward L.   FB 32,33,34
    FB 39
Klewicki, Herman A.   BS 60,62
Klewicki, Wesley L.   BS 96
Kling, Frederick J.   TN 34,36
Klunzinger, Willard R.   BS 07
Knapp, William W.   TR 09,10C
Knecht, John W.   FB 53
Knight, Dale W.   BS 67,68,69
Knight, Marvin   BS 29,30
Knisel, Wendell O.   WR 52,53
Knotts, James D.   SW 43
Knox, Robert D.   SW 61
Kobel, Robert J.   BX 58
Koehn, Jack L.   WR 58
Kolbe, Joseph W.   SW 62,64
Kolodziej, Anthony M.   FB 55,56,57
Konrad, Ignatius J.   WR 43,46C,47
Kopriva, Donald   CC 69M
    TR 69M,70M
Korkiala, Raimo   SO 69
Korten, Donald H.   SW 47,48,49,50
Kortge, Ralph M.   GO 42
Korwek, Jerome L.   BS 57,58,59
Kositcheck, Leonard   TN 39
Kostegian, Vanar A.   BS 45
Kough, Stephen J.   FB 69
Kovacich, George T.   BS 37
    FB 36,37,38

Koverly, George T.	BS 37	Lafayette, Kenneth F.	TR 31,32
	FB 36,37,38	Lafayette, Lee	BK 67,68,69C
Kowal, Stanley J.	GO 39,40	Lafever, Albert M.	BS 13
Kowalczyk, Walter J.	FB 55,56,57	Laforge, Richard W.	BX 52
Kowalk, Clayton J.	BK 43	LaFrance, Leonard B.	SW 40
Kowatch, Joseph	FB 30,31,32	Lagrou, Alfred J.	TR 46,48
Kozikowski, Renaldo	FB 50	Laitner, Cass B.	FB 96
Kraft, Howard A.	BK 36,37,38C		TR 96,97
Krajczinski, Alex A.	SW 47	Lake, Robert L.	CC 57,58,59
Krakora, J. G.	BK 45		TR 58,59,60C
Krall, William R.	BK 45,46	Laking, Allen	HO 70
Krasman, John R.	BS 65,66	Lamers, John G.	BK 61,62,63C
Krat, Nick	SO 64,65	Lampel, Thomas R.	TR 46
Kratz, Frank J.	FB 01,02,03C,04	Lampke, Louis J.	FB 03
	TR 03,04,05	Lamssies, Robert R.	FB 44,45
Kratz, Oscar A.	FB 05	Lancour, Harvard L.	BX 57,58
	BS 06,07	Lande, Lars O.	BS 63
Krause, Floyd J.	TN 41	Landman, Jack E.	SW 53
Kreft, Thomas W.	SO 66,67,68	Landsburg, George	WR 28C
Krehl, Edward C.	BK 05,06C,07C,08	Lane, Ray	BS 51,52
Kreiner, Jack B.	WR 47,48,49	Lang, Forrest J.	TR 27,28,29
Kreitsch, Robert	FC 69,70	Lange, Robert	FB 67
Krental, Adorf B.	BS 96,97	Langer, C. A.	BS 31,32,33
Krental, Alexander C.	BS 95,96,97,98,99	Langley, Gary	SW 67,68
	TR 95	Lanini, Jeffrey	SW 70
Krental, Christian M.	BS 97M	Lanker, James E.	SW 56,57,58
Krestel, Robert D.	BS 48,49	LaRose, Clifford E.	FB 56,57,58
	FB 47,48	Larsen, Thomas H.	WR 56
Kreuger, Richard	BS 70	Larson, Edward Lee	BK 34M
Kritzer, Robert J.	TR 48	Larson, Fran	WR 66
Kroll, William H.	TR 27,28	Larson, Orlin C.	CC 62
Kronbach, Allan J.	BS 34,35	Laska, Melvin E.	FC 65,66
Kronk, Charles	LA 70	Lassila, Gordon A.	HO 56
Krueger, Warren	CC 69	Lattimer, Earl B.	FB 61,62,63
Krushak, Donald H.	FC 43	Lau, William F.	TN 61,62
Krzemienski, Thomas C.	FB 63,64	Lautenschlager, Edmund H.	TR 39
Kuczerepa, George	GY 50,51	Law, Donald	FB 67,68,69
Kuester, Fred R.	WR 55	Lawless, Richard J.	FC 59,60,61
Kuh, Richard E.	FB 50,51	Lawrence, James G.	HO 63,64,65
Kuhl, Kenneth Robert	FB 55M	Lawrence, Wendell B.	BS 48,49,50
Kuhlman, John P.	GY 67M, 68M	Lawrie, Wayne L.	BS 51,52,53,54
Kuhlman, Thomas	GY 70	Lawson, Paul	FB 67
Kuhn, Bernard D.	BS 21,22,23C	Lawson, Thomas J.	BS 50,51,52
Kuhn, George W.	BS 24,25,26	Lay, Russell M.	FB 32,33
Kuhne, Kurt H.	BS 36	Lazar, Dennis	BS 69
	FB 35	Lean, David F.	CC 57,58C
Kuk, John E.	BS 37,38		TR 56,57,58C
Kulesza, Bruce A.	FB 68,69	Learned, William L.	BS 87
Kumiega, Anthony L.	FB 59,60,61	Leas, Donald E.	GY 55,56,57
	TR 61		SW 55,56
Kuper, George	GY 50,51	LeClair, Donald D.	FB 41,42,46
Kupper, James	BK 65,66	Lee, Andre L.	FC 66
Kurrle, Harry A.	FB 26,27,28	Lee, Dwight	FB 65,66,67
	WR 29C	Lee, Martin E.	FB 08
Kurtz, Lawrence D.	BK 18, 19C,20	Lee, Stephen	LA 70
	TR 18C,19	LeFevre, Neil	FB 41M
Kurtz, Lloyd B.	TR 24,25C,26	Leffler, Martin J.	FB 17,19,20
Kurtz, Raymond L.	FB 08M	Lehnhardt, Milton O.	BS 35,36,37C
Kush, Frank J.	FB 50,51,52		FB 35,36
Kutchins, Bryon A.	FC 63,64,65	Lekenta, Eugene E.	FB 52
Kutchins, Henry K.	FB 34,35,36	Lemmon, Charles A.	FB 08,09
Kutchins, Walter S.	FB 39,40	Lenardson, Faunt V.	FB 10,11,12,13
Kutschinski, Tom	FB 68,69	Lennox, Theodore R.	WR 54,55
Kuzma, Theodore R.	GO 48	Leonard, Lewis R.	FC 64
Kwasney, Thomas A.	SW 56,57,58	Leonard, Terry G.	WR 64,65
		Leonowicz, Kenneth	CC 67,68C,69C
			TR 68,69,70
		Lepard, Olin L.	WR 33
		Lesnik, Mike	SO 65
		Levagood, George E.	BS 38,39
L		Levin, Harvey A.	BK 65M
		Levine, Frederick A.	TN 55
		Lewin, Dennis	HO 63M,64M,65M
Lacey, William H.	FC 47,48,49,50C	Lewis, Ben	WR 70
Lackey, Carl K.	HO 62,63,64	Lewis, Dwight	HO 70
Lackey, Thomas W.	HO 61,62,63	Lewis, Floyd W.	FB 29
LaCoste, Andre	HO 59,60,61	Lewis, John	FB 53,54,55
Ladd, Donald B.	SW 39,40C,41		
Ladd, John C.	SW 65		
Ladue, Howard A.	BS 41,42,43		

Lewis, Sherman P.	FB 61,62,63C TR 62,63C	Lynn, Geoffrey	GO 66
		Lytle, Gary	BS 65
Libbers, Arthur J.	BS 37,38,39		
Liberty, Clifford P.	TR 31,32,33	**M**	
Lick, Thomas W.	BK 67,68,69		
Lickley, Ralph M.	FB 99M		
Lickman, Ronald F.	TN 62	Maas, Kirk	BS 69,70
Lieberman, Albert G.	BK 49M	MacArthur, Duncan C.	BS 90
Liggett, John A.	TR 42,43	Macauley, William A.	CC 33M
Lillyblad, Robert B.	TR 57	MacDonald, Glenn H.	HO 57,59
Limber, Peter E.	FB 44M	MacDonald, Robert B.	TR 38M
Lincoln, Dewey R.	FB 61,62,63	MacDonell, Dennis A.	GO 63
Lincoln, James E.	TR 52,53	MacDougall, Everett R.	BK 40M
Lindeman, Edward C.	FB 10M	MacGrain, Donald	BS 36,37
Lindley, Darrell E.	BS 51	Macier, George W.	BS 28,29
Link, Arthur B.	CC 65,66 TR 66	MacInnes, Donald E.	TR 39
		Mack, Walter C.	CC 41,45C,46C TR 42,46,47
Link, Donald	TN 34		
Linne, William V.	BS 67,68,69	Mack, William G.	CC 48,49C TR 49,50
Lioret, Ernest L.	FB 22,23,24		
Lische, Charles H.	TR 29	MacKenzie, Thomas W.	HO 57,58,59
Little, Kenneth E.	FB 67,68,69	Mackey, Frederick	GO 65,66
Little, Kenneth R.	BS 33	Mackey, Lawrence L.	FB 64
Little, Stephen H.	TR 51,52,53	MacKinnon, Arthur C.	BS 93,94,95
Litwhiler, Richard W.	BS 67	MacMaster, Hugh D.	BK 52
Livensparger, Donald E.	BS 61	MacMillan, James A.	SW 65,66
Lobaugh, Leslie L.	SW 56,57,58	MacMillan, Roy A.	BS 21,23,24C BK 23,25 FB 20,22
Lofgren, Bruce E.	FB 56M		
Logan, John M.	CC 53		
Logan, Leonard N.	FB 31M	Macomber, Ronald M.	FC 63
Lohri, Jean	SO 60,61,62	Macon, David C. Jr.	TR 40
Loney, Glenn	TR 67M	Macuga, Edward J.	FB 64
Long, John E.	FC 38C	Mader, Kurt E.	TR 38,40,41
Lonigro, Aldo F.	SO 58	Madonna, John	BS 30,31,32C
Lonsbury, Pierre B.	TR 26M	Madura, Mike	TN 70
Look, Bruce	BS 64	Maedo, Dennis	BS 65,66
Look, Dean Z.	BS 58,59 FB 57,58,59	Maekawa, Choken	BX 54,55,56
		Magi, Vincent	BS 49,50,51C
Loomis, Ladd N.	SW 38,40	Mahaney, Robert C.	BK 51M
Loose, William S.	TN 34	Mahoney, Earl L.	FB 46
Lopes, Roger	FB 61,62,63	Maichoss, Arthur F.	BS 42,43
Lord, Charles S.	TR 10,11,12	Maidlow, James	WR 65,66
Lord, Richard L.	HO 51,52,53	Maidlow, Kenneth A.	WR 56,57,58,59
Lord, Russell R.	TR 26,27,28	Mailbach, Allan	TR 67
Lothamer, Edward D.	FB 62,63	Maki, Alfred W.	HO 51
Loulakis, Nickolas M.	BS 45	Maki, Edwin C.	TR 40M
Loutzenhiser, Rodger	FC 66,67	Makielski, Donald J.	TR 49,50,51 CC 49,50
Love, Thomas E.	FB 68		
Loveland, Clarence W.	FB 14 TR 12,13,14,15	Makielski, Edward L.	TR 49
		Malaga, Robert S.	TN 47,48,49C
Loveland, Harold V.	TR 09	Maldegan, Robert G.	WR 46,47,48,49C
Lowe, Gary R.	FB 54,55	Malecek, Gerald	WR 70
Lowe, Richard V.	SW 62,63,64	Maliskey, Donald C.	FB 38
Lowrance, Keith	WR 68,69,70	Malley, Mark	WR 70
Lowther, Charles	FB 66	Mallory, William E.	TR 49
Lucas, Harold W.	FB 63,64,65	Maloney, Maurice E.	CC 49
Lucas, Leslie	SO 68,69	Mancour, David A.	GO 53,54
Luce, Francis Alan	BS 55,56,57C	Manders, David	FB 59,60,61
Luchenbill, Dave	WR 69M, 70M	Mangan, Albert J.	CC 39,40 TR 39,40,41
Ludwig, Robert H.	BS 46 FB 45		
		Mangrum, Richard W.	FB 41,42C
Lueck, Walter H.	FB 36,37	Maniere, Robert C.	BS 63,64,65
Lukasik, Larry	FB 64,66	Manion, Edward J.	BS 40
Luke, Edwin E.	FB 50,51,52	Mann, William Alfred	TR 61,62
Lukins, Darle J.	TR 16,17	Manning, George H.	TR 04
Lumianski, Jeremy P.	BS 59,60,62C	Mannor, Richard L.	CC 57M,58M TR 58M
Lumsden, David H.	FB 48,49 BK 47,48		
		Manrique, Dennis R.	SW 66
Lund, Donald	FC 65,66	Mansfield, William C.	BS 54,57
Lundy, Charles B.	FB 98	Mansfield, William H.	CC 39 TR 38,39,40
Luoto, Lauri	SW 42,43		
Luplow, Alvin D.	FB 58	Manwell, Arthur R.	SW 59
Lustik, Donald P.	TR 57	Marchal, Joseph H.	WR 59
Lutz, Harry J.	FC 35C	Marchini, Donald E.	GY 57
Lux, Harry J.	BK 56,57	Marek, Gabriel	BX 49,50
Lyke, Wardell H.	TR 43	Marin, Nels V.	FC 63,64,65
Lyman, Richard P. Jr.	FB 23,24,25	Marion, Louis W.	FC 45

Mark, Forrest	FC 58	McCann, William C.	BS 32,33,34
Markham, Arthur G.	FB 11	McCarthy, Robert J.	TR 41,42,43
Marks, Cornelius E.	TR 18	McCarthy, William E.	BS 11
Marlatt, Ronald G.	BS 60	McCaslin, Garold E.	BS 31,32,33
Maronick, Gregory D.	SW 56		BK 31,32,33C
Marr, Richard C.	GO 64	McCauley, Robert H.	BS 28,29,30
Marrs, John	WR 42	McClain, Jack	TR 45
Marsa, Lee A.	WR 33	McClain, Joseph	LA 70
Marsh, Donald F.	TR 57,59	McCleary, Eugene J.	BS 40M
Marsh, Jack D.	SW 65,66,67	McClelland, Albert L.	BK 15,16,17C
Marsh, Robert G.	GY 55,56C		FB 16
Marshall, Donald B.	SW 40M	McClelland, Robert L.	TR 51
Marshall, Eric R.	FB 67	McClure, Homer R.	WR 63,64
Marshall, Harvey	TR 41M	McCollam, Paul	TR 65
Marshall, Merrill G.	WR 30		CC 65
Marshall, Philip T.	BX 47,48	McComb, J. Robert	FB 37
Marston, Phillip C.	GO 63C,64	McCook, Jack	BS 61
Martens, Michael J.	TR 65,66	McCool, Paul F.	FB 17
Martin, Arthur D.	FB 20	McCormick, Norman F.	BS 45
Martin, Blanche	FB 56,57,59	McCormick, William E.	HO 50,51,52C
Martin, Dave	TR 70	McCosh, James A.	FB 25,26,27
Martin, George E.	TR 03,04	McCoy, Julius	BK 54,55,56
Martin, John E.	BK 33M		TR 54,55
Martin, Michael L.	HO 63M	McCrary, James L.	FB 33,34
Martin, Robert E.	TR 51	McCray, John L.	WR 59,61,62
Martin, Stanley A.	FB 11	McCue, Charles A.	FB 98,99C,00C,01M
Martin, Thomas F.	TN 49	McCulloch, Robert W.	BS 86,87
Martin, William P.	WR 39,40		TR 87
Martin, Wilton	FB 68,69	McCullum, Albert D.	FC 61
Martinek, Julius A.	FB 48M	McCurdy, Russell J.	FB 12,13
Marvin, Virgil I.	FB 29M	McCurry, Robert B. Jr.	FB 46C,47C,48C
Marx, Boyer H.	BK 25	McDaniel, Lewis E.	GO 61,62
Maskill, William R.	FB 44	McDermid, Frank H.	FB 11
	TR 45,46	McDermid, H. B.	FB 04,05
Masny, Myron	FB 38		TR 04
Mason, Donald L.	FB 47,48,49	McDonald, Malcolm E.	WR 47,48
Mason, Elwood M.	BK 25	McDurmon, Clare J.	TR 36,37,38
Mason, John D.	SW 56,57	McElroy, Edward M.	BS 93
Massuch, Richard C.	BS 46,47	McFadden, Marvin G.	FB 50,51
	FB 44,45	McFarland, Jerome	FB 58
Masters, Norman D.	FB 53,54,55	McFetters, Douglas S.	TR 52
Mather, Richard R.	TR 63,64	McGaw, Donald	FC 70
Mathews, Charles L.	BS 52,53,54,55	McGilliaray, Lodowic A.	FB 08
Mathieson, Roderick R.	BK 12	McGilliard, Michael	WR 68,69
Matsko, John	FB 54,55,56C	McGillicuddy, Robert J.	BK 28
Matsock, John J.	BS 54,55C	McGowen, Leon W.	TR 49
	FB 53,54	McGrath, John E.	SW 45
Matson, Edward I.	BK 21,22	McInnis, Frank G.	BS 24
	FB 20,21	McIntyre, Malcolm M.	FB 00
Matsos, Archie G.	FB 55,56,58	McKay, Raymond F.	TR 51,52,53
Matt, Juergen H.	SW 60,61,62	McKenna, Edward B.	BS 05M
Matthews, Wallace B.	BK 25M		FB 03,04,05C
Mattson, Jeffrey P.	SW 61,62,63C		TR 02,04,05C
Maupin, Theodore	BS 49,50	McKenna, George F.	TR 36,37
Maxwell, John William	TN 42,43	McKenna, Parnell G.	BK 06,07,08,09C,1(
	WR 41,42,43		FB 06,07,08,09C
Maxwell, Mark A.	CC 69	McKenzie, Richard D.	BS 57
May, Floyd Earl	TN 42,43	McKillop, Edward A.	TR 55
	BK 43	McKinnon, Peter A.	SO 58,59
May, Frank O.	FB 47M	McKoy, Frederick G.	TR 64,65,66
Mayer, Rudolph	SO 69	McLachlan, Robert H.	SW 51,52,53C
Mayes, John W.	HO 52,53,55	McLaughlin, Ernest L.	TR 36,37,38
Mayhew, Harold D.	TR 46,47	McLaughry, DeArmond	FB 11
Mazza, Matthew A.	BK 46,47	McLee, Bradley M.	FB 69
Mazza, Orlando J.	FB 51	McLoud, Eddy W.	FB 67,68
McAndrew, Brian	GO 65,66,67	McLouth, Aldrich L.	FB 98,99
	HO 65,66,67	McLouth, John D.	BS 96,97C
McAtee, Harold A.	TR 27,28,29	McLucas, Edwin	FB 59
McAuliffe, Donald F.	FB 50,51,52C	McMillen, Larry D.	GO 61
McAuliffe, Thomas	BK 51	McNamara, B. Edward	SW 36,37C
McBrady, Gary	SO 65,66,67	McNamara, William J.	FC 61
McBride, Dunbar	TR 24M	McNeely, Thomas W.	BX 58
McCabe, Albert M.	TR 27	McNeil, Robert A.	FB 40,41,42
McCaffree, David Lee	SW 58,59	McNutt, Bernard G.	FB 32,33C
McCaffree, Donald C.	SW 65M, 66M		TR 32,33
McCalla, Donald F.	FC 57,58C	McRae, R. H.	BX 48
McCallum, Albert D.	FC 61	McRae, Stanley P.	FB 38,39

McShannock, Thomas	FB 37,38
McWilliams, James E.	FB 10,11
McWilliams, Robert H.	BS 15,16,17
Meadows, Clinton L.	FB 67
Means, Clarence T.	BK 50,51,52C
Meek, Harry C.	FB 01,02
	TR 03
Meiers, Francis H.	FB 30,31,32
Mekules, Frank A.	BS 40,41
	BK 41
Melhorn, Wilton N.	BS 42M
Mellencamp, Burton C.	BS 22
Mellinger, Stephen T.	FB 61,62,64
Melnitsky, Peter T.	SW 50M
Mencotti, Ido	BX 43
	FB 42
Mendyk, Dennis A.	BS 57
	FB 55,56
Menzel, Richard G.	TN 54,55,56
Mercer, Ralph E.	SW 45
Merchant, Roger T.	TR 67,68,69
	CC 66,67,68C
Merkel, William J.	FB 97M
Merrill, Leland G. Jr.	WR 40,41,42C
Mervin, Clyde E.	FB 07M
Merz, Elmer H.	BK 08,09
Mescall, Ronald T.	TN 57,59,60
Mesler, Leon L.	CC 55
Meyer, Donald H.	FB 54M, 55M
Meyer, Robert F.	GO 63,64C
Michaud, Lewis E.	SW 52,53,54,55M
Michelutti, Robert	HO 70
Middleton, John L.	FB 56,57,58
Migiaccio, Nicolo L.	TR 43
Migyanka, Charles Jr.	FB 62,63,64C
Miketinac, Michael N.	FB 42
Mikkola, Thomas M.	HO 65,66,67
Mikles, Gale	WR 45,46,47,48C
Miknavich, Norbert A.	FB 36,37
Mikulich, Robert L.	TR 51M
Milbourn, John D.	TR 52
Milkovich, Tom	WR 70
Millar, Wilson F.	BS 02,03,04C
	FB 03
	TR 02,03,04
	BK 03M,04M
Millard, Forrest G.	BS 17,19
Miller, Carl F.	BK 16
Miller, Carl P.	TR 49,50
Miller, Charles D.	FB 23M
Miller, Costa	BK 60M
Miller, Donald E.	SW 48,49,50
Miller, Douglas L.	BS 63
Miller, Ellwood J.	HO 56,59
Miller, G. Devere	FB 96
Miller, Henry R.	GY 60
Miller, Hiram H.	BK 13,14
	FB 13,14,15
Miller, Howard D.	BS 64,65
Miller, Lyle W.	HO 64
Miller, Oscar R.	FB 13,14
	BK 14,15C
Miller, Patrick F.	FB 69
	BK 70
Miller, Peter T.	SW 50M
Miller, Richard	BS 68,69
Miller, Robert E. II	BK 65,66
Miller, Robert T.	SW 50M
Miller, Roger B.	SW 47,48,49,50
Miller, Roger L.	FB 66M
Miller, Stephen H.	GO 58
Miller, Wilbert E.	FB 17,19
Miller, William A.	CC 55
Miller, William B.	BS 13,14,15
	FB 12,13,14,15C
	BK 13,15
Milliken, William F.	FB 41,42

Milliman, Douglas G.	WR 62
Mills, David B.	TN 50,51
Mills, Edward L.	CC 39,40C
	TR 39,40
Mills, George H.	BS 17,20
Mills, Herbert	BS 07,08,09C,10
	BK 07,08,09
Mills, William H.	BS 56,57
Milne, James A.	TR 41,42,43,47
Minarik, Henry J.	FB 48,49,50
Miner, Elmer F.	TR 25
Mineweaser, Richard L.	BS 45,46,47,48
	FB 44
Minier, Howard G.	GO 31
Mitchell, Dave	TN 69
Mitchell, Robert B.	FB 58M
Mittelberg, Victor	FB 69
	WR 70
Mock, John	FC 65
Mock, John A.	TR 69,70
	CC 68
Modine, Franklin	SW 59,60C
Moeller, William	FB 26,27,28
Moffat, Alexander	SO 69
Moffett, John C.	FC 53,54
Mogge, Norton W.	BS 11,12,13,14C
Monan, Richard	TN 66,67,68
Monczka, Robert M.	BS 59,60
Monnett, Robert C.	FB 30,31,32C
Monroe, George C.	BS 38,39,40C
Monroe, George C.	TR 91,92
Monroe, Ralph B. Jr.	CC 40,41C,42C
	TR 41,42
Monroe, W. R.	FB 42
Montalvo, Sergio	FC 67
Monte, Raymond L.	FC 53
Montford, Roy M.	FB 10
Montgomery, Gregory H.	FB 57,58
Montgomery, Russell F.	FB 17M
Moody, Michael	LA 70
Moon, Harry E.	TR 02,03,04C,05C
Moore, Clyde D.	FB 06,07,08,09
Moore, Cyril F.	TR 38
Moore, Donald Dean	BS 57
Moore, Gerald	GY 66,67,68
Moore, Glenn B.	FB 45M
Moore, John I.	BK 50
Moore, John R.	TR 41
Moore, Rex W.	FB 44
Moore, Walter J.	TN 64M,65M,66M
Morabito, Daniel L.	FB 40
Morant, Frank	SO 68,69
Morehouse, Robert B.	WR 58M,59M
Moreland, Gary S.	GY 61
Moreland, Robert L.	TR 63,64
Morey, Donald E.	SW 53,54,57
Morgan, Jack	FB 50,51,52
Morgan, Rodney S.	BS 47
Morgan, William R.	TR 40
Moroney, Terrance B.	HO 58,59,60
Morrall, Earl E.	BS 54,55,56
	FB 53,54,55
Morris, Robert M.	BK 39,40,41
Morris, Thomas W.	SW 34,35C,36
Morrison, Bolton	GO 65
Morrison, John	TR 70
Morrison, Robert J.	FB 32M
Morrison, Russell A.	FB 20,21,22
Morrison, William R.	BS 40
Morrissey, Harry T.	FB 53M
Morrow, Robert E.	BS 98M
Morse, Charles	GY 70
Morse, Floyd	BS 32,33,34
Mosack, Carl L.	GO 51,52,53C
Moser, Richard J.	BS 51,52
Moser, Robert O.	WR 58,59,60C
Mosher, Joseph D.	BS 28M

Mosher, Richard W.	FB 46M
Moulthrop, Maurice J.	TR 32
Mounteer, Jack E.	GO 47,48C
Moyes, Paul L.	BS 37,38
Mroz, Vincent P.	FB 42
Mueller, Carl T.	TR 35,36,37C
Mueller, John H.	TR 47,48,49,50
Mueller, Joseph F.	SW 45
Mueller, William F.	FB 28
Muir, Thomas G.	WR 69,70
Mulcahy, Matthew	HO 65,66
Mulder, Thomas	WR 62
Mulheron, Hugh M.	TR 91,92
Mullen, John	FB 64,66
Mullinneux, Thomas H.	GY 52M
Mullins, Robert D.	BX 54,55
Munce, Donald C.	BS 59
Munn, Arthur H.	BS 91
Munn, John S.	TR 34
Murahata, Richard	GY 68,69,70
Murphy, Edwin	GO 67
Murphy, Fred M.	BS 99,00
Murphy, Jack H.	FC 29,33
Murphy, Larry	GO 68,69C
Murphy, Michael J.	TR 68
Murphy, Mike	TR 70
Murphy, Morley R.	FB 52,53,54
Murphy, Tom	GO 70
Murray, Byron M.	BK 17,18C
	TR 17
Murray, Jerry	SO 69
Musat, Nicholaus P.	HO 62,63,64
Musetti, Gerald A.	FB 54,55
Mustonen, Tom	HO 59,60,61
Musulin, John	SW 66,67,68
Mutchler, David G.	TR 62,63,64
Muth, Charles K.	BK 33
	FB 33
Muzyczko, Thaddeus	GY 58
Myers, Garry	TN 68
Myles, Reggie H. Jr.	GO 51

N

Naab, Leonard G.	TR 42,43,46
Nagel, Robert F.	BK 50
	TR 50
Neal, James E.	FB 52.53
Needham, George W.	FB 27
Neitzert, Kent D.	FC 70
Nelke, Richard	SO 65,66,67
Neller, Elton G.	FB 22,23,24
Nelson, Arnold P.	GY 48,49
Nelson, C. Walter	FB 36,37,38
Nelson, J. Harold	BS 06,07,08
Nelson, Joseph E.	BS 42
Nelson, Roy P.	GO 38,39
Nern, Carl R.	FB 02
Nestor, Carl	FB 47
Neubert, Bernard E.	FB 42
Neumann, Allan W.	TR 59
Neumann, Harrison H.	FB 35,36
Neumann, James R.	GO 62
Nevulis, Kazimer E.	BS 37
Newman, Harold C.	BK 24M
Newman, Joseph M.	TR 25M
Newman, Raymond A.	GO 48,49,50C
Newman, Mitchell	FB 61
Newton, Ralph J.	SW 41,42,43
Nichols, Donald H.	SW 57,58
Nichols, John W.	SW 43
Nicholson, Elmer	TR 05
Nicoli, Derio J.	HO 52,53,54,55C
Niemeyer, Roy K.	TR 47
Niemi, John A.	CC 53M
Nies, Eric E.	BS 05,06,07

Ninowski, James A. Jr.	FB 55,56,57
Niswander, James E.	BS 94M
Noack, William M.	BS 64
Noble, Chester John	GY 63,64
Noblet, Ubald J.	FB 19,20,21
Nock, William M.	BK 64
Nodus, Robert J.	GO 55,56,57
Norcutt, Larry	FC 69
Nordberg, Carl A.	FB 28,29,30
Norman, David A.	SW 51,52
Norman, Robert F.	HO 58,59,60
	SO 57
Northcross, David C.	FB 57,58,59
Northey, Richard H.	HO 51,52,53
Norton, Roy M.	BS 98,99,00
Novak, Greg	BS 69M,70M
Nowak, Gary W.	FB 68,69
Nower, Arthur	BS 32M
Nutter, Jack W.	BS 61,62,63C
Nuttila, Matt E.	BK 23,24,25C
Nuznov, Sam	BS 37,38,39
Nyquist, Richard L.	CC 47M
Nystie, Charles V.	FB 48,49
Nystrom, Carl W.	FB 53,54,55C

O

Oas, Reginald G.	BS 17,20,21
	FB 17
O'Brien, Francis J.	FB 56,57,58
O'Brien, Richard W.	GY 55,56,57
O'Callaghan, Jack W.	BS 16M
Ocean, Edward J.	SW 38,39
O'Connell, Kevin	SO 66
O'Conner, Robert L.	CC 29
	TR 29,31
O'Connor, Daniel	HO 69
O'Connor, Michael J.	HO 69,70
Odom, Herbert D.	BX 52,53,54,55
O'Connell, Eugene A.	TN 63,64
Odorico, Armando L.	FC 54,55,56
O'Gara, Francis	FB 06M
O'Leary, Robert	BK 45
	TR 45
Olexa, Russell E.	TR 52,53
Olin, Bruff W.	TR 03
Oliver, Thomas W.	TR 60M
Olman, Norman A.	FB 36,37
Olmstead, Clifford G.	FB 00
Olmstead, James L.	FC 63
Olsen, Robert C.	TR 27,30,31
Olsen, William R.	CC 52M
Olson, Chester M.	TN 38,39,40C
Olson, Duane E.	BK 54
Olson, Franklin E.	TR 99
Olson, Hilding C.	TN 32C
Olson, Lance	BK 58,59,60C
Olson, Michael	HO 68,69,70
	BS 69
Olson, Richard	HO 70
Olson, Weldon H.	HO 52,53,54,55C
Omans, Glenn A.	SW 49,50,51
O'Neill, Lawrence	SW 70
Onopa, William	SO 61,62
Orme, Malcolm L.	HO 63,64
Orr, James B.	FB 66M
Orr, John J.	WR 40
Orr, Stephen T.	BS 09,10
Orr, Wesley B.	TR 35,36,37
Osborn, George E.	TR 46,48,49
Osborn, Ralph H.	BS 96
Osborn, Raymond L.	TR 37,39
Osgood, Richard A.	SW 65M
Osterink, Leonard	BK 37
Oswald, Garth B.	FC 40
Oswalt, Ferris H.	TR 30

Oswalt, Stanley M.	TR 31
Oswalt, William L.	TR 58
Ott, Rodney R.	WR 66,67,68
Ottey, Thomas C.	CC 32,33C,34C
Otting, Robert W.	FB 42,46
Ottmar, Dale N.	GO 46
Ouellet, Ron	WR 68,69,70
Overgard, Jon T.	GO 62
Oviatt, Charles J.	TR 07,08,09C
Oviatt, Clarence R.	FB 15
Owen, Forrest F.	SW 39
Owen, Frank M.	BS 97
Owen, George E.	BS 38,39,40
Owen, Robert H.	TR 39M
Owens, Alton L.	FB 63,64,65
Oxendine, Richard C.	FB 60
Ozybko, Edward	HO 59,60,61

P

Pacynski, Stanley L.	BS 21,22
	BK 22
Paganini, Frank T.	SW 54,55,56
Page, Jerry M.	CC 42
	TR 41,42,43
Page, William W.	BS 45,46
Pagel, William L.	FB 45
Paior, John J.	FB 54
Pajakowski, Joseph A.	FB 45
Palamara, Frank	BS 56,57,58C
Palm, Wayne V.	BK 19,20,21
Palmateer, Bernard B.	FB 62
Palmer, Russell E.	SW 54
Pangborn, Daniel	SW 66,67,68
Panin, Lewis R.	FB 50,51,52
Panitch, Michael B.	FB 56,57,58
Panks, Gary A.	GO 63
Panter, Robert B.	TR 60M
Papachristou, Gerald	SO 60,61,62
Parke, Ross A.	HO 56,57,58
Parker, Arnold P.	BS 33,34,35
Parker, Delmer G.	CC 53
Parker, Jack B.	GY 48
Parker, John D.	TR 62,63
Parker, Ward H.	FB 06,07
Parks, Warren A.	FB 21
Parks, William T.	FB 97,98,99
Parmalee, Charles H.	TR 03
Parmentier, Gary	FB 68
Parrish, Frank B.	SW 55,56,57
Parrish, Harry R.	BS 95
Parrott, Roy	FB 61
Parsell, Rex J.	FB 47,48,49
Passerini, M. Harold	HO 52
Passink, Clarence	TR 27,29
Pataconi, Ronald J.	TR 56M
Patchett, Wendell T.	BK 32,33,34C
Paterra, Herbert E.	FB 62
Paton, Henry D. Jr.	SW 47,48,49,50
Patten, Ronald J.	TR 56M
Patrick, J. Cuthbert	BS 93
Patridge, Ernest D.	TR 95
Patterson, Donald W.	SW 57,58,59
Patterson, Howard F.	SW 46,48,49,50
Pattison, Benjamin P.	BS 09,10
	BK 11
	FB 09,10
Patton, David C.	SW 51
Pattullo, Robert	HO 68,69,70
Paul Russell L.	GY 52,57,58C
Paull, Richard A.	TR 68,69
Paulson, Donald H.	BK 49M
Pavlick, George R.	BS 48
Pawlik, Eugene P.	FC 63
Pawlowski, Walter L.	FB 40,41,42C
Paxson, Avery B.	FB 33

Payette, Thomas M.	TR 52
	SW 52,53,54,55C
Payne, Wade	FB 67
Payton, Gerald L.	FC 49
Peaks, Clarence E.	FB 54,55,56
Pearce, Edward J.	FB 37,38,39
Pearsall, Gilson P.	TR 34,35
Pearsall, Ropha V.	TR 04,05,06,07
Pearson, Helge E.	FB 37
Peck, Clair B.	FB 03
Peckham, Thomas J.	TR 61,62,63
Pellerin, Frank E.	BS 41,42,43
Pelletier, John R.	FC 62,63C
Pemberton, T. Berwyn	BS 31,32,33
Peppard, David L.	BK 17
	TR 14,16,17C
Peppard, David L.	TR 48,49,50
Peppler, Albert P.	BS 46,47,48
	BK 43,46,47
Perillo, Daniel R.	TN 49,50
Perkins, Charles H.	TR 09
Perkins, Fred E.	TN 39,40,41C
Perkins, John W.	BS 35M
Perles, George	FB 58
Perne, Donald C.	GO 49,50,51C
Perranoski, Ronald P.	BS 56,57,58
Perrin, Arthur C.	BS 89
Perrone, Vito	WR 52,53C,54
Perry, J. Carleton	TR 21
Petela, Stanley F.	BK 48
Peters, Arthur D.	FB 01,02C,03
Peters, Dale	BS 63,64,65
Peters, Howard F.	BS 18
Peterson, Carl H.	BS 13,14
	FB 14M
Peterson, Donald L.	HO 55M,56M
Peterson, Duane	BK 54,55,56
Peterson, Ernest E.	BS 15M
Peterson, Harry S.	BS 08,09
Peterson, John H.	BK 42M
Peterson, John	GO 70
Peterson, Lorwyn E.	TR 29
Peterson, Melvin O.	BK 40,41,42
Peterson, Robert L.	BS 66,67
Petley, James R.	TR 93,94
Petroff, George J.	BS 69,70
Petroski, Carl F.	BK 41,42,43
Pettibone, R. Bruce	BS 64,65
Pettyjohn, Fred M.	BX 57
Petzold, Rudolf H.	FB 54M,55M
Pevic, Charles Vincent	BS 28,29,30
Pfeil, Richard J.	FC 54
Pflug, Melville M.	TR 30,31,32C
Philips, David P.	TN 41,45,46
Phillips, Charles W.	HO 67,68,69
Phillips, Donald F.	WR 54
Phillips, Frank G.	TR 02,03
Phillips, James	TN 65,66,67
Phillips, Jess Jr.	FB 65,66
Phillips, Richard K.	GY 55,57M
Phillips, Robert H.	BK 39,40,41C
Picciuto, Nicholas T.	BS 42
Pickens, Bob	WR 65
Pickering, H. Lee	TR 45
Pierson, William R.	FC 50,52
Pilitsis, Angelos	SO 57
Pingel, John S.	FB 36,37,38
	TR 37
Pinnance, Edward W.	BS 03
Pinneo, Dee W.	BK 31,32C
Piro, Steven P.	FB 69
Pirronello, William G.	FB 44
Pisano, Vincent F.	FB 50,51,52
Pitts, Jack	FB 67
Pjesky, Daniel D.	BK 43,46
Plagenhoef, Roger D.	TN 59,60,61
Planutis, Gerald R.	FB 53,54,55

Pletz, John E. — FB 46
Plotts, James — BS 67,68
Pogor, Edmund F. — FB 39
Polano, Joseph — HO 57,58,59
Polhamus, Edward H. — TR 91
Polisar, Steve — BS 66
Pollard, Charles N. — TR 67,68,70
Pollesel, Bruno — HO 57,58,59
Pollesel, Edward — HO 57,58,59
Polomsky, John — BS 54,55,56
HO 54,55,56C
Polonchek, John N. — FB 47,48,49
Pomerleau, Bertrand T. — HO 54,55,56
Pongrace, Otto W. — CC 32,33
TR 32,33,34C
Pontius, Larry L. — SW 59
Popejoy, Kenneth L. — TR 70
Popp, Robert T. — FB 57
Popper, Edward — FC 47,48
Pore, James H. — TN 52,53,54C
Porrevecchio, Joseph S. — BS 62,63,64
Porteous, William L. — TR 40M
Poss, Frank R. — TR 91,92,93,94
Postula, Victor A. — FB 54
Postula, William J. — FB 53
Pound, Howard E. — FB 39
Powell, James H. — BS 49M
Powell, Robert L. — BS 53,54,55
Prashaw, Milton L. — FB 44
Pratt, Leon A. — BS 17
Pratt, Robert M. — BS 33M
Prebel, Merle L. — WR 61
Preston, Ronald J. — TR 24
Price, David L. — GY 63,64,65C
Price, H. Eugene — FB 96,97
Price, Robert E. — CC 44C
TR 45C
Prieskorn, George W. — GO 55
Proctor, John E. — CC 54
Proebstle, James M. — FB 65
Proebstle, Richard J. — BS 62,64
FB 61,63,64
Pruiett, Mitchell — FB 65,66,67
Pruitt, Ronald — BS 70
Przybycki, Joseph R. — FB 65,66,67
Pyle, William P. — FB 57,58,59

Q

Quayle, Donald E. — BS 51,52
Quiggle, Jack E. — BK 56,57,58
Quigley, Arlon B. — SW 47M
Quigley, Fred K. Jr. — FB 39
Quigley, James L. — SW 46,49,50,51
Quigley, John R. — SW 51,52
Quinlan, William D. — FB 52,53
Quirk, Martin W. — HO 61,62C

R

Rabias, Robert J. — BS 57,58
Radatz, Richard R. — BS 57,58,59C
Radewald, Carl B. — FB 20
Radford, Fred — FB 00M
Radman, George — WR 66,67
Radman, Richard — WR 70
Radulescu, George — FB 42
Rae, George H. — TR 02
Raines, Richard C. — TN 69
Rains, Ralph J. — BS 10
Rajkovich, Nick J. — WR 33
Ralph, Donald — FB 55M
Ralston, Merle C. — BK 24
Ralston, Milo J. — BS 23M
Ramsey, C. F. — FB 16,17,19

Rand, Thomas A. — BK 58,59
TR 57
Randall, Clyde J. — BS 36,37,38
Ranieri, Ron — FB 66,67
Rankin, Glenn B. — BS 38
Ranney, Ellis W. — BS 97,98,99C,00
FB 97,98C,99C
Ranney, Frederick — BS 24
Rapchak, William M. — BK 45,48,49,50
Rapes, Anthony L. — TR 36,37
Rashead, Philip — BS 69,70
Rasmussen, Rasmus — BS 02,03,04M,05C
Rauch, Donald M. — SW 67,68,69CoC
Ray, Harlan C. — FB 27M
Raye, James — FB 65,66,67
Raymond, James A. — GO 55
BK 55
Raz, Steve — HO 52,54
Rea, William M., III — SW 64M,65M
Reader, Russell B. — FB 45,46
TR 46
Reading, Shannon — BK 66,67
Reading, Willard L. — BK 48M
Reavely, Gordon — FB 32,33,34
WR 32,33,35C
Reavely, William H. — BS 43
Reck, Daniel J. — BK 34,35,36C
Redd, Keith L. — FB 66
Redfern, Scott J. — FB 96M
Reed, Oswald H. — BS 95
Reid, Delmar Tice — HO 50,51,52
Reid, Earl W. — BX 43M
Reid, John D. — CC 29
Reid, Michael T. — TR 39
Reiff, Peter A. — CC 69
Reinke, Paul G. — SW 55,56,57
Rendon, George — SO 62,63
Renwick, Howard M. — BS 20M
Rettenmund, Larry — BS 69,70
Revou, Robert C. — HO 51,52,53
Reynolds, Albert S., Jr. — TN 47,48C
Reynolds, Bruce W. — BK 54M
Reynolds, Frank E. — SW 53
Reynolds, John C. — GO 58,59,60
Reynolds, Russell H. — FB 33,34C
Reynolds, William T. — CC 58,59,60
TR 60,61C
Rhodes, Eugene N. — BK 53
Rhoades, Ralph — TN 70
Riblett, William R. — FB 10,11,12C
Ricamore, Wilford W. — FB 99,00,01
Richard, Shepard A. — GO 63,64
Richards, Bruce Warren — SW 68,69,70
Richards, James M. — SW 47,49
Richards, Roland G. — BS 24
BK 24,25
FB 22,23,24
Richardson, Gerald C. — FC 39,40C
Richardson, Jeff — WR 65,66,67
FB 66
Richardson, Kenneth — LA 70
Richey, William K. — BX 47
Richmond, Ernest A. — SW 24C
Richter, Richard R. — GY 49,50,51
Rickard, James B. — SW 54,55
Rickens, Ronald F. — FB 56,57,58
Ricker, Fred G. — BX 15,16
Ricketts, Neil H. — BS 48
Ricucci, Robert J. — FB 59
Ridgway, Ronald D. — SW 53
Ridler, Donald G. — FB 28,29,30
Riedesel, Henry K. — GY 55M
Rieger, Richard H. — TN 50,51,52C
Rigby, Cyril P. — BK 16
Riggs, Benjamin F. — WR 39,40C,41
Riley, Thomas E. — BS 60,61
Rinehart, Forrest — BS 26,27,28C

Rintz, Carlton L.	GY 52,53,54,55C
Riordan, Edward D.	BK 33
Riordan, Sidney R.	TR 41
Ripmaster, Peter E.	FB 40,42
Ripper, C. E.	TR 24,25,26
Rippberger, Donald R.	WR 43
Risch, John I.	BS 52,53,54
Rittenger, Charles F.	BS 87,89,90C,91
Rittenger, John W.	BS 93C,94
Ritz, Alfred H.	BX 36
Rivest, Robert N.	GO 54
Rivich, Joseph N.	BS 50,51,52
Roach, Marty E.	GY 65
Robbins, Robert D.	BK 47,48,49,50C
Roberts, David	HO 70
Roberts, Douglas W.	FB 63,64
	HO 63,64,65C
Roberts, Floyd T.	CC 27,28
Roberts, Irving M.	TN 40
Roberts, John A.	HO 58,59,60
Roberts, Richard K.	TN 53
Roberts, Richard W.	TN 52
	CC 50
Roberts, Robin	BK 45,46,47C
	BS 46,47
Roberts, Wesley W.	SW 60
Roberts, William W.	TR 43
Robie, Richard R.	SW 52
Robinson, David K.	BK 20
Robinson, Embry L.	FB 54,55
Robinson, Gayle B.	TR 37,38,39
Robinson, Hugh A.	BK 23,25
	FB 22,23,24
Robinson, Lennox	SO 69
Robinson, Theodore K.	FB 59M
Robuck, John	GY 49,50
Rochester, Paul G.	FB 58,59
Roche, Thomas	HO 66
Rockefeller, Van	SW 69
Rockenbach, Lyle J.	FB 37,38,39C
Rodewald, Kenneth G.	GO 54,56,57
Rody, Fred A.	FB 53,54
Roe, James W.	TR 61
Rogers, Spencer W.	BK 35
Rogge, Harry E.	BS 11,12
Rogula, Michael G.	TR 48,49
Rohs, John D.	GY 63,66
Roland, Charles B.	TR 52
Rolen, Edward C.	BK 35,36,37
Rollin, Arthur S.	FC 54C
Ronan, Arthur P.	BS 50
Ronan, Kenneth M.	BS 17
Ronberg, Gary M.	BS 61,62
Ronie, Andrew M.	BX 55
Roossien, Elmer J.	CC 27,28,29
	TR 28,29
Rork, Frank C.	FB 99,01
Rosa, Robert J.	TN 36C,37
Rosen, Robert	TR 13
Rosenbaum, Daniel M.	TR 39,40,41
Rosenberg, W. Dean	TR 67
	CC 66,67
Roskopp, B. G.	FB 42,46,47
Ross, Arthur F.	FB 34,35
Ross, Daniel M.	TR 39,40,41
Ross, Donald L.	FB 63,64
Ross, Henry, T.	TR 03M
Ross, Loren S.	BS 21,22,23
Ross, Robert H.	BS 59,60,61
Ross, Robert William	FB 52,53
Ross, Ronald R.	FB 62
Ross, Ward F.	FB 25,26,27
Ross, William L.	FB 52,53
Rossi, Don A.	BX 38
	FB 38,39
Rossi, Robert A.	TR 53
Rossman, Victor H.	TR 27,28,29

Rossow, William C.	SW 63
Roth, Donald	HO 65
Rouse, Arthur K.	BS 33,34,35C
Rouse, Milo M.	BK 34,35C
Rowe, Douglas E.	SW 61,62
Rowley, Gail A.	BS 26,27
Rowley, Glenn E.	BS 14
Roy, Errol A.	FB 69
Roy, Robert L.	HO 53M,54M,55M
Rubick, Ronald R.	FB 61,62,63
Rugg, Gary L.	FB 64
Ruhl, Jack W.	FB 28
Ruminski, Roger J.	FB 66
Rummel, Martin F.	FB 24,25,26C
Rupp, Vernon W.	TR 25
Rupp, William, Jr.	FB 39,40,41C
Ruppart, Dennis	SW 60,61
Ruscheinski, Emanuel	SO 64,65
Rush, Jerry	FB 62,63,64
Russel, Jack J.	TR 15,16C
Russell, John G.	BS 57,58,59C
Russell, Robert K.	TR 29,30,31
Russell, William E.	FB 97,98,99
	TR 98,99C
Russo, Leroy G.	BK 28,29
Russo, Patrick	HO 68,69,70
Russow, Walter F.	TN 29,30
Rutenbar, George H.	BS 46,47,48,49
Rutledge, Leslie E.	FB 55,56,57
Ryan, Barry A.	TR 39,40
Ryan, Edward J.	FB 60,61C
Rymal, Steven A.	BK 66,67,68
	BS 66,67,68
Ryon, Edgar C.	TR 30

S

Sabo, Ronald J.	BK 61
Sachs, Albert W.	BS 28,29,30C
Sack, James F.	BS 54,55,56
Sackett, Donald K.	BS 59,60
Sackrider, Thomas C.	BK 55M,56M
Saffran, William S.	BS 53
Safran, Paul	LA 70
Sagendorph, William K.	TR 92
Sahratian, John	TN 51,52,53
Saidock, Thomas	FB 55,56
Saimes, George	FB 60,61,62C
Salamone, Louis P.	FC 63,64C
Salling, Carl L.	BS 63
Salmon, David A.	TR 28,29,30
Sanabria, Zenon A.	SO 57
Sanders, Lonnie	FB 60,61,62
	BK 62
Sanders, Marcus L.	BK 63,64,65C
Sanders, Terry A.	SO 66,67,68
Saperstein, Melvin D.	TN 60
Sarenac, Bosko	SW 57M
Sarria, Paz Alvaro	SO 57,58
Sartorius, Patrick J.	BS 59,60,61
Sasanko, Alvin M.	SO 58
Sass, Robert C.	GY 58M
Sassack, Robert S.	TN 58,59
Satchell, Donald P.	FC 68,69C
Saul, Richard	FB 67,68,69CoC
Saul, Ronald R.	FB 67,68,69
Saunders, Luther	SO 60,61
Sauve, Joseph L.	HO 54,55
Savoldi, Joseph A.	TR 54,55,56
Sawyer, Charles M.	TN 34M
Scales, John J.	TR 38,39,40
Scales, R. Wilson	TR 39
Schafer, Steve	TN 67
Schaffer, John E.	BK 03,04,05
Schau, Henry W.	BK 28
	FB 27,28,29

Schaubel, Ray C.	SW 30,31
Scheid, Charles G.	SW 30
Schelb, Michael W.	FB 39,40,41
	TR 40,41
Schenck, Ray M.	TR 19
Schepers, Robert E.	TR 46,47,48
Schiefler, Lee Roy M.	BS 37,38,39
Schiesel, Richard J.	BS 58
Schiesswohl, Don	FB 52,53
	TR 52
Schiller, Edward A.	HO 54,55,56C
Schinderle, Jack W.	FB 64,65
Schlaeger, David P.	TR 38
Schlatter, G. James	BK 52,53,54
Schloemer, Richard L.	FC 61,62C,63
Schluter, Robert C.	WR 60,61
Schmidt, Tad B.	GO 59,60,61
Schmitter, Charles Jr.	FC 59,60,61
Schmyser, Verne	FB 23,24
Schneider, Bert L.	BS 19
Schneider, John	WR 68,69
Schneider, Robert	TN 67
Schoenegge, Walter	TR 51
Scholes, Clarke C.	SW 50,51,52C
Scholtz, Harold C.	BK 35,36,37
	TN 36,37C
Schrader, Nelson A.	FB 36,37
Schrag, Truman F.	FC 58
Schrecengost, Randall P.	FB 52,53,54
Schroeder, Fred A.	FB 36,37
Schroeder, Robert E.	FB 44
Schroeter, Herbert R.	BS 50,51
Schubel, Otto	GO 56,57,58
Schubert, Frank A.	FC 67
Schudlich, William H.	BS 59,60,61
Schuler, Donald	BS 45
Schulgen, George F.	FB 20,21
Schultz, Carl F.	FB 23,24
Schultz, Harry W.	TR 00,01
Schumacher, Robert G.	SW 50,52,53
Schuster, John H.	HO 65,66,67
Schwarm, Arthur V.	BK 60,61,62C
Schwartz, Ira	FC 70
Schwartz, Ronald	SW 61
Schwartz, William R.	BK 62,63,64
	SO 63
Schwei, John J.	FB 18,19,20
	TR 19,20,21,22
Scialli, Vince	HO 67M,68M
Scott, David A.	BK 57,60
Scott, Edward W.	BK 29,30,31C
Scott, Harper	BS 36,37,38C
Scott, William	SW 70
Scott, William J.	CC 40,42
	TR 41,42,43C
Scott, William W.	SW 66
Scutt, Wayne E.	CC 50,51,52
	TR 51,52
Sebo, Stephen	BS 35,36,37C
	FB 34,35,36
Sedelbauer, N. J.	FB 56M
Seibold, David H.	SW 46,47,48,49C,50
Seibold, Jack D.	SW 47,50
Seibold, Paul A.	SW 46,47,48
Selinger, Joe	HO 57,58,59
Sell, Joseph P.	FB 40M
Selz, John C.	BX 56
Senzig, Michael J.	WR 60,61
Sepaneck, Jack A.	BS 22,23,24C
Sepetys, George N.	SO 57,58,59
Sergeant, Dale L.	HO 54
Serlin, Joel	FC 63,64,65C
Serr, Gordon H.	FB 50,51,52
Servis, Lawrence R.	FB 12
Severance Roy W.	TR 27
Sewell, Robert A.	CC 46,47,48C,49
	TR 47,48,49,50
Seyfarth, Theodore H.	SO 61,62
Shaar, Carl J.	SW 60,61,62C
Shackelford, John H.	HO 52,53
Shaffer, John R.	BS 05
Shananhan, Robert E.	BS 09M
Shannon, Harlow G.	TR 22
Sharkey, Richard	CC 65,66
	TR 65,66,67
Sharp, John E.	FB 59,61
	TR 59,61
Shaw, George W.	TR 10
Shaw, Harold T.	FB 03
Shaw, Steven J.	FB 36,37,38
Sheathelm, Russell W.	BK 30
Shedd, Bert	FB 05,06,07,08C,09
Shedd, John G.	FB 39M
Shedd, Robert W.	FB 42M
Shedd, Ward R.	FB 00,01
Sheffield, Arthur R.	BK 16,17
Shehigian, John	WR 55
Shehigian, Ruben B.	WR 51,52,53
Shek, Paul P.	TR 50
Sheldon, Earl B.	TR 15,16
Shelley, Roger	SW 70
Shelton, Dwight J.	TN 63,64,65
Sheppard, Holly C.	BS 87
Sherman, Martin J.	WR 51
Sherman, Robert G.	FB 39,40,41
Sherwood, Robert O.	SW 64
Shick, John	BK 65
Shidler, Frank J.	BK 38,39
Shields, Edmund H.	TR 47
Shingleton, John D.	TN 47,48
Shomin, George H.	TR 47,48
Shorr, Harold D.	GY 59,60
Shoup, Harold A.	SW 50,51,52
Shulak, Frederick B.	FC 56
Shumway, Guy C.	FB 19
Shuttleworth, Earl H.	FB 11
Sibbald, John H.	HO 52
Siebert, William N.	FC 65,66
Sieminski, Adam C.	FB 55
Sieradski, Stephen H.	BS 47
	FB 46,47
Sierra, Lawrence	SO 58
Siler, William M.	FB 44
Silka, Frank	HO 60,61,62C
Silvia, Thomas V.	CC 69
Simcox, Harry	BS 50
Simeck, Daniel	CC 68
Simmons, David C.	FC 63
Simmons, George E.	BS 93,94C
Simmons, Irving L.	BS 96
Simmons, Walter H.	TR 19
Simonds, Harold E.	FC 58
Simonson, Ronald W.	FB 50M
Simpson, Nathan D.	BS 13M
Simpson, Ralph	BK 70
Simpson, William D.	SW 49,50
Sims, Albert G.	SW 37,38
Sims, Marion	TR 69
Sinadinos, James P.	WR 54,55C,56C
Sinclair, Norman	TR 65
Singleton, William	SW 59,60,61
Sinks, Michael G.	BS 59,60,61
Sipola, William	HO 70
Sirhal, Charles M.	BX 49
Sisinni, George J.	BX 54,55,56
Skinner, J. Hackley	FB 98,99
Skinner, Ralph	FB 67
Skokos, Zachary G.	TR 49
Skotarek, Alex	SO 67,68,69
Skotarek, Edward	SO 66,67,68
Skrocki, Joseph	BS 41,42,46
Skuce, Thomas W.	FB 21M
Slamkowski, Barney X.	SW 39
Slank, Ronald J.	FB 69

Slater, Eugene B.	FB 34M
Slayton, Philip W.	FC 62,63
Sleder, Julius C.	FB 34,35,36
Slezak, Steve M.	WR 38,39C
Slonac, Evan J.	FB 51,52,53
Small, Ralph E.	CC 32
	TR 32
Small, Walter H.	FB 03,04,05,06,07C
	TR 04,05,06,08
Smead, Harold E.	FB 28,29,30C
Smedley, Ernest Leo	WR 56
Smieska, Paul	BS 67
Smiley, Lewis N.	FB 39,40,41
	TR 40
Smith, Arnold W.	TR 51,52
Smith, Ben T.	SW 59M
Smith, C. A. III	GO 59,60,61
Smith, Charles A.	FB 64,65,66
Smith, Chester	FB 27
Smith, Cleon L.	TR 40,41,42
Smith, Daniel R.	BK 50
Smith, Dennis	GY 66,67,69
Smith, Denton L.	CC 41M
Smith, Earl I.	FB 97,98
Smith, Gary	BS 65,67
Smith, George B.	BX 48
	FB 47,48,49
Smith, George W.	BS 54,55
Smith, Gideon E.	FB 13,14,15
Smith, Hal D.	TN 57,58,59,60
Smith, Horace	FB 46,47,48,49
	TR 48,49C,50
Smith, Howard B.	FB 02
Smith, Jeff	WR 68,69
Smith, Joseph F.	BK 35,36
Smith, J. Gary	WR 63,64,65C
Smith, Kermit	FB 67,68,69
Smith, Lawrence J.	FB 37M
Smith, Lawrence J.	FB 66,67
Smith, Louis A.	FB 51
Smith, Louis J.	BK 26,27
Smith, Nicholas	WR 53
	GY 53
Smith, Nile C.	BS 86,87,89
Smith, Norman E.	TR 31,33
Smith, Paul M.	FB 25,26,27C
	TR 26,27,28
Smith, Peter	BS 62
	FB 61,62
Smith, Webb Anthony	CC 57m58,59
	TR 59,60
Smith, William	HO 66M,67M
Smith, William E.	FB 52M
Smith, William H.	TR 35,36,37
Smolinski, Theodore C.	FB 41
Snider, Irving J.	BS 18,19,20
	BK 18,19
	FB 17,18,19
Snodgrass, James A.	BK 49,50,51C
Snorton, H. Matthew	FB 61,62,63
Soave, John	FB 57
Sobczak, Edward F.	BS 46,47,48,49
	FB 46,48
Sohacki, Edward	FB 47
Sokoll, Randy	HO 69,70
Sorensen, Harry	FC 70
Sorg, Herbert	GY 69,70
Southan, Arthur H.	SO 57,58
Southan, John R.	SO 58,59
Southworth, Fred M.	TR 41M
Spalink, John	WR 42
Sparks, Harold L.	TR 36,37,38
	CC 35,36,37
Sparling, William J.	TR 27M
Sparvero, Robert P.	BK 62
Spauling, Donald	BK 69M
Speare, Almus R.	TR 95

Speelman, Harry E.	FB 35,36,37C
Speer, Robert H.	BS 65,66
Speerstra, Herbert A.	FB 44,48
	TR 45
Spencer, Norman M.	BS 11,12
	BK 10,12,13
Spiedel, Fred C.	TR 19
Spiegel, William S. Jr.	FB 46,47,48
Spiekerman, Roy P.	BS 25,26
	FB 23,24,25
Spieser, Charles	BX 50,51,52
Spinner, Robert W.	BS 39M
Springer, Dale R.	TR 37,38
Springer, Harold A.	BS 15,20
	FB 15,19,20
Springer, Ron	HO 70
Squier, George G.	FB 32
Squire, Dana D.	TN 53,54
Stachow, Theodore	SO 62
Stack, J. R.	BS 89
Stanick, Kenneth J.	BS 53
Stanley, Dale E.	CC 66
Starck, Paul W.	BS 40
Stark, Elbert J.	FB 42
Stark, George W. Jr.	BS 39
Starkey, Charles W.	FB 69
	TR 69,70
Staser, Joe A.	GY 53,54C
Stauffer, Gordon C.	BK 50,51,52
Stead, Ronald S.	BS 54,55
Steckley, William	BS 65,66,67
Steele, Rex B.	TR 31,33,34
Steele, Robert	TR 65,66,67
Steenken, Thomas A.	GO 68
Steffee, Donald K.	BK 45,46
Steffen, Raymond B.	BK 49,50,51
Steffen, William	TR 49,50
Steimle, David H.	SW 52,53
Steimle, Earl H.	TR 31
Steimle, John E.	GO 54,55
Stelamashenko, Stanley	SO 61,62,63
Stemm,, Merle R.	BS 36,37
Stepanovic, George	TN 55,56,57C
Stephens, Wallace T.	BS 22,23
Stephenson, Mark T.	TR 31,32
Stepter, Harrison	BS 68,69
Sterling, Tom	TR 68,69,70
Sterner, Keith	GY 66,67
Steuart, William	SW 58,59,61
Stevens, Dewey D.	FB 50
Stevens, Donald E.	GO 52,53
Stevens, Earl L.	FB 39
	TR 40,41
Stevens, Frederick D.	TR 02
Stevens, John B. Jr.	TR 43
Stevens, Patrick L.	CC 61
Stevens, Richard A.	CC 67
	TR 68
Stevens, Robert L.	BK 48,49
Stevenson, George A.	FB 60
Stevenson, Robert	LA 70
Stewart, Donald M.	FB 45
Stewart, Donald W.	FB 59,60,61
Stewart, Frank	TR 16
Stewart, Guy L.	BS 95M
Stewart, James F.	TR 66,67
Stewart, John B.	TR 00,01C
Stifler, Gerald R.	BS 57,58
Stillman, Fred	SW 45C
Stobinski, Frank	LA 70
Stockwell, Frederick B.	BS 89
Stone, Fred A.	FB 09,10,11C
Stone, Fred A. Jr.	BK 42,43,47
Stonebraker, Guy W.	TN 34
Stonebraker, Louis V.	TN 36,37
Stoner, N. H.	WR 28,30,32
Stouffer, James	BK 58,59

Stout, Melvin L.	GY 49,50,51C	TeRoller, Henry	BS 10
Stow, Arthur F.	BS 91	Tetzlaff, Ted J.	TR 55,56,57
Straight, Herbert D.	FB 14,15,16	Teufer, Philip H.	FB 22
Strand, William C.	FB 02	Thalken, Francis R.	FC 41C,42C
Strauch, Clark M.	FB 24M	Thatcher, Fent E.	BS 06,07
Strautnieks, Gundars	SO 59,60	Thayer, Robert F.	FB 24
Streb, Claude R.	FB 29,30	Theurer, John	SW 70
Streder, Erich	SO 58,59	Thiele, Earl O.	SO 62,63,64
Strickland, Kenneth R.	TR 52M	Thiess, Albert A. Jr.	GO 66,67,68
Strobel, Ray	GY 66	Thomann, Frederick J.	BK 62,63,64
Stroia, Eugene J.	FB 50	Thomas, Arthur	HO 61,62,63
Strong, Charles E.	SW 62,63,64C	Thomas, David W.	FB 68,69
Strong, Lawrence F.	BK 58M	Thomas, Deane A.	FB 50
Stroud, Donald E.	WR 56,57,58	Thomas, George C.	TR 30,31,32
Struck, Herman R.	TN 39C,40	Thomas, George H.	FC 55C,56,57
Stuart, James L.	SW 53	Thomas, Gordon G.	GY 48
Stutsman, Richard R.	TR 54	Thomas, Horace L.	TR 26
Suarez, Joseph E.	HO 50,51	Thomas, James P.	SW 43
Suci, Robert L.	FB 59,60,61	Thomas, Jesse L.	FB 48,49,50
Suess, Ronald D.	TR 54,55		TR 49,50,51
Sullivan, Charles P.	WR 48,49	Thomas, John E.	HO 52,53,54C
Sullivan, James E.	GO 55,56,57	Thomas, LaMarr	FB 67
Sullivan, T. Brady	FB 44C	Thomas, Reinhold	SW 27
Summers, James III	FB 65,66	Thomas, Robert C.	SW 59
	TR 65,66	Thomas, Walter P.	BS 15,16
Sumners, Roger K.	TR 62,63	Thompson, Arthur R.	SW 53
Sunnen, August	TR 41,43	Thompson, Donald	HO 70
Super, Robert	FB 66,67,68	Thompson, Earl C.	BX 39
Surato, Leslie C.	TR 23	Thompson, Charles F.	GY 59,60,61
Sutherland, Donald R.	BK 53M	Thompson, Herbert J.	WR 43
Sutilla, Edward D.	FB 58	Thompson, Kelly A.	TR 57
Sutton, Jerry	BS 62,63,64	Thompson, Robert C.	TR 42
Sveden, Ronald F.	HO 54,55		CC 41
Swanson, Al	HO 68,69,70C	Thomson, Charles J.	FB 17,19,20
Swanson, David W.	TR 30	Thomson, Elmer L.	FB 96
Swanson, Hugo T.	FB 20,21,22	Thor, David	GY 66,67,68
	BK 22	Thorburn, Robert	GY 67M
Swanson, Thomas L.	CC 69	Thornhill, Charles E.	FB 64,65,66
Swartz, Douglas	GO 65	Thornton, Richard L.	WR 52
Swartz, Howard R.	FB 35,36,37	Thorpe, Gustave A.	FB 20,21,22
Swartz, Douglas O.	GO 64,66	Thrower, Willie L.	FB 52
Sykes, Phil	SO 68M	Thurston, Lloyd M.	TR 20,21
Symington, Jim	TN 70	Thurtell, Herbert	BS 87
Syria, Donald L.	SW 61	Tichnor, Jack R.	TR 33M
Szasz, Stephen J.	FB 36,37,38	Tiemann, Barry R.	SO 66,67,69
Szilagyi, Mickey	TN 66,67,68	Tierney, Jack	BX 48,50
Szwast, Robert F.	FB 60,61	Tillotson, Ivan G.	TR 26,27,28
Szymke, Theodore J.	FC 36	Timmerman, Edward G.	FB 50,51,52
		Tinnick, John F.	FB 64

T

		Tipton, Norman E.	FB 45
		Toan, John W.	TR 88
Tallefson, Willard T.	TR 34	Tobin, John F.	FB 48,49,50
Tambo, William	WR 54	Tobin, Michael G.	FB 68,69
Tamburo, Richard P.	FB 50,51,52	Todd, Douglas	SW 67,68
Tanner, Kinsey H.	TR 46,48	Tolles, Albert R.	BS 26,27
Tansey, Robert L.	GO 47,48,49	Tompkins, Chandler Z.	TR 98
Tansey, Warren E.	GO 38	Tompkins, Richard S.	WR 30,31
Tarshis, Stanley G.	GY 58,59,60	Totte, Raymond, Jr.	FC 50,51,52
Tate, Charles G.	FB 97	Totten, Edward C.	BK 28,29
Tate, Mark T.	FB 58	Tower, Gordon E.	FB 99
Tatter, Jordan B.	SO 57,58	Tower, Ray R.	BS 02,03C
Tatu, George W.	CC 58,60		BK 02,03
Tavenner, Roger C.	WR 60		TR 03M
Taylor, Clifford A.	GO 48,49,50	Towner, John H.	BK 48M
Taylor, Dean R.	SW 57,58	Towner, Wilford S.	BS 03,04,05
Taylor, Maurice R.	FB 22,23C	Towns, Ivan A.	GY 48,49C
Taylor, Neal C.	BK 37M	Townsend, Clinton D.	GO 62
Teale, George W.	GO 46	Townsend, Edward E.	CC 55,56
Techlin, David G.	FB 65,66	Towson, Toby W.	GY 67,68,69
Teifer, Gerald E.	TN 49	Trace, David R.	SO 67,68,69
Telder, Robert A.	BS 42	Tracy, John E.	TR 94
Temple, P. F.	TR 22	Trahan, John Carroll	BX 55
Temple, Thomas D.	GY 58,60	Trapp, Donald G.	SW 34
TenEyck, Rex C.	TR 35,36	Travis, William E.	FB 99
Terlaak, Robert T.	FB 32,33	Traylor, Frank	FB 67
Terpay, Alexander	HO 64,65	Trier, Howard E.	TN 53
		Triplett, William L.	FB 68,69

Trowbridge, Charles L.	BS 13
Trueman, John J.	FB 59
Trull, Donald B.	CC 47M
Trull, Richard T.	CC 50M
	TR 50M
Tryon, Donald J.	FB 65M
Tryon, Edward C.	TR 92
Tryon, James H.	TR 05
Tsakiris, Alex	BX 52,53
Tuber, Gary H.	BS 65M
Tuchscherer, Ernest	SO, 67,68,69
Tungate, Paul S.	BS 63
Tuomi, Roger L.	GY 58
Turchan, Manuel C.	GY 63
Turcotte, Real J.	HO 60,61,62
Turnbull, Richard J.	WR 64
Turner, Joseph E.	FB 16,17
Turner, Kenneth E.	SW 40
Turner, Stanley A.	BS 53
Tuttle, H. Foley	BK 03,04,05C
Twellman, Steven	SO 69
Tyler, Bobby	FC 69,70
Tyrrell, Milford A.	FB 22M
Tyson, James	BS 21M

U

Uckele, William E.	TR 35
Ulmer, Jack D.	BK 59M,60M
Ulrich, Rudolph	TR 37,38,39
Underwood, Daniel D.	FB 61,62,63C
Uram, Michael	GY 69,70
Urbanik, Daniel A.	BS 48,49C

V

Valcanoff, Alex	WR 61,62,63
Vallier, Donald J.	FC 53
Van Arman, John P.	TR 25,26
Van Auken, E. W.	TR 39
Van Buren, Earl	FB 25
Vance, Walter E.	BS 08,09
Van Dagens, John L.	FC 50,51
Vandenburg, Vincent I.	FB 34,35,36
Vanderhoef, Wilfred R.	FB 95C,96C
VanderHorst, Leo	SO 57,58
VanderJagt, Mark	BK 65
Vandermeer, Myrton L.	FB 30,31,32
VanderMeiden, John	GO 70
Van Der Roest, Nick A.	BK 32,33,34
Vanderstolp, John H.	FB 96,97,98
Vandervoort, Adelbert D.	FB 14,15,16,19
Van Elst, Gary L.	FB 69
Van Elst, G. David	FB 68,69
Van Faasen, Arnold B.	BK 33,34,35C
Van Havel, John J.	BS 58M
Van Meter, Clifford W.	HO 58M
Van Noppen, D. M.	TR 24,25,26
Van Orden, Richard	FB 18,19
Van Poppelen, John W.	BX 51M
Van Sciever, Craig W.	BS 59,60
Van Spybrook, Eldon	HO 60
Vantine, Donald E.	GO 47
Van Wormer, Michael	GY 68
Van Zylen, James H.	BK 28,29,30C
Vargha, Louis A.	TR 52,53,54
Vary, Richard	BS 68,69,70
Vass, Denny	GO 69,70
Vatz, Abe M.	BS 13
	BK 12,13,14
Vaughn, Ernest	BS 07,08
	FB 07
	TR 07
Vaughn, Lawrence F.	FB 13,14
Vandik, Frank J.	BK 35
Vela, Luis F.	TN 55,56,57

Venema, Jacob G.	FC 47
Venia, James	LA 70
Ventura, Mabricio	SO 61,62
Verity, Gordon L.	SW 49,50
Verran, Garfield C.	TR 02,03
Vershinski, Thomas F.	FB 59
Vest, Donald S.	GY 52
Vetter, Frederick J.	TN 70
Vevia, Paul J.	BK 16,17
Vezmar, Walter	FB 45
Vincent, Wendell C.	CC 56M
	TR 57M
Viney, Robert W.	FB 63,64,65
Vissing, Paul R.	BK 47M
Vissing, William C.	FB 42M
Voelker, Arthur F.	TR 29
Vogel, Alfred R.	FB 24,25
Vogler, Harold	FB 47,48,49C
Vogt, Raymond A.	FB 50,51,52
Vollweiler, Andy	TN 69
Volmar, Douglas	HO 65,66,67
Vondette, Roy W.	BK 06,07,08MC
Vondette, William L.	BK 32,33
Von Eberstein, John A.	TR 43
Voorheis, Donald N.	TR 61,63
Vore, Stephen	FC 64,65,66
Vosburg, Robert L.	TR 46,47
Vosper, Richard H.	TR 10
Vrablec, John	SO 60,61
Vrooman, James	TR 52,53,54,55

W

Wagner, Sidney P.	FB 33,34,35C
Wagner, Thomas F.	TR 56
Wagonlander, Edward	BK 51
Waite, Kenneth A.	CC 35,36,37C
	TR 36,37,38C
Waite, Roy H.	TR 04,05,06,07C
Wakefield, Harry K.	BS 24,25,26
Waks, Charles A.	HO 54
Wakulsky, George T.	GO 56,57,58
Walcott, Roland	BS 65,66
Waldron, Donald	BK 46,47,48
	FB 46
	TN 48
Walker, Alan N.	FC 52
Walker, George M.	FB 58,59,60
Walker, Horace	BK 59,60C
Walker, Jerry	BS 64,65,66
Walker, John C.	GY 51,52,53C
Walsh, Eugene G.	SW 48
Walsh, Eugene J.	BS 46,47
Walsh, John J.	FB 63,64
Walsh, Kenneth	SW 65,66,67CoC
Walsh, Robert D.	GO 58
Walter, John P.	CC 50,52
	TR 51,52,53
Walters, John	BS 66,67
Walters, Warren P.	BS 36
Ward, George R.	TR 57,58,59
Ward, James C.	HO 53,54,55
Ward, Lloyd	BK 68,69,70
Ward, Morgan C.	CC 59,60
	TR 61
Ware, Harold W.	GO 52,53,54
Ware, William H. Jr.	FB 67
Wareham, Earl D.	TR 27
Warmbein, Kurt C.	FB 33,34,35
Warner, Arthur E.	TR 12,13
Warner, Frank E.	TR 41
Warner, Frank T.	TR 16
Warner, John A.	TR 46M,47M
Warner, Gary	BS 57,58
Warner, Laird	TN 64,65,66
Warner, Robert E.	TR 23

Name	Ref
Warner, Roy C.	BS 29
Warren, Carl L.	TR 20
Warren, Charles K.	TR 32,33,34
Warren, Frank V.	BS 96,97,98C
Warren, John L. III	BK 66M,67M
Washburne, Chandler	FC 48C
Washington, Eugene	FB 64,65,66
	TR 65,66,67
Washington, Herb	TR 70
Washington, Stan	BK 64,65,66
Waters, Frank D. III	FB 66,67,68
Waters, Franklin D. Jr.	FB 46,47,48,49
Watkins, Douglas A.	BS 28,29
Watkins, L. Whitney	BS 93M
Watkins, Ronald	FB 62
	TR 62
Watson, George G.	TR 49
Watson, Joseph A. Jr.	GO 42C
Watt, James	HO 70
Watt, William	HO 69,70
Watts, Neil S.	SW 62,63,64
Watts, Robert	BK 52M
Waver, Hal C.	TR 03
Wawzysko, John H.	GO 46
Weamer, Philip E.	TR 22,23
Weaver, Dee Lee	TR 35
Weaver, Douglas W.	FB 50,51,52
Weaver, Frank J.	CC 60
Webster, George	FB 64,65,66CoC
Webster, William R.	TR 39,40,41
Weckler, C. A.	FB 21
Wedemeyer, Charlie	FB 66,68
Wedemeyer, Harry P.	TR 99,00C
Wedgworth, George H.	BK 50M
Weed, Stanley E.	BS 28,29
Weeder, Maurice G.	BS 14,15
Weeks, Fred H.	BX 51
Weeks, Kenneth B.	FB 27
Weening, Bertrand T.	TR 48M
Wehrwein, Bill	TR 68,69,70
Weideman, Charles H.	BS 90,91
Weil, Norman O.	FB 60M
Weimer, L. Austin	BS 35,36
Weinacker, Adolph J.	TR 47,48,50
Weinland, Arthur A.	TR 30
Weissblum, Herbert	BX 57
Weissengruber, Max E.	TR 59
Weitz, Stanley E.	TN 32,33,34C
Weitzmann, James	SW 51,52
Welch, Harold I.	BS 34,35,36
Welfare, Ronald E.	SW 60
Wells, George B.	FB 96,97
	TR 97,98
Wells, Stephen	GY 65
Wells, William P.	FB 51,52,53
Wenger, Ralph D.	FB 45,48,49
Wenner, Elywyn A.	FB 26
Wenner, George	BS 22,23,24
Wenner, Jack H.	BS 54,55
Werner, Daniel L.	FB 69
Werner, Edward R.	HO 54
Werthmann, Thomas	GY 57,58
Wesling, Richard M.	BK 52,53
Wessells, Phillipp H.	BK 05
West, Jerry	FB 64,65,66
Westerman, Leslie B.	BK 06,07
Weston, Gerald W.	BS 10
Weston, James W.	BS 14M
Weyland, Robert L.	BK 43M
Wheeler, Burr	FB 02M
Wheeler, John P. Jr.	FB 46
Wheeler, Joseph R.	TR 50
Wheeler, Philip R.	TR 56
	CC 56,57
Wheeler, Roy S.	FB 07,08
	TR 07,08
Wherley, James R.	HO 61
Whetter, Lloyd A.	TR 43,46
White, Curtis W.	BK 35,36
White, Grover C.	TR 08
White, James L.	SW 62
White, Oliver G.	BK 43,46,47
White, Thorpe	TN 42M
Whiteford, Frederick G.	SW 66,67
Whitlock, Stanley C.	SW 26C
Whittemore, Olin S.	FB 51M
Wickering, Jack	SW 60
Wieleba, Ralph C.	FB 69
Wierman, Thomas H.	TN 62,63,64
Wietecha, Raymond W.	FB 46
Wightman, Robert R.	SW 53
Wilcox, Ernest A.	BS 02,03,05
Wilcox, Fred E.	BK 22
	FB 20,21
Wiley, Carroll E.	WR 57
Wilkinson, Dorian C.	BK 36,37
Wilkinson, Harry G.	GY 53
Wilkinson, Harry V.	BK 43M
Wilks, John J.	FB 57,59
Willard, William D.	TR 24,25
	CC 23
Williams, Bill	TR 53
Williams, Chester I.	BS 24M
Williams, David S.	BS 67,68,69
Williams, Dean E.	BS 15,16
Williams, Edward L.	BK 61,62,63
Williams, Fred J.	BS 23,24
Williams, Fred T.	FB 97
	TR 97
Williams, Glenn	FC 68,69
Williams, J. C.	FB 48,49,50
Williams, Mark L.	HO 63
Williams, Pete	SW 66,67,68
Williams, Raymond P.	SW 47,48,49,50
Williams, Robert C.	BS 53,54
Williams, Sam F.	FB 56,57,58C
Williams, William G.	SW 61
Williamson, Herbert H.	FB 34
Williamson, Leon M.	SW 38
Willis, George E.	FC 41C,42C
Willman, Walter K.	BS 17,20,21C
Willmarth, Theodore	CC 27,28,29C
	TR 27,28,29
Willoughby, Theodore C.	TR 22M
Wilson, Edward B.	GY 65,66
Wilson, Howard D.	SW 48
Wilson, Howard H.	TR 20,22
Wilson, James A.	BS 90,91
Wilson, John B.	TR 29,30
	FB 27
Wilson, John D.	FB 50,51,52
Wilson, Miles M.	FB 34,35
Wilson, Patrick	CC 66
	TR 67
Wilson, Patrick J.	BK 55,56,57
	FB 54,55,56
Wilson, Robert P.	TR 33
Wilson, Tom R.	FB 58,59,60
Wines, Thomas J.	SW 55
Winfield, Kenneth J.	SW 70
Winiecki, Thomas	FB 60,61
Winger, Norman	FC 55,57
Winther, Paul C.	SO 58,59
Wirs, Nick	SO 66
Wiseman, Donald R.	FB 34,35
Wissner, Walter F.	CC 32C
	TR 31,32,33
Witherill, Thomas	GY 62M
Witter, Gordon L.	BS 27
Witzke, Edward S.	GY 67,68,69
Wohlfert, Duane G.	WR 59,61
Wolf, Clyde, M.	BS 99,
	FB 98
Wolf, Robert H.	SW 65,66,67

Wolfe, David A.   HO 52M
Wolff, Charles R.   TN 63,64,65C
Wolkowicz, Leo R.   BS 40,41
Wonch, Ted N.   TR 41,42,43,46C
Wood, J. Edward   BX 43
Wood, Michael J.   SW 61,62,63C
Wood, William L. Jr.   SW 61,62,63
Wood, William W.   BK 16
Woodin, George B.   WR 58,59
Woods, Stanley H.   TR 25
Woodstra, Harvey P.   TR 38
Woodworth, Fred L.   FB 97
Wooley, Bill Jr.   BS 66M,67M
Woolf, Harry R.   HO 63,64,65C
Workman, Robert   GO 66
Woulfe, Richard T.   GO 69,70
Wren, Leon P.   TR 41
Wright, Donald M.   FB 57,58,59C
Wright, Harry A.   FB 05
Wright, James H.   CC 35
   TR 35,36,37
Wulf, John V.   BK 47,48,49C
Wulff, James F.   FB 55,56,58
Wycinsky, Craig   FB 68,69
Wylie, Henry   CC 27C
   TR 26,27,28C

Y

Yamamoto, Steven M.   SW 67
Yarger, Kenneth W.   TR 29,30,31
Yarian, Stephen E.   FB 64
Yatchman, Michael W.   TN 49
Yerkes, Donald P.   BS 86,87C
   TR 86,87
Yewcic, Thomas   BS 53,54
   FB 51,52,53
Yocca, John   FB 48,50
York, Eugene A.   TR 49M
Young, Barney C.   CC 69
Young, Edmund C.   FB 18
Young, Gerald A.   TR 62
Young, H. Earl   FB 01M
Young, Hendricks M.   FB 58
Young, John L.   BK 60
Young, Michael S.   FB 67,68
Young, Norman   WR 59,60,61

Young, Robert G.   BS 41,42
Youngs, Edward W.   FB 61,62,63
Youngs, Michael   TN 65,66C
Yuhse, Frank J.   FB 13M

Z

Zacks, Kenneth W.   HO 59M,60M,61M
Zagers, Bert A.   FB 52,53,54
Zalar, Edward J.   FB 55
Zaremba, Michael F.   RN 57
Zarza, Louis F.   FB 33,34,35
Zbiciak, Ed   BS 48,49
Zeitler, John W.   BS 52,53,54C
Zemper, Eric   CC 66
   TR 64,65,67
Zensen, John   SO 68
Zerbe, Jerry A.   CC 50,51,52
   TR 51,52
Ziegel, Frederick K.   BS 34,35,36
   FB 34,35,36
   SW 34,35,36
Ziegenfus, Gilbert A.   SW 39C
   TR 39
Ziegert, Dave   GY 70
Ziegler, Nickolas J.   FB 45
Ziemann, Frederick S.   TN 43
Zimmerman, Delmar R.   BS 25,26,27
   TR 25
Zindel, Barry L.   FB 59
Zindel, Bruce   WR 70
Zindel, Howard C.   FB 34,35,36
Zindel, Jack D.   FB 68
   WR 68,69,70
Zinn, Jack   GO 50,51,52C
Zito, James J.   FB 46,47
   TR 47,48,49
Zobel, Richard J.   TR 46
Zoppa, Ralph M.   CC 69
   TR 68,69,70
Zorn, William   FB 62
Zucco, Victor   FB 56
Zurakowski, William   BX 41,42,43C
Zvoda, Alvin P.   BS 51
Zylstra, William H.   GO 40,41C
Zysk, Donald H.   FB 55,56,57